The TRUMAN
ADMINISTRATION:

A Documentary History

The TRUMAN ADMINISTRATION:

A Documentary History

EDITED BY

Barton J. Bernstein and Allen J. Matusow

HARPER COLOPHON BOOKS
Harper & Row, Publishers
New York, Evanston and London

TO
Frank Freidel
our teacher and friend

First HARPER COLOPHON edition published 1968 by Harper &
Row, Publishers.

Library of Congress Catalog Card Number: 66-13938

Contents

Illustrations

Preface

Not enough time has elapsed nor has sufficient research been done to permit historians to pass considered judgment on the presidency of Harry S. Truman. Contemporary scholars have come to admire the little man who rose from dirt farmer at the age of thirty-three to President of the United States less than thirty years later. They have respected his capacity for growth, his struggle on behalf of progressive legislation, and his resolution in the conduct of foreign policy. While some of this praise is merited, it obscures certain less happy aspects of Truman's tenure. How much, for instance, did political and administrative incompetence within the administration contribute to the election of the Republican Eightieth Congress in 1946? Too few have investigated whether Truman's failure to win acceptance for most of his Fair Deal program was not partly the result of his own lack of political skill. Much of Truman's current reputation rests on his conduct of foreign affairs, but even here it is not yet clear whether he halted the spread of Communism in Europe or seriously misjudged the expansionary intentions of Marshal Stalin, thereby contributing unnecessarily to the deterioration of Russian-American relations.

After the advent of the Korean War, when the onslaughts of Senator Joseph R. McCarthy of Wisconsin and General Douglas MacArthur threatened the administration with political ruin, Truman proved unable to rally the public behind his policies. It is possible that his lack of personal stature and magnetism added significantly to this failure. Unresolved doubts about the administration cannot detract, however, from its moments of real greatness. The Marshall Plan did, after all, save Europe. The President's advocacy of civil rights did help to prepare the way for the revolution of the 1950's. And most students of the episode have come to view his measured use of power in Korea as both wise and courageous. Because the eight years of the Truman presidency were crammed with events of extraordinary variety and importance and were marked by wide fluctuations of public mood, it is little wonder that the period has so far defied intelligent generalization. The purpose of this book is to permit students to read for themselves some of the important documents of the Truman administration and to make, if they can, judgments of their own.

BARTON J. BERNSTEIN
ALLEN J. MATUSOW

Editors' Note

Footnotes preceded by a symbol (*†) represent material contained in the documents. The editors' footnotes are preceded by a number.

The editors' interpolations are within brackets and followed by "—Eds." Other bracketed matter is to be found in the original source.

The editors have altered spelling, hyphenation, and capitalization in several of the documents for the sake of internal consistency; minor errors have also been corrected. In no case has the editing changed the meaning of a document.

1 • The A-Bomb Decision

On July 16, 1945, a huge ball of fire rose out of the New Mexico desert. As he watched the first atomic explosion a line from the Bhagavad-Gita flashed through the mind of Dr. J. Robert Oppenheimer, then a little-known physicist. "Now I am become death, destroyer of worlds." At Potsdam, where they learned the news of the successful test, President Truman, Prime Minister Winston Churchill, and Secretary of War Henry L. Stimson, knowing that an event of unsurpassed importance had occurred, debated whether to tell Marshal Joseph Stalin their secret.

Ten days after that mushroom cloud over Alamogordo ushered in a new era, Truman and Churchill issued a declaration for Japan's unconditional surrender—despite Stimson's earlier plea that the proclamation guarantee the Emperor his throne. When Japan seemed to reject the ultimatum of the Allies, the first bomb was dropped on Hiroshima. On August 8, two days later, Russia declared war on Japan, and the next day the United States dropped a second atomic bomb. Japan quickly capitulated.

The history of those two bombs can be traced back to 1938. The news that a German laboratory had produced nuclear fission that year electrified the scientific world and alarmed those few who thought Nazi Germany might build a nuclear bomb. Fearful scientists resolved that the United States had to defeat Germany in the likely race. Dr. Leo Szilard, an impetuous and imaginative physicist, soon enlisted Albert Einstein to alert President Franklin D. Roosevelt to the danger and the possibility. The President shunted the subject to a committee, whose recommendations led to paltry federal assistance for an atomic project. Not until Pearl Harbor did the government lose its timidity about spending money on a mere theory. Soon placed under the Army, the project cost $2 billion, but in the end it produced the explosives for Hiroshima and Nagasaki.

The story of how the government decided to drop the atomic bomb on Japan is a jumbled one and raises questions both of strategy and of morals. For many the issues have been resolved simply—the choice was to use nuclear weapons or to sacrifice as many as a million Americans in the invasion of Japan. But in July and August these were not the only alternatives open to Truman and Stimson. They knew that the invasion was not scheduled until November, and they also knew that General MacArthur, their Pacific commander, had estimated very light casualties during the few months before the assault. Time existed, therefore, to seek and use alternatives. But the President and the Secretary of War had come to assume that the bomb would be dropped, and seemed never to have questioned that position.

According to Major General Leslie R. Groves, commanding general of the Manhattan District (code name for the A-bomb project), Truman "was like a little boy on a toboggan," who perhaps never even had an opportunity to say yes. A few critics, however, have found a careful design behind America's action. They have charged that Truman was anxious to end the war speedily—before Russia could enter the conflict, gain territory, and demand a role in postwar occupation. Some have even suggested that the bomb was not intended primarily to end the Japanese war but to demonstrate the weapon to Russia: "The dropping of the atomic bombs was not so much the last military act of the Second World War, as the first major operation of the cold diplomatic war," P. M. S. Blackett, a Nobel laureate in physics, later argued. However, many scholars of the period have pointed out that the United States could have offered conditional surrender, made peace before Russia entered the war, and found other ways to demonstrate the bomb to the Japanese. The weapons were used against Japan, most studies conclude, simply to end the war. A demonstration of the bomb for Japanese observers would have been a dangerous gamble: "Nothing would have been more damaging to our efforts to obtain surrender than a warning or demonstration followed by a dud," Stimson later explained. Moreover, the United States, with only two completed bombs, was unwilling to use one of them for a demonstration that might not even convince the divided Japanese government to yield. Though the two bombs brought death to more than 100,000 Japanese, Stimson and others have emphasized that they actually saved Japanese lives by ending the fire raids, halting the strangling blockade, and preventing the "ghastly . . . clash of great land armies."

STIMSON MEMO ON THE A-BOMB

1 ✑ AS A SENATOR, Truman had not known of the atomic-bomb project. On an occasion when the Senate Committee to Investigate the National Defense Program, of which he was chairman, was about to probe part of the Manhattan District, he had backed off at Secretary Stimson's request. Not until April 12, 1945, just after the new President's first cabinet meeting, did Stimson tell Truman about the bomb. Roosevelt's former "assistant President," James F. Byrnes, probably informed the new President more fully when they conferred the next day. On April 25 Stimson "discussed with President Truman the broader aspects of the subject." The memorandum that Stimson used for this conference with the President follows:[1]

1. Within four months we shall in all probability have completed the most terrible weapon ever known in human history, one bomb of which could destroy a whole city.

2. Although we have shared its development with the U.K., physically the U.S. is at present in the position of controlling the resources with which to construct and use it and no other nation could reach this position for some years.

3. Nevertheless it is practically certain that we could not remain in this position indefinitely.

a. Various segments of its discovery and production are widely known among many scientists in many countries, although few scientists are now acquainted with the whole process which we have developed.

b. Although its construction under present methods requires great scientific and industrial effort and raw materials, which are temporarily mainly within the possession and knowledge of U.S. and U.K., it is extremely probable that much easier and cheaper methods of production will be discovered by scientists in the future, together with the use of materials of much wider distribution. As a result, it is extremely probable that the future will make it pos-

[1] Reprinted from Henry Stimson, "The Decision to Use the Atomic Bomb," *Harper's Magazine*, February 1947, pp. 99–100; hereafter cited as Stimson, "A-Bomb." Reprinted by permission of *Harper's Magazine*. Later reprinted in Chapter XXIII of *On Active Service in Peace and War*, by Henry L. Stimson and McGeorge Bundy (Harper & Brothers, 1948). See Editors' Note, p. viii.

sible for atomic bombs to be constructed by smaller nations or even groups, or at least by a larger nation in a much shorter time.

4. As a result, it is indicated that the future may see a time when such a weapon may be constructed in secret and used suddenly and effectively with devastating power by a wilful nation or group against an unsuspecting nation or group of much greater size and material power. With its aid even a very powerful unsuspecting nation might be conquered within a very few days by a very much smaller one. . . .*

5. The world in its present state of moral advancement compared with its technical development would be eventually at the mercy of such a weapon. In other words, modern civilization might be completely destroyed.

6. To approach any world peace organization of any pattern now likely to be considered, without an appreciation by the leaders of our country of the power of this new weapon, would seem to be unrealistic. No system of control heretofore considered would be adequate to control this menace. Both inside any particular country and between the nations of the world, the control of this weapon will undoubtedly be a matter of the greatest difficulty and would involve such thoroughgoing rights of inspection and internal controls as we have never heretofore contemplated.

7. Furthermore, in the light of our present position with reference to this weapon, the question of sharing it with other nations and, if so shared, upon what terms, becomes a primary question of our foreign relations. Also our leadership in the war and in the development of this weapon has placed a certain moral responsibility upon us which we cannot shirk without very serious responsibility for any disaster to civilization which it would further.

8. On the other hand, if the problem of the proper use of this weapon can be solved, we would have the opportunity to bring the world into a pattern in which the peace of the world and our civilization can be saved.

9. As stated in General Groves' report, steps are under way looking towards the establishment of a select committee of particular qualifications for recommending action to the executive and legislative branches of our government when secrecy is no longer in full effect. The committee would also recommend the actions to be taken by the War Department prior to that time in anticipation of the postwar

---

* A brief reference to the estimated capabilities of other nations is here omitted; it in no way affects the course of the argument.

problems. All recommendations would of course be first submitted to the President.

JOINT CHIEFS' STRATEGY RECOMMENDATIONS

2 ◄§ BY LATE APRIL 1945, before the atomic bomb became operational, the American military decided, in the words of a Department of Defense study, that "early invasion of the Japanese home islands represented the most suitable strategy to accomplish unconditional surrender." On June 18 Truman met with the Joint Chiefs of Staff to discuss the details of the campaign against Japan. Prior to the meeting, Admiral William Leahy, chief of staff, informed the Joint Chiefs of the President's aims: "It is his intention to make his decisions on the campaign with the purpose of economizing to the maximum extent possible in the loss of American lives. Economy in the use of time and in money cost is comparatively unimportant."

Though the published minutes of the special White House meeting of June 18 do not record any mention of the atomic bomb, John J. McCloy, assistant secretary of war, recalled that it had been discussed. There was a suggestion, according to McCloy, that the Japanese should be warned that America had an atomic bomb before it was used against them. Both Secretary of War Stimson and the Joint Chiefs, fearing that the bomb might be unsuccessful, opposed the proposal.

At the meeting General George Marshall, chief of staff of the Army, read the President a digest of a memorandum prepared by the Joint Chiefs describing current strategy. Excerpts from the digest of the memo and part of the resulting discussion follow:[2]

Our air and sea power has already greatly reduced movement of Jap shipping south of Korea and should in the next few months cut it to a trickle if not choke it off entirely. Hence, there is no need for seizing further positions in order to block Japanese communications south of Korea.

General MacArthur and Admiral [Chester W.—Eds.] Nimitz are in agreement with the Chiefs of Staff in selecting 1 November as the target date to go into Kyushu because by that time:

[2] Reprinted from *Foreign Relations of the United States: Conference of Berlin (Potsdam), 1945* (Washington, D.C., 1960), I, 904–9; hereafter cited as *Potsdam Papers*.

a. If we press preparations we can be ready.

b. Our estimates are that our air action will have smashed practically every industrial target worth hitting in Japan as well as destroying huge areas in the Jap cities.

c. The Japanese Navy, if any still exists, will be completely powerless.

d. Our sea action and air power will have cut Jap reinforcement capabilities from the mainland to negligible proportions.

Important considerations bearing on the 1 November date rather than a later one are the weather and cutting to a minimum Jap time for preparation of defenses. If we delay much after the beginning of November the weather situation in the succeeding months may be such that the invasion of Japan, and hence the end of the war, will be delayed for up to 6 months. . . .

The Kyushu operation is essential to a strategy of strangulation and appears to be the least costly worthwhile operation following Okinawa. The basic point is that a lodgement in Kyushu is essential, both to tightening our strangle hold of blockade and bombardment on Japan, and to forcing capitulation by invasion of the Tokyo Plain.

We are bringing to bear against the Japanese every weapon and all the force we can employ and there is no reduction in our maximum possible application of bombardment and blockade, while at the same time we are pressing invasion preparations. It seems that if the Japanese are ever willing to capitulate short of complete military defeat in the field they will do it when faced by the completely hopeless prospect occasioned by (1) destruction already wrought by air bombardment and sea blockade, coupled with (2) a landing on Japan indicating the firmness of our resolution, and also perhaps coupled with (3) the entry or threat of entry of Russia into the war.

With reference to clean-up of the Asiatic mainland, our objective should be to get the Russians to deal with the Japs in Manchuria (and Korea if necessary) and to vitalize the Chinese to a point where, with assistance of American air power and some supplies, they can mop out their own country.

Casualties. Our experience in the Pacific war is so diverse as to casualties that it is considered wrong to give any estimate in numbers. Using various combinations of Pacific experience, the War Department staff reaches the conclusion that the cost of securing a worthwhile position in Korea would almost certainly be greater than the cost of the Kyushu operation. Points on the optimistic side of the Kyushu operation are that: General MacArthur has not yet accepted responsibility for going ashore where there would be disproportionate casualties. The nature of the objective area gives room for maneuver, both on the land and by sea. As to any discussion of specific operations, the following data are pertinent:

Campaign	U.S. casualties killed, wounded, missing	Jap casualties killed and prisoners (not including wounded)	Ratio to Jap U.S.
Leyte	17,000	78,000	1:4.6
Luzon	31,000	156,000	1:5.0
Iwo Jima	20,000	25,000	1:1.25
Okinawa	34,000 (Ground)	81,000	1:2
	7,700 (Navy)	(not a complete	
Normandy (1st		count)	
30 days)	42,000	—	—

The record of General MacArthur's operations from 1 March 1944 through 1 May 1945 shows 13,742 U.S. killed compared to 310,165 Japanese killed, or a ratio of 22 to 1.

There is reason to believe that the first 30 days in Kyushu should not exceed the price we have paid for Luzon. It is a grim fact that there is not an easy, bloodless way to victory in war and it is the thankless task of the leaders to maintain their firm outward front which holds the resolution of their subordinates. Any irresolution in the leaders may result in costly weakening and indecision in the subordinates. . . .

An important point about Russian participation in the war is that the impact of Russian entry on the already hopeless Japanese may well be the decisive action levering them into capitulation at that time or shortly thereafter if we land in Japan.

In considering the matter of command and control in the Pacific war which the British wish to raise at the next conference, we must bear in mind the point that anything smacking of combined command in the Pacific might increase the difficulties with Russia and perhaps with China. Furthermore the obvious inefficiencies of combined command may directly result in increased cost in resources and American lives.

General Marshall said that he had asked General MacArthur's opinion on the proposed operation and had received from him the following telegram, which General Marshall then read:

"I believe the operation presents less hazards of excessive loss than any other that has been suggested and that its decisive effect will eventually save lives by eliminating wasteful operations of nondecisive character. I regard the operation as the most economical one in effort and lives that is possible. In this respect it must be remembered that the several preceding months will involve practically no losses in ground troops and that sooner or later a decisive ground attack must be made. The hazard and loss will be greatly lessened if an attack is launched from Siberia sufficiently ahead of our target date to commit the enemy to major combat. I most earnestly recommend no change in OLYMPIC [the plan for invasion of Kyushu on November 1—Eds.]. Additional subsidiary attacks will simply build up our final total casualties."

General Marshall said that it was his personal view that the operation against Kyushu was the only course to pursue. He felt that air power alone was not sufficient to put the Japanese out of the war. It was unable alone to put the Germans out. General [Ira C.—Eds.] Eaker and General [Dwight D.—Eds.] Eisenhower . . . agreed to this. . . .

The President stated that one of his objectives in connection with the coming conference would be to get from Russia all the assistance in the war that was possible. To this end he wanted to know all the decisions that he would have to make in advance in order to occupy the strongest possible position in the discussions.

Admiral Leahy said that he could not agree with those who said to him that unless we obtain the unconditional surrender of the Japanese that we will have lost the war. He feared no menace from Japan in the foreseeable future, even if we were unsuccessful in forcing unconditional surrender. What he did fear was that our insistence on unconditional surrender would result only in making the Japanese desperate and thereby increase our casualty lists. He did not think that this was at all necessary.

The President stated that it was with that thought in mind that he had left the door open for Congress to take appropriate action with reference to unconditional surrender. However, he did not feel that he could take any action at this time to change public opinion on the matter. . . .

INTERIM COMMITTEE ON USE OF BOMB

3 ◄§ AS STIMSON had suggested on April 25, the President created a special advisory committee on atomic energy. Designed

largely to deal with postwar problems, the board, known as the Interim Committee, was composed of Stimson as chairman; George Harrison, president of the New York Life Insurance Company, who served as alternate chairman; James Byrnes (future Secretary of State but then a private citizen), representing the President; Dr. Vannevar Bush, director of the Office of Scientific Research and Development (OSRD) and president of the Carnegie Institution; Dr. Karl Compton, president of the Massachusetts Institute of Technology and an official in OSRD; Dr. James Conant, president of Harvard University and chairman of the National Defense Research Committee; and Ralph Bard, Under Secretary of the Navy.

To assist this group, the Scientific Advisory Committee—Doctors Arthur H. Compton, Enrico Fermi, Ernest Lawrence, and J. Robert Oppenheimer—had been appointed. On May 31 this scientific panel had conferred with the Interim Committee to consider use of the atomic bomb. Eleven years later, in his account of the meeting, Compton recalled that it was "the occasion for [the—Eds.] fullest consideration of whether and in what manner the bomb should be used." "Throughout the morning's discussion," continued Compton, "it seemed to be a foregone conclusion that the bomb would be used." Ralph Bard later remarked that he had the impression that the committee "approved a decision that had already been made." But Bard denied that the meeting had been the scene of an "intensive exploration" of the use of the bomb. Nor did he recall that anyone had discussed the possibility of a nonmilitary demonstration of the bomb for Japan's benefit. According to Oppenheimer, the "recommendations which the [Interim—Eds.] Committee adopted on June 1st were not based upon discussion with the [Scientific—Eds.] panel at that first meeting."

As closely as the story can be pieced together from fragmentary and sometimes contradictory recollections, it appears that the question of an alternative use of the bomb was never discussed at the meeting of the two groups. But at lunch Compton had raised the issue with Stimson, and some members of the two committees had briefly discussed it. After lunch the Interim Committee met alone, and the next day it resolved that there was no alternative to using the bomb. A year later Stimson discussed his version of the process of decision-making:[3]

[3] Reprinted from Stimson, "A-Bomb," pp. 100–1.

On June 1, after its discussions with the Scientific Panel, the Interim Committee unanimously adopted the following recommendations:

(1) The bomb should be used against Japan as soon as possible.

(2) It should be used on a dual target—that is, a military installation or war plant surrounded by or adjacent to houses and other buildings most susceptible to damage, and

(3) It should be used without prior warning [of the nature of the weapon]. One member of the committee, Mr. Bard, later changed his view and dissented from recommendation (3).

In reaching these conclusions the Interim Committee carefully considered such alternatives as a detailed advance warning or a demonstration in some uninhabited area. Both of these suggestions were discarded as impractical. They were not regarded as likely to be effective in compelling a surrender of Japan, and both of them involved serious risks. Even the New Mexico test would not give final proof that any given bomb was certain to explode when dropped from an airplane. Quite apart from the generally unfamiliar nature of atomic explosives, there was the whole problem of exploding a bomb at a predetermined height in the air by a complicated mechanism which could not be tested in the static test of New Mexico. Nothing would have been more damaging to our effort to obtain surrender than a warning or a demonstration followed by a dud—and this was a real possibility. Furthermore, we had no bombs to waste. It was vital that a sufficient effect be quickly obtained with the few we had.

FRANCK COMMITTEE REPORT

4 ⊷§ ON JUNE 12, nearly two weeks after the Interim Committee's recommendation, James Franck, a Nobel laureate, tried to present a report to the Secretary of War from the Committee on Social and Political Implications. This committee, composed of seven scientists in Chicago who had worked on the preparation of the nuclear explosive, plutonium, had been created at the suggestion of Arthur H. Compton of the University of Chicago, one of the four scientific advisers to the Interim Committee. Though his report expressed the unanimous opinion of the seven committee members, Franck managed to see only a lieutenant in the office of George Harrison, alternate chairman of the Interim Committee. One of the signers of the report, Eugene

Rabinowitch, later explained why the document had been couched in political rather than in moral terms: "We did not think in the necessarily a-moral climate in which wartime decisions have to be made these would be effective." Excerpts from the committee's report follow:[4]

. . . We feel compelled to take a more active stand now because the success which we have achieved in the development of nuclear power is fraught with infinitely greater dangers than were all the inventions of the past. All of us, familiar with the present state of nucleonics, live with the vision before our eyes of sudden destruction visited on our own country, of a Pearl Harbor disaster repeated in thousand-fold magnification in every one of our major cities. . . .

. . . The certainty that German scientists were working on this weapon and that their government would certainly have no scruples against using it when available, was the main motivation of the initiative which American scientists took in urging the development of nuclear power for military purposes on a large scale in this country. In Russia, too, the basic facts and implications of nuclear power were well understood in 1940, and the experience of Russian scientists in nuclear research is entirely sufficient to enable them to retrace our steps within a few years, even if we should make every attempt to conceal them. Even if we can retain our leadership in basic knowledge of nucleonics for a certain time by maintaining secrecy as to all results achieved on this and associated Projects, it would be foolish to hope that this can protect us for more than a few years.

It may be asked whether we cannot prevent the development of military nucleonics in other countries by a monopoly on the raw materials of nuclear power. The answer is that even though the largest now known deposits of uranium ores are under the control of powers which belong to the "western" group (Canada, Belgium and British India), the old deposits in Czechoslovakia are outside this sphere. Russia is known to be mining radium on its own territory; and even if we do not know the size of the deposits discovered so far in the USSR, the probability that no large reserves of uranium will be found in a country which covers one-fifth of the land area of the earth (and whose sphere of influence takes in additional territory), is too small

[4] Reprinted from "A Report to the Secretary of War," later published in *Bulletin of the Atomic Scientists*, May 1, 1946, pp. 2–4, 16.

to serve as a basis for security. **Thus, we cannot hope to avoid a nuclear armament race either by keeping secret from the competing nations the basic scientific facts of nuclear power or by cornering the raw materials required for such a race.** . . .

One possible way to introduce nuclear weapons to one world— which may particularly appeal to those who consider nuclear bombs primarily as a secret weapon developed to help win the present war —is to use them without warning on appropriately selected objects in Japan.

Although important tactical results undoubtedly can be achieved by a sudden introduction of nuclear weapons, we nevertheless think that the question of the use of the very first available atomic bombs in the Japanese war should be weighed very carefully, not only by military authorities, but by the highest political leadership of this country.

Russia, and even allied countries which bear less mistrust of our ways and intentions, as well as neutral countries may be deeply shocked by this step. It may be very difficult to persuade the world that a nation which was capable of secretly preparing and suddenly releasing a new weapon, as indiscriminate as the rocket bomb and a thousand times more destructive, is to be trusted in its proclaimed desire of having such weapons abolished by international agreement. We have large accumulations of poison gas, but do not use them, and recent polls have shown that public opinion in this country would disapprove of such a use even if it would accelerate the winning of the Far Eastern war. It is true that some irrational element in mass psychology makes gas poisoning more revolting than blasting by explosives, even though gas warfare is in no way more "inhuman" than the war of bombs and bullets. Nevertheless, it is not at all certain that American public opinion, if it could be enlightened as to the effect of atomic explosives, would approve of our own country being the first to introduce such an indiscriminate method of whole-sale destruction of civilian life.

Thus, from the "optimistic" point of view—looking forward to an international agreement on the prevention of nuclear warfare—the military advantages and the saving of American lives achieved by the sudden use of atomic bombs against Japan may be outweighed by the ensuing loss of confidence and by a wave of horror and repulsion sweeping over the rest of the world and perhaps even dividing public opinion at home.

From this point of view, a demonstration of the new weapon might best be made, before the eyes of representatives of all the United Nations, on the desert or a barren island. The best possible atmosphere for the achievement of an international agreement could be achieved if America could say to the world, "You see what sort of a weapon we had but did not use. We are ready to renounce its use in the future if other nations join us in this renunciation and agree to the establishment of an efficient international control."

After such a demonstration the weapon might perhaps be used against Japan if the sanction of the United Nations (and of public opinion at home) were obtained, perhaps after a preliminary ultimatum to Japan to surrender or at least to evacuate certain regions as an alternative to their total destruction. This may sound fantastic, but in nuclear weapons we have something entirely new in order of magnitude of destructive power, and if we want to capitalize fully on the advantage their possession gives us, we must use new and imaginative methods.

It must be stressed that if one takes the pessimistic point of view and discounts the possibility of an effective international control over nuclear weapons at the present time, then the advisability of an early use of nuclear bombs against Japan becomes even more doubtful— quite independently of any humanitarian considerations. If an international agreement is not concluded immediately after the first demonstration, this will mean a flying start toward an unlimited armaments race. If this race is inevitable, we have every reason to delay its beginning as long as possible in order to increase our head start still further.

OPPENHEIMER AND SCIENTIFIC ADVISORY COMMITTEE

5 ⋖§ PARTLY AS A RESULT of the Franck report, the government referred the problem of considering alternatives to using the bomb to the Scientific Advisory Committee. The members of the committee—Compton, Fermi, Lawrence, and Oppenheimer— made their report on June 16, 1945. Uninformed that the invasion of Japan was not planned until November, and otherwise ignorant of the military situation, the scientists believed that the only real alternative to dropping the bomb was an imminent invasion of Japan. In 1954, at the hearings on his security status, Oppenheimer

recalled his participation in the June meetings that led to the fateful decision:[5]

. . . Lawrence, Fermi, and Arthur Compton were the other members of this panel. We met with the Interim Committee I think on the 1st of June—I am not certain—of 1945 for a very prolonged discussion which was attended by all members of the committee, all members of the panel, and for most of the time General Marshall.

Apart from trying to make as vivid as we could the novelty, the variety, and the dynamic quality of this field, which we thought very important to get across, that this was not a finished job and there was a heck of a lot we didn't know, much of the discussion revolved around the question raised by Secretary Stimson as to whether there was any hope at all of using this development to get less barbarous relations with the Russians.

The other two assignments which the panel had—one was quite slight. We were asked to comment on whether the bomb should be used. I think the reason we were asked for that comment was because a petition had been sent in from a very distinguished and thoughtful group of scientists: "No, it should not be used." It would be better for everything that they should not. We didn't know beans about the military situation in Japan. We didn't know whether they could be caused to surrender by other means or whether the invasion was really inevitable. But in back of our minds was the notion that the invasion was inevitable because we had been told that. I have not been able to review this document, but what it said I think is characteristic of how technical people should answer questions.

We said that we didn't think that being scientists especially qualified us as to how to answer this question of how the bombs should be used or not; opinion was divided among us as it would be among other people if they knew about it. We thought the two overriding considerations were the saving of lives in the war and the effect of our actions on the stability, on our strength and the stability of the postwar world. We did say that we did not think exploding one of these things as a firecracker over a desert was likely to be very impressive. This was before we had actually done that.

---

[5] Excerpt reprinted from Atomic Energy Commission, *In the Matter of J. Robert Oppenheimer* (Washington, D.C., 1954), p. 34.

SCIENTIFIC ADVISORY COMMITTEE REPORT

6 ◄§ THOUGH MUCH of the June 16 report of the Scientific
Advisory Committee remains classified, a portion of the
conclusion is available:[6]

The opinions of our scientific colleagues on the initial use of these
weapons are not unanimous: they range from the proposal of a purely
technical demonstration to that of the military application best designed to induce surrender. Those who advocate a purely technical
demonstration would wish to outlaw the use of atomic weapons, and
have feared that if we use the weapons now our position in future
negotiations will be prejudiced. Others emphasize the opportunity of
saving American lives by immediate military use, and believe that
such use will improve the international prospects, in that they are
more concerned with the prevention of war than with the elimination
of this special weapon. We find ourselves closer to these latter views;
*we can propose no technical demonstration likely to bring an end to
the war; we see no acceptable alternative to direct military use.* [Italics
mine]

With regard to these general aspects of the use of atomic energy,
it is clear that we, as scientific men, have no proprietary rights. It
is true that we are among the few citizens who have had occasion
to give thoughtful consideration to these problems during the past few
years. We have, however, no claim to special competence in solving
the political, social, and military problems which are presented by
the advent of atomic power.

NAVY UNDER SECRETARY'S OBJECTIONS TO BOMB

7 ◄§ ON JUNE 27, nearly a month after the Interim Committee
had unanimously ratified use of the bomb against Japan,
Under Secretary of the Navy Bard reversed his earlier decision and
explained his objections in a memorandum:

Ever since I have been in touch with this program I have had a
feeling that before the bomb is actually used against Japan that Japan
should have some preliminary warning for say two or three days in
advance of use. The position of the United States as a great humani-

[6] Reprinted from Stimson, "A-Bomb," p. 101.

tarian nation and the fair play attitude of our people generally is responsible in the main for this feeling.

During recent weeks I have also had the feeling very definitely that the Japanese Government may be searching for some opportunity which they could use as a medium of surrender. Following the three-power conference emissaries from this country could contact representatives from Japan somewhere on the China Coast and make representations with regard to Russia's position and at the same time give them some information regarding the proposed use of atomic power, together with whatever assurances the President might care to make with regard to the Emperor of Japan and the treatment of the Japanese nation following unconditional surrender. It seems quite possible to me that this presents the opportunity which the Japanese are looking for.

I don't see that we have anything in particular to lose in following such a program. The stakes are so tremendous that it is my opinion very real consideration should be given to some plan of this kind. I do not believe under present circumstances existing that there is anyone in this country whose evaluation of the chances of the success of such a program is worth a great deal. The only way to find out is to try it out.

SZILARD'S PETITION AGAINST DROPPING BOMB

8 ⋖§ IN JULY, believing that the Franck report of June 12 had not been enough, scientists in Chicago prepared a petition addressed this time to the President and containing sixty-nine signatures. Dr. Leo Szilard, who helped bring the possibility of the atomic bomb to Roosevelt's attention, was the moving spirit behind the July petition. On July 3 Szilard circulated a strongly worded statement concluding, "We the undersigned respectfully petition that you exercise your power as commander in chief to rule that the United States shall not, in the present phase of the war, resort to the use of atomic bombs." To attract more signers, Szilard discarded this petition and substituted a milder version, which, on July 17, he submitted to Washington.

The second Szilard petition, along with at least two others, never reached the President. Major General Leslie Groves, director of the Manhattan project, kept them in his office for about two weeks. Nearly a year later an assistant prepared a memorandum of explanation for the files: Since questions of the bomb's use "had already been fully considered and settled by the proper authorities," and since the Interim Committee's scientific panel had provided a channel for such views, "no useful purpose would be served by transmitting either the petition or the attached documents to the White House, particularly since the President was not in the country." Earlier Szilard had tried to see the President about the problems of atomic energy, and he had been shunted off to Byrnes, who was about to become Secretary of State. On the basis of their May 28 meeting, he was appalled by Byrnes's ignorance and insensitivity; according to Szilard, Byrnes seemed to feel that the bomb was a nice thing to have when you meet the Russians. The complete text of Szilard's July 17 petition follows:[7]

Discoveries of which the people of the United States are not aware may affect the welfare of this nation in the near future. The liberation of atomic power which has been achieved places atomic bombs in the hands of the Army. It places in your hands, as Commander-in-Chief, the fateful decision whether or not to sanction the use of such bombs in the present phase of the war against Japan.

We, the undersigned scientists, have been working in the field of atomic power. Until recently we have had no fear that the United States might be attacked by atomic bombs during this war and that her only defense might lie in a counterattack by the same means. Today, with the defeat of Germany, this danger is averted and we feel impelled to say what follows:

The war has to be brought speedily to a successful conclusion and attacks by atomic bombs may very well be an effective method of warfare. We feel, however, that such attacks on Japan could not be justified, at least not unless the terms which will be imposed after the war on Japan were made public in detail and Japan were given an opportunity to surrender.

If such public announcement gave assurance to the Japanese that they could look forward to a life devoted to peaceful pursuits in their homeland and if Japan still refused to surrender, our nation might then, in certain circumstances, find itself forced to resort to the use of atomic bombs. Such a step, however, ought not to be made at

[7] From "A Petition to the President of the United States," in The Atomic Age, eds. Morton Grodzins and Eugene Rabinowitch (New York: Basic Books, 1963), pp. 28–9. Reprinted by permission of the Bulletin of the Atomic Scientists.

any time without seriously considering the moral responsibilities which are involved.

The development of atomic power will provide the nations with new means of destruction. The atomic bombs at our disposal represent only the first step in this direction and there is almost no limit to the destructive power which will become available in the course of their future development. Thus a nation which sets the precedent of using these newly liberated forces of nature for purposes of destruction may have to bear the responsibility of opening the door to an era of devastation on an unimaginable scale.

If after this war a situation is allowed to develop in the world which permits rival powers to be in uncontrolled possession of these new means of destruction, the cities of the United States as well as the cities of other nations will be in continuous danger of sudden annihilation. All the resources of the United States, moral and material, may have to be mobilized to prevent the advent of such a world situation. Its prevention is at present the solemn responsibility of the United States—singled out by virtue of her lead in the field of atomic power.

The added material strength which this lead gives to the United States brings with it the obligation of restraint, and if we were to violate this obligation our moral position would be weakened in the eyes of the world and in our own eyes. It would then be more difficult for us to live up to our responsibility of bringing the unloosened forces of destruction under control.

In view of the foregoing, we, the undersigned, respectfully petition: first, that you exercise your power as Commander-in-Chief to rule that the United States shall not resort to the use of atomic bombs in this war unless the terms which will be imposed upon Japan have been made public in detail and Japan, knowing these terms, has refused to surrender; second, that in such an event the question whether or not to use atomic bombs be decided by you in the light of the considerations presented in this petition as well as all the other moral responsibilities which are involved.

CHICAGO SCIENTISTS' PETITION

9 ⋅⋟ AMONG THE OTHER PETITIONS which never reached the President were one from sixty-eight scientists at Oak Ridge and one from eighteen in Chicago. Before using the weapon in the war, the Oak Ridge group recommended, the bomb's "powers

should be adequately described and demonstrated, and the Japanese nation should be given the opportunity to consider the consequences of further refusal to surrender." The eighteen scientists, though generally agreeing with the Szilard petition, chose other words to express their doubts:[8]

We respectfully petition that the use of atomic bombs, particularly against cities, be sanctioned by you as Chief Executive only under the following conditions:

1. Opportunity has been given the Japanese to surrender on terms assuring them the possibility of peaceful development in their homeland.

2. Convincing warnings have been given that a refusal to surrender will be followed by use of a new weapon.

3. Responsibility for use of atomic bombs is shared with our allies.

POLL OF 150 CHICAGO SCIENTISTS

10 ⚹ A POLL OF 150 scientists at Chicago was also buried in the files:[9]

In a wartime poll taken among the scientists at the Metallurgical Laboratory at the University of Chicago, 15 per cent favored full military use of the atomic bomb, 46 per cent favored its limited use, 26 per cent wanted an experimental demonstration before military use and 13 per cent preferred to avoid any military use whatever. . . .

The scientists working in their laboratories at Chicago on July 12, 1945 were asked, one at a time, to vote in this poll by secret ballot without previous discussion. The poll was entirely voluntary and informal. It read as follows:

"Which of the following five procedures comes closest to your choice as to the way in which any new weapons that we may develop should be used in the Japanese war:

"1. Use them in the manner that is from the military point of view most effective in bringing about prompt Japanese surrender at minimum human cost to our armed forces.

"2. Give a military demonstration in Japan to be followed by a

[8] Reprinted from Fletcher Knebel and Charles Bailey, "The Fight Over the A-Bomb," *Look*, August 13, 1963, p. 23.

[9] Excerpts reprinted from Arthur Compton and Farrington Daniels, "A Poll of Scientists at Chicago, July 1945," *Bulletin of the Atomic Scientists*, February 1948, p. 44. Reprinted by permission of the *Bulletin*.

renewed opportunity for surrender before full use of the weapons is employed.

"3. Give an experimental demonstration in this country, with representatives of Japan present; followed by a new opportunity for surrender before full use of the weapon is employed.

"4. Withhold military use of the weapons, but make public experimental demonstration of their effectiveness.

"5. Maintain as secret as possible all developments of our new weapons and refrain from using them in this war."

After reading the questions, each of the scientists placed a number in an envelope expressing his opinion. The poll did not reach everyone, but all those who were approached voted and the number comprised more than half of the scientists.

The scientists were physicists, chemists, biologists, and metallurgists who had received an academic degree. The results were as follows:

Procedure indicated above	1	2	3	4	5
Number voting	23	69	39	16	3
Per cent of votes	15	46	26	11	2

These five procedures were undoubtedly interpreted differently by different scientists, as they undoubtedly will be by present readers, but no definition or amplification of these procedures was made at the time of the poll.

OPPENHEIMER AND PRESSURE TO PRODUCE BOMB

11 ☙ DESPITE THE FERMENT at Chicago and the concern elsewhere in the Manhattan District, progress on the bomb continued. In 1954, at his security hearing, Oppenheimer answered questions about this period of feverish activity:[10]

Q. As the work progressed, you began to get goals and deadlines, I suppose, against which to produce the bomb, if you could?

A. The deadline never changed. It was as soon as possible. This depends on when we were ready, when the stuff was ready, and how much stuff we needed.

Q. Wasn't there a particular effort to get it done before the Potsdam Conference?

A. Yes, that was of course quite late. After the collapse of Germany, we understood that it was important to get this ready for the

[10] Excerpt reprinted from *In the Matter of J. Robert Oppenheimer*, p. 31.

war in Japan. We were told that it would be very important—I was told I guess by Mr. Stimson—that it would be very important to know the state of affairs before the meeting at Potsdam at which the future conduct of the war in the Far East would be discussed.

Q. Discussed with the Russians?

A. I don't want to overstate that. It was my understanding, and on the morning of July 16, I think Dr. Bush told me, that it was the intention of the United States statesmen who went to Potsdam to say something about this to the Russians. I never knew how much. Mr. Stimson explained later that he had planned to say a good deal more than what was said, but when they saw what the Russians looked like and how it felt, he didn't know whether it was a good idea. The historical record as it is published indicates that the President said no more than we had a new weapon which we planned to use in Japan, and it was very powerful. I believe we were under incredible pressure to get it done before the Potsdam meeting and Groves and I bickered for a couple of days.

MESSAGES TO STIMSON AT POTSDAM

12 &§ ON JULY 16 AND 17 the alternate chairman of the Interim Committee, George Harrison, sent two messages to Stimson at Potsdam. Truman, Stimson, and Byrnes were delighted by the news of "Little Boy," one of the code names for the bomb. The texts of the secret messages follow:[11]

Operated on this morning. Diagnosis not yet complete but results seem satisfactory and already exceed expectations. Local press release necessary as interest extends great distance. Dr. Groves pleased. He returns tomorrow. I will keep you posted.

Doctor has just returned most enthusiastic and confident that the LITTLE BOY is as husky as his big brother. The light in his eyes discernible from here to Highhold * and I could have heard his screams from here to my farm.†

[11] Reprinted from *Potsdam Papers*, II, 1360-1.

* Stimson's home on Long Island.

† At Upperville, Virginia.

Stimson's diary entry for July 18 includes the following: "Harrison's second message came, giving a few of the far reaching details of the test. I at once took it to the President who was highly delighted. . . . The President was evidently very greatly reenforced over the message from Harrison and said he was very glad I had come to the meeting. . . ."

GENERAL GROVES ON ALAMOGORDO TEST

13 ❧ ON JULY 18 Stimson received a more complete and very enthusiastic report of the Alamogordo test from General Groves:[12]

1. This is not a concise, formal military report but an attempt to recite what I would have told you if you had been here on my return from New Mexico.*

2. At 0530, 16 July 1945, in a remote section of the Alamogordo Air Base, New Mexico, the first full scale test was made of the implosion type atomic fission bomb. For the first time in history there was a nuclear explosion. And what an explosion! . . . The bomb was not dropped from an airplane but was exploded on a platform on top of a 100-foot high steel tower.

3. The test was successful beyond the most optimistic expectations of anyone. Based on the data which it has been possible to work up to date, I estimate the energy generated to be in excess of the equivalent of 15,000 to 20,000 tons of TNT; and this is a conservative estimate. Data based on measurements which we have not yet been able to reconcile would make the energy release several times the conservative figure. There were tremendous blast effects. For a brief period there was a lighting effect within a radius of 20 miles equal to several suns in midday; a huge ball of fire was formed which lasted for several seconds. This ball mushroomed and rose to a height of over ten thousand feet before it dimmed. The light from the explo-

---

[12] Excerpts, *ibid.*, pp. 1361–8.

* Stimson's diary entry for July 21 contains the following information relating to this document:

". . . At eleven thirty-five General Groves' special report was received by special courier. It was an immensely powerful document, clearly and well written and with supporting documents of the highest importance. It gave a pretty full and eloquent report of the tremendous success of the test and revealed far greater destructive power than we expected in S–1. . . .

"At three o'clock I found that Marshall had returned from the Joint Chiefs of Staff, and to save time I hurried to his house and had him read Groves' report and conferred with him about it.

"I then went to the 'Little White House' and saw President Truman. I asked him to call in Secretary Byrnes and then I read the report in its entirety and we then discussed it. They were immensely pleased. The President was tremendously pepped up by it and spoke to me of it again and again when I saw him. He said it gave him an entirely new feeling of confidence and he thanked me for having come to the Conference and being present to help him in this way."

sion was seen clearly at Albuquerque, Santa Fe, Silver City, El Paso and other points generally to about 180 miles away. The sound was heard to the same distance in a few instances but generally to about 100 miles. Only a few windows were broken although one was some 125 miles away. A massive cloud was formed which surged and billowed upward with tremendous power, reaching the substratosphere at an elevation of 41,000 feet, 36,000 feet above the ground, in about five minutes, breaking without interruption through a temperature inversion at 17,000 feet which most of the scientists thought would stop it. Two supplementary explosions occurred in the cloud shortly after the main explosion. The cloud contained several thousand tons of dust picked up from the ground and a considerable amount of iron in the gaseous form. Our present thought is that this iron ignited when it mixed with the oxygen in the air to cause these supplementary explosions. Huge concentrations of highly radioactive materials resulted from the fission and were contained in this cloud. . . .

11. Brigadier General Thomas F. Farrell was at the control shelter located 10,000 yards south of the point of explosion. His impressions are given below:

. . . "Just after . . . Groves left, announcements began to be broadcast of the interval remaining before the blast. They were sent by radio to the other groups participating in and observing the test. As the time interval grew smaller and changed from minutes to seconds, the tension increased by leaps and bounds. Everyone in that room knew the awful potentialities of the thing that they thought was about to happen. The scientists felt that their figuring must be right and that the bomb had to go off but there was in everyone's mind a strong measure of doubt. The feeling of many could be expressed by 'Lord, I believe; help Thou mine unbelief.' We were reaching into the unknown and we did not know what might come of it. It can be safely said that most of those present—Christian, Jew and Atheist—were praying and praying harder than they had ever prayed before. If the shot was successful, it was a justification of the several years of intensive effort of tens of thousands of people— statesmen, scientists, engineers, manufacturers, soldiers, and many others in every walk of life.

"In that brief instant in the remote New Mexico desert the tremendous effort of the brains and brawn of all these people came suddenly and startlingly to the fullest fruition. Dr. Oppenheimer, on whom had rested a very heavy burden, grew tenser as the last seconds ticked off. He scarcely breathed. He held on to a post to steady himself. For the last few seconds, he stared directly ahead and then when the announcer shouted 'Now!' and there came this tremendous burst of light followed shortly thereafter by the deep growling roar of the explosion, his face relaxed into an expression of tremendous relief. Several of the observers standing back of the shelter to watch the lighting effects were knocked flat by the blast.

"The tension in the room let up and all started congratulating each other. Everyone sensed 'This is it!' No matter what might happen now all knew that the impossible scientific job had been done. Atomic fission would no longer be hidden in the cloisters of the theoretical physicists' dreams. It was almost full grown at birth. It was a great new force to be used for good or for evil. There was a feeling in that shelter that those concerned with its nativity should dedicate their lives to the mission that it would always be used for good and never for evil.

"Dr. Kistiakowsky, the impulsive Russian, threw his arms around Dr. Oppenheimer and embraced him with shouts of glee. Others were equally enthusiastic. All the pent-up emotions were released in those few minutes and all seemed to sense immediately that the explosion had far exceeded the most optimistic expectations and wildest hopes of the scientists. All seemed to feel that they had been present at the birth of a new age—The Age of Atomic Energy—and felt their profound responsibility to help in guiding into right channels the tremendous forces which had been unlocked for the first time in history.

CHURCHILL'S REACTION TO THE GROVES REPORT

14 ✑ AT POTSDAM Stimson showed Groves's report to Churchill, who immediately recognized that the bomb "would redress the balance with the Russians." On July 22 Stimson recorded in his diary Churchill's reaction to the report from Groves:[13]

At ten-forty Bundy and I again went to the British headquarters and talked to the Prime Minister and Lord Cherwell for over an hour. Churchill read Groves' report in full. He told me that he had noticed at the meeting of the Three yesterday that Truman was evidently much fortified by something that had happened and that he stood up to the Russians in a most emphatic and decisive manner, telling them as to certain demands that they absolutely could not

13 *Ibid.*, p. 225.

have and that the United States was entirely against them. He said 'Now I know what happened to Truman yesterday. I couldn't understand it. When he got to the meeting after having read this report he was a changed man. He told the Russians just where they got on and off and generally bossed the whole meeting.' Churchill said he now understood how this pepping up had taken place and that he felt the same way. His own attitude confirmed this admission. He now not only was not worried about giving the Russians information on the matter but was rather inclined to use it as an argument in our favor in the negotiations. The sentiment of the four of us was unanimous in thinking that it was advisable to tell the Russians at least that we were working on that subject and intended to use it if and when it was successfully finished.

ORDER FOR DROPPING THE BOMB

15 ◆§ ON JULY 21 Stimson received a message from George Harrison of the Interim Committee: "Patient progressing rapidly and will be ready for final operation first good break in August." Two days later Stimson replied, expressing delight "with apparent improvement in timing" of patient's progress. He assumed that the "operation may be any time after the first of August." The decision, he added, "has been confirmed by highest authority" —the President. At Potsdam, Churchill later wrote, there was no discussion of whether the bomb should be used. The decision "was never an issue. . . ." On July 24 the War Department instructed General Carl Spaatz, commanding general of Army Strategic Air Forces, that the first bomb could be dropped on Japan after August 3. The text of the authorized message (from General Thomas Handy) to General Spaatz follows:[14]

1. The 509 Composite Group, 20th Air Force will deliver its first special bomb as soon as weather will permit visual bombing after about 3 August 1945 on one of the targets: Hiroshima, Kokura, Niigata and Nagasaki. To carry military and civilian scientific personnel from the War Department to observe and record the effects of the explosion of the bomb, additional aircraft will accompany the airplane carrying the bomb. The observing planes will stay several miles distant from the point of impact of the bomb.

[14] From *The Army Air Forces in World War II*, eds. Wesley F. Craven and James L. Cate (Chicago: University of Chicago Press, 1953), V, 696–7.

2. Additional bombs will be delivered on the above targets as soon as made ready by the project staff. Further instructions will be issued concerning targets other than those listed above.

3. Dissemination of any and all information concerning the use of the weapon against Japan is reserved to the Secretary of War and the President of the United States. No communique on the subject or release of information will be issued by Commanders in the field without specific prior authority. Any news stories will be sent to the War Department for special clearance.

4. The foregoing directive is issued to you by direction and with the approval of the Secretary of War and the Chief of Staff, U.S.A. It is desired that you personally deliver one copy of this directive to General MacArthur and one copy to Admiral Nimitz for their information.

TOGO TO SATO ON ATTEMPT TO END WAR

16 ᵉᵇ　AS EARLY AS MAY 30, 1945, the American government knew that the Japanese were putting out peace feelers to the Russians. The United States had cracked the Japanese secret code earlier in the war and was presumably able to follow much of the tentative negotiations. At Potsdam Stalin told Truman of recent feelers from Japan, and Truman revealed that he was aware of the Japanese note of July 25 from Naotake Sato, the Japanese ambassador in the Soviet Union, to Shigenori Togo, the Japanese minister of foreign affairs. There is no reason why the American delegation would not have known the contents of a note Togo sent on July 21 to Sato. Part of the July 21 note follows:[15]

1. We cannot accept unconditional surrender (understood fully your telegram No. 1416) in any situation. Although it is apparent that there will be more casualties on both sides in case the war is prolonged, we will stand united as one nation against the enemy if the enemy forcibly demands our unconditional surrender. It is, however, our intention to achieve, with Soviet assistance, a peace which is not of unconditional nature, in order to avoid such a situation as mentioned above in accordance with His Majesty's desire. It will be necessary for us to exert our utmost efforts to have the United States and Great Britain understand thoroughly this intention. Thus, it is impossible at this time to ask the Soviet Union uncondi-

15 Reprinted from *Potsdam Papers*, II, 1258.

tionally for assistance in obtaining peace; at the same time, it is also impossible and to our disadvantage to indicate the concrete conditions immediately at this time on account of internal and external relations. Under such delicate circumstances, we hope to have Prince Konoye transmit to the Soviet Union our concrete intentions based on the Emperor's wishes and following a conference to have the Soviets deal with the United States and Great Britain, while considering the Soviet demands in Asia.

PROCLAMATION FOR UNCONDITIONAL SURRENDER

17 ⮔ EVEN BEFORE THE Japanese note of July 21, Stimson and Under Secretary of State Joseph C. Grew, a former ambassador to Japan, had urged Truman to announce that he would allow the Emperor to remain on his throne. Following the pattern of Truman's May 8 demand for unconditional surrender, however, the United States, the United Kingdom, and China issued on July 26, 1945, their proclamation for the unconditional surrender of Japan:[16]

(1) We, the President of the United States, the President of the National Government of the Republic of China and the Prime Minister of Great Britain, representing the hundreds of millions of our countrymen, have conferred and agree that Japan shall be given an opportunity to end this war.

(2) The prodigious land, sea and air forces of the United States, the British Empire and of China, many times reinforced by their armies and air fleets from the west are poised to strike the final blows upon Japan. This military power is sustained and inspired by the determination of all the Allied nations to prosecute the war against Japan until she ceases to resist.

(3) The result of the futile and senseless German resistance to the might of the aroused free peoples of the world stands forth in awful clarity as an example to the people of Japan. The might that now converges on Japan is immeasurably greater than that which, when applied to the resisting Nazis, necessarily laid waste to the lands, the industry and the method of life of the whole German people. The full application of our military power, backed by our resolve, *will* mean the inevitable and complete destruction of the Japanese armed

---

[16] Excerpt, *ibid.*, pp. 1474–6.

forces and just as inevitably the utter devastation of the Japanese homeland.

(4) The time has come for Japan to decide whether she will continue to be controlled by those self-willed milita[r]istic advisers whose unintelligent calculations have brought the Empire of Japan to the threshold of annihilation, or whether she will follow the path of reason.

(5) Following are our terms. We will not deviate from them. There are no alternatives. We shall brook no delay.

(6) There must be eliminated for all time the authority and influence of those who have deceived and misled the people of Japan into embarking on world conquest, for we insist that a new order of peace, security and justice will be impossible until irresponsible militarism is driven from the world.

(7) Until such a new order is established and until there is convincing proof that Japan's war-making power is destroyed, points in Japanese territory to be designated by the Allies shall be occupied to secure the achievement of the basic objectives we are here setting forth.

(8) The terms of the Cairo Declaration shall be carried out and Japanese sovereignty shall be limited to the islands of Honshu, Hokkaido, Kyushu, Shikoku and such minor islands as we determine.

(9) The Japanese military forces, after being completely disarmed, shall be permitted to return to their homes with the opportunity to lead peaceful and productive lives.

(10) We do not intend that the Japanese shall be enslaved as a race or destroyed as [a] nation, but stern justice shall be meted out to all war criminals, including those who have visited cruelties upon our prisoners. The Japanese government shall remove all obstacles to the revival and strength[en]ing of democratic tendencies among the Japanese people. Freedom of speech, of religion, and of thought, as well as respect for the fundamental human rights shall be established.

(11) Japan shall be permitted to maintain such industries as will sustain her economy and permit the exaction of just reparations in kind, but not those industries which would enable her to re-arm for war. To this end, access to, as distinguished from control of raw materials shall be permitted. Eventual Japanese participation in world trade relations shall be permitted.

(12) The occupying forces of the Allies shall be withdrawn from

Japan as soon as these objectives have been accomplished and there has been established in accordance with the freely expressed will of the Japanese people a peacefully inclined and responsible government.

(13) We call upon the Government of Japan to proclaim now the unconditional surrender of all the Japanese armed forces, and to provide proper and adequate assurances of their good faith in such action. The alternative for Japan is prompt and utter destruction.

SATO MESSAGE ON PEACE PROSPECTS

18 ⟨⟩ ON JULY 28 the Japanese Prime Minister, Admiral Baron Kantaro Suzuki, apparently rejected the three-power demand for unconditional surrender. Asked at an afternoon press conference about the proclamation, he replied that it was "nothing but a rehash of the Cairo Declaration." The government "does not find any important value in it, and there is no other recourse but to ignore it entirely and resolutely fight for the successful conclusion of this war." There is some controversy about whether the Prime Minister intended to reject it "entirely." The dispute hinges on the use of the word "mokusatsu," which can also mean "wait and see." At the time the American government seemed unaware of the ambiguity of Suzuki's response, and plans to use the bomb continued unchecked. The President probably knew of the July 30 message from Sato to Togo:[17]

1. There is no reason to believe that Stalin was not informed beforehand on the Potsdam joint declaration and this must be considered only natural, judging from the present relationship among the three countries—the United States, Great Britain, and the Soviet Union. Also, for the most part, we can surmise that the above-mentioned joint declaration had some connection with our plan to send the special envoy, i.e., our first request to the Soviet Union on the 13th regarding the dispatch of a special envoy. It can be suspected that the subject was casually mentioned to the leaders of the United States and Great Britain at Potsdam. I believe we can conclude that the recent joint declaration was based on this information and that the three countries—the United States, Great Britain, and China—made a proclamation in an effort to make their stand clear and definite.

17 Excerpt, *ibid.*, pp. 1296-7.

As to whether or not the declaration of the 26th was made after the leaders of the United States and Great Britain were informed of the first request which I made to [Solomon A.—Eds.] Lozovsky [acting Soviet foreign minister—Eds.] on the 25th and also regarding the second request (my telegram No. 1449) on sending the special envoy, all this is not actually too important. Also, in reality, we believe that a discussion was held with Chiang Kai-shek prior to our presentation of the request on the 25th. Nevertheless, it is possible that they have already ferreted out signs of our overtures to conclude a negotiated peace at that time. The only ones who knew the circumstances of that period are Stalin and Molotov, and it is a difficult task to find out the truth. As for our side, I believe there is nothing we can do but to reason as indicated above.

2. In connection with the above problems, one important point is that by issuing the joint declaration, the United States and Great Britain made persistent demands on Japan to surrender unconditionally immediately, and another important point which they made clear is that they have no intention of relaxing the terms as stated in the declaration. If Stalin sees that it is impossible to shake the will of the United States and Great Britain regarding the above points, it would mean that our request to send the special envoy cannot be accepted and will be futile, regardless of how we explain that our desire to terminate the miserable war is in accordance with the will of our gracious Emperor and that Stalin will be called the advocate of world peace, etc. As for the United States and Great Britain, their contention will be that the only way for Japan to avoid the bloodshed of war is to surrender immediately. Stalin will also exert sufficient heavy pressure on the United States, Great Britain, and China regarding Manchuria, China, Korea, etc., in the event that Japan surrenders. He is also believed to have made up his mind to push through his claim and actually holds the power to do so. Therefore I believe that Stalin feels there is absolutely no necessity for making a voluntary agreement with Japan. On this point I see a serious discrepancy between your view and the actual state of affairs.

Also, attention should be paid to Australian Foreign Minister [Herbert V.—Eds.] Evatt's announcement, as reported by the B.B.C. on the 30th, that he was opposed to the attitude of the joint declaration against Japan since it tends to be more lenient toward Japan than the stand taken by the Allied nations against Germany in the past.

STIMSON DEFENSE OF USE OF A-BOMB

19 ⋘ Japanese rejection of the Potsdam ultimatum meant that the government would use the atomic bomb. Secretary of War Stimson, who, more than any other man, was responsible for this decision, summarized his reasons in the now-famous article in *Harper's Magazine*, February 1947. Part of Stimson's article follows:[18]

. . . The ultimate responsibility for the recommendation to the President rested upon me, and I have no desire to veil it. The conclusions of the committee were similar to my own, although I reached mine independently. I felt that to extract a genuine surrender from the Emperor and his military advisers, they must be administered a tremendous shock which would carry convincing proof of our power to destroy the Empire. Such an effective shock would save many times the number of lives, both American and Japanese, that it would cost.

The facts upon which my reasoning was based and steps taken to carry it out now follow.

The principal political, social, and military objective of the United States in the summer of 1945 was the prompt and complete surrender of Japan. Only the complete destruction of her military power could open the way to lasting peace.

Japan, in July 1945, had been seriously weakened by our increasingly violent attacks. It was known to us that she had gone so far as to make tentative proposals to the Soviet government, hoping to use the Russians as mediators in a negotiated peace. These vague proposals contemplated the retention by Japan of important conquered areas and were therefore not considered seriously. There was as yet no indication of any weakening in the Japanese determination to fight rather than accept unconditional surrender. If she should persist in her fight to the end, she had still a great military force.

In the middle of July 1945, the intelligence section of the War Department General Staff estimated Japanese military strength as follows: in the home islands, slightly under 2,000,000; in Korea, Manchura, China proper, and Formosa, slightly over 2,000,000; in French Indo-China, Thailand, and Burma, over 200,000; in the East Indies area, including the Philippines, over 500,000; in the by-passed Pacific

[18] Reprinted from Stimson, "A-Bomb," pp. 101–7.

islands, over 100,000. The total strength of the Japanese Army was estimated at about 5,000,000 men. These estimates later proved to be in very close agreement with official Japanese figures.

The Japanese Army was in much better condition than the Japanese Navy and Air Force. The Navy had practically ceased to exist except as a harrying force against an invasion fleet. The Air Force had been reduced mainly to reliance upon Kamikaze, or suicide, attacks. These latter, however, had already inflicted serious damage on our seagoing forces, and their possible effectiveness in a last ditch fight was a matter of real concern to our naval leaders.

As we understood it in July, there was a very strong possibility that the Japanese government might determine upon resistance to the end, in all the areas of the Far East under its control. In such an event the Allies would be faced with the enormous task of destroying an armed force of five million men and five thousand suicide aircraft, belonging to a race which had already amply demonstrated its ability to fight literally to the death.

The strategic plans of our armed forces for the defeat of Japan, as they stood in July, had been prepared without reliance upon the atomic bomb, which had not yet been tested in New Mexico. We were planning an intensified sea and air blockade, and greatly intensified strategic air bombing, through the summer and early fall, to be followed on November 1 by an invasion of the southern island of Kyushu. This would be followed in turn by an invasion of the main island of Honshu in the spring of 1946. The total U.S. military and naval force involved in this grand design was of the order of 5,000,000 men; if all those indirectly concerned are included, it was larger still.

We estimated that if we should be forced to carry this plan to its conclusion, the major fighting would not end until the latter part of 1946, at the earliest. I was informed that such operations might be expected to cost over a million casualties, to American forces alone. Additional large losses might be expected among our allies, and, of course, if our campaign were successful and if we could judge by previous experience, enemy casualties would be much larger than our own.

It was already clear in July that even before the invasion we should be able to inflict enormously severe damage on the Japanese homeland by the combined application of "conventional" sea and air power. The critical question was whether this kind of action would induce surrender. It therefore became necessary to consider very carefully the probable state of mind of the enemy, and to assess with accuracy the line of conduct which might end his will to resist.

With these considerations in mind, I wrote a memorandum for the President, on July 2, which I believe fairly represents the thinking of the American government as it finally took shape in action. This memorandum was prepared after discussion and general agreement with Joseph C. Grew, Acting Secretary of State, and Secretary of the Navy Forrestal, and when I discussed it with the President, he expressed his general approval.

July 2, 1945

Memorandum for the President

PROPOSED PROGRAM FOR JAPAN

1. The plans of operation up to and including the first landing have been authorized and the preparations for the operation are now actually going on. This situation was accepted by all members of your conference on Monday, June 18.

2. There is reason to believe that the operation for the occupation of Japan following the landing may be a very long, costly, and arduous struggle on our part. The terrain, much of which I have visited several times, has left the impression on my memory of being one which would be susceptible to a last ditch defense such as has been made on Iwo Jima and Okinawa and which of course is very much larger than either of those two areas. According to my recollection it will be much more unfavorable with regard to tank maneuvering than either the Philippines or Germany.

3. If we once land on one of the main islands and begin a forceful occupation of Japan, we shall probably have cast the die of last ditch resistance. The Japanese are highly patriotic and certainly susceptible to calls for fanatical resistance to repel an invasion. Once started in actual invasion, we shall in my opinion have to go through with an even more bitter finish fight than in Germany. We shall incur the losses incident to such a war and we shall have to leave the Japanese islands even more thoroughly destroyed than was the case with Germany. This would be due both to the difference in the Japanese and German personal character and the differences in the size and character of the terrain through which the operations will take place.

4. A question then comes: Is there any alternative to such a forceful occupation of Japan which will secure for us the equivalent of an unconditional surrender of her forces and a permanent destruction of her power again to strike an aggressive blow at the "peace of the Pacific"? I am inclined to think that there is enough such chance to make it well worthwhile our giving them a warning of what is to come and a definite opportunity to capitulate. As above suggested, it should be tried before the actual forceful occupation of the homeland islands is begun and furthermore the warning should be given in ample time to permit a national reaction to set in.

We have the following enormously favorable factors on our side— factors much weightier than those we had against Germany:

Japan has no allies.

Her navy is nearly destroyed and she is vulnerable to a surface and underwater blockade which can deprive her of sufficient food and supplies for her population.

She is terribly vulnerable to our concentrated air attack upon her crowded cities, industrial and food resources.

She has against her not only the Anglo-American forces but the rising forces of China and the ominous threat of Russia.

We have inexhaustible and untouched industrial resources to bring to bear against her diminishing potential.

We have great moral superiority through being the victim of her first sneak attack.

The problem is to translate these advantages into prompt and economical achievement of our objectives. I believe Japan *is* susceptible to reason in such a crisis to a much greater extent than is indicated by our current press and other current comment. Japan is not a nation composed wholly of mad fanatics of an entirely different mentality from ours. On the contrary, she has within the past century shown herself to possess extremely intelligent people, capable in an unprecedentedly short time of adopting not only the complicated technique of Occidental civilization but to a substantial extent their culture and their political and social ideas. Her advance in all these respects during the short period of sixty or seventy years has been one of the most astounding feats of national progress in history— a leap from the isolated feudalism of centuries into the position of one of the six or seven great powers of the world. She has not only built up powerful armies and navies. She has maintained an honest and effective national finance and respected position in many of the sciences in which we pride ourselves. Prior to the forcible seizure of power over her government by the fanatical military group in 1931, she had for ten years lived a reasonably responsible and respectable international life.

My own opinion is in her favor on the two points involved in this question:

a. I think the Japanese nation has the mental intelligence and versatile capacity in such a crisis to recognize the folly of a fight to the finish and to accept the proffer of what will amount to an unconditional surrender; and

b. I think she has within her population enough liberal leaders (although now submerged by the terrorists) to be depended upon for her reconstruction as a responsible member of the family of nations. I think she is better in this last respect than Germany was. Her liberals yielded only at the point of the pistol and, so far as I am aware, their liberal attitude has not been personally subverted in the way which was so general in Germany.

On the other hand, I think that the attempt to exterminate her armies and her population by gunfire or other means will tend to produce a fusion of race solidity and antipathy which has no analogy in the case of Germany. We have a national interest in creating, if possible, a condition wherein the Japanese nation may live as a peaceful and useful member of the future Pacific community.

5. It is therefore my conclusion that a carefully timed warning be given to Japan by the chief representatives of the United States, Great Britain, China, and, if then a belligerent, Russia by calling upon Japan to surrender and permit the occupation of her country in order to insure its complete demilitarization for the sake of the future peace.

This warning should contain the following elements:

The varied and overwhelming character of the force we are about to bring to bear on the islands.

The inevitability and completeness of the destruction which the full application of this force will entail.

The determination of the Allies to destroy permanently all authority and influence of those who have deceived and misled the country into embarking on world conquest.

The determination of the Allies to limit Japanese sovereignty to her main islands and to render them powerless to mount and support another war.

The disavowal of any attempt to extirpate the Japanese as a race or to destroy them as a nation.

A statement of our readiness, once her economy is purged of its militaristic influence, to permit the Japanese to maintain such industries, particularly of a light consumer character, as offer no threat of aggression against their neighbors, but which can produce a sustaining economy, and provide a reasonable standard of living. The statement should indicate our willingness, for this purpose, to give Japan trade access to external raw materials, but no longer any control over the sources of supply outside her main islands. It should also indicate our willingness, in accordance with our now established foreign trade policy, in due course to enter into mutually advantageous trade relations with her.

The withdrawal from their country as soon as the above objectives of the Allies are accomplished, and as soon as there has been established a peacefully inclined government, of a character representative of the masses of the Japanese people. I personally think that if in saying this we should add that we do not exclude a constitutional monarchy under her present dynasty, it would substantially add to the chances of acceptance.

6. Success of course will depend on the potency of the warning which we give her. She has an extremely sensitive national pride and, as we are now seeing every day, when actually locked with the enemy will fight to the very death. For that reason the warning must be tendered before the actual invasion has occurred and while the impending destruction, though clear beyond peradventure, has not yet reduced her to fanatical despair. If Russia is a part of the threat, the Russian attack, if actual, must not have progressed too far. Our own bombing should be confined to military objectives as far as possible.

It is important to emphasize the double character of the suggested warning. It was designed to promise destruction if Japan resisted, and hope, if she surrendered.

It will be noted that the atomic bomb is not mentioned in this memorandum. On grounds of secrecy the bomb was never mentioned except when absolutely necessary, and furthermore, it had not yet been tested. It was of course well forward in our minds, as the memorandum was written and discussed, that the bomb would be the best possible sanction if our warning were rejected.

The adoption of the policy outlined in the memorandum of July 2 was a decision of high politics; once it was accepted by the President, the position of the atomic bomb in our planning became quite clear. I find that I stated in my diary, as early as June 19, that "the last chance warning . . . must be given before an actual landing of the ground forces in Japan, and fortunately the plans provide for enough time to bring in the sanctions to our warning in the shape of heavy ordinary bombing attack and an attack of S-1." S-1 was a code name for the atomic bomb.

There was much discussion in Washington about the timing of the warning to Japan. The controlling factor in the end was the date already set for the Potsdam meeting of the Big Three. It was President Truman's decision that such a warning should be solemnly issued by the U.S. and the U.K. from this meeting, with the concurrence of the head of the Chinese government, so that it would be plain that *all* of Japan's principal enemies were in entire unity. This was done, in the Potsdam ultimatum of July 26, which very closely followed the above memorandum of July 2, with the exception that it made no mention of the Japanese Emperor.

On July 28 the Premier of Japan, Suzuki, rejected the Potsdam ultimatum by announcing that it was "unworthy of public notice." In the face of this rejection we could only proceed to demonstrate that the ultimatum had meant exactly what it said when it stated that if the Japanese continued the war, "the full application of our military power, backed by our resolve, will mean the inevitable and complete destruction of the Japanese armed forces and just as inevitably the utter devastation of the Japanese homeland."

For such a purpose the atomic bomb was an eminently suitable weapon. The New Mexico test occurred while we were at Potsdam, on July 16. It was immediately clear that the power of the bomb measured up to our highest estimates. We had developed a weapon of such a revolutionary character that its use against the enemy might well be expected to produce exactly the kind of shock on the Japanese ruling oligarchy which we desired, strengthening the position of those who wished peace, and weakening that of the military party.

Because of the importance of the atomic mission against Japan, the detailed plans were brought to me by the military staff for approval. With President Truman's warm support I struck off the list of suggested targets the city of Kyoto. Although it was a target of considerable military importance, it had been the ancient capital of Japan and was a shrine of Japanese art and culture. We determined that it should be spared. I approved four other targets including the cities of Hiroshima and Nagasaki.

Hiroshima was bombed on August 6, and Nagasaki on August 9. These two cities were active working parts of the Japanese war effort. One was an army center; the other was naval and industrial. Hiroshima was the headquarters of the Japanese Army defending southern Japan and was a major military storage and assembly point. Nagasaki was a major seaport and it contained several large industrial plants of great wartime importance. We believed that our attacks had struck cities which must certainly be important to the Japanese military leaders, both Army and Navy, and we waited for a result. We waited one day.

Many accounts have been written about the Japanese surrender. After a prolonged Japanese cabinet session in which the deadlock was broken by the Emperor himself, the offer to surrender was made on August 10. It was based on the Potsdam terms, with a reservation concerning the sovereignty of the Emperor. While the Allied reply made no promises other than those already given, it implicity recognized the Emperor's position by prescribing that his power must be subject to the orders of the Allied Supreme Commander. These terms were accepted on August 14 by the Japanese, and the instrument of surrender was formally signed on September 2, in Tokyo Bay. Our great objective was thus achieved, and all the evidence I have seen indicates that the controlling factor in the final Japanese decision to accept our terms of surrender was the atomic bomb.*

The two atomic bombs which we had dropped were the only ones we had ready, and our rate of production at the time was very small. Had the war continued until the projected invasion on November 1, additional fire raids of B-29's would have been more destructive of life and property than the very limited number of atomic raids which we could have executed in the same period. But the atomic bomb was more than a weapon of terrible destruction; it was a psychological weapon. In March 1945 our Air Force had launched its first great incendiary raid on the Tokyo area. In this raid more damage was done and more casualties were inflicted than was the case at Hiroshima. Hundreds of bombers took part and hundreds of tons of incendiaries

* Report of United States Strategic Bombing Survey, "Japan's Struggle to End the War"; "If the Atomic Bomb Had Not Been Used," by K. T. Compton, *Atlantic Monthly*, December 1946; unpublished material of historical division, War Department Special Staff, June 1946.

were dropped. Similar successive raids burned out a great part of the urban area of Japan, but the Japanese fought on. On August 6 one B-29 dropped a single atomic bomb on Hiroshima. Three days later a second bomb was dropped on Nagasaki and the war was over. So far as the Japanese could know, our ability to execute atomic attacks, if necessary by many planes at a time, was unlimited. As Dr. Karl Compton has said, "it was not one atomic bomb, or two, which brought surrender; it was the experience of what an atomic bomb will actually do to a community, *plus the dread of many more*, that was effective."

The bomb thus served exactly the purpose we intended. The peace party was able to take the path of surrender, and the whole weight of the Emperor's prestige was exerted in favor of peace. When the Emperor ordered surrender, and the small but dangerous group of fanatics who opposed him were brought under control, the Japanese became so subdued that the great undertaking of occupation and disarmament was completed with unprecedented ease.

TRUMAN'S ANNOUNCEMENT ON HIROSHIMA

20 ◂§ SECRETARY OF STATE James F. Byrnes "was most anxious to get the Japanese affair over with before the Russians got in," James Forrestal, secretary of the Navy, confided to his diary on July 28, 1945. Byrnes, according to Forrestal, was worried that the Russians would move into Dairen and Port Arthur. "Once in there, he felt, it would not be easy to get them out." Answering questions in 1960, Byrnes acknowledged that he had been eager to end the war in the Pacific before the Russians became too deeply involved. If Byrnes believed that an atomic attack in Japan in August would thwart all Russian designs in the Far East, events proved him mistaken. On August 8, 1945, three days after the United States dropped the atomic bomb on Hiroshima, Russia entered the war. On August 9 the United States dropped a second bomb, this one on Nagasaki. A third bomb would have been ready by August 17 or 18, but the Japanese started negotiations for peace and surrendered on August 14, 1945. On August 6 President Truman issued the following statement:[19]

Sixteen hours ago an American airplane dropped one bomb on Hiroshima, an important Japanese Army base. That bomb had more

[19] Excerpts reprinted from *Potsdam Papers*, II, 1376-8.

power than 20,000 tons of T.N.T. It had more than two thousand times the blast power of the British "Grand Slam" which is the largest bomb ever yet used in the history of warfare.

The Japanese began the war from the air at Pearl Harbor. They have been repaid many fold. And the end is not yet. With this bomb we have now added a new and revolutionary increase in destruction to supplement the growing power of our armed forces. In their present form these bombs are now in production and even more powerful forms are in development.

It is an atomic bomb. It is a harnessing of the basic power of the universe. The force from which the sun draws its power has been loosed against those who brought war to the Far East. . . .

We are now prepared to obliterate more rapidly and completely every productive enterprise the Japanese have above ground in any city. We shall destroy their docks, their factories, and their communications. Let there be no mistake; we shall completely destroy Japan's power to make war.

It was to spare the Japanese people from utter destruction that the ultimatum of July 26 was issued at Potsdam. Their leaders promptly rejected that ultimatum. If they do not now accept our terms they may expect a rain of ruin from the air, the like of which has never been seen on this earth. Behind this air attack will follow sea and land forces in such numbers and power as they have not yet seen and with the fighting skill of which they are already well aware.

U.S. WARNING TO JAPAN

21 ◄§ ON AUGUST 9, 1945, the day the United States dropped an atomic bomb on Nagasaki, President Truman threatened Japan with continued destruction until it surrendered:[20]

The British, Chinese, and United States Governments have given the Japanese people adequate warning of what is in store for them. We have laid down the general terms on which they can surrender. Our warning went unheeded; our terms were rejected. Since then the Japanese have seen what our atomic bomb can do. They can foresee what it will do in the future.

The world will note that the first atomic bomb was dropped on Hiroshima, a military base. That was because we wished in this first attack to avoid, insofar as possible, the killing of civilians. But that

[20] Excerpt reprinted from *Public Papers of the Presidents, Harry S. Truman, 1945* (Washington, D.C., 1960), p. 212; hereafter cited as *Truman Papers.*

attack is only a warning of things to come. If Japan does not surrender, bombs will have to be dropped on her war industries and, unfortunately, thousands of civilian lives will be lost. I urge Japanese civilians to leave industrial cities immediately, and save themselves from destruction.

I realize the tragic significance of the atomic bomb.

Its production and its use were not lightly undertaken by this Government. But we knew that our enemies were on the search for it. We know now how close they were to finding it. And we knew the disaster which would come to this Nation, and to all peace loving nations, to all civilization, if they had found it first.

That is why we felt compelled to undertake the long and uncertain and costly labor of discovery and production.

We won the race of discovery against the Germans.

Having found the bomb we have used it. We have used it against those who attacked us without warning at Pearl Harbor, against those who have starved and beaten and executed American prisoners of war, against those who have abandoned all pretense of obeying international laws of warfare. We have used it in order to shorten the agony of war, in order to save the lives of thousands and thousands of young Americans.

We shall continue to use it until we completely destroy Japan's power to make war. Only a Japanese surrender will stop us.

STRATEGIC BOMBING SURVEY

22 ◁§   FOLLOWING THE SURRENDER, the Strategic Bombing Survey,
         a group of experts, studied the Japanese situation of early
August and judged the impact of the atomic bombs. The conclusions of their survey follow:[21]

Japan's will to resist, the core target of our assault, was supported mainly by military potential, production potential, morale of the people, and such political considerations of the leadership as the preservation of the Tenno system, etc. So long as these factors supported resistance they operated, of course, as impediments to surrender. Thus affecting the determination of Japan's leaders to continue the war was not alone the actual loss of an air force capable of defending the home islands, but the loss of hope that this air force could be replaced, let alone enlarged. It was not necessary for us to

[21] Excerpts reprinted from United States Strategic Bombing Survey, *Japan's Struggle to End the War* (Washington, D.C., 1946), pp. 10–13.

burn every city, to destroy every factory, to shoot down every airplane or sink every ship, and starve the people. It was enough to demonstrate that we were capable of doing all this—that we had the power and the intention of continuing to the end. In this fashion, those responsible for the decision to surrender felt the twin-impact of our attack which made them not only impotent to resist, but also destroyed any hope of future resistance.

The will of the political leaders to resist collapsed well before the will of the people as a whole. The leaders were, however, unwilling to move too far in advance of public opinion. At the time of surrender, even though there was little pressure toward surrender from the people, their confidence in victory had been thoroughly undermined and they accepted the Imperial rescript, perhaps with surprise, but not with active resistance as some of the leaders had feared.

One further point should be developed and stressed here. The political objective which existed in Japan lay exposed and vulnerable to air attack, which fact goes far toward explaining the true basis for unconditional surrender without invasion of the home islands. That vulnerability to air attack derived in part from the basic character of the war in its decisive phases. It turned out to be essentially a war to win air control over the Japanese homeland. This concept was not merely central to much of the strategy guiding our operations, but was thoroughly understood and feared by an effective sector of Japanese leaders who sought and achieved political power to terminate the war. By the summer and fall of 1944, and throughout the remainder of the war, the validity of their fear was being persuasively demonstrated by the application of our air power in its several roles. Loss of fleet and air forces, without which, as the leaders knew, no effective defense could be mounted, was almost entirely the result of air superiority. . . .

. . . Thus the Japanese leaders lost both power and hope of resistance as our air weapons exploited air control over the home islands. . . .

1. Blockade of Japan's sea communications exploited the basic vulnerability of an island enemy which, with inherently second-power resources, was struggling to enlarge its capabilities by milking the raw materials of a rich conquered area. . . .

. . . The special feeling of vulnerability to blockade, to which a dependent island people are ever subject, increased and dramatized, especially to the leaders, the hopelessness of their position and favored the growing conviction that the defeat was inevitable.

2. While the blockade was definitive in strangling Japan's war mobilization and production, it cannot be considered separately from the pressure of our concurrent military operations, with which it formed a shears that scissored Japan's military potential into an ineffectual remnant. . . .

3. Fear of home island bombing was persuasive to the political leaders even before its direct effects could be felt. News of the B-29 and its intended capabilities reached Japan in 1943. . . . After the Marianas were lost but before the first attacks were flown in November 1944, [General Hideki—Eds.] Tojo had been unseated and peacemakers introduced into the Government as prominent elements. The war economy had already passed its peak, fleet and air forces had been critically weakened, confidence of the "intelligentsia" in the Government and the military had been deflated, and confidence of the people in eventual victory was weakening. . . .

4. When Japan was defeated without invasion, a recurrent question arose as to what effect the threat of a home island invasion had had upon the surrender decision. It was contended that the threat of invasion, if not the actual operation, was a requirement to induce acceptance of the surrender terms. On this tangled issue the evidence and hindsight are clear. The fact is, of course, that Japan did surrender without invasion, and with its principal armies intact. Testimony before the Survey shows that the expected "violation of the sacred homeland" raised few fears which expedited the decision to surrender beforehand. . . . But in Japan's then depleted state, the diversion was not significant. The responsible leaders in power read correctly the true situation and embraced surrender well before invasion was expected. . . .

6. The Hiroshima and Nagasaki atomic bombs did not defeat Japan, nor by the testimony of the enemy leaders who ended the war did they persuade Japan to accept unconditional surrender. The Emperor, the Lord Privy Seal, the Prime Minister, the Foreign Minister, and the Navy Minister had decided as early as May of 1945 that the war should be ended even if it meant acceptance of defeat on allied terms. The War Minister and the two chiefs of staff opposed unconditional surrender. The impact of the Hiroshima attack was to bring further urgency and lubrication to the machinery of achieving peace, primarily by contributing to a situation which permitted the Prime Minister to bring the Emperor overtly and directly into a position where his decision for immediate acceptance of the Potsdam

Declaration could be used to override the remaining objectors. Thus, although the atomic bombs changed no votes of the Supreme War Direction Council concerning the Potsdam terms, they did foreshorten the war and expedite the peace.

Events and testimony which support these conclusions are blue-printed from the chronology established in the first sections of this report:

(a) The mission of the Suzuki government, appointed 7 April 1945, was to make peace. An appearance of negotiating for terms less onerous than unconditional surrender was maintained in order to contain the military and bureaucratic elements still determined on a final Bushido [code of chivalry in feudal Japan—Eds.] defense, and perhaps even more importantly to obtain freedom to create peace with a minimum of personal danger and internal obstruction. It seems clear however that in extremis the peacemakers would have peace, and peace on any terms. This was the gist of advice given to [Emperor —Eds.] Hirohito by the Jushin [senior statesmen—Eds.] in February, the declared conclusion of Kido in April, the underlying reason for Koiso's fall in April, the specific injunction of the Emperor to Suzuki on becoming premier which was known to all members of his cabinet.

(b) A series of conferences of the Supreme War Direction Council before Hirohito on the subject of continuing or terminating the war began on 8 June and continued through 14 August. At the 8 June meeting the war situation was reviewed. On 20 June the Emperor, supported by the Premier, Foreign Minister, and Navy Minister, declared for peace; the Army Minister and the two Chiefs of Staff did not concur. On 10 July the Emperor again urged haste in the moves to mediate through Russia, but Potsdam intervened. While the Government still awaited a Russian answer, the Hiroshima bomb was dropped on 6 August.

(c) Consideration of the Potsdam terms within the Supreme War Direction Council revealed the same three-to-three cleavage which first appeared at the Imperial conference on 20 June. On the morning of 9 August Premier Suzuki and Hirohito decided at once to accept the Potsdam terms; meetings and moves thereafter were designed to legalize the decision and prepare the Imperial rescript. At the con-clusive Imperial conference, on the night of 9–10 August, the Supreme War Direction Council still split three-to-three. It was necessary for the Emperor finally to repeat his desire for acceptance of the Potsdam terms.

(d) Indubitably the Hiroshima bomb and the rumor derived from interrogation of an American prisoner (B-29 pilot) who stated that an atom bomb attack on Tokyo was scheduled for 12 August introduced urgency in the minds of the Government and magnified the pressure behind its moves to end the war.

7. The sequence of events just recited also defines the effect of Russia's entry into the Pacific war on 8 August 1945. Coming 2 days after the Hiroshima bomb, the move neither defeated Japan nor materially hastened the acceptance of surrender nor changed the votes of the Supreme War Direction Council. Negotiation for Russia to intercede began the forepart of May 1945 in both Tokyo and Moscow. Konoye, the intended emissary to the Soviets, stated to the Survey that while ostensibly he was to negotiate, he received direct and secret instructions from the Emperor to secure peace at any price, notwithstanding its severity. Sakomizu, the chief cabinet secretary, alleged that while awaiting the Russian answer on mediation, Suzuki and Togo decided that were it negative direct overtures would be made to the United States. Efforts toward peace through the Russians, forestalled by the imminent departure of Stalin and Molotov for Potsdam, were answered by the Red Army's advance into Manchuria. The Kwantung army, already weakened by diversion of its units and logistics to bolster island defenses in the South and written off for the defense of Japan proper, faced inescapable defeat.

There is little point in attempting more precisely to impute Japan's unconditional surrender to any one of the numerous causes which jointly and cumulatively were responsible for Japan's disaster. Concerning the absoluteness of her defeat there can be no doubt. The time lapse between military impotence and political acceptance of the inevitable might have been shorter had the political structure of Japan permitted a more rapid and decisive determination of national policies. It seems clear, however, that air supremacy and its later exploitation over Japan proper was the major factor which determined the timing of Japan's surrender and obviated any need for invasion.

Based on a detailed investigation of all the facts and supported by the testimony of the surviving Japanese leaders involved, it is the Survey's opinion that certainly prior to 31 December 1945, and in all probability prior to 1 November 1945, Japan would have surrendered even if the atomic bombs had not been dropped, even if Russia had not entered the war, and even if no invasion had been planned or contemplated.

2 · Inflation and Politics,
1945-1946

*I*n November 1946 the voters turned against the Democratic party and elected the first Republican Congress in eighteen years. The destruction of the Roosevelt coalition, which made possible the Republican victory, was partly the result of the politics of inflation. Hoping to restrain the upward push of prices and wages, the Truman administration could not bestow the favors necessary to keep the interest groups loyal to the Democratic party, and in fact was forced to oppose the rising aspirations of Roosevelt's old supporters. Labor, mainstay of the New Deal coalition, was irritated by continued wage controls, and in the spring of 1946 turned bitterly against the President when he threatened to draft strikers. Farmers had been drifting away from the Democrats since 1937, but the efforts of the Office of Price Administration (OPA) to keep down farm prices hastened the mass exodus from the party in 1946. Ironically Truman also lost the support of the minority of liberal farmers (whose spokesman was the National Farmers Union) partly because he failed to give the OPA full support. When cattle growers declared a meat strike in the autumn of 1946 to kill price control, a meat famine developed in the cities, and the urban masses, blaming the Democrats for the shortage of pork and beef, also deserted in large numbers to the Republicans.

As the administration's response to the problem of inflation grew more hesitant and confused, the liberal intellectuals who had followed Roosevelt grew ever more alienated and began to cast about for a new leader. By the end of 1946 the administration's economic troubles at home had multiplied so alarmingly and its successes were so few that the favorite quip of the day became, "To err is Truman."

EMPLOYMENT ACT OF 1946

1 ⧫ THE INTELLECTUAL ORIGINS of the Employment Act of 1946 can easily be traced to the economic theories of John Maynard Keynes and the famed Beveridge Plan in Britain. Using the World War II economy as their example, economists tried to show that federal fiscal policy could avoid the familiar and painful "boom-and-bust" cycle. The theory that government action could promote full employment finally won Roosevelt's support, and the measure became a prominent plank in the 1944 platform. President Truman formally gave the proposal his blessing in 1945. That year Senator James Murray, a Democrat of Montana, and Senator Robert Wagner, a well-known New Dealer from New York, joined by many cosponsors, introduced the original measure, called the Full Employment Act. It asserted the federal government's responsibility "to provide Federal investment . . . to assure continuing full employment."

Despite Truman's open endorsement, the bill received wavering support from the administration. Economic conservatives, though subscribing to the goal of economic stability, amended the measure to make it more palatable to proponents of laissez faire. The final result, which some original sponsors rejected, was a weak version of the initial proposal. Signed into law on February 20, 1946, it directed the President to appoint a three-member Council of Economic Advisers "to analyze and interpret economic developments"; required him to present an economic report to Congress; and provided for a Joint Congressional Committee on the Economic Report. The heart of the measure is Section 2:[1]

The Congress hereby declares that it is the continuing policy and responsibility of the Federal Government to use all practicable means consistent with its needs and obligations and other essential considerations of national policy, with the assistance and cooperation of industry, agriculture, labor, and State and local governments, to coordinate and utilize all its plans, functions, and resources for the purpose of creating and maintaining, in a manner calculated to foster and promote free competitive enterprise and the general welfare, conditions under which there will be afforded useful employment

[1] Reprinted from *United States Statutes at Large*, 1946, Vol. LX, Part I, pp. 23–6.

opportunities, including self-employment, for those able, willing, and seeking to work, and to promote maximum employment, production, and purchasing power.

TRUMAN'S REVISION OF PRICE-WAGE RULES

2 ✦§ TWO DAYS after the surrender of Japan President Truman began revising the wartime stabilization program. On August 18 he issued Executive Order 9599, which modified wartime controls over prices, wages, and materials. His August 16 statement, which was designed to ensure industrial peace, quickly created problems that the President had not foreseen. Parts of the statement follow:[2]

Our national welfare requires that during the reconversion period production of civilian goods and services go forward without interruption, and that labor and industry cooperate to keep strikes and lockouts at a minimum. We must work out means for the peaceful settlement of disputes that might adversely affect the transition to a peacetime economy. . . .

1. In the near future I shall call a conference of representatives of organized labor and industry, for the purpose of working out by agreement means to minimize the interruption of production by labor disputes in the reconversion period.

2. Pending the completion of the conference and until some new plan is worked out and made effective, disputes which cannot be settled by collective bargaining and conciliation, including disputes which threaten a substantial interference with the transition to a peacetime economy, should be handled by the War Labor Board under existing procedures. For that interim period I call upon the representatives of organized labor and industry to renew their no-strike and no-lockout pledges, and I shall expect both industry and labor in that period to continue to comply voluntarily, as they have in the past, with the directive orders of the War Labor Board.

3. The Stabilization Act is effective until June 30, 1946. During its continuance wage adjustments which might affect prices must continue to be subject to stabilization controls. With the ending of war production, however, there is no longer any threat of an inflationary bidding up of wage rates by competition in a short labor market. I am therefore authorizing the War Labor Board to release proposed vol-

---

[2] Reprinted from *Truman Papers, 1946* (Washington, D.C., 1961), pp. 220-2.

untary wage increases from the necessity of approval upon condition that they will not be used in whole or in part as the basis for seeking an increase in price ceilings. Proposed wage increases requiring price relief must continue to be passed upon by the Board.

TREASURY SECRETARY VINSON'S ECONOMIC ANALYSIS

3 ⮜⮞ MOST ECONOMISTS had predicted a serious depression after the war's end. Unless the government compensated for the anticipated decline in private spending, they forecast between 8 and 10 million unemployed. But the depression did not come.

In the months following V-J Day, economists in and out of government slowly became uncertain about whether the future would bring inflation or depression. If inflation were to appear, then the government's wartime tax structure might perform a peacetime function by absorbing some of the excess money supply. But in early September 1945, when depression was still feared, President Truman proposed tax reductions, and in November an enthusiastic Congress responded by slashing taxes $5.9 billion. Congress repealed the excess-profits levy and granted other relief to corporations and individuals. On October 1, 1945, while the tax bill was still before the House Ways and Means Committee, Secretary of the Treasury Fred M. Vinson presented the administration's views and voiced the uncertainty that made the task of policy formulation so difficult. Excerpts from Secretary Vinson's testimony follow:[3]

During the coming year we shall find ourselves in a somewhat paradoxical situation. The rate of government expenditures—and particularly those expenditures which find their way currently into the pockets of consumers—will be declining rapidly. Millions of workers will be laid off and forced to seek new jobs. As the labor market loosens, the workers' total income will decline. Overtime pay will rapidly diminish. Many workers who have been promoted to well-paid classifications will find themselves reclassified into less remunerative jobs. Workers, in many instances, will have to move long distances in search of new jobs. In many States, unemployment compensation, under existing legislation, will not prove adequate to sustain mass purchasing power.

All these are deflationary factors. They do not result, however, from

[3] Excerpts reprinted from *Annual Report of the Secretary of the Treasury on the State of the Finance*, 1946 (Washington, D.C., 1946), pp. 326–32.

any fundamental deflationary situation—that is to say, they do not result from a deficiency of total purchasing power in the hands of individual consumers and business investors. On the contrary, both business and consumers have more money in reserve than at any time in our history. Rather, such deflationary dangers as we face are the byproducts—many of them inevitable byproducts—of a titanic physical change-over from war production to peace production.

In other words, we should have adequate demand if we were able to mobilize our physical resources quickly enough to satisfy it. Therefore, one of the primary objectives of our fiscal policy must be to encourage the boldest, the quickest and most venturesome expansion of peacetime enterprise by business investors.

So long as we remain in this period of physical transition, we shall continue to be faced with inflationary pressures. There is an enormous pent-up demand, particularly for capital and consumers' durable goods. The budgetary deficit will be large. Accumulated individual and corporate savings are enormous. We are starved for new houses, new cars, new radios, and the like.

We must, therefore, at present keep up our guards against inflation, not only through price and other direct controls, but through taxation. It would be pathetic if, after besting the enemy of inflation all through the war, we allowed it to overtake us on the homestretch. In other words, I am convinced that, in considering how much room there is for tax reduction your Committee will be well advised to keep a weather eye to the storm signals of inflation.

At the same time, we cannot overlook the deflationary dangers to which I have already alluded. If the physical change-over of our economy is delayed or hampered, by fiscal or other impediments, the temporary phenomena of deflation may take on a more permanent and inflexible character. If business lacks confidence in the future, enterprise will be timid. If workers and consumers lack confidence, they will contract their purchases and hoard their savings. In either of these events, the prompt expansion of our peacetime economy will be endangered. . . .

Hence after considering all factors, economic and budgetary, it is my considered judgment that total reductions should not exceed $5,000 million for 1946.

This is a time when rapid reconversion and business expansion are of the utmost importance to the maintenance of a high level of employment and income. Tax reduction for 1946 should be designed to afford the maximum aid and stimulus to reconversion and expansion that is compatible with our revenue needs. Therefore, I suggest that the Committee should view the primary function of this bill to be the removal from the tax law of serious impediments which it may present to the swift transition from a war economy to a prosperous peacetime era for which we are preparing. If, as I believe, we can do this without an unwarranted sacrifice in revenues, then the present problem will be successfully met.

In this connection, I wish to discuss with you the excess profits tax because I consider it to be in a class by itself in its relation to postwar business expansion. . . .

Despite its importance as a source of revenue, the excess profits tax was not imposed merely as a revenue measure and has never been viewed primarily as such. The primary purpose of the tax has been to prevent war profiteering. Although it has not altogether succeeded in that purpose, there can be no doubt of its great value in recapturing war profits.

The excess profits tax has been a control measure, one of a large group of control measures which were absolutely necessary to the effective conduct of the war and to the maintenance of economic stability and a fair distribution of the sacrifices of war. It is the fixed policy of this Administration that every war control over American business and American life shall be dropped as soon as conditions make it possible to do so. . . .

The case against the excess profits tax for 1946 goes beyond the fact that it is primarily a wartime control. It is also an obstacle to that reconversion and expansion of business, which are so necessary for a high level of employment and income. The testimony of businessmen is that they are unable to take the risk of full peacetime business expansion until this tax has been removed. Their attitude is not difficult to understand when we re-examine the nature of the excess profits tax and observe the erratic character of its measurement of excessive profits. . . .

Let us never forget the human side of the taxation problem. No system of taxation is an inanimate thing. Directly or indirectly, it inevitably touches the pocketbooks and influences the lives of every man, woman, and child in our country.

In this connection I urge that in distributing the limited amount of tax reduction now possible, you give full consideration to relieving the direct pressure of wartime taxes upon lower income groups.

Whatever relief can be given in reducing personal income taxes will be most beneficial, in sustaining mass purchasing power, when given to the individuals and families to whom a dollar means most. And beyond this economic argument is the overpowering logic of equity.

I direct your particular attention to the so-called normal individual income tax. This tax is normal in name only. . . .

. . . For example, in the case of a married taxpayer with two dependent children, receiving $3,000 of net income before personal exemption, the repeal of the normal tax would reduce his tax from $275 to $200, a reduction of $75. This is very substantial relief and goes to the kinds of taxpayers needing it the most. I recommend that you repeal this special wartime normal tax levy as of January 1, 1946. The revenue loss from repeal is estimated at $2,085 million.

Additional relief to individuals which would be particularly helpful to the lower and middle income groups can be given also by setting an effective date for the excise tax reductions now provided in the law. The industries involved in the excise taxes have pointed out the disadvantages arising from uncertainty in the effective date for these automatic reductions. I recommend that the effective date for the reductions be made July 1, 1946, which is at the end of the fiscal year. This would result in a reduction of excise tax liabilities for the calendar year 1946 estimated at $547 million.

TRUMAN'S WAGE-PRICE PROGRAM

4 &3 AS COLLECTIVE BARGAINING began to break down under the administration's first wage-price program, the government moved hastily to revise the stabilization framework. On October 30 President Truman explained a new policy to the American people:[4]

On August 18, 1945, four days after the surrender of Japan, I issued Executive Order 9599 which laid down the guiding policies of your Government during the transition from war to peace.

Briefly stated these policies are:

First, to assist in the maximum production of civilian goods.

Second, as rapidly as possible to remove Government controls and restore collective bargaining and free markets.

Third, to avoid both inflation and deflation.

Those are still our policies.

[4] Excerpts reprinted from *Truman Papers*, 1945, pp. 439–49.

One of the major factors determining whether or not we shall succeed in carrying out those policies is the question of wages and prices. If wages go down substantially, we face deflation. If prices go up substantially, we face inflation. We must be on our guard, and steer clear of both these dangers to our security.

What happens to wages is important to all of us—even to those of us who do not work for wages.

It is important to business, for example, not only because wages represent an essential item in the cost of producing goods, but because people cannot buy the products of industry unless they earn enough wages generally.

What happens to wages is also important to the farmer. The income he earns depends a great deal on the wages and purchasing power of the workers in our factories and shops and stores. They are the customers of the farmer and cannot buy farm products unless they earn enough wages.

The fact is that all of us are deeply concerned with wages, because all of us are concerned with the well-being of all parts of our economic system.

That is a simple truth. But like all simple truths, it is too often forgotten. Management sometimes forgets that business cannot prosper without customers who make good wages and have money in their pockets; labor sometimes forgets that workers cannot find employment and that wages cannot rise unless business prospers and makes profits.

Like most of you, I have been disturbed by the labor difficulties of recent weeks. These difficulties stand in the way of reconversion; they postpone the day when our veterans and displaced war workers can get back into good peacetime jobs. We need more of the good sense, the reasonableness, the consideration for the position of the other fellow, the teamwork which we had during the war. . . .

You do know that sudden total victory caused millions of war workers to be laid off with very short notice or none at all. While we hope to overcome that condition before too many months have passed, unemployment is hardly a suitable reward for the contribution which veterans and war workers have made to victory.

Several months ago, I urged the Congress to amend the unemployment compensation law so as to help workers through the difficult months of unemployment until reconversion could be effected. The Congress has not yet passed that legislation.

The responsibility for that is solely up to Congress—and specifically

I mean the Ways and Means Committee of the House of Representatives. I hope that this Committee will fulfill its obligation to the people of the Nation, and will give the Members of the House an early chance to vote on this important legislation. We must all recognize that legislation which will help sustain the purchasing power of labor until reconversion is completed, benefits not labor alone but all of us—business, agriculture, white-collar workers, and every member of our economic society. . . .

But quite as important as these problems of unemployment is the fact that the end of the war has meant a deep cut in the pay envelopes of many millions of workers. I wonder how many of you know that many war workers have already had to take, or will soon have to take, a cut in their wartime pay by one quarter or more. Think of what such a decrease in your own income would mean to you and to your families. . . .

It has been estimated that, unless checked, the annual wage and salary bill in private industry will shrink by over twenty billions of dollars. That is not going to do anybody any good—labor, business, agriculture, or the general public.

It is a sure road to wide unemployment.

This is what is known as deflation, and it is just as dangerous as inflation.

However, we must understand that we cannot hope, with a reduced work week, to maintain now the same take-home pay for labor generally that it has had during the war. There will have to be a drop. But the Nation cannot afford to have that drop too drastic.

Wage increases are therefore imperative—to cushion the shock to our workers, to sustain adequate purchasing power and to raise the national income.

There are many people who have said to me that industry cannot afford to grant any wage increases, however, without obtaining a corresponding increase in the price of its products. And they have urged me to use the machinery of Government to raise both.

This proposal cannot be accepted under any circumstances. To accept it would mean but one thing—inflation. And that invites disaster. An increase in wages if it were accompanied by an increase in the cost of living would not help even the workers themselves. Every dollar that we put in their pay envelopes under those circumstances would be needed to meet the higher living expenses resulting from increased prices.

Obviously, such a juggling of wages and prices would not settle anything or satisfy anyone. . . . runaway inflation would be upon us. . . .

If these twin objectives of ours—stability of prices and higher wage rates—were irreconcilable, if one could not be achieved without sacrificing the other, the outlook for all of us—labor, management, the farmer, and the consumer—would be very black indeed.

Fortunately, this is not so. While the positions of different industries vary greatly, there is room in the existing price structure for business as a whole to grant increases in wage rates. . . .

Let me now turn to the question of just how wages are to be increased. Many people have asked the Government to step in and decide who is to increase wages and by exactly how much. I have, indeed, been criticised because I have not stepped in to lay down the law to business and labor. My refusal to do so has been deliberate.

I am convinced that we must get away as quickly as possible from Government controls, and that we must get back to the free operation of our competitive system. Where wages are concerned, this means that we must get back to free and fair collective bargaining.

As a free people, we must have the good sense to bargain peaceably and sincerely. We must be determined to reach decisions based upon our long-range interest.

Let me emphasize, however, that the decisions that are reached in collective bargaining must be kept within the limits laid down by the wage-price policy of the Government. . . .

This policy was described in the order of last August which I have already mentioned.

Briefly, it allows management to make wage increases without Government approval, but requires Government approval before the wage increase can be reflected in higher price ceilings. That is still the policy of the United States.

To guide labor and management in their interpretation of this Executive order, I have today issued an amendment—which I hope every one of you will read carefully in your newspapers tomorrow—amplifying the order and setting forth three classes of cases in which wage increases may be granted even though price ceiling increases may result.

They are all situations where wage increases are necessary, irrespective of price consequences. They will not cause many price increases.

In addition, the amendment makes two points of importance which I wish to emphasize here.

The first point has been true all along, but it has not been generally understood. If management does grant a wage increase, it is not prevented from coming in thereafter and requesting Government approval to have the wage increase considered for purposes of increasing prices. Whether such approval is sought before or after the wage increase is given, it receives the same consideration. . . .

The second point is new and is very important. It is something which I am sure will help industry get over this very difficult period of readjustment. In cases where no approval of the wage increase has been requested by management, or even where a request has been made and denied by the Government, industry will not be asked by the Government to take an unreasonable chance in absorbing such wage increases. After a reasonable test period which, save in exceptional cases, will be six months, if the industry has been unable to produce at a fair profit, the entire wage increase will be taken into account in passing upon applications for price ceiling increases.

The Office of Price Administration will have to give its prompt consideration to all applications for price increases.

This is your Government's wage-price policy. For the time being, the machinery that administers it will remain the same as during the war.

But, as you know, I have called a conference here in Washington of the representatives of management and labor. It will start next week. One of their jobs is to recommend machinery for mediating or arbitrating differences wherever collective bargaining fails to work.

GENERAL MOTORS' OBJECTIONS TO FACT-FINDING BOARDS

5 ◄৪৳ THE GOVERNMENT, desperately seeking to restore healthy collective bargaining, had called a labor-management conference for early November. After a few weeks the delegates departed without any solution to the short-run problems posed by postwar adjustment. While the conference was still in session the United Automobile Workers (UAW-CIO) called for a strike against General Motors for November 21, 1945. Walter Reuther, the intelligent and bold leader of the union's GM division, wanted a 30-percent increase in wages—from $1.12 to $1.46 an hour— without any price rise. When the company balked, the workers walked out. To prevent strikes, Truman had asked Congress on December 3 to enact a law (like the Railway Labor Act of 1916) to authorize him to appoint fact-finding boards in labor-manage-

Instrument of Surrender

of

All German armed forces in HOLLAND, in

northwest Germany including all islands,

and in DENMARK.

1. The German Command agrees to the surrender of all German armed
forces in HOLLAND, in northwest Germany including the FRISIAN
ISLANDS and HELIGOLAND and all other islands, in SCHLESWIG-
HOLSTEIN, and in DENMARK, to the C.-in-C. 21 Army Group.
This to include all naval ships in these areas.
These forces to lay down their arms and to surrender unconditionally.

2. All hostilities on land, on sea, or in the air by German forces
in the above areas to cease at 0800 hrs. British Double Summer Time
on Saturday 5 May 1945.

3. The German command to carry out at once, and without argument or
comment, all further orders that will be issued by the Allied
Powers on any subject.

4. Disobedience of orders, or failure to comply with them, will be
regarded as a breach of these surrender terms and will be dealt
with by the Allied Powers in accordance with the accepted laws
and usages of war.

5. This instrument of surrender is independent of, without prejudice
to, and will be superseded by any general instrument of surrender
imposed by or on behalf of the Allied Powers and applicable to Germany
and the German armed forces as a whole.

6. This instrument of surrender is written in English and in German.

The English version is the authentic text.

7. The decision of the Allied Powers will be final if any doubt or
dispute arises as to the meaning or interpretation of the surrender
terms.

B. L. Montgomery
Field-Marshal

4 May 1945
1830 hrs.

One of the first German documents of surrender, May 4, 1945 (*UPI*)

Site of first A-bomb test, Alamogordo, N. Mex.; J. Robert Oppenheimer (*left*), director of Los Alamos A-bomb laboratory, and Major General Leslie R. Groves, head of Manhattan District, Sept. 11, 1945 (*UPI*)

Truman and Secretary of War Henry L. Stimson, Aug. 8, 1945 (*UPI*)

Signing of UN Charter, San Francisco, June 6, 1945; *left to right*: Truman, U.S. representative Edward R. Stettinius, Jr., U.S. delegate Harold E. Stassen (*Truman Library*)

Churchill, Truman, and Stalin, Potsdam, July 31, 1945 (*Wide World*)

Signing of cease-fire, Chinese civil war, Chungking, Feb. 1, 1946; *left to right:* General Chou En-lai, Governor Chan Chun, General George C. Marshall (*Wide World*)

Andrei Gromyko (*left*), Soviet delegate to UN, and Bernard M. Baruch, U.S. delegate to UN Atomic Energy Commission, New York City, May 24, 1946 (*UPI*)

Soviet Foreign Minister Vyacheslav Molotov (*left*) and Secretary of State James F. Byrnes, Council of Foreign Ministers, Paris, May 13, 1946 (*UPI*)

Churchill's "iron curtain" speech, Westminster College, Fulton, Mo., March 5, 1946 (*UPI*)

Secretary of State Marshall before delivering Marshall Plan speech at Harvard University commencement, June 5, 1947 (*UPI*)

Senate Foreign Relations Committee hearings on Truman Doctrine, March 24, 1947; Arthur H. Vandenberg (*left*), chairman, and Acting Secretary of State Dean Acheson (*UPI*)

Left to right: Truman; Under Secretary of State Robert A. Lovett; George F. Kennan, director of State Department's Policy Planning Staff; Charles E. Bohlen, special assistant to Secretary Marshall, Nov. 13, 1947 (*UPI*)

Warren R. Austin, U.S. delegate, informing UN Security Council of U.S. plans to send troops to Korea, June 30, 1950 (UPI)

General Douglas MacArthur, after ouster by Truman, before defending his Far East policy at joint session of Congress, April 19, 1951; at rear, Vice President Alben W. Barkley (*left*) and House Speaker Sam Rayburn (*UPI*)

ment disputes and to bar walkouts during the panel's investigation. Labor protested the threatened infringement of its right to strike, and Congress blocked the President's request. However, Truman appointed his own fact-finding groups for the major strikes. At first he did not spell out their functions. But the GM-union conflict over "ability to pay" soon compelled the President to become specific. When he decided that the question of "ability to pay" was within the domain of his panel to investigate, the company withdrew from fact-finding sessions. On December 29 Alfred P. Sloan, Jr., chairman of the GM board, and Charles Erwin Wilson, president of the firm, explained their objections to the President's decision:[5]

Is American business in the future as in the past to be conducted as a competitive system? Or is the determination of the essential economic factors such as costs, prices, profits, etc., upon which business success and progress depend, to be made politically by some governmental agency instead of by the management appointed by the owners of the business for that purpose?

America is at the crossroads. It must preserve the freedom of each unit of American business to determine its own destinies. Or it must transfer to some governmental bureaucracy or agency, or to a union, the responsibility of management that has been the very keystone of American business. Shall this responsibility be surrendered? That is the decision the American people face. America must choose!

General Motors has made its choice. It refuses to subscribe to what it believes will ultimately become, through the process of evolution, the death of the American system of competitive enterprise. It will not participate voluntarily in what stands out crystal clear as the end of the road—a regimented economy. If this is what the American people want, they must make that choice through their accredited representatives in Congress. General Motors declines for itself to take such a great responsibility.

It may be said that this is an exaggeration. It is not! All business questions are interrelated. Costs, prices, wages, profits, schedules, investments must be the responsibility of management. Political determination of such relationships means regimentation.

The idea of ability to pay, whatever its validity may be, is not

5 Excerpt reprinted from General Motors press release, December 29, 1945.

applicable to an individual business within an industry as a basis for raising its wages beyond the going rate.

REUTHER TO TRUMAN DURING UAW STRIKE

6 ◄ἐⳡ THOUGH REUTHER had formulated the program of a wage increase without a compensatory price increase when the stabilization program was encouraging such tactics, the union leader soon found that he was not receiving support from the White House. Feeling betrayed as the strike dragged on, Reuther telegraphed the President on February 2, 1946, and tried to enlist his support for the workers:[6]

Wages are no longer the major issue in the dispute which is holding up reconversion to civilian production and our progress toward the goals of full employment, full production and full consumption. The major issue now is prices.

The General Motors Corporation and other large corporations engaged in disputes with their employees are resigned to granting wage increases at least to the extent recommended by you and your fact-finding boards. Labor is ready to accept those recommendations as a down payment on what it is justly and equitably entitled to.

But industry, spearheaded by steel and the General Motors Corporation, is determined to hijack the American people and the American Government into accepting unjustified price increases that would provide the most outrageous profits in history.

Industry bases its holdup on the false pretext that higher prices are needed to pay the higher wage rates necessary to maintain take-home pay, sustain purchasing power during reconversion and provide a bridge to a peacetime economy of full consumption, full production and full employment.

The conspiracy of big business to wreck price control, to which GM is a party, is the reason that no progress has been made in negotiations to settle the General Motors strike. . . .

The American people are entitled to know all the facts with respect to current industrial pressure campaign to smash price control. We believe it is your duty, Mr. President, to inform them fully and frankly and in complete detail.

The overwhelming majority of the people of this country are determined to hold prices down. They favor retention of rigorous

[6] Excerpts reprinted from UAW-GM press release, February 2, 1946.

price controls until we are safely past the danger of inflation, and they favor increased purchasing power through the combination of increased wages and maintenance of price levels.

Now is the time for you to speak out and to call upon the American people to rally behind you in support of price control. Their response will be overwhelming. . . .

The fight of the General Motors workers is your fight and the fight of every American. It demands your immediate and militant support.

TAFT'S CRITICISM OF OPA

7 ◆§   THE GOVERNMENT'S chief weapon against a price inflation was the Office of Price Administration, which had successfully held the price line since 1943. After the end of the war the OPA came under growing attack from businessmen and conservatives in Congress. Senator Robert A. Taft, a leading Republican conservative, was an ardent critic of the price-control agency and its director, Chester Bowles. On November 6, 1945, speaking to a group of businessmen, he assailed the OPA:[7]

I believed in the principle of price control during time of war.

Any Government bureau is inclined to perpetuate itself. The OPA has released a few unimportant articles from price control such as sleigh bells in Hawaii, but it has made no important modifications as yet. Apparently, Mr. Bowles' view is that an article of any importance must return to normal conditions of demand and supply before price control is removed. In many fields such normal conditions may not be wholly restored for years. In others, supply can perhaps only be obtained by permitting the price to rise. I do not think the OPA can be trusted with the decision as to what articles must still be controlled after July 1, 1946.

My criticism of the OPA administration is of the methods it has pursued. I believe it has entirely departed from the original purpose of the Price Control Act and is gradually setting up a complete control of profits instead of prices. . . .

In order to maintain the fetish of a retail price freeze, the OPA has resorted to every possible device to make industry absorb increased costs. Its price fixing is based on the profits of the largest manufac-

---

[7] Excerpts reprinted from *Commercial and Financial Chronicle*, December 13, 1945.

turers so that many others are forced to sell at a loss. Special adjustments are then made for individual concerns. This means that each concern has a different price. This means that the OPA is fixing profits for each company and not fixing a general price level. The tighter the squeeze becomes, the closer the margin, the more we have profit control and not price control. . . .

Today we have an entirely different condition. The problem now is to get production and employment. If we can get production, prices will come down by themselves to the lowest point justified by increased costs. If we hold prices at a point where no one can make a profit, there will be no expansion of existing industry and no new industry in that field. We must adopt a policy which, while preventing the skyrocketing of prices, recognizes that some increase is necessary to bring about their ultimate production.

Unfortunately, President Truman has now endorsed the policy of the OPA of making industry absorb increased costs. He has advocated higher wages at the same time. . . .

. . . OPA admits . . . they are compelling many lines of commodities to be sold at a loss and that some industries are compelled by regulation to do business at cost. But the fetish of an absolutely frozen retail level has been maintained in the face of conditions which necessarily forced higher costs. . . .

In the third place, the whole attitude of the price administration is hypocritical. It pretends that it desires to make adjustments, but it does not intend to do so and seldom does. Applications for increases lie for months in the different sections of the OPA. They are granted by one section and refused by its superior. If one is finally granted it is probably half the increase justified by the evidence and often admitted to be fair by officials in the OPA itself. By that time costs have again increased. One Senator said that OPA has a defense in depth. Certainly, it has made it effective.

I do not mean to say that OPA rulings are always wrong or that the businessmen are always right, but I do say that the general policy of the OPA has been so tight as to squeeze many businesses, discourage production and reconversion and new projects and cause particular distress to the thousands of small industries which ought to be encouraged.

The executive order approved by the President on Oct. 30 is a snare and a delusion. It authorizes increases in wages, as if such increases had not been taking place ever since VJ-Day. It graciously permits an employer to grant an increase and then apply for an increase in prices which he can be sure he will not get. The Price Administrator cannot take the increase into account until after a test period of six months after the increase has been made. By the time the Price Administrator got around to granting an increase, if he ever did, there would be a full year of operation on increased wages and no increase in price.

Long before the increase is granted, I trust his office will be abolished.

LETTERS OF BOWLES TO TRUMAN

8 ⊷§   CHESTER BOWLES, the embattled chief of the OPA, struggled to secure firm support from the President. On December 17, 1945, he sent a letter to the President, outlining some of the difficulties he had encountered:[8]

In September I told you why I would like to be relieved of my present responsibilities by the first of the year. My desire for relief is even greater today. As you know, I have been carrying this difficult assignment for nearly thirty months. The pressures today are at their peak. Like many others I feel the need for a rest.

In addition to these rather personal reasons, I have been disturbed over my relationship, and the relationship of the Office of Price Administration, to John Snyder [director of the Office of War Mobilization and Reconversion] and some of his staff. While I like John personally and respect his sincerity, we often fail to see eye to eye on the most effective ways to meet the problems which we face.

Under the circumstances John might feel more comfortable to have a man in my position with whom he was in more fundamental agreement. . . .

While my own personal desires are clear, I can assure you I will not let this program down, if it is your sincere conviction that it is to your own interest and the interest of the Administration that I should stay on at least until the first of July. If this were the case, I would, however, want to make certain proposals which seem to me vitally important if my own effectiveness is to be maintained.

(1) I feel that it is a bad mistake from everyone's standpoint to leave me alone as almost the sole Administration spokesman for the

---

[8] Excerpts reprinted from letter of Bowles to Truman, December 17, 1945, Bowles Papers. Published by permission of Chester Bowles.

anti-inflation program. We will be faced from now on with an increasingly bitter fight on the part of reactionary groups, such as the National Association of Manufacturers, the National Retail Dry Goods Association, the National Association of Real Estate Boards, and others. While these people have been on the wrong side of every public issue for the last several years, they still carry a lot of influence in some quarters.

If the job is to be done successfully, it must be an all out fight by the Administration as a whole. It must be made clear to the country, as well as to myself, that the various department heads are solidly behind the Office of Price Administration, and that our fight is their fight.

As part of this program I would feel it most essential for you to make an emphatic statement in the immediate future that price and rent controls must be renewed after June 30 for one more year. If this statement is not forthcoming, there will be a rapidly growing belief, on the part of business, that it will pay to hold back production. This can only result in a slowing down in reconversion and cause unnecessary unemployment.

I feel that it should also be made clear to the leaders of Congress of the Administration's determination to see this issue through. My relationships with Sam Rayburn, John McCormack, and Alben Barkley have always been excellent.

My relationships with Senator McKellar, on the other hand, in spite of my very best efforts, have been consistently bad. In any case, it is a fact in recent months that on Capitol Hill we have been left alone to fight the entire battle as far as the Senate and House leaders are concerned, and with very few exceptions, as far as the Administration itself is concerned.

I think I am right in saying that no top Administration leader has defended the OPA anti-inflation program on the floor of either house since last June. This program is far too important for the country as a whole, as well as for the future strength of the Administration to leave its defense to one individual.

(2) Since I have been in Washington I have been handicapped by a feeling that the price administrator was not really a part of the Administration's policy-making "team."

While the head of every other major agency attends Cabinet Meetings, OPA has been excluded. For this reason I have had no opportunity to keep myself currently familiar with your own thinking on top policy matters nor have I had an opportunity to keep in touch with the thinking of your immediate advisors—except through occasional personal contacts. Operating more or less as a "lone wolf" I do not feel that I can be as effective as I might if I were thoroughly familiar at all times with the basic Administration thinking.

9 ☙ ON JANUARY 20, 1946, about 750,000 steelworkers joined nearly 200,000 meat-packing workers, 200,000 electrical workers, and 320,000 General Motors employees on the picket lines. To avert the steel strike, the President had appointed a fact-finding panel, and he had acted on the basis of their preliminary findings to propose a settlement. Without first checking whether the industry would accept his compromise, he publicly recommended specific terms, which the steel industry rejected. After the industry had refused to grant the 18.5 cents per hour wage increase Truman had proposed, he tried to rally public opinion against the recalcitrant industry. Again Truman failed.

On January 24, as he was about to leave Washington for a vacation, Bowles lectured the President on the perils menacing the stabilization program:[9]

If we should fail in the job you have set for us, no economic miracle could save the country from soaring living costs. Yet, as I write this letter, I am convinced that we are on the brink of failure—not because this agency is unequal to its task, not because we lack public support, not because the policies you have declared are weak or unwise, but simply because repeated statements and actions of responsible officials are leading business, labor, and the public to believe that the Administration does not really intend to hold to the position it has officially taken.

I have reviewed for you a number of the issues on which a weak course, rather than a firm course, has been taken over the objection of the Office of Price Administration. . . . But these cases have not been isolated; they merely exemplify a trend that has been growing since V-J Day. In its day-to-day operations, OPA encounters chronic reluctance and frequent refusal by other agencies to exercise the powers they possess to aid the stabilization program. Instead of vigor-

[9] Excerpts reprinted from letter of Bowles to Truman, January 24, 1946, Bowles Papers. Published by permission of Chester Bowles.

ous, constructive action, they have one solution to suggest to OPA for almost every problem: Increase the ceilings or remove the controls. Moreover, not infrequently they are willing to share their price-raising views with industry and even the public at large. "Eighteen cents more a pound for butter" is a conspicuous but far from an unprecedented instance.

The cumulative effects of such a state of mind and the actions which accompany it are soon felt. For the industry seeking the relaxation of some control or in quest of a price increase, it does not take long to learn where to go to get results. As a consequence, in addition to resisting the usual pressures from industry groups and from members of Congress, we in OPA have had to fight off the still more effective pressures from the very agencies of the Government on whose cooperation we should have the greatest reason to rely. . . .

The steel situation is a case in point. As you know, I opposed the $4 a ton proposal as inconsistent with our standards and as unfairly discriminatory. However, although I thought the increase weakened our position enormously, when I was overruled I was willing to try to live with it. Last night, however, Mr. Fairless announced over the radio that his offer of a 15 cent wage increase was made after he was "informed from Washington by a high Government official that the government was willing to sanction some price increase over the promised $4 a ton, if the labor dispute could be settled." Naturally I cannot know the accuracy of this assertion. So long as such a statement stands, however, it seems a public advertisement that price increases will be doled out measured by no other yardstick than what an employer insists he must have.

That a major industry can obtain a concession by pressure tactics is bad enough, but I believe the Government simply cannot stand the common knowledge that an industry's blunt rejection of the first concession will extract a better one. . . .

The fact that we are dealing with vast industries and powerful unions is no reason for retreat or surrender. The Government has the legal power to carry out a firm policy. Never in the history of price control has it had stronger public support. For the first time the people have come to realize that their standard of living and their savings are really in danger. They will back wholeheartedly a determined Administration which, when confronted by concerted opposition, whether from business or from labor, will show by its actions that it means what it says.

To be sure, the situation has now drifted so far that seizure in steel as well as in meat seems essential. Conceivably die-hards in the steel industry would protract the seizure over a period of months, but a much more realistic estimate would be a matter of weeks or even days. The industry, which for a time was close to settlement, has little to gain from defying a resolute Government and a hostile public. Even the Washington *Times-Herald* has denounced Ben Fairless editorially for his unstatesmanlike stand.

The fear that management might strike against the Government and frustrate the seizure should not in my opinion deter us from acting. First, public opinion would be overwhelmingly against such tactics. Second, I believe that the sanctions under the War Labor Disputes Act could effectively be used. Finally, in the unlikely event that a management strike can tie up steel production, the situation is no worse than at present when a labor-management wage dispute is doing the same thing. Moreover, the Government would be in the strong position of moving vigorously to keep reconversion from stalling instead of the weak one of standing by and confessing its helplessness.

The industries engaged in the present wage controversies have drawn the lines for a decisive battle. It cannot be escaped except by surrender. But by thus forcing the issue these industries have made our course easier. By pushing through to victory in this crisis, the Administration can win the freedom to develop its policies, not in response to business and other group pressures, but rather to meet the changing economic conditions of the transition period. . . .

Above all there is this very practical question: How can I effectively go before Congress seeking extension of price and subsidy legislation when the declared policies of the Administration which I am charged with executing are constant targets for attack in public statements, in conferences with industry, and even before Congressional committees by high officials of other Government agencies and departments? My concern does not rise from any personal embarrassment. I am concerned by the embarrassment to the Administration if it is fairly open to the charge that it has no clear-cut policy to which its leaders subscribe.

I am afraid the conviction is growing in the public mind and on Capitol Hill that the Government's stabilization policy is not what you have stated it to be, but is instead one of improvising on a day-to-day, case-by-case basis, as one crisis leads to another—in short, that there is really no policy at all. It is not yet too late to stamp out this belief, but it is rapidly becoming too late. It can not be stamped out by words, however firm, but only by decisive action. If you make it clear to the responsible officials of the Government that a positive program of action must promptly be substituted for the policy of "retreat," I am confident that the Government can ride successfully through this crisis and emerge with its prestige enormously enhanced. Otherwise the stabilization policy will, I believe, progressively disintegrate.

I am sorry if I have added to your own personal problems in any way by my stand on what seems to me to be the all-important issue of the transition period. No one can know better than I how completely you believe in stabilization. Nothing in my Washington experience heartened me so much as your forthright public support when, shortly after V-E Day, we were battling against a tide of pressures that threatened to engulf us, and for that I am everlastingly grateful. Never since that day have you failed either in public statement or private conversation with me to give the stabilization program or me personally the fullest of support. It is for this very reason that I have felt free to write to you with such candor.

THIRD WAGE-PRICE PROGRAM

10 ◢§   REBUFFED BY THE STEEL INDUSTRY and unwilling to seize the mills, Truman followed the advice of John Snyder, his loyal friend and the director of the Office of War Mobilization and Reconversion, and yielded to the steel management. Under the new stabilization policy of February 14, 1946, the steel industry received more than $5.30 a ton in price compensation for the additional 18.5 cents an hour workers gained. Meanwhile on March 13 the United Automobile Workers finally ended its 113-day strike against General Motors, also winning a wage increase of 18.5 cents. Soon after, the company raised prices. Though Truman had allowed a "bulge in the line" to settle the steel and auto strikes and others besides, he still hoped to restrain inflation. On February 14 the President explained his revised wage-price program:[10]

I am now modifying our wage-price policy to permit wage increases within certain limits and to permit any industry placed in a hardship

---

[10] Excerpts reprinted from *Truman Papers*, 1946, pp. 117–19.

position by an approved increase to seek price adjustments without waiting until the end of a six months' test period, as previously required. . . .

I am authorizing the National Wage Stabilization Board to approve any wage or salary increase, or part thereof, which is found to be consistent with the general pattern of wage or salary adjustments established in the industry or local labor market area since August 18, 1945. Where there is no such general pattern, provision is made for the approval of increases found necessary to eliminate gross inequities' as between related industries, plants, or job classifications, or to correct substandards of living, or to correct disparities between the increase in wage or salary rates since January, 1941, and the increase in the cost of living between that date and September, 1945.

PRESIDENT ON WORLD FAMINE

11 ◄§   IN ADDITION TO labor-management problems, a worldwide famine developed, which added to the inflationary pressures menacing the economy. Uninformed about European conditions, the nation suddenly learned the sad truth on February 6, 1946, when the President addressed the people:[11]

For the world as a whole, a food crisis has developed which may prove to be the worst in modern times. More people face starvation and even actual death for want of food today than in any war year and perhaps more than in all the war years combined.

The United States and other countries have moved food into war-torn countries in record amounts, but there has been a constantly widening gap between essential minimum needs and available supplies.

Although this country enjoyed a near-record production of food and a record crop of wheat, the wheat crops of Europe and North Africa and the rice crops of the Far East have proved to be much shorter than anticipated; in fact some areas have experienced the shortest crops in fifty years because of extreme droughts and the disruption of war.

We in this country have been consuming about 3,300 calories per person per day. In contrast, more than 125 million people in Europe will have to subsist on less than 2,000 calories a day; 28 million will

[11] Excerpts reprinted from White House press release, February 6, 1946, Truman Papers, Truman Library.

get less than 1,500 calories a day and in some parts of Europe, large groups will receive as little as 1,000 calories.

Under these circumstances it is apparent that only through super-human efforts can mass starvation be prevented. . . .

I am sure that the American people are in favor of carrying their share of the burden. . . .

9. The Department of Agriculture will develop additional ways in which grain now being used in the feeding of livestock and poultry could be conserved for use as human food. These steps may include means to obtain the rapid marketing of heavy hogs, preferably all those over 225 pounds, and of beef cattle with a moderate rather than a high degree of finish; to encourage the culling of poultry flocks; to prevent excessive chick production; and to encourage more economical feeding of dairy cattle. Regulations to limit wheat inventories of feed manufacturers and to restrict . . . use of wheat in feed will be prepared. . . .

In attempting to alleviate the shortages abroad, this country will adhere to the policy of giving preference to the liberated peoples and to those who have fought beside us, but we shall also do our utmost to prevent starvation among our former enemies.

I am confident that every citizen will cooperate wholeheartedly in the complete and immediate mobilization of this country's tremendous resources to win this world-wide war against mass starvation.

BUDGET DIRECTOR SMITH ON ADMINISTRATION'S WEAKNESSES

12 ✑ ON FEBRUARY 8, two days after the President's speech, he conferred with Harold Smith, director of the Bureau of the Budget. Smith, who had served throughout the war as chief of the Budget, was an expert on governmental administration. In his entry for February 8 in his diary, he recorded his conversation with the President:[12]

I said, "Mr. President, there are some serious administrative difficulties today which are accumulative. While you, yourself, are an orderly person, there is disorder all around you and it is becoming worse. There are a couple of points—and not many more—at the

[12] Excerpt reprinted from Record of Smith Conference with the President, February 8, 1946, Smith Papers, Bureau of the Budget. Published by permission of Mrs. Lillian M. Riley.

center of these difficulties. For one thing, you need good, continuous, organized staff work and you are not getting it." The President said, "I know it, and the situation is pretty serious."

I continued by saying, "I will give you just one example, but I could give you many others. Not more than three or four weeks ago top people in Agriculture were making speeches which indicated their worry about a possible food surplus in this country. Now you are issuing a statement about black bread. Of course the international picture was not taken into consideration, but I doubt that a food surplus would have existed even for this country alone. At any rate, if that sort of thing continues, Mr. President, the people of the country will think that the Administration has gone completely crazy. It was entirely possible to know precisely the situation months ago, rather than weeks ago. The only excuse for not knowing is the lack of careful putting together of all the pieces.

"Frankly, I don't know who does what around here," I added, "and that is a rather dangerous situation for all of us to be in. You would be interested in my recent wisecrack that the top people in the Government are solving problems in a vacuum and the vacuum is chiefly in their heads."

BOWLES'S REQUEST FOR FURTHER RATIONING

13 ⋙ ON NOVEMBER 2, 1945, three months before the rest of the administration was ready to acknowledge the famine, Bowles had written to Truman about the food needs of Europe:[13]

I have no first-hand knowledge of the food situation in Europe and other foreign countries. However, according to all public reports the situation in many areas is desperate indeed with tens of millions of people close to the starvation line. . . .

Unless my estimate of the American people is wholly incorrect, I believe they would cheerfully accept a reduction of 10 per cent in the total amount of meat, fats and oils which are now being made available to civilians. . . . And it would provide roughly 160 million more pounds of meat each month for the next six to eight months to meet the desperate demands of people of foreign countries.

If you should decide to take this step, and if you clearly explained

[13] Excerpts reprinted from letter of Bowles to Truman, November 2, 1945, Bowles Papers. Published by permission of Chester Bowles.

it to the public, I believe it would be met by widespread approval. Your move would offer dramatic testimony to the fact that America feels deeply her responsibilities as a world power.

It would indicate our willingness to share our food abundance with undernourished people in foreign lands who are facing a desperate winter. It would bring hope into the lives of tens of millions of people whose outlook today is bleak indeed. It might spell the difference between life and death to tens of thousands of individual men, women and children. . . .

If you consider this proposal either unwise or unnecessary, and if it is decided that the American people should continue to consume the present high levels of meats, fats and oils, I can see no further reason for rationing of these products.

With the present and anticipated supplies available for American civilian consumption, rationing constitutes only a hollow gesture. It may make us appear to be making sacrifices in order to carry out foreign commitments abroad. But it will not fool anyone who knows the facts.

Obviously from my own selfish standpoint and for the good of our overall OPA program I would be glad of an opportunity to drop these rationing problems tomorrow. They represent a severe drain on our manpower and on our energies.

But I admit that I have a distinctly uneasy feeling as I compare our overflowing food abundance to the privation faced by people of other lands. I cannot believe it is right and I am confident that if the great majority of our people had the facts they would feel as I do.

BOWLES'S APPEAL FOR PUBLIC SUPPORT OF OPA

14 ‹§   BY LATE NOVEMBER and early December 1945 it was becoming clear that price inflation was the immediate menace to the United States economy. In January the administration disappointed Secretary of Agriculture Anderson and the organized farm groups by announcing that food subsidies, paid to farmers to increase returns without raising prices, would have to continue for another year. But in spite of this victory for its point of view, the OPA remained on the defensive and received only weak support from the White House. On April 17, 1946, the House went on a rampage and mutilated the price-control bill to continue the life of the OPA for one year beyond June 30. Hoping to obtain more favorable treatment from the Senate, Bowles appealed to the public

for support. On the evening of April 17 he discussed the action of the House:[14]

For weeks I have been deeply concerned over the possibility—the very real possibility—that your country and my country is stumbling toward an economic disaster. I have been fearful that we are about to throw away all the fruits of our four year battle against higher rents and prices, and embark on an inflationary joy-ride—a joy-ride that will eventually result in the same wave of unemployment—the same epidemic of bankruptcies and foreclosures—that swept this country in 1920—and again in 1929.

Tonight this danger seems closer than ever. This afternoon on Capitol Hill the House of Representatives took a long step—a step, however, which fortunately is not final—toward starting us on just such a joy-ride to disaster. . . .

But here is the question—the ten—twenty—fifty—the *hundred billion dollar* question—what will happen *after* July 1? Will Congress provide the continued authority necessary to fight off the greatest inflationary forces which have ever threatened our country? Or will our legal authority to hold down prices and rents be watered down—weakened—compromised away—until it is meaningless and ineffective?

That is the issue which is being debated in Congress right now. That is the issue which must be settled either one way or the other way during the next few weeks. That issue—let me emphasize and re-emphasize—is the most important single economic issue of our generation.

There are some people, notably the leaders of the National Manufacturers Association, who take the fantastic stand that price and rent controls should be eliminated entirely when our present legislative powers come to an end on July 1. That proposal runs so completely contrary to the interest and the convictions of the great mass of our people that I will not even bother to discuss it.

Some kind of price control act will be passed. I have no question about that. But what kind of a price and rent control act will it be? Will it be merely an empty gesture toward continued economic stabilization—or will it offer us the opportunity to really protect ourselves against runaway inflation?

Let me briefly outline for you some of the changes in the Price

[14] Excerpts reprinted from Office of Economic Stabilization press release, April 17, 1946.

Control Act which right now are being seriously proposed to Congress. I urge you to listen carefully—and then consider what the effect of each one would be on your own family budget.

ANDERSON ON CONTROLS

15 ◄§   THE AMERICAN FARM BUREAU FEDERATION, long a reluctant supporter of price control, refused to back legislation extending the life of the price-control agency if subsidies were not eliminated by December 30, 1946. "This unwarranted expenditure from the federal treasury must be stopped," Edward O'Neal, the Farm Bureau president, told the Senate Banking and Currency Committee. As long as prices were artificially reduced, O'Neal argued, "supply will be very slow to come into balance with demand." The National Grange, which frequently followed the lead of the more powerful bureau, also refused to endorse renewed price control unless the government ended subsidies.

The OPA, while incurring the wrath of these two farm organizations over subsidies, was also struggling with farmers over another problem—a meat shortage. After the abandonment of slaughter controls (which channeled livestock to legitimate slaughterers), the major packers had been unable to purchase their normal share of the market. Crooked new slaughterers were violating OPA ceilings and supplying the growing black markets. The OPA had wanted to reimpose slaughtering controls, but Secretary Anderson had blocked the agency for almost a month. Finally he yielded, and controls were restored at the end of April. On May 1 Secretary Anderson appeared before the Senate Banking and Currency Committee, which was considering the OPA bill:[15]

SENATOR BARKLEY: These statements that come to me all head up to the suggestion finally that the way to cure this whole situation in meat is to take off all controls and ceilings, on the theory that meat might run up for 30 days in price, but it would level off, so that there would not be any of this artificial situation. I do not know whether that is the answer or not. I am seeking the answer.

[15] Excerpt reprinted from Senate Banking and Currency Committee, *Hearings, 1946 Extension of the Emergency Price Control and Stabilization Acts of 1942, as amended*, Seventy-ninth Congress, second session, pp. 1075–6.

I say this: that I do not see how this committee can write in here, into the law itself, an exemption of every industry and every activity that wants to be exempted from ceilings; but it seems that those facts, if they are facts, ought to be taken into consideration by the administrative agency that has the power to deal with it.

MR. ANDERSON: Well, Senator, if I may, I would say to you that there have been many times when I have debated with myself very seriously as to whether or not the removal of many of these controls on meat might not be a good thing in view of the surplus population of our ranches. I would say that about as far as I have been able to persuade myself to go is to regard this present period when we are trying to reestablish slaughter controls as about the last effort to see if it will work. If with slaughter controls and with the increased force that OPA is now putting on this we are not able to direct these cattle back into decent channels, if we are not able to persuade people that they have got to buy in compliance, and if we are not able to get food for the American people at decent prices, then we surely ought to try something else; and the only other "something else" is an abandonment of these controls. I would hate to see that happen until we again have made a vigorous effort.

A year ago when the conditions were pretty bad, the OPA greatly increased its enforcement and greatly changed the picture, threw a lot of this meat back into normal channels and preserved price control, and still preserved a decent operation.

SENATOR BANKHEAD: Mr. Secretary, right there you have made a very important statement—it impresses me—about your views. How long do you think it will take to make a fair test of whether the new program will be effective?

MR. ANDERSON: That is an awfully hard question for me to answer, Senator. They should do something with it in 90 days or abandon it.

SENATOR BANKHEAD: Ninety days?

SENATOR BARKLEY: Ninety, did you say?

MR. ANDERSON: Ninety days, or abandon it; yes. I say to you if you cannot stop the black market that exists, if you cannot stop the situation that the large packers upon whom we have to depend for a good deal of the meat that we ship in export—and that is my principal interest just now—if they cannot handle something like a normal volume of it, if it all goes out where it is wasted, then something is wrong.

FARMERS UNION ATTACK ON ANDERSON

16 ◆§ BOWLES, WHO HAD BEEN advanced to the head of the Office
of Economic Stabilization, and Paul Porter, the new OPA
chief, were enraged by Anderson's statement. Along with the press,
they believed that he had recommended elimination of price controls, not just slaughter controls, after a ninety-day trial. They tried
to get the President to repudiate the Secretary's testimony, but at
first they failed. Indeed, Truman seemed to be endorsing Anderson's judgment when he told his press conference on May 2, "If it is
necessary to do that [take controls off meat in ninety days—Eds.],
we will do it." Stabilization officials, placed on the defensive by
these comments, pleaded with the President to modify his statement. The next day the White House issued a clarification: "Both
the President and the Secretary took the term [meat controls—Eds.]
to mean, not price controls, but rather . . . slaughter controls. . . ."
But the belief that Anderson favored an end to price control of
meat remained widespread and contributed to the determination
of cattle growers to end controls through a producers' strike, which
began on May 2. James Patton, president of the Farmers Union,
wrote to Truman and demanded Anderson's dismissal:[16]

The testimony of Secretary of Agriculture Anderson to the Senate
Banking and Currency Committee yesterday constitutes so flagrant
a disregard of the welfare of the people of the Nation and of the
policies of your administration that I am forced to write you that,
in my view, his usefulness as Secretary is at an end.

The statements that Mr. Anderson made under questioning yesterday are the culmination of a long series of actions, which I will cite
in detail farther in this letter, that force me to urge you to ask for
his resignation from your Cabinet.

This recommendation is not made hastily or in heat of emotion.
For many months, I have been distressed by the course of the Department of Agriculture. . . .

Equally shocking was the Secretary's statement that "you are talking
to the wrong man" when Senator Taft criticized the payment of
bonuses to obtain corn to aid in the foreign food relief program. This
of course was an invitation to Senator Taft to attack Chester Bowles,

[16] Excerpt from letter of Patton to Truman, May 2, 1946, Official File (OF)
227, Truman Papers, Truman Library. Published by permission of James Patton.

the Economic Stabilization Administrator, as were the Secretary's specific references to his own advocacy of higher meat prices, higher wheat and corn prices, the end of meat subsidies by June 30, and of a different line of action on citrus fruit ceilings from that taken by OPA.

Obviously, the Secretary is unwilling to accept the obligations as well as the benefits of membership in the Cabinet and in your Administration. Senator Taft put his finger on the matter when he observed that the Administration "can't divide itself up into compartments." In the light of his attempt to shift responsibility, it appears obvious that there is no room in the same Administration for Mr. Anderson and those who are still seeking to control inflation.

The second major count against Secretary Anderson is that his fumbling, fluctuating policies regarding American food production and the relief of suffering abroad are directly responsible for the present disastrous situation of the United States in relation to helping to avoid revolutionary developments in Europe and Asia.

It is quite true that more could have been done than was done before the Secretary assumed his present position. It is also true that during the past year he has been principally responsible for the failure of the United States to produce enough and to procure enough food to fulfill its responsibilities abroad. It was the Secretary who was directly responsible for ending food rationing, a step that not only ended any possibility of stockpiling for relief but that also destroyed the machinery for doing anything about it later. It was he who demanded an end to food subsidies. It was he who reduced production goals for oil crops, now so badly needed. His policy and opinion have wavered for months. One day he is quoted as saying, at the time when the flour set aside was ordered, that nothing more could be done if that did not work. Immediately afterward, he is quoted as saying that more must be done. One month he says that the food emergency is a 90-day emergency, and another month he discovers it may last for years.

TRUMAN'S DEFENSE OF ANDERSON

17 ◆⩤ ON MAY 4 TRUMAN responded to Patton's letter with a sharp note. Soon Patton and his liberal farm organization announced opposition to the administration. Truman's letter follows:[17]

[17] Letter of Truman to Patton, May 4, 1946, OF 1, Truman Papers, Truman Library.

I read your letter of the second with a great deal of interest and I regret very much that you are at odds with my able Secretary of Agriculture.

You know, as far as Cabinet positions are concerned, they belong to the President and, as long as Secretary Anderson is satisfactory to me, I'll keep him.

I think you are entirely misinformed on his attitude. I think he is as able a Secretary of Agriculture as the Country has ever had and I intend to keep him.

TRUMAN AND SMITH ON FOOD PROBLEMS

18 ◄§ DESPITE BOWLES's earlier concern about adequate meat supplies for Europe, the real problem was a shortage of grain. Farmers, rather than sell grain for foreign shipments, were feeding it to livestock. To tempt farmers to put the grain on the market, the government either had to lower livestock prices or raise grain prices. When bonuses and pleas failed, the government finally yielded to the farmers on May 8, 1946, and raised the price of corn and wheat. By the end of June the administration had met its foreign commitment of 225 million bushels for the first half of 1946, but the price rise for grain had weakened the stabilization program. Concessions, once offered, as Bowles had warned, only lead interest groups to demand greater benefits.

On May 15 Budget Director Smith discussed the problems with the President:[18]

At this point, the President mentioned the food situation and his concern about it. I commented, "That is an example of where you need a lot better staff work." He said, "I know it and I am not getting it." I pointed out that I knew a little about the situation both officially and as a farmer, that I felt that a very blundering job was being done by the Department of Agriculture, and that I agreed with Jim Patton's criticism (National Farmers' Union). I said that Anderson was a most likable person, but that he was in a very dangerous position and that in many ways the Department of Agriculture, in my judgment, was the worst it has ever been. The President seemed a little surprised at this, but not as surprised as I expected him to be. I stated that

[18] Excerpt reprinted from Record of Smith Conference with the President, May 15, 1946, Smith Papers, Bureau of the Budget. Published by permission of Mrs. Lillian M. Riley.

I liked Anderson personally and that when he was appointed Secretary of Agriculture, I thought that the President had made a good choice, but that now I was far from certain of this. I expressed the feeling that a most confused situation was developing. I went on to say that as a farmer I had outguessed the Department before on the raising of hogs and that I was going to do so again because I was thoroughly convinced that the playing around carelessly with such a delicate matter as the relation between feed and livestock would completely upset the meat situation to a point where shortages would accumulate.

The President asked, "What do you think is the trouble?" I replied, "The trouble gets right down to very poor staff work. Either Anderson does not have a staff under him to tell him the facts, or he does not use the Bureau of Agricultural Economics, or the Bureau of Agricultural Economics has itself fallen down on the job." I continued by pointing out that for one thing, eating habits have probably changed radically, and I stressed again my belief that the whole subject should be thoroughly explored. The President said that he was certain that rationing would be a terrible headache. I told him that I was not at all certain of this—in fact, that I was rather convinced that we should have started rationing in the beginning.

I admitted to the President that I was involved in a certain amount of emotionalism in discussing the subject because I was so completely convinced that our international relations depended more on what we did about the food situation than on all of the negotiations of the State Department put together. I said that our stature in the world would certainly be diminished in the eyes of nations suffering severe food shortages if we did not make some real sacrifices on their behalf, and that I had no confidence whatever in voluntary effort.

Then the President asked, "What do you think Anderson needs to do?" I replied, "Well, I don't know whether he will see just what he will need to do, and I have thought that I have not done my duty because I have not gone over and talked with him about the situation." The President said, "I wish you would do that. He is a good guy and he wants to be the best Secretary of Agriculture ever, and you might be helpful. Don't do it on the basis of my suggestion, but do it on your own because you think you can do some good." I indicated that I would be very glad to do anything I could because I felt greatly concerned. The President suggested, "Slip me a memorandum on the food situation. See what you think it looks like."

The President went on to express concern about Lehman's activities on the food front. He said that Lehman (recently resigned as director of the United Nations Relief and Rehabilitation Administration) objected to his sending Herbert Hoover around the world to check on the major famine areas. However the President was convinced that Hoover had come through with X million tons of food as a result of the trip. Lehman, who had botched up UNRRA and who now was apparently running for the Senate from New York, was taking it out on him. The President commented that Lehman had "sat on his fanny" for several years, but now he is showing a great burst of activity over the international food situation about which he should have been doing something all along. The President apparently did not consider his activity to be very helpful.

PRESIDENTIAL STATEMENT ON RAILROAD STRIKE

19 ⇜ DURING THE SPRING of 1946 trouble was again brewing in labor. When the operators refused to grant the United Mine Workers a health-and-welfare fund, the miners walked out in April. By May a government agency declared that the shortage of coal was creating a "national disaster." Fearful of growing anti-labor antagonism in Congress, John L. Lewis, head of the Mine Workers, declared a two-week truce in mid-May, and the men returned to the pits. When contract negotiations again broke down, Truman, to protect the nation, seized the mines on May 21. A week later the government, as a contracting party, granted the union handsome terms, which added another "bulge" to the stabilization line. While making concessions to Lewis, the administration had not been able to halt a walkout by two railroad brotherhoods. At first, at the President's request, the brotherhoods of the trainmen and the engineers had postponed the strike for five days. But when Truman later offered a settlement of 18.5 cents more an hour and a postponement of all rules changes, the two brotherhoods decided to strike against the government, which had seized the railroads.

On May 23 the railroads stopped running. Two days later the President addressed a joint session of Congress:[19]

. . . For the past two days the Nation has been in the grip of a railroad strike which threatens to paralyze all our industrial, agricultural, commercial, and social life.

[19] Excerpts reprinted from *Truman Papers*, 1946, pp. 277–9.

Last night I tried to point out to the American people the bleak picture which we face at home and abroad if the strike is permitted to continue.

The disaster will spare no one. Hundreds of thousands of liberated people of Europe and Asia will die who could be saved if the railroads were not now tied up.

As I stated last night, unless the railroads are manned by returning strikers, I shall immediately undertake to run them by the Army of the United States.

I assure you that I do not take this action lightly. But there is no alternative. This is no longer a dispute between labor and management. It has now become a strike against the Government of the United States itself. That kind of strike can never be tolerated. If allowed to continue, the Government will break down. Strikes against the Government must stop. I appear before you to request immediate legislation designed to help stop them.

I am sure that some of you may think that I should have taken this action earlier, and that I should have made this appearance here before today. The reason I did not do so, was that I was determined to make every possible human effort to avoid this strike against the Government and to make unnecessary the kind of legislation which I am about to request. . . .

This particular crisis has been brought about by the obstinate arrogance of two men. They are Mr. Alvanley Johnston, president of the Brotherhood of Locomotive Engineers, and Mr. A. F. Whitney, president of the Brotherhood of Railway Trainmen. Eighteen other unions and all of the railroad companies of the Nation are ready to run the railroads, and these two men have tried to stop them. . . .

We are dealing with a handful of men who have it within their power to cripple the entire economy of the Nation.

I request temporary legislation to take care of this immediate crisis. I request permanent legislation leading to the formulation of a long-range labor policy designed to prevent the recurrence of such crises and generally to reduce stoppages of work in all industries for the future.

I request that the temporary legislation be effective only for a period of 6 months after the declaration by the President or by the Congress of the termination of hostilities. It should be applicable only to those few industries in which the President by proclamation declares that an emergency has arisen which affects the entire economy of the United States. It should be effective only in those situations where the President of the United States has taken over the operation of the industry. In such situations where the President has requested the men either to remain at work or to return to work and where such a request is ignored, the legislation should:

(a) authorize the institution of injunctive or mandatory proceedings against any union leader forbidding him from encouraging or inciting members of the union to leave their work or to refuse to return to work; subjecting him to contempt proceedings for failure to obey any order of the Court made in such proceedings;

(b) deprive workers of their seniority rights who, without good cause, persist in striking against the Government;

(c) provide criminal penalties against employers and union leaders who violate the provisions of the act.

The legislation should provide that after the Government has taken over an industry and has directed the men to remain at work or return to work, the wage scale be fixed either by negotiation or by arbitrators appointed by the President and when so fixed, it shall be retroactive.

This legislation must be used in a way that is fair to capital and to labor alike. The President will not permit either side—industry or workers—to use it to further their own selfish interest, or to foist upon the Government the carrying out of their selfish aims.

Net profits of Government operation, if any, should go to the Treasury of the United States.

As a part of this temporary emergency legislation, I request the Congress immediately to authorize the President to draft into the Armed Forces of the United States all workers who are on strike against their Government.

[*At this point the President was handed a message by Leslie L. Biffle, Secretary of the Senate.*]

Word has just been received that the railroad strike has been settled, on terms proposed by the President!

These measures may appear to you to be drastic. They are. I repeat that I recommend them only as temporary emergency expedients. . . .

VETO OF OPA BILL

20 ◄§ THOUGH POLLS STILL indicated popular support for the OPA, Truman, agreeing with Bowles that the final bill was

bad, on June 29, 1946, vetoed it. Excerpts from his veto message follow:[20]

The choice which H. R. 6042 presents is not a choice between continued price stability and inflation. It is a choice between inflation with a statute and inflation without one. The bill continues the Government's responsibility to stabilize the economy and at the same time it destroys the Government's power to do so.

If this bill were allowed to become law, the American people would believe that they were protected by a workable price-control law. But they would not be protected and they would soon come to a bitter realization of that truth. It is only fair to tell them the facts now.

The lesson from our own experience after the last war, disastrous as it was to our farmers, our workers, our manufacturers, our distributors, and our consumers, has been too easily obscured by the annoyances and irritations and the occasional inequities of price control. The fact that inflation has already gutted the economy of country after country all over the world should shake our comfortable assurance that such a catastrophe cannot happen here. . . .

I wish it were possible to tell you exactly how many billions of dollars the American people would eventually have to pay for the Taft amendment and its companion pieces. To attempt to do so, however, would be like trying to estimate the cost of a fire about to sweep a city before the first building had started to burn. Even to estimate the total amount of all the first round of price increases is not now possible.

Here, however, are a few examples which would enter into such a total.

The first impact of the Taft and Wherry amendments in the crucial field of housing would be little short of devastating. The prices of nearly all building materials would be affected. The average increases of such materials, excluding lumber, would be approximately 20 percent. This would completely disrupt the program recently approved by the Congress to provide veterans' housing at reasonable cost.

Ceilings for steel would have to be raised an average of $4 to $8 a ton. These increases would in turn be reflected in the ceilings of everything made of steel.

[20] Reprinted from *Congressional Record*, Seventy-ninth Congress, second session, pp. 7973–5.

The average price of low-priced automobiles would be increased $225 to $250 on top of the substantial increases already granted.

The spectacular increases in the prices of manufactured goods which the Taft amendment and its companion amendments would cause, right at the beginning, are far in excess of anything which industry needs to earn generous profits and obtain full production. The increases are so large because the formulas for computing them are bonanza formulas.

The Taft amendment puts into prices the profit per unit of sales which the industry received for the particular product in the year 1941. That was a year in which manufacturers and processors received a much greater profit out of each dollar of sales than in any one of the five peacetime years which preceded 1941. . . .

. . . As industry after industry accepts the invitation of the Taft amendment in an attempt to make good profits better, prices will go up and up.

In addition, the industries in real need of relief will tend to be lost in the shuffle. The OPA, already criticized for delay in these deserving cases, will be increasingly unable to act promptly to break production bottlenecks.

There is a grim irony in the fact that the Taft amendment is defended as a stimulant to production when in fact it will greatly impede production. . . .

As far back as September 6, 1945, I urged the Congress to pass an extension of the Price Control Act at an early date so as to avoid the uncertainties which have made control more difficult for the last few months. Had this been done there would now be no necessity for these last-minute decisions. I repeated my request to the Congress to extend price-control legislation without crippling amendments again and again—on January 21, 1946, May 22, 1946, May 25, 1946, and June 11, 1946.

Nevertheless, just before the expiration of all price control there has been presented to me by the Congress an impossible bill.

I cannot bring myself to believe, however, that the Representatives of the American people will permit the great calamity which will befall this country if price and rent controls end at midnight Sunday. On behalf of the people I request the Congress to continue by resolution the present controls for the short period of time necessary to write a workable bill.

The fight against inflation is never easy. We are battling against economic forces which have caused us untold misery after every previous war and which have overcome or are threatening to overwhelm many of the nations engaged in this war.

We shall not win this fight by soft measures.

All of us who must play a part in the decision of this issue face a solemn responsibility. We stand at an historic moment. Our actions will be judged by the American people and judged again by history.

END OF MEAT CONTROLS

21 ⤶ ON JULY 25 the President signed the new price-control bill "with reluctance." The measure contained a watered-down version of the Taft amendment and left dairy products, grain, livestock, and meat without controls until at least August 20. Then the special three-member Price Control Board, appointed by the President, could decide whether controls should be reimposed. After lengthy deliberation the board authorized controls on livestock and meat. Paul Porter of the OPA and Secretary Anderson squabbled about the new price ceilings on meat and Anderson raised them about 15 percent above June levels. Despite this concession, meat quickly disappeared from the markets. Congressmen protested and the executive committee of the Democratic party begged the President to declare a sixty-day holiday—until after the election—on meat controls. Defeated by the cattlemen, Truman, on October 14, explained his decision to the nation:[21]

I wish to report to you this evening on a subject which I am sure has concerned you as much as it has me—the meat shortage and our general stabilization program.

I recognize the hardship that many of you have undergone because of the lack of meat. I sympathize with the millions of housewives who have been hard pressed to provide nourishing meals for their families. I sympathize particularly with our thousands of veterans and other patients in hospitals throughout the country. I know that our children, as well as those persons engaged in manual labor, need meat in their diet. . . .

Many of us have asked the same question: Why should there be a meat shortage when there are millions of cattle and hogs on the ranges and farms and in feed lots in this country? Who are the persons

[21] Excerpts reprinted from *Truman Papers*, 1946, pp. 451–5.

responsible for this serious condition? Why doesn't the Government
do something about it? . . .

The responsibility rests squarely on a few men in the Congress who,
in the service of selfish interests, have been determined for some time
to wreck price controls no matter what the cost might be to our
people. . . .

During this period, selfish men rushed unfattened cattle to the
slaughter houses in order to get in under the wire and make high
profits. That inevitably caused a shortage later. If price control had
been enacted by the Congress in time—if this lag of two months had
not occurred—this wasteful slaughter of unfattened cattle would not
have taken place. . . .

The real blame, however, lies at the door of the reckless group of
selfish men who, in the hope of gaining political advantage, have
encouraged sellers to gamble on the destruction of price controls.

This group, today as in the past, is thinking in terms of millions
of dollars instead of millions of people. This same group has opposed
every effort of this administration to raise the standard of living and
increase the opportunity for the common man. This same group
hated Franklin D. Roosevelt and fought everything he stood for.
This same group did its best to discredit his efforts to achieve a
better life for our people. . . .

For many months representatives of the livestock and meat industry
have insistently demanded the lifting of controls from their products.
They have made the definite promise that the lifting of controls on
livestock and meat would bring to market the meat which our people
want, at reasonable prices. The American people will know where
the responsibility rests if profiteering on meat raises prices so high
that the average American cannot buy it.

TRUMAN ON END OF MOST CONTROLS

22 ❦§   ON NOVEMBER 9, 1946, after the debacle at the polls, President Truman announced the end of all wage and most
price controls:[22]

There is no virtue in control for control's sake. When it becomes
apparent that controls are not furthering the purposes of the stabilization laws but would, on the contrary, tend to defeat these purposes,
it becomes the duty of the Government to drop the controls. . . .

[22] Excerpts, *ibid.*, pp. 475–7.

. . . the situation is far more favorable for the return to a free economy today than it was when the present badly weakened stabilization law was finally enacted by the Congress.

Nevertheless, some shortages remain and some prices will advance sharply when controls are removed. We have, however, already seen what consumer resistance can do to excessive prices. The consumers of America know that if they refuse to pay exorbitant prices, prices will come down. . . .

Today's action places squarely upon management and labor the responsibility for working out agreements for the adjustment of their differences without interruption of production.

3 · The Fair Deal, 1945-1953

*F*rom one point of view Truman's domestic program, known as the Fair Deal, can be judged a failure. After almost eight years in office Truman could point to only a few tangible accomplishments: his executive orders ending discrimination in the armed services and in the federal government, the public-housing act of 1949, a rise in minimum wages passed that same year, and a social-security measure in 1950 that increased benefits and extended coverage to ten million more Americans. But his boldest proposals were ignored or defeated by Congress: civil-rights legislation, national health insurance, the Brannan Plan for agriculture, rational and humane immigration laws, federal aid to education. His achievements, then, seem mainly negative. In a conservative era he helped prevent repeal of the New Deal and preserved its vision of mild welfare capitalism.

This judgment, while true, is also incomplete. Truman's best proposals proved to be a form of public education that prepared the way for enactment of similar programs in more favorable times. Beyond its educational function, the Fair Deal served still another purpose: it elected its author to the presidency in his own right in 1948. Though the temper of the country was perhaps even more illiberal during Truman's second term than it had been during his first, a series of lucky accidents and shrewd campaigning by the Democrats managed to revive for a short time in the autumn of 1948 the electoral coalition that had won so many victories for the New Deal. Though the coalition quickly collapsed again, its brief resurrection was partly the result of Truman's Fair Deal rhetoric. By aligning himself with the party's liberal wing, by attempting to assume Roosevelt's mantle —in short, by advocating the Fair Deal—Truman achieved electoral success and earned his reputation in history as a progressive President.

86

TRUMAN'S TWENTY-ONE POINTS

1 ⤙§ ON SEPTEMBER 6, 1945, President Truman sent Congress a
twenty-one point message spelling out his domestic program.
This message, Truman wrote later, "symbolizes for me my assumption of the office of President in my own right." While many of
his points dealt with reconversion problems facing the nation in
the immediate future—decontrol of the economy, impending labor
disputes, selective service in peacetime, tax reductions for 1946,
disposal of war plants, veterans' benefits—the message also declared
the President's determination to expand the welfare programs of
the New Deal. Excerpts from Truman's message follow:[1]

I regret that you have been compelled to cut short your recess
period. I know, however, that you have been just as eager as any of
us to meet the problems which naturally have crowded down upon us
with the surrender of the Japanese. . . .

The end of the war came more swiftly than most of us anticipated.
Widespread cut-backs in war orders followed promptly. As a result,
there has already been a considerable number of workers who are
between jobs as war industries convert to peace. Other workers are
returning to a 40-hour week and are faced with a corresponding
reduction in take-home pay. . . .

On May 28, 1945, I recommended to the Congress that the Federal
Government immediately supplement the unemployment insurance
benefits now provided by the several States. That is the only feasible
way to provide at least a subsistence payment in all parts of the United
States during this coming unemployment period.

As I pointed out then, the existing State laws relative to unemployment insurance are inadequate in three respects:

(1) Only about 30,000,000 of our 43,000,000 nonagricultural workers are protected by unemployment insurance. Federal Government
employees, for example, such as Federal shipyard and arsenal workers,
are not covered. Nor are employees of small businesses and small
industrial establishments. Nor are the officers and men of the mer-
chant marine who have braved enemy torpedoes and bombs to deliver
supplies and the implements of war to our armed services and our
allies.

---

[1] Reprinted from *Truman Papers*, 1945, pp. 263–309.

(2) The weekly benefit payments under many of the State laws are now far too low to provide subsistence and purchasing power for the workers and their families. Almost half of the States have the clearly inadequate maximum of $15 to $18 a week.

(3) Many of the States pay benefits for too short a period. In more than one-third of the States, for example, 18 weeks is the maximum.

I recommended then, and I urgently renew my recommendation now, that the Congress take immediate action to make good these deficiencies for the present emergency period of reconversion. . . .

The foundations of a healthy national economy cannot be secure so long as any large section of our working people receive substandard wages. The existence of substandard wage levels sharply curtails the national purchasing power and narrows the market for the products of our farms and factories.

In the Fair Labor Standards Act of 1938, the Congress adopted a program intended to provide a minimum wage standard for a large number of American workers.

In that statute, the Congress declared it to be our national policy to eliminate, from interstate industry, wage levels detrimental to the maintenance of minimum standards of living. The establishment then of a minimum wage of 25 cents per hour represented a first step toward the realization of that policy. The goal of 40 cents per hour, which under the act was to be made effective by 1945, was actually made fully effective more than a year ago by the voluntary action of the industry committees.

I believed that the goal of a 40 cent minimum was inadequate when established. It has now become obsolete.

Increases in the cost of living since 1938 and changes in our national wage structure, require an immediate and substantial upward revision of this minimum. Only in that way can the objectives of the Fair Labor Standards Act be realized, the national purchasing power protected, and an economy of full production and abundance preserved and maintained for the American people.

The high prosperity which we seek in the postwar years will not be meaningful for all our people if any large proportion of our industrial wage earners receive wages as low as the minimum now sanctioned by the Fair Labor Standards Act.

I therefore recommend that the Congress amend the Fair Labor Standards Act by substantially increasing the minimum wage specified therein to a level which will eliminate substandards of living, and assure the maintenance of the health, efficiency, and general well-being of workers. . . .

I am confident that, with the cooperation of American industry, labor, and agriculture, we can bridge the gap between war and peace.

When we have reconverted our economy to a peacetime basis, however, we shall not be satisfied with merely our prewar economy. The American people have set high goals for their own future. They have set these goals high because they have seen how great can be the productive capacity of our country.

The levels of production and income reached during the war years have given our citizens an appreciation of what a full production peacetime economy can be.

They are not interested in boom prosperity—for that only too often leads to panic and depression. But they are interested in providing opportunity for work and for ultimate security.

Government must do its part and assist industry and labor to get over the line from war to peace.

That is why I have asked for unemployment compensation legislation.

That is why I now ask for full-employment legislation.

The objectives for our domestic economy which we seek in our long-range plans were summarized by the late President Franklin D. Roosevelt over a year and a half ago in the form of an economic bill of rights. Let us make the attainment of those rights the essence of postwar American economic life.

I repeat the statement of President Roosevelt:

> In our day these economic truths have become accepted as self-evident. We have accepted, so to speak, a second bill of rights under which a new basis of security and prosperity can be established for all— regardless of station, race, or creed.
>
> Among these are:
>
> The right to a useful and remunerative job in the industries, or shops or farms or mines of the Nation.
>
> The right to earn enough to provide adequate food and clothing and recreation.
>
> The right of every farmer to raise and sell his products at a return which will give him and his family a decent living.
>
> The right of every businessman, large and small, to trade in an

atmosphere of freedom from unfair competition and domination by monopolies at home or abroad.

The right of every family to a decent home.

The right to adequate medical care and the opportunity to achieve and enjoy good health.

The right to adequate protection from the economic fears of old age, sickness, accident, and unemployment.

The right to a good education.

All of these rights spell security. And after this war is won we must be prepared to move forward, in the implementation of these rights, to new goals of human happiness and well-being.

America's own rightful place in the world depends in large part upon how fully these and similar rights have been carried into practice for our citizens. For unless there is security here at home there cannot be lasting peace in the world.

I shall from time to time communicate with the Congress on some of the subjects included in this enumeration of economic rights.

Most of them, in the last analysis, depend upon full production and full employment at decent wages.

There has been much discussion about the necessity of continuing full employment after the war if we hope to continue in substantial degree the prosperity which came with the war years. The time has come for action along these lines.

To provide jobs we must look first and foremost to private enterprise—to industry, agriculture, and labor. Government must inspire enterprise with confidence. That confidence must come mainly through deeds, not words.

But it is clear that confidence will be promoted by certain assurances given by the Government:

Assurance that all the facts about full employment and opportunity will be gathered periodically for the use of all.

Assurance of stability and consistency in public policy, so that enterprise can plan better by knowing what the Government intends to do.

Assurance that every governmental policy and program will be pointed to promote maximum production and employment in private enterprise.

Assurance that priority will be given to doing those things first which stimulate normal employment most.

A national reassertion of the right to work for every American citizen able and willing to work—a declaration of the ultimate duty of Government to use its own resources if all other methods should fail to prevent prolonged unemployment—these will help to avert fear and establish full employment. The prompt and firm acceptance of this bedrock public responsibility will reduce the need for its exercise.

I ask that full-employment legislation to provide these vital assurances be speedily enacted. Such legislation should also provide machinery for a continuous full-employment policy—to be developed and pursued in cooperation among industry, agriculture, and labor, between the Congress and the Chief Executive, between the people and their Government. . . .

During the years of war production we made substantial progress in overcoming many of the prejudices which had resulted in discriminations against minority groups.

Many of the injustices based upon considerations of race, religion, and color were removed. Many were prevented. Perfection was not reached, of course, but substantial progress was made.

In the reconversion period and thereafter, we should make every effort to continue this American ideal. It is one of the fundamentals of our political philosophy, and it should be an integral part of our economy.

The Fair Employment Practice Committee is continuing during the transition period. I have already requested that legislation be enacted placing the Fair Employment Practice Committee on a permanent basis. I repeat that recommendation.

The Government now must be prepared to carry out the Nation's responsibility to aid farmers in making their necessary readjustments from a wartime to a peacetime basis. The Congress already has provided postwar supports against price collapse for many farm products. This was a provision of wisdom and foresight.

After the First World War farm prices dropped more than 50 percent from the spring of 1920 to the spring of 1921. We do not intend to permit a repetition of the disaster that followed the First World War. The Secretary of Agriculture [Charles F. Brannan—Eds.] has assured me that he will use all means now authorized by the Congress to carry out the price-support commitments. . . .

Within recent years the Congress has enacted various measures which have done much to improve the economic status of this country's farmers and to make rural living more attractive. In enacting individual pieces of legislation it has not been possible to make adjustments in existing measures in keeping with the changing pattern of needs. The Secretary of Agriculture is now reexamining existing agricultural programs in the light of peacetime needs in order that they [may—Eds.] make the fullest contribution to the welfare of farmers and the people as a whole. I hope that the Congress also, through its appropriate committees, will give careful consideration to this problem with a view to making such adjustments as are necessary to strengthen the effectiveness of these various measures.

The largest single opportunity for the rapid postwar expansion of private investment and employment lies in the field of housing, both urban and rural. The present shortage of decent homes and the enforced widespread use of substandard housing indicate vital unfulfilled needs of the Nation. These needs will become more marked as veterans begin to come back and look for places to live.

There is wide agreement that, over the next ten years, there should be built in the United States an average of from a million to a million and a half homes a year.

Such a program would provide an opportunity for private capital to invest from six to seven billion dollars annually. Private enterprise in this field could provide employment for several million workers each year. A housing program of this realistic size would, in turn, stimulate a vast amount of business and employment in industries which make house furnishings and equipment of every kind, and in the industries which supply the materials for them. It would provide an impetus for new products, and would develop new markets for a variety of manufactured articles to be made by private enterprise.

Housing is high on the list of matters calling for decisive Congressional action. This is reflected in recommendations contained in reports recently issued by the postwar committees of the Senate and of the House of Representatives. While differing opinions may be held as to detail, these proposals for action already developed in the Congress appear to me sound and essential.

I urgently recommend that the Congress, at an early date, enact broad and comprehensive housing legislation.

The cardinal principle underlying such legislation should be that house construction and financing for the overwhelming majority of our citizens should be done by private enterprise.

We should retain and improve upon the present excellent Government facilities which permit the savings of the people to be channeled voluntarily into private house construction on financing terms that will serve the needs of home owners of moderate income.

The present principles of insurance of housing investment—now tested by years of experience—should be retained and extended, so as to encourage direct investment in housing by private financing institutions.

The Government, in addition to providing these facilities to help private enterprise and private capital build homes, should take effective measures to stimulate research in methods and materials of housing construction. In this way, better and cheaper methods may be developed to build homes.

In addition to this type of research, the Government might well undertake to assist communities in making recurrent community studies in matters relating to housing and real estate generally. Such a program would contribute in great degree to the progress of private initiative and private capital investment in housing.

We must go on. We must widen our horizon even further. We must consider the redevelopment of large areas of the blighted and slum sections of our cities so that in the truly American way they may be remade to accommodate families not only of low-income groups as heretofore, but of every income group. We must make it possible for private enterprise to do the major part of this job. In most cases, it is now impossible for private enterprise to contemplate rebuilding slum areas without public assistance. The land cost generally is too high.

The time has come for the Government to begin to undertake a program of Federal aid to stimulate and promote the redevelopment of these deteriorating areas. Such Federal aid should be extended only to those communities which are willing to bear a fair part of the cost of clearing their blighted city areas and preparing them for redevelopment and rebuilding.

The rebuilding of these areas should conform to broad city plans, provide adequately for displaced families and make maximum use of private capital. Here lies another road toward establishing a better standard of city living, toward increasing business activity and providing jobs.

During the war special attention was paid to small business. The American small business is the backbone of our free-enterprise system. The efforts of the Congress in protecting small business during the war paid high dividends, not only in protecting small business enterprise, but also in speeding victory. In spite of the fact, however, that many businesses were helped and saved, it is true that many thousands of them were obliged to close up because of lack of materials or manpower or inability to get into war production.

It is very important to the economy of the United States that these small businesses and many more of them be given opportunity to become a part of American trade and industry. To do this, assistance should be given to small businesses to enable them to obtain adequate materials, private financing, technological improvements, and surplus property.

While some special facilities for small business are required, the greatest help to it will come from the maintenance of general prosperity and full employment. It is much more difficult for small business to survive the hazards which come from trade recessions and widespread unemployment. What small business needs chiefly is a steady supply of customers with stable purchasing power.

I am sure that the Congress will see to it that in its legislation adequate protection and encouragement will be given to the small business of the Nation. . . .

We should build and improve our roads—the arteries of commerce; we must harness our streams for the general welfare; we must rebuild and reclaim our land; we must protect and restore our forests.

This is not only to provide men and women with work, it is to assure to the Nation the very basis of its life. It is to play the part of a good businessman who insists carefully on maintaining and rebuilding his plant and machinery.

We know that by the investment of Federal funds we can, within the limits of our own Nation, provide for our citizens new frontiers —new territories for the development of industry, agriculture, and commerce.

We have before us the example of the Tennessee Valley Authority, which has inspired regional resource development throughout the entire world. . . .

We know that we have programs, carefully considered and extensively debated, for regional development of the Columbia River in the great Northwest, the Missouri River, the Central Valley of California, and the Arkansas River. . . .

I hope that the Congress will proceed as rapidly as possible to authorize regional development of the natural resources of our great river valleys.

COMMITTEE ON CIVIL RIGHTS REPORT

2 ⋖§ PRESIDENT TRUMAN'S most notable addition to the liberal program of the Democratic party was his occasional advocacy of civil rights for Negroes. Though Roosevelt had successfully wooed the Negro vote away from its traditional Republicanism with his welfare and recovery programs, the New Deal had done virtually nothing during the depression to fight racial discrimination. Truman, though wavering, moved slowly to fight discrimination, but liberals frequently questioned his motives and criticized his actions, which were hesitant and sometimes contradictory. Shortly after becoming President, he allowed Congress to strangle the special wartime Fair Employment Practices Commission. Though he unsuccessfully asked Congress to create a permanent FEPC, he also restricted the powers of the temporary commission. But Truman also affirmed his commitment to legal equality for the Negro. On December 5, 1946, he created the President's Committee on Civil Rights to determine "in what respect current law enforcement measures may be strengthened and improved to safeguard the civil rights of the people." Within a year, civil rights became a major issue for the Truman administration. In October 1947 the Committee on Civil Rights released its famous report, To Secure These Rights. Though the report discussed a wide range of problems, its major concern was racial discrimination. A few excerpts from the report and some of its recommendations follow:[2]

THE RIGHT TO EDUCATION

The United States has made remarkable progress toward the goal of universal education for its people. The number and variety of its schools and colleges are greater than ever before. Student bodies have become increasingly representative of all the different peoples who make up our population. Yet we have not finally eliminated prejudice and discrimination from the operation of either our public or our private schools and colleges. Two inadequacies are extremely serious. We have failed to provide Negroes and, to a lesser extent,

[2] Reprinted from President's Committee on Civil Rights, To Secure These Rights (Washington, D.C., 1947), pp. 62–5, 67–9, 166–71.

other minority group members with equality of educational opportunities in our public institutions, particularly at the elementary and secondary school levels. We have allowed discrimination in the operation of many of our private institutions of higher education, particularly in the North with respect to Jewish students.

Discrimination in public schools.—The failure to give Negroes equal educational opportunities is naturally most acute in the South, where approximately 10 million Negroes live. The South is one of the poorer sections of the country and has at best only limited funds to spend on its schools. With 34.5 percent of the country's population, 17 southern states and the District of Columbia have 39.4 percent of our school children. Yet the South has only one-fifth of the taxpaying wealth of the nation. Actually, on a percentage basis, the South spends a greater share of its income on education than do the wealthier states in other parts of the country. For example, Mississippi, which has the lowest expenditure per school child of any state, is ninth in percentage of income devoted to education. A recent study showed Mississippi spending 3.41 percent of its income for education as against New York's figure of only 2.61 percent. But this meant $400 per classroom unit in Mississippi, and $4,100 in New York. Negro and white school children both suffer because of the South's basic inability to match the level of educational opportunity provided in other sections of the nation.

But it is the South's segregated school system which most directly discriminates against the Negro. This segregation is found today in 17 southern states and the District of Columbia. Poverty-stricken though it was after the close of the Civil War, the South chose to maintain two sets of public schools, one for whites and one for Negroes. With respect to education, as well as to other public services, the Committee believes that the "separate but equal" rule has not been obeyed in practice. There is a marked difference in quality between the educational opportunities offered white children and Negro children in the separate schools. Whatever test is used— expenditure per pupil, teachers' salaries, the number of pupils per teacher, transportation of students, adequacy of school buildings and educational equipment, length of school term, extent of curriculum— Negro students are invariably at a disadvantage. Opportunities for Negroes in public institutions of higher education in the South— particularly at the professional graduate school level—are severely limited.

Statistics in support of these conclusions are available. Figures provided by the United States Office of Education for the school year, 1943–44, show that the average length of the school term in the areas having separate schools was 173.5 days for whites, and 164 for Negroes; the number of pupils per teacher was 28 for white and 34 for Negroes; and the average annual salary for Negro teachers was lower than that for white teachers in all but three of the 18 areas. Salary figures are as follows:

State or District of Columbia	Average annual salary of principals, supervisors, and teachers In schools for—	
	Whites	Negroes
Alabama	$1,158	$ 661
Arkansas	924	555
Delaware	1,953	1,814
Florida	1,530	970
Georgia	1,123	515
Louisiana	1,683	828
Maryland	2,085	2,002
Mississippi	1,107	342
Missouri	1,397	1,590[a]
North Carolina	1,380	1,249
Oklahoma	1,428	1,438
South Carolina	1,203	615
Tennessee	1,071	1,010
Texas	1,395	946
Virginia	1,364	1,129
District of Columbia	2,610	2,610

[a] Higher salaries due to the fact that most Negro schools are located in cities where all salaries are higher.

The South has made considerable progress in the last decade in narrowing the gap between educational opportunities afforded the white children and that afforded Negro children. For example, the gap between the length of the school year for whites and the shorter one for Negroes has been narrowed from 14.8 days in 1939–40 to 9.5 days in 1943–44. Similarly, the gap in student load per teacher in white and Negro schools has dropped from 8.5 students in 1939–40 to 6 students in 1943–44.

In spite of the improvement which is undoubtedly taking place, the Committee is convinced that the gap between white and Negro schools can never be completely eliminated by means of state funds alone. The cost of maintaining separate, but truly equal, school systems would seem to be utterly prohibitive in many of the southern states. It seems probable that the only means by which such a goal can finally be won will be through federal financial assistance. The extension of the federal grant-in-aid for educational purposes, already available to the land-grant colleges and, for vocational education, to the secondary school field, seems both imminent and desirable.

Whether the federal grant-in-aid should be used to support the maintenance of separate schools is an issue that the country must soon face.

In the North, segregation in education is not formal, and in some states is prohibited. Nevertheless, the existence of residential restrictions in many northern cities has had discriminatory effects on Negro education. In Chicago, for example, the schools which are most crowded and employ double shift schedules are practically all in Negro neighborhoods. . . .

THE RIGHT TO HOUSING

Equality of opportunity to rent or buy a home should exist for every American. Today, many of our citizens face a double barrier when they try to satisfy their housing needs. They first encounter a general housing shortage which makes it difficult for any family without a home to find one. They then encounter prejudice and discrimination based upon race, color, religion or national origin, which places them at a disadvantage in competing for the limited housing that is available. The fact that many of those who face this double barrier are war veterans only underlines the inadequacy of our housing record.

Discrimination in housing results primarily from business practices. These practices may arise from special interests of business groups, such as the profits to be derived from confining minorities to slum areas, or they may reflect community prejudice. One of the most common practices is the policy of landlords and real estate agents to prevent Negroes from renting outside of designated areas. Again, it is "good business" to develop exclusive "restricted" suburban developments which are barred to all but white gentiles. When Negro veterans seek "GI" loans in order to build homes, they are likely to find that credit from private banks, without whose services there is no possibility of taking advantage of the GI Bill of Rights, is less freely available to members of their race. Private builders show a tendency not to construct new homes except for white occupancy. These interlocking business customs and devices form the core of our discriminatory policy. But community prejudice also finds expression in open public agitation against construction of public housing projects for Negroes, and by violence against Negroes who seek to occupy public housing projects or to build in "white" sections.

The restrictive covenant.—Under rulings of the Supreme Court, it is legally impossible to segregate housing on a racial or religious basis by zoning ordinance. Accordingly, the restrictive covenant has become the most effective modern method of accomplishing such segregation. Restrictive covenants generally take the form of agreements written into deeds of sale by which property owners mutually bind themselves not to sell or lease to an "undesirable." These agreements have thus far been enforceable by court action. Through these covenants large areas of land are barred against use by various classes of American citizens. Some are directed against only one minority group, others against a list of minorities. These have included Armenians, Jews, Negroes, Mexicans, Syrians, Japanese, Chinese and Indians.

While we do not know how much land in the country is subject to such restrictions, we do know that many areas, particularly large cities in the North and West, such as Chicago, Cleveland, Washington, D. C., and Los Angeles, are widely affected. The amount of land covered by racial restrictions in Chicago has been estimated at 80 percent. Students of the subject state that virtually all new subdivisions are blanketed by these covenants. Land immediately surrounding ghetto areas is frequently restricted in order to prevent any expansion in the ghetto. Thus, where old ghettos are surrounded by restrictions, and new subdivisions are also encumbered by them, there is practically no place for the people against whom the restrictions are directed to go. Since minorities have been forced into crowded slum areas, and must ultimately have access to larger living areas, the restrictive covenant is providing our democratic society with one of its most challenging problems. . . .

V. *To strengthen the right to equality of opportunity, the President's Committee recommends:*
1. **In general:**
   The elimination of segregation, based on race, color, creed, or national origin, from American life.

The separate but equal doctrine has failed in three important respects. First, it is inconsistent with the fundamental equalitarianism of the American way of life in that it marks groups with the brand of inferior status. Secondly, where it has been followed, the results have been separate and unequal facilities for minority peoples. Finally, it has kept people apart despite incontrovertible evidence that an environment favorable to civil rights is fostered whenever groups are permitted to live and work together. There is no adequate defense of segregation.

The conditioning by Congress of all federal grants-in-aid and other forms of federal assistance to public or private agencies for any purpose on the absence of discrimination and segregation based on race, color, creed, or national origin.

We believe that federal funds, supplied by taxpayers all over the nation, must not be used to support or perpetuate the pattern of segregation in education, public housing, public health services, or other public services and facilities generally. We recognize that these services are indispensable to individuals in modern society and to further social progress. It would be regrettable if federal aid, conditioned on nonsegregated services, should be rejected by sections most in need of such aid. The Committee believes that a reasonable interval of time may be allowed for adjustment to such a policy. But in the end it believes that segregation is wrong morally and practically and must not receive financial support by the whole people.

A minority of the Committee favors the elimination of segregation as an ultimate goal but opposes the imposition of a federal sanction. It believes that federal aid to the states for education, health, research and other public benefits should be granted provided that the states do not discriminate in the distribution of the funds. It dissents, however, from the majority's recommendation that the abolition of segregation be made a requirement, until the people of the states involved have themselves abolished the provisions in their state constitutions and laws which now require segregation. Some members are against the nonsegregation requirement in educational grants on the ground that it represents federal control over education. They feel, moreover, that the best way ultimately to end segregation is to raise the educational level of the people in the states affected; and to inculcate both the teachings of religion regarding human brotherhood and the ideals of our democracy regarding freedom and equality as a more solid basis for genuine and lasting acceptance by the peoples of the states.

2. For employment:

The enactment of a federal Fair Employment Practice Act prohibiting all forms of discrimination in private employment, based on race, color, creed, or national origin.

A federal Fair Employment Practice Act prohibiting discrimination in private employment should provide both educational machinery and legal sanctions for enforcement purposes. The administration of the act should be placed in the hands of a commission with power to receive complaints, hold hearings, issue cease-and-desist orders and seek court aid in enforcing these orders. The Act should contain definite fines for the violation of its procedural provisions. In order to allow time for voluntary adjustment of employment practices to the new law, and to permit the establishment of effective enforcement machinery, it is recommended that the sanction provisions of the law not become operative until one year after the enactment of the law.

The federal act should apply to labor unions and trade and professional associations, as well as to employers, insofar as the policies and practices of these organizations affect the employment status of workers.

The enactment by states of similar laws;

A federal fair employment practice statute will not reach activities which do not affect interstate commerce. To make fair employment a uniform national policy, state action will be needed. The successful experiences of some states warrant similar action by all of the others.

The issuance by the President of a mandate against discrimination in government employment and the creation of adequate machinery to enforce this mandate.

The Civil Service Commission and the personnel offices of all federal agencies should establish on-the-job training programs and other necessary machinery to enforce the nondiscrimination policy in government employment. It may well be desirable to establish a government fair employment practice commission, either as a part of the Civil Service Commission, or on an independent basis with authority to implement and enforce the Presidential mandate.

3. For education:

Enactment by the state legislatures of fair educational practice laws for public and private educational institutions, prohibiting discrimination in the admission and treatment of students based on race, color, creed, or national origin.

These laws should be enforced by independent administrative commissions. These commissions should consider complaints and hold hearings to review them. Where they are found to be valid, direct negotiation with the offending institution should be undertaken to secure compliance with the law. Wide publicity for the commission's findings would influence many schools and colleges sensitive to public opinion to abandon discrimination. The final sanction for such a body would be the cease-and-desist order enforceable by court action. The Committee believes that educational institutions supported by churches and definitely identified as denominational should be exempted.

There is a substantial division within the Committee on this recommendation. A majority favors it.

4. For housing:

The enactment by the states of laws outlawing restrictive covenants;

Renewed court attack, with intervention by the Department of Justice, upon restrictive covenants.

The effectiveness of restrictive covenants depends in the last analysis on court orders enforcing the private agreement. The power of the state is thus utilized to bolster discriminatory practices. The Committee believes that every effort must be made to prevent this abuse. We would hold this belief under any circumstances; under present conditions, when severe housing shortages are already causing hardship for many people of the country, we are especially emphatic in recommending measures to alleviate the situation.

5. For health services:

The enactment by the states of fair health practice statutes forbidding discrimination and segregation based on race, creed, color, or national origin, in the operation of public or private health facilities.

Fair health practice statutes, following the pattern of fair employment practice laws, seem desirable to the Committee. They should cover such matters as the training of doctors and nurses, the admission of patients to clinics, hospitals and other similar institutions, and the right of doctors and nurses to practice in hospitals. The administration of these statutes should be placed in the hands of commissions, with authority to receive complaints, hold hearings, issue cease-and-desist orders and engage in educational efforts to promote the policy of these laws.

6. For public services:

The enactment by Congress of a law stating that discrimination and segregation, based on race, color, creed, or national origin, in the rendering of all public services by the national government is contrary to public policy;

The enactment by the states of similar laws;

The elimination of discrimination and segregation depends largely on the leadership of the federal and state governments. They can make a great contribution toward accomplishing this end by affirming in law the principle of equality for all, and declaring that public funds, which belong to the whole people, will be used for the benefit of the entire population.

The establishment by act of Congress or executive order of a unit in the federal Bureau of the Budget to review the execution of all government programs, and the expenditures of all government funds, for compliance with the policy of nondiscrimination;

Continual surveillance is necessary to insure the nondiscriminatory execution of federal programs involving use of government funds. The responsibility for this task should be located in the Bureau of the Budget which has the duty of formulating the executive budget and supervising the execution of appropriation acts. The Bureau already checks the various departments and agencies for compliance with announced policy. Administratively, this additional function is consistent with its present duties and commensurate with its present powers.

The enactment by Congress of a law prohibiting discrimination or segregation, based on race, color, creed, or national origin, in interstate transportation and all the facilities thereof, to apply against both public officers and the employees of private transportation companies;

Legislation is needed to implement and supplement the Supreme Court decision in *Morgan v. Virginia*. There is evidence that some state officers are continuing to enforce segregation laws against interstate passengers. Moreover, carriers are still free to segregate such passengers on their own initiative since the *Morgan* decision covered only segregation based on law. Congress has complete power under the Constitution to forbid all forms of segregation in interstate commerce. We believe it should make prompt use of it.

The enactment by the states of laws guaranteeing equal access to places of public accommodation, broadly defined, for persons of all races, colors, creeds, and national origins.

Since the Constitution does not guarantee equal access to places of public accommodation, it is left to the states to secure that right. In the 18 states that have already enacted statutes, we hope that enforcement will make practice more compatible with theory. The civil suit for damages and the misdemeanor penalty have proved to be inadequate sanctions to secure the observance of these laws. Additional means, such as the revocation of licenses, and the issuance of cease-and-desist orders by administrative agencies are needed to bring about wider compliance. We think that all of the states should enact such legislation, using the broadest possible definition of public accommodation.

PRESIDENTIAL CIVIL-RIGHTS MESSAGE

3 ·§ ON FEBRUARY 2, 1948, President Truman sent a special message to Congress on civil rights. His strong stand at that particular moment was in part inspired by fear of Henry Wallace, who had recently announced his candidacy for President on the Progressive party ticket and who seemed likely to lure five million liberal voters from the Democrats. Excerpts from Truman's message follow:[3]

In the State of the Union Message on January 7, 1948, I spoke of five great goals toward which we should strive in our constant effort to strengthen our democracy and improve the welfare of our people. The first of these is to secure fully our essential human rights. I am now presenting to the Congress my recommendations for legislation to carry us forward toward that goal.

This Nation was founded by men and women who sought these shores that they might enjoy greater freedom and greater opportunity than they had known before. The founders of the United States proclaimed to the world the American belief that all men are created equal, and that governments are instituted to secure the inalienable rights with which all men are endowed. In the Declaration of Independence and the Constitution of the United States, they eloquently expressed the aspirations of . . . mankind for equality and freedom. . . .

We believe that all men are created equal and that they have the right to equal justice under law.

We believe that all men have the right to freedom of thought and of expression and the right to worship as they please.

We believe that all men are entitled to equal opportunities for jobs, for homes, for good health and for education.

We believe that all men should have a voice in their government

[3] Reprinted from *Truman Papers*, 1948, pp. 121–6.

and that government should protect, not usurp, the rights of the people.

These are the basic civil rights which are the source and the support of our democracy.

Today, the American people enjoy more freedom and opportunity than ever before. Never in our history has there been better reason to hope for the complete realization of the ideals of liberty and equality. . . .

The Federal Government has a clear duty to see that Constitutional guarantees of individual liberties and of equal protection under the laws are not denied or abridged anywhere in our Union. That duty is shared by all three branches of the Government, but it can be fulfilled only if the Congress enacts modern, comprehensive civil rights laws, adequate to the needs of the day, and demonstrating our continuing faith in the free way of life.

I recommend, therefore, that the Congress enact legislation at this session directed toward the following specific objectives:

1. Establishing a permanent Commission on Civil Rights, a Joint Congressional Committee on Civil Rights, and a Civil Rights Division in the Department of Justice.

2. Strengthening existing civil rights statutes.

3. Providing Federal protection against lynching.

4. Protecting more adequately the right to vote.

5. Establishing a Fair Employment Practice Commission to prevent unfair discrimination in employment.

6. Prohibiting discrimination in interstate transportation facilities.

7. Providing home-rule and suffrage in Presidential elections for the residents of the District of Columbia.

8. Providing Statehood for Hawaii and Alaska and a greater measure of self-government for our island possessions.

9. Equalizing the opportunities for residents of the United States to become naturalized citizens.

10. Settling the evacuation claims of Japanese-Americans.

Strengthening the Government Organization

As a first step, we must strengthen the organization of the Federal Government in order to enforce civil rights legislation more adequately and to watch over the state of our traditional liberties.

I recommend that the Congress establish a permanent Commission on Civil Rights reporting to the President. The Commission should continuously review our civil rights policies and practices, study specific problems, and make recommendations to the President at frequent intervals. It should work with other agencies of the Federal Government, with state and local governments, and with private organizations.

I also suggest that the Congress establish a Joint Congressional Committee on Civil Rights. This Committee should make a continuing study of legislative matters relating to civil rights and should consider means of improving respect for and enforcement of those rights. . . .

A specific Federal measure is needed to deal with the crime of lynching—against which I cannot speak too strongly. It is a principle of our democracy, written into our Constitution, that every person accused of an offense against the law shall have a fair, orderly trial in an impartial court. We have made great progress toward this end, but I regret to say that lynching has not yet finally disappeared from our land. So long as one person walks in fear of lynching, we shall not have achieved equal justice under law. I call upon the Congress to take decisive action against this crime.

Protecting the Right to Vote

Under the Constitution, the right of all properly qualified citizens to vote is beyond question. Yet the exercise of this right is still subject to interference. Some individuals are prevented from voting by isolated acts of intimidation. Some whole groups are prevented by outmoded policies prevailing in certain states or communities.

We need stronger statutory protection of the right to vote. I urge the Congress to enact legislation forbidding interference by public officers or private persons with the right of qualified citizens to participate in primary, special and general elections in which Federal officers are to be chosen. This legislation should extend to elections for state as well as Federal officers insofar as interference with the right to vote results from discriminatory action by public officers based on race, color, or other unreasonable classification.

Requirements for the payment of poll taxes also interfere with the right to vote. There are still seven states which, by their constitutions, place this barrier between their citizens and the ballot box. The American people would welcome voluntary action on the part of these states to remove this barrier. Nevertheless, I believe the Congress should enact measures insuring that the right to vote in elections for Federal officers shall not be contingent upon the payment of taxes.

I wish to make it clear that the enactment of the measures I have recommended will in no sense result in Federal conduct of elections. They are designed to give qualified citizens Federal protection of their right to vote. The actual conduct of elections, as always, will remain the responsibility of State governments.

Fair Employment Practice Commission

We in the United States believe that all men are entitled to equality of opportunity. Racial, religious and other invidious forms of discrimination deprive the individual of an equal chance to develop and utilize his talents and to enjoy the rewards of his efforts.

Once more I repeat my request that the Congress enact fair employment practice legislation prohibiting discrimination in employment based on race, color, religion or national origin. The legislation should create a Fair Employment Practice Commission with authority to prevent discrimination by employers and labor unions, trade and professional associations, and government agencies and employment bureaus. The degree of effectiveness which the wartime Fair Employment Practice Committee attained shows that it is possible to equalize job opportunity by government action and thus to eliminate the influence of prejudice in employment.

Interstate Transportation

The channels of interstate commerce should be open to all Americans on a basis of complete equality. The Supreme Court has recently declared unconstitutional state laws requiring segregation on public carriers in interstate travel. Company regulations must not be allowed to replace unconstitutional state laws. I urge the Congress to prohibit discrimination and segregation, in the use of interstate transportation facilities, by both public officers and the employees of private companies. . . .

The position of the United States in the world today makes it especially urgent that we adopt these measures to secure for all our people their essential rights.

The peoples of the world are faced with the choice of freedom or enslavement, a choice between a form of government which harnesses the state in the service of the individual and a form of government which chains the individual to the needs of the state. . . .

We know that our democracy is not perfect. But we do know that it offers a fuller, freer, happier life to our people than any totalitarian nation has ever offered.

If we wish to inspire the peoples of the world whose freedom is in jeopardy, if we wish to restore hope to those who have already lost their civil liberties, if we wish to fulfill the promise that is ours, we must correct the remaining imperfections in our practice of democracy.

We know the way. We need only the will.

SOUTHERN RESPONSE TO CIVIL-RIGHTS SPEECH

4 ⋅⋅⋅§   PRESIDENT TRUMAN'S civil-rights message provoked a revolt in the Southern wing of the Democratic party that led ultimately to the Dixiecrat secession. On April 8, 1948, Representative William M. Colmer of Mississippi addressed the House:[4]

Mr. Speaker, not since the first gun was fired on Fort Sumter, resulting as it did in the greatest fratricidal strife in the history of the world, has any message of any President of these glorious United States provoked so much controversy, and resulted in the driving of a schism in the ranks of our people, as did President Truman's so-called civil-rights message, sent to the Congress several weeks ago. Not only did that message provoke serious racial controversies, but it raised anew the issue of the rights of the sovereign States as against a strong centralized government and drove a devastating wedge into the unity of the Democratic Party at a time when that party was riding high on a wave of popularity in the entire country.

It revived the age-old controversy which flourished at the very beginning of our Government, the controversy of a strong centralized government as advocated by Alexander Hamilton on the one hand, and a government of the people as opposed to a government by the rulers, as advocated by the greatest of all exponents of civil rights, possibly the greatest Democrat of them all, Thomas Jefferson. For, after all, it was Jefferson's theory that that people is best governed who is least governed, and the closer the government is to the people, the better the government is.

And while it is freely admitted and generally understood that this

---

[4] Excerpts reprinted from *Congressional Record*, Eightieth Congress, second session, pp. 4270–1.

message was conceived as a political maneuver, at a time when that erstwhile Republican and Democrat, Henry Wallace, who echoes the voice of the Kremlin in Moscow, was attempting to form a third party, it must also be recognized that this proposed program would adversely affect the rights, privileges, and freedom of the people of all sections and of all walks of life in this country. It stabs at the very heart of the rights and freedom of all races, colors, and sections of our great country. For, if the Federal Government can repeal the poll tax in Mississippi and several other Southern States, regulate employment under the FEPC, punish innocent taxpayers under the antilynch bill, and abolish segregation in the several States by usurpation of the sovereign rights of the several States of the Union, then we have indeed witnessed an end of constitutional government as conceived by the founding fathers. . . .

Is it any wonder then, Mr. Speaker, that a revolt has arisen all over our country, from Mississippi on the shores of the Gulf-kissed coast in the South to the stony crags of Maine in the North, and from the Atlantic to the Pacific Oceans, by southern Democrats and those freedom-loving Americans everywhere, at this attempt to destroy the true civil rights of the citizens of our great and common country? For, I again call to the attention of my northern colleagues what I have often repeated upon the floor of this House, namely, that the South is not the only section aggrieved by these proposed unconstitutional laws. The small- as well as the large-business man in the North, the East, and the West, will find the heavy hand of the Federal Government just as oppressive in the operation of his business under FEPC as will the southern employer. The citizens of other sections of this country will feel, under these politically expedient laws, the same sharp resentment at the interference by a powerful Federal Government with their individual liberties as the people of the South.

Does any fair-minded American find amazement, however, that the people of the South are in revolt against the leadership of the Democratic Party? Is it necessary to remind any student of political history in this country that it was the section from which I hail that has cradled, nourished, and sustained the Democratic Party throughout its lean as well as its prosperous years? The South has ever been a strong believer in and contender for the Jeffersonian theory of democracy. It has ever been ready to fight for those principles. Many of its most gallant sons shed their precious blood upon the altar of States' rights. Certainly it is not surprising, therefore, that it should take the lead in the battle against this program, which would destroy the last vestige of the rights of the sovereign States. . . .

But now, for the first time in the history of the country, and the loyalty of my section to the Democratic Party, a President of the United States has asked the Congress to enact such a devastating, obnoxious, and repugnant program to the people of that section and their Jeffersonian conception of democracy as this so-called civil-rights program. No President, either Democrat or Republican, has ever seen fit heretofore to make such recommendations.

And what, I ask you, my colleagues, has this message of our President, calling for the enactment of this program, accomplished to date? So far as I have been able to observe its accomplishments have been two-fold. First, it has inflicted an apparently fatal blow, not only to the unity of the party, but to the unity of the country, at a time when that unity is so highly desirable in a fight to the death with the enemy of free men—communism. Secondly, it has encouraged the arrogant demands of these minority groups to whom it was designed to appeal. Witness, Mr. Speaker, the sorry spectacle of an erstwhile pullman porter, William Randolph, a Negro labor leader, defiantly telling the membership of a committee of this Congress that unless segregation in the armed forces should be abolished that he would call upon the Negroes of this country to ignore the call of their country in the event of a war with Russia. Such ingratitude, such arrogance, such treason can only be attributed to such political bargaining as this proposed program.

DESEGREGATION OF ARMED FORCES

5 ◆§ SINCE CONGRESS FAILED to enact any part of his program, Truman's major concrete civil-rights achievements resulted from the issuance of two executive orders in the summer preceding the elections of 1948. On July 26, 1948, the President ordered that "All personnel actions taken by Federal appointing officers shall be based solely on merit and fitness; and such officers are authorized and directed to take appropriate steps to insure that in all such actions there shall be no discrimination because of race, color, religion, or national origin." On the same day he issued a second

order, which began the desegregation of the armed services. An excerpt from this second order follows:[5]

EXECUTIVE ORDER 9981

ESTABLISHING THE PRESIDENT'S COMMITTEE ON EQUALITY OF TREAT-
MENT AND OPPORTUNITY IN THE ARMED SERVICES

WHEREAS it is essential that there be maintained in the armed services of the United States the highest standards of democracy, with equality of treatment and opportunity for all those who serve in our country's defense:

NOW, THEREFORE, by virtue of the authority vested in me as President of the United States, by the Constitution and the statutes of the United States, and as Commander in Chief of the armed services, it is hereby ordered as follows:

1. It is hereby declared to be the policy of the President that there shall be equality of treatment and opportunity for all persons in the armed services without regard to race, color, religion or national origin. This policy shall be put into effect as rapidly as possible, having due regard to the time required to effectuate any necessary changes without impairing efficiency or morale.

2. There shall be created in the National Military Establishment an advisory committee to be known as the President's Committee on Equality of Treatment and Opportunity in the Armed Services, which shall be composed of seven members to be designated by the President.

3. The Committee is authorized on behalf of the President to examine into the rules, procedures and practices of the armed services in order to determine in what respect such rules, procedures and practices may be altered or improved with a view to carrying out the policy of this order. The Committee shall confer and advise with the Secretary of Defense, the Secretary of the Army, the Secretary of the Navy, and the Secretary of the Air Force, and shall make such recommendations to the President and to said Secretaries as in the judgment of the Committee will effectuate the policy hereof.

4. All executive departments and agencies of the Federal Government are authorized and directed to cooperate with the Committee in its work, and to furnish the Committee such information or the

[5] Reprinted from *Federal Register* (Washington, D.C., 1948), XVIII, 722.

services of such persons as the Committee may require in the performance of its duties.

1948 DEMOCRATIC CIVIL-RIGHTS PLANK

6 ⋖§   AT THE DEMOCRATIC convention of 1948, which reluctantly
nominated Harry Truman, the big issue was civil rights.
The platform committee, with Truman's support, drafted a plank
calling on Congress to help achieve equal protection of the law
for racial minorities. From the convention floor, liberals and big-
city bosses then proposed a somewhat stronger and more explicit
civil-rights statement. After a bitter fight the liberal plank won the
convention's approval, and several southern delegations walked out.
The final Democratic civil-rights plank of 1948 follows:[6]

The Democratic Party is responsible for the great civil rights gains
made in recent years in eliminating unfair and illegal discrimination
based on race, creed or color.

The Democratic Party commits itself to continuing its efforts to
eradicate all racial, religious and economic discrimination.

We again state our belief that racial and religious minorities must
have the right to live, the right to work, the right to vote, the full
and equal protection of the laws, on a basis of equality with all citizens
as guaranteed by the Constitution.

We highly commend President Harry S. Truman for his courageous
stand on the issue of civil rights.

We call upon the Congress to support our President in guaranteeing
these basic and fundamental American Principles: (1) the right of
full and equal political participation; (2) the right to equal opportunity of employment; (3) the right of security of person; (4) and
the right of equal treatment in the service and defense of our nation.

VETO OF SEGREGATION BILL

7 ⋖§   THOUGH CONGRESS CONTINUED to thwart Truman's repeated
appeals for the civil-rights legislation he had requested first
in 1948, he was still reluctant to use his executive authority during
the Korean War to create a Fair Employment Practice Committee.
When he acceded finally to demands by liberals, Truman established a commission that was weaker than the body President
Roosevelt had authorized nearly ten years before.

[6] Reprinted from *The New York Times*, July 15, 1948, p. 8.

Despite Truman's reluctance on this front, the federal government was still active in the struggle to extend the benefits of legal equality to the Negro. It was during his administration that the Department of Justice, as *amicus curiae*, submitted briefs arguing the unconstitutionality of restrictive covenants and segregation in public schools. In the United States of the early fifties, when illiberalism seemed likely to triumph, it was Harry S. Truman who refused to abandon the Negro. Though his actions did not match his words, he did advance the cause of the Negro, and he battled those who sought to extend segregation. On November 2, 1951, he explained his pocket veto of a bill expanding segregation:[7]

I am withholding my approval of H.R. 5411, a bill to amend Public Laws No. 815 and 874 of the 81st Congress with respect to schools in critical defense housing areas and for other purposes.

The basic purpose of this bill is meritorious. It would provide for the construction, maintenance, and operation of elementary and secondary schools in those localities where defense activities of the Federal Government have created unusual burdens. Thus, this bill would complete the plan of Federal assistance now operating under the Defense Housing and Community Facilities and Services Act of September 1951. In addition, it contains perfecting amendments which would improve the administration of an established program supporting the operation of local school facilities, where they are inadequate to meet the impact of expanded defense activities.

Unfortunately, however, the Congress has included one provision in this bill which I cannot approve. This provision would require a group of schools on Federal property which are now operating successfully on an integrated basis to be segregated. It would do so by requiring Federal schools on military bases and other Federal property to conform to the laws of the States in which such installations are located. This is a departure from the provisions of Public Laws 815 and 874, which required only that the education provided under these circumstances should be comparable to that available to other children in the State. The purpose of the proposed change is clearly to require that schools operated solely by the Federal Government on Federally-owned land, if located in any of seventeen States, shall be operated on a segregated basis "to the maximum extent practicable."

[7] Excerpt from White House press release, November 2, 1951, Truman Papers, Truman Library.

This proposal, if enacted into law, would constitute a backward step in the efforts of the Federal Government to extend equal rights and opportunities to all our people. During the past few years, we have made rapid progress toward equal treatment and opportunity in those activities of the Federal Government where we have a direct responsibility to follow national rather than local interpretations of nondiscrimination. Two outstanding examples are the Federal civil service and our armed forces, where important advances have been made toward equalizing treatment and opportunity.

Not every school operated on a Federal reservation has been integrated. It is never our purpose to insist on integration without considering pertinent local factors; but it is the duty of the Federal Government to move forward in such locations and in such fields of activity as seem best and appropriate under individual conditions and circumstances.

We have assumed a role of world leadership in seeking to unite people of great cultural and racial diversity for the purpose of resisting aggression, protecting their mutual security and advancing their own economic and political development. We should not impair our moral position by enacting a law that requires a discrimination based on race. Step by step we are discarding old discriminations; we must not adopt new ones.

TRUMAN'S HEALTH MESSAGE

8 ANOTHER AREA in which the President went beyond the New Deal was medical care, and here there were even fewer tangible achievements than in the field of civil rights. In November 1945 Truman sent his first message recommending a comprehensive health program to Congress, and on many occasions thereafter he pleaded with the legislators to enact his program, but always without success. In his November message Truman asked for federal funds for hospital construction, federal grants to assist medical research, extension of the social insurance system to include payment of benefits to replace at least part of a worker's earnings lost because of illness, and expansion of federal-state cooperative health programs. The heart of his program, however, was a proposal for compulsory national health insurance. After his election in 1948 Truman redoubled his efforts to win approval of his health program, but the conservative forces in Congress and the skillful opposition of the American Medical Association proved too strong. Excerpts

from the Special Message to the Congress Recommending a Comprehensive Health Program, November 19, 1945, follow:[8]

In my message to the Congress of September 6, 1945, there were enumerated in a proposed Economic Bill of Rights certain rights which ought to be assured to every American citizen.

One of them was: "The right to adequate medical care and the opportunity to achieve and enjoy good health." Another was the "right to adequate protection from the economic fears of . . . sickness. . . ."

Millions of our citizens do not now have a full measure of opportunity to achieve and enjoy good health. Millions do not now have protection or security against the economic effects of sickness. The time has arrived for action to help them attain that opportunity and that protection.

The people of the United States received a shock when the medical examinations conducted by the Selective Service System revealed the widespread physical and mental incapacity among the young people of our nation. We had had prior warnings from eminent medical authorities and from investigating committees. The statistics of the last war had shown the same condition. But the Selective Service System has brought it forcibly to our attention recently—in terms which all of us can understand. . . .

People with low or moderate incomes do not get the same medical attention as those with high incomes. The poor have more sickness, but they get less medical care. People who live in rural areas do not get the same amount or quality of medical attention as those who live in our cities.

Our new Economic Bill of Rights should mean health security for all, regardless of residence, station, or race—everywhere in the United States.

We should resolve now that the health of this Nation is a national concern; that financial barriers in the way of attaining health shall be removed; that the health of all its citizens deserves the help of all the Nation. . . .

. . . The principal reason why people do not receive the care they need is that they cannot afford to pay for it on an individual basis at the time they need it. This is true not only for needy persons. It is also true for a large proportion of normally self-supporting persons. . . .

---

[8] Reprinted from *Truman Papers, 1945*, pp. 475ff.

For some persons with very low income or no income at all we now use taxpayers' money in the form of free services, free clinics, and public hospitals. Tax-supported, free medical care for needy persons, however, is insufficient in most of our cities and in nearly all of our rural areas. This deficiency cannot be met by private charity or the kindness of individual physicians.

Everyone should have ready access to all necessary medical, hospital and related services.

I recommend solving the basic problem by distributing the costs through expansion of our existing compulsory social insurance system. This is not socialized medicine.

Everyone who carries fire insurance knows how the law of averages is made to work so as to spread the risk, and to benefit the insured who actually suffers the loss. If instead of the costs of sickness being paid only by those who get sick, all the people—sick and well—were required to pay premiums into an insurance fund, the pool of funds thus created would enable all who do fall sick to be adequately served without overburdening anyone. That is the principle upon which all forms of insurance are based. . . .

A system of required prepayment would not only spread the costs of medical care, it would also prevent much serious disease. Since medical bills would be paid by the insurance fund, doctors would more often be consulted when the first signs of disease occur instead of when the disease has become serious. Modern hospital, specialist and laboratory services, as needed, would also become available to all, and would improve the quality and adequacy of care. Prepayment of medical care would go a long way toward furnishing insurance against disease itself, as well as against medical bills.

Such a system of prepayment should cover medical, hospital, nursing and laboratory services. It should also cover dental care—as fully and for as many of the population as the available professional personnel and the financial resources of the system permit.

The ability of our people to pay for adequate medical care will be increased if, while they are well, they pay regularly into a common health fund, instead of paying sporadically and unevenly when they are sick. This health fund should be built up nationally, in order to establish the broadest and most stable basis for spreading the costs of illness, and to assure adequate financial support for doctors and hospitals everywhere. If we were to rely on state-by-state action only, many years would elapse before we had any general coverage. Meanwhile health service would continue to be grossly uneven, and disease would continue to cross state boundary lines. . . .

People should remain free to choose their own physicians and hospitals. The removal of financial barriers between patient and doctor would enlarge the present freedom of choice. The legal requirement on the population to contribute involves no compulsion over the doctor's freedom to decide what services his patient needs. People will remain free to obtain and pay for medical service outside of the health insurance system if they desire, even though they are members of the system; just as they are free to send their children to private instead of to public schools, although they must pay taxes for public schools.

Likewise physicians should remain free to accept or reject patients. They must be allowed to decide for themselves whether they wish to participate in the health insurance system full time, part time, or not at all. A physician may have some patients who are in the system and some who are not. Physicians must be permitted to be represented through organizations of their own choosing, and to decide whether to carry on in individual practice or to join with other doctors in group practice in hospitals or in clinics. . . .

None of this is really new. The American people are the most insurance-minded people in the world. They will not be frightened off from health insurance because some people have misnamed it "socialized medicine."

I repeat—what I am recommending is not socialized medicine.

Socialized medicine means that all doctors work as employees of government. The American people want no such system. No such system is here proposed.

Under the plan I suggest, our people would continue to get medical and hospital services just as they do now—on the basis of their own voluntary decisions and choices. Our doctors and hospitals would continue to deal with disease with the same professional freedom as now. There would, however, be this all-important difference: whether or not patients get the services they need would not depend on how much they can afford to pay at the time.

I am in favor of the broadest possible coverage for this insurance system. I believe that all persons who work for a living and their dependents should be covered under such an insurance plan. This would include wage and salary earners, those in business for themselves, professional persons, farmers, agricultural labor, domestic employees, government employees and employees of non-profit institutions and their families.

In addition, needy persons and other groups should be covered through appropriate premiums paid for them by public agencies. Increased Federal funds should also be made available by the Congress under the public assistance programs to reimburse the States for part of such premiums, as well as for direct expenditures made by the States in paying for medical services provided by doctors, hospitals and other agencies to needy persons. . . .

We are a rich nation and can afford many things. But ill-health which can be prevented or cured is one thing we cannot afford.

AMA OPPOSITION TO HEALTH-INSURANCE BILL

9 ৶ৼ৾ THE FOLLOWING EDITORIAL in the *Journal of the American Medical Association* (January 15, 1949) expresses the attitude of organized medicine toward the President's health program:[9]

The Drift Toward a Socialist Democracy

The consensus of editorial writers whose opinions have become available on the address given by President Truman to the Congress on January 5 indicates their point of view that the President is considerably left of what used to be called the New Deal. The Congress, if it should adopt any considerable number of the recommendations made, would move the nation away from its present status as a republic or a true democracy into a condition which resembles what is called in Europe a socialist democracy. Adhering to the pattern followed by other nations in this drift, President Truman said:

> We must spare no effort to raise the general level of health in this country. In a nation as rich as ours it is a shocking fact that tens of millions lack adequate medical care. We are short of doctors, hospitals and nurses. We must remedy these shortages. Moreover we need, and we must have without further delay, a system of prepaid medical insurance which will enable every American to afford good medical care.

A careful analysis of the statement quoted indicates the necessity for an absolute denial of the statement made that "tens of millions

[9] From the *Journal of the American Medical Association*, January 15, 1949, pp. 156–7. Reprinted by permission of the *Journal*.

lack adequate medical care." Such statements should not be made without the ability to produce the evidence in their support. As far as can be determined by all available studies, and particularly recent studies, that statement is not supported by competent evidence.

The President says that we are short of doctors, hospitals and nurses. Actually the United States, as was proved in a statement published in these columns recently, has more doctors in proportion to the population than any other country in the world, whether with or without a system of socialized medicine. True, there are faults of distribution of physicians which need to be remedied. The faults, however, are related to economic rather than other factors. The Congress has passed and the government has implemented the Hill-Burton Act for increasing hospitals about as rapidly as they can be increased. The chief difficulty at present is the difficulty of finding personnel to staff such hospitals and the economic conditions sufficient to support such hospitals.

The American Nurses' Association, the American Red Cross, the American Surgical Association, the American College of Surgeons, the American Medical Association and, in fact, all organizations in this country interested in the utilization of nurses have been working on technics for increasing the available supply of nurses, and enrolments were 5,000 more in 1948 than in 1947; the total answer is not yet apparent. If the federal government or any of its agencies has an answer to the problem of the nurse supply, that answer will be welcomed by the medical profession. Many of the nurses themselves insist that it is simply a question of adequate remuneration in comparison with what other employees, particularly those affiliated with unions, are paid for their services.

The final sentence of Mr. Truman's recommendation brings some interesting thoughts. The first time he uses the words "adequate medical care" and the second time "good medical care," whereas Mr. [Oscar—Eds.] Ewing [Federal Security Agency administrator—Eds.] usually says "proper medical care." What is needed at this time is a definition by some appropriate agency of these terms "adequate," "good" and "proper." There is plenty of evidence that the kind of medical care given in other countries under such systems as that proposed for the United States has no resemblance to the quality of medical service that now prevails in the United States. When diagnosis is made on the basis of one or two questions and when therapy is provided on the same basis, when doctors try to see from 40 to 100 patients a day in order to give the kind of medical care that can be given under such circumstances—and that is the case in many of the countries that have these systems—the medical care cannot be characterized as "adequate," "good" or "proper." Apparently what the proponents need is some adequate, good or proper term to characterize the kind of medical care that they refer to. The medical profession contends that it is inadequate, bad and improper. The one positive characteristic that it has is the fact that it is provided by the government following taxation of all of the workers of the country; a proper term would be nationalized, bureaucratic, governmental or socialized medical care.

Following the address by President Truman, a bill was introduced into the Senate bearing the names of Senators [James—Eds.] Murray, [Howard—Eds.] McGrath, [Robert—Eds.] Wagner, [Dennis—Eds.] Chavez, [Glen—Eds.] Taylor and [Claude—Eds.] Pepper and into the House of Representatives by Congressman [John—Eds.] Dingell, which assurance from Senator Murray's office indicates is identical with Senate Bill 1320 except for the change in date and a new number, which is Senate Bill 5. As far as can be determined, there is no cry for this type of government medical service from the vast majority of the middle class people of the United States. Ours apparently is the only nation in the world still possessing a large middle class. Nor is there any insistent demand for this legislation from rural groups. In the meantime, moreover, statements just made available from competent sources indicate that at the present time 52,000,000 Americans are insured against the costs of hospitalization, 31,000,000 against loss of income due to disability, 26,000,000 against surgical expense and 9,000,000 against medical expense. This is the most rapid rate of growth of any form of prepaid medical insurance on a voluntary basis that the world has ever known. It answers the President's request—but it is not compulsory!

SOUTHERN ATTACK ON ORGANIZED LABOR

10 ◄§ TO RE-ESTABLISH the old Roosevelt coalition, which by Election Day 1946 lay in ruins, Truman had first of all to win back labor. His successful courtship of unions, beginning in 1947, was the indispensable first step toward his electoral triumph in 1948. In the postwar period public hostility toward organized labor mounted rapidly, and conservatives decided that the time had come to curb the power of the unions. In the South bitterness was

particularly acute, as is revealed in the following speech to the House of Representatives on April 30, 1946, by Judge Howard W. Smith of Virginia:[10]

Mr. Speaker, the utter indifference of the Government, the people, and the press to the economic calamity that is about to engulf the Nation in a few days is amazing and frightening. The coal strike which has been in progress for a month, with no signs of settlement, has so depleted the Nation's supply of coal that industry and transportation are today breaking down all over the country. In a matter of days the wheels of industry will stop turning for lack of coal, and the Nation will suffer a paralysis that will bring about utter chaos. In the face of this calamity, negotiations for settlement of the strike have broken up and apparently no serious effort is being made to avert the pending crisis.

Stranger still, there is at the moment no demand by the mine workers for additional wages or improved working conditions. The sole issue is the demand of the United Mine Workers that the labor union be paid a royalty of 10 cents a ton on all coal mined and consumed by the American people. The issue is whether the American public shall be subjected to a special tax levied by and paid to a private labor organization. The principle involved is vital. If the miners' union can levy a public tax for private purposes on the coal used by the consuming public, then every other labor union can and naturally will levy a tax on the American people for their private use on every other commodity consumed by the public. And so we shall soon have every minority pressure group, that has the power to deprive the public of essential commodities, levying its own private tax upon the American people.

Such a spectacle should have the effect of finally arousing a people steeped in lethargy to a sense of danger and responsibility—a responsibility to demand in no uncertain voice that the Congress and the administration adopt a firm, decisive policy to prohibit this new and revolutionary type of extortion. . . .

Six years ago, as chairman of the Committee to Investigate the National Labor Relations Board, I conducted an investigation that disclosed that certain radical elements of organized labor working in conjunction with equally radical agencies of the Federal Govern-

[10] Excerpts reprinted from *Congressional Record*, Seventy-ninth Congress, second session, p. 4257.

ment, both tinged with communistic theories, were slowly but surely fastening upon the Nation a labor dictatorship intended to control and run the Government of the United States in the interest of minority pressure groups. The evidence was so clear and the findings of that committee so specific, that the House of Representatives adopted the remedial legislation which we recommended. Unfortunately that legislation, like other legislation I have since proposed, failed of final passage. The disclosures of the threatened labor dictatorship made by the committee of which I was chairman 6 years ago were so clear and the proof so positive that these radical units of organized labor have, in three different campaigns, promoted opposition to me and have sought my defeat. The fourth attempt to eliminate me from Congress by these radical groups, headed by the CIO Political Action Committee, is now being threatened. I defy them now as I have done in the past.

I do not desire a seat in the Congress at the price of supine submission to any minority pressure group, particularly the CIO Political Action Committee.

If the people of this Nation are so indifferent to the American system of government under which we have lived and prospered that they are willing to submit supinely to the yoke being fitted to their necks by a small group of labor dictators, I have at least done my part to sound the warning.

In recent days the CIO Political Action Committee has announced its purpose in the present primary campaigns throughout the Southern States to seek to eliminate from public life every Congressman who has shown an unwillingness to submit to their dictatorship. This is no secret. They have published it boldly and boastfully under large headlines in every daily newspaper in the country. They have even had the temerity to announce in these publications the huge sums of money that they have set aside to buy the elections of Congressmen in the Southern States who will do their will. They propose to conduct this nefarious enterprise openly and boldly from their head offices in New York and Washington.

Are the southern people become so supine and spineless that they will meekly submit to another carpetbagger invasion without raising a voice in protest? Such is the scheme that has been cooked up, dished, and is ready to be served by persons who are not even citizens of the States they propose to invade and conquer.

The carpetbaggers who invaded the South after the Civil War were at least American-born citizens with American names. The communistic designs of today had not then been brought to our shores.

Today this new swarm of carpetbaggers who are invading the Southern States to take over our political affairs are impregnated and indoctrinated with communism. They seek and have long sought to destroy the American system of government as we have known it and to fasten upon us the fetters of political and economic dictatorship.

There is not an American-born citizen in the top-flight leadership of this model 1946 carpetbag invasion. The swarm of minor hirelings who propose to do the actual field work are but the puppets of a foreign-born and foreign-conceived plot to spread the fearsome specter of communism over the face of the globe.

On my part, I shall fight this invasion openly and aboveboard with all the energy I possess. Expecting no quarter and asking none, I shall be content if I can bring to public notice an awareness of the destructive purposes of this CIO Political Action Committee campaign to destroy the system of government under which we have lived and grown strong.

Impregnated with communistic aims, purposes, and personnel, as has been proved time and again from both inside and outside the CIO, this un-American organization seeks absolute domination and control over the economic life of the Nation. Only an aroused public opinion can stem this tide. No Member of Congress who knows the fact and seeks re-election is worthy of a seat in this body who will temporize or compromise with the nefarious aims of these selfish groups.

VETO OF TAFT-HARTLEY BILL

11 ◄§ NOTHING DID MORE to win for Truman the gratitude and support of organized labor than his veto of the Taft-Hartley bill in 1947. In the previous year the President had vetoed one stringent labor measure (the Case bill), and Congress had been unable to override the veto. In 1947, however, the new Republican majority, backed by a public still fuming over the great strikes of 1946, determined to redress the balance between labor and management allegedly upset by the prolabor Wagner Act (National Labor Relations Act) of 1935.

The resulting Taft-Hartley bill permitted unions to be sued by employers for breach of contract and by third parties suffering from jurisdictional disputes and secondary boycotts. The bill outlawed the closed shop but permitted union-shop contracts unless state law held these also illegal. It prohibited labor from exacting pay for work not performed and from contributing to campaign funds. It ended the checkoff system, by which employers collected union dues. It allowed employers to present their side during organizational campaigns and to ask the National Labor Relations Board to hold elections to determine bargaining agents. Before a union could engage in collective bargaining, its officers had to sign affidavits that they were not members of the Communist party, and unions were required to register with and submit financial reports to the Secretary of Labor. By the terms of the bill, when either labor or management intended to terminate a contract, it had to give sixty days' notice. It empowered the President to ask for court injunctions that could forestall for eighty days a strike that he thought would endanger national welfare. Finally, the bill created a special labor conciliation service outside the jurisdiction of the Department of Labor, which Congress believed favored unions. Excerpts from Truman's belligerent veto message, issued on June 20, 1947, follow:[11]

I find that this bill is completely contrary to that national policy of economic freedom. It would require the Government, in effect, to become an unwanted participant at every bargaining table. It would establish by law limitations on the terms of every bargaining agreement, and nullify thousands of agreements mutually arrived at and satisfactory to the parties. It would inject the Government deeply into the process by which employers and workers reach agreement. It would superimpose bureaucratic procedures on the free decisions of local employers and employees.

At a time when we are determined to remove, as rapidly as practicable, Federal controls established during the war, this bill would involve the Government in free processes of our economic system to a degree unprecedented in peacetime. . . .

The bill prescribes unequal penalties for the same offense. It would require the National Labor Relations Board to give priority to charges against workers over related charges against employers. It would discriminate against workers by arbitrarily penalizing them for all critical strikes.

[11] Reprinted from *Truman Papers*, 1947, pp. 288–97.

Much has been made of the claim that the bill is intended simply to equalize the positions of labor and management. Careful analysis shows that this claim is unfounded. Many of the provisions of the bill standing alone seem innocent but, considered in relation to each other, reveal a consistent pattern of inequality. . . .

4. *The bill would deprive workers of vital protection which they now have under the law*

(1) The bill would make it easier for an employer to get rid of employees whom he wanted to discharge because they exercised their right of self-organization guaranteed by the act. It would permit an employer to dismiss a man on the pretext of a slight infraction of shop rules, even though his real motive was to discriminate against this employee for union activity.

(2) The bill would also put a powerful new weapon in the hands of employers by permitting them to initiate elections at times strategically advantageous to them. It is significant that employees on economic strike who may have been replaced are denied a vote. An employer could easily thwart the will of his employees by raising a question of representation at a time when the union was striking over contract terms.

(3) It would give employers the means to engage in endless litigation, draining the energy and resources of unions in court actions, even though the particular charges were groundless.

(4) It would deprive workers of the power to meet the competition of goods produced under sweatshop conditions by permitting employers to halt every type of secondary boycott, not merely those for unjustifiable purposes.

(5) It would reduce the responsibility of employers for unfair labor practices committed in their behalf. The effect of the bill is to narrow unfairly employer liability for antiunion acts and statements made by persons who, in the eyes of the employees affected, act and speak for management, but who may not be "agents" in the strict legal sense of that term.

(6) At the same time it would expose unions to suits for acts of violence, wildcat strikes and other actions, none of which were authorized or ratified by them. By employing elaborate legal doctrine, the bill applies a superficially similar test of responsibility for employers and unions—each would be responsibile for the acts of his "agents." But the power of an employer to control the acts of his subordinates

is direct and final. This is radically different from the power of unions to control the acts of their members—who are, after all, members of a free association. . . .

6. *The bill would establish an ineffective and discriminatory emergency procedure for dealing with major strikes affecting the public health or safety*

This procedure would be certain to do more harm than good, and to increase rather than diminish widespread industrial disturbances. I am convinced that the country would be in for a bitter disappointment if these provisions of the bill became law.

The procedure laid down by the bill is elaborate. Its essential features are a Presidential board of inquiry, a waiting period of approximately 80 days (enforced by injunction), and a secret ballot vote of the workers on the question of whether or not to accept their employer's last offer. . . .

After this elaborate procedure the injunction would then have to be dissolved, the parties would be free to fight out their dispute, and it would be mandatory for the President to transfer the whole problem to the Congress, even if it were not in session. Thus, major economic disputes between employers and their workers over contract terms might ultimately be thrown into the political arena for disposition. One could scarcely devise a less effective method for discouraging critical strikes.

This entire procedure is based upon the same erroneous assumptions as those which underlay the strike-vote provision of the War Labor Disputes Act, namely, that strikes are called in haste as the result of inflamed passions, and that union leaders do not represent the wishes of the workers. We have learned by experience, however, that strikes in the basic industries are not called in haste, but only after long periods of negotiation and serious deliberation; and that in the secret-ballot election the workers almost always vote to support their leaders.

Furthermore, a fundamental inequity runs through these provisions. The bill provides for injunctions to prohibit workers from striking, even against terms dictated by employers after contracts have expired. There is no provision assuring the protection of the rights of the employees during the period they are deprived of the right to protect themselves by economic action. . . .

9. *The bill raises serious issues of public policy which transcend labor-management difficulties*

(1) In undertaking to restrict political contributions and expendi-

tures, the bill would prohibit many legitimate activities on the part of unions and corporations. This provision would prevent the ordinary union newspaper from commenting favorably or unfavorably upon candidates or issues in national elections. I regard this as a dangerous intrusion on free speech, unwarranted by any demonstration of need, and quite foreign to the stated purposes of this bill.

Furthermore, this provision can be interpreted as going far beyond its apparent objectives, and as interfering with necessary business activities. It provides no exemption for corporations whose business is the publication of newspapers or the operation of radio stations. It makes no distinctions between expenditures made by such corporations for the purpose of influencing the results of an election, and other expenditures made by them in the normal course of their business "in connection with" an election. Thus it would raise a host of troublesome questions concerning the legality of many practices ordinarily engaged in by newspapers and radio stations.

(2) In addition, in one important area the bill expressly abandons the principle of uniform application of national policy under Federal law. The bill's stated policy of preserving some degree of union security would be abdicated in all States where more restrictive policies exist. In other respects the bill makes clear that Federal policy would govern insofar as activities affecting commerce are concerned. This is not only an invitation to the States to distort national policy as they see fit, but is a complete forsaking of a long-standing constitutional principle.

(3) In regard to Communists in unions, I am convinced that the bill would have an effect exactly opposite to that intended by the Congress. Congress intended to assist labor organizations to rid themselves of Communist officers. With this objective I am in full accord. But the effect of this provision would be far different. The bill would deny the peaceful procedures of the National Labor Relations Act to a union unless all its officers declared under oath that they were not members of the Communist Party and that they did not favor the forceful or unconstitutional overthrow of the Government. The mere refusal by a single individual to sign the required affidavit would prevent an entire national labor union from being certified for purposes of collective bargaining. Such a union would have to win all its objectives by strike, rather than by orderly procedure under the law. The union and the affected industry would be disrupted for perhaps a long period of time while violent electioneering, charges and counter-

charges split open the union ranks. The only result of this provision would be confusion and disorder, which is exactly the result the Communists desire.

This provision in the bill is an attempt to solve difficult problems of industrial democracy by recourse to oversimplified legal devices. I consider that this provision would increase, rather than decrease, disruptive effects of Communists in our labor movement.

The most fundamental test which I have applied to this bill is whether it would strengthen or weaken American democracy in the present critical hour. This bill is perhaps the most serious economic and social legislation of the past decade. Its effects—for good or ill— would be felt for decades to come.

I have concluded that the bill is a clear threat to the successful working of our democratic society.

One of the major lessons of recent world history is that free and vital trade unions are a strong bulwark against the growth of totalitarian movements. We must, therefore, be everlastingly alert that in striking at union abuses we do not destroy the contribution which unions make to our democratic strength.

This bill would go far toward weakening our trade-union movement. And it would go far toward destroying our national unity. By raising barriers between labor and management and by injecting political considerations into normal economic decisions, it would invite them to gain their ends through direct political action. I think it would be exceedingly dangerous to our country to develop a class basis for political action.

TAFT'S REPLY TO VETO

12 ⊷ ON THE EVENING of Truman's veto of the Taft-Hartley bill, Senator Robert A. Taft of Ohio went on the radio to attack the President's message. The next day Congress overrode the veto. Excerpts from Senator Taft's speech of June 20, 1947, follow:[12]

The President's message vetoing the labor bill is a complete misrepresentation, both of the general character of the bill and of most of its detailed provisions. . . .

Following the lead of labor union leaders, the President does not

[12] Reprinted from *Congressional Record*, Eightieth Congress, first session, pp. A3043–4.

find a single good provision in the entire bill. He ignores every abuse by labor unions which fill the record of evidence before the committees. While he gives lip service to the idea of labor reform by saying that he heartily condemns abuses on the part of unions and employers, he nowhere recognizes the existence of any specific abuse. He wants a commission to study a matter carefully studied for months by committees of Congress with the best expert advice. This is the standard device of those who wish to delay and defeat action. He assumes that every power given to the labor union leaders is for the benefit of the members of labor unions—and utterly ignores the fact that these members and their wives and families are the real sufferers from unjustified strikes and arbitrary closed-shop agreements. No workingman is deprived of any fundamental right as the President stated this evening. Only the arbitrary power of the labor bosses are curbed.

If there is one subject upon which every unprejudiced person is agreed, it is that unions must be made responsible for their acts, that collective bargaining cannot continue to be an important factor in our labor relations unless both parties are bound by their contracts. The President criticizes every provision designed to make unions responsible. He criticizes the requirement that they file financial and other reports with the Department of Labor. Corporations have long been required to file reports, both with State and local authorities. Why not unions?

He attacks the provisions that unions may be sued for breach of collective-bargaining agreements—on the ground that they should not be bothered with having to defend lawsuits regardless of what they do. He says they might be harassed by an employer. Everybody else in the United States is subject to harassment by lawsuits. Why not unions? In any event, the purpose of this provision is to induce them to live up to their contracts, and if they do, few suits will ever be filed.

Perhaps the most extraordinary provision of the message is the President's attack on the section permitting an injunction against a Nation-wide strike affecting the national health and safety. It was through such a procedure that he secured an injunction against John L. Lewis last fall. Last year when faced by a Nation-wide strike, it was the President himself who recommended Government seizure and the drafting of all the strikers into the United States Army. Because Congress now gives him a carefully drafted authority to delay such a strike, to attempt mediation and finally to conduct a strike vote when other remedies have been exhausted, he says the procedure will do more harm than good. He prefers to let the Smith-Connally Act expire on June 30 without any protection whatever for the people against Nation-wide strikes. . . .

The President says an employer can discharge a man on the pretext of a slight infraction, even though his real motive is to discriminate against the employee for union activity. This is not so. The Board decides under the new law, as under the former law, whether the man was really discharged for union activity or for good cause.

The President says the law would expose unions to suits for acts of violence, wildcat strikes, and other actions, none of which were authorized or ratified by them. This is not so. We have simply provided that unions are subject to the same general laws or agency as any other corporation or citizen in determining their liability for the acts of the agents.

The President attacks the provision giving freedom of speech to employers. The need for such a provision was the one thing admitted even by labor union leaders. The Bill simply provides that views, argument, or opinion shall not be evidence of an unfair labor practice unless they contain in themselves a threat of coercion or a promise of benefit. Without these provisions there would be no freedom of speech on the part of employers any more than there has been for the last 10 years.

The President criticizes the provision that State laws prohibiting union shops are to remain in effect. He does not tell you that this is the provision of the Wagner Act, which has never undertaken to authorize closed-shop agreements if the state law prohibits them.

It is astonishing to find the President objecting to the section which attempts to prevent Communists from being officers of labor unions. We have merely required that every officer of a labor union seeking certification must file an affidavit that he is not a member of the Communist Party and does not favor the forceable overthrow of the Government. . . .

There is hardly a sentence in the President's message which is not open to direct challenge, and there are many others besides those I have cited which misrepresent the meaning of the new bill. The committees of Congress who wrote this bill had no antiunion prejudice. They have tried to restore equality in collective bargaining, and correct only those abuses against employers, union members and third parties which were clearly shown to exist by bona fide evidence. The campaign carried on against the bill by the labor unions has been a complete tissue of falsification, to support the contention of the last 10 years that unions are above criticism and above the law, that there must be no legislation on the pain of political execution. It is discouraging to find the President of the United States yielding to their pressure, adopting their arguments and blocking the effort of the great majority of the people's representatives including a large majority of the Democratic Party to secure a reasonable reform.

PRESIDENT'S APPEAL FOR LABOR VOTE

13 ◄ᗡ§ TRUMAN'S APPEAL for the labor vote in 1948 was eminently successful. On Labor Day (September 6), 1948, he made a speech in Cadillac Square, Detroit, Michigan:[13]

Two years ago the people of this country, and many workingmen among them, seemed to feel that they wanted a change. They elected the Republican 80th Congress—and they got their change. That Congress promptly fell into the familiar Republican pattern of aid for big business and attack on labor. The Republicans promptly voted themselves a cut in taxes, and voted you a cut in freedom.

That 80th Republican Congress failed to crack down on prices but it cracked down on labor all right!

The Republicans failed to give the consumers of America protection against the rising cost of living, but at the same time they put a dangerous weapon into the hands of the big corporations in the shape of the Taft-Hartley law which I vetoed, but which was passed over my veto.

The union men with whom I have talked tell me that labor is just beginning to feel the effects of the Taft-Hartley law. And you and I know that the Taft-Hartley law is only a foretaste of what you will get if the Republican reaction is allowed to . . . grow. . . .

If the congressional elements that made the Taft-Hartley law are allowed to remain in power, and if these elements are further encouraged by the election of a Republican President, you men of labor can expect to be hit by a steady barrage of body blows. And if you stay at home, as you did in 1946, and keep these reactionaries in power, you will deserve every blow you get.

Not only the labor unions, but all men and women who work are

[13] Excerpts reprinted from *Truman Papers, 1948*, pp. 475-9.

in danger, and the danger is greatest for those who do not belong to unions. If anything, the blows will fall most severely on the white-collar workers and the unorganized workers.

And that is not all!

If this Taft-Hartley law remains in effect, labor's position will be bad enough. But suppose, while that law is in effect, a reactionary Republican administration were to bring upon us another "boom and bust" cycle similar to that which struck us during the last Republican administration? . . .

If you let the Republican administration reactionaries get complete control of this Government, the position of labor will be so greatly weakened that I would fear, not only for the wages and living stand-ards of the American workingman, but even for our Democratic institutions of free labor and free enterprise. . . .

If you place the Government of this country under the control of those who hate labor, who can you blame if measures are thereafter adopted to destroy the powers, prestige, and earning power of labor?

I tell you that labor must fight now harder than ever before to make sure that its rights are kept intact. In practical terms, this means a powerful political effort which must culminate in an all-out vote on election day. Anything short of an all-out vote would be a betrayal by labor of its own interests.

TRUMAN'S APPEAL TO FARMERS

14 ◄§   THE DEFECTION of midwestern farmers from the New Deal coalition had begun in 1937 and by November 1946 was complete. Antagonized by the administration's efforts to enact new price controls, freed from depression anxieties by inflated farm prices, and unhappy with Truman's attempt to ally himself with labor, farmers in the Midwest were expected to support overwhelm-ingly the Republican ticket in 1948. But in the summer of that year grain prices began to slide, and during October corn in some areas fell beneath the government's support price. The Democrats shrewdly tried to blame the faltering performance of the price-support mechanism on the Republicans, for the Eightieth Congress had included a provision in the new charter of the Commodity Credit Corporation inhibiting the government's ability to acquire storage facilities for support operations.

As fear of a new agricultural depression spread in the farm belt, an undetected shift to the Democrats took place. In November a temporary revival of the old farmer-labor coalition, which in the 1930's had given Roosevelt his great victories, made possible Truman's amazing upset. The Brannan Plan, unveiled by the administration in 1949, was in part an attempt to reward farmers for their support. Truman's major farm speech in the 1948 campaign was made on September 18, 1948, at the National Plowing Match at Dexter, Iowa:[14]

The Wall Street reactionaries are not satisfied with being rich. They want to increase their power and their privileges, regardless of what happens to the other fellow. They are gluttons of privilege.

These gluttons of privilege are now putting up fabulous sums of money to elect a Republican administration.

Why do you think they are doing that? For the love of the Republican candidate? Or do you think it is because they expect a Republican administration to carry out their will, as it did in the days of Harding, Coolidge, and Hoover?

I think we know the answer. I think we know that Wall Street expects its money this year to elect a Republican administration that will listen to the gluttons of privilege first, and to the people not at all.

Republican reactionaries want an administration that will assure privilege for big business, regardless of what may happen to the rest of the Nation.

The Republican strategy is to divide the farmer and the industrial worker—to get them to squabbling with each other—so that big business can grasp the balance of power and take the country over, lock, stock, and barrel.

To gain this end, they will stop at nothing. On the one hand, the Republicans are telling industrial workers that the high cost of food in the cities is due to this Government's farm policy. On the other hand, the Republicans are telling the farmers that the high cost of manufactured goods on the farm is due to this Government's labor policy.

That's plain hokum. It's an old political trick. "If you can't convince 'em, confuse 'em." But this time it won't work.

The farmer and the worker know that their troubles have been coming from another source. Right here I would like to cite you an example of the situation that they were faced with not so long ago. In 1932, under the Republicans, we had 12,500,000 unemployed, with

[14] Excerpts reprinted from *Truman Papers*, 1948, pp. 503–8.

average hourly wages at 45 cents, and we had 15 cent corn and 3 cent hogs. In fact, you burnt up some of your corn, because you couldn't market it, it was too cheap. . . .

The Democratic Party puts human rights and human welfare first.

But the attitude of the Republican gluttons of privilege is very different. The big-money Republican looks on agriculture and labor merely as expense items in a business venture. He tries to push their share of the national income down as low as possible and increase his own profits. And he looks upon the Government as a tool to accomplish this purpose.

These Republican gluttons of privilege are cold men. They are cunning men. And it is their constant aim to put the Government of the United States under the control of men like themselves. They want a return of the Wall Street economic dictatorship.

You have had a sample of what the Republican administration would mean to you. Two years ago, in the congressional elections, many Americans decided that they would not bother to vote. Well, others thought they would like to have a change. And they brought into power a Republican Congress—that notorious "do-nothing" 80th Republican Congress.

Let us look at the results of that change. This Republican Congress has already stuck a pitchfork in the farmer's back.

They have already done their best to keep the price supports from working. Many growers have sold wheat this summer at less than the support price, because they could not find proper storage.

When the Democratic administration had to face this problem in the past, the Government set up grain bins all over the wheat and corn belts to provide storage.

Now the farmers need such bins again. But when the Republican Congress rewrote the charter of the Commodity Credit Corporation this year, there were certain lobbyists in Washington representing the speculative grain trade—your old friend.

These big-business lobbyists and speculators persuaded the Congress not to provide the storage bins for the farmers. They tied the hands of the administration. They are preventing us from setting up storage bins that you will need in order to get the support price for your grain.

When the farmers have to sell their wheat below the support price, because they have no place to store it, they can thank this same Republican 80th Congress that gave the speculative grain trade a rakeoff at your expense.

The Republican reactionaries are not satisfied with that. Now they are attacking the whole structure of price supports for farm products.

This attack comes at a time when many farm prices are dropping and the price support program is of the greatest importance to the farmer.

The Democratic Party originated the farm support program. We built the price support plan out of hard experience. We built it for the benefit of the entire Nation—not only for the farmer, but for the consumer as well.

Republican spokesmen are now complaining that my administration is trying to keep farm prices up. They have given themselves away. They have given you a plain hint of what they have in store for you if they come into power. They are obviously ready to let the bottom drop out of farm prices.

Your best protection is to elect a Democratic Congress and a President that will play fair with the farmer—an administration that will reinforce soil conservation, provide adequate storage facilities for grain, encourage production, and help the farmer make enough on his crop to meet the cost of living, and have something left over.

I don't need to tell you how long it takes to get a good crop, and how big the dangers are. You can work a year, plowing and cultivating, and then at the last minute, a sudden drought or flood can wipe you out. You all know how terrible these disasters of nature can be.

Now you are faced with the danger of another kind of disaster—a man-made disaster bearing the Republican trademark. For 16 years the Democrats have been working on a crop of prosperity for the farmer. We have been plowing, and seeding, and cultivating the soil of the American economy in order to get a crop of prosperity that you have been enjoying for the past several years.

The question is: Are you going to let another Republican blight wipe out that prosperity?

BRANNAN PLAN

15 ⋟ ON APRIL 7, 1949, Secretary of Agriculture Brannan proposed a new farm program to Congress. Since the administration had advocated the flexible price supports (ranging from 60 percent to 90 percent of parity, according to supply) enacted by the Republican Eightieth Congress, the level of farm supports was not an issue in the 1948 campaign. After the election the administration's two principal farm supporters in the Midwest—the

National Farmers Union and the Agricultural Adjustment Administration (AAA) farmer committees set up in the days of the New Deal—indicated preference for high, rigid price supports. In his new program Brannan not only embraced high supports; he offered a sweeping revision of the old farm program that made farm policy a major center of controversy during Truman's second term. Brannan called, first of all, for discarding the old notion of parity and for price supports henceforth to be determined on the basis of the Income Support Standard—a moving ten-year average of gross farm income adjusted for inflation. Since the years since 1940 had been good ones on the farm, the Support Standard and consequently support prices would be high for some time to come. On behalf of what Brannan called the family-sized farm, he proposed that no farmer receive supports on more than $26,100 worth of his crop. The most controversial part of Brannan's testimony dealt with production payments on perishable commodities.

Determined opposition from southern Democrats, Republicans, and the giant among farm organizations—the American Farm Bureau Federation—assured the defeat of the Brannan Plan. But in the first months after Brannan's testimony Democrats believed that his production payments would prove the device that would make permanent the tentative farmer-labor alliance formed in 1948. An excerpt from his testimony of April 7, 1949, follows:[15]

I recommend that the Congress designate those commodities which should have first priority on the funds available for price-support purposes. This list should include the agricultural commodities of prime importance, both from the standpoint of their contribution to farm income and their importance to the American consumer family.

This list should include, at least, the following commodities: Corn, cotton, wheat, tobacco, whole milk, eggs, farm chickens, and the meat animals—hogs, beef cattle, and lambs.

I recommend that the prices or returns of these first priority, group 1, commodities be maintained at not less than the full support price standard. It should be clearly understood that the support price standard is not a ceiling.

Those commodities not included in the group 1 or priority list should be supported in line with or in relation to group 1 commodi-

[15] Reprinted from *Congressional Record*, Eighty-first Congress, first session, pp. 4035–40.

ties, taking into account the available funds and authorities, the ability of producers to keep supplies in line with demand and other relevant factors. There will also need to be discretionary authority available for adjusting supports for these commodities in order to maintain desirable commodity relationships, especially in order to maintain normal feeding ratios or feed-value relationships.

It may also on occasion, be necessary to recommend to the Congress certain adjustments in support prices for one or more of the group 1 commodities in order to maintain feed ratios or feed-value relationships.

The authority should be available to support any commodity at whatever level is required to increase supplies or meet national emergencies.

Price support methods: Commodity loans and purchase agreements are methods well adapted to the support of storable commodities which can be carried over without processing for a number of market ing years if necessary. Storables account for roughly 25 percent of our annual cash receipts from farm marketings and include cotton, corn, wheat, and other grains, tobacco, the oilseed crops, dry beans and peas, wool, and peanuts. These are not all equally storable, but experience has shown that loans and purchase agreements are effective for all the commodities on this list. Nevertheless, it would be desirable to have available, as a supplementary method, the authority to make production payments under certain circumstances.

The nonstorables—products which are either highly perishable or which can be stored only at heavy expense—include fruits, vegetables, meat animals, milk, butterfat, poultry and eggs, and account for roughly 75 percent of cash farm receipts. Production of these commodities is geared largely to domestic demand, and this demand fluctuates with employment, wages and other factors which change mass purchasing power. We can hope to increase per capita consumption of all or most of these products in a healthy economic climate.

When it is necessary to apply supports to any of these nonstorable commodities, I recommend that we rely mainly upon production payments.

The term "production payment" means exactly what it says—a payment to the farmer to go on producing to meet genuine consumer need, rather than restricting output short of that need.

Under this system the farmer would be paid in cash the difference between the support standard for commodities which he produced and the average selling price for those commodities in the market place. Because the payment would go directly to the farmer it would be an efficient support operation.

Another big advantage is that the system would induce efficient production and marketing, because any farmer who could exceed the average market price by quality of product or good bargaining would benefit to the extent that his selling price exceeded the average market price.

A third advantage of this system is that it would allow farm income to remain at a high enough level to sustain abundant production while retail prices sought their supply-and-demand level in the market place. This level is bound to be reasonable for consumers because of the larger supplies brought out.

It is obvious, of course, that the use of production payments must be qualified in such a manner as to avoid extremely depressed prices in the market place or a wasteful use of soil resources.

The payment method is not new. It has been used for various purposes before and during the war and we know it is administratively feasible. We know it is a method which not only protects farmers but gives consumers a real break.

I want to make it clear that I believe production payments should be used to encourage increased consumption as well as to support farm returns. Let me illustrate. In some of our larger cities, milk consumption per capita was much higher in 1947 than in 1940. The increases ranged from 15 percent to nearly 50 percent. Since 1947, in some of these same cities, the average person has been using less and less milk. Consumers have not simply decided they want or need less milk. The decision to buy less was forced upon them for the most part by the rising cost of the commodity. The result is bad for both consumer and producer.

Through production payments, we can keep the market price within reach of more people and maintain returns to the dairy farmers at a level which will bring forth the necessary production. As we indicated in our long-range testimony in 1947, we should be producing and consuming 150,000,000,000 pounds of milk by now instead of something less than 120,000,000,000. If it is necessary to get milk down to the area of 15 cents a quart at retail in order to have maximum consumption, and use production payments to assure farmers of fair returns, I think both farmers and consumers will want to do it.

I believe the production payment authority should be so written as to allow it to be used as a supplement to our milk marketing agreements and orders.

The same principle should apply to other commodities to which marketing agreements and orders are adapted.

Parenthetically, I believe authority to support hog and milk prices through direct payments should be available before January 1, 1950. If it becomes necessary to support prices of hogs and milk this year as now required by law, authority to make payments will facilitate the job.

TRUMAN ON NATIONAL HOUSING ACT

16 ◈§   AT THE CLOSE of the war the nation faced a serious housing shortage caused by returning veterans and pent-up wartime demand. Some estimates placed at ten million the number of Americans searching for homes. Accordingly President Truman took certain belated emergency measures in 1945, and in 1946 he asked Congress to authorize subsidies to spur construction ("starts") of 1.2 million homes in that year and 1.5 million in 1947. The resulting Patman Act seemed to give Truman what he had requested, but interagency warfare and the disorder of the construction industry were largely responsible for the government's failure to achieve more than half of its goal for veterans' emergency housing. Truman continued to demand legislation to provide adequate housing, and in 1949 Congress finally responded with one of the major achievements of the Fair Deal: the National Housing Act. This act provided for 810,000 low-cost housing units to be built in the next six years and provided loans and grants for slum clearance and rural housing. On July 15, 1949, President Truman issued a statement expressing his satisfaction with the new law:[16]

I have today approved the Housing Act of 1949.

This far-reaching measure is of great significance to the welfare of the American people. It opens up the prospect of decent homes in wholesome surroundings for low-income families now living in the squalor of the slums. It equips the Federal Government, for the first time, with effective means for aiding cities in the vital task of clearing slums and rebuilding blighted areas. It authorizes a comprehensive program of housing research aimed at reducing housing costs and

[16] Reprinted from *Truman Papers*, 1949, pp. 381–2.

raising housing standards. It initiates a program to help farmers obtain better homes.

The Housing Act of 1949 also establishes as a national objective the achievement as soon as feasible of a decent home and a suitable living environment for every American family, and sets forth the policies to be followed in advancing toward that goal. These policies are thoroughly consistent with American ideals and traditions. They recognize and preserve local responsibility, and the primary role of private enterprise, in meeting the Nation's housing needs. But they also recognize clearly the necessity for appropriate Federal aid to supplement the resources of communities and private enterprise.

I take deep satisfaction in the successful conclusion of the long fight for this legislation. I know this satisfaction is shared by the Members of Congress of both political parties, and by the many private groups and individuals, who have supported this legislation over the past 4 years against ill-founded opposition.

The task before us now is to put this legislation into operation with speed and effectiveness. That task presents a great challenge to the executive branch of the Federal Government, to local governments, and to industry and labor. While this act authorizes programs which will take a number of years to complete, in the light of the present serious needs for low-cost housing and slum clearance, and of the present period of economic transition, we should cut to a minimum the time necessary to initiate these programs.

Accordingly, I have directed the Housing and Home Finance Administrator [Raymond M. Foley—Eds.] and the Secretary of Agriculture to make special efforts to place these programs into operation as rapidly as possible. I am submitting to the Congress immediately a request for the additional appropriations which will be required in the present fiscal year.

Furthermore, since the low-rent housing and slum clearance programs depend upon local initiative, I urge State and local authorities to act speedily.

This legislation permits us to take a long step toward increasing the well-being and happiness of millions of our fellow citizens. Let us not delay in fulfilling that high purpose.

TRUMAN ON DISPLACED PERSONS ACT

17 ⚬§ THE DESCENDANTS of the immigrants who came to the
United States in the late nineteenth and early twentieth

centuries lived and worked in the great urban centers, and it was there that Roosevelt had found his staunchest and most numerous supporters. Truman appealed to these same voters with his welfare programs and his stand in behalf of labor. He also championed a just immigration policy, still a matter of importance to certain ethnic and religious minorities.

The 1.2 million Europeans living in displaced-persons camps after World War II posed a worldwide problem. In 1945 Truman found a way to admit 42,000 of these people and asked Congress to admit 400,000 more. Not until 1948 did Congress act, and then, according to the President, it was in a discriminatory and inhumane manner. During the campaign of 1948 Truman reminded city audiences that the Republican Congress had discriminated against Catholics and Jews. After signing the Displaced Persons Act on June 25, 1948, the President made the following statement:[17]

It is with very great reluctance that I have signed S. 2242, the Displaced Persons Act of 1948.

If the Congress were still in session, I would return this bill without my approval and urge that a fairer, more humane bill be passed. In its present form this bill is flagrantly discriminatory. It mocks the American tradition of fair play. Unfortunately, it was not passed until the last day of the session. If I refused to sign this bill now, there would be no legislation on behalf of displaced persons until the next session of the Congress.

It is a close question whether this bill is better or worse than no bill at all. After careful consideration I have decided, however, that it would not be right to penalize the beneficiaries of this bill on account of the injustices perpetrated against others who should have been included within its provisions. I have therefore signed the bill in the hope that its injustices will be rectified by the Congress at the first opportunity.

Americans of all religious faiths and political beliefs will find it hard to understand, as I do, why the 80th Congress delayed action on this subject until the end of this session, with the result that most attempts to improve the bill were frustrated. . . .

I have analyzed closely the bill which was sent to me for signature. Its good points can be stated all too briefly: At long last, the principle

---

[17] Excerpts reprinted from *Truman Papers, 1948*, pp. 382–4.

is recognized that displaced persons should be admitted to the United States. Two hundred thousand displaced persons may be admitted in the next 2 years, as well as 2,000 recent Czech refugees and 3,000 orphans.

The bad points of the bill are numerous. Together they form a pattern of discrimination and intolerance wholly inconsistent with the American sense of justice.

The bill discriminates in callous fashion against displaced persons of the Jewish faith. This brutal fact cannot be obscured by the maze of technicalities in the bill or by the protestations of some of its sponsors.

The primary device used to discriminate against Jewish displaced persons is the provision restricting eligibility to those displaced persons who entered Germany, Austria, or Italy on or before December 22, 1945. Most of the Jewish displaced persons who had entered Germany, Austria, or Italy by that time have already left; and most of the Jewish displaced persons now in those areas arrived there after December 22, 1945, and hence are denied a chance to come to the United States under this bill. By this device more than 90 percent of the remaining Jewish displaced persons are definitely excluded. Even the eligible 10 percent are beset by numerous additional restrictions written into the bill.

For all practical purposes, it must be frankly recognized, therefore, that this bill excludes Jewish displaced persons, rather than accepting a fair proportion of them along with other faiths.

The bill also excludes many displaced persons of the Catholic faith who deserve admission. Many anti-Communist refugees of Catholic faith fled into the American zones after December 22, 1945, in order to escape persecution in countries dominated by a Communist form of government. These too are barred by the December 22, 1945, dateline.

It is inexplicable, except upon the abhorrent ground of intolerance, that this date should have been chosen instead of April 21, 1947, the date on which General Clay closed the displaced persons camps to further admissions.

The Jewish and Catholic displaced persons who found asylum in our zones between December 22, 1945, and April 21, 1947, who are wrongly excluded by this bill, fled their native countries for the same basic reasons as Balts who came before December 22, 1945, and Czechs who came after January, 1948, who are rightly included. I sincerely hope that the Congress will remedy this gross discrimination at its earliest opportunity. . . .

I know what a bitter disappointment this bill is—to the many displaced victims of persecution who looked to the United States for hope; to the millions of our citizens who wanted to help them in the finest American spirit; to the many Members of the Congress who fought hard but unsuccessfully for a decent displaced persons bill. I hope that this bitter disappointment will not turn to despair.

VETO OF MCCARRAN-WALTER BILL

18 ◄§ IN 1952 CONGRESS passed the McCarran-Walter Immigration and Nationality Act. The act codified existing legislation, retaining the 1924 quota system based on national origins. The new law did, however, modify the old restriction on Asiatic peoples by granting each nation an annual quota of 100. The act also set up elaborate screening procedures to keep out "subversives" and other undesirables and empowered the Attorney General to deport immigrants for Communist affiliations even after they had received citizenship. On June 25, 1952, President Truman vetoed the bill, but the veto was overridden by Congress. Excerpts from the veto message follow:[18]

In one respect, this bill recognizes the great international significance of our immigration and naturalization policy, and takes a step to improve existing laws. All racial bars to naturalization would be removed, and at least some minimum immigration quota would be afforded to each of the free nations of Asia. . . .

But now this most desirable provision comes before me embedded in a mass of legislation which would perpetuate injustices of long standing against many other nations of the world, hamper the efforts we are making to rally the men of east and west alike to the cause of freedom, and intensify the repressive and inhumane aspects of our immigration procedures. The price is too high, and in good conscience I cannot agree to pay it.

I want all our residents of Japanese ancestry, and all our friends throughout the Far East, to understand this point clearly. I cannot take the step I would like to take and strike down the bars that prejudice has erected against them, without, at the same time, estab-

[18] Reprinted from *Congressional Record*, Eighty-second Congress, second session, pp. 8082–5.

lishing new discriminations against the peoples of Asia and approving harsh and repressive measures directed at all who seek a new life within our boundaries. I am sure that with a little more time and a little more discussion in this country the public conscience and the good sense of the American people will assert themselves, and we shall be in a position to enact an immigration and naturalization policy that will be fair to all. . . .

The bill would continue, practically without change, the national origins quota system, which was enacted into law in 1924, and put into effect in 1929. This quota system—always based upon assumptions at variance with our American ideals—is long since out of date and more than ever unrealistic in the face of present world conditions.

This system hinders us in dealing with current immigration problems, and is a constant handicap in the conduct of our foreign relations. As I stated in my message to Congress on March 24, 1952, on the need for an emergency program of immigration from Europe:

> Our present quota system is not only inadequate to meet present emergency needs, it is also an obstacle to the development of an enlightened and satisfactory immigration policy for the long-run future.

. . . The greatest vice of the present quota system . . . is that it discriminates, deliberately and intentionally, against many of the peoples of the world. The purpose behind it was to cut down and virtually eliminate immigration to this country from southern and eastern Europe. A theory was invented to rationalize this objective. The theory was that in order to be readily assimilable, European immigrants should be admitted in proportion to the numbers of persons of their respective national stocks already here as shown by the census of 1920. Since Americans of English, Irish, and German descent were most numerous, immigrants of those three nationalities got the lion's share—more than two-thirds—of the total quota. The remaining third was divided up among all the other nations given quotas.

The desired effect was obtained. Immigration from the newer sources of southern and eastern Europe was reduced to a trickle. The quotas allotted to England and Ireland remained largely unused, as was intended. Total quota immigration fell to a half or third—and sometimes even less—of the annual limit of 154,000. People from such countries as Greece or Spain or Latvia were virtually deprived of any opportunity to come here at all, simply because Greeks or

Spaniards or Latvians had not come here before 1920 in any substantial numbers.

The idea behind this discriminatory policy was, to put it baldly, that Americans with English or Irish names were better people and better citizens than Americans with Italian or Greek or Polish names. It was thought that people of west European origin made better citizens than Rumanians or Yugoslavs or Ukrainians or Hungarians or Balts or Austrians. Such a concept is utterly unworthy of our traditions and our ideals. It violates the great political doctrine of the Declaration of Independence that "all men are created equal." It denies the humanitarian creed inscribed beneath the Statue of Liberty proclaiming to all nations, "Give me your tired, your poor, your huddled masses yearning to breathe free."

It repudiates our basic religious concepts, our belief in the brotherhood of man, and in the words of St. Paul "there is neither Jew nor Greek, there is neither bond nor free, for ye are all one in Christ Jesus."

The basis of this quota system was false and unworthy in 1924. It is even worse now. At the present time, this quota system keeps out the very people we want to bring in. It is incredible to me that, in this year of 1952, we should again be enacting into law such a slur on the patriotism, the capacity, and the decency of a large part of our citizenry.

Today, we have entered into an alliance, the North Atlantic Treaty, with Italy, Greece, and Turkey against one of the most terrible threats mankind has ever faced. We are asking them to join with us in protecting the peace of the world. We are helping them to build their defenses, and train their men, in the common cause. But, through this bill, we say to their people: You are less worthy to come to this country than Englishmen or Irishmen; you Italians, who need to find homes abroad in the hundreds of thousands—you shall have a quota of 5,645; you Greeks, struggling to assist the helpless victims of a Communist civil war—you shall have a quota of 308; and you Turks, you are brave defenders of the eastern flank, but you shall have a quota of only 225.

Today we are protecting ourselves, as we were in 1924, against being flooded by immigrants from Eastern Europe. This is fantastic. The countries of Eastern Europe have fallen under the Communist yoke; they are silenced, fenced off by barbed wire and mine fields; no one passes their borders but at the risk of his life. We do not need to be protected against immigrants from these countries; on the contrary, we want to stretch out a helping hand, to save those who have managed to flee into Western Europe, to succor those who are brave enough to escape from barbarism, to welcome and restore them against the day when their countries will, as we hope, be free again. But this we cannot do, as we would like to do, because the quota for Poland is only 6,500, as against the 138,000 exiled Poles all over Europe, who are asking to come to these shores; because the quota for the now subjugated Baltic countries is little more than 700, against the 23,000 Baltic refugees imploring us to admit them to a new life here; because the quota for Rumania is only 289, and some 30,000 Rumanians who have managed to escape the labor camps and the mass deportations of their Soviet masters, have asked our help. These are only a few examples of the absurdity, the cruelty of carrying over into this year of 1952 the isolationist limitations of our 1924 law.

In no other realm of our national life are we so hampered and stultified by the dead hand of the past as we are in this field of immigration. We do not limit our cities to their 1920 boundaries; we do not hold corporations to their 1920 capitalizations; we welcome progress and change to meet changing conditions in every sphere of life except in the field of immigration. . . .

I am asked to approve the reenactment of highly objectionable provisions now contained in the Internal Security Act of 1950—a measure passed over my veto shortly after the invasion of South Korea. Some of these provisions would empower the Attorney General to deport any alien who has engaged or has had a purpose to engage in activities "prejudicial to the public interest" or "subversive to the national security." No standards or definitions are provided to guide discretion in the exercise of powers so sweeping. To punish undefined "activities" departs from traditional American insistence on established standards of guilt. To punish an undefined "purpose" is thought control.

These provisions are worse than the infamous Alien Act of 1798, passed in a time of national fear and distrust of foreigners, which gave the President power to deport any alien deemed "dangerous to the peace and safety of the United States." Alien residents were thoroughly frightened and citizens much disturbed by that threat to liberty.

Such powers are inconsistent with our democratic ideals. Conferring powers like that upon the Attorney General is unfair to him as well as to our alien residents. Once fully informed of such vast discretionary powers vested in the Attorney General, Americans now would and should be just as alarmed as Americans were in 1798 over less drastic powers vested in the President.

Heretofore, for the most part, deportation and exclusion have rested upon findings of fact made upon evidence. Under this bill, they would rest in many instances upon the "opinion" or "satisfaction" of immigration or consular employees. The change from objective findings to subjective feelings is not compatible with our system of justice. The result would be to restrict or eliminate judicial review of unlawful administrative action.

PROPOSAL FOR SPECIAL SESSION OF CONGRESS

19 ⊷ TRUMAN'S STRATEGY in 1948 was to run against Herbert Hoover and the Republican Eightieth Congress. At the Democratic convention in July Truman told the cheering delegates that in order to demonstrate the gap between Republican platform promises and Republican deeds, he was going to call Congress back to Washington for a special session. As the results testify, Truman's strategy worked.

Judge Samuel I. Rosenman, an adviser to both Roosevelt and Truman, is most likely the author of an unsigned memorandum, dated June 29, 1948, that is to be found among his papers in the Truman Library. The document argues in behalf of the special session:[19]

Subject: *Should the President call Congress back?*

This election can only be won by bold and daring steps, calculated to reverse the powerful trend now running against us. The boldest and most popular step the President could possibly take would be to call a special session of Congress early in August. We make the following points:

1. This would focus attention on the rotten record of the 80th Congress, which [Thomas E.—Eds.] Dewey, [Earl—Eds.] Warren and the press will try to make the country forget.

2. It would force Dewey and Warren to defend the actions of Congress, and make them accept the Congress as a basic issue.

3. It would keep a steady glare of publicity on the Neanderthal

[19] Reprinted from unsigned memorandum of June 29, 1948, in the Truman Library.

men of the Republican Party, the reactionary men such as [Congress-men Joseph—Eds.] Martin, [Charles—Eds.] Halleck, [Jesse—Eds.] Wolcott, [Les—Eds.] Allen, who will embarrass Dewey and Warren. The press is with us on the 80th Congress issue, and the Martins, Hallecks, Wolcotts, [John—Eds.] Tabers are bound to stir up severe criticism.

4. It would split the Republican Party on the major questions of how to deal with housing, inflation, foreign policy, social security, etc.

5. It would give President Truman a chance to follow through on the fighting start he made on his Western tour. It would show the President *in action on Capitol Hill,* fighting for the people, delivering messages to Congress at joint sessions in person, broadcasting his messages, leading his party in a crusade for the millions of Americans ignored by the "rich man's Congress."

This course may be hazardous politically, but we cannot shut our eyes to the fact that President Truman faces an uphill fight to win the coming election—and the American people love a fighting leader who takes bold action to help the ordinary citizens against the lobbies and the corporations.

Here are the objections to the special-session plan, and the answers as we see them:

1. *The Danger:*

Republicans may invite a Southern filibuster by introducing strong civil rights legislation.

The Answer:

The President or Senator [Alben W.—Eds.] Barkley, after the President's nomination, could call in the Southern members of Con-gress and make it plain to them that they stand in extreme danger of losing their patronage, their positions of power in the party, and their prestige in the event of a Republican victory.

If the Southerners are recalcitrant at this meeting, the President might announce that he will call for a coalition of liberal Democrats and liberal Republicans to pass moderate civil rights legislation, and that he will ask Senator [Joseph—Eds.] O'Mahoney to introduce a bill embodying his recommendations to the Congress. He might tell the Southerners that he will go on the radio to announce his position, to explain that he feels that the majority of Democrats and the majority of Americans support his position against a stubborn few.

The chances are that the President will never have to take these extreme measures. The Republicans may have to go easy on civil rights bills. Joe Grundy and other powerful Republicans are opposed to such legislation.

The election will be won or lost in the Northern, Midwestern and Western states. The South cannot win or lose the election for the Democratic Party. If the President supports the introduction of moderate legislation, beating the Republicans to the punch, the credit would go to Mr. Truman and the Democratic Party even if a few diehard Southern senators try to start a filibuster. Filibusters can be broken.

2. *The Danger:*

In spite of the Martins, the Tabers, and the Wolcotts, Congress may pass some genuinely good legislation, for which Dewey and Warren would seize credit.

The Answer:

This Congress is so closely controlled by reactionaries and lobbyists that it cannot pass satisfactory bills to stop the disastrous inflation which is frightening the people, or to start construction of the millions of homes needed, or to initiate a more enlightened policy on ERP [European Recovery Program, or Marshall Plan—Eds.], or to extend social security.

If one or two good bills are passed under the President's personal prodding, it will be up to the Democratic Publicity Department and campaign speakers to pound it home to the people that the President deserves credit. The President would be leading the fight. Dewey would be standing in the wings, saying: "Yes, we should have some housing legislation. Yes, we should stop inflation. Yes, we should extend social security. Me, too. Me, too!"

3. *The Danger:*

Congress might pass phony bills on housing, price control, aid to education, national health, etc., which might fool the people.

The Answer:

On the issue of price control, which will be the hottest issue of this campaign, the Congress cannot possibly act. The present Congress cannot take any steps to curb prices or to prevent the people from watching the cost of living go higher and higher and higher. This Congress is run by men who cannot pass price-control legislation without losing their financial backers and incurring the wrath of the N.A.M. [National Association of Manufacturers—Eds.], the U.S. Chamber of Commerce, and other such groups.

On housing, education, social security, health—the answer is the same. This Congress cannot meet the critical needs of the country. It is tied up by the rich interests which expect to make a killing after the Republican victory in November—if they get that victory.

ADDRESS TO DEMOCRATIC CONVENTION

20 ⌇ EXCERPTS FROM TRUMAN's address to the Democratic convention, July 15, 1948, follow:[20]

I am sorry that the microphones are in the way, but I must leave them the way they are because I have got to be able to see what I am doing—as I am always able to see what I am doing.

I can't tell you how very much I appreciate the honor which you have just conferred upon me. I shall continue to try to deserve it.

I accept the nomination.

And I want to thank this convention for its unanimous nomination of my good friend and colleague, Senator Barkley of Kentucky. He is a great man, and a great public servant. Senator Barkley and I will win this election and make these Republicans like it—don't you forget that!

We will do that because they are wrong and we are right, and I will prove it to you in just a few minutes.

This convention met to express the will and reaffirm the beliefs of the Democratic Party. There have been differences of opinion, and that is the democratic way. Those differences have been settled by a majority vote, as they should be. . . .

Confidence and security have been brought to the people by the Democratic Party. Farm income has increased from less than $2½ billion in 1932 to more than $18 billion in 1947. Never in the world were the farmers of any republic or any kingdom or any other country as prosperous as the farmers of the United States; and if they don't do their duty by the Democratic Party, they are the most ungrateful people in the world!

Wages and salaries in this country have increased from $29 billion in 1933 to more than $128 billion in 1947. That's labor, and labor never had but one friend in politics, and that is the Democratic Party and Franklin D. Roosevelt.

And I say to labor what I have said to the farmers: they are the most ungrateful people in the world if they pass the Democratic Party by this year.

[20] Reprinted from *Truman Papers*, 1948, pp. 406–11.

The total national income has increased from less than $40 billion in 1933 to $203 billion in 1947, the greatest in all the history of the world. These benefits have been spread to all the people, because it is the business of the Democratic Party to see that the people get a fair share of these things.

This last, worst 80th Congress proved just the opposite for the Republicans. . . .

Way back 4½ years ago, while I was in the Senate, we passed a housing bill in the Senate known as the Wagner-Ellender-Taft bill. It was a bill to clear the slums in the big cities and to help to erect low-rent housing. That bill, as I said, passed the Senate 4 years ago. It died in the House. That bill was reintroduced in the 80th Congress as the Taft-Ellender-Wagner bill. The name was slightly changed, but it is practically the same bill. And it passed the Senate, but it was allowed to die in the House of Representatives; and they sat on that bill, and finally forced it out of the Banking and Currency Committee, and the Rules Committee took charge, and it still is in the Rules Committee.

But desperate pleas from Philadelphia in that convention that met here 3 weeks ago couldn't get that housing bill passed. They passed a bill they called a housing bill, which isn't worth the paper it's written on.

In the field of labor we needed moderate legislation to promote labor-management harmony, but Congress passed instead that so-called Taft-Hartley Act, which has disrupted labor-management relations and will cause strife and bitterness for years to come if it is not repealed, as the Democratic platform says it ought to be repealed.

On the Labor Department, the Republican platform of 1944 said, if they were in power, that they would build up a strong Labor Department. They have simply torn it up. Only one bureau is left that is functioning, and they cut the appropriation of that so it can hardly function.

I recommended an increase in the minimum wage. What did I get? Nothing. Absolutely nothing.

I suggested that the schools in this country are crowded, teachers underpaid, and that there is a shortage of teachers. One of our greatest national needs is more and better schools. I urged the Congress to provide $300 million to aid the States in the present educational crisis. Congress did nothing about it. Time and again I have recommended improvements in the social security law, including extending protection to those not now covered, and increasing the amount of benefits, to reduce the eligibility age of women from 65 to 60 years. Congress studied the matter for 2 years, but couldn't find the time to extend or increase the benefits. But they did find time to take social security benefits away from 750,000 people, and they passed that over my veto.

I have repeatedly asked the Congress to pass a health program. The Nation suffers from lack of medical care. That situation can be remedied any time the Congress wants to act upon it.

Everybody knows that I recommended to the Congress the civil rights program. I did that because I believed it to be my duty under the Constitution. Some of the members of my own party disagree with me violently on this matter. But they stand up and do it openly! People can tell where they stand. But the Republicans all professed to be for these measures. But Congress failed to act. They had enough men to do it, they could have had cloture, they didn't have to have a filibuster. They had enough people in that Congress that would vote for cloture.

Now everybody likes to have low taxes, but we must reduce the national debt in times of prosperity. And when tax relief can be given, it ought to go to those who need it most and not those who need it least, as this Republican rich man's tax bill did when they passed it over my veto on the third try.

The first one of these was so rotten that they couldn't even stomach it themselves. They finally did send one that was somewhat improved, but it . . . helps the rich and sticks a knife into the back of the poor. . . .

Now listen! This is equally as bad, and as cynical. The Republican platform comes out for slum clearance and low-rental housing. I have been trying to get them to pass that housing bill ever since they met the first time, and it is still resting in the Rules Committee, that bill.

The Republican platform favors educational opportunity and promotion of education. I have been trying to get Congress to do something about that ever since they came there, and that bill is at rest in the House of Representatives.

The Republican platform is for extending and increasing social security benefits. Think of that! Increasing social security benefits! Yet when they had the opportunity, they took 750,000 off the social security rolls!

I wonder if they think they can fool the people of the United States with such poppycock as that!

There is a long list of these promises in that Republican platform. If it weren't so late, I would tell you all about them. I have discussed a number of these failures of the Republican 80th Congress. Every one of them is important. Two of them are of major concern to nearly every American family. They failed to do anything about high prices, they failed to do anything about housing.

My duty as President requires that I use every means within my power to get the laws the people need on matters of such importance and urgency.

I am therefore calling this Congress back into session July 26th.

On the 26th day of July, which out in Missouri we call "Turnip Day," I am going to call Congress back and ask them to pass laws to halt rising prices, to meet the housing crisis—which they are saying they are for in their platform.

At the same time I shall ask them to act upon other vitally needed measures such as aid to education, which they say they are for; a national health program; civil rights legislation, which they say they are for; an increase in the minimum wage, which I doubt very much they are for; extension of the social security coverage and increased benefits, which they say they are for; funds for projects needed in our program to provide public power and cheap electricity. By indirection, this 80th Congress has tried to sabotage the power policies the United States has pursued for 14 years. That power lobby is as bad as the real estate lobby, which is sitting on the housing bill. . . .

1949 STATE OF UNION MESSAGE

21 ◄§   ON JANUARY 5, 1949, President Truman delivered his annual State of the Union address to Congress. The message was a full statement of the domestic program of his administration.[21]

During the last 16 years, our people have been creating a society which offers new opportunities for every man to enjoy his share of the good things of life. . . .

The Government must work with industry, labor, and the farmers in keeping our economy running at full speed. The Government must see that every American has a chance to obtain his fair share of our increasing abundance. These responsibilities go hand in hand.

[21] Excerpts reprinted from *Truman Papers*, 1949, pp. 1–7.

We cannot maintain prosperity unless we have a fair distribution of opportunity and a widespread consumption of the products of our factories and farms.

Our Government has undertaken to meet these responsibilities.

We have made tremendous public investments in highways, hydro-electric power projects, soil conservation, and reclamation. We have established a system of social security. We have enacted laws protecting the rights and the welfare of our working people and the income of our farmers. These Federal policies have paid for themselves many times over. They have strengthened the material foundations of our democratic ideals. Without them, our present prosperity would be impossible.

Reinforced by these policies, our private enterprise system has reached new heights of production. Since the boom year of 1929, while our population has increased by only 20 percent, our agricultural production has increased by 45 percent, and our industrial production has increased by 75 percent. We are turning out far more goods and more wealth per worker than we have ever done before.

This progress has confounded the gloomy prophets—at home and abroad—who predicted the downfall of American capitalism. The people of the United States, going their own way, confident in their own powers, have achieved the greatest prosperity the world has ever seen.

But, great as our progress has been, we still have a long way to go.

As we look around the country, many of our shortcomings stand out in bold relief.

We are suffering from excessively high prices.

Our production is still not large enough to satisfy our demands.

Our minimum wages are far too low.

Small business is losing ground to growing monopoly.

Our farmers still face an uncertain future. And too many of them lack the benefits of our modern civilization.

Some of our natural resources are still being wasted.

We are acutely short of electric power, although the means for developing such power are abundant.

Five million families are still living in slums and firetraps. Three million families share their homes with others.

Our health is far behind the progress of medical science. Proper medical care is so expensive that it is out of the reach of the great majority of our citizens.

Our schools, in many localities, are utterly inadequate.

Our democratic ideals are often thwarted by prejudice and intolerance.

Each of these shortcomings is also an opportunity—an opportunity for the Congress and the President to work for the good of the people.

Our first great opportunity is to protect our economy against the evils of "boom and bust."

This objective cannot be attained by government alone. Indeed, the greater part of the task must be performed by individual efforts under our system of free enterprise. We can keep our present prosperity, and increase it, only if free enterprise and free government work together to that end.

We cannot afford to float along ceaselessly on a postwar boom until it collapses. It is not enough merely to prepare to weather a recession if it comes. Instead, government and business must work together constantly to achieve more and more jobs and more and more production—which mean more and more prosperity for all the people.

The business cycle is man-made; and men of good will, working together, can smooth it out.

So far as business is concerned, it should plan for steady, vigorous expansion—seeking always to increase its output, lower its prices, and avoid the vices of monopoly and restriction. So long as business does this, it will be contributing to continued prosperity, and it will have the help and encouragement of the Government.

The Employment Act of 1946 pledges the Government to use all its resources to promote maximum employment, production, and purchasing power. This means that the Government is firmly committed to protect business and the people against the dangers of recession and against the evils of inflation. This means that the Government must adapt its plans and policies to meet changing circumstances.

One of the most important factors in maintaining prosperity is the Government's fiscal policy. At this time, it is essential not only that the Federal budget be balanced, but also that there be a substantial surplus to reduce inflationary pressures, and to permit a sizable reduction in the national debt, which now stands at $252 billion. I recommend, therefore, that the Congress enact new tax legislation to bring in an additional $4 billion of Government revenue. This should come principally from additional corporate taxes. A portion should come from revised estate and gift taxes. Consideration should be given to raising personal income [tax—Eds.] rates in the middle and upper brackets.

If we want to keep our economy running in high gear, we must be sure that every group has the incentive to make its full contribution to the national welfare. At present, the working men and women of the Nation are unfairly discriminated against by a statute that abridges their rights, curtails their constructive efforts, and hampers our system of free collective bargaining. That statute is the Labor-Management Relations Act of 1947, sometimes called the Taft-Hartley Act.

That act should be repealed!

The Wagner Act should be reenacted. However, certain improvements, which I recommended to the Congress 2 years ago, are needed. Jurisdictional strikes and unjustified secondary boycotts should be prohibited. The use of economic force to decide issues arising out of the interpretation of existing contracts should be prevented. Without endangering our democratic freedoms, means should be provided for setting up machinery for preventing strikes in vital industries which affect the public interest.

The Department of Labor should be rebuilt and strengthened and those units properly belonging within that department should be placed in it.

The health of our economy and its maintenance at high levels further require that the minimum wage fixed by law should be raised to at least 75 cents an hour. . . .

Our national farm program should be improved—not only in the interest of the farmers, but for the lasting prosperity of the whole Nation. Our goals should be abundant farm production and parity income for agriculture. Standards of living on the farm should be just as good as anywhere else in the country. . . .

We should give special attention to extending modern conveniences and services to our farms. Rural electrification should be pushed forward. And in considering legislation relating to housing, education, health, and social security, special attention should be given to rural problems. . . .

In all this we must make sure that the benefits of these public undertakings are directly available to the people. Public power should be carried to consuming areas by public transmission lines where necessary to provide electricity at the lowest possible rates. Irrigation waters should serve family farms and not land speculators.

The Government has still other opportunities—to help raise the standard of living of our citizens. These opportunities lie in the fields of social security, health, education, housing, and civil rights.

The present coverage of the social security laws is altogether inadequate; the benefit payments are too low. . . .

We must spare no effort to raise the general level of health in this country. . . .

It is . . . shocking that millions of our children are not receiving a good education. . . . I cannot repeat too strongly my desire for prompt Federal financial aid to the States to help them operate and maintain their school systems.

The governmental agency which now administers the programs of health, education, and social security should be given full departmental status.

The housing shortage continues to be acute. As an immediate step, the Congress should enact the provisions for low-rent public housing, slum clearance, farm housing, and housing research which I have repeatedly recommended. . . .

The authority which I have requested, to allocate materials in short supply and to impose price ceilings on such materials, could be used, if found necessary, to channel more materials into homes large enough for family life at prices which wage earners can afford. . . .

The fulfillment of this promise is among the highest purposes of government. The civil rights proposals I made to the 80th Congress, I now repeat to the 81st Congress. They should be enacted in order that the Federal Government may assume the leadership and discharge the obligations clearly placed upon it by the Constitution.

4 • The Cold War, 1945-1953

*I*n 1945 Americans looked forward to peace among the Allies and hoped for a new world order based on justice and law. But events soon dashed their optimism. Forced to abandon their prewar indifference to foreign affairs, Americans slowly learned again that incidents in Poland or Czechoslovakia could deeply affect their lives. Reluctantly they supported a large military establishment and growing defense expenditures, and slowly they adjusted to life in a world divided into armed camps.

The roots of the Cold War can be traced to nearly a quarter century of antagonism between the United States and Great Britain on the one side and Russia on the other. Though the war had temporarily submerged animosities, during the Grand Alliance fears and doubts lingered. England's great wartime leader, Prime Minister Winston Churchill, an enemy of the Russian Revolution, never lost his suspicion of the Soviets. Despite the carnage of Russia's armies and her war-torn economy, Churchill's apprehensions grew. He envisaged Russia as a behemoth threatening war-wracked Europe. President Franklin D. Roosevelt, though more optimistic about the future, had sufficient doubts to conceal the atomic-bomb project from Marshal Joseph Stalin, the Soviet leader. In turn, Stalin, perhaps the most mistrusting, feared that his wartime allies planned to surround Russia with anti-Soviet pro-West states, and he contrived to create only friendly governments in Eastern Europe.

During most of the war, the Allies, at Roosevelt's insistence, had restricted negotiations largely to military affairs and so postponed divisive issues. Perhaps at the cost of placing the future in bondage, they had maintained a superficial harmony. Even the fear of a split on the question of Eastern Europe was temporarily reduced in February 1945 at the Yalta Conference. Though some State Department officials had already consigned that area to the Soviet orbit, Roosevelt believed that a free Eastern Europe had been obtained at the conference table. "We were absolutely certain that we had won the first great victory of peace," Harry Hopkins, Roosevelt's close aide, later recalled. But shortly before his death, Roosevelt feared that Soviet defiance of wartime agreements might destroy the Grand Alliance.

Roosevelt's policy for dealing with the Soviets had been based on his belief in the willingness of Stalin to cooperate with the West. Truman, though promising to follow Roosevelt's policies, quickly discontinued them. As early as his April 23, 1945, cabinet meeting, the new President complained that settlements with Russia "had so far been a one-way street, and this could not continue." The same day, at a meeting with the Soviet Foreign Minister, Vyacheslav Molotov, Truman accused Russia of violating the Yalta accord and spoke sharply to the diplomat. "FDR's appeasement is over," concluded a happy Senator Arthur Vandenberg. American policy seemed more firm, and on August 25 the United States cut off Lend-Lease. That cancellation did not make the Russians more tractable, but Truman hoped that the atomic bomb would give him "a hammer on those boys."

Not until the Potsdam Conference did international politics become bipolar. Despite brief hopes, the conference did not settle basic disputes. Though the Big Three seemed to agree on Germany, the issues of Eastern Europe remained largely unresolved. Soon after the meeting, the Alliance openly crumbled under the burden of accusations and hostilities. The Cold War was beginning.

American policy, though growing progressively more firm, remained sensitive to Republican charges that the Democrats were risking moral principles. As the administration yielded to its critics on the right, those on the left, such as Secretary of Commerce Henry Wallace, challenged emerging policy. But their suggestions for bold concessions were rebuffed. As the two blocs quarreled over Eastern Europe, Iran, Germany, and control of atomic energy, the East-West cleavage deepened. Despite the settlement of the Iran problem, the disputes became rancorous and the struggle menacing.

By 1947 the administration openly subscribed to the doctrine of containment. Despite brief hopes that the Marshall Plan would act as a bridge between East and West, that proposal ultimately widened the split. In the next few years the coup in Czechoslovakia, the Berlin blockade and the airlift, NATO, and the Warsaw Pact left Europe a divided continent.

ACT OF MILITARY SURRENDER

1 ⋖⸱ ON MAY 7, 1945, after nearly six years of war, Germany surrendered. The Act of Military Surrender follows:[1]

1. We the undersigned, acting by authority of the German High Command, hereby surrender unconditionally to the Supreme Commander, Allied Expeditionary Force and simultaneously to the Soviet High Command all forces on land, sea, and in the air who are at this date under German control.

2. The German High Command will at once issue orders to all German military, naval and air authorities and to all forces under German control to cease active operations at 2301 hours Central European time on 8 May and to remain in the positions occupied at that time. No ship, vessel, or aircraft is to be scuttled, or any damage done to their hull, machinery or equipment.

3. The German High Command will at once issue to the appropriate commanders, and ensure the carrying out of any further orders issued by the Supreme Commander, Allied Expeditionary Force and by the Soviet High Command.

4. This act of military surrender is without prejudice to, and will be superseded by any general instrument of surrender imposed by, or on behalf of the United Nations and applicable to GERMANY and the German armed forces as a whole.

5. In the event of the German High Command or any of the forces under their control failing to act in accordance with this Act of Surrender, the Supreme Commander, Allied Expeditionary Force and the Soviet High Command will take such punitive or other action as they deem appropriate.

STATE DEPARTMENT MEMO TO TRUMAN

2 ⋖⸱ THE END OF THE WAR in Europe emphasized the need to establish a firm and lasting peace. Just weeks before victory in Europe, in a memorandum of April 13, 1945, the State Department sketched for the new President the troubling problems he would face:[2]

[1] Reprinted from *Department of State Bulletin*, July 22, 1945, p. 105.
[2] Reprinted from *The Memoirs by Harry S. Truman* (New York: Doubleday & Co., Inc., 1955), I, 14–17. Copyright © 1955 Time Inc. Reprinted by permission.

UNITED KINGDOM. Mr. Churchill's policy is based fundamentally upon cooperation with the United States. It is based secondarily on maintaining the unity of the three great powers but the British Government has been showing increasing apprehension of Russia and her intentions. Churchill fully shares this Government's interpretation of the Yalta [Crimea—Eds.] Agreements on Eastern Europe and liberated areas. He is inclined however to press this position with the Russians with what we consider unnecessary rigidity as to detail. The British long for security but are deeply conscious of their decline from a leading position to that of the junior partner of the Big Three and are anxious to buttress their position vis-a-vis United States and Russia both through exerting leadership over the countries of Western Europe and through knitting the Commonwealth more closely together.

FRANCE. The best interests of the United States require that every effort be made by this Government to assist France, morally as well as physically, to regain her strength and her influence.

It is recognized that the French Provisional Government [government of Charles de Gaulle, president of the Council of Ministers —Eds.] and the French people are at present unduly preoccupied, as a result of the military defeat of 1940 and the subsequent occupation of their country by the enemy, with questions of national prestige. They have consequently from time to time put forward requests which are out of all proportion to their present strength and have in certain cases, notably in connection with Indochina, showed unreasonable suspicions of American aims and motives. It is believed that it is in the interest of the United States to take full account of this psychological factor in the French mind and to treat France in all respects on the basis of her potential power and influence rather than on the basis of her present strength. Positive American contributions toward the rebuilding of France include: present and future rearming of the French Army; support of French participation in the European Advisory Commission [composed of representatives from the U.S., U.K., U.S.S.R., and France for consultations during the war—Eds.], the control and occupation of Germany, the Reparations Commission and other organizations; and the conclusion of a Lend-Lease Agreement. De Gaulle has recently stated his appreciation of the necessity for the closest possible cooperation between France and the United States.

SOVIET UNION. Since the Yalta Conference the Soviet Government has taken a firm and uncompromising position on nearly every major question that has arisen in our relations. The more important of these are the Polish question, the application of the Crimea agreement on liberated areas, the agreement on the exchange of liberated prisoners of war and civilians, and the San Francisco Conference [Conference on United Nations—Eds.]. In the liberated areas under Soviet control, the Soviet Government is proceeding largely on a unilateral basis and does not agree that the developments which have taken place justify application of the Crimea agreement. Permission for our contact teams to go into Poland to assist in the evacuation of liberated prisoners of war has been refused although in general our prisoners have been reasonably well treated by Soviet standards. The Soviet Government appears to desire to proceed with the San Francisco Conference but was unwilling to send their Foreign Minister. They have asked for a large postwar credit and pending a decision on this matter have so far been unwilling to conclude an agreement providing for the orderly liquidation of lend-lease aid. In the politico-military field, similar difficulties have been encountered in collaboration with the Soviet authorities. . . .

GERMANY. The policy of the United States toward Germany was outlined in a memorandum approved by President Roosevelt on March 23, 1945. The principal features of that policy are: destruction of National Socialist organizations and influence, punishment of war criminals, disbandment of the German military establishment, military government administered with a view to political decentralization, reparation from existing wealth and future production, prevention of the manufacture of arms and destruction of all specialized facilities for their production, and controls over the German economy to secure these objectives.

Agreements have been reached with the United Kingdom and the Soviet Union on the text of the instrument of unconditional surrender on control machinery for Germany, and on zones of occupation. France has approved the first two agreements. The War Department is now studying the zone originally allocated to the United States with a view to transferring a portion of it to France in conformity with the Crimea undertaking.

No tripartite or quadripartite agreement on the treatment of Germany during the period of military government has been reached. This Government, however, has submitted the memorandum of

March 23 for negotiations in the European Advisory Commission meeting in London. This Government has prepared a program of reparation for presentation to the forthcoming conference in Moscow on that subject. . . .

SUPPLIES FOR LIBERATED AREAS. A problem of urgent importance to the U.S. is that of supplies for areas liberated from enemy occupation. The chaos and collapse which may result in these countries from starvation, unemployment and inflation can be averted principally by making available essential civilian supplies. Political stability and the maintenance of democratic governments which can withstand the pressures of extremist groups depend on the restoration of a minimum of economic stability. To do our part we must carefully analyze the needs and reserves of all claimants, military and civilian, domestic and foreign, and insist that they be reduced to absolute essentials. This will involve a reexamination both of U.S. military requirements and supply procedures and of U.S. civilian consumption. The British Cabinet Members are here to discuss critical food and other supply problems with the U.S. and Canada and have authority to reach decisions. It is essential that we organize ourselves at once to meet this problem. The Department is prepared to play its full role in this matter.

TRUMAN'S RADIO ADDRESS TO UN CONFERENCE

3 ⌒§ DESPITE ROOSEVELT'S DEATH just two weeks before the opening of the United Nations Conference on International Organization, President Truman decided that the conference should proceed as planned. Though he did not journey to the meeting at San Francisco, he addressed the opening session over the radio from Washington, D.C., on April 25, 1945:[3]

. . . The world has experienced a revival of an old faith in the everlasting moral force of justice. At no time in history has there been a more important conference, nor a more necessary meeting, than this one in San Francisco, which you are opening today. . . .

In the name of a great humanitarian—one who surely is with us today in spirit—I earnestly appeal to each and every one of you to rise above personal interests and adhere to those lofty principles which benefit all mankind.

[3] Excerpts reprinted from *Department of State Bulletin,* April 29, 1945, pp. 789–94, 798.

Franklin D. Roosevelt gave his life while trying to perpetuate these high ideals. This Conference owes its existence, in a large part, to the vision and foresight and determination of Franklin Roosevelt.

Each of you can remember other courageous champions, who also made the supreme sacrifice, serving under your flag. They gave their lives so that others might live in security. They died to insure justice. We must work and live to guarantee justice—for all.

You members of this Conference are to be the architects of the better world. In your hands rests our future. By your labors at this Conference, we shall know if suffering humanity is to achieve a just and lasting peace. . . .

We hold a powerful mandate from our people. They believe we will fulfil this obligation. We must prevent, if human mind, heart, and hope can prevent it, the repetition of the disaster from which the entire world will suffer for years to come.

If we should pay merely lip service to inspiring ideals, and later do violence to simple justice, we would draw down upon us the bitter wrath of generations yet unborn.

We must not continue to sacrifice the flower of our youth merely to check madmen, those who in every age plan world domination. The sacrifices of our youth today must lead, through your efforts, to the building for tomorrow of a mighty combination of nations founded upon justice for peace.

Justice remains the greatest power on earth. . . .

We must, once and for all, reverse the order, and prove by our acts conclusively that Right Has Might.

If we do not want to die together in war, we must learn to live together in peace.

With firm faith in our hearts, to sustain us along the hard road to victory, we will find our way to a secure peace, for the ultimate benefit of all humanity.

We must build a new world—a far better world—one in which the eternal dignity of man is respected.

YALTA PROTOCOL

4 ⁊ IN THE SPRING OF 1945 Churchill and Truman felt that another meeting of the Big Three was necessary. During the early days of May, Churchill and Truman communicated on their plans for the conference, their understanding of the Yalta agreement, and their appraisal of Russian intentions. Churchill,

predicting that "the gravest matters in the world will be decided" in the next two months, advised that the British and American armies "should hold firmly" to their positions in Yugoslavia, Austria, Czechoslovakia, and on the main front reaching to Lübeck. Then, explained Churchill, "we must . . . show them [the Russians —Eds.] how much we have to offer or withhold."

Churchill was delighted that Truman agreed "to adhere to our rightful interpretation of the Yalta agreements and to stand firmly on our present announced attitude towards all questions at issue." The particular portion of the Yalta pact leading to dispute was the provision dealing with countries liberated from Nazi Germany. In the protocol, Roosevelt, Churchill, and Stalin had jointly pledged:[4]

. . . to concert during the temporary period of instability in liberated Europe the policies of their three governments in assisting the peoples liberated from the domination of Nazi Germany and the peoples of the former Axis satellite states of Europe to solve by democratic means their pressing political and economic problems.

The establishment of order in Europe and the re-building of national economic life must be achieved by processes which will enable the liberated peoples to destroy the last vestiges of Nazism and Fascism and to create democratic institutions of their own choice. This is a principle of the Atlantic Charter—the right of all peoples to choose the form of government under which they will live—the restoration of sovereign rights and self-government to those peoples who have been forcibly deprived of them by the aggressor nations.

To foster the conditions in which the liberated peoples may exercise these rights, the three governments will jointly assist the people in any European liberated state or former Axis satellite state in Europe where in their judgment conditions require (a) to establish conditions of internal peace; (b) to carry out emergency measures for the relief of distressed peoples; (c) to form interim governmental authorities broadly representative of all democratic elements in the population and pledged to the earliest possible establishment through free elections of governments responsive to the will of the people; and (d) to facilitate where necessary the holding of such elections.

The three governments will consult the other United Nations and

[4] Excerpts reprinted from *Potsdam Papers*, II, 1569.

provisional authorities or other governments in Europe when matters of direct interest to them are under consideration.

When, in the opinion of the three governments, conditions in any European liberated state or any former Axis satellite state in Europe make such action necessary, they will immediately consult together on the measures necessary to discharge the joint responsibilities set forth in this declaration.

By this declaration we reaffirm our faith in the principles of the Atlantic Charter, our pledge in the Declaration by the United Nations, and our determination to build in co-operation with other peace-loving nations world order under law, dedicated to peace, security, freedom and general well-being of all mankind.

MESSAGES FROM CHURCHILL TO TRUMAN

5 ⋙ ON MAY 11, 1945, Churchill sent a telegram to President Truman:[5]

The Polish problem may be easier to settle when set in relation to the now numerous outstanding questions of the utmost gravity which require urgent settlement with the Russians. I fear terrible things have happened during the Russian advance through Germany to the Elbe. The proposed withdrawal of the United States Army to the occupational lines which were arranged with the Russians and Americans in Quebec and which were marked in yellow on the maps we studied there, would mean the tide of Russian domination sweeping forward 120 miles on a front of 300 or 400 miles. This would be an event which, if it occurred, would be one of the most melancholy in history. After it was over and the territory occupied by the Russians, Poland would be completely engulfed and buried deep in Russian-occupied lands. What would in fact be the Russian frontier would run from the North Cape in Norway along the Finnish-Swedish frontier, across the Baltic to a point just east of Lübeck along the at present agreed line of occupation and along the frontier between Bavaria to Czechoslovakia to the frontiers of Austria which is nominally to be in quadruple occupation, and half-way across that country to the Isonzo River behind which Tito and Russia will claim everything to the east. Thus the territories under Russian control would include the Baltic provinces, all of Germany to the occupational line, all Czechoslovakia, a large part of Austria, the whole of Yugoslavia,

[5] Excerpts, *ibid.*, I, 5–6.

Hungary, Roumania, Bulgaria until Greece in her present tottering condition is reached. It would include all the great capitals of middle Europe including Berlin, Vienna, Budapest, Belgrade, Bucharest and Sofia. The position of Turkey and Constantinople will certainly come immediately into discussion.

This constitutes an event in the history of Europe to which there has been no parallel, and which has not been faced by the Allies in their long and hazardous struggle. The Russian demands on Germany for reparations alone will be such as to enable her to prolong the occupation almost indefinitely, at any rate for many years during which time Poland will sink with many other states into the vast zone of Russian-controlled Europe, not necessarily economically Sovietised but police-governed.

It is just about time that these formidable issues were examined between the principal powers as a whole. We have several powerful bargaining counters on our side, the use of which might make for a peaceful agreement. First, the Allies ought not to retreat from their present positions to the occupational line until we are satisfied about Poland and also about the temporary character of the Russian occupation of Germany, and the conditions to be established in the Russianised or Russian-controlled countries in the Danube valley particularly Hungary, Austria and Czechoslovakia and the Balkans. Secondly, we may be able to please them about the exits from the Black Sea and the Baltic as part of a general settlement. All these matters can only be settled before the United States armies in Europe are weakened. If they are not settled before the United States armies withdraw from Europe and the Western world folds up its war machines, there are no prospects of a satisfactory solution and very little of preventing a third world war. It is to this early and speedy showdown and settlement with Russia that we must now turn our hopes. Meanwhile I am against weakening our claim against Russia on behalf of Poland in any way. I think it should stand where it was put in the telegrams from the President and me.

6 ⋐§   CHURCHILL SENT a message to Truman on May 12, 1945:[6]

. . . Anyone can see that in a very short space of time our armed power on the Continent will have vanished except for moderate forces to hold down Germany.

[6] Excerpt, *ibid.*, pp. 8–9.

Meanwhile what is to happen about Russia? I have always worked for friendship with Russia, but like you, I feel deep anxiety because of their misinterpretation of the Yalta decisions, their attitude towards Poland, their overwhelming influence in the Balkans excepting Greece, the difficulties they make about Vienna, the combination of Russian power and the territories under their control or occupied, coupled with the Communist technique in so many other countries, and above all their power to maintain very large armies in the field for a long time. What will be the position in a year or two, when the British and American armies have melted and the French has not yet been formed on any major scale, when we may have a handful of divisions mostly French, and when Russia may choose to keep two or three hundred on active service?

An iron curtain is drawn down upon their front. We do not know what is going on behind. There seems little doubt that the whole of the regions east of the line Lübeck–Trieste–Corfu will soon be completely in their hands. To this must be added the further enormous area conquered by the American armies between Eisenach and [the] Elbe, which will I suppose in a few weeks be occupied, when the Americans retreat, by the Russian power. All kinds of arrangements will have to be made by General Eisenhower to prevent another immense flight of the German population westward as this enormous Muscovite advance into the centre of Europe takes place. And then the curtain will descend again to a very large extent if not entirely. Thus a broad band of many hundreds of miles of Russian-occupied territory will isolate us from Poland.

Meanwhile the attention of our peoples will be occupied in inflicting severities upon Germany, which is ruined and prostrate, and it would be open to the Russians in a very short time to advance if they chose to the waters of the North Sea and the Atlantic.

Surely it is vital now to come to an understanding with Russia, or see where we are with her, before we weaken our armies mortally or retire to the zones of occupation. This can only be done by a personal meeting. I should be most grateful for your opinion and advice. Of course we may take the view that Russia will behave impeccably and no doubt that offers the most convenient solution. To sum up, this issue of a settlement with Russia before our strength has gone seems to me to dwarf all others.

BOHLEN MEMO ON STALIN-HOPKINS MEETING

7 ◄◄§ BEFORE THE POTSDAM MEETING Truman, still feeling very
     inexperienced in foreign affairs, sent Harry Hopkins, one
of Roosevelt's close advisers on foreign policy, to meet with Marshal
Stalin. Hopkins and Stalin held five conversations; other officials,
including W. Averell Harriman, the American ambassador to the
Soviet Union, attended the meetings. Charles Bohlen, assistant to
the secretary of state, took notes on the meetings and prepared
memoranda. Bohlen's memorandum on the first meeting, May 26,
1945, follows:[7]

Mr. Hopkins said . . . Two months ago there had been overwhelming sympathy among the American people for the Soviet Union and
complete support for President Roosevelt's policies which the Marshal
knew so well. This sympathy and support came primarily because of
the brilliant achievements of the Soviet Union in the war and partly
from President Roosevelt's leadership and the magnificent way in
which our two countries had worked together to bring about the
defeat of Germany. The American people at that time hoped and
confidently believed that the two countries could work together in
peace as well as they had in war. Mr. Hopkins said there had always
been a small minority, the Hearsts and the McCormicks, who had
been against the policy of cooperation with the Soviet Union. These
men had also been bitter political enemies of President Roosevelt
but had never had any backing from the American people as was
shown by the fact that against their bitter opposition President Roosevelt had been four times elected President. He said he did not intend
to discuss this small minority but to discuss the general state of
American opinion and particularly the present attitude of the millions
of Americans who had supported President Roosevelt's policy in
regard to the Soviet Union and who believed that despite different
political and economic ideology of the two countries, the United
States and the Soviet Union could work together after the war in
order to bring about a secure peace for humanity. He said he wished
to assure the Marshal with all the earnestness at his command that
this body of American public opinion who had been the constant
support of the Roosevelt policies were seriously disturbed about their

[7] Excerpts, *ibid.*, pp. 26–9.

relations with Russia. In fact, in the last six weeks deterioration of public opinion had been so serious as to affect adversely the relations between our two countries. He said he wished to emphasize that this change had occurred in the very people who had supported to the hilt Roosevelt's policy of cooperation with the Soviet Union. . . .

Mr. Hopkins said that it was not simple or easy to put a finger on the precise reasons for this deterioration but he must emphasize that without the support of public opinion and particularly of the supporters of President Roosevelt it would be very difficult for President Truman to carry forward President Roosevelt's policy. He said that, as the Marshal was aware, the cardinal basis of President Roosevelt's policy which the American people had fully supported had been the concept that the interests of the United States were world wide and not confined to North and South America and the Pacific Ocean and it was this concept that had led to the many conferences concerning the peace of the world which President Roosevelt had had with Marshal Stalin. President Roosevelt had believed that the Soviet Union had likewise world-wide interests and that the two countries could work out together any political or economic considerations at issue between them. After the Yalta Conference it looked as though we were well on the way to reaching a basic understanding on all questions of foreign affairs of interest to our respective countries, in regard to the treatment of Germany; Japan and the question of setting up a world security organization, to say nothing of the long term interests between the United States and the U.S.S.R. He said in a country like ours public opinion is affected by specific incidents and in this case the deterioration in public opinion in regard to our relations with the Soviet Union had been centered in our inability to carry into effect the Yalta Agreement on Poland. There were also a train of events, each unimportant in themselves, which had grown up around the Polish question, which contributed to the deterioration in public opinion. President Truman feels, and so does the American public, although they are not familiar with all the details, a sense of bewilderment at our inability to solve the Polish question. . . .

Marshal Stalin replied that the reason for the failure on the Polish question was that the Soviet Union desired to have a friendly Poland, but that Great Britain wanted to revive the system of *cordon sanitaire* on the Soviet borders.

Mr. Hopkins replied that neither the Government nor the people of the United States had any such intention.

Marshal Stalin replied he was speaking only of England and said that the British conservatives did not desire to see a Poland friendly to the Soviet Union.

Mr. Hopkins stated that the United States would desire a Poland friendly to the Soviet Union and in fact desired to see friendly countries all along the Soviet borders.

Marshal Stalin replied if that be so we can easily come to terms in regard to Poland.

Mr. Hopkins said that during his visit here there were a number of specific questions that he and Mr. Harriman hoped to discuss with Marshal Stalin and Mr. Molotov but that the general statement he had just made concerning public opinion in the United States was the principal reason for his coming and the principal cause of anxiety at the present time. He said he had wished to state frankly and as forcibly as he knew how to Marshal Stalin the importance that he, personally, attached to the present trend of events and that he felt that the situation would get rapidly worse unless we could clear up the Polish matter. He had therefore been glad to hear the Marshal say that he thought the question could be settled.

Marshal Stalin replied that in his opinion it was best to settle it but not if the British conservatives attempted to revive the *cordon sanitaire.*

BOHLEN MEMO ON SECOND MEETING

8 ⋅∘§   BOHLEN'S MEMORANDUM on the second meeting, May 27, 1945, follows:[8]

Marshal Stalin said he would not attempt to use Soviet public opinion as a screen but would speak of the feeling that had been created in Soviet governmental circles as a result of recent moves on the part of the United States Government. He said these circles felt a certain alarm in regard to the attitude of the United States Government. It was their impression that the American attitude towards the Soviet Union had perceptibly cooled once it became obvious that Germany was defeated, and that it was as though the Americans were saying that the Russians were no longer needed. He said he would give the following examples:

. . . (2) The question of . . . Reparations Commission. At Yalta it had been agreed that the three powers would sit on this Commission

[8] Excerpts, *ibid.*, pp. 32–41.

in Moscow and subsequently the United States Government had insisted that France should be represented on the same basis as the Soviet Union. This he felt was an insult to the Soviet Union in view of the fact that France had concluded a separate peace with Germany and had opened the frontier to the Germans. It was true that this had been done by [Marshal Henri Philippe—Eds.] Pétain's Government [the Vichy government—Eds.] but nevertheless it was an action of France. To attempt to place France on the same footing as the Soviet Union looked like an attempt to humiliate the Russians.

(3) The attitude of the United States Government towards the Polish question. He said that at Yalta it had been agreed that the existing government was to be reconstructed and that anyone with common sense could see that this meant that the present government was to form the basis of the new. He said no other understanding of the Yalta Agreement was possible. Despite the fact that they were simple people the Russians should not be regarded as fools, which was a mistake the West frequently made, nor were they blind and could quite well see what was going on before their eyes. It is true that the Russians are patient in the interests of a common cause but that their patience has its limits.

(4) The manner in which Lend Lease had been curtailed. He said that if the United States was unable to supply the Soviet Union further under Lend Lease that was one thing but that the manner in which it had been done had been unfortunate and even brutal. For example, certain ships had been unloaded and while it was true that this order had been cancelled the whole manner in which it had been done had caused concern to the Soviet Government. If the refusal to continue Lend Lease was designed as pressure on the Russians in order to soften them up then it was a fundamental mistake. He said he must tell Mr. Hopkins frankly that [if] the Russians were approached frankly on a friendly basis much could be done but that reprisals in any form would bring about the exact opposite effect. . . .

. . . Mr. Harriman said that he, personally, felt that if Mr. Molotov had not introduced the question of an invitation to the present Polish Government we might have been successful in persuading the Latin American countries to postpone the question of Argentina, but that once Mr. Molotov had connected the question of Argentina with that of an invitation to the present Polish Government, Mr. [Edward —Eds.] Stettinius [Secretary of State and head of American delegation to UN—Eds.] felt that because of the willingness of the South American countries to support the Crimea Decision and the invitation to the Ukraine and White Russia, he was committed to vote for the admission of Argentina.

. . . The Government and people of the United States were disturbed because the preliminary steps towards the reestablishment of Poland appeared to have been taken unilaterally by the Soviet Union together with the present Warsaw Government and that in fact the United States was completely excluded. He said he hoped that Stalin would believe him when he said that this feeling was a fact. Mr. Hopkins said he urged that Marshal Stalin would judge American policy by the actions of the United States Government itself and not by the attitudes and public expressions of the Hearst newspapers and the *Chicago Tribune.* He hoped that the Marshal would put his mind to the task of thinking up what diplomatic methods could be used to settle this question, keeping in mind the feeling of the American people. . . .

Marshal Stalin replied that he wished Mr. Hopkins would take into consideration the following factors: He said it may seem strange although it appeared to be recognized in United States circles and Churchill in his speeches also recognized it, that the Soviet Government should wish for a friendly Poland. In the course of twenty-five years the Germans had twice invaded Russia via Poland. Neither the British nor American people had experienced such German invasions which were a horrible thing to endure and the results of which were not easily forgotten. He said these German invasions were not warfare but were like the incursions of the Huns. He said that Germany had been able to do this because Poland had been regarded as a part of the *cordon sanitaire* around the Soviet Union and that previous European policy had been that Polish Governments must be hostile to Russia. In these circumstances either Poland had been too weak to oppose Germany or had let the Germans come through. Thus Poland had served as a corridor for the German attacks on Russia. He said Poland's weakness and hostility had been a great source of weakness to the Soviet Union and had permitted the Germans to do what they wished in the East and also in the West since the two were mixed together. It is therefore in Russia's vital interest that Poland should be both strong and friendly. He said there was no intention on the part of the Soviet Union to interfere in Poland's internal affairs, that Poland would live under the parliamentary system which is like Czechoslovakia, Belgium and Holland and that any talk of an intention to Sovietize Poland was stupid. He said even the Polish leaders, some of whom were communists, were against the Soviet system since the Polish people did not desire collective farms or other aspects of the Soviet system. In this the Polish leaders were right since the Soviet system was not exportable—it must develop from within on the basis of a set of conditions which were not present in Poland. He said all the Soviet Union wanted was that Poland should not be in a position to open the gates to Germany and in order to prevent this Poland must be strong and democratic. . . .

. . . He said it was contrary to the Soviet policy to set up [a] Soviet administration on foreign soil since this would look like occupation and be resented by the local inhabitants. It was for this reason that some Polish administration had to be established in Poland and this could be done only with those who had helped the Red Army. He said he wished to emphasize that these steps had not been taken with any desire to eliminate or exclude Russia's Allies. He must point out however that Soviet action in Poland had been more successful than British action in Greece and at no time had they been compelled to undertake the measures which they had done in Greece. Stalin then turned to his suggestion for the solution of the Polish problem.

Marshal Stalin said that he felt that we should examine the composition of the future Government of National Unity. He said there were eighteen or twenty ministries in the present Polish Government and that four or five of these portfolios could be given representatives of other Polish groups taken from the list submitted by Great Britain and the United States (Molotov whispered to Stalin who then said he meant four and not five posts in the government). He said he thought the Warsaw Poles would not accept more than four ministers from other democratic groups.

BOHLEN MEMO ON FOURTH MEETING

9 ↰↰↰ BOHLEN'S MEMORANDUM on the fourth meeting, May 30, 1945, follows:[9]

Mr. Hopkins said he would like to accent once again the reasons for our concern in regard to Poland, and indeed, in regard to other countries which were geographically far from our borders. He said

[9] Excerpt, *ibid.*, pp. 54–6.

there were certain fundamental rights which, when impinged [in-fringed?] upon or denied caused concern in the United States. These were cardinal elements which must be present if a parliamentary system is to be established and maintained. He said for example:

(1) There must be the right of freedom of speech so that people could say what they wanted to, right of assembly, right of movement and the right to worship at any church that they desired;

(2) All political parties[,] except the fascist party and fascist elements[,] who represented or could represent democratic governments should be permitted the free use, without distinction, of the press, radio, meetings and other facilities of political expression;

(3) All citizens should have the right of public trial, defense by council [counsel] of their own choosing, and the right of habeas corpus. . . .

Marshal Stalin replied that these principles of democracy are well known and would find no objection on the part of the Soviet Government. He was sure that the Polish Government, which in its declaration had outlined just such principles, would not only not oppose them but would welcome them. He said, however, that in regard to the specific freedoms mentioned by Mr. Hopkins, they could only be applied in full in peace time, and even then with certain limitations. He said for example the fascist party, whose intention it was to overthrow democratic governments, could not be permitted to enjoy to the full extent these freedoms. He said secondly there were the limitations imposed by war. All states when they were threatened by war on [or] their frontiers were not secure had found it necessary to introduce certain restrictions. . . .

CHURCHILL TO TRUMAN ON USSR

10 ◄§ CHURCHILL CONTINUED to express his fears of Russia to Truman, this time in a telegram of June 4, 1945:[10]

. . . I view with profound misgivings the retreat of the American Army to our line of occupation in the Central Sector, thus bringing Soviet power into the heart of Western Europe and the descent of an iron curtain between us and everything to the eastward.

I hoped that this retreat, if it has to be made, would be accompanied by the settlement of many great things which would be the

[10] Excerpt, *ibid.*, p. 92.

true foundation of world peace. Nothing really important has been settled yet and you and I will have to bear great responsibility for the future.

JOSEPH DAVIES' REPORT ON CHURCHILL

11 ⤟ IN PREPARATION for the forthcoming Potsdam Conference, Truman, who did not know Churchill, sent Joseph Davies, chairman of the President's War Relief Board, as a special representative to explore pressing issues. Davies reported in a telegram of June 12 on his conversations of May 26 and 27, 1945, with Churchill:[11]

[Churchill—Eds.] . . . was even more bitter towards Tito. He could not be permitted arbitrarily to stake out and occupy, and assert dominion over parts of Austria and the Trieste District. That was for the Peace Conference. Tito, he said, was thoroughly unreliable, a communist, and completely under the domination of Moscow.

As to the rest of the Balkans, he complained bitterly that there was no joint cooperation or "fifty fifty" control as to Yugoslavia, nor "eighty twenty" in Bulgaria or Rumania, nor "tripartite" control in Austria. As he saw it, Tito's attitude was a reflection of the Soviet policy and action, and failure of cooperation elsewhere disclosed what Europe had to confront and expect from the Soviets.

As the Prime Minister went on, he became vehement and even violent in his criticisms of the Soviet Armies and officials in the re-occupied areas. What was more horrible to him than Communism, was the imposition of the Secret Police and Gestapo methods. He spoke with much feeling of the "steel curtain" of the Soviets being "clamped down" on Eastern liberated areas, the horror of such a black out, etc. etc.

When Stalin, he said, had asked him recently why he feared the Soviets in Europe, he had replied that it was because they were sending, in advance of the Red Army, Communist propagandists and leaders, "like locusts," to establish communist cells. Stalin's attitude seemed to be that he had given his assurances as to his real purpose not to try to communize Europe; that this should be sufficient, particularly as an army had to take every precaution to protect itself in hostile, invaded territory.

[11] Excerpt, *ibid.*, pp. 65–9.

What he elaborated upon at length, and with great emphasis and emotion, were the grave dangers which would arise with the withdrawal of American troops from Europe. It would be a "terrible thing" if the American Army were vacated from Europe. Europe would be prostrate and at the mercy of the Red Army and of Communism. Moreover, it would never do to permit those American Forces which had advanced some 120 miles east of the lines of the American occupational zones to retire now. The present lines, through Central Germany, of the British and U.S. Armies should be maintained, lest Communism should dominate and control all of Western Europe. The positions were strategic. They should be held to serve for bargaining purposes with the Soviets, despite the fact that they were in advance of the areas of occupancy agreed upon. When I suggested that there had been an express agreement as to these zones, he said that conditions had greatly changed. . . .

The Prime Minister did not demur, but resumed again his elaboration upon what a desperate situation Europe confronted at the hands of the Soviets if American forces were withdrawn from Europe. If his fears were justified, England, he proclaimed, would stand her ground alone, if she had to. England was not a negligible factor in world affairs. England could still protect herself. The difficulties of crossing the Channel and her mastery of the air, made her still invulnerable to attack. If need be, England would stand alone. She had done it before, etc. It was in line with his address to the House of Commons two weeks ago. I checked back in my files and quote it here. It is an authoritative definition of the classic policy of England as to Europe.

> We have had to hold out from time to time all alone, or to be the mainspring of coalitions, against a continental tyrant or dictator, and we have had to hold out for quite a long time . . . In all these world wars our islands *kept the lead of Europe or else held out alone.*

The Prime Minister is one of the greatest men of our time, and the greatest Englishman of this or any other time, in my opinion. But he is first and foremost an Englishman. He is still the King's Minister who will not liquidate the Empire. He is still the great Briton of Runnymede and Dunkirk. He is superbly endowed and is a great advocate. He would be equally great in a courtroom, on the stage, or in any intellectual or fighting field. He was at his oratorical and powerful best.

12 ✑ PRESIDENT TRUMAN, on recognizing Poland on July 5, 1945, announced that the new Polish Provisional Government of National Unity "has informed me . . . that it has recognized in their entirety the decisions of the Crimea [Yalta—Eds.] Conference on the Polish question. The new Government has thereby confirmed its intention to carry out the provisions of the Crimea decisions with respect to the holding of elections." The Yalta agreement had pledged the new government "to the holding of free and unfettered elections as soon as possible on the basis of universal suffrage and secret ballot."

A briefing paper of June 29 outlined future American policy toward Poland:[12]

. . . The prestige and democratic functioning of any government at Warsaw meeting our requirements will adversely be affected by the continuing presence in Poland of large Soviet forces. These elections should likewise be supervised by representatives of the Three Great Powers, otherwise, the presence of Soviet officials and troops in Poland would result in supervision by the Soviet Government alone and in possible undue and undesirable Soviet influence on the outcome of the elections.

We should support actively those elements in the new Government which oppose Poland's becoming a Soviet satellite. Such support should not become open interference in internal Polish affairs but it should be effective enough to enable the democratic Polish leaders to carry out the pledge we have made to the Polish nation. Their task and our task will be greatly simplified if we can use this to foster the maintenance of freedom of expression, freedom of the press and information and personal liberty in reconstructed Poland. The free exchange of information between Poland and the Western World, accompanied by a wide interchange of visitors which is impossible at the present time, should be among our chief objectives, since contact between Poland and the Western World will be reestablished thereby. It is chiefly through support of [Stanislaw—Eds.] Mikołajczyk and his fellow democratic ministers in the new government that we can hope to end the present "blackout" in Poland.

[12] Excerpt, *ibid.*, p. 716.

STIMSON ON U.S.-SOVIET DIFFICULTIES

13 ◄§ CONTINUED DIFFERENCES between the Soviet Union and the United States and fears of a postwar schism among these allies led Secretary of War Stimson to analyze the difficulties in a memorandum of July 19. Two days later he presented the paper to the President, explaining that it was in "no way" official. Ambassador Harriman agreed with the analysis but was pessimistic about getting Russia to change her system. Truman, after reading the paper, told Stimson that he agreed with its contents. The text of the memorandum follows:[13]

1. With each International Conference that passes and, in fact, with each month that passes between conferences, it becomes clearer that the great basic problem of the future is the stability of the relations of the Western democracies with Russia.

2. With each such time that passes it also becomes clear that that problem arises out of the fundamental differences between a nation of free thought, free speech, free elections, in fact, a really free people with a nation which is not basically free but which is systematically controlled from above by Secret Police and in which free speech is not permitted.

3. It also becomes clear that no permanently safe international relations can be established between two such fundamentally different national systems. With the best of efforts we cannot understand each other. Furthermore, in an autocratically controlled system, policy cannot be permanent. It is tied up with the life of one man. Even if a measure of mental accord is established with one head the resulting agreement is liable to be succeeded by an entirely different policy coming from a different successor.

4. Daily we find our best efforts for coordination and sympathetic understanding with Russia thwarted by the suspicion which basically and necessarily must exist in any controlled organization of men.

5. Thus every effort we make at permanent organization of such a world composed of two such radically different systems is subject to frustration by misunderstandings arising out of mutual suspicion.

6. The great problem ahead is how to deal with this basic difference which exists as a flaw in our desired accord. I believe we must not

[13] Excerpt, *ibid.*, pp. 1155-7.

accept the present situation as permanent for the result will then almost inevitably be a new war and the destruction of our civilization.

I believe we should direct our thoughts constantly to the time and method of attacking the basic difficulty and the means we may have in hand to produce results. That something can be accomplished is not an idle dream. Stalin has shown an indication of his appreciation of our system of freedom by his proposal of a free constitution to be established among the Soviets. To read this Constitution would lead one to believe that Russia had in mind the establishing of free speech, free assembly, free press and the other essential elements of our Bill of Rights and would not have forever resting upon every citizen the stifling hand of autocracy. He has thus given us an opening.

The questions are:

a. When can we take any steps without doing more harm than good?

b. By what means can we proceed?

1. By private diplomatic discussion of the reasons for our distrust.

2. By encouraging open public discussions.

3. By setting conditions for any concessions which Russia may ask in respect to—

(a) Territorial concessions

(b) Loans

(c) Bases

(d) Any other concessions.

How far these conditions can extend is a serious problem. At the start it may be possible to effect only some amelioration of the local results of Russia's Secret Police State.

7. The foregoing has a vital bearing upon the control of the vast and revolutionary discovery of . . . [atomic energy—Eds.] which is now confronting us. Upon the successful control of that energy depends the future successful development or destruction of the modern civilized world. The Committee appointed by the War Department which has been considering that control has pointed this out in no uncertain terms and has called for an international organization for that purpose. After careful reflection I am of the belief that no world organization containing as one of its dominant members a nation whose people are not possessed of free speech but whose governmental action is controlled by the autocratic machinery of a secret political

police, cannot [can] give effective control of this new agency with its devastating possibilities.

I therefore believe that before we share our new discovery with Russia we should consider carefully whether we can do so safely under any system of control until Russia puts into effective action the proposed constitution which I have mentioned. If this is a necessary condition, we must go slowly in any disclosures or agreeing to any Russian participation whatsoever and constantly explore the question how our head-start in . . . [atomic energy—Eds.] and the Russian desire to participate can be used to bring us nearer to the removal of the basic difficulties which I have emphasized.

FOREIGN MINISTERS' MEETING

14 ◄§ THE POTSDAM CONFERENCE opened on July 16, 1945. In addition to the meetings of the heads of state, with the new British Prime Minister, Clement R. Atlee, replacing Churchill midway through the sessions, there were also conferences of the foreign ministers. Secretary of State Byrnes represented the United States; Foreign Secretary Anthony Eden, and then Ernest Bevin, the United Kingdom; and Foreign Minister Vyacheslav Molotov, the Soviet Union. At their third meeting, on July 20, they discussed the problems of Eastern Europe:[14]

Mr. Molotov then raised the question of the Yalta declaration on liberated Europe and circulated the Soviet draft.

Mr. Eden, with some warmth, stated that he would like to say at once that the description of Greece given in the Soviet proposal is a complete travesty of fact. The Soviet Government had no representatives in Greece, although they were free to go there. The press of the whole world was free to go to Greece and see for themselves and tell the world without censorship what was going on. Unfortunately this was not possible in either Rumania or Bulgaria. The Greeks proposed regular elections open to all parties. The present Greek Government had invited international observers to regulate these elections. Unfortunately the situation in Rumania and Bulgaria was not the same.

Mr. Molotov stated that there were missions in Rumania and Bulgaria, including British representatives.

Mr. Eden replied that these representatives had few facilities to

14 Excerpt, *ibid.*, pp. 150–3.

see anything and still less to get anything done. In addition, the press was not permitted freely to operate in these countries.

Mr. Molotov remarked that the number of British representatives in Rumania and Bulgaria was greater than the number of Soviet representatives. It was true that there were no British troops, but there were many political representatives. It was his understanding that the British Government had enough people there to keep it informed. In addition, Mr. Eden knew that the Soviet representatives had recently made proposals for greater cooperation.

Mr. Eden replied that he now hoped that the situation would improve.

Mr. Molotov asked what suggestions there were.

Mr. Byrnes stated that so far as the United States was concerned it had hoped that the spirit of the Yalta declaration would be carried into effect. However, the governments in the countries concerned have restricted the movement of our representatives and the press has been denied admission. This had become a source of great irritation among our people. They believe that the Yalta agreement contemplated early elections. Mr. Byrnes considered that the determination of policy in these countries should not be the sole burden of one of the three powers but should be shared by all of them, and he felt that steps should be taken to see that the governments in question should not discriminate against either the Soviet, British, or American Governments. In view of the attitude of the governments concerned, we could not recognize them at this time. At Yalta we agreed in the declaration on liberated Europe, among other things, to form interim governments broadly representative of all democratic elements of the people and pledged to the earliest possible establishment of a government through free elections. If such elections were held, the United States would gladly recognize any governments resulting therefrom. It cannot do so now. As long as the governments in question deny to American representatives and press an opportunity to observe and report on conditions, recognition will be difficult.

Mr. Molotov stated that there were no excesses in Bulgaria or Rumania comparable to those taking place in Greece. He cited the American and British press as authority for this statement. He went on to say that there was no trouble in Bulgaria or Rumania. He admitted restrictions on British and American representatives during the war but stated that things will be different now. The Soviet representatives in the countries in question have therefore already made suggestions in Hungary, Bulgaria, and Rumania to the American and British representatives regarding the future operation of the control councils. He was willing to discuss the matter at this meeting. He pointed out that no elections had been held in Italy despite the fact that Italy had been out of the war for some time. Nevertheless, the United States has diplomatic representatives there. It was therefore difficult to understand why the United States should not recognize Bulgaria and Rumania, which gave greater assistance to the war effort than Italy. In any event, the Soviet Government can no longer delay diplomatic recognition of these countries. He suggested the consideration of a draft either in the present meeting or in a subcommittee.

Mr. Byrnes pointed out that our press was able to get an account of conditions in Greece but was unable to do so in Bulgaria and Rumania. Many misunderstandings might disappear if the press was permitted to operate in these countries.

Mr. Molotov stated that there was no objection to this.

Mr. Byrnes replied that he was sure that the Soviet Union did not object but the governments of these countries do. In Greece the United States is impressed by the fact that the Greeks invite us to supervise their elections. He had just this morning addressed to Mr. Molotov a letter inviting Russia to participate in the supervision of these elections.

Mr. Molotov stated that there was no doubt of free elections in Rumania and Bulgaria, which would be held as soon as candidates could be nominated.

Mr. Byrnes asked whether the British Empire had been consulted regarding elections in Rumania and Bulgaria.

Mr. Eden replied that it had not.

Mr. Molotov confirmed this statement.

Mr. Eden pointed out the difference between Greece, where all parties would participate in the elections, and Bulgaria, where the vote would be only for or against a set list. This did not meet the British idea of democracy. The press of the world could send anything out of Greece, and this included the TASS representative. On the other hand, British press representatives could send nothing out of Rumania or Bulgaria without extremely heavy censorship.

Mr. Molotov said that censorship had been hard during the war but would be better now.

Mr. Byrnes recalled that at Yalta we, and particularly President

Roosevelt, had wanted to see Poland and other governments bordering Russia friendly to the Soviet Union. The United States has no interest in the Governments of Rumania and Bulgaria except that they be representative of the people and permit our representatives and press to observe conditions freely.

Mr. Molotov suggested that methods be discussed.

Mr. Byrnes pointed out that if elections are held without asking for supervision by the Big Three, and governments were established which were distrusted generally by the people of our country, it will affect our relations. If the Big Three will see to it that free elections are held, the United States would recognize any government formed. We are interested in having governments friendly toward Russia.

Mr. Molotov stated that there was no reason to fear delay or that elections would not be free. However, the situation in Greece was different. The situation was dangerous. Mr. Molotov cited warlike speeches made in Greece against neighboring countries.

Mr. Eden interjected that he was aware that the Yugoslav press and radio were accusing Greece of aggressive intentions. The same charges were contained in the document presented this morning by the Soviet delegation.

Mr. Molotov insisted that there is no connection between the Soviet document and the Yugoslav Government.

Mr. Eden replied that he had only said that the language was the same. He pointed out that the Prime Minister yesterday had given figures proving that it was ludicrous to talk about an aggressive Greece. This was quite apart from the presence of British troops in Greece. He could only suppose that our Soviet Allies do not accept British assurances regarding the number of Greek troops. Greece has neither the intention nor the means to be aggressive.

Mr. Molotov remarked that Mr. Eden's logic was correct, but the facts were that warlike speeches were being made.

MEMO ON SOVIET ATTITUDES

15 ◄§ AT THE POTSDAM MEETINGS much of the discussion continued to center on Eastern Europe. Churchill, at the July 24 meeting, charged that an "iron fence" was being built in Eastern Europe. "All fairy tales," replied Stalin. Despite Stalin's retort, State Department officials in Eastern Europe continued to report on the suppression of civil liberties, the rise of Communist

parties, and marauding activities by alleged Communists. After the conclusion of the conference, on August 2, Charles Yost, the secretary-general of the American delegation at Potsdam, in a memorandum of August 8, 1945, summarized Soviet attitudes toward Romania, Bulgaria, Hungary, and Finland:[15]

A number of aspects of Soviet policy toward these countries were brought out during the Conference. Stalin indicated that the basic objective of his policy in this regard was to separate these countries permanently from Germany. The first method for accomplishing this aim had of course been the use of force but he felt that if the Allies confined themselves to the use of force alone these countries might ultimately be driven back into the arms of Germany. He therefore maintained that in order to detach these countries permanently from Germany it was necessary to forget thoughts of revenge and to take all appropriate measures to bring these countries into free collaboration with the Allies.

As far as their present governments are concerned, the Soviet position was that these governments are "democratic" and are such as to have fulfilled the Yalta Declaration on Liberated Areas. (Light is shed on this characterization by Stalin's remark that "if a government is not Fascist it is democratic".) Stalin on one occasion referred to them as "closer to the people" than the present Government of Italy. Molotov maintained that in all these governments the Communist Party formed only a small minority. The Soviets urged at great length that these governments be recognized either at once or in the very near future by the United States and Great Britain. They were unwilling to accord to Italy more favorable treatment in the easing of the armistice terms and other matters than to Rumania, Bulgaria, Hungary and Finland, which they claimed had made a greater contribution to the Allied war effort.

The Soviets took the position that it was superfluous and undesirable for the Great Powers either to supervise or to observe the elections in those countries. They stated that the elections in Finland had been "free and unfettered" and that it therefore followed that they would also be so in the other three countries. The Soviets agreed that it was desirable, in view of the termination of the war, to revise the procedures of the Control Commissions in these countries but stated that the proposals which their representatives on these Com-

15 Excerpt, ibid., pp. 736–7.

missions had just put forward constituted a satisfactory revision. They would not admit that United States and British representatives in these countries had been unduly restricted in the past and in fact Stalin described Churchill's catalog of their difficulties as "all fairy tales."

POTSDAM PROTOCOL

16 ⁀§ THE HEADS OF GOVERNMENT at Potsdam did not agree on the western frontier of Poland, and final determination of the Polish-German border was postponed until the peace treaty. Other major decisions appear in the excerpts from the "Protocol of the Proceedings of the Berlin Conference," August 1, 1945:[16]

I. ESTABLISHMENT OF A COUNCIL OF FOREIGN MINISTERS

The Conference reached the following agreement for the establishment of a Council of Foreign Ministers to do the necessary preparatory work for the peace settlements:

(1) There shall be established a Council composed of the Foreign Ministers of the United Kingdom, the Union of Soviet Socialist Republics, China, France and the United States.

(2) (i) The Council shall normally meet in London, which shall be the permanent seat of the joint Secretariat which the Council will form. Each of the Foreign Ministers will be accompanied by a high-ranking Deputy, duly authorized to carry on the work of the Council in the absence of his Foreign Minister, and by a small staff of technical advi[s]ers.

(ii) The first meeting of the Council shall be held in London not later than September 1st 1945. Meetings may be held by common agreement in other capitals as may be agreed from time to time.

(3) (i) As its immediate important task, the Council shall be authorized to draw up, with a view to their submission to the United Nations, treaties of peace with Italy, Rumania, Bulgaria, Hungary and Finland, and to propose settlements of territorial questions outstanding on the termination of the war in Europe. The Council shall be utilized for the preparation of a peace settlement for Germany to be accepted by the Government of Germany when a government adequate for the purpose is established.

(ii) For the discharge of each of these tasks the Council will be composed of the Members representing those States which were

[16] Excerpts, *ibid.*, pp. 1478-9, 1483-5, 1490ff.

signatory to the terms of surrender imposed upon the enemy State concerned. For the purposes of the peace settlement for Italy, France shall be regarded as a signatory to the terms of surrender for Italy. Other Members will be invited to participate when matters directly concerning them are under discussion. . . .

III. GERMAN REPARATION

1. Reparation claims of U.S.S.R. shall be met by removals from the zone of Germany occupied by the U.S.S.R., and from appropriate German external assets.

2. The U.S.S.R. undertakes to settle the reparation claims of Poland from its own share of reparations.

3. The reparations claims of the United States, the United Kingdom and other countries entitled to reparations shall be met from the Western Zones and from appropriate German external assets.

4. In addition to the reparations to be taken by the U.S.S.R. from its own zone of occupation, the U.S.S.R. shall receive additionally from the Western Zones:

(a) 15 per cent of such usable and complete industrial equipment, in the first place from the metallurgical, chemical and machine manufacturing industries as is unnecessary for the German peace economy and should be removed from the Western Zones of Germany, in exchange for an equivalent value of food, coal, potash, zinc, timber, clay products, petroleum products, and such other commodities as may be agreed upon.

(b) 10 per cent of such industrial capital equipment as is unnecessary for the German peace economy and should be removed from the Western Zones, to be transferred to the Soviet Government on reparations account without payment or exchange of any kind in return.

Removals of equipment as provided in (a) and (b) above shall be made simultaneously.

5. The amount of equipment to be removed from the Western Zones on account of reparations must be determined within six months from now at the latest.

6. Removals of industrial capital equipment shall begin as soon as possible and shall be completed within two years from the determination specified in paragraph 5. The delivery of products covered by 4 (a) above shall begin as soon as possible and shall be made by the U.S.S.R. in agreed installments within five years of the date

hereof. The determination of the amount and character of the industrial capital equipment unnecessary for the German peace economy and therefore available for reparation shall be made by the Control Council under policies fixed by the Allied Commission on Reparations, with the participation of France, subject to the final approval of the Zone Commander in the Zone from which the equipment is to be removed.

7. Prior to the fixing of the total amount of equipment subject to removal, advance deliveries shall be made in respect to such equipment as will be determined to be eligible for delivery in accordance with the procedure set forth in the last sentence of paragraph 6.

8. The Soviet Government renounces all claims to shares of German enterprises which are located in the Western Zones of Germany as well as to German foreign assets in all countries except those specified in paragraph 9 below.

9. The Governments of the U.K. and U.S.A. renounce their claims to shares of German enterprises which are located in the Eastern Zone of occupation in Germany, as well as to German foreign assets in Bulgaria, Finland, Hungary, Rumania and Eastern Austria. . . .

IX. POLAND

A. Declaration

We have taken note with pleasure of the agreement reached among representative Poles from Poland and abroad which has made possible the formation, in accordance with the decisions reached at the Crimea Conference, of a Polish Provisional Government of National Unity recognised by the Three Powers. The establishment by the British and United States Governments of diplomatic relations with the Polish Provisional Government has resulted in the withdrawal of their recognition from the former Polish Government in London, which no longer exists.

The Three Powers note that the Polish Provisional Government in accordance with the decisions of the Crimea Conference has agreed to the holding of free and unfettered elections as soon as possible on the basis of universal suffrage and secret ballot in which all democratic and anti-Nazi parties shall have the right to take part and to put forward candidates; and that representatives of the Allied Press shall enjoy full freedom to report to the world upon developments in Poland before and during the elections. . . .

X. CONCLUSION OF PEACE TREATIES AND ADMISSION TO THE UNITED NATIONS ORGANISATION

The Three Governments consider it desirable that the present anomalous position of Italy, Bulgaria, Finland, Hungary and Roumania should be terminated by the conclusion of Peace Treaties. They trust that the other interested Allied Governments will share these views.

For their part the Three Governments have included the preparation of a Peace Treaty with Italy as the first among the immediate important tasks to be undertaken by the new Council of Foreign Ministers. Italy was the first of the Axis Powers to break with Germany, who [to] whose defeat she has made a material contribution, and has now joined with the Allies in the struggle against Japan. Italy has freed herself from the Fascist regime and is making good progress towards reestablishment of a democratic government and institutions. The conclusion of such a Peace Treaty with a recognised and democratic Italian Government will make it possible for the Three Governments to fulfil their desire to support an application from Italy for membership of the United Nations.

The Three Governments have also charged the Council of Foreign Ministers with the task of preparing Peace Treaties for Bulgaria, Finland, Hungary and Roumania. The conclusion of Peace Treaties with recognised democratic Governments in these States will also enable the Three Governments to support applications from them for membership of the United Nations. The Three Governments agree to examine each separately in the near future, in the light of the conditions then prevailing, the establishment of diplomatic relations with Finland, Roumania, Bulgaria, and Hungary to the extent possible prior to the conclusion of peace treaties with those countries. . . .

STIMSON ON BYRNES BEFORE LONDON CONFERENCE

17 ⫿ᔆ   TWO DAYS BEFORE Secretary Byrnes sailed for the London conference of foreign ministers, he discussed with Secretary Stimson the important role of the atomic bomb in his diplomacy. In his diary entry for September 4, 1945, Stimson summarized their conversation:[17]

[17] From Stimson Diary, entry for September 4, 1945, Yale University Library. Published by permission of the Stimson Literary Trust.

Jim Byrnes had not yet gone abroad and I had a very good talk with him afterwards sitting in the White House hall . . . I took up the question which I had been working at with McCloy up in St. Hubert's, namely how to handle Russia with the big bomb. I found that Byrnes was very much against any attempt to cooperate with Russia. His mind is full of his problems with the coming meeting of foreign ministers and he looks to having the presence of the bomb in his pocket, so to speak, as a great weapon to get through the thing. . . .

BYRNES REPORT ON COUNCIL OF FOREIGN MINISTERS

18 ◄§ THE FIRST SESSION of the Council of Foreign Ministers (September 11 to October 2, 1945) dashed hopes for an easy agreement on the question of peace treaties. In the United States, Secretary Byrnes went on the radio, on October 5, 1945, to tell the nation of his difficulties at the London conference:[18]

The first session of the Council of Foreign Ministers closed in a stalemate. But that need not, and should not, deprive us of a second and better chance to get on with the peace.

In the past I have been both criticized and commended for being a compromiser. I confess that I do believe that peace and political progress in international affairs as in domestic affairs depend upon intelligent compromise. The United States Delegation acted in that spirit at Berlin. We acted in that spirit at London. And we shall continue to act in that spirit at future conferences. . . .

Compromise, however, does not mean surrender, and compromise unlike surrender requires the assent of more than one party.

The difficulties encountered at the London conference will, I hope, impress upon the peoples of all countries, including our own people, the hard reality that none of us can expect to write the peace in our own way. If this hard reality is accepted by statesmen and peoples at an early stage of the peacemaking process, it may at later stages save us and save the peace of the world from the disastrous effects of disillusionment and intransigencies. . . .

Substantial progress was also made on the directives for the preparatory work on the Finnish treaty and the treaties with Rumania and

[18] Excerpts reprinted from *Department of State Bulletin*, October 17, 1945, pp. 507–12.

Bulgaria. The principles suggested by the American Delegation and accepted for the Italian treaty for the safeguarding of human rights and fundamental freedoms are also to be incorporated in these treaties.

The directives concerning the limitation of armament for Rumania and Bulgaria are expected to follow the same general line as those accepted for Italy.

Before work could be commenced upon the directives for the Hungarian treaty the Soviet Delegation announced they felt obliged to withdraw their assent to the procedure previously accepted by the Council for dealing with peace treaties.

Before taking up these procedural difficulties I should say a few words about the Soviet Delegation's disappointment with the failure of Great Britain and the United States to recognize the Bulgarian and Rumanian Governments.

The thought apparently exists in their mind that our government objects to these governments because they are friendly to the Soviet Union and that our unwillingness to recognize these governments is a manifestation of unfriendliness to the Soviet Union.

There could be no greater misconception of our attitude. I was at Yalta. The Yalta declaration on the liberated and ex-satellite countries was based on a proposal submitted by President Roosevelt. Under it the Allied Powers, including the Soviet Union, assumed the responsibility of concerting their policies to assist in the establishment of interim governments broadly representative of all important democratic elements in the population and pledged to the earliest possible establishment through free elections of governments responsive to the will of the people. That pledge cannot be fulfilled in countries where freedom of speech and of assembly are denied.

That policy sponsored by President Roosevelt was America's policy and remains America's policy.

We are well aware that no government is perfect and that the representative character of any provisional government will always be subject to debate. We do not demand perfection where perfection is unobtainable.

In an effort to concert our policies with our Allies we have tried to show a spirit of conciliation. Certainly we did not make unduly exacting the requirements we set before we recognized the Provisional Polish Government or the conditions which we have proposed as a basis for the recognition of the Provisional Hungarian Government.

And I hope that as the result of efforts now being made by the Provisional Austrian Government to broaden its representation, we may soon be able to recognize that Government.

At Berlin we stated we would examine in the near future, in the light of prevailing conditions, the question of recognition of Rumania and Bulgaria. We have investigated and we shall continue to investigate. But we cannot know whether conditions justify recognition unless our political representatives are fully informed and unless our news correspondents are permitted freely to enter countries and freely to send their stories uncensored.

We do not seek to dictate the internal affairs of any people. We only reserve for ourselves the right to refuse to recognize governments if after investigation we conclude they have not given to the people the rights pledged to them in the Yalta agreement and in the Atlantic Charter.

The peace of Europe depends upon the existence of friendly relations between the Soviet Union and its European neighbors, and two wars in one generation have convinced the American people that they have a very vital interest in the maintenance of peace in Europe. . . .

It certainly never occurred to President Truman or myself that any of the five members of the Council who are also the five permanent members of the United Nations Security Council, which is charged with the responsibility for maintaining the peace which the Council of Foreign Ministers is preparing, would not be invited to be present during the discussions of the treaties.

Such exclusion of two permanent members of the Security Council would not promote the harmonious relations essential to the success of the United Nations Organization.

The Soviet Delegation's position was not simply that they wished to withdraw the invitation to China and France to participate without right to vote. Their position was that it was beyond the authority of the States signatory to the surrender terms to extend the invitation.

Although this construction of the Berlin agreement did not accord with the understanding of the American Delegation or the British Delegation or the President of the United States or the Prime Minister of Great Britain, the Soviet Delegation insisted that they could no longer discuss treaty matters in the presence of members who were not parties to the surrender terms. . . .

The Soviet Delegation stated, however, that they could not agree to the American proposal for a peace conference until they had returned to Moscow and had personal consultations with their Government.

It therefore became obvious that there could be no agreement unless the other delegations were prepared to yield their views and convictions to those of the Soviet Delegation. This none of the other delegations was prepared to do.

The United States is willing to dictate terms of peace to an enemy but is not willing to dictate terms of peace to its Allies.

Our task then became one of arranging an adjournment until the Soviet Delegation could return to Moscow. It is customary before adjournment to adopt and have all conferees to sign a protocol containing a record of the agreed decisions of a conference. The Soviet Delegation would not agree to the inclusion in the protocol of the decision of September 11 that the five members should participate in all meetings, even though it included a statement of the action taken by the Soviet Delegation on September 22 to withdraw their assent to that decision.

On the last day of the session the Soviet Delegation announced it would offer a compromise proposal. The proposal was that there should be four separate protocols without recording in any of them the decision of September 11 which had been agreed to by them but which they later wished to rescind. This was the same position that they had urged for days. The only thing new about it was the suggestion that on the following day they would discuss unsettled questions including the American proposal for a peace conference and the disputed September 11 decision.

TRUMAN'S NAVY DAY SPEECH

19✑§   AS THE DIFFERENCES between East and West emerged more clearly, President Truman chose the Navy Day celebration, October 27, 1945, for a speech that one adviser described as "getting tough with the Russians":[19]

Now we are in the process of demobilizing our naval force. We are laying up ships. We are breaking up aircraft squadrons. We are rolling up bases, and releasing officers and men. But when our demobilization is all finished as planned, the United States will still be the greatest naval power on earth. . . .

[19] Excerpts reprinted from *Truman Papers*, 1945, pp. 431–8.

Why do we seek to preserve this powerful Naval and Air Force, and establish this strong Army reserve? Why do we need to do that? . . .

We . . . need this kind of armed might . . . for four principal tasks:

First, our Army, Navy, and Air Force, in collaboration with our allies, must enforce the terms of peace imposed upon our defeated enemies.

Second, we must fulfill the military obligations which we are undertaking as a member of the United Nations Organization—to support a lasting peace, by force if necessary.

Third, we must cooperate with other American nations to preserve the territorial integrity and the political independence of the nations of the Western Hemisphere.

Fourth, in this troubled and uncertain world, our military forces must be adequate to discharge the fundamental mission laid upon them by the Constitution of the United States—to "provide for the common defense" of the United States.

These four military tasks are directed not toward war—not toward conquest—but toward peace. . . .

Let me restate the fundamentals of that foreign policy of the United States:

1. We seek no territorial expansion or selfish advantage. We have no plans for aggression against any other state, large or small. We have no objective which need clash with the peaceful aims of any other nation.

2. We believe in the eventual return of sovereign rights and self-government to all peoples who have been deprived of them by force.

3. We shall approve no territorial changes in any friendly part of the world unless they accord with the freely expressed wishes of the people concerned.

4. We believe that all peoples who are prepared for self-government should be permitted to choose their own form of government by their own freely expressed choice, without interference from any foreign source. That is true in Europe, in Asia, in Africa, as well as in the Western Hemisphere.

5. By the combined and cooperative action of our war allies, we shall help the defeated enemy states establish peaceful democratic governments of their own free choice. And we shall try to attain a world in which Nazism, Fascism, and military aggression cannot exist.

6. We shall refuse to recognize any government imposed upon any nation by the force of any foreign power. In some cases it may be impossible to prevent forceful imposition of such a government. But the United States will not recognize any such government.

7. We believe that all nations should have the freedom of the seas and equal rights to the navigation of boundary rivers and waterways and of rivers and waterways which pass through more than one country.

8. We believe that all states which are accepted in the society of nations should have access on equal terms to the trade and the raw materials of the world.

9. We believe that the sovereign states of the Western Hemisphere, without interference from outside the Western Hemisphere, must work together as good neighbors in the solution of their common problems.

10. We believe that full economic collaboration between all nations, great and small, is essential to the improvement of living conditions all over the world, and to the establishment of freedom from fear and freedom from want.

11. We shall continue to strive to promote freedom of expression and freedom of religion throughout the peace-loving areas of the world.

12. We are convinced that the preservation of peace between nations requires a United Nations Organization composed of all the peace-loving nations of the world who are willing jointly to use force if necessary to insure peace. . . .

The atomic bomb does not alter the basic foreign policy of the United States. It makes the development and application of our policy more urgent than we could have dreamed 6 months ago. It means that we must be prepared to approach international problems with greater speed, with greater determination, with greater ingenuity, in order to meet a situation for which there is no precedent.

We must find the answer to the problems created by the release of atomic energy—we must find the answers to the many other problems of peace—in partnership with all the peoples of the United Nations. For their stake in world peace is as great as our own.

As I said in my message to the Congress, discussion of the atomic bomb with Great Britain and Canada and later with other nations cannot wait upon the formal organization of the United Nations. These discussions, looking toward a free exchange of fundamental

scientific information, will be begun in the near future. But I emphasize again, as I have before, that these discussions will not be concerned with the processes of manufacturing the atomic bomb or any
other instruments of war.

In our possession of this weapon, as in our possession of other new
weapons, there is no threat to any nation. The world, which has seen
the United States in two great recent wars, knows that full well. The
possession in our hands of this new power of destruction we regard as
a sacred trust. Because of our love of peace, the thoughtful people of
the world know that that trust will not be violated, that it will be
faithfully executed.

Indeed, the highest hope of the American people is that world
cooperation for peace will soon reach such a state of perfection that
atomic methods of destruction can be definitely and effectively outlawed forever.

LETTER OF TRUMAN TO BYRNES

20 ·⊰ WHEN SECRETARY BYRNES returned from a conference in
Moscow late in December 1945, he planned to address the
nation before reporting to the President. Truman, angered by the
Secretary's independence, demanded that Byrnes first discuss the
Moscow conference with him. According to Truman's recollection,
Byrnes "sought to put the blame mostly on his subordinates" for
not keeping the President properly informed. Studying the documents Byrnes presented to him, Truman concluded "that the
successes of the Moscow conference were unreal," and prepared a
letter which he claims (and Byrnes denies) he read at their meeting
of January 3, 1946:[20]

I have been considering some of our difficulties. As you know, I
would like to pursue a policy of delegating authority to the members
of the Cabinet in their various fields and then back them up in the
results. But in doing that and in carrying out that policy I do not
intend to turn over the complete authority of the President nor to
forgo the President's prerogative to make the final decision.

Therefore it is absolutely necessary that the President should be
kept fully informed on what is taking place. This is vitally necessary
when negotiations are taking place in a foreign capital, or even in
another city than Washington. This procedure is necessary in domes-

[20] Reprinted from *The Memoirs by Harry S. Truman* (New York: Doubleday &
Co., Inc., 1955), I, 551–2. Copyright © 1955 Time Inc. Reprinted by permission.

tic affairs and it is vital in foreign affairs. At San Francisco no agreements or compromises were ever agreed to without my approval. At London you were in constant touch with me and communication was established daily if necessary. I only saw you for a possible thirty minutes the night before you left after your interview with the Senate committee.

I received no communication from you directly while you were in Moscow. The only message I had from you came as a reply to one which I had Under Secretary Acheson send to you about my interview with the Senate Committee on Atomic Energy.

The protocol was not submitted to me, nor was the communiqué. I was completely in the dark on the whole conference until I requested you to come to the Williamsburg and inform me. The communiqué was released before I ever saw it.

Now I have infinite confidence in you and in your ability but there should be a complete understanding between us on procedure. Hence this memorandum.

For the first time I read the Ethridge letter this morning. It is full of information on Rumania and Bulgaria and confirms our previous information on those two police states. I am not going to agree to the recognition of those governments unless they are radically changed.

I think we ought to protest with all the vigor of which we are capable against the Russian program in Iran. There is no justification for it. It is a parallel to the program of Russia in Latvia, Estonia and Lithuania. It is also in line with the high-handed and arbitrary manner in which Russia acted in Poland.

At Potsdam we were faced with an accomplished fact and were by circumstances almost forced to agree to Russian occupation of Eastern Poland and the occupation of that part of Germany east of the Oder River by Poland. It was high-handed outrage.

At the time we were anxious for Russian entry into the Japanese War. Of course we found later that we didn't need Russia there and that the Russians have been a headache to us ever since.

When you went to Moscow you were faced with another accomplished fact in Iran. Another outrage if I ever saw one.

Iran was our ally in the war. Iran was Russia's ally in the war. Iran agreed to the free passage of arms, ammunition and other supplies running into the millions of tons across her territory from the Persian Gulf to the Caspian Sea. Without these supplies furnished by the

United States, Russia would have been ignominiously defeated. Yet now Russia stirs up rebellion and keeps troops on the soil of her friend and ally—Iran.

There isn't a doubt in my mind that Russia intends an invasion of Turkey and the seizure of the Black Sea Straits to the Mediterranean. Unless Russia is faced with an iron fist and strong language another war is in the making. Only one language do they understand—"how many divisions have you?"

I do not think we should play compromise any longer. We should refuse to recognize Rumania and Bulgaria until they comply with our requirements; we should let our position on Iran be known in no uncertain terms and we should continue to insist on the internationalization of the Kiel Canal, the Rhine-Danube waterway and the Black Sea Straits and we should maintain complete control of Japan and the Pacific. We should rehabilitate China and create a strong central government there. We should do the same for Korea.

Then we should insist on the return of our ships from Russia and force a settlement of the Lend-Lease debt of Russia.

I'm tired of babying the Soviets.

KENNAN'S CABLE ON CONTAINMENT

21 ◄§ BY THE BEGINNING of 1946 reassessment of American policy toward Russia was well advanced. On February 22 George F. Kennan, the scholarly chargé d'affaires in Moscow, sent a now-famous and an influential cable to the State Department, attempting to explain Soviet behavior and proposing an appropriate Western response. A primitive statement of the policy later called containment, Kennan's cable was the basis for his anonymous article "The Sources of Soviet Conduct," *Foreign Affairs* (July 1947), which clearly enunciated the containment doctrine. In the spring of 1947 Secretary of State Marshall appointed Kennan head of the department's newly formed Policy Planning Staff. The full text of Kennan's cable follows:[21]

Answer to Dept's 284, Feb 3 involves questions so intricate, so delicate, so strange to our form of thought, and so important to analysis of our international environment that I cannot compress answers into single brief message without yielding to what I feel would

---

[21] Reprinted from a photocopy of the original telegram.

be dangerous degree of over-simplification. I hope, therefore, Dept will bear with me if I submit in answer to this question five parts, subjects of which will be roughly as follows:

(One) Basic features of post-war Soviet outlook.

(Two) Background of this outlook.

(Three) Its projection in practical policy on official level.

(Four) Its projection on unofficial level.

(Five) Practical deductions from standpoint of US policy.

I apologize in advance for this burdening of telegraphic channel; but questions involved are of such urgent importance, particularly in view of recent events, that our answers to them, if they deserve attention at all, seem to me to deserve it at once. THERE FOLLOWS PART ONE: BASIC FEATURES OF POST-WAR SOVIET OUTLOOK, AS PUT FORWARD BY OFFICIAL PROPAGANDA MACHINE, ARE AS FOLLOWS:

(A) USSR still lives in antagonistic "capitalist encirclement" with which in the long run there can be no permanent peaceful coexistence. As stated by Stalin in 1927 to a delegation of American Workers:

"In course of further development of international revolution there will emerge two centers of world significance: a socialist center, drawing to itself the countries which tend toward socialism, and a capitalist center, drawing to itself the countries that incline toward capitalism. Battle between these two centers for command of world economy will decide fate of capitalism and of communism in entire world."

(B) Capitalist world is beset with internal conflicts, inherent in nature of capitalist society. These conflicts are insoluble by means of peaceful compromise. Greatest of them is that between England and US.

(C) Internal conflicts of capitalism inevitably generate wars. Wars thus generated may be of two kinds: intra-capitalist wars between two capitalist states, and wars of intervention against socialist world. Smart capitalists, vainly seeking escape from inner conflicts of capitalism, incline toward latter.

(D) Intervention against USSR, while it would be disastrous to those who undertook it, would cause renewed delay in progress of Soviet socialism and must therefore be forestalled at all costs.

(E) Conflicts between capitalist states, though likewise fraught with danger for USSR, nevertheless hold out great possibilities for advancement of socialist cause, particularly if USSR remains militarily powerful, ideologically monolithic and faithful to its present brilliant leadership.

(F) It must be borne in mind that capitalist world is not all bad. In addition to hopelessly reactionary and bourgeois elements, it includes (one) certain wholly enlightened and positive elements united in acceptable communistic parties and (two) certain other elements (now described for tactical reasons as progressive or democratic) whose reactions, aspirations and activities happen to be "objectively" favorable to interests of USSR. These last must be encouraged and utilized for Soviet purposes.

(G) Among negative elements of bourgeois-capitalist society, most dangerous of all are those whom Lenin called false friends of the people, namely moderate-socialist or social-democratic leaders (in other words, non-communist left-wing). These are more dangerous than out-and-out reactionaries, for latter at least march under their true colors, whereas moderate left-wing leaders confuse people by employing devices of socialism to serve interests of reactionary capital.

So much for premises. To what deductions do they lead from standpoint of Soviet policy? To following:

(A) Everything must be done to advance relative strength of USSR as factor in international society. Conversely, no opportunity must be missed to reduce strength and influence, collectively as well as individually, of capitalist powers.

(B) Soviet efforts, and those of Russia's friends abroad, must be directed toward deepening and exploiting of differences and conflicts between capitalist powers. If these eventually deepen into an "imperialist" war, this war must be turned into revolutionary upheavals within the various capitalist countries.

(C) "Democratic-progressive" elements abroad are to be utilized to maximum to bring pressure to bear on capitalist governments along lines agreeable to Soviet interests.

(D) Relentless battle must be waged against socialist and social-democratic leaders abroad.

PART TWO: BACKGROUND OF OUTLOOK

Before examining ramifications of this party line in practice there are certain aspects of it to which I wish to draw attention.

First, it does not represent natural outlook of Russian people. Latter are, by and large, friendly to outside world, eager for experience of it, eager to measure against it talents they are conscious of possessing, eager above all to live in peace and enjoy fruits of their own labor. Party line only represents thesis which official propaganda machine puts forward with great skill and persistence to a public often remarkably resistant in the stronghold of its innermost thoughts. But party line is binding for outlook and conduct of people who make up apparatus of power—party, secret police and government—and it is exclusively with these that we have to deal.

Second, please note that premises on which this party line is based are for most part simply not true. Experience has shown that peaceful and mutually profitable coexistence of capitalist and socialist states is entirely possible. Basic internal conflicts in advanced countries are no longer primarily those arising out of capitalist ownership of means of production, but are ones arising from advanced urbanism and industrialism as such, which Russia has thus far been spared not by socialism but only by her own backwardness. Internal rivalries of capitalism do not always generate wars, and not all wars are attributable to this cause. To speak of possibility of intervention against USSR today, after elimination of Germany and Japan and after example of recent war, is sheerest nonsense. If not provoked by forces of intolerance and subversion "capitalist" world of today is quite capable of living at peace with itself and with Russia. Finally, no sane person has reason to doubt sincerity of moderate socialist leaders in western countries. Nor is it fair to deny success of their efforts to improve conditions for working population whenever, as in Scandinavia, they have been given chance to show what they could do.

Falseness of these premises, every one of which pre-dates recent war, was amply demonstrated by that conflict itself. Anglo-American differences did not turn out to be major differences of western world. Capitalist countries, other than those of Axis, showed no disposition to solve their differences by joining in crusade against USSR. Instead of imperialist war turning into civil wars and revolution, USSR found itself obliged to fight side by side with capitalist powers for an avowed community of aims.

Nevertheless, all these theses, however baseless and disproven, are being boldly put forward again today. What does this indicate? It indicates that Soviet party line is not based on any objective analysis of situation beyond Russia's borders; that it has, indeed, little to do with conditions outside of Russia; that it arises mainly from basic inner-Russian necessities which existed before recent war and exist today.

At bottom of Kremlin's neurotic view of world affairs is traditional and instinctive Russian sense of insecurity. Originally, this was insecurity of a peaceful agricultural people trying to live on vast exposed plain in neighborhood of fierce nomadic peoples. To this was added, as Russia came into contact with economically advanced west, fear of more competent, more powerful, more highly organized societies in that area. But this latter type of insecurity was one which afflicted rather Russian rulers than Russian people; for Russian rulers have invariably sensed that their rule was relatively archaic in form, fragile and artificial in its psychological foundation, unable to stand comparison or contact with political systems of western countries. For this reason they have always feared foreign penetration, feared direct contact between western world and their own, feared what would happen if Russians learned truth about world without or if foreigners learned truth about world within. And they have learned to seek security only in patient but deadly struggle for total destruction of rival power, never in compacts and compromises with it.

It was no coincidence that Marxism, which had smouldered ineffectively for half a century in Western Europe, caught hold and blazed for first time in Russia. Only in this land which had never known a friendly neighbor or indeed any tolerant equilibrium of separate powers, either internal or international, could a doctrine thrive which viewed economic conflicts of society as insoluble by peaceful means. After establishment of Bolshevist regime, Marxist dogma, rendered even more truculent and intolerant by Lenin's interpretation, became a perfect vehicle for sense of insecurity with which Bolsheviks, even more than previous Russian rulers, were afflicted. In this dogma, with its basic altruism of purpose, they found justification for their instinctive fear of outside world, for the dictatorship without which they did not know how to rule, for cruelties they did not dare not to inflict, for sacrifices they felt bound to demand. In the name of Marxism they sacrificed every single ethical value in their methods and tactics. Today they cannot dispense with it. It is fig leaf of their moral and intellectual respectability. Without it they would stand before history, at best, as only the last of that long succession of cruel and wasteful Russian rulers who have relentlessly forced country on to ever new heights of military power in order to guarantee external security of their internally weak regimes. This is why Soviet purposes must always be solemnly clothed in trappings of Marxism, and why no one should underrate importance of dogma in Soviet affairs. Thus Soviet leaders are driven necessities of their own past and present position to put forward a dogma which [views—Eds.] outside world as evil, hostile and menacing; but as bearing within itself germs of creeping disease and destined to be wracked with growing internal convulsions until it is given final coup de grace by rising power of socialism and yields to new and better world. This thesis provides justification for that increase of military and police power of Russian state, for that isolation of Russian population from outside world, and for that fluid and constant pressure to extend limits of Russian police power which are together the natural and instinctive urges of Russian rulers. Basically this is only the steady advance of uneasy Russian nationalism, a centuries old movement in which conceptions of offense and defense are inextricably confused. But in new guise of international Marxism, with its honeyed promises to a desperate and war torn outside world, it is more dangerous and insidious than ever before.

It should not be thought from above that Soviet party line is necessarily disingenuous and insincere on part of all those who put it forward. [Many—Eds.] of them are too ignorant of outside world and mentally too dependent to question . . . self-hypnotism, and who have no difficulty making themselves believe what they find it comforting and convenient to believe. Finally we have the unsolved mystery as to who, if anyone, in this great land actually receives accurate and unbiased information about outside world. In atmosphere of oriential secretiveness and conspiracy which pervades this government, possibilities for distorting or poisoning sources and currents of information are infinite. The very disrespect of Russians for objective truth —indeed, their disbelief in its existence—leads them to view all stated facts as instruments for furtherance of one ulterior purpose or another. There is good reason to suspect that this government is actually a conspiracy within a conspiracy; and I for one am reluctant to believe that Stalin himself receives anything like an objective picture of outside world. Here there is ample scope for the type of subtle intrigue at which Russians are past masters. Inability of foreign governments to place their case squarely before Russian policy makers—extent to which they are delivered up in their relations with Russia to good graces of obscure and unknown advisers whom they never see and cannot influence—this to my mind is most disquieting feature of diplomacy in Moscow, and one which western statesmen would do well to keep in mind if they would understand nature of difficulties encountered here.

PART THREE: PROJECTION OF SOVIET OUTLOOK IN
PRACTICAL POLICY ON OFFICIAL LEVEL

We have now seen nature and background of Soviet program. What may we expect by way of its practical implementation?

Soviet policy, as Department implies in its query under reference, is conducted on two planes: (one) official plane represented by actions undertaken officially in name of Soviet Government; and (two) subterranean plane of actions undertaken by agencies for which Soviet Government does not admit responsibility.

Policy promulgated on both planes will be calculated to serve basic policies (A) to (D) outlined in part one. Actions taken on different planes will differ considerably, but will dovetail into each other in purpose, timing and effect.

On official plane we must look for following:

(A) Internal policy devoted to increasing in every way strength and prestige of Soviet state's intensive military-industrialization; maximum development of armed forces; great displays to impress outsiders; continued secretiveness about internal matters, designed to conceal weaknesses and to keep opponents in dark.

(B) Wherever it is considered timely and promising, efforts will be made to advance official limits of Soviet power. For the moment, these efforts are restricted to certain neighboring points conceived of here as being of immediate strategic necessity, such as Northern Iran, Turkey, possibly Bornholm. However, other points may at any time come into question, if and as concealed Soviet political power is extended to new areas. Thus a "friendly" Persian Government might be asked to grant Russia a port on Persian Gulf. Should Spain fall under communist control, question of Soviet base at Gibraltar Strait might be activated. But such claims will appear on official level only when unofficial preparation is complete.

(C) Russians will participate officially in international organizations where they see opportunity of extending Soviet power or of inhibiting or diluting power of others. Moscow sees in UNO not the mechanism for a permanent and stable world society founded on mutual interest and aims of all nations, but an arena in which aims just mentioned can be favorably pursued. As long as UNO is considered here to serve this purpose, Soviets will remain with it. But if at any time they come to conclusion that it is serving to embarrass or frustrate their aims for power expansion and if they see better prospects for pursuit of these aims along other lines, they will not hesitate to abandon UNO. This would imply, however, that they felt themselves strong enough to split unity of other nations by their withdrawal, to render UNO ineffective as a threat to their aims or security, and to replace it with an international weapon more effective from their viewpoint. Thus Soviet attitude toward UNO will depend largely on loyalty of other nations to it, and on degree of vigor, decisiveness and cohesion with which these nations defend in UNO the peaceful and hopeful concept of international life, which that organization represents to our way of thinking. I reiterate, Moscow has no abstract devotion to UNO ideals. Its attitude to that organization will remain essentially pragmatic and tactical.

(D) Toward colonial areas and backward or dependent peoples, Soviet policy, even on official plane, will be directed toward weakening of power and influence and contacts of advanced western nations, on theory that in so far as this policy is successful, there will be created a vacuum which will favor communist-Soviet penetration. Soviet pressure for participation in trusteeship arrangements thus represents, in my opinion, a desire to be in a position to complicate and inhibit exertion of western influence at such points rather than to provide major channel for exerting of Soviet power. Latter motive is not lacking, but for this Soviets prefer to rely on other channels than official trusteeship arrangements. Thus we may expect to find Soviets asking for admission everywhere to trusteeship or similar arrangements and using levers thus acquired to weaken western influence among such peoples.

(E) Russians will strive energetically to develop Soviet representation in, and official ties with, countries in which they sense strong possibilities of opposition to western centers of power. This applies to such widely separated points as Germany, Argentina, Middle Eastern countries, etc.

(F) In international economic matters, Soviet policy will really be dominated by pursuit of autarchy for Soviet Union and Soviet-dominated adjacent areas taken together. That, however, will be underlying policy. As far as official line is concerned, position is not yet clear. Soviet Government has shown strange reticence since termination hostilities on subject foreign trade. If large scale long term credits should be forthcoming, I believe Soviet Government may eventually again do lip service, as it did in nineteen-thirties to desirability of building up international economic exchange in general.

Otherwise I think it possible Soviet foreign trade may be restricted largely to Soviet's own security sphere, including occupied areas in Germany, and that a cold official shoulder may be turned to principle of general economic collaboration among nations.

(G) With respect to cultural collaboration, lip service will likewise be rendered to desirability of deepening cultural contacts between peoples, but this will not in practice be interpreted in any way which could weaken security position of Soviet peoples. Actual manifestations of Soviet policy in this respect will be restricted to arid channels of closely shepherded official visits and functions, with super-abundance of vodka and speeches and dearth of permanent effects.

(H) Beyond this, Soviet official relations will take what might be called "correct" course with individual foreign governments, with great stress being laid on prestige of Soviet Union and its representatives and with punctilious attention to protocol, as distinct from good manners.

PART FOUR: FOLLOWING MAY BE SAID AS TO WHAT WE MAY EXPECT BY WAY OF IMPLEMENTATION OF BASIC SOVIET POLICIES ON UNOFFICIAL, OR SUBTERRANEAN PLANE, i.e. ON PLANE FOR WHICH SOVIET GOVERNMENT ACCEPTS NO RESPONSIBILITY

Agencies utilized for promulgation of policies on this plane are following:

One. Inner central core of communist parties in other countries. While many of persons who compose this category may also appear and act in unrelated public capacities, they are in reality working closely together as an underground operating directorate of world communism, a concealed Comintern tightly coordinated and directed by Moscow. It is important to remember that this inner core is actually working on underground lines, despite legality of parties with which it is associated.

Two. Rank and file of communist parties. Note distinction is drawn between these and persons defined in paragraph one. This distinction has become much sharper in recent years. Whereas formerly foreign communist parties represented a curious (and from Moscow's standpoint often inconvenient) mixture of conspiracy and legitimate activity, now the conspiratorial element has been neatly concentrated in inner circle and ordered underground, while rank and file—no longer even taken into confidence about realities of movement—are thrust forward as bona fide internal partisans of certain political tendencies within their respective countries, genuinely innocent of conspiratorial connection with foreign states. Only in certain countries where communists are numerically strong do they now regularly appear and act as a body. As a rule they are used to penetrate, and to influence or dominate, as case may be, other organizations less likely to be suspected of being tools of Soviet Government, with a view to accomplishing their purposes through [these—Eds.] organizations, rather than by direct action as a separate political party.

Three. A wide variety of national associations or bodies which can be dominated or influenced by such penetration. These include: labor unions, youth leagues, womens organizations, racial societies, religious societies, social organizations, cultural groups, liberal magazines, publishing houses, etc.

Four. International organizations which can be similarly penetrated through influence over various national components. Labor, youth and womens organizations are prominent among them. Particular, almost vital, importance is attached in this connection to international labor movement. In this, Moscow sees possibility of sidetracking western governments in world affairs and building up international lobby capable of compelling governments to take actions favorable to Soviet interests in various countries and of paralyzing actions disagreeable to USSR.

Five. Russian Orthodox Church, with its foreign branches, and through it the Eastern Orthodox Church in general.

Six. Pan-Slav movement and other movements (Azerbaijan, Armenian, Turcoman, etc.) based on racial groups within Soviet Union.

Seven. Governments or governing groups willing to lend themselves to Soviet purposes in one degree or another, such as present Bulgarian and Yugoslav governments, North Persian regime, Chinese Communists, etc. Not only propaganda machines but actual policies of these regimes can be placed extensively at disposal of USSR.

It may be expected that component parts of this far-flung apparatus will be utilized, in accordance with their individual suitability, as follows:

(A) To undermine general political and strategic potential of major western powers. Efforts will be made in such countries to disrupt national self-confidence, to hamstring measures of national defense, to increase social and industrial unrest, to stimulate all forms of disunity. All persons with grievances, whether economic or racial, will be urged to seek redress not in mediation and compromise, but in defiant violent struggle for destruction of other elements of society. Here poor will be set against rich, black against white, young against old, newcomers against established residents, etc.

(B) On unofficial plane particularly violent efforts will be made to weaken power and influence of western powers of colonial, backward, or dependent peoples. On this level, no holds will be barred. Mistakes and weaknesses of western colonial administration will be mercilessly exposed and exploited. Liberal opinion in western countries will be mobilized to weaken colonial policies. Resentment among dependent peoples will be stimulated. And while latter are being encouraged to seek independence of western powers, Soviet dominated puppet political machines will be undergoing preparation to take over domestic power in respective colonial areas when independence is achieved.

(C) Where individual governments stand in path of Soviet purposes pressure will be brought for their removal from office. This can happen where governments directly oppose Soviet foreign policy aims (Turkey, Iran), where they seal their territories off against Communist penetration (Switzerland, Portugal), or where they compete too strongly, like Labor Government in England, for moral domination among elements which it is important for Communists to dominate. (Sometimes, two of these elements are present in a single case. Then Communist opposition becomes particularly shrill and savage.)

(D) In foreign countries Communists will, as a rule, work toward destruction of all forms of personal independence, economic, political or moral. Their system can handle only individuals who have been brought into complete dependence on higher power. Thus, persons who are financially independent—such as individual businessmen, estate owners, successful farmers, artisans and all those who exercise local leadership or have local prestige, such as popular local clergymen or political figures, are anathema. It is not by chance that even in USSR local officials are kept constantly on move from one job to another, to prevent their taking root.

(E) Everything possible will be done to set major western powers against each other. Anti-British talk will be plugged among Americans, anti-American talk among British. Continentals, including Germans, will be taught to abhor both Anglo-Saxon powers. Where suspicions exist, they will be fanned; where not, ignited. No effort will be spared to discredit and combat all efforts which threaten to lead to any sort of unity or cohesion among other [nations—Eds.] from which Russia might be excluded. Thus, all forms of international organization not amenable to communist penetration and control, whether it be the Catholic [Church's—Eds.] international economic concerns, or the international fraternity of royalty and aristocracy, must expect to find themselves under fire. . . .

(F) In general, all Soviet efforts on unofficial international plane will be negative and destructive in character, designed to tear down sources of strength beyond reach of Soviet control. This is only in line with basic Soviet instinct that there can be no compromise with rival power and that constructive work can start only when communist power is dominant. But behind all this will be applied insistent, unceasing pressure for penetration and command of key positions in administration and especially in police apparatus of foreign countries. The Soviet regime is a police regime par excellence, reared in the dim half world of Tsarist police intrigue, accustomed to think primarily in terms of police power. This should never be lost sight of in gauging Soviet motives.

PART FIVE

In summary, we have here a political force committed fanatically to the belief that with US there can be no permanent modus vivendi, that it is desirable and necessary that the internal harmony of our society be disrupted, our traditional way of life be destroyed, the international authority of our state be broken, if Soviet power is to be secure. This political force has complete power of disposition over energies of one of world's greatest peoples and resources of world's richest national territory, and is borne along by deep and powerful currents of Russian nationalism. In addition, it has an elaborate and far flung apparatus for exertion of its influence in other countries, an apparatus of amazing flexibility and versatility, managed by people whose experience and skill in underground methods are presumably without parallel in history. Finally, it is seemingly inaccessible to considerations of reality in its basic reactions. For it, the vast fund of objective fact about human society is not, as with us, the measure against which outlook is constantly being tested and re-formed, but a grab bag from which individual items are selected arbitrarily and tendenciously to bolster an outlook already preconceived. This is admittedly not a pleasant picture. Problem of how to cope with this force is undoubtedly greatest task our diplomacy has ever faced and probably greatest it will ever have to face. It should be point of departure from which our political general staff work at present juncture should proceed. It should be approached with same thoroughness and care as solution of major strategic problem in war, and if necessary, with no smaller outlay in planning effort. I cannot attempt to suggest all answers here. But I would like to record my conviction that problem is within our power to solve—and that without recourse to any general military conflict. And in support of this conviction there are certain observations of a more encouraging nature I should like to make:

(One) Soviet power, unlike that of Hitlerite Germany, is neither schematic nor adventuristic. It does not work by fixed plans. It does not take unnecessary risks. Impervious to logic of reason, and it is highly sensitive to logic of force. For this reason it can easily withdraw—and usually does—when strong resistance is encountered at any point. Thus, if the adversary has sufficient force and makes clear his readiness to use it, he rarely has to do so. If situations are properly handled there need be no prestige engaging showdowns.

(Two) Gauged against western world as a whole, Soviets are still by far the weaker force. Thus, their success will really depend on degree of cohesion, firmness and vigor which western world can muster. And this is factor which it is within our power to influence.

(Three) Success of Soviet system, as form of internal power, is not yet finally proven. It has yet to be demonstrated that it can survive supreme test of successive transfer of power from one individual or group to another. Lenin's death was first such transfer, and its effects wracked Soviet state for 15 years after. Stalin's death or retirement will be second. But even this will not be final test. Soviet internal system will now be subjected, by virtue of recent territorial expansions, to series of additional strains which once proved severe tax on Tsardom. We here are convinced that never since termination of civil war have mass of Russian people been emotionally farther removed from doctrines of communist party than they are today. In Russia, party has now become a great and—for the moment—highly successful apparatus of dictatorial administration, but it has ceased to be a source of emotional inspiration. Thus, internal soundness and permanence of movement need not yet be regarded as assured.

(Four) All Soviet propaganda beyond Soviet security sphere is basically negative and destructive. It should therefore be relatively easy to combat it by any intelligent and really constructive program.

For these reasons I think we may approach calmly and with good heart problem of how to deal with Russia. As to how this approach should be made, I only wish to advance, by way of conclusion, following comments:

(One) Our first step must be to apprehend, and recognize for what it is, the nature of the movement with which we are dealing. We must study it with same courage, detachment, objectivity, and same determination not to be emotionally provoked or unseated by it, with which doctor studies unruly and unreasonable individual.

(Two) We must see that our public is educated to realities of Russian situation. I cannot over-emphasize importance of this. Press cannot do this alone. It must be done mainly by government, which is necessarily more experienced and better informed on practical problems involved. In this we need not be deterred by [ugliness —Eds.] of picture. I am convinced that there would be far less hysterical anti-Sovietism in our country today if realities of this situation were better understood by our people. There is nothing as dangerous or as terrifying as the unknown. It may also be argued that to reveal more information on our difficulties with Russia would reflect unfavorably on Russian American relations. I feel that if there is any real risk here involved, it is one which we should have courage to face, and sooner the better. But I cannot see what we would be risking. Our stake in this country, even coming on heels of tremendous demonstrations of our friendship for Russian people, is remarkably small. We have here no investments to guard, no actual trade to lose, virtually no citizens to protect, few cultural contacts to preserve. Our only stake lies in what we hope rather than what we have; and I am convinced we have better chance of realizing those hopes if our public is enlightened and if our dealings with Russians are placed entirely on realistic and matter of fact basis.

(Three) Much depends on health and vigor of our own society. World communism is like malignant parasite which feeds only on diseased tissue. This is point at which domestic and foreign policies meet. Every courageous and incisive measure to solve internal problems of our own society, to improve self-confidence, discipline, morale and community spirit of our own people, is a diplomatic victory over Moscow worth a thousand diplomatic notes and joint communiqués.

If we cannot abandon fatalism and indifference in face of deficiencies of our own society, Moscow will profit—Moscow cannot help profiting by them in its foreign policies.

(Four) We must formulate and put forward for other nations a much more positive and constructive picture of sort of world we would like to see than we have put forward in past. It is not enough to urge people to develop political processes similar to our own. Many foreign peoples, in Europe at least, are tired and frightened by experiences of past, and are less interested in abstract freedom than in security. They are seeking guidance rather than responsibilities. We should be better able than Russians to give them this. And unless we do, Russians certainly will.

(Five) Finally we must have courage and self-confidence to cling to our own methods and conceptions of human society. After all, the greatest danger that can befall us in coping with this problem of Soviet Communism, is that we shall allow ourselves to become like those with whom we are coping.

BYRNES STATEMENT ON RUSSIA

22 ⋖§ SHORTLY AFTER RECEIPT of Kennan's cable, Secretary Byrnes moved openly toward a harder policy. On February 28, 1946, after complaining privately of attacks by Republicans John Foster Dulles and Senator Arthur Vandenberg, Byrnes responded to their charges of appeasement with a firm speech on Russia:[22]

I should be lacking in candor if I said to you that world conditions today are sound or reassuring. All around us there is suspicion and distrust, which in turn breeds suspicion and distrust.

Some suspicions are unfounded and unreasonable. Of some others that cannot be said. That requires frank discussion between great powers of the things that give rise to suspicion. At the Moscow conference there was such frank discussion. It was helpful. But the basis of some suspicions persists and prompts me to make some comments as to our position. . . .

Unless the great powers are prepared to act in the defense of law, the United Nations cannot prevent war. We must make it clear in advance that we do intend to act to prevent aggression, making it clear at the same time . . . we will not use force for any other purpose. . . .

[22] Excerpts reprinted from *Department of State Bulletin*, March 10, 1946, pp. 355-8.

The present power relationships of the great states preclude the domination of the world by any one of them. Those power relationships cannot be substantially altered by the unilateral action of any one great state without profoundly disturbing the whole structure of the United Nations.

Therefore, if we are going to do our part to maintain peace in the world we must maintain our power to do so; and we must make it clear that we will stand united with other great states in defense of the Charter. . . .

Much as we desire general disarmament and much as we are prepared to participate in a general reduction of armaments, we cannot be faithful to our obligations to ourselves and to the world if we alone disarm.

While it is not in accord with our traditions to maintain a large professional standing army, we must be able and ready to provide armed contingents that may be required on short notice. We must also have a trained citizenry able and ready to supplement those armed contingents without unnecessarily prolonged training.

I am convinced that there is no reason for war between any of the great powers. Their present power relationships and interests are such that none need or should feel insecure in relation to the others, as long as each faithfully observes the purposes and principles of the Charter. . . .

Our diplomacy must not be negative and inert. It must be capable of adjustment and development in response to constantly changing circumstances. It must be marked by creative ideas, constructive proposals, practical and forward-looking suggestions.

Though the status quo is not sacred and unchangeable, we cannot overlook a unilateral gnawing away at the status quo. The Charter forbids aggression, and we cannot allow aggression to be accomplished by coercion or pressure or by subterfuges such as political infiltration. . . .

In our relations with the other great powers there are many problems which concern two or three of us much more than the others of us. I see no objection to conferences between the big three or the big four or the big five.

Even conferences between ourselves and the Soviet Union alone, conferences between ourselves and Britain alone, or conferences between ourselves and France or China alone, can all help to further general accord among the great powers and peace with the smaller powers.

But in such conferences, so far as the United States is concerned, we will gang up against no state. We will do nothing to break the world into exclusive blocs or spheres of influence. In this atomic age we will not seek to divide a world which is one and indivisible. . . .

But in the interest of world peace and in the interest of our common and traditional friendship we must make plain that the United States intends to defend the Charter.

Great powers as well as small powers have agreed under the United Nations Charter not to use force or the threat of force except in defense of law and the purposes and principles of the Charter.

We will not and we cannot stand aloof if force or the threat of force is used contrary to the purposes and principles of the Charter.

We have no right to hold our troops in the territories of other sovereign states without their approval and consent freely given.

We must not unduly prolong the making of peace and continue to impose our troops upon small and impoverished states.

No power has a right to help itself to alleged enemy properties in liberated or ex-satellite countries before a reparation settlement has been agreed upon by the Allies. We have not and will not agree to any one power deciding for itself what it will take from these countries.

We must not conduct a war of nerves to achieve strategic ends.

We do not want to stumble and stagger into situations where no power intends war but no power will be able to avert war.

We must not regard the drawing of attention to situations which might endanger the peace, as an affront to the nation or nations responsible for those situations. . . .

We must live by the Charter. That is the only road to peace. . . .

Loose talk of the inevitability of war casts doubt on our own loyalty to the Charter and jeopardizes our most cherished freedoms, both at home and abroad.

There are ideological differences in the world. There always have been. But in this world there is room for many people with varying views and many governments with varying systems. None of us can foresee the far-distant future and the ultimate shape of things to come. But we are bound together as part of a common civilization. . . .

Great states and small states must work together to build a friendlier and happier world. If we fail to work together there can be no peace, no comfort, and little hope for any of us.

23 ◦§ WINSTON CHURCHILL, accompanied by President Truman, delivered the famous "iron curtain" speech at Fulton, Missouri, on March 5, 1946. Though Churchill was no longer the leader of Britain, and Truman claimed he had not known in advance the contents of the address, some accepted it as a statement of the developing American position:[23]

The United States stands at this time at the pinnacle of world power. It is a solemn moment for the American democracy. With primacy in power is also joined an awe-inspiring accountability to the future. As you look around you, you feel not only the sense of duty done but also feel anxiety lest you fall below the level of achievement. Opportunity is here now, clear and shining, for both our countries. To reject it or ignore it or fritter it away will bring upon us all the long reproaches of the after time. It is necessary that constancy of mind, persistency of purpose, and the grand simplicity of decision shall guide and rule the conduct of the English-speaking peoples in peace as they did in war. We must and I believe we shall prove ourselves equal to this severe requirement. . . .

. . . Before we cast away the solid assurances of national armaments for self-preservation, we must be certain that our temple is built, not upon shifting sands or quagmires, but upon the rock. Anyone with his eyes open can see that our path will be difficult and also long, but if we persevere together as we did in the two World Wars—though not, alas, in the interval between them—I cannot doubt that we shall achieve our common purpose in the end.

I have, however, a definite and practical proposal to make for action. Courts and magistrates cannot function without sheriffs and constables. The United Nations Organization must immediately begin to be equipped with an international armed force. In such a matter we can only go step by step; but we must begin now. I propose that each of the powers and states should be invited to dedicate a certain number of air squadrons to the service of the world organization. These squadrons would be trained and prepared in their own countries but would move around in rotation from one country to another. They

[23] Excerpts reprinted from *Congressional Record*, Seventy-ninth Congress, second session, pp. A1145–7.

would wear the uniform of their own countries with different badges. They would not be required to act against their own nation but in other respects they would be directed by the world organization. This might be started on a modest scale and a grow [sic—Eds.] as confidence grew. I wished to see this done after the First World War and trust it may be done forthwith.

It would nevertheless be wrong and imprudent to entrust the secret knowledge or experience of the atomic bomb, which the United States, Great Britain, and Canada now share, to the world organization, while it is still in its infancy. It would be criminal madness to cast it adrift in this still agitated and ununited world. No one in any country has slept less well in their beds because this knowledge and the method and the raw materials to apply it are at present largely retained in American hands. I do not believe we should all have slept so soundly had the positions been reversed and some Communist or neo-Fascist state monopolized, for the time being, these dread agencies. The fear of them alone might easily have been used to enforce totalitarian systems upon the free democratic world, with consequences appalling to human imagination. . . .

. . . We cannot be blind to the fact that the liberties enjoyed by individual citizens throughout the United States and British Empire are not valid in a considerable number of countries, some of which are very powerful. In these states control is enforced upon the common people by various kinds of all-embracing police governments, to a degree which is overwhelming and contrary to every principle of democracy. The power of the state is exercised without restraint, either by dictators or by compact oligarchies operating through a privileged party and a political police. It is not our duty at this time, when difficulties are so numerous, to interfere forcibly in the internal affairs of countries whom we have not conquered in war, but we must never cease to proclaim in fearless tones the great principles of freedom and the rights of man, which are the joint inheritance of the English-speaking world and which, through Magna Carta, the Bill of Rights, the habeas corpus, trial by jury, and the English common law find their . . . expression in the Declaration of Independence. . . .

A shadow has fallen upon the scenes so lately lighted by the Allied victory. Nobody knows what Soviet Russia and its Communist international organization intends to do in the immediate future, or what are the limits, if any, to their expansive and proselytizing tendencies. I have a strong admiration and regard for the valiant Russian people

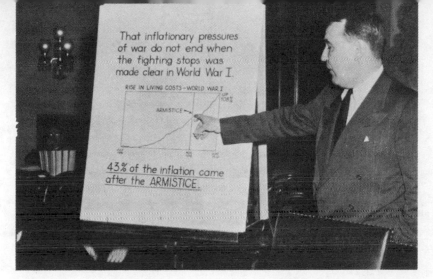

That inflationary pressures of war do not end when the fighting stops was made clear in World War I.

RISE IN LIVING COSTS – WORLD WAR I

UP 108%

ARMISTICE

43% of the inflation came after the ARMISTICE.

Chester Bowles, OPA director, before Senate Small Business Committee, Dec. 4, 1945 (*Wide World*)

Truman and Secretary of Agriculture Clinton P. Anderson (*UPI*)

Secretary of Agriculture Charles F. Brannan, March 3, 1951 (*UPI*)

Harold Smith, director, Bureau of the Budget (*UPI*)

After settlement of coal strike announced, May 28, 1946; foreground, *left to right*: Truman, Secretary of the Interior Julius A. Krug, John L. Lewis, president, United Mine Workers (*UPI*)

Railway workers reading about Truman's seizure of the railroads, May 17, 1946 (*UPI*)

After passage of controversial Taft-Hartley bill, June 20, 1947; *left to right*: Representative Fred A. Hartley, Jr., Senate secretary Carl Loeffler, Senator Robert A. Taft (*UPI*)

Seated, left to right: George Meany, AFL secretary-treasurer; Eric Johnston, director, Economic Stabilization Agency; George Leighty, chairman, Railway Labor Executives Association; *standing*: A. J. Hayes, president, International Association of Machinists; Charles Murphy, presidential counsel; Arthur J. Goldberg, CIO counsel, Washington, D.C., March 6, 1951 (*UPI*)

Truman announcing decision to seize steel mills, April 9, 1952 (UPI)

Truman after announcing settlement of steel strike, with Benjamin F. Fairless (left), president, U.S. Steel, and Philip Murray, president, CIO and CIO United Steelworkers, July 24, 1952 (UPI)

Civil Rights Congress demonstration in behalf of 11 top Communists convicted under Smith Act, Sept. 27, 1949 (*UPI*)

Communist leaders indicted for violation of Smith Act; *left to right:* Henry Winston, Eugene Dennis, Benjamin Davis, Carl Winter, Gil Green, John Williamson, Gus Hall, Sept. 15, 1948 (*UPI*)

Whittaker Chambers, June 2, 1949
(UPI)

Alger Hiss, Aug. 3, 1948
(Wide World)

Hiss confronted by Chambers at House Un-American Activities Committee hearing, Aug. 17, 1948 (Wide World)

Senators Joseph R. McCarthy and Everett M. Dirksen, Sept. 25, 1952
(*UPI*)

McCarthy with one of his famous "documents," attacking Adlai E.
Stevenson, Chicago telecast, Oct. 27, 1952 (*Wide World*)

and for my wartime comrade, Marshal Stalin. There is sympathy and good will in Britain—and I doubt not here also—toward the peoples of all the Russias and a resolve to persevere through many differences and rebuffs in establishing lasting friendships.

We understand the Russian need to be secure on her western frontiers from all renewal of German aggression. We welcome her to her rightful place among the leading nations of the world. Above all, we welcome constant, frequent, and growing contacts between the Russian people and our own people on both sides of the Atlantic. It is my duty, however, to place before you certain facts about the present position in Europe.

From Stettin in the Baltic to Trieste in the Adriatic, an iron curtain has descended across the continent. Behind that line lie all the capitals of the ancient states of central and eastern Europe. Warsaw, Berlin, Prague, Vienna, Budapest, Belgrade, Bucharest, and Sofia, all these famous cities and the populations around them lie in the Soviet sphere and all are subject, in one form or another, not only to Soviet influence but to a very high and increasing measure of control from Moscow. Athens alone, with its immortal glories, is free to decide its future at an election under British, American, and French observation.

The Russian-dominated Polish Government has been encouraged to make enormous and wrongful inroads upon Germany, and mass expulsions of millions of Germans on a scale grievous and undreamed of are now taking place. The Communist parties, which were very small in all these eastern states of Europe, have been raised to pre-eminence and power far beyond their numbers and are seeking everywhere to obtain totalitarian control. Police governments are prevailing in nearly every case, and so far, except in Czechoslovakia, there is not true democracy.

Turkey and Persia are both profoundly alarmed and disturbed at the claims which are made upon them and at the pressure being exerted by the Moscow government. An attempt is being made by the Russians in Berlin to build up a quasi-Communist party in their zone of occupied Germany by showing special favors to groups of left-wing German leaders. At the end of the fighting last June, the American and British Armies withdrew westward, in accordance with an earlier agreement, to a depth at some points of 150 miles on a front of nearly 400 miles, to allow the Russians to occupy this vast expanse of territory which the western democracies ... conquered....

In front of the iron curtain which lies across Europe are other causes for anxiety. In Italy the Communist Party is seriously hampered by having to support the Communist-trained Marshal Tito's claims to former Italian territory at the head of the Adriatic. Nevertheless, the future of Italy hangs in the balance. Again, one cannot imagine a regenerated Europe without a strong France. All my public life I have worked for a strong France and I never lost faith in her destiny, even in the darkest hours. I will not lose faith now.

However, in a great number of countries, far from the Russian frontiers and throughout the world, Communist fifth columns are established and work in complete unity and absolute obedience to the directions they receive from the Communist center. Except in the British Commonwealth, and in the United States, where communism is in its infancy, the Communist parties or fifth columns constitute a growing challenge and peril to Christian civilization. These are somber facts for anyone to have to recite on the morrow of a victory gained by so much splendid comradeship in arms and in the cause of freedom and democracy, and we should be most unwise not to face them squarely while time remains.

The outlook is also anxious in the Far East and especially in Manchuria. The agreement which was made at Yalta, to which I was a party, was extremely favorable to Soviet Russia, but it was made at a time when no one could say that the German war might not extend all through the summer and autumn of 1945 and when the Japanese war was expected to last for a further 18 months from the end of the German war. In this country you are all so well informed about the Far East and such devoted friends of China that I do not need to expatiate on the situation there.

On the other hand, I repulse the idea that a new war is inevitable, still more that it is imminent. It is because I am so sure that our fortunes are in our own hands and that we hold the power to save the future, that I feel the duty to speak out now that I have an occasion to do so. I do not believe that Soviet Russia desires war. What they desire is the fruits of war and the indefinite expansion of their power and doctrines. But what we have to consider here today while time remains, is the permanent prevention of war and the establishment of conditions of freedom and democracy as rapidly as possible in all countries.

Our difficulties and dangers will not be removed by closing our eyes to them; they will not be removed by mere waiting to see what happens; nor will they be relieved by a policy of appeasement. What is needed is a settlement, and the longer this is delayed, the more difficult it will be and the greater our dangers will become. From what I have seen of our Russian friends and allies during the war, I am convinced that there is nothing they admire so much as strength, and there is nothing for which they have less respect than for military weakness. For that reason the old doctrine of a balance of power is unsound. We cannot afford, if we can help it, to work on narrow margins, offering temptations to a trial of strength. If the western democracies stand together in strict adherence to the principles of the United Nations Charter, their influence for furthering these principles will be immense and no one is likely to molest them. If, however, they become divided or falter in their duty, and if these all-important years are allowed to slip away, then indeed catastrophe may overwhelm us all.

Last time I saw it all coming, and cried aloud to my own fellow countrymen and to the world, but no one paid any attention. Up till the year 1933 or even 1935, Germany might have been saved from the awful fate which has overtaken her and we might all have been spared the miseries Hitler let loose upon mankind.

There never was a war in all history easier to prevent by timely action than the one which has just desolated such great areas of the globe. It could have been prevented without the firing of a single shot, and Germany might be powerful, prosperous, and honored today, but no one would listen and one by one we were all sucked into the awful whirlpool.

We surely must not let that happen again. This can only be achieved by reaching now, in 1946, a good understanding on all points with Russia under the general authority of the United Nations and by the maintenance of that good understanding through many peaceful years, by the world instrument, supported by the whole strength of the English speaking world and all its connections.

STIMSON MEMOS ON A-BOMB CONTROL

24 ◄§   IN THE SPRING OF 1946 American diplomacy achieved mixed results. At Potsdam Stalin had pledged to withdraw his forces from Iran within six months after the end of the war, and though for a time he seemed reluctant to abide by the agreement, he yielded in April and promised to remove his army within a month. But in Eastern Europe matters became worse. In June, for instance, the United States protested Romania's failure to schedule

promised elections and during the rest of the year continued to send moralistic and ineffectual notes lamenting the fate of the satellite nations. It had become painfully clear that the American nuclear monopoly had not made Russia more tractable and in fact had fostered dangerous distrust and fear. As early as September 1945, Secretary of War Stimson had foreseen some of the problems the bomb posed.

On September 12, 1945, Stimson, about to retire after arduous wartime service, submitted to the President two memoranda on control of atomic bombs. Stimson's proposals led to a discussion in mid-September at two cabinet meetings. Secretary of Commerce Henry Wallace, Secretary of Labor Lewis Schwellenbach, and Postmaster-General Robert Hannegan supported Stimson, as did representatives from the State and War departments. But the President and the rest of the cabinet rejected the recommendation. The text of Stimson's brief memorandum of September 11, which introduces his more lengthy note of September 11, follows:[24]

In handing you today my memorandum about our relations with Russia in respect to the atomic bomb, I am not unmindful of the fact that when in Potsdam I talked with you about the question whether we could be safe in sharing the atomic bomb with Russia while she was still a police state and before she put into effect provisions assuring personal rights of liberty to the individual citizen.

I still recognize the difficulty and am still convinced of the ultimate importance of a change in Russian attitude toward individual liberty but I have come to the conclusion that it would not be possible to use our possession of the atomic bomb as a direct lever to produce the change. I have become convinced that any demand by us for an internal change in Russia as a condition of sharing in the atomic weapon would be so resented that it would make the objective we have in view less probable.

I believe that the change in attitude towards the individual in Russia will come slowly and gradually and I am satisfied that we should not delay our approach to Russia in the matter of the atomic bomb until that process has been completed. My reasons are set forth in the memorandum I am handing you today. Furthermore, I believe that this long process of change in Russia is more likely to be

[24] Reprinted from Stimson Diary, entry for September 11, 1945, Yale University Library. Published by permission of the Stimson Literary Trust.

expedited by the closer relationship in the matter of the atomic bomb which I suggest and the trust and confidence that I believe would be inspired by the method of approach which I have outlined.

25 ᴥᴗ STIMSON'S OTHER MEMORANDUM of September 11 appears below:[25]

Subject: Proposed Action for Control of Atomic Bombs

The advent of the atomic bomb has stimulated great military and probably even greater political interest throughout the civilized world. In a world atmosphere already extremely sensitive to power, the introduction of this weapon has profoundly affected political considerations in all sections of the globe.

In many quarters it has been interpreted as a substantial offset to the growth of Russian influence on the continent. We can be certain that the Soviet government has sensed this tendency and the temptation will be strong for the Soviet political and military leaders to acquire this weapon in the shortest possible time. Britain in effect already has the status of a partner with us in the development of this weapon. Accordingly, unless the Soviets are voluntarily invited into the partnership upon a basis of cooperation and trust, we are going to maintain the Anglo-Saxon bloc over against the Soviet [Union—Eds.] in the possession of this weapon. Such a condition will almost certainly stimulate feverish activity on the part of the Soviet toward the development of this bomb in what will in effect be a secret armament race of a rather desperate character. There is evidence to indicate that such activity may have already commenced.

If we feel, as I assume we must, that civilization demands that some day we shall arrive at a satisfactory international arrangement respecting the control of this new force, the question then is how long we can afford to enjoy our momentary superiority in the hope of achieving our immediate peace council objectives.

Whether Russia gets control of the necessary secrets of production in a minimum of say four years or a maximum of twenty years is not nearly as important to the world and civilization as to make sure

[25] Reprinted from carbon copy in the Stimson Papers, Yale University Library. Published by permission of the Stimson Literary Trust. The parts in italics are those sections that Stimson later judged most important. The italics did not appear in the original.

that when they do get it they are willing and cooperative partners among the peace loving nations of the world. It is true that if we approach them now, as I would propose, we may be gambling on their good faith and risk their getting into production of bombs a little sooner than they would otherwise.

To put the matter concisely, I consider the problem of our satisfactory relations with Russia as not merely connected with but as virtually dominated by the problem of the atomic bomb. Except for the problem of the control of that bomb, those relations, while vitally important, might not be immediately pressing. The establishment of relations of mutual confidence between her and us could afford to await the slow progress of time. But with the discovery of the bomb, they became immediately emergent. *Those relations may be perhaps irretrievably embittered by the way in which we approach the solution of the bomb with Russia. For if we fail to approach them now and merely continue to negotiate with them, having this weapon rather ostentatiously on our hip, their suspicions and their distrust of our purposes and motives will increase.* It will inspire them to greater efforts in an all out effort to solve the problem. If the solution is achieved in that spirit, it is much less likely that we will ever get the kind of covenant we may desperately need in the future. This risk is, I believe, greater than the other, inasmuch as our objective must be to get the best kind of international bargain we can—one that has some chance of being kept and saving civilization not for five or for twenty years, but forever.

The chief lesson I have learned in a long life is that the only way you can make a man trustworthy is to trust him; and the surest way to make him untrustworthy is to distrust him and show your distrust.

If the atomic bomb were merely another though more devastating military weapon to be assimilated into our pattern of international relations, it would be one thing. We could then follow the old custom of secrecy and nationalistic military superiority relying on international caution to prescribe the future use of the weapon as we did with gas. But I think the bomb instead constitutes merely a first step in a new control by man over the forces of nature too revolutionary and dangerous to fit into the old concepts. I think it really caps the climax of the race between man's growing technical power for destructiveness and his psychological power of self-control and group control—his moral power. If so, our method of approach to the

Russians is a question of the most vital importance in the evolution of human progress.

Since the crux of the problem is Russia, any contemplated action leading to the control of this weapon should be primarily directed *to* [italicized in the original—Eds.] Russia. It is my judgment that the Soviet [Union—Eds.] would be more apt to respond sincerely to a direct and forthright approach made by the United States on this subject than would be the case if the approach were made as a part of a general international scheme, or if the approach were made after a succession of express or implied threats or near threats in our peace negotiations.

My idea of an approach to the Soviets would be a direct proposal after discussion with the British that we would be prepared in effect to enter an arrangement with the Russians, the general purpose of which would be to control and limit the use of the atomic bomb as an instrument of war and so far as possible to direct and encourage the development of atomic power for peaceful and humanitarian purposes. Such an approach might more specifically lead to the proposal that we would stop work on the further improvement in, or manufacture of, the bomb as a military weapon, provided the Russians and the British would agree to do likewise. It might also provide that we would be willing to impound what bombs we now have in the United States provided the Russians and the British would agree with us that in no event will they or we use a bomb as an instrument of war unless all three Governments agree to that use. We might also consider including in the arrangement a covenant with the U.K. and the Soviets providing for the exchange of benefits of future developments whereby atomic energy may be applied on a mutually satisfactory basis for commercial or humanitarian purposes.

I would make such an approach just as soon as our immediate political considerations make it appropriate.

I emphasize perhaps beyond all other considerations the importance of taking this action with Russia as a proposal of the United States— backed by Great Britain—but peculiarly the proposal of the United States. Action of any international group of nations, including many small nations who have not demonstrated their potential power or responsibility in this war would not, in my opinion, be taken seriously by the Soviets. The loose debates which would surround such [a— Eds.] proposal, if put before a conference of nations, would provoke but scant favor from the Soviet [Union—Eds.]. As I say, I think this is the most important point in the program.

After the nations which have won this war have agreed to it, there will be ample time to introduce France and China into the covenants and finally to incorporate the agreement into the scheme of the United Nations. The use of this bomb has been accepted by the world as the result of the initiative and productive capacity of the United States, and I think this factor is a most potent lever toward having our proposals accepted by the Soviets, whereas I am most skeptical of obtaining any tangible results by way of any international debate. I urge this method as the most realistic means of accomplishing this vitally important step in the history of the world.

BARUCH PLAN FOR CONTROL

26 ◅§ THOUGH HE HAD spoken about international control of atomic energy, Truman had let slip to reporters in the autumn of 1945 that the United States would not disclose the secret of the bomb. On November 15 the heads of state of the United States, Canada, and the United Kingdom agreed to continue the availability of "basic scientific information essential to the development of atomic energy for peaceful purposes. . . ." However, until enforceable safeguards were created by a UN commission (which the three nations had proposed), they decided to restrict all information "regarding the practical application of atomic energy. . . ." Industrial use, they explained, was too closely related to military exploitation of atomic energy.

At the Moscow conference in December 1945 the Big Three recommended that the General Assembly establish a UN commission on atomic energy. The United States did not offer any plan for international control. Dr. J. Robert Oppenheimer, then a government consultant on atomic energy, later recalled: "I got the impression that we did not know what international control was or what we could say to the Russians. . . ." David E. Lilienthal, then head of the Tennessee Valley Authority and later the first chairman of the Atomic Energy Commission, observed in his diary entry for January 16, 1946, that Under Secretary of State Dean Acheson was disturbed by the ignorance of Truman and Byrnes about international control of atomic energy.

Truman, at Acheson's behest, appointed a committee in January to formulate a position on control of the bomb secret. On March

17, 1946, the committee, chaired by Lilienthal, submitted the so-called Acheson-Lilienthal report. According to Acheson, it was "a rough sketch," "a sort of working paper." Bernard M. Baruch said that the report "laid the basis for a system of international control of atomic energy [and—Eds.] proved indispensable in formulating specific plans." Baruch became the United States representative on the UN Atomic Energy Commission. Appointed on March 16, the financier and long-time adviser to Democratic Presidents began working on a plan that emphasized "the crucial problem of enforcement," which the Acheson-Lilienthal proposal had neglected. After only brief consultation with the State Department, Baruch, on June 14, presented the American plan to the UN Atomic Energy Commission:[26]

. . . we are here to make a choice between the quick and the dead. That is our business.

Behind the black portent of the new atomic age lies a hope which, seized upon with faith, can work our salvation. If we fail, then we have damned every man to be the slave of fear. Let us not deceive ourselves: We must elect world peace or world destruction. . . .

When an adequate system of atomic energy, including the renunciation of the bomb as a weapon, has been agreed upon and put into effective operation and condign punishments set up for violations of the rules of control which are to be stigmatized as international crimes, we propose that:

1. Manufacture of atomic bombs shall stop;

2. Existing bombs shall be disposed of pursuant to the terms of the treaty; and

3. The authority shall be in possession of full information as to the know-how for the production of atomic energy.

Let me repeat, so as to avoid misunderstanding: My country is ready to make its full contribution toward the end we seek, subject, of course, to our constitutional processes, and to an adequate system of control becoming fully effective as we finally work it out.

Now as to violations: In the agreement, penalties of as serious a nature as the nations may wish and as immediate and certain in their execution as possible, should be fixed for:

1. Illegal possession or use of an atomic bomb;

[26] Excerpts reprinted from The United States and The United Nations: United States Atomic Energy Proposals, series 2 (Washington, D.C., 1946), pp. 1–12.

2. Illegal possession or separation of atomic material suitable for use in an atomic bomb;

3. Seizure of any plant or other property belonging to or licensed by the authority;

4. Willful interference with the activities of the authority;

5. Creation or operation of dangerous projects in a manner contrary to, or in the absence of, a license granted by the international control body.

It would be a deception, to which I am unwilling to lend myself, were I not to say to you and to our peoples that the matter of punishment lies at the very heart of our present security system. It might as well be admitted, here and now, that the subject goes straight to the veto power contained in the Charter of the United Nations so far as it relates to the field of atomic energy. The Charter permits penalization solely by concurrence of each of the five great powers—Union of Soviet Socialist Republics, the United Kingdom, China, France, and the United States.

I want to make this very plain that I am concerned here with the veto power only as it affects this particular problem. There must be no veto to protect those who violate their solemn agreements not to develop or use atomic energy for destructive purposes. . . .

1. General: The authority should set up a thorough plan for control of the field of atomic energy, through various forms of ownership, dominion, licenses, operation, inspection, research, and management by competent personnel. After this is provided for there should be as little interference as may be with the economic plans and the present private, corporate, and state relationships in the several countries involved. . . .

4. Atomic explosives: The authority should be given sole and exclusive right to conduct research in the field of atomic explosives. Research activities in the field of atomic explosives are essential in order that the authority may keep in the forefront of knowledge in the field of atomic energy and fulfill the objective of preventing illicit manufacture of bombs. Only by maintaining its position as the best informed agency will the authority be able to determine the line between intrinsically dangerous and nondangerous activities. . . .

9. Inspection: By assigning intrinsically dangerous activities exclusively to the authority, the difficulties of inspection are reduced. If the authority is the only agency which may lawfully conduct dangerous

activities, then visible operation by others than the authority will constitute an unambiguous danger signal. Inspection will also occur in connection with the licensing functions of the authority.

10. Freedom of access: Adequate ingress and egress for all qualified representatives of the authority must be assured. Many of the inspection activities of the authority should grow out of, and be incidental to, its other functions.

Important measures of inspection will be associated with the tight control of raw materials, for this is a keystone of the plan. The continuing activities of prospecting, survey, and research in relation to raw materials will be designed not only to serve the affirmative development functions of the authority, but also to assure that no surreptitious operations are conducted in the raw materials field by nations or their citizens.

11. Personnel: The personnel of the authority should be recruited on a basis of proven competence, but also so far as possible on an international basis.

12. Progress by stages: A primary step in the creation of the system of control is the setting forth, in comprehensive terms of the functions, responsibilities, powers, and limitations of the authority. Once a charter for the authority has been adopted, the authority and the system of control for which it will be responsible will require time to become fully organized and effective. The plan of control will, therefore, have to come into effect in successive stages. These should be specifically fixed in the Charter or means should be otherwise set forth in the Charter for transition from one stage to another, as contemplated in the resolution of the United Nations Assembly which created this commission.

13. Disclosures: In the deliberations of the United Nations Commission on Atomic Energy, the United States is prepared to make available the information, essential to a reasonable understanding of the proposals which it advocates. Further disclosures must be dependent, in the interest of all, upon the effective ratification of the treaty. When the authority is actually created, the United States will join the other nations in making available the further information essential to that organization for the performance of its functions. As the successive stages of international control are reached, the United States will be prepared to yield, to the extent required by each stage, national control of activities in this field to the authority.

GROMYKO'S OBJECTIONS TO BARUCH PLAN

27 ✑§ FIVE DAYS AFTER Baruch's proposal, at the second UN
      Atomic Energy Commission meeting, Andrei Gromyko,
the Soviet delegate, raised what would become a persistent problem
in international negotiations: Which ought to be first—a commitment to disarm or provisions for enforcement of the commitment?
Excerpts from Gromyko's speech follow:[27]

As one of the first measures to be carried out, in order to carry out
the decision of the General Assembly of the 24th of January, the
Soviet delegation proposes a study of the question of the conclusions
of international agreements forbidding the production and use of
weapons based upon the use of atomic energy for the purposes of
mass destruction. The purpose of such an agreement should be to
forbid the production and use of atomic weapons, the destruction of
existing stocks of atomic weapons, and the punishment of all activities
undertaken with a view to the violation of such agreements. The
elaboration and conclusion of such agreements would be, in the
opinion of the Soviet delegation, only one of the primordial measures
which must be taken to prevent the use of atomic energy to harm
humanity. It should be followed by other measures designed to introduce means of assuring a strict supervision of the observance of
undertakings entered into, the conclusion in connection with the
above-mentioned agreements, the setting up of a system of supervision
and control to see that the conventions and agreements are observed,
and measures concerning sanctions against unlawful use of atomic
energy. . . .

The proposals are as follows:

The first one concerns the conclusion of an international agreement
for the outlawing of the production and application of a weapon
based upon the use of atomic energy for the purposes of mass
destruction.

The second concerns an organization of the work of the commission
for the control of atomic energy.

I will read the text of the first proposal:

Draft international agreement to forbid the production and use of
weapons based upon the use of atomic energy for the purposes of
mass destruction. There follows after this a list of the signatory states,

[27] Reprinted from *The New York Times*, June 20, 1946, p. 4.

and the text continues: "Deeply aware of the extreme importance of the great scientific discoveries connected with the splitting of the atom and with a view to the use of atomic energy for the purposes of raising the welfare and standard of life of the peoples of the world, and also for the development of culture and science for the good of humanity; unanimously desiring universal co-operation as wide as possible for the use of all people of scientific discoveries in the field of atomic energy, for the improvement of the conditions of the life of the peoples of the whole world, the raising of their standard of welfare and further progress of human culture; taking account clearly of the fact that the great scientific discoveries in the field of atomic energy contain a great danger first and foremost for the peaceful towns and civilian populations in case such a discovery were used as a means of applying an atomic weapon for the purposes of mass destruction; taking note also of the great importance of the fact that through international agreements, the use in time of war of suffocating, poisonous and other similar gases and also similar liquids, substances and processes, and also bacteriological methods have already been outlawed by common accord between the civilized peoples; and considering that the international outlawry of the use of the atomic weapon for mass destruction would correspond in still greater measure to the aspirations and the conscience of the peoples of the whole world; animated by an intense desire to remove the threat of the use of these scientific discoveries for the harm of humanity and against the interests of humanity; the high contracting parties decided to conclude an agreement to forbid the production and use of a weapon based upon the use of atomic energy, and for this purpose appointed as their plenipotentiaries"—and here the list of plenipotentiaries will follow, whose credentials are found to be in due form—"agree as follows:

"ARTICLE 1: The high contracting parties solemnly declare that they will forbid the production and use of a weapon based upon the use of atomic energy, and with this in view take upon themselves the following obligations:

"(a) Not to use, in any circumstances, an atomic weapon;

"(b) To forbid the production and keeping of a weapon based upon the use of atomic energy;

"(c) To destroy within a period of three months from the entry into force of this agreement all stocks of atomic energy weapons whether in a finished or semifinished condition.

"ARTICLE 2: The high contracting parties declare that any violation of Article 1 of this agreement shall constitute a serious crime against humanity.

"ARTICLE 3: The high contracting parties, within six months of the entry into force of the present agreement, shall pass legislation providing severe punishment for the violation of the terms of this assignment.

"ARTICLE 4: The present agreement shall be of indefinite duration.

"ARTICLE 5: The present agreement is open for signature to all states whether or not they are members of the United Nations.

"ARTICLE 6: The present agreement shall come into force after approval by the Security Council, and after ratification by half the signature states, including all states members of the United Nations, as under Article 23 of the Charter. The ratification shall be placed for safe keeping in the hands of the Secretary-General of the United Nations.

"ARTICLE 7: After the entry into force of the present agreement, it shall be an obligation upon all states whether members or not of the United Nations.

"ARTICLE 8: The present agreement of which the Russian, Chinese, French, English and Spanish texts shall be authentic, is drawn up in one copy and will be in the safe-keeping of the Secretary-General of the United Nations. The Secretary-General shall communicate to all signatories a duly certified copy thereof."

I would like now to read the text of the second proposal. . . .

1. The setting up of committees of the commission, pursuing the aims indicated in the decision of the General Assembly to "proceed with the utmost dispatch and inquire into all phases of the problems and make such recommendations from time to time with respect to that as it finds possible."

In connection with this item, it seems quite necessary to establish two committees which as auxiliary organs of the commission would be responsible for a general study of the problem of atomic energy and the elaboration of recommendations which the commission might make for the carrying out of the decision of the General Assembly and other organs of the United Nations.

It is proposed that there should be set up two committees, the first a committee for the exchange of scientific information. This committee would be set up for the purpose of studying point (a) of Article 5 of the decision of the General Assembly of the 24th of January, 1946. Among the tasks of this committee would be that of elaborating recommendations concerning practical measures for the organization of the exchange of information. (1) Concerning the contents of scientific discoveries connected with the splitting of the atom and other discoveries connected with the obtaining and use of atomic energy, and (2) concerning the technology and the organization of technological processes for obtaining and using atomic energy. (3) Concerning the organization and method of industrial production of atomic energy and the use of such energy. (4) Concerning forms, sources, and the location of raw materials necessary for obtaining atomic energy.

I come now to the second proposed committee whose task would be to prevent the use of atomic energy for the harm of humanity. This committee should be set up in order to attain the aims set forth in points (b), (c) and (d) of Article 5 of the decision of the General Assembly. The task of this committee would be to prepare recommendations on the following subjects:

(1). The preparation of a draft international agreement for the outlawing of weapons based upon the use of atomic energy and forbidding the production and use of such weapons and all similar forms of weapons destined for mass destruction.

(2). The elaboration and creation of methods to forbid the production of weapons based upon the use of atomic energy and to prevent the use of atomic weapons and all other similar weapons of mass destruction.

(3). Measures, systems and organizations of control in the use of atomic energy to insure the observance of the conditions abovementioned in the international agreement for the outlawing of atomic weapons.

(4). The elaboration of a system of sanctions for application against the unlawful use of atomic energy.

Part 2: The composition of the committees. Each committee would be composed of one representative of each state represented in the commission. Each representative may have advisers.

3. Rules of procedure of the committees. The rules of procedure of committee shall be drawn up by the commission. . . .

In conclusion, I wish to say that in this statement I aimed chiefly at underlining the extreme importance to be attributed to the conclusion of the above-mentioned agreement for the outlawry of the production and use of atomic weapons. The conclusion of such an agreement would constitute an important practical step in the direction of fulfilling the task which lies before the commission.

OPPENHEIMER ON EARLY U.S. CONTROL PLANS

28 ᴥ§   AT HIS SECURITY HEARINGS in 1954 Oppenheimer discussed the early American programs for international control of atomic energy:[28]

. . . I think that any attempt at that time to establish control along these lines would, if accepted by the Soviets, have so altered their whole system and so altered their whole relations with the Western World that the threat which has been building up year after year since could not have existed. I think that no one at that time could with much confidence believe that they would accept these proposals. I think it was important to put them forward, and it was also important not to express too much doubt that they might be accepted.

In the U.N. we hammered away at this line, but there are some intervening complications.

Q. The central idea of this scheme, I take it, was that there should be not merely inspection of atomic-energy production and atomic-energy armaments, but actual ownership and control of that whole process by an international agency, so that purely national development of these atomic-energy programs would be ruled out, and that would have entailed in Russia as in other countries the actual ownership of productive facilities in that land, as in others, by an international agency, is that correctly stated?

A. That is correctly stated. I think it is part of the story. It would have meant that the Russian Government gave up control over things going on involving their citizens on their territory. It would have permitted free intercourse between Russian nationals and people of the rest of the world. It would have meant that there could be no Iron Curtain. How radical it was I may indicate by a comment that came much later. General [Matthew B.—Eds.] Ridgway was on the Military Staff Committee at the U.N. at the time when I was on Mr. Brook's staff, and our people had looked at this proposal and said if it were to go through, they would recommend that all secret military establishments be abolished. This was quite a slug.

[28] Excerpt reprinted from *In the Matter of J. Robert Oppenheimer*, p. 38.

BYRNES'S STUTTGART SPEECH

29 ◄§ PROBLEMS OF GERMANY'S future and the organization of
the economy and government during the occupation
widened the split between the United States and Soviet Russia.
On September 6, 1946, at Stuttgart, Secretary of State Byrnes
reinterpreted American policy:[29]

We have learned, whether we like it or not, that we live in one
world, from which world we cannot isolate ourselves. We have learned
that peace and well-being are indivisible and that our peace and
well-being cannot be purchased at the price of the peace or the well-
being of any other country.

I hope that the German people will never again make the mistake
of believing that because the American people are peace-loving they
will sit back hoping for peace if any nation uses force or the threat
of force to acquire dominion over other peoples and other governments.

In 1917 the United States was forced into the first World War.
After that war we refused to join the League of Nations. . . .

We will not again make that mistake. We intend to continue our
interest in the affairs of Europe and of the world. We have helped
to organize the United Nations. We believe it will stop aggressor
nations from starting wars. Because we believe it, we intend to support
the United Nations organization with all the power and resources
we possess. . . .

In agreeing at Potsdam that Germany should be disarmed and
demilitarized and in proposing that the four major powers should
by treaty jointly undertake to see that Germany is kept disarmed
and demilitarized for a generation, the United States was not unmindful of the responsibility resting upon it and its major Allies to
maintain and enforce peace under the law.

Freedom from militarism will give the German people the opportunity, if they will but seize it, to apply their great energies and
abilities to the works of peace. It will give them the opportunity to
show themselves worthy of the respect and friendship of peace-loving
nations, and in time, to take an honorable place among the members
of the United Nations.

It is not in the interest of the German people or in the interest of

[29] Excerpts reprinted from *Department of State Bulletin*, September 15, 1946,
pp. 496–501.

world peace that Germany should become a pawn or a partner in a military struggle for power between the East and the West.

German militarism and Nazism have devastated twice in our generation the lands of Germany's neighbors. It is fair and just that Germany should do her part to repair that devastation. Most of the victims of Nazi aggression were before the war less well off than Germany. They should not be expected by Germany to bear, unaided, the major costs of Nazi aggression.

The United States, therefore, is prepared to carry out fully the principles outlined in the Postdam Agreement on demilitarization and reparations. However, there should be changes in the levels of industry agreed upon by the Allied Control Commission if Germany is not to be administered as an economic unit as the Potsdam Agreement contemplates and requires.

The basis of the Potsdam Agreement was that, as part of a combined program of demilitarization and reparations, Germany's war potential should be reduced by elimination and removal of her war industries and the reduction and removal of heavy industrial plants. It was contemplated this should be done to the point that Germany would be left with levels of industry capable of maintaining in Germany average European living standards without assistance from other countries. . . .

The carrying out of the Potsdam Agreement has, however, been obstructed by the failure of the Allied Control Council to take the necessary steps to enable the German economy to function as an economic unit. Essential central German administrative departments have not been established, although they are expressly required by the Potsdam Agreement. . . .

The United States is firmly of the belief that Germany should be administered as an economic unit and that zonal barriers should be completely obliterated so far as the economic life and activity in Germany are concerned.

The conditions which now exist in Germany make it impossible for industrial production to reach the levels which the occupying powers agreed were essential for a minimum German peacetime economy. Obviously, if the agreed levels of industry are to be reached, we cannot continue to restrict the free exchange of commodities, persons, and ideas throughout Germany. The barriers between the four zones of Germany are far more difficult to surmount than those between normal independent states.

The time has come when the zonal boundaries should be regarded as defining only the areas to be occupied for security purposes by the armed forces of the occupying powers and not as self-contained economic or political units.

That was the course of development envisaged by the Potsdam Agreement, and that is the course of development which the American Government intends to follow to the full limit of its authority. It has formally announced that it is its intention to unify the economy of its own zone with any or all of the other zones willing to participate in the unification.

So far only the British Government has agreed to let its zone participate. We deeply appreciate their cooperation. Of course, this policy of unification is not intended to exclude the governments not now willing to join. The unification will be open to them at any time they wish to join.

We favor the economic unification of Germany. If complete unification cannot be secured, we shall do everything in our power to secure the maximum possible unification. . . .

So far as many vital questions are concerned, the Control Council is neither governing Germany nor allowing Germany to govern itself.

A common financial policy is essential for the successful rehabilitation of Germany. Runaway inflation accompanied by economic paralysis is almost certain to develop unless there is a common financial policy directed to the control of inflation. A program of drastic fiscal reform to reduce currency and monetary claims, to revise the debt structure, and to place Germany on a sound financial basis is urgently required.

The United States has worked hard to develop such a program, but fully coordinated measures must be accepted and applied uniformly to all zones if ruinous inflation is to be prevented. A central agency of finance is obviously necessary to carry out any such program effectively.

It is also essential that transportation, communications, and postal services should be organized throughout Germany without regard to zonal barriers. The nation-wide organization of these public services was contemplated by the Potsdam Agreement. Twelve months have passed and nothing has been done. . . .

Similarly, there is urgent need for the setting up of a central German administrative agency for industry and foreign trade. While Germany must be prepared to share her coal and steel with the liberated countries of Europe dependent upon those supplies, Germany must be enabled to use her skills and her energies to increase her industrial production and to organize the most effective use of her raw materials.

Germany must be given a chance to export goods in order to import enough to make her economy self-sustaining. Germany is a part of Europe, and recovery in Europe, and particularly in the states adjoining Germany, will be slow indeed if Germany with her great resources of iron and coal is turned into a poorhouse. . . .

The Potsdam Agreement, concluded only a few months after the surrender, bound the occupying powers to restore local self-government and to introduce elective and representative principles into the regional, provincial, and state administration as rapidly as was consistent with military security and the purposes of the military occupation.

The principal purposes of the military occupation were and are to demilitarize and de-Nazify Germany but not to raise artificial barriers to the efforts of the German people to resume their peacetime economic life.

The Nazi war criminals were to be punished for the suffering they brought to the world. The policy of reparations and industrial disarmament prescribed in the Potsdam Agreement was to be carried out. But the purpose of the occupation did not contemplate a prolonged foreign dictatorship of Germany's peacetime economy or a prolonged foreign dictatorship of Germany's internal political life. The Potsdam Agreement expressly bound the occupying powers to start building a political democracy from the ground up.

The Potsdam Agreement did not provide that there should never be a central German government; it merely provided that for the time being there should be no central German government. Certainly this only meant that no central government should be established until some sort of democracy was rooted in the soil of Germany and some sense of local responsibility developed.

The Potsdam Agreement wisely provided that administration of the affairs of Germany should be directed toward decentralization of the political structure and the development of local responsibility. This was not intended to prevent progress toward a central government with the powers necessary to deal with matters which would be dealt with on a nation-wide basis. But it was intended to prevent the establishment of a strong central government dominating the

German [s—Eds.] . . . instead of being responsible to their democratic will. . . .

But of course the question for us will be: What force is needed to make certain that Germany does not rearm as it did after the first World War? Our proposal for a treaty with the major powers to enforce for 25 or even 40 years the demilitarization plan finally agreed upon in the peace settlement would have made possible a smaller army of occupation. For enforcement we could rely more upon a force of trained inspectors and less upon infantry. . . .

It is the view of the American Government that the provisional government should not be handpicked by other governments. It should be a German national council composed of the democratically responsible minister presidents or other chief officials of the several states or provinces which have been established in each of the four zones.

Subject to the reserved authority of the Allied Control Council, the German National Council should be responsible for the proper functioning of the central administrative agencies. Those agencies should have adequate power to assure the administration of Germany as an economic unit, as was contemplated by the Potsdam Agreement.

The German National Council should also be charged with the preparation of a draft of a federal constitution for Germany which, among other things, should insure the democratic character of the new Germany and the human rights and fundamental freedoms of all its inhabitants.

After approval in principle by the Allied Control Council, the proposed constitution should be submitted to an elected convention for final drafting and then submitted to the German people for ratification. . . .

At Potsdam specific areas which were part of Germany were provisionally assigned to the Soviet Union and to Poland, subject to the final decisions of the Peace Conference. At that time these areas were being held by the Soviet and Polish armies. We were told that Germans in large numbers were fleeing from these areas and that it would in fact, because of the feelings aroused by the war, be difficult to reorganize the economic life of these areas if they were not administered as integral parts in the one case of the Soviet Union and in the other case of Poland. . . .

The Soviets and the Poles suffered greatly at the hands of Hitler's invading armies. As a result of the agreement at Yalta, Poland ceded

to the Soviet Union territory east of the Curzon Line. Because of
this, Poland asked for revision of her northern and western frontiers.
The United States will support a revision of these frontiers in Poland's
favor. However, the extent of the area to be ceded to Poland must
be determined when the final settlement is agreed upon.

The United States does not feel that it can deny to France, which
has been invaded three times by Germany in 70 years, its claim to
the Saar territory, whose economy has long been closely linked with
France. Of course, if the Saar territory is integrated with France she
should readjust her reparation claims against Germany. . . .

The United States will favor such control over the whole of Germany, including the Ruhr and the Rhineland, as may be necessary
for security purposes. It will help to enforce those controls. But it
will not favor any controls that would subject the Ruhr and the Rhineland to political domination or manipulation of outside powers. . . .

The United States has returned to Germany practically all prisoners
of war that were in the United States. We are taking prompt steps
to return German prisoners of war in our custody in other parts of
the world.

The United States cannot relieve Germany from the hardships
inflicted upon her by the war her leaders started. But the United
States has no desire to increase those hardships or to deny the
German people an opportunity to work their way out of those
hardships so long as they respect human freedom and follow the
paths of peace.

The American people want to return the government of Germany
to the German people. The American people want to help the
German people to win their way back to an honorable place among
the free and peace-loving nations of the world.

CONFIDENTIAL LETTER OF WALLACE TO TRUMAN

30 ◄§ AMERICAN LIBERALS were divided over what stance the
nation should assume toward Russia. Leader of those who
favored conciliation was Secretary of Commerce Henry A. Wallace.
Wallace had been Secretary of Agriculture during Roosevelt's first
two terms and his choice for Vice-President in 1940. In 1944
pressure from conservative Democrats forced Wallace from the
national ticket, and he moved to the Commerce Department. On
July 23, 1946, Wallace wrote a confidential letter to Truman:[30]

30 Excerpts reprinted from The New York Times, September 18, 1946, p. 2.

How do American actions since V-J Day appear to other nations? I mean by actions the concrete things like $13,000,000,000 for the War and Navy Departments, the Bikini tests of the atomic bomb and continued production of bombs, the plan to arm Latin America with our weapons, production of B-29's and planned production of B-36's and the effort to secure air bases spread over half the globe from which the other half of the globe can be bombed. I cannot but feel that these actions must make it look to the rest of the world as if we were only paying lip service to peace at the conference table.

These facts rather make it appear either (1) that we are preparing ourselves to win the war which we regard as inevitable or (2) that we are trying to build up a predominance of force to intimidate the rest of mankind. How would it look to us if Russia had the atomic bomb and we did not, if Russia had 10,000-mile bombers and air bases within 1,000 miles of our coastlines, and we did not?

Some of the military men and self-styled "realists" are saying: "What's wrong with trying to build up a predominance of force. The only way to preserve peace is for this country to be so well armed that no one will dare attack us. We know that America will never start a war."

The flaw in this policy is simply that it will not work. In a world of atomic bombs and other revolutionary weapons, such as radio-active poison gases and biological warfare, a peace maintained by a predominance of force is no longer possible.

There is, however, a fatal defect in the Moscow statement, in the Acheson report and in the American plan recently presented to the United Nations Atomic Energy Commission. That defect is the scheme, as it is generally understood, of arriving at international agreements by "many stages," of requiring other nations to enter into binding commitments not to conduct research into the military uses of atomic energy and to disclose their uranium and thorium resources while the United States retains the right to withhold its technical knowledge of atomic energy until the international control and inspection system is working to our satisfaction.

In other words, we are telling the Russians that if they are "good boys" we may eventually turn over our knowledge of atomic energy to them and to the other nations. But there is no objective standard of what will qualify them as being "good" nor any specified time for sharing our knowledge.

Is it any wonder that the Russians did not show any great enthusiasm for our plan? Would we have been enthusiastic if the Russians had a monopoly of atomic energy, and offered to share the information with us at some indefinite time in the future at their discretion if we agreed now not to try to make a bomb and give them information on our secret resources of uranium and thorium? I think we would react as the Russians appear to have done. We would have put up counter-proposals for the record, but our real efforts would go into trying to make a bomb so that our bargaining position would be equalized. That is the essence of the Russian position, which is very clearly stated in the Pravda article of June 24, 1946.

It is perfectly clear that the "step-by-step plan" in any such one-sided form is not workable. The entire agreement will have to be worked out and wrapped up in a single package. This may involve certain steps or stages, but the timing of such steps must be agreed to in the initial master treaty. . . .

Insistence on our part that the game must be played our way will only lead to a deadlock. The Russians will redouble their efforts to manufacture bombs, and they may also decide to expand their "security zone" in a serious way. Up to now, despite all our outcries against it, their efforts to develop a security zone in Eastern Europe and in the Middle East are small change from the point of view of military power as compared with our air bases in Greenland, Okinawa and many other places thousands of miles from our shores. We may feel very self-righteous if we refuse to budge on our plan and the Russians refuse to accept it, but that means only one thing—the atomic armament race is on in deadly earnest.

I am convinced therefore that if we are to achieve our hopes of negotiating a treaty which will result in effective international atomic disarmaments we must abandon the impractical form of the "step-by-step" idea which was presented to the United Nations Atomic Energy Commission. We must be prepared to reach an agreement which will commit us to disclosing information and destroying our bombs at a specified time or in terms of specified actions by other countries, rather than at our unfettered discretion. If we are willing to negotiate on this basis, I believe the Russians will also negotiate seriously with a view to reaching an agreement.

There can be, of course, no absolute assurance the Russians will finally agree to a workable plan if we adopt this view. They may prefer to stall until they also have bombs and can negotiate on a more equal basis, not realizing the danger to themselves as well as the rest of the world in a situation in which several nations have atomic bombs.

But we must make the effort to head off the atomic bomb race. We have everything to gain by doing so, and do not give up anything by adopting this policy as the fundamental basis for our negotiation. During the transition period toward full-scale international control, we retain our technical know-how, and the only existing production plants for fissionable materials and bombs remain within our borders.

The Russian counter-proposal itself is an indication that they may be willing to negotiate seriously if we are. In some respects their counter-proposal goes even further than our plan and is in agreement with the basic principles of our plan, which is to make violations of the proposed treaty a national and international crime for which individuals can be punished.

I should list the factors which make for Russian distrust of the United States and of the Western world as follows:

The first is Russian history, which we must take into account because it is the setting in which Russians see all actions and policies of the rest of the world. Russian history for over a thousand years has been a succession of attempts, often unsuccessful, to resist invasion and conquest—by the Mongols, the Turks, the Swedes, the Germans and the Poles.

The scant thirty years of the existence of the Soviet Government has in Russian eyes been a continuation of their historical struggle for national existence. The first four years of the new regime, from 1917 through 1921, were spent in resisting attempts at destruction by the Japanese, the British and French, with some American assistance, and by the several White Russian armies encouraged and financed by the Western powers.

Then, in 1941, the Soviet state was almost conquered by the Germans after a period during which the Western European powers had apparently acquiesced in the rearming of Germany in the belief that the Nazis would seek to expand eastward rather than westward. The Russians, therefore, obviously see themselves as fighting for their existence in a hostile world.

Second, it follows that to the Russians all of the defense and security measures of the Western powers seem to have an aggressive intent. Our actions to expand our military security system—such steps as extending the Monroe Doctrine to include the arming of the Western Hemisphere nations, our present monopoly of the atomic bomb, our interest in outlying bases and our general support of the British Empire—appear to them as going far beyond the requirements of defense.

I think we might feel the same if the United States were the only capitalistic country in the world, and the principal socialistic countries were creating a level of armed strength far exceeding anything in their previous history. From the Russian point of view, also, the granting of a loan to Britain and the lack of tangible results on their request to borrow for rehabilitation purposes may be regarded as another evidence of strengthening of an anti-Soviet bloc.

Finally, our resistance to her attempts to obtain warm water ports and her own security system in the form of "friendly" neighboring states seems, from the Russian point of view, to clinch the case. After twenty-five years of isolation and after having achieved the status of a major power, Russia believes that she is entitled to recognition of her new status. Our interest in establishing democracy in Eastern Europe, where democracy by and large has never existed, seems to her an attempt to re-establish the encirclement of unfriendly neighbors which was created after the last war and which might serve as a springboard of still another effort to destroy her.

If this analysis is correct, and there is ample evidence to support it, the action to improve the situation is clearly indicated. The fundamental objective of such action should be to allay any reasonable Russian grounds for fear, suspicion and distrust. We must recognize that the world has changed and that today there can be no "One World" unless the United States and Russia can find some way of living together.

For example, most of us are firmly convinced of the soundness of our position when we suggest the internationalization and defortification of the Danube or of the Dardanelles, but we would be horrified and angered by any Russian counter-proposal that would involve also the internationalizing and disarming of Suez or Panama. We must recognize that to the Russians these seem to be identical situations.

We should ascertain from a fresh point of view what Russia believes to be essential to her own security as a prerequisite to the writing of the peace and to cooperation in the construction of a world order. We should be prepared to judge her requirements against the background of what we ourselves and the British have insisted upon as essential to our respective security. We should be prepared, even at the expense of risking epithets of appeasement, to agree to reasonable

Russian guarantees of security. The progress made during June and July on the Italian and other treaties indicates that we can hope to arrive at understanding and agreement on this aspect of the problem.

We should not pursue further the question of the veto in connection with atomic energy, a question which is irrelevant and should never have been raised. We should be prepared to negotiate a treaty which will establish a definite sequence of events for the establishment of international control and development of atomic energy. This, I believe, is the most important single question, and the one on which the present trend is definitely toward deadlock rather than ultimate agreement.

We should make an effort to counteract the irrational fear of Russia which is being systematically built up in the American people by certain individuals and publications. The slogan that communism and capitalism, regimentation and democracy, cannot continue to exist in the same world is, from a historical point of view, pure propaganda. . . .

It is of the greatest importance that we should discuss with the Russians in a friendly way their long-range economic problems and the future of our cooperation in matters of trade. The reconstruction program of the U.S.S.R. and the plans for the full development of the Soviet Union offer tremendous opportunities for American goods and American technicians. . . .

I think that progressive leadership along the lines suggested above would represent and best serve the interests of the large majority of our people, would reassert the forward-looking position of the Democratic party in international affairs, and finally, would arrest the new trend toward isolationism and a disastrous atomic world war.

WALLACE ADDRESS ON FOREIGN POLICY

31 ⊷§   WHILE SECRETARY BYRNES was in Paris at the meeting of
        the Council of Foreign Ministers, Wallace, on September
12, delivered an address on foreign policy:[31]

. . . We must not let British balance-of-power manipulations determine whether and when the United States gets into war. . . .

In this connection, I want one thing clearly understood. I am neither anti-British nor pro-British—neither anti-Russian nor pro-

[31] Excerpts from speech by Secretary Wallace, September 12, 1946, Schindler Papers, Truman Library.

Russian. And just two days ago, when President Truman read these words, he said that they represented the policy of his administration.

I plead for an America vigorously dedicated to peace—just as I plead for opportunities for the next generation throughout the world to enjoy the abundance which now, more than ever before, is the birthright of man.

To achieve lasting peace, we must study in detail just how the Russian character was formed—by invasions of Tartars, Mongols, Germans, Poles, Swedes, and French; by the czarist rule based on ignorance, fear and force; by the intervention of the British, French and Americans in Russian affairs from 1919 to 1921; by the geography of the huge Russian land mass situated strategically between Europe and Asia; and by the vitality derived from the rich Russian soil and the strenuous Russian climate. Add to all this the tremendous emotional power which Marxism and Leninism gives to the Russian leaders—and then we can realize that we are reckoning with a force which cannot be handled successfully by a "Get tough with Russia" policy. "Getting tough" never bought anything real and lasting— whether for schoolyard bullies or businessmen or world powers. The tougher we get, the tougher the Russians will get.

Throughout the world there are numerous reactionary elements which had hoped for Axis victory—and now profess great friendship for the United States. Yet, these enemies of yesterday and false friends of today continually try to provoke war between the United States and Russia. They have no real love of the United States. They only long for the day when the United States and Russia will destroy each other.

We must not let our Russian policy be guided or influenced by those inside or outside the United States who want war with Russia. This does not mean appeasement.

We most earnestly want peace with Russia—but we want to be met half way. We want cooperation. And I believe that we can get cooperation once Russia understands that our primary objective is neither saving the British Empire nor purchasing oil in the Near East with the lives of American soldiers. We cannot allow national oil rivalries to force us into war. All of the nations producing oil, whether inside or outside of their own boundaries, must fulfill the provisions of the United Nations Charter and encourage the development of world petroleum reserves so as to make the maximum amount of oil available to all nations of the world on an equitable peaceful basis—and not on the basis of fighting the next war.

For her part, Russia can retain our respect by cooperating with the United Nations in a spirit of openminded and flexible give-and-take.

The real peace treaty we now need is between the United States and Russia. On our part, we should recognize that we have no more business in the *political* affairs of Eastern Europe than Russia has in the *political* affairs of Latin America, Western Europe and the United States. We may not like what Russia does in Eastern Europe. Her type of land reform, industrial expropriation, and suppression of basic liberties offends the great majority of the people of the United States. But whether we like it or not the Russians will try to socialize their sphere of influence just as we try to democratize our sphere of influence. This applies also to Germany and Japan. We are striving to democratize Japan and our area of control in Germany, while Russia strives to socialize eastern Germany. . . .

The Russians have no more business in stirring up native communists to political activity in Western Europe, Latin America and the United States than we have in interfering in the politics of Eastern Europe and Russia. We know what Russia is up to in Eastern Europe, for example, and Russia knows what we are up to. We cannot permit the door to be closed against our trade in Eastern Europe any more than we can in China. But at the same time we have to recognize that the Balkans are closer to Russia than to us—and that Russia cannot permit either England or the United States to dominate the politics of that area.

China is a special case and although she holds the longest frontier in the world with Russia, the interests of world peace demand that China remain free from any sphere of influence, either politically or economically. . . .

Under friendly peaceful competition the Russian world and the American world will gradually become more alike. The Russians will be forced to grant more and more of the personal freedoms; and we shall become more and more absorbed with the problems of social-economic justice.

Russia must be convinced that we are not planning for war against her and we must be certain that Russia is not carrying on territorial expansion or world domination through native communists faithfully following every twist and turn in the Moscow party line. But in this competition, we must insist on an open door for trade throughout the world. There will always be an ideological conflict—but that is no reason why diplomats cannot work out a basis for both systems to live safely in the world side by side.

Once the fears of Russia and the United States Senate have been allayed by practical regional political reservations, I am sure that concern over the veto power would be greatly diminished. Then the United Nations would have a really great power in those areas which are truly international and not regional. In the world-wide, as distinguished from the regional field, the armed might of the United Nations should be so great as to make opposition useless. Only the United Nations should have atomic bombs and its military establishment should give special emphasis to air power. It should have control of the strategically located air bases with which the United States and Britain have encircled the world. And not only should individual nations be prohibited from manufacturing atomic bombs, guided missiles and military aircraft for bombing purposes, but no nation should be allowed to spend on its military establishment more than perhaps 15 per cent of its budget. . . .

In brief, as I see it today, the World Order is bankrupt—and the United States, Russia and England are the receivers. These are the hard facts of power politics on which we have to build a functioning, powerful United Nations and a body of international law. And as we build, we must develop fully the doctrine of the rights of small peoples as contained in the United Nations Charter. This law should ideally apply as much to Indonesians and Greeks as to Bulgarians and Poles—but practically, the application may be delayed until both British and Russians discover the futility of their methods.

DISMISSAL OF WALLACE

32 ✑ ON THE AFTERNOON of Wallace's scheduled speech, a correspondent at the news conference asked the President whether he had approved it, as Wallace claimed in the text. "I approved the whole speech," responded Truman. Commentators correctly judged the address a repudiation of recent foreign policy and an attack on Byrnes. Truman, retreating from his earlier claim that he had read and agreed with the speech, told newsmen on September 14 that he had intended only to approve "the right of the Secretary of Commerce to deliver the speech. I did not intend to indicate that I approved the speech as constituting a

statement of the foreign policy of this country." The President promised that there would be no "significant change in that policy" without consultation with Byrnes and congressional leaders. Wallace, refusing to be rebuffed, asserted that he would continue to fight to return the nation to the road of peace. Byrnes threatened to resign unless the President fired the Secretary of Commerce. On September 20 the President announced his dismissal of Wallace:[32]

The foreign policy of this country is the most important question confronting us today. Our responsibility for obtaining a just and lasting peace extends not only to the people of this country but to the nations of the world.

The people of the United States may disagree freely and publicly on any question, including that of foreign policy, but the Government of the United States must stand as a unit in its relations with the rest of the world.

I have today asked Mr. Wallace to resign from the Cabinet. It had become clear that between his views on foreign policy and those of the administration—the latter being shared, I am confident, by the great body of our citizens—there was a fundamental conflict. We could not permit this conflict to jeopardize our position in relation to other countries. I deeply regret the breaking of a long and pleasant official association, but I am sure that Mr. Wallace will be happier in the exercise of his right to present his views as a private citizen. I am confirmed in this belief by a very friendly conversation I had with Mr. Wallace on the telephone this morning.

Our foreign policy as established by the Congress, the President, and the Secretary of State, remains in full force and effect without change. No change in our foreign policy is contemplated. No member of the Executive branch of the Government will make any public statement as to foreign policy which is in conflict with our established foreign policy. Any public statement on foreign policy shall be cleared with the Department of State. In case of disagreement, the matter will be referred to me.

As I have frequently said, I have complete confidence in Mr. Byrnes and his delegation now representing this country at the Paris Peace Conference.

[32] Reprinted from *Truman Papers*, 1946, p. 431.

Mr. Byrnes consults with me often, and the policies which guide him and his delegation have my full endorsement.

BYRNES ON U.S.-SOVIET SPLIT

33 ✌ AFTER THE PARIS CONFERENCE, July 29 to October 5, 1946, Secretary Byrnes discussed the cleavage between Russia and America on a national broadcast on October 18:[33]

We must guard against the belief that deep-rooted suspicions can be dispelled and far-reaching differences can be reconciled by any single act of faith. . . .

But if the temple of peace is to be built the idea of the inevitability of conflict must not be allowed to dominate the minds of men and tear asunder a world which God made one.

It is that idea of the inevitability of conflict that is throttling the economic recovery of Europe. It is that idea that is causing artificial tensions between states and within states.

The United States stands for freedom for all nations and for friendship among all nations. We shall continue to reject the idea of exclusive alliances. We shall refuse to gang up against any state.

We stand with all peace-loving, law-abiding states in defense of the principles of the Charter of the United Nations.

Any nation that abides by those principles can count upon the friendship and cooperation of the United States, irrespective of national differences or possible conflict of interests.

No country desires unity among the principal powers more than we or has done more to achieve it. But it must be unity founded on the Charter and not unity purchased at its expense.

We deplore the tendency upon the part of the Soviet Union to regard states which are friendly to us as unfriendly to the Soviet Union and to consider as unfriendly our efforts to maintain traditionally friendly relations with states bordering on the Soviet Union.

We deplore the talk of the encirclement of the Soviet Union. We have it from no less authority than Generalissimo Stalin himself that the Soviet Union is in no danger of encirclement.

During the war the Baltic states were taken over by the U.S.S.R. The Polish frontier and the Finnish frontier have been substantially modified in Russia's favor. Königsberg, Bessarabia, Bukovina, and

[33] Excerpts reprinted from *Department of State Bulletin*, October 27, 1946, pp. 742–3.

Ruthenia are to be given to her. In the Pacific, the Kuriles, Port Arthur, and Sakhalin have been assigned to her. Certainly the Soviet Union is not a dispossessed nation.

We know the suffering and devastation which Nazi aggression brought to the Soviet Union. The American people came to the support of the Soviet Union even before the United States was attacked and entered the war. Our people were allies of the Soviet people during the war. And the American people in time of peace desire to live on terms of friendship, mutual helpfulness, and equality with the Soviet people.

Before the Paris Peace Conference the United States spared no effort to reconcile its views of the proposed treaties with the views of the Soviet Union. Indeed it was the Soviet Union which insisted that our views be reconciled on all questions which the Soviet Union regarded as fundamental before they would consent to the holding of the Conference.

If, therefore, in the Conference we differed on some questions, they were not questions that were fundamental from the Soviet viewpoint.

While there were many issues which attracted little public attention on which the Soviet Union and the United States voted together, it was regrettable that on many issues which did command public attention the Soviet Union and the newly established governments in central and southeastern Europe voted consistently together against all the other states.

Whatever considerations caused this close alignment of the Soviet Union and her Slav neighbors on these issues, other states were not constrained to vote as they did by any caucus or bloc action.

It requires a very imaginative geographic sense to put China or Ethiopia into a Western bloc. And it was quite evident to discerning observers at Paris that not only China and Ethiopia, but Norway and France were particularly solicitous to avoid not only the fact, but the suspicion, of alliance with any Western bloc.

If the voting cleavage at Paris was significant, its significance lies in the fact that the cleavage is not between the United States and the Soviet Union, or between a Western bloc and the Soviet Union. The cleavage is based upon conviction and not upon strategy or hidden design.

I should be less than frank if I did not confess my bewilderment at the motives which the Soviet Delegation attributed to the United

States at Paris. Not once, but many times, they charged that the
United States had enriched itself during the war, and, under the
guise of freedom for commerce and equality of opportunity for the
trade of all nations, was now seeking to enslave Europe economically.

Coming from any state these charges would be regrettable to us.
They are particularly regrettable when they are made by the Soviet
Government to whom we advanced more than 10 billion dollars of
lend-lease during the war and with whom we want to be friendly
in time of peace.

TRUMAN ADDRESS TO UN

34 ◆§   ON OCTOBER 23, 1946, President Truman, retreating from
         the harshness of Byrnes's October speech, minimized East-
West differences in his address to the UN General Assembly:[34]

I have been reading reports from many parts of the world. These
reports all agree on one major point—the people of every nation are
sick of war. They know its agony and its futility. No responsible
government can ignore this universal feeling.

The United States of America has no wish to make war, now or
in the future, upon any people anywhere in the world. The heart
of our foreign policy is a sincere desire for peace. This nation will
work patiently for peace by every means consistent with self-respect
and security. Another world war would shatter the hopes of mankind
and completely destroy civilization as we know it.

I am sure that every delegate in this hall will join me in rejecting
talk of war. No nation wants war. Every nation needs peace.

To avoid war and rumors and danger of war, the peoples of all
countries must not only cherish peace as an ideal but they must
develop means of settling conflicts between nations in accordance
with principles of law and justice. . . .

The war has left many parts of the world in turmoil. Differences
have arisen among the Allies. It will not help us to pretend that this
is not the case. But it is not necessary to exaggerate the differences.

For my part, I believe there is no difference of interest that need
stand in the way of settling these problems and settling them in
accordance with the principles of the United Nations Charter. Above

[34] Excerpts reprinted from *Department of State Bulletin*, November 3, 1946,
pp. 809–11.

all, we must not permit differences in economic and social systems to stand in the way of peace, either now or in the future. To permit the United Nations to be broken into irreconcilable parts by different political philosophies would bring disaster to the world. . . .

Two of the greatest obligations undertaken by the United Nations toward the removal of the fear of war remain to be fulfilled.

First, we must reach an agreement establishing international controls of atomic energy that will ensure its use for peaceful purposes only, in accordance with the Assembly's unanimous resolution of last winter.

Second, we must reach agreements that will remove the deadly fear of other weapons of mass destruction, in accordance with the same resolution.

Each of these obligations is going to be difficult to fulfil. Their fulfilment will require the utmost in perseverance and good faith, and we cannot succeed without setting fundamental precedents in the law of nations. Each will be worth everything in perseverance and good faith that we can give to it. The future safety of the United Nations, and of every member nation, depends upon the outcome.

TRUMAN DOCTRINE

35 ⋖§ THE ECONOMIC BURDENS of the Cold War were heavy. The British government, struggling to restore economic stability, notified the State Department in mid-February that it would have to withdraw all troops and end all military and economic aid to Greece and economic assistance to Turkey by March 31, 1947. President Truman addressed Congress on March 12, 1947, and requested $400 million for the beleaguered nations. His pledge of American aid to contain Communism in Europe became known as the Truman Doctrine. Excerpts from Truman's address follow:[35]

The foreign policy and the national security of this country are involved.

One aspect of the present situation, which I wish to present to you at this time for your consideration and decision, concerns Greece and Turkey.

[35] Reprinted from *Congressional Record*, Eightieth Congress, first session, pp. 1980–1.

The United States has received from the Greek Government an urgent appeal for financial and economic assistance. Preliminary reports from the American economic mission now in Greece and reports from the American Ambassador in Greece corroborate the statement of the Greek Government that assistance is imperative if Greece is to survive as a free nation.

I do not believe that the American people and the Congress wish to turn a deaf ear to the appeal of the Greek Government.

Greece is not a rich country. Lack of sufficient natural resources has always forced the Greek people to work hard to make both ends meet. Since 1940, this industrious and peace-loving country has suffered invasion, 4 years of cruel enemy occupation, and bitter internal strife. . . .

As a result of these tragic conditions, a militant minority, exploiting human want and misery, was able to create political chaos which, until now, has made economic recovery impossible.

Greece is today without funds to finance the importation of those goods which are essential to bare subsistence. Under these circumstances the people of Greece cannot make progress in solving their problems of reconstruction. Greece is in desperate need of financial and economic assistance to enable it to resume purchases of food, clothing, fuel, and seeds. These are indispensable for the subsistence of its people and are obtainable only from abroad. Greece must have help to import the goods necessary to restore internal order and security so essential for economic and political recovery. . . .

The very existence of the Greek state is today threatened by the terrorist activities of several thousand armed men, led by Communists, who defy the Government's authority at a number of points, particularly along the northern boundaries. A commission appointed by the United Nations Security Council is at present investigating disturbed conditions in northern Greece and alleged border violations along the frontier between Greece on the one hand and Albania, Bulgaria, and Yugoslavia on the other.

Meanwhile, the Greek Government is unable to cope with the situation. The Greek Army is small and poorly equipped. It needs supplies and equipment if it is to restore the authority of the Government throughout Greek territory.

Greece must have assistance if it is to become a self-supporting and self-respecting democracy.

The United States must supply this assistance. We have already extended to Greece certain types of relief and economic aid but these are inadequate.

There is no other country to which democratic Greece can turn.

No other nation is willing and able to provide the necessary support for a democratic Greek Government.

The British Government, which has been helping Greece, can give no further financial or economic aid after March 31. Great Britain finds itself under the necessity of reducing or liquidating its commitments in several parts of the world, including Greece.

We have considered how the United Nations might assist in this crisis. But the situation is an urgent one requiring immediate action, and the United Nations and its related organizations are not in a position to extend help of the kind that is required.

. . . It is of the utmost importance that we supervise the use of any funds made available to Greece, in such a manner that each dollar spent will count toward making Greece self-supporting, and will help to build an economy in which a healthy democracy can flourish.

No government is perfect. One of the chief virtues of a democracy, however, is that its defects are always visible and under democratic processes can be pointed out and corrected. The Government of Greece is not perfect. Nevertheless it represents 85 percent of the members of the Greek Parliament who were chosen in an election last year. Foreign observers, including 692 Americans, considered this election to be a fair expression of the views of the Greek people.

The Greek Government has been operating in an atmosphere of chaos and extremism. It has made mistakes. The extension of aid by this country does not mean that the United States condones everything that the Greek Government has done or will do. We have condemned in the past, and we condemn now, extremist measures of the right or the left. We have in the past advised tolerance, and we advise tolerance now.

Greece's neighbor, Turkey, also deserves our attention.

The future of Turkey as an independent and economically sound state is clearly no less important to the freedom-loving peoples of the world than the future of Greece. The circumstances in which Turkey finds itself today are considerably different from those of Greece. Turkey has been spared the disasters that have beset Greece.

And during the war, the United States and Great Britain furnished Turkey with material aid.

Nevertheless, Turkey now needs our support.

Since the war, Turkey has sought financial assistance from Great Britain and the United States for the purpose of effecting that modernization necessary for the maintenance of its national integrity.

That integrity is essential to the preservation of order in the Middle East.

The British Government has informed us that, owing to its own difficulties, it can no longer extend financial or economic aid to Turkey.

As in the case of Greece, if Turkey is to have the assistance it needs, the United States must supply it. We are the only country able to provide that help.

I am fully aware of the broad implications involved if the United States extends assistance to Greece and Turkey, and I shall discuss these implications with you at this time.

One of the primary objectives of the foreign policy of the United States is the creation of conditions in which we and other nations will be able to work out a way of life free from coercion. This was a fundamental issue in the war with Germany and Japan. Our victory was won over countries which sought to impose their will, and their way of life, upon other nations.

To insure the peaceful development of nations, free from coercion, the United States has taken a leading part in establishing the United Nations. The United Nations is designed to make possible lasting freedom and independence for all its members. We shall not realize our objectives, however, unless we are willing to help free peoples to maintain their free institutions and their national integrity against aggressive movements that seek to impose upon them totalitarian regimes. [Applause.] This is no more than a frank recognition that totalitarian regimes imposed on free peoples, by direct or indirect aggression, undermine the foundations of international peace and hence the security of the United States.

The peoples of a number of countries of the world have recently had totalitarian regimes forced upon them against their will. The Government of the United States has made frequent protests against coercion and intimidation, in violation of the Yalta agreement, in Poland, Rumania, and Bulgaria. I must also state that in a number of other countries there have been similar developments.

At the present moment in world history nearly every nation must choose between alternative ways of life. The choice is too often not a free one.

One way of life is based upon the will of the majority, and is distinguished by free institutions, representative government, free elections, guarantees of individual liberty, freedom of speech and religion, and freedom from political oppression.

The second way of life is based upon the will of a minority forcibly imposed upon the majority. It relies upon terror and oppression, a controlled press and radio, fixed elections, and the suppression of personal freedoms.

I believe that it must be the policy of the United States to support free peoples who are resisting attempted subjugation by armed minorities or by outside pressures.

I believe that we must assist free peoples to work out their own destinies in their own way.

I believe that our help should be primarily through economic and financial aid, which is essential to economic stability and orderly political processes.

The world is not static and the status quo is not sacred. But we cannot allow changes in the status quo in violation of the Charter of the United Nations by such methods as coercion, or by such subterfuges as political infiltration. In helping free and independent nations to maintain their freedom, the United States will be giving effect to the principles of the Charter of the United Nations.

It is necessary only to glance at a map to realize that the survival and integrity of the Greek nation are of grave importance in a much wider situation. If Greece should fall under the control of an armed minority, the effect upon its neighbor, Turkey, would be immediate and serious. Confusion and disorder might well spread throughout the entire Middle East.

Moreover, the disappearance of Greece as an independent state would have a profound effect upon those countries in Europe whose peoples are struggling against great difficulties to maintain their freedoms and their independence while they repair the damages of war.

It would be an unspeakable tragedy if these countries, which have struggled so long against overwhelming odds, should lose that victory for which they sacrificed so much. Collapse of free institutions and loss of independence would be disastrous not only for them but for the world. Discouragement and possibly failure would quickly be the lot of neighboring peoples striving to maintain their freedom and independence.

Should we fail to aid Greece and Turkey in this fateful hour, the effect will be far reaching to the West as well as to the East.

We must take immediate and resolute action.

I therefore ask the Congress to provide authority for assistance to Greece and Turkey in the amount of $400,000,000 for the period ending June 30, 1948. In requesting these funds, I have taken into consideration the maximum amount of relief assistance which would be furnished to Greece out of the $350,000,000 which I recently requested that the Congress authorize for the prevention of starvation and suffering in countries devastated by the war.

In addition to funds, I ask the Congress to authorize the detail of American civilian and military personnel to Greece and Turkey, at the request of those countries, to assist in the tasks of reconstruction, and for the purpose of supervising the use of such financial and material assistance as may be furnished. I recommend that authority also be provided for the instruction and training of selected Greek and Turkish personnel. . . .

The seeds of totalitarian regimes are nurtured by misery and want. They spread and grow in the evil soil of poverty and strife. They reach their full growth when the hope of a people for a better life has died.

We must keep that hope alive.

The free peoples of the world look to us for support in maintaining their freedoms.

If we falter in our leadership, we may endanger the peace of the world—and we shall surely endanger the welfare of our own Nation.

Great responsibilities have been placed upon us by the swift movement of events.

I am confident that the Congress will face these responsibilities squarely.

MARSHALL PLAN

36 ◄§ DURING THE WINTER and spring of 1947 the State Department had slowly become aware of Europe's economic collapse. Reports of deterioration and misery soon dashed the hopes for speedy recovery. The Policy Planning Staff started to formulate a plan for European assistance. On May 8 Under Secretary of State Dean Acheson had warned a southern audience that

America might have to support the reconstruction of Europe. The next month, at the Harvard commencement on June 5, the new Secretary of State, George C. Marshall, delivered the momentous address that launched the Marshall Plan (European Recovery Program):[36]

I need not tell you gentlemen that the world situation is very serious. That must be apparent to all intelligent people. I think one difficulty is that the problem is one of such enormous complexity that the very mass of facts presented to the public by press and radio make it exceedingly difficult for the man in the street to reach a clear appraisement of the situation. Furthermore, the people of this country are distant from the troubled areas of the earth and it is hard for them to comprehend the plight and consequent reactions of the long-suffering peoples, and the effect of those reactions on their governments in connection with our efforts to promote peace in the world.

In considering the requirements for the rehabilitation of Europe the physical loss of life, the visible destruction of cities, factories, mines, and railroads was correctly estimated, but it has become obvious during recent months that this visible destruction was probably less serious than the dislocation of the entire fabric of European economy. For the past 10 years conditions have been highly abnormal. The feverish preparation for war and the more feverish maintenance of the war effort engulfed all aspects of national economies. Machinery has fallen into disrepair or is entirely obsolete. Under the arbitrary and destructive Nazi rule, virtually every possible enterprise was geared into the German war machine. Long-standing commercial ties, private institutions, banks, insurance companies and shipping companies disappeared through loss of capital, absorption through nationalization or by simple destruction. In many countries, confidence in the local currency has been severely shaken. The breakdown of the business structure of Europe during the war was complete. Recovery has been seriously retarded by the fact that 2 years after the close of hostilities a peace settlement with Germany and Austria has not been agreed upon. But even given a more prompt solution of these difficult problems, the rehabilitation of the economic structure of Europe quite

36 *Ibid.*, p. A3248.

evidently will require a much longer time and greater effort than had been foreseen.

There is a phase of this matter which is both interesting and serious. The farmer has always produced the foodstuffs to exchange with the city dweller for the other necessities of life. This division of labor is the basis of modern civilization. At the present time it is threatened with breakdown. The town and city industries are not producing adequate goods to exchange with the food-producing farmer. Raw materials and fuel are in short supply. Machinery is lacking or worn out. The farmer or the peasant cannot find the goods for sale which he desires to purchase. So the sale of his farm produce for money which he cannot use seems to him an unprofitable transaction. He, therefore, has withdrawn many fields from crop cultivation and is using them for grazing. He feeds more grain to stock and finds for himself and his family an ample supply of food, however short he may be on clothing and the other ordinary gadgets of civilization. Meanwhile people in the cities are short of food and fuel. So the governments are forced to use their foreign money and credits to procure these necessities abroad. This process exhausts funds which are urgently needed for reconstruction. Thus a very serious situation is rapidly developing which bodes no good for the world. The modern system of the division of labor upon which the exchange of products is based is in danger of breaking down.

The truth of the matter is that Europe's requirements for the next 3 or 4 years of foreign food and other essential products—principally from America—are so much greater than her present ability to pay that she must have substantial additional help, or face economic, social, and political deterioration of a very grave character.

The remedy lies in breaking the vicious circle and restoring the confidence of the European people in the economic future of their own countries and of Europe as a whole. The manufacturer and the farmer throughout wide areas must be able and willing to exchange their products for currencies the continuing value of which is not open to question.

Aside from the demoralizing effect on the world at large and the possibilities of disturbances arising as a result of the desperation of the people concerned, the consequences to the economy of the United States should be apparent to all. It is logical that the United States should do whatever it is able to do to assist in the return of normal economic health in the world, without which there can be no political stability and no assured peace. Our policy is directed not against any country or doctrine but against hunger, poverty, desperation, and chaos. Its purpose should be the revival of a working economy in the world so as to permit the emergence of political and social conditions in which free institutions can exist. Such assistance, I am convinced, must not be on a piecemeal basis as various crises develop. Any assistance that this Government may render in the future should provide a cure rather than a mere palliative. Any government that is willing to assist in the task of recovery will find full cooperation, I am sure, on the part of the United States Government. Any government which maneuvers to block the recovery of other countries cannot expect help from us. Furthermore, governments, political parties, or groups which seek to perpetuate human misery in order to profit therefrom politically or otherwise will encounter the opposition of the United States.

It is already evident that, before the United States Government can proceed much further in its efforts to alleviate the situation and help start the European world on its way to recovery, there must be some agreement among the countries of Europe as to the requirements of the situation and the part those countries themselves will take in order to give proper effect to whatever action might be undertaken by this Government. It would be neither fitting nor efficacious for this Government to undertake to draw up unilaterally a program designed to place Europe on its feet economically. This is the business of the Europeans. The initiative, I think, must come from Europe. The role of this country should consist of friendly aid in the drafting of a European program and of later support of such a program so far as it may be practical for us to do so. The program should be a joint one, agreed to by a number, if not all European nations.

An essential part of any successful action on the part of the United States is an understanding on the part of the people of America of the character of the problem and the remedies to be applied. Political passion and prejudice should have no part. With foresight, and a willingness on the part of our people to face up to the vast responsibility which history has clearly placed upon our country, the difficulties I have outlined can and will be overcome.

SOVIET OBJECTIONS TO MARSHALL PLAN

37 ◄§   THE SOVIET UNION, though invited to participate in the Marshall Plan, soon withdrew from negotiations with other

major European powers and also prevented its satellites from joining the program. Czechoslovakia, which had indicated strong interest, yielded to Russian pressure and retreated.

On July 2, 1947, Foreign Minister Molotov explained some of his nation's objections to the Marshall Plan:[37]

The Soviet government, considering that the Anglo-French plan to set up a special organization for the co-ordination of the economies of European states would lead to interference in the internal affairs of European countries, particularly those which have the greatest need for outside aid, and believing that this can only complicate relations between the countries of Europe and hamper their co-operation, rejects this plan as being altogether unsatisfactory and incapable of yielding any positive results.

On the other hand, the Soviet Union favors the fullest development of economic collaboration between European and other countries on a healthy basis of equality and mutual understanding. . . .

What would the implementation of the Franco-British proposal concerning the setting up of a special organization or of a "steering committee" for the elaboration of a comprehensive European economic program lead to?

It would lead to no good results.

It would lead to Great Britain, France and that group of countries which follows them separating themselves from the other European states and thus dividing Europe into two groups of states and creating new difficulties in the relations between them.

In that case American credits would serve not to facilitate the economic rehabilitation of Europe, but to make use of some European countries against other European countries in whatever way certain strong powers seeking to establish their domination should find it profitable to do so.

The Soviet government considers it necessary to caution the governments of Great Britain and of France against the consequences of such action, which would be directed not toward the unification of the efforts of the countries of Europe in the task of their economic rehabilitation after the war, but would lead to opposite results, which have nothing in common with the real interests of the peoples of Europe.

[37] Excerpts reprinted from The New York Times, July 3, 1947, p. 4.

VISHINSKY'S ATTACK ON U.S. POLICY

38 ✒ ON SEPTEMBER 18, 1947, Andrei Vishinsky, chairman of the Soviet delegation to the UN General Assembly, lashed out at American policy:[38]

A number of newspapers and magazines, mostly American, cry every day and in every way about a new war, systematically promoting this baneful psychological coaxing of public opinion of their countries. The warmongers indulge in propaganda under a smokescreen of cries about strengthening of national defense and the necessity to fight against a war danger which allegedly comes from other countries.

The war-mongering propagandists try by hook and crook to frighten people poorly versed in politics by the fables and vicious fabrications about alleged preparations on the part of the Soviet Union to attack America. They certainly know only too well that they are telling lies, that the Soviet Union is not threatening in any way an attack on any country, that the Soviet Union devotes all its forces to the cause of rehabilitation of the areas that either were destroyed by the war or suffered general damage in the course of war, that the Soviet Union devotes all its efforts to the cause of rehabilitation and further development of its national economy. . . .

As one can judge by a number of signs, the preparation for a new war has already passed the stage of a sheer propaganda, psychological coaxing and war of nerves. Numerous facts prove that in some countries—and this is particularly the case of the United States—the war psychosis is being warmed up by putting into effect practical measures of military and strategical characters together with such organizational and technical measures as the construction of new military bases, relocation of armed forces in accordance with plans of future military operations, expansion of manufacture of new armaments and feverish work for the purpose of improving weapons. . . .

It should be noted that the capitalist monopolies, having secured a decisive influence during the war, retained this influence on the termination of the war, skillfully utilizing for this purpose governmental subsidies and grants of billions of dollars as well as the protection they enjoyed and still are enjoying from the various governmental agencies and organizations. This is facilitated by the close connections

[38] Excerpts reprinted from The New York Times, September 19, 1947, pp. 18–19.

of the monopolies with Senators, members of the government, many of whom very often are either officials or partners in the monopolistic corporations.

Such a state of affairs affects also industrial scientific activity concentrated in the laboratories of various large corporations.

The same can be said with regard to the research in the field of the use of atomic energy. Such capitalistic monopolies like du Pont chemical trust, Monsanto Chemical Company, Westinghouse Company, General Electric, Standard Oil and others are most closely connected with this research work, being complete masters in this field.

Before the war they maintained the closest cartel connections with German trusts, and many cartel agreements contained a clause on the renewal of the exchange of information after the war.

. . . It is by no means accidental that the particularly violent warmongers among them are those who are closely connected with commercial, industrial and financial trusts, concerns and monopolies.

There is no need to name too many of them. It is sufficient to mention some of them, having in view certainly, not their personalities, personal convictions, personal merits and so on—but mainly those social groups, enterprises, industrial, technical, scientific societies whose views and interests these persons represent.

1. Dorn, member of the House of Representatives on May 7 . . .

2. Jordan, the president of the National Industrial Conference . . .

3. Earle, former United States Minister in Hungary and Bulgaria . . .

4. Eaton, chairman of the House of Representatives Committee on Foreign Affairs . . .

5. McMahon, Senator, former Chairman of Congressional Committee on Atomic Energy . . .

6. Brooks, Senator, from Illinois . . .

7. General Deane [former head of U.S. Military Mission in the U.S.S.R.] . . .

9. John Foster Dulles, in a speech delivered on Feb. 10, 1947, in Chicago, urged "a tough foreign policy toward the Soviet Union," declaring that if the U.S.A. does not take up such a course counting on possibility of reaching a compromise with the Soviet Union, then the war is inevitable. In the same speech Dulles boasted that since the collapse of the Roman Empire no nation ever possessed such great superiority of material power as the United States, and urged the United States to utilize this power to promote its ideals.

The meaning of these statements is clear. They are poorly camouflaged instigation for war against the U.S.S.R. This is a provocative attempt to divert attention from the true war-mongers to camouflage their war-mongering activity with a slanderous demagogy about a "social revolution in the whole world" and other rot, expecting the simpletons easily to believe it.

REPORT ON MARSHALL PLAN

39 BY THE FALL OF 1947 the State Department realized that Europe needed immediate economic relief if there was to be any hope for later plans of recovery. The President called a special session of Congress, which appropriated $540 million to rescue Europe. At the same time the elaborate program to win congressional support for the Marshall Plan continued. Shortly after Marshall's Harvard address Truman had appointed three special committees to study the impact on America of the proposed aid to Europe. All three submitted favorable reports. The most important group, the President's Committee on Foreign Aid (chaired by Harriman), consisted of leading citizens, including prominent businessmen. The committee enthusiastically endorsed the Marshall Plan in its report of November 7, 1947:[39]

We believe that the future of Western Europe lies very much in its own hands. No amount of outside aid, however generous, can by itself restore to health the economies of the sixteen nations which met at Paris in July. Except in western Germany, where the United States has direct governmental responsibility, the success of any aid program depends ultimately on hard work and straight thinking by the people and the governments of the European nations themselves. The sixteen nations, and western Germany, comprise over 270,000,000 men and women. They possess great agricultural and industrial resources. Even in its present depressed state, the production of this area is vastly greater than any aid which this country can provide. Such aid must be viewed not as a means of supporting Europe, but as a spark which can fire the engine. . . .

. . . We, who as a nation are enjoying comparative luxury, cannot in good conscience do otherwise [than give aid to Europe—Eds.]. To

[39] Excerpts reprinted from *European Recovery and American Aid: A Report by the President's Committee on Foreign Aid* (Washington, D.C., 1947), pp. 3, 18–21.

withhold our aid would be to violate every moral precept associated with our free government and free institutions.

This moral obligation does not mean blind, unlimited assistance to all who ask for it; nor does it mean that need must be the sole criterion. Aid in any form, public or private, always involves many practical considerations and limitations which temper its kind and quantity. . . .

Our economic self-interest is closely related to the fate of Europe. . . .

The deterioration of the European economy for lack of means to obtain essential imports would force European countries to resort to trade by government monopoly—not only for economic but for political ends. The United States would almost inevitably have to follow suit. The resulting system of state controls, at first relating to foreign trade, would soon have to be extended into the domestic economy to an extent that would endanger the survival of the American system of free enterprise. . . .

But these countries of Western Europe cannot continue unaided to play this role. Their peoples are sorely dissatisfied with their present plight. If by democratic means they do not soon obtain an improvement in their affairs, they may be driven to turn in the opposite direction. Therein lies the strength of the Communist tactic: It wins by default when misery and chaos are great enough. That is why any program for the democratic rehabilitation of Western Europe must overcome not only the complex economic problems resulting from the ravages of war, but also the deliberate sabotage by the Communists who see in the continuance of misery and chaos their best chance for an ultimate victory.

Open ideological war has been declared already by the totalitarian nations and their satellites upon all other nations and peoples believing in individual liberty. It has been called a "cold war." The first major battle in the cold war is being fought now in Western Europe. It is cold only in the sense that guns are not smoking and bombs and guided missiles are not exploding. In every other respect the ideological war of the Communists is as ruthless and as determined a drive to achieve world domination as a hot war. . . .

The quick response of the Western European nations to Secretary Marshall's suggestion is an indication that they regard this economic recovery as necessary to the achievement of these ideals. It is likewise the most recent demonstration that by tradition and inclination West-

crn Europe desires to maintain the democratic concepts of government. But tradition and inclination are not enough. We know that the
democratic system must provide the basic necessities of life now, and
that it must quickly rekindle the hope that by hard work a higher
standard of living is attainable. . . .

Thus broadly the United States' political interest may be defined.
An objective analysis of the situation points conclusively to the need
for courageous constructive action to aid Western Europe, both for its
sake and for our own enlightened self-interest.

CONSERVATIVE ATTACK ON FOREIGN AID

40 ◄§   MUCH OF THE OPPOSITION in Congress to the Marshall Plan
was rooted in fears that the American economy could not
bear the financial burden and that American money was being
poured into the "rat holes" of Europe. Opposed to socialism and
even to government planning, some conservatives concluded that
America was being asked to support alien ways and to "make good
the ruin caused not by war, but by Socialist politicians." Shortly
after Marshall's speech at Harvard, Representative Hubert Ellis of
West Virginia expressed his suspicion and hostility in an address
to the House on July 16, 1947:[40]

. . . Speaker, if there ever was a time when the American people
were justified in yelling with all their might "Stop, thief; police,"
it is at this moment.

The fantastic foreign spending program of this administration is
completely out of hand and going at a pace beyond the comprehension
of the average citizen. The sums are so tremendous and the dangerous
situation is so cleverly hidden by the propaganda methods of the State
Department in its effort to launch a new multi-billion-dollar proposal
for the relief of Europe that what has occurred up until this time
seemingly goes unnoticed.

The fact is, in addition to the lend-lease program of $50,000,000,000
during the war, we have since VJ-day extended credits and relief grants
to foreign governments of approximately $15,000,000,000. This means
merchandise out of the American market. For all this, the result seems
to be that we find Europe in a worse condition than it was at the end
of the war. . . .

[40] Excerpts reprinted from *Congressional Record*, Eightieth Congress, first
session, p. 9049.

A bankrupt and demoralized America can make no contribution to the suffering people of this world.

Before we consider this new proposal, the conduct of our foreign operations by this administration should be fully explored, the facts made known to our people, and the hand of guilt laid on those responsible for the maladministration of our affairs and the ignominious failure of our foreign activities.

TRUMAN'S REQUEST FOR MARSHALL PLAN

41 &§ ON DECEMBER 19, 1947, President Truman, backed by bipartisan support and endorsements by three special committees, asked Congress for the Marshall Plan:[41]

It is of vital importance to the United States that European recovery be continued to ultimate success. The American tradition of extending a helping hand to people in distress, our concern for the building of a healthy world economy which can make possible ever-increasing standards of living for our people, and our overwhelming concern for the maintenance of a civilization of freemen and free institutions, all combine to give us this great interest in European recovery.

The people of the United States have shown, by generous contributions since the end of hostilities, their great sympathy and concern for the many millions in Europe who underwent the trials of war and enemy occupation. Our sympathy is undiminished, but we know that we cannot give relief indefinitely, and so we seek practical measures which will eliminate Europe's need for further relief.

Considered in terms of our own economy, European recovery is essential. The last two decades have taught us the bitter lesson that no economy, not even one so strong as our own, can remain healthy and prosperous in a world of poverty and want.

In the past, the flow of raw materials and manufactured products between western Europe, Latin America, Canada, and the United States has integrated these areas in a great trading system. In the same manner, Far Eastern exports to the United States have helped pay for these goods shipped from Europe to the Far East. Europe is thus an essential part of a world trading network. The failure to revive fully this vast trading system, which has begun to function again since the end of the war, would result in economic deterioration throughout

41 Excerpt, *ibid.*, p. 11749.

the world. The United States, in common with other nations, would suffer.

Our deepest concern with European recovery, however, is that it is essential to the maintenance of the civilization in which the American way of life is rooted. It is the only assurance of the continued independence and integrity of a group of nations who constitute a bulwark for the principles of freedom, justice, and the dignity of the individual.

The economic plight in which Europe now finds itself has intensified a political struggle between those who wish to remain freemen living under the rule of law and those who would use economic distress as a pretext for the establishment of a totalitarian state.

Such a turn of events would constitute a shattering blow to peace and stability in the world. It might well compel us to modify our own economic system and to forego, for the sake of our own security, the enjoyment of many of our freedoms and privileges.

It is for these reasons that the United States has so vital an interest in strengthening the belief of the people of Europe that freedom from fear and want will be achieved under free and democratic governments.

The next few years can determine whether the free countries of Europe will be able to preserve their heritage of freedom. If Europe fails to recover, the peoples of these countries might be driven to the philosophy of despair—the philosophy which contends that their basic wants can be met only by the surrender of their basic rights to totalitarian control.

FINLETTER COMMISSION'S REPORT

42 ◄§   EVEN DURING THE FIRST YEARS of peace, military expenditures exceeded a quarter of the federal budget. Though millions of troops had returned to civilian life and many ships had been put in mothballs, the United States had approximately 1,380,000 men in uniform at the end of 1947. Some in the government, greatly impressed by the atomic bomb and persuaded that the United States would retain its nuclear monopoly for some years, wanted to rely even more heavily on the Air Force for strategic deterrence and so opposed the "balanced-force" concept of Secretary of Defense James V. Forrestal. The President's Air Policy Commission (the Finletter Commission) issued its recommendations on January 1, 1948. The committee, predicting that Russia would not develop an atomic bomb before 1953, called the period

of U.S. nuclear monopoly Phase I and the following period Phase II. Excerpts from the Finletter Commission report follow:[42]

We also must have in being and ready for immediate action a counteroffensive force built around a fleet of bombers, accompanying planes, and long-range missiles which will serve notice on any nation which may think of attacking us that if it does, it will see its factories and cities destroyed and its war machine crushed. The strength of the counteroffensive force must be such that it will be able to make an aggressor pay a devastating price for attacking us. It must, if possible, be so strong that it will be able to silence the attack on the United States mainland and give us the time again to build up our industrial machine and our manpower to go on to win the war. . . .

On first impression it might seem that a major war during this Phase I is unlikely; and this opinion has been expressed to this Commission by high military authorities. The argument is persuasive. Our monopoly of the atomic bomb may make any aggression-minded nation wait until it also has the atomic bomb before it takes on the United States. Moreover, the unrepaired devastation and the fatigue from World War II is a powerful force working for a breathing period from war. There usually is such a breathing period in the unending procession of wars throughout history. Great wars usually happen after the nations have recovered from their wounds and a new generation has forgotten the horror of the previous battles.

However, we cannot be sure. The world situation is dangerous, and our foreign policy is not running away from the danger. This is not to criticize our foreign policy. A nation in the position in which the United States finds itself today has no choice but to follow policies which may lead to friction with other nations. . . .

In neither phase can we have in being a counteroffensive force capable of winning the war outright in the first counterblow. We cannot support in peace a force capable of dominating the enemy's mainland. That would require a nation in arms—a nation as dedicated to war as the United States was at the peak of World War II. What we must have and can support is a reasonably strong defensive establishment to minimize the enemy's blow, but above all a counteroffensive air force in being which will be so powerful that if an aggressor does attack, we will be able to retaliate with the utmost violence and to

[42] Reprinted from *Survival in the Air Age: A Report by the President's Air Policy Commission* (Washington, D.C., 1948), pp. 20-3.

seize and hold the advanced positions from which we can divert the destruction from our homeland to his.

GENERAL CLAY'S PREDICTION OF WAR

43 ◄§ IN 1948 TWO EVENTS widened the East-West split and frightened the United States. The first was the Communist coup d'état in Czechoslovakia in late February. Though Soviet influence on the Czech government had long been strong, and the nation had refused to participate in the Marshall Plan, the coup was shocking. On March 5, in the midst of growing official alarm, General Lucius D. Clay sent a secret message to Washington, D.C., from Berlin:[43]

For many months, based on logical analysis, I have felt and held that war was unlikely for at least ten years. Within the last few weeks, I have felt a subtle change in Soviet attitude which I cannot define but which now gives me a feeling that it may come with dramatic suddenness. I cannot support this change in my own thinking with any data or outward evidence in relationships other than to describe it as a feeling of a new tenseness in every Soviet individual with whom we have official relations. I am unable to submit any official report in the absence of supporting data but my feeling is real. You may advise the Chief of Staff of this for whatever it may be worth if you feel it advisable.

PRESIDENT'S ADDRESS TO CONGRESS

44 ◄§ CLAY'S MESSAGE had provoked a hasty reappraisal of Soviet intentions. Not until ten days later could the Central Intelligence Agency inform the President that war was unlikely in the next sixty days. On March 17, 1948, Truman addressed a joint session of Congress:[44]

Until the free nations of Europe have regained their strength, and so long as Communism threatens the very existence of democracy, the United States must remain strong enough to support those countries of Europe which are threatened with Communist control and police-state rule.

[43] From *The Forrestal Diaries*, ed. Walter Millis (New York: Viking, 1951), p. 387. Reprinted by permission of Princeton University.
[44] Excerpt reprinted from *Department of State Bulletin*, March 28, 1948, p. 420.

I believe that we have learned the importance of maintaining military strength as a means of preventing war. We have found that a sound military system is necessary in time of peace if we are to remain at peace. Aggressors in the past, relying on our apparent lack of military force, have unwisely precipitated war. Although they have been led to destruction by their misconception of our strength, we have paid a terrible price for our unpreparedness.

Universal training is the only feasible means by which the civilian components of our armed forces can be built up to the strength required if we are to be prepared for emergencies. Our ability to mobilize large numbers of trained men in time of emergency could forestall future conflict and, together with other measures of national policy, could restore stability to the world.

The adoption of universal training by the United States at this time would be unmistakable evidence to all the world of our determination to back the will to peace with the strength for peace. I am convinced that the decision of the American people, expressed through the Congress, to adopt universal training would be of first importance in giving courage to every free government in the world.

Third, I recommend the temporary reenactment of selective-service legislation in order to maintain our armed forces at their authorized strength.

Our armed forces lack the necessary men to maintain their authorized strength. They have been unable to maintain their authorized strength through voluntary enlistments, even though such strength has been reduced to the very minimum necessary to meet our obligations abroad and is far below the minimum which should always be available in the continental United States.

We cannot meet our international responsibilities unless we maintain our armed forces. It is of vital importance, for example, that we keep our occupation forces in Germany until the peace is secure in Europe.

There is no conflict between the requirements of selective service for the regular forces and universal training for the reserve components. Selective service is necessary until the solid foundation of universal training can be established. Selective service can then be terminated and the regular forces may then be maintained on a voluntary basis.

The recommendations I have made represent the most urgent steps toward securing the peace and preventing war.

We must be ready to take every wise and necessary step to carry out this great purpose. This will require assistance to other nations. It will require an adequate and balanced military strength. We must be prepared to pay the price of peace, or assuredly we shall pay the price of war.

We in the United States remain determined to seek, by every possible means, a just and honorable basis for the settlement of international issues. We shall continue to give our strong allegiance to the United Nations as the principal means for international security based on law, not on force. We shall remain ready and anxious to join with all nations—I repeat, with all nations—in every possible effort to reach international understanding and agreement.

The door has never been closed, nor will it ever be closed, to the Soviet Union or any other nation which will genuinely cooperate in preserving the peace.

At the same time, we must not be confused about the central issue which confronts the world today.

The time has come when the free men and women of the world must face the threat to their liberty squarely and courageously.

The United States has a tremendous responsibility to act according to the measure of our power for good in the world. We have learned that we must earn the peace we seek just as we earned victory in war, not by wishful thinking but by realistic effort.

At no time in our history has unity among our people been so vital as it is at the present time.

Unity of purpose, unity of effort, and unity of spirit are essential to accomplish the task before us.

Each of us here in this chamber today has a special responsibility. The world situation is too critical, and the responsibilities of this country are too vast, to permit party struggles to weaken our influence for maintaining peace.

The American people have the right to assume that political considerations will not affect our working together. They have the right to assume that we will join hands, whole-heartedly and without reservation, in our efforts to preserve peace in the world.

With God's help we shall succeed.

MARSHALL'S PROTEST ON BERLIN BLOCKADE

45 ⸭ THE SECOND CRISIS of the spring of 1948 occurred in Berlin, the West German outpost one hundred miles behind the

Iron Curtain. A dispute over currency reform in late March led, in April, to Russian harassment of traffic between the city and West Germany. After the United States, Great Britain, and France instituted a new currency on June 23, Russia, in retaliation, closed the routes to the Western zones of Berlin. To bring in needed supplies, the United States started the Berlin airlift, which continued until May 12, 1949, when the Soviets ended the blockade. On July 6, 1948, Secretary Marshall formally protested to Russia:[45]

The United States Government wishes to call to the attention of the Soviet Government the extremely serious international situation which has been brought about by the actions of the Soviet Government in imposing restrictive measures on transport which amount now to a blockade against the sectors in Berlin occupied by the United States, United Kingdom and France. The United States Government regards these measures of blockade as a clear violation of existing agreements concerning the administration of Berlin by the four occupying powers. . . .

These agreements implied the right of free access to Berlin. This right has long been confirmed by usage. It was directly specified in a message sent by President Truman to Premier Stalin on June 14, 1945, which agreed to the withdrawal of United States forces to the zonal boundaries, provided satisfactory arrangements could be entered into between the military commanders, which would give access by rail, road and air to United States forces in Berlin. Premier Stalin replied on June 16 suggesting a change in date but no other alteration in the plan proposed by the President. Premier Stalin then gave assurances that all necessary measures would be taken in accordance with the plan. Correspondence in a similar sense took place between Premier Stalin and Mr. Churchill. In accordance with this understanding, the United States, whose armies had penetrated deep into Saxony and Thuringia, parts of the Soviet zone, withdrew its forces to its own area of occupation in Germany and took up its position in its own sector in Berlin. Thereupon the agreements in regard to the occupation of Germany and Berlin went into effect. The United States would not have so withdrawn its troops from a large area now occupied by the Soviet Union had there been any doubt whatsoever about the observance of its agreed right of free access to its sector of Berlin. The right of the United States to its position in Berlin thus stems from precisely the same source as the right of the Soviet Union. It is impossible to assert the latter and deny the former.

It clearly results from these undertakings that Berlin is not a part of the Soviet zone, but is an international zone of occupation. Commitments entered into in good faith by the zone commanders, and subsequently confirmed by the Allied Control Authority, as well as practices sanctioned by usage, guarantee the United States together with other powers, free access to Berlin for the purpose of fulfilling its responsibilities as an occupying power. The facts are plain. Their meaning is clear. Any other interpretation would offend all the rules of comity and reason.

In order that there should be no misunderstanding whatsoever on this point, the United States Government categorically asserts that it is in occupation of its sector in Berlin with free access thereto as a matter of established right deriving from the defeat and surrender of Germany and confirmed by formal agreements among the principal Allies. It further declares that it will not be induced by threats, pressures or other actions to abandon these rights. It is hoped that the Soviet Government entertains no doubts whatsoever on this point. . . .

The United States Government is therefore obliged to insist that in accordance with existing agreements the arrangements for the movement of freight and passenger traffic between the western zones and Berlin be fully restored. There can be no question of delay in the restoration of these essential services, since the needs of the civilian population in the Berlin area are imperative.

Holding these urgent views regarding its rights and obligations in the United States sector of Berlin, yet eager always to resolve controversies in the spirit of fair consideration for the viewpoints of all concerned, the Government of the United States declares that duress should not be invoked as a method of attempting to dispose of any disagreements which may exist between the Soviet Government and the Government of the United States in respect of any aspect of the Berlin situation.

Such disagreements if any should be settled by negotiation or by any of the other peaceful methods provided for in Article 33 of the Charter in keeping with our mutual pledges as copartners in the United Nations. For these reasons the Government of the United States is ready as a first step to participate in negotiations in Berlin among the four Allied Occupying Authorities for the settlement of any question in dispute arising out of the administration of the city of Berlin. It is, however, a prerequisite that the lines of communication and the movement of persons and goods between the United Kingdom, the United States and the French sectors in Berlin and the Western Zones shall have been fully restored.

VANDENBERG RESOLUTION

46 ⊲§ REKINDLED FEARS of Soviet aggression prodded Great Britain, France, and the Benelux nations to sign a defensive alliance in mid-March 1948. These nations, encouraged by the State Department, then approached the United States for formal support. Truman, already committed to the defense of Western Europe, asked the Senate to "extend to the free nations the support which the situation requires." Since the alliance was militarily impotent (and seemed provocative to Russia), the State Department decided that the new union vitally needed an American endorsement. Though Senator Vandenberg was reluctant to propose a military alliance to the Eightieth Congress, he offered a moderate resolution (Senate Resolution 239), which the Senate overwhelmingly approved on June 11, 1948:[46]

Whereas peace with justice and the defense of human rights and fundamental freedoms require international cooperation through more effective use of the United Nations: Therefore be it

Resolved, That the Senate reaffirm the policy of the United States to achieve international peace and security through the United Nations, so that armed force shall not be used except in the common interest, and that the President be advised of the sense of the Senate that this Government, by constitutional process, should particularly pursue the following objectives within the United Nations Charter:

(1) Voluntary agreement to remove the veto from all questions involving pacific settlements of international disputes and situations, and from the admission of new members.

(2) Progressive development of regional and other collective arrangements for individual and collective self-defense in accordance with the purposes, principles, and provisions of the Charter.

(3) Association of the United States, by constitutional process, with such regional and other collective arrangements as are based on

[46] Reprinted from Congressional Record, Eightieth Congress, second session, pp. 6053-4.

continuous and effective self-help and mutual aid, and as affect its national security.

(4) Contributing to the maintenance of peace by making clear its determination to exercise the right of individual or collective self-defense under article 51 should any armed attack occur affecting its national security.

(5) Maximum efforts to obtain agreements to provide the United Nations with armed forces as provided by the Charter, and to obtain agreement among member nations upon universal regulation and reduction of armaments under adequate and dependable guarantee against violation.

(6) If necessary, after adequate effort toward strengthening the United Nations, review of the Charter at an appropriate time by a general conference called under article 109 or by the General Assembly.

ACHESON ON NATO

47 ⋲§   IN HIS INAUGURAL ADDRESS on January 20, 1949, the President presented a four-point program for foreign policy, including a suggestion (Point Four) for technical assistance to underdeveloped nations. More than a year later Congress lamely responded with an appropriation for $27 million. In his speech Truman had also endorsed arrangements for collective defense, a policy proposal that met a happier fate. In March 1949 the United States successfully brought into being the North Atlantic Treaty Organization (NATO). The signatory nations were those already adhering to the Brussels treaty, plus Canada, Denmark, Iceland, Italy, Portugal, Norway, and the United States. The parties agreed in Article 3 "to maintain and develop their individual and collective capacity to resist armed attack." More important, Article 5 provided "that an armed attack against one or more . . . shall be considered an attack against . . . all"; each "in exercise of the right of individual or collective self-defense recognized by Article 51 [UN Charter —Eds.] . . . will assist . . . by taking . . . such action as it deems necessary, including the use of armed force." On March 18, 1949, Dean Acheson, the new secretary of state, defended the NATO plan of collective security:[47]

[47] Excerpts reprinted from *Department of State Bulletin*, March 27, 1949, pp. 384–8.

The very basis of western civilization, which we share with the other nations bordering the North Atlantic, and which all of us share with many other nations, is the ingrained spirit of restraint and tolerance. This is the opposite of the Communist belief that coercion by force is a proper method of hastening the inevitable. Western civilization has lived by mutual restraint and tolerance. This civilization permits and stimulates free inquiry and bold experimentation. It creates the environment of freedom, from which flows the greatest amount of ingenuity, enterprise, and accomplishment.

These principles of democracy, individual liberty, and the rule of law have flourished in this Atlantic community. They have universal validity. They are shared by other free nations and find expression on a universal basis in the Charter of the United Nations; they are the standards by which its members have solemnly agreed to be judged. They are the elements out of which are forged the peace and welfare of mankind.

Added to this profoundly important basis of understanding is another unifying influence—the effect of living on the sea. The sea does not separate people as much as it joins them, through trade, travel, mutual understanding, and common interests.

For this second reason, as well as the first, North America and Western Europe have formed the two halves of what is in reality one community, and have maintained an abiding interest in each other.

It is clear that the North Atlantic pact is not an improvisation. It is the statement of the facts and lessons of history. We have learned our history lesson from two world wars in less than half a century. That experience has taught us that the control of Europe by a single aggressive, unfriendly power would constitute an intolerable threat to the national security of the United States. We participated in those two great wars to preserve the integrity and independence of the European half of the Atlantic community in order to preserve the integrity and independence of the American half. It is a simple fact, proved by experience, that an outside attack on one member of this community is an attack upon all members. . . .

Successful resistance to aggression in the modern world requires modern arms and trained military forces. As a result of the recent war, the European countries joining in the pact are generally deficient in both requirements. The treaty does not bind the United States to any arms program. But we all know that the United States is now the only democratic nation with the resources and the productive capacity to help the free nations of Europe to recover their military strength.

Therefore, we expect to ask the Congress to supply our European partners some of the weapons and equipment they need to be able to resist aggression. We also expect to recommend military supplies for other free nations which will cooperate with us in safeguarding peace and security.

In the compact world of today, the security of the United States cannot be defined in terms of boundaries and frontiers. A serious threat to international peace and security anywhere in the world is of direct concern to this country. Therefore it is our policy to help free peoples to maintain their integrity and independence, not only in Western Europe or in the Americas, but wherever the aid we are able to provide can be effective. Our actions in supporting the integrity and independence of Greece, Turkey, and Iran are expressions of that determination. Our interest in the security of these countries has been made clear, and we shall continue to pursue that policy.

In providing military assistance to other countries, both inside and outside the North Atlantic pact, we will give clear priority to the requirements for economic recovery. We will carefully balance the military assistance program with the capacity and requirements of the total economy, both at home and abroad.

But to return to the treaty, article 5 deals with the possibility, which unhappily cannot be excluded, that the nations joining together in the pact may have to face the eventuality of an armed attack. In this article, they agree that an armed attack on any of them, in Europe or North America, will be considered an attack on all of them. In the event of such an attack, each of them will take, individually and in concert with the other parties, whatever action it deems necessary to restore and maintain the security of the North Atlantic area, including the use of armed force.

This does not mean that the United States would be automatically at war if one of the nations covered by the pact is subjected to armed attack. Under our Constitution, the Congress alone has the power to declare war. We would be bound to take promptly the action which we deemed necessary to restore and maintain the security of the North Atlantic area. That decision would be taken in accordance with our constitutional procedures. The factors which would have to be considered would be, on the one side, the gravity of the armed attack, on the other, the action which we believed necessary to restore and maintain the security of the North Atlantic area. That is the end to be achieved. We are bound to do what in our honest judgment is necessary to reach that result. If we should be confronted again with a calculated armed attack such as we have twice seen in the twentieth century, I should not suppose that we would decide any action other than the use of armed force effective either as an exercise of the right of collective self-defense or as necessary to restore the peace and security of the North Atlantic area. That decision will rest where the Constitution has placed it.

This is not a legalistic question. It is a question we have frequently faced, the question of faith and principle in carrying out treaties. Those who decide it will have the responsibility for taking all appropriate action under the treaty. Such a responsibility requires the exercise of will—a will disciplined by the undertaking solemnly contracted to do what they decide is necessary to restore and maintain the peace and security of the North Atlantic area. That is our obligation under this article 5. It is equally our duty and obligation to the security of our own country. . . .

Allegations that aggressive designs lie behind this country's signature of the Atlantic pact can rest only on a malicious misrepresentation or a fantastic misunderstanding of the nature and aims of American society. It is hard to say which of these attitudes is more irresponsible and more dangerous to the stability of international life. For misunderstanding on a question so vital to world progress and so easily susceptible of clarification could only be willful or the product of a system that imprisons the human mind and makes it impervious to facts. It is the duty of all those who seriously and realistically wish for peace to refuse to be misled by this type of falsehood and to prevent it from poisoning the atmosphere in which the quest of a happier world must be conducted.

This treaty is designed to help toward the goal envisioned by President Truman when he said:

> . . . As our stability becomes manifest, as more and more nations come to know the benefits of democracy and to participate in growing abundance, I believe that those countries which now oppose us will abandon their delusions and join with the free nations of the world in a just settlement of international differences.

To bring that time to pass, we are determined, on the one hand, to make it unmistakably clear that immediate and effective counter measures will be taken against those who violate the peace and, on the other, to wage peace vigorously and relentlessly.

Too often peace has been thought of as a negative condition—the mere absence of war. We know now that we cannot achieve peace by taking a negative attitude. Peace is positive, and it has to be waged with all our thought, energy and courage, and with the conviction that war is not inevitable. . . .

The United States is waging peace by throwing its full strength and energy into the struggle, and we shall continue to do so.

We sincerely hope we can avoid strife, but we cannot avoid striving for what is right. We devoutly hope we can have genuine peace, but we cannot be complacent about the present uneasy and troubled peace.

A secure and stable peace is not a goal we can reach all at once and for all time. It is a dynamic state, produced by effort and faith, with justice and courage. The struggle is continuous and hard. The prize is never irrevocably ours.

To have this genuine peace we must constantly work for it. But we must do even more. We must make it clear that armed attack will be met by collective defense, prompt and effective.

That is the meaning of the North Atlantic pact.

WALLACE'S ATTACK ON NATO TREATY

48 ✍ HENRY WALLACE, defeated by the voters in 1948 when he ran for the presidency on the Progressive party ticket, continued his criticism of American foreign policy. Opposing the NATO treaty, he spoke on March 27, 1949:[48]

Americans are rightly worried. They sense that the pact, as one writer has put it, is "superseding a one-world organization with a military alliance looking toward the possibility of war in a world split in two."

The first victim of the pact is the United Nations—the one hope for peace.

When Secretary of State Acheson claimed the pact is an essential instrument for strengthening the United Nations, the New York

[48] Excerpt reprinted from *Congressional Record*, Eighty-first Congress, first session, p. A1866.

Post called this the most absurd of all claims, and one columnist called it nauseating. For the clear intention of the pact is to take the place of the United Nations. Mr. [Ernest—Eds.] Bevin and Mr. Churchill have been more frank about this than Acheson. The pact sets up an Atlantic council with a military staff committee in Europe with more power than the UN Security Council. The Atlantic Pact substitutes the divided nations for the United Nations. The military men and the diplomats who put over the pact try to justify it as a regional arrangement under the United Nations Charter.

What kind of region is it that covers everything from the Aleutian Islands in the North Pacific to Africa? Can this hard dividing of the world into two armed camps bring peace?

Stripped of legal verbiage, the North Atlantic military pact gives the United States Army military bases up to the very borders of the Soviet Union.

Recently a national conference was held by the Federal Council of Churches of Christ in America, representing all the Protestant denominations. These Protestant leaders said about the North Atlantic Pact, "No defense alliance should be entered into which might validly appear as aggressive to Russia, as a Russian alliance would undoubtedly appear to us."

As we ponder these words and think of the bases which the Atlantic Pact will set up so close to Russia we cannot afford to forget Russian history. In the last 25 years they have been attacked by foreign armies five separate times. Does anyone imagine that, as they stare across their borders at our jet bombers and our cannon, calm visions of peace will be born in their minds? If we apply Christian behavior and try for a moment to put ourselves in their place the true meaning of the Atlantic Pact will be clear to us. Supposing the Soviets had military bases on the Mexican border? The Canadian border? On Cuba? Could the treaty which put guns in our faces be called a pact of peace? . . .

TAFT'S OBJECTIONS TO THE PACT

49 ◄§ SOME SENATORS, fearful of entanglements and further polarization of the two blocs, opposed NATO. Despite their efforts, only thirteen voted against the treaty, which easily passed on July 21, 1949. Four days later President Truman requested $1.45 billion for military aid to the friends and new allies of the United States; in September Congress granted $1.3 billion. On

July 11, 1949, before the vote on NATO, Senator Robert A. Taft, an old isolationist known fondly as "Mr. Republican," expressed his objections to the treaty:[49]

It is with great regret that I have come to my conclusion, but I have come to it because I think the pact carries with it an obligation to assist in arming, at our expense, the nations of western Europe, because with that obligation I believe it will promote war in the world rather than peace, and because I think that with the arms plan it is wholly contrary to the spirit of the obligations we assumed in the United Nations Charter. I would vote for the pact if a reservation were adopted denying any legal or moral obligation to provide arms.

The purpose of American foreign policy, as I see it, is to maintain the freedom of the people of this country and, insofar as consistent with that purpose, to keep this country at peace. We are, of course, interested in the welfare of the rest of the world because we are a humane nation. Our huge economic aid, however, is based on the belief that a world which is prosperous and well off is less likely to engage in war than one in which there are great inequities in the economic condition of different people. . . .

. . . The present treaty obligates us to go to war if certain facts occur. The Monroe Doctrine imposed no obligation whatever to assist any American Nation by giving it arms or even economic aid. We were free to fight the war in such a manner as we might determine, or not at all. This treaty imposes on us a continuous obligation for 20 years to give aid to all the other members of the pact, and, I believe, to give military aid to all the other members of the pact.

All kinds of circumstances may arise which will make our obligation most inconvenient. The government of one of these nations may be taken over by the Communist Party of that nation. The distinguished Senator from Michigan [Vandenberg—Eds.] says that we are then released from our obligation, but I see no basis whatever for such a conclusion. If that were true of a Communist government, it might also be true of a Socialist government if we did not happen to approve of socialism at the time. Presumably, it could be true of a Fascist government, one similar, perhaps, to that existing in Spain which has been denounced recently by the Secretary of State, and which is not very different from the dictatorship of Portugal, which

[49] Excerpts, ibid., pp. 9205–10.

is a member of the pact and which has not a truly democratic form of government.

I cannot find anything in this treaty which releases us because we do not happen to like the officials in charge of the member nations at the particular moment.

Second. The pact standing by itself would clearly be a deterrent to war. If Russia knows that if it starts a war it will immediately find itself at war with the United States, it is much less likely to start a war. I see and believe in the full force of that argument. That is why I would favor the extension of the Monroe Doctrine to Europe. But if Russia sees itself ringed about gradually by so-called defensive arms, from Norway and Denmark to Turkey and Greece, it may form a different opinion. It may decide that the arming of western Europe, regardless of its present purpose, looks to an attack upon Russia. Its view may be unreasonable, and I think it is. But from the Russian standpoint it may not seem unreasonable. They may well decide that if war is the certain result, that war might better occur now rather than after the arming of Europe is completed. . . .

ACHESON ON GERMANY

50 ◁§ GERMANY CONTINUED to be a major divisive issue throughout the Cold War. Though the Berlin blockade ended in May, unification of Germany still seemed impossible. The United States and its allies in Germany sponsored the formation of a government in West Germany. On May 8, 1949, the German Parliamentary Council at Bonn accepted the basic law prescribing a federal system of government. Four months later, on September 7, the West German Parliament convened. The American military government ended later in September, and was replaced by the German High Commission. Early in October, Russia responded by creating the German Democratic Republic in East Germany. Secretary Acheson, speaking on April 28, 1949, explained past differences over Germany and discussed the agreement of the United States, Great Britain, and France that had been reached earlier that month on the German question:[50]

. . . it is the ultimate objective of the United States that the German people, or as large a part of them as possible, be integrated into a

[50] Excerpts reprinted from *Department of State Bulletin*, May 8, 1949, pp. 585–8.

new common structure of the free peoples of Europe. We hope that the Germans will share in due time as equals in the obligations, the economic benefits, and the security of the structure which has been begun by the free peoples of Europe. . . .

This Government made earnest efforts for two and a half years after the war to resolve the major issues arising from the defeat of Germany and to achieve a general settlement. During that period we participated in the four-power machinery for control of Germany established by international agreement in 1945.

By the end of 1947 it appeared that the Soviet Union was seeking to thwart any settlement which did not concede virtual Soviet control over German economic and political life. This was confirmed in two futile meetings of the Council of Foreign Ministers in Moscow and London. It was emphasized in the Allied Control Authority in Berlin, where the Soviet veto power was exercised three times as often as by the three Western Powers combined.

The resultant paralysis of interallied policy and control created an intolerable situation. Germany became divided into disconnected administrative areas and was rapidly being reduced to a state of economic chaos, distress, and despair. Disaster was averted primarily by American economic aid.

The German stalemate heightened the general European crisis. The European Recovery Program could not succeed without the raw materials and finished products which only a revived German economy could contribute.

By 1948 it became clear that the Western Powers could no longer tolerate an impasse which made it impossible for them to discharge their responsibilities for the organization of German administration and for the degree of German economic recovery that was essential for the welfare of Europe as a whole. These powers determined to concert their policies for the area of Germany under their control, which embraced about two thirds of the territory and three fourths of the population of occupied Germany.

These common policies were embodied in the London agreements, announced on June 1, 1948. This joint program, I wish to emphasize, is in no sense a repudiation of our international commitments on Germany, embodied in the Potsdam protocol and other agreements. It represents a sincere effort to deal with existing realities in the spirit of the original Allied covenants pertaining to Germany. . . .

The Germans were authorized to establish a provisional government, democratic and federal in character, based upon a constitution of German inception. It would be subject, in accordance with an occupation statute, to minimum supervision by the occupation authorities in the interest of the general security and of broad Allied purposes for Germany. Coordinated three-power control was to be established, with the virtual abolition of the zonal boundaries.

Of exceptional importance were the guarantees of security against a German military revival, a point sometimes overlooked in present-day talk about the hazards inherent in rebuilding German economic and political life. The London agreement provided that there is to be consultation among the three occupying powers in the event of any threat of German military resurgence; that their armed forces are to remain in Germany until the peace of Europe is secure; that a joint Military Security Board should be created with powers of inspection to insure against both military and industrial rearrangement; that all agreed disarmament and demilitarization measures should be maintained in force; and that long-term demilitarization measures should be agreed upon prior to the end of the occupation. It should be observed that these far reaching safeguards are to accompany the more constructive aspects of the program and assure that the new powers and responsibilities assumed by the Germans may not be abused. . . .

The agreement in Washington on the text of an occupation statute has removed one of the major obstacles to the establishment of the German Federal Republic. The Parliamentary Council met at Bonn on September 1, and has been working diligently to draft a basic law or provisional constitution for a Federal German Government. Since last December its leaders have requested the text of the occupation statute which had been promised to the Parliamentary Council before completion of its work.

The three occupying powers have been discussing the occupation statute since last August. In the course of these many months the draft occupation statute had become a very heavy, complicated, and legalistic document. The three Foreign Ministers approved the text of an occupation statute in a new and simpler form, which was then transmitted to the German Parliamentary Council at Bonn. According to latest reports, all the controversial issues with respect to the basic law have been settled, all differences between the occupying powers and the Germans and among the Germans themselves have been resolved, and a constitution is expected to be approved by the Parliamentary Council by May 15.

The establishment of a German Government does not, and cannot at this time, mean the end of the occupation of Germany. If democratic self-government is to be introduced in Germany it must be given a chance to live. It cannot thrive if its powers are in question, or if it is subject to arbitrary intervention. The occupation statute defines the powers to be retained by the occupying authorities upon the establishment of the German Federal Republic and sets forth the basic procedures for the operation of Allied supervision. . . .

The key issue for the future will be the manner and extent to which the Allied authorities exercise their powers. A practicable basis for cooperation between the Western Allies and the future federal Western government will have to be sought, through which the German people may exercise democratic self-government under the statute.

. . . How long must we be satisfied with interim measures when the people of all countries desperately desire a genuine and lasting peace? Will the moves we are making in Western Germany contribute to a permanent settlement of the German problem? What are the possibilities of renewed four-power talks on Germany? Has the possibility of such talks or the success of their outcome been prejudiced?

In the communiqué announcing the London agreements, released June 6, 1948, it was emphasized that the agreed recommendations in no way precluded, and on the contrary would facilitate, eventual four-power agreement on the German problem. They were designed, it was stated, to solve the urgent political and economic problems arising out of the present situation in Germany.

When this Government embarked, together with its Western Allies, on the discussion of new arrangements for Western Germany, it did not mean that we had abandoned hope of a solution which would be applicable to Germany as a whole or that we were barring a resumption of discussions looking toward such a solution whenever it might appear that there was any chance of success. It did mean that this Government was not prepared to wait indefinitely for four-power agreement before endeavoring to restore healthy and hopeful conditions in those areas of Germany in which its influence could be exerted.

Should it prove possible to arrange for renewed four-power discussions, this Government will do its utmost, as it has in the past, to arrive at a settlement of what is plainly one of the most crucial problems in world affairs. . . .

The people of Europe may rest assured that this Government will agree to no arrangements concerning Germany which do not protect the security interests of the European community.

The people of the United States may rest assured that in any discussions relating to the future of Germany, this Government will have foremost in mind their deep desire for a peaceful and orderly solution of these weighty problems which have been the heart of so many of our difficulties in the postwar period.

TRUMAN ON SOVIET NUCLEAR EXPLOSION

51 ◄§ THE NUCLEAR MONOPOLY of the United States, which some prominent Western scientists had predicted would end between four and five years after Hiroshima, terminated on August 26, 1949. After some hesitation President Truman, on September 23, 1949, announced that there had been an atomic explosion in the Soviet Union:[51]

I believe the American people, to the fullest extent consistent with national security, are entitled to be informed of all developments in the field of atomic energy. That is my reason for making public the following information.

We have evidence that within recent weeks an atomic explosion occurred in the U.S.S.R.

Ever since atomic energy was first released by man, the eventual development of this new force by other nations was to be expected. This probability has always been taken into account by us.

Nearly 4 years ago I pointed out that "scientific opinion appears to be practically unanimous that the essential theoretical knowledge upon which the discovery is based is already widely known. There is also substantial agreement that foreign research can come abreast of our present theoretical knowledge in time." And, in the Three-Nation Declaration of the President of the United States and the Prime Ministers of the United Kingdom and of Canada, dated November 15, 1945, it was emphasized that no single nation could in fact have a monopoly of atomic weapons.

This recent development emphasizes once again, if indeed such

[51] Reprinted from *Truman Papers,* 1949, p. 485.

emphasis were needed, the necessity for that truly effective enforceable international control of atomic energy which this Government and the large majority of the members of the United Nations support.

OPPENHEIMER ON HYDROGEN BOMB

52 ⸗§   THE ADMINISTRATION, fearful once it had lost the nuclear monopoly, considered building a more powerful bomb. After a few months, on January 31, 1950, President Truman announced that he had directed the U.S. Atomic Energy Commission "to continue its work on all forms of atomic weapons, including the so-called hydrogen or super-bomb." As Commander in Chief, Truman explained, it "is part of my responsibility . . . to see to it that our country is able to defend itself against any possible aggressor." J. Robert Oppenheimer, then chairman of the General Advisory Committee (a scientific panel) to the AEC, later discussed the decision to build the hydrogen bomb. His recollections are from testimony given during his security hearings in 1954:[52]

. . . No serious controversy arose about the super until the Soviet explosion of an atomic bomb in the autumn of 1949.

Shortly after that event, in October 1949, the Atomic Energy Commission called a special session of the General Advisory Committee and asked us to consider and advise on two related questions: First, whether in view of the Soviet success the Commission's program was adequate, and if not, in what way it should be altered or increased; second, whether a crash program for the development of the super should be a part of any new program. The committee considered both questions, consulting various officials from the civil and military branches of the executive departments who would have been concerned, and reached conclusions which were communicated in a report to the Atomic Energy Commission in October 1949.

This report, in response to the first question that had been put to us, recommended a great number of measures that the Commission should take to increase in many ways our overall potential in weapons.

As to the super itself, the General Advisory Committee stated its unanimous opposition to the initiation by the United States of a crash program of the kind we had been asked to advise on. The report of that meeting, and the Secretary's notes, reflect the reasons which

[52] Excerpt reprinted from In the Matter of J. Robert Oppenheimer, pp. 81, 87.

moved us to this conclusion. The annexes, in particular, which dealt more with political and policy considerations—the report proper was essentially technical in character—indicated differences in the views of members of the committee. There were two annexes, one signed by [Isadore I.—Eds.] Rabi and Fermi, the other by Conant, [Lee—Eds.] DuBridge, [Henry DeWolf—Eds.] Smyth, [Hartley—Eds.] Rowe, [Oliver E.—Eds.] Buckley and myself. (The ninth member of the committee, [Glenn T.—Eds.] Seaborg, was abroad at the time.)

It would have been surprising if eight men considering a problem of extreme difficulty had each had precisely the same reasons for the conclusion in which we joined. But I think I am correct in asserting that the unanimous opposition we expressed to the crash program was based on the conviction, to which technical considerations as well as others contributed, that because of our overall situation at that time such a program might weaken rather than strengthen the position of the United States.

KENNAN ON NUCLEAR ARSENAL

53 ◀§ AT OPPENHEIMER'S SECURITY HEARINGS, George F. Kennan also discussed his attitudes toward the improvement of the U.S. nuclear arsenal:[53]

[Mr. Gordon Gray, chairman, Personnel Security Board—Eds.]: I would like to move back to the question of your attitudes toward the development of the hydrogen bomb in the period before the President's decision to proceed in January of 1950. Had you been told, Mr. Kennan, in 1949, for example, by a scientist whose judgment and capability you respected that it was probable that a thermonuclear weapon could be developed which would be more economical in terms of the use of material and cost and the rest of it than the equivalent number of atom bombs, would you have then been in favor of developing the hydrogen bomb?

The WITNESS: I would not have favored developing it at least until a real decision had been made in this Government about the role which atomic weapons were to play generally in its arsenal of weapons. I would have had great doubts then about the soundness of doing it. That comes from philosophic considerations partly which I exposed to the Secretary of State, which did not I might say meet with his agreement or with that of most of my colleagues and the

53 Excerpt, ibid., pp. 366–7.

future will have to tell, but it seemed to me at the end of this atomic weapons race, if you pursued it to the end, we building all we can build, they building all they can build, stands the dilemma which is the mutually destructive quality of these weapons, and it was very dangerous for us to get our public before the dilemma, that the public mind will not entertain the dilemma, and people will take refuge in irrational and unsuitable ideas as to what to do.

For that reason I have always had the greatest misgivings about the attempt to insure the security of this country by an unlimited race in the cultivation of these weapons of mass destruction and have felt that the best we could do in a world where no total security is possible is to hold just enough of these things to make it a very foolish thing for the Russians or anybody else to try to use them against us.

Mr. GRAY: So you would have been in favor of stopping production of the A bomb after we had reached a certain point with respect to the stockpile?

The WITNESS: That is correct.

Mr. GRAY: Whatever that might have been?

The WITNESS: No; and I didn't consider myself competent to determine exactly what that point was. I have never known the number of our bombs nor the real facts of their destructiveness or any of those things.

Mr. GRAY: Knowing the Russians as you do—perhaps as well as any American—would you have expected them to continue to improve whatever weapons they may have within limitations of economy, scientific availability and so forth?

The WITNESS: My estimate is that they would have cultivated these weapons themselves primarily for the purpose of seeing that they were not used, and would have continued to lay their greatest hopes for the expansion of their power on the police weapons, the capacity to absorb contiguous areas, and on the conventional armaments as a means of intimidating other people and perhaps fighting if they have to fight.

ACHESON'S DISCUSSION OF SOVIET POLICY

54 ↭ ON MARCH 16, 1950, just three months before the Korean War, Secretary Acheson outlined the changes in Soviet policy that the American government desired:[54]

[54] Excerpts reprinted from Department of State, *Strengthening the Forces of Freedom* (Washington, D.C., 1950), pp. 21–8.

We can see no moral compromise with the contrary theses of international Communism: that the end justifies the means, that any and all methods are therefore permissible, and that the dignity of the human individual is of no importance as against the interests of the state. . . .

· It is now nearly 5 years since the end of hostilities, and the victorious Allies have been unable to define the terms of peace with the defeated countries. This is a grave, a deeply disturbing fact. For our part, we do not intend nor wish, in fact we do not know how, to create satellites. Nor can we accept a settlement which would make Germany, Japan, or liberated Austria satellites of the Soviet Union. The experience in Hungary, Rumania, and Bulgaria has been one of bitter disappointment and shocking betrayal of the solemn pledges by the wartime Allies. The Soviet leaders joined in the pledge at Tehran that they looked forward "with confidence to the day when all peoples of the world may live free lives, untouched by tyranny, and according to their varying desires and their own consciences." We can accept treaties of peace which would give reality to this pledge and to the interests of all in security.

With regard to Germany, unification under a government chosen in free elections under international observation is a basic element in an acceptable settlement. With that need recognized and with a will to define the terms of peace, a German treaty could be formulated which, while not pretending to solve all of the complex and bitter problems of the German situation, would, nevertheless, go far toward a relaxation of a set of major tensions. . . .

In the Far East, generally, there are many points where the Soviet leaders could, if they chose, relax tensions. They could, for example, permit the United Nations Commission in Korea to carry out its duties by allowing the Commission's entry into North Korea and by accepting its report as the basis for a peaceful settlement of that liberated country's problems. They could repatriate Japanese prisoners of war from Siberian camps. They could refrain from subverting the efforts of the newly independent states of Asia and their native leaders to solve their problems in their own way.

With regard to the whole group of countries which we are accustomed to think of as the satellite area, the Soviet leaders could withdraw their military and police force and refrain from using the shadow of that force to keep in power persons or regimes which do not command the confidence of the respective peoples, freely expressed through orderly representative processes. In other words, they could elect to observe, in practice, the declaration to which they set their signatures at Yalta concerning liberated Europe.

In this connection, we do not insist that these governments have any particular political or social complexion. What concerns us is that they should be truly independent national regimes, with a will of their own and with a decent foundation in popular feeling. We would like to feel, when we deal with these governments, that we are dealing with something representative of the national identity of the peoples in question. We cannot believe that such a situation would be really incompatible with the security of the Soviet Union. . . .

Their policy of walk-out and boycott is a policy that undermines the concept of majority decision. Indeed, they seem deliberately to entrench themselves in a minority position in the United Nations. This was illustrated last fall when they voted against the Essentials of Peace resolution which solemnly restated and reaffirmed the principles and purposes of the United Nations Charter and which pointed to practical steps which members should take to support the peace.

Let the Soviet Union put forward in the United Nations genuine proposals conducive to the work of peace, respectful of the real independence of other governments, and appreciative of the role which the United Nations could and should play in the preservation of world stability and the cooperation of nations. They will, then, doubtless have a majority with them. We will rejoice to see them in such a majority. We will be pleased to be a member of it ourselves.

The Soviet leaders could join us in seeking realistic and effective arrangements for the control of atomic weapons and the limitation of armaments in general. We know that it is not easy for them, under their system, to contemplate the functioning on their territory of an authority in which people would participate who are not of their political persuasion.

If we have not hesitated to urge that they as well as we accept this requirement, it is because we believe that a spirit of genuine responsibility to mankind is widely present in this world. Many able administrators and scientists could be found to operate such an authority who would be only too happy, regardless of political complexion, to take an elevated and enlightened view of the immense responsibility which would rest upon them. There are men who would scorn to use their powers for the negative purpose of intrigue and destruction. We believe that an authority could be established which would not be controlled or subject to control by either ourselves or the Soviet Union.

The Kremlin could refrain from using the Communist apparatus controlled by it throughout the world to attempt to overthrow, by subversive means, established governments with which the Soviet Government stands in an outward state of friendship and respect. In general, it could desist from, and could cooperate in efforts to prevent, indirect aggression across national frontiers—a mode of conduct which is inconsistent with the spirit and the letter of the United Nations Charter. . . .

In general, the Soviet leaders could refrain, I think, from systematically distorting to their own peoples the picture of the world outside their borders, and of our country, in particular. . . .

What are we now to conclude from the morbid fancies which their propaganda exudes of a capitalist encirclement, of a United States craftily and systematically plotting another world war? They know, and the world knows, how foreign is the concept of aggressive war to our philosophy and our political system. They know that we are not asking to be the objects of any insincere and effusive demonstrations of sentimental friendship. But we feel that the Soviet leaders could at least permit access to the Soviet Union of persons and ideas from other countries so that other views might be presented to the Russian people.

These are some of the things which we feel that the Soviet leaders could do which would permit the rational and peaceful development of the coexistence of their system and ours. They are not things that go to the depths of the moral conflict. They are not things that promise the Kingdom of Heaven. They have been formulated by us, not as moralists but as servants of government, anxious to get on with the practical problems that lie before us and to get on with them in a manner consistent with mankind's deep longing for a respite from fear and uncertainty.

Nor have they been formulated as a one-sided bargain. A will to achieve binding, peaceful settlements would be required of all participants. All would have to produce unmistakable evidence of their good faith. All would have to accept agreements in the observance of which all nations could have real confidence.

We want peace, but not at any price. We are ready to negotiate, but not at the expense of rousing false hopes which would be dashed by new failures. We are equally determined to support all real efforts for peaceful settlements and to resist aggression.

The times call for a total diplomacy equal to the task of defense against Soviet expansion and to the task of building the kind of world in which our way of life can flourish. We must continue to press ahead with the building of a free world which is strong in its faith and in its material progress. The alternative is to allow the free nations to succumb, one by one, to the erosive and encroaching processes of Soviet expansion.

We must not slacken, rather we must reinvigorate, the kind of democratic efforts which are represented by the European Recovery Program, the North Atlantic and Rio Pacts, the Mutual Defense Assistance Program, the Point Four Program for developing the world's new workshops, and assistance in creating the conditions necessary to a growing, many-sided exchange of the world's products.

We must champion an international order based on the United Nations and on the abiding principles of freedom and justice, or accept an international society increasingly torn by destructive rivalries.

We must recognize that our ability to achieve our purposes cannot rest alone on a desire for peace but that it must be supported by the strength to meet whatever tasks Providence may have in store for us.

We must not make the mistake, in other words, of using Soviet conduct as a standard for our own. Our efforts cannot be merely reactions to the latest moves by the Kremlin. The bipartisan line of American foreign policy has been and must continue to be the constructive task of building, in cooperation with others, the kind of world in which freedom and justice can flourish. We must not be turned aside from this task by the diversionary thrusts of the Soviet Union. And if it is necessary, as it sometimes is, to deal with such a thrust or the threat of one, the effort should be understood as one which, though essential, is outside the main stream of our policy.

EISENHOWER'S STATEMENT ON "LIBERATION"

55 ◆§   WITHIN A FEW MONTHS the eyes of America again turned to the East, when North Korea invaded South Korea. As American fortunes in the war sagged, Republicans resumed their attacks on the administration's conduct of foreign policy both in Asia and in Europe. Convinced that containment was failing, John

Foster Dulles, chief adviser on foreign policy to General Dwight D. Eisenhower, the Republican nominee in 1952, criticized the response of Truman's government to Russia. The GOP foreign-policy plank, prepared by Dulles, promised that a Republican administration would "mark the end of the negative, futile and immoral policy of 'containment' which abandons countless human beings to a despotism and godless terrorism. . . ." Eisenhower accepted Dulles' thesis, including the future Secretary of State's proposal of "liberation," and on August 25, in an address before the American Legion, the future President expressed his views:[55]

Seven years ago this very month I left the Army with no possible thought that I should ever enter politics. But seven years ago today no one in our whole country would have dreamed that today we would be prey to fear.

Who would have thought as we disbanded that great Army, a great Navy and a great Air Force, that only seven years later America would have to be studying and analyzing the world in terms of fear and concern? We are threatened by a great tyranny—a tyranny that is brutal in its primitiveness. It is a tyranny that has brought thousands, millions of people into slave camps and is attempting to make all humankind its chattel.

Now let America, saddened by the tragedy of lost opportunity, etch in its memory the roll of countries once independent now suffocating under this Russian pall.

Latvia and her million people.

Estonia and her million and a quarter, and Lithuania with more than twice that number.

Poland and her twenty-five million, a country that for centuries has been the bulwark against Tartar savages.

East Germany and her more than seventeen million.

East Austria and her two million.

Czechoslovakia and her twelve million—a nation that was born in the Czechoslovakian councils in America.

Albania and her twelve hundred thousand.

Bulgaria and Rumania and their twenty-three million.

All these people are blood kin to us. How many people today live in a great fear that never again shall they hear from a mother, a grand-

[55] Excerpt reprinted from *The New York Times*, August 26, 1952, p. 12.

father, a brother or a cousin? Dare we rest while these millions of our kinsmen remain in slavery? I can almost hear your answer.

The American conscience can never know peace until these people are restored again to being masters of their own fate.

Not only in Eastern Europe has Communist barbarism broken forth beyond its own borders. On its Asiatic periphery the Kremlin has made captive China and Tibet, Inner Mongolia, Northern Korea, Northern Japan, the northern half of Indo-China its slaves. It has added five hundred million people to its arsenal manpower. . . .

Again I can hear you say the conscience of America shall never be free until these people have opportunity to choose their own paths.

The lands and the millions made captive to the Kremlin are fresh evidence that dire peril stalks every free nation today. Tyranny must feed on new conquests, else it withers away. Using force here and propaganda there, its purpose is conquest. . . .

Still the Soviets have not yet attained a position from which they can accomplish the most important of their objectives. This objective is the economic containment and gradual strangulation of America because the Communists both fear and respect our productive power. Now they know that our productive power, our economic strength is chiefly dependent upon vast quantities of critical materials that we import from other sections of the globe. Their method, therefore, is to infiltrate those areas, to seize them, control them and so deny us those materials that we so badly need in order to sustain our economy and our kind of civilization in order to keep up the American prosperity.

They are therefore preparing this whole great mass of people and of material so that they may surpass our own productive capacity. They are preparing those people psychologically and materially for whatever decision the Kremlin makes—even global war, should war appear to them to be profitable. . . .

We can never rest—and we must so inform all the world, including the Kremlin—that until the enslaved nations of the world have in the fullness of freedom the right to choose their own path, that then, and then only, can we say that there is a possible way of living peacefully and permanently with communism in the world.

We must tell the Kremlin that never shall we desist in our aid to every man and woman of those shackled lands who seeks refuge with us, any man who keeps burning among his own people the flame of freedom or who is dedicated to the liberation of his fellows.

STEVENSON'S CRITICISM OF "LIBERATION"

56 ◄§ ADLAI STEVENSON, the Democratic candidate for the presidency, soon responded to the challenge of Dulles and Eisenhower. On Labor Day, September 1, 1952, speaking before a crowd containing many Americans of Polish descent, he warned the nation of the dangers of "liberation:"[56]

. . . Last week the Republican candidate for President made a speech to the American Legion in New York. His speech aroused speculation here and abroad that if he were elected, some reckless action might ensue in an attempt to liberate the peoples of Eastern Europe from Soviet tyranny.

Many of you here in Hamtramck and in other cities across the country have friends and relatives who are suffering behind the Iron Curtain. Last Thursday I discussed their plight with Representative Machrowicz and others. We agreed that we would all deeply regret it if a false campaign issue were to be built on the hopes and fears of these suffering people and on the anxieties of all Americans for their liberation.

The freedom of the descendants of [Thaddeus—Eds.] Kosciusko and [Jan—Eds.] Masaryk and other heroes of the fight for liberty in Eastern Europe is an issue between all the free nations and the Soviet Union. It should never be an issue between Americans, for we are all united in our desire for their liberation from the oppressor and in confidence that freedom will again be theirs.

But I want to make one thing very plain: Even if votes could be won by it, I would not say one reckless word on this matter during this campaign. Some things are more precious than votes.

The cruel grip of Soviet tyranny upon your friends and relatives cannot be loosened by loose talk or idle threats. It cannot be loosened by awakening false hopes which might stimulate intemperate action that would only lead your brothers to the execution squads; we remember only too well how thousands went to their death in Warsaw but a few short years ago.

It cannot be loosened by starting a war which would lead to untold suffering for innocent people everywhere; such a course could liberate only broken, silent, and empty lands.

[56] Excerpt, *ibid.*, September 2, 1952, p. 11.

We have a responsibility to these suffering peoples. We must continue our efforts to outlaw genocide. We must review our immigration policies. We must help provide better care for those who succeed in escaping from behind the Iron Curtain.

Above all, we must work with others to build strong and healthy societies in the free nations, for we know that the future freedom of Poland, Czechoslovakia, Hungary, Eastern Germany, and the other peoples who have fallen under Soviet rule depends on the outcome of the vast worldwide struggle in which we are engaged.

Not in the ashes of another world war; only in the atmosphere of a peaceful world can the reaffirmation of the right of self-determination have any meaning, or can the enslaved nations be free and independent again.

I have hoped that this political campaign might reaffirm America's dedication to the ideal of freedom and independence for all nations as the only solid foundation for a just and durable peace.

Stalin pledged his word to us to grant these countries liberty after World War Two. He has violated that pledge. But we have not forgotten his pledge and we shall not forget his violation. We will continue to work for the day when all peoples will be free to choose their own government and to walk again erect and unafraid.

I tell you now that I will never fear to negotiate in good faith with the Soviet Union, for to close the door to the conference room is to open a door to war. Man's tragedy has all too often been that he has grown weary in the search for an honorable alternative to war, and, in desperate impatience, has turned to violence.

Action for action's sake is the last resort of mentally and morally exhausted men. The free nations must never tire in their search for peace. They must always be ready to sit down at the conference table, insisting only that any agreement must conform to the spirit of our great wartime pledges and the Charter of the United Nations.

With our friends we will seek patiently and tirelessly for the rule of law among nations. That law has been written. It is the Charter of the United Nations. It remains for every nation to respect it. That is the goal.

I think that progress toward that goal depends more on action than on angry words. I think the Soviet Union will be influenced only by a steady, serious, undeviating determination to build up the strength of the free world—not with a view toward war but with a view toward preventing war and negotiating the conditions of peace. . . .

Defeat begins in the heart. The peoples of Eastern Europe will never lose heart. They have kept their faith alive before, through long periods of darkness. We too must keep faith. We must not allow the recklessness of despair to find any lodging in our hearts. With indomitable faith and courage, with unfaltering determination, we must continue to strive for a future in which all peoples will know the joys of liberty for which their fathers have bled and died so often in the eternal struggle between freedom and tyranny.

5 · China Policy, 1945-1950

Since Secretary John Hay dispatched the first Open Door notes in 1899, U.S. diplomacy had pursued large aims in its China policies, and many Americans had regarded the Chinese with special affection. The United States had, in fact, hoped to extend to China Western religion and government and looked forward to the day when China would be the great power in Asia. But whatever hopes this country had for the Chinese suffered a fatal blow in December 1949, when Mao Tse-tung's soldiers drove Chiang Kai-shek and his Nationalist government from the mainland onto Formosa.

The Japanese invasion of China in 1937 had created the conditions that made possible later Communist successes. By 1943 disorganization in the country and the demoralization of the ruling Kuomintang party permitted Mao's guerrillas to emerge as China's most dynamic force. While the U.S. government supported Chiang in the common struggle against Japan, it discouraged the Nationalists from suppressing their Communist opponents at home and hoped that the impending civil war could be averted. Believing that a united China could make a significant contribution to the war effort, and convinced that Mao was more an agrarian reformer than a real Communist, American policy-makers undertook in 1944 to bring about a coalition government in China that would include both Nationalists and Communists. When the atomic bomb ended the war, Americans were still attempting to mediate between the factions.

After V-J Day General Albert C. Wedemeyer, American commander in China, gave invaluable assistance to Chiang by transporting between 400,000 and 500,000 Nationalists to key points in east and north China to insure that they, rather than the Communists, would receive the Japanese surrender. In addition, American marines were sent to Peiping (Peking), Tientsin, and other cities until Chiang's troops could occupy them. Meanwhile, abetted by the Russian occupation, the Chinese Communists made deep inroads into Manchuria and took possession of large stores of Japanese weapons. By the end of 1945 China again seemed bent on civil war.

Unwilling to intervene with further military assistance on the side of the Nationalists, and equally reluctant to withdraw entirely from China, the administration in December 1945 resumed the policy of mediation. As the documents in this chapter indicate, the policy was doomed from the start, and in mid-1946 the civil war began again. Chiang failed to make necessary internal reforms, lost popular support, and saw his armies fall apart or defect. By 1949 Mao's victories forced the Nationalists to retreat to Formosa.

In retrospect it seems that only massive American military intervention, including the commitment of ground troops, could have prevented the disaster. But such a policy would not have commanded support from a war-weary public, was impossible in view of the small size of the American armies in the late 1940's, and was, in fact, never suggested by even the staunchest of Chiang's American friends. Some critics of the Truman administration still argue, however, that if the government had only heeded the advice of General Wedemeyer, and of other friends of Chiang, China could have been saved. That the tragedy did immeasurable damage to the Democrats during Truman's second term and that it fed the anxieties that culminated in McCarthyism are sad facts beyond dispute. Unwilling to believe that U.S. desires could not shape the postwar world, and unprepared for the triumph of the Communists in China, most Americans became easy victims of simple explanations. They were ready to believe the hysterical charges of treason and subversion, that the Democrats had "sold out" Chiang and that Communists in the State Department had engineered the take-over.

ACHESON'S SUMMARY OF CHINA POLICY

1 ◄§ WHEN CHIANG'S COLLAPSE became a certainty, the State Department undertook to prepare a defense of its policies in China since Pearl Harbor. Throughout the spring and summer of 1949 a large number of officials worked on a lengthy document, later popularly called the White Paper on China. Consisting of a long historical essay and relevant diplomatic documents, *United States Relations with China*, released to the public on August 5, 1949, also contained a letter by Dean Acheson that was at once an

able explanation of government policies and a short summary of this unhappy chapter in U.S. diplomatic history:[1]

From the wartime cooperation with the Soviet Union and from the costly campaigns against the Japanese came the Yalta Agreement. The American Government and people awaited with intense anxiety the assault on the main islands of Japan which it was feared would cost up to a million American casualties before Japan was conquered. The atomic bomb was not then a reality and it seemed impossible that the war in the Far East could be ended without this assault. It thus became a primary concern of the American Government to see to it that the Soviet Union enter the war against Japan at the earliest possible date in order that the Japanese Army in Manchuria might not be returned to the homeland at the critical moment. It was considered vital not only that the Soviet Union enter the war but that she do so before our invasion of Japan, which already had been set for the autumn of 1945.

At Yalta, Marshal Stalin not only agreed to attack Japan within two or three months after V-E Day but limited his "price" with reference to Manchuria substantially to the position which Russia had occupied there prior to 1904. We for our part, in order to obtain this commitment and thus to bring the war to a close with a consequent saving of American, Chinese and other Allied lives, were prepared to and did pay the requisite price. Two facts must not, however, be lost sight of in this connection. First, the Soviet Union when she finally did enter the war against Japan, could in any case have seized all the territories in question and considerably more regardless of what our attitude might have been. Second, the Soviets on their side in the Sino-Soviet Treaty arising from the Yalta Agreement, agreed to give the National Government of China moral and material support and moreover formalized their assurances of noninterference in China's internal affairs. Although the unexpectedly early collapse of Japanese resistance later made some of the provisions of the Yalta Agreement seem unnecessary, in the light of the predicted course of the war at that time they were considered to be not only justified but clearly advantageous. Although dictated by military necessity, the Agreement and the subsequent Sino-Soviet Treaty in fact imposed limita-

[1] Excerpt reprinted from Department of State, *United States Relations with China*, August 1950, pp. viii–xvi.

tions on the action which Russia would, in any case, have been in a position to take.

For reasons of military security, and for those only, it was considered too dangerous for the United States to consult with the National Government regarding the Yalta Agreement or to communicate its terms at once to Chungking. We were then in the midst of the Pacific War. It was felt that there was grave risk that secret information transmitted to the Nationalist capital at this time would become available to the Japanese almost immediately. Under no circumstances, therefore, would we have been justified in incurring the security risks involved. It was not until June 15, 1945, that General [Patrick J.—Eds.] Hurley was authorized to inform Chiang Kai-shek of the Agreement.

In conformity with the Russian agreement at Yalta to sign a treaty of friendship and alliance with Nationalist China, negotiations between the two nations began in Moscow in July 1945. During their course, the United States felt obliged to remind both parties that the purpose of the treaty was to implement the Yalta Agreement—no more, no less—and that some of the Soviet proposals exceeded its provisions. The treaty, which was signed on August 14, 1945, was greeted with general satisfaction both in Nationalist China and in the United States. It was considered that Russia had accepted definite limitations on its activities in China and was committed to withhold all aid from the Chinese Communists. On September 10, however, our embassy in Moscow cautioned against placing undue confidence in the Soviet observance of either the spirit or letter of the treaty. The subsequent conduct of the Soviet Government in Manchuria has amply justified this warning.

When peace came the United States was confronted with three possible alternatives in China: (1) it could have pulled out lock, stock and barrel; (2) it could have intervened militarily on a major scale to assist the Nationalists to destroy the Communists; (3) it could, while assisting the Nationalists to assert their authority over as much of China as possible, endeavor to avoid a civil war by working for a compromise between the two sides.

The first alternative would, and I believe American public opinion at the time so felt, have represented an abandonment of our international responsibilities and of our traditional policy of friendship for China before we had made a determined effort to be of assistance. The second alternative policy, while it may look attractive theoretically and in retrospect, was wholly impracticable. The Nationalists had been unable to destroy the Communists during the 10 years before the war. Now after the war the Nationalists were, as indicated above, weakened, demoralized, and unpopular. They had quickly dissipated their popular support and prestige in the areas liberated from the Japanese by the conduct of their civil and military officials. The Communists on the other hand were much stronger than they had ever been and were in control of most of North China. Because of the ineffectiveness of the Nationalist forces which was later to be tragically demonstrated, the Communists probably could have been dislodged only by American arms. It is obvious that the American people would not have sanctioned such a colossal commitment of our armies in 1945 or later. We therefore came to the third alternative policy whereunder we faced the facts of the situation and attempted to assist in working out a *modus vivendi* which would avert civil war but nevertheless preserve and even increase the influence of the National Government.

As the record shows, it was the Chinese National Government itself which, prior to General Hurley's mission, had taken steps to arrive at a working agreement with the Communists. As early as September 1943 in addressing the Kuomintang Central Executive Committee, the Generalissimo said, "we should clearly recognize that the Communist problem is a purely political problem and should be solved by political means." He repeated this view on several occasions. Comprehensive negotiations between representatives of the Government and of the Communists, dealing with both military cooperation and civil administration, were opened in Sian in May 1944. These negotiations, in which Ambassador Hurley later assisted at the invitation of both parties between August 1944 and September 1945, continued intermittently during a year and a half without producing conclusive results and culminated in a comprehensive series of agreements on basic points on October 11, 1945, after Ambassador Hurley's departure from China and before General Marshall's arrival. Meanwhile, however, clashes between the armed forces of the two groups were increasing and were jeopardizing the fulfillment of the agreements. The danger of wide-spread civil war, unless the negotiations could promptly be brought to a successful conclusion, was critical. It was under these circumstances that General Marshall left on his mission to China at the end of 1945.

As the account of General Marshall's mission and the subsequent years in chapters V and VI of the underlying record reveals, our policy at that time was inspired by the two objectives of bringing peace to China under conditions which would permit stable government and progress along democratic lines, and of assisting the National Government to establish its authority over as wide areas of China as possible. As the event proved, the first objective was unrealizable because neither side desired it to succeed: the Communists because they refused to accept conditions which would weaken their freedom to proceed with what remained consistently their aim, the communization of all China; the Nationalists because they cherished the illusion, in spite of repeated advice to the contrary from our military representatives, that they could destroy the Communists by force of arms.

The second objective of assisting the National Government, however, we pursued vigorously from 1945 to 1949. The National Government was the recognized government of a friendly power. Our friendship, and our right under international law alike, called for aid to the Government instead of to the Communists who were seeking to subvert and overthrow it. The extent of our aid to Nationalist China is set forth in detail in chapters V, VI, VII and VIII of the record and need not be repeated here. The National Government had in 1945, and maintained until the early fall of 1948, a marked superiority in manpower and armament over their rivals. Indeed during that period, thanks very largely to our aid in transporting, arming and supplying their forces, they extended their control over a large part of North China and Manchuria. By the time General Marshall left China at the beginning of 1947, the Nationalists were apparently at the very peak of their military successes and territorial expansion. The following year and a half revealed, however, that their seeming strength was illusory and that their victories were built on sand.

The crisis had developed around Manchuria, traditional focus of Russian and Japanese imperialism. On numerous occasions, Marshal Stalin had stated categorically that he expected the National Government to take over the occupation of Manchuria. In the truce agreement of January 10, 1946, the Chinese Communists agreed to the movement of Government troops into Manchuria for the purpose of restoring Chinese sovereignty over this area. In conformity with this understanding the United States transported sizable government armies to the ports of entry into Manchuria. Earlier the Soviet Army had expressed a desire to evacuate Manchuria in December 1945, but had remained an additional two or three months at the request of the

Chinese Government. When the Russian troops did begin their evacuation, the National Government found itself with extended lines of communications, limited rolling stock and insufficient forces to take over the areas being evacuated in time to prevent the entry of Chinese Communist forces, who were already in occupation of the countryside. As the Communists entered, they obtained the large stocks of matériel from the Japanese Kwantung Army which the Russians had conveniently "abandoned." To meet this situation the National Government embarked on a series of military campaigns which expanded the line of its holdings to the Sungari River. Toward the end of these campaigns it also commenced hostilities within North China and succeeded in constricting the areas held by the Communists.

In the spring of 1946 General Marshall attempted to restore peace. This effort lasted for months and during its course a seemingly endless series of proposals and counterproposals were made which had little effect upon the course of military activities and produced no political settlement. During these negotiations General Marshall displayed limitless patience and tact and a willingness to try and then try again in order to reach agreement. Increasingly he became convinced, however, that twenty years of intermittent civil war between the two factions, during which the leading figures had remained the same, had created such deep personal bitterness and such irreconcilable differences that no agreement was possible. The suspicions and the lack of confidence were beyond remedy. He became convinced that both parties were merely sparring for time, jockeying for military position and catering temporarily to what they believed to be American desires. General Marshall concluded that there was no hope of accomplishing the objectives of his mission.

Even though for all practical purposes General Marshall, by the fall of 1946, had withdrawn from his efforts to assist in a peaceful settlement of the civil war, he remained in China until January 1947. One of the critical points of dispute between the Government and the Communists had been the convocation of the National Assembly to write a new constitution for China and to bring an end to the period of political tutelage and of one-party government. The Communists had refused to participate in the National Assembly unless there were a prior military settlement. The Generalissimo was determined that the Assembly should be held and the program carried out. It was the hope of General Marshall during the late months of 1946 that his presence in China would encourage the liberal elements in non-Communist China to assert themselves more forcefully than they had in the past and to exercise a leavening influence upon the absolutist control wielded by the reactionaries and the militarists. General Marshall remained in China until the Assembly had completed its work. Even though the proposed new framework of government appeared satisfactory, the evidence suggested that there had been little shift in the balance of power.

In his farewell statement, General Marshall announced the termination of his efforts to assist the Chinese in restoring internal peace. He described the deep-seated mutual suspicion between the Kuomintang and the Chinese Communist Party as the greatest obstacle to a settlement. He made it clear that the salvation of China lay in the hands of the Chinese themselves and that, while the newly adopted constitution provided the framework for a democratic China, practical measures of implementation by both sides would be the decisive test. He appealed for the assumption of leadership by liberals in and out of the Government as the road to unity and peace. With these final words he returned to Washington to assume, in January 1947, his new post as Secretary of State.

As the signs of impending disaster multiplied, the President in July 1947, acting on the recommendation of the Secretary of State, instructed Lt. Gen. Albert C. Wedemeyer to survey the Chinese scene and make recommendations. In his report, submitted on September 19, 1947, the General recommended that the United States continue and expand its policy of giving aid to Nationalist China, subject to these stipulations:

1. That China inform the United Nations of her request for aid.

2. That China request the United Nations to bring about a truce in Manchuria and request that Manchuria be placed under a Five-Power guardianship or a trusteeship.

3. That China utilize her own resources, reform her finances, her Government and her armies, and accept American advisers in the military and economic fields.

General Wedemeyer's report, which fully recognized the danger of Communist domination of all China and was sympathetic to the problems of the National Government, nevertheless listed a large number of reforms which he considered essential if that Government were to rehabilitate itself.

It was decided that the publication at that time of a suggestion for the alienation of a part of China from the control of the National Government, and for placing that part under an international administration to include Soviet Russia, would not be helpful. In this record, the full text of that part of General Wedemeyer's report which deals with China appears as an annex to chapter VI.

The reasons for the failures of the Chinese National Government appear in some detail in the attached record. They do not stem from any inadequacy of American aid. Our military observers on the spot have reported that the Nationalist armies did not lose a single battle during the crucial year of 1948 through lack of arms or ammunition. The fact was that the decay which our observers had detected in Chungking early in the war had fatally sapped the powers of resistance of the Kuomintang. Its leaders had proved incapable of meeting the crisis confronting them, its troops had lost the will to fight, and its Government had lost popular support. The Communists, on the other hand, through a ruthless discipline and fanatical zeal, attempted to sell themselves as guardians and liberators of the people. The Nationalist armies did not have to be defeated; they disintegrated. History has proved again and again that a regime without faith in itself and an army without morale cannot survive the test of battle.

The record obviously cannot set forth in equal detail the inner history and development of the Chinese Communist Party during these years. The principal reason is that, while we had regular diplomatic relations with the National Government and had the benefit of voluminous reports from our representatives in their territories, our direct contact with the Communists was limited in the main to the mediation efforts of General Hurley and General Marshall.

Fully recognizing that the heads of the Chinese Communist Party were ideologically affiliated with Moscow, our Government nevertheless took the view, in the light of the existing balance of forces in China, that peace could be established only if certain conditions were met. The Kuomintang would have to set its own house in order and both sides would have to make concessions so that the Government of China might become, in fact as well as in name, the Government of all China and so that all parties might function within the constitutional system of the Government. Both internal peace and constitutional development required that the progress should be rapid from one party government with a large opposition party in armed rebellion, to the participation of all parties, including the moderate non-Communist elements, in a truly national system of government.

None of these conditions has been realized. The distrust of the leaders of both the Nationalist and Communist Parties for each other proved too deep-seated to permit final agreement, notwithstanding temporary truces and apparently promising negotiations. The Nationalists, furthermore, embarked in 1946 on an over-ambitious military campaign in the face of warnings by General Marshall that it not only would fail but would plunge China into economic chaos and eventually destroy the National Government. General Marshall pointed out that though Nationalist armies could, for a period, capture Communist-held cities, they could not destroy the Communist armies. Thus every Nationalist advance would expose their communications to attack by Communist guerrillas and compel them to retreat or to surrender their armies together with the munitions which the United States has furnished them. No estimate of a military situation has ever been more completely confirmed by the resulting facts.

The historic policy of the United States of friendship and aid toward the people of China was, however, maintained in both peace and war. Since V-J Day, the United States Government has authorized aid to Nationalist China in the form of grants and credits totaling approximately 2 billion dollars, an amount equivalent in value to more than 50 percent of the monetary expenditures of the Chinese Government and of proportionately greater magnitude in relation to the budget of that Government than the United States has provided to any nation of Western Europe since the end of the war. In addition to these grants and credits, the United States Government has sold the Chinese Government large quantities of military and civilian war surplus property with a total procurement cost of over 1 billion dollars, for which the agreed realization to the United States was 232 million dollars. A large proportion of the military supplies furnished the Chinese armies by the United States since V-J Day has, however, fallen into the hands of the Chinese Communists through the military ineptitude of the Nationalist leaders, their defections and surrenders, and the absence among their forces of the will to fight.

It has been urged that relatively small amounts of additional aid—military and economic—to the National Government would have enabled it to destroy communism in China. The most trustworthy military, economic, and political information available to our Government does not bear out this view.

A realistic appraisal of conditions in China, past and present, leads to the conclusion that the only alternative open to the United States was full-scale intervention in behalf of a Government which had lost the confidence of its own troops and its own people. Such intervention would have required the expenditure of even greater sums than have been fruitlessly spent thus far, the command of Nationalist armies by American officers, and the probable participation of American armed forces—land, sea, and air—in the resulting war. Intervention of such a scope and magnitude would have been resented by the mass of the Chinese people, would have diametrically reversed our historic policy, and would have been condemned by the American people.

It must be admitted frankly that the American policy of assisting the Chinese people in resisting domination by any foreign power or powers is now confronted with the gravest difficulties. The heart of China is in Communist hands. The Communist leaders have foresworn their Chinese heritage and have publicly announced their subservience to a foreign power, Russia, which during the last 50 years, under czars and Communists alike, has been most assiduous in its efforts to extend its control in the Far East. In the recent past, attempts at foreign domination have appeared quite clearly to the Chinese people as external aggression and as such have been bitterly and in the long run successfully resisted. Our aid and encouragement have helped them to resist. In this case, however, the foreign domination has been masked behind the façade of a vast crusading movement which apparently has seemed to many Chinese to be wholly indigenous and natural. Under these circumstances, our aid has been unavailing.

The unfortunate but inescapable fact is that the ominous result of the civil war in China was beyond the control of the government of the United States. Nothing that this country did or could have done within the reasonable limits of its capabilities could have changed that result; nothing that was left undone by this country has contributed to it. It was the product of internal Chinese forces, forces which this country tried to influence but could not. A decision was arrived at within China, if only a decision by default.

ROBERTSON INDICTMENT OF U.S. POLICIES

2 ⊷§   WALTER S. ROBERTSON was a businessman who accepted his first diplomatic assignment in 1943. In 1945 the State

Department sent him to China, where he served as minister and counselor on economic affairs and as chargé d'affaires. For his work as a member of the Truce Commission in 1946, General Marshall awarded him the Medal for Merit. In September 1946 Robertson quit the Foreign Service. While in China and afterward Robertson was critical of the Truman administration's China policies, and in 1953 President Eisenhower appointed him Assistant Secretary of State for Far Eastern Affairs. On October 8, 1949, Robertson wrote a letter to the U.S. Ambassador at large, Philip C. Jessup, indicating in broad terms U.S. conduct in China:

In justice to ourselves as well as to whatever friends we may have left in Asia, it would seem to be imperative that we clarify our objectives and pursue them with fidelity. Chiang Kai-shek has now been made the official scapegoat not only for China's sins but for ours as well. His back is hardly broad enough to bear such a burden. China's economic ills and appalling social problems will remain to plague whatever Government follows him and, in my opinion at least, it can be fairly demonstrated that the confused and confusing inconsistencies of our own vacillating policy, however well-meaning it might have been, contributed directly and indirectly to the debacle which engulfed him and his Government, our ally, and brought to power the Communists, our long-avowed enemies.

That great confusion existed is attested by the fact that both the National Government and the Communist Party can make out a case against us of having run with the hare and ridden with the hounds. The confusion is explicable. Officially we were committed to a policy of expediency which was constantly being challenged by reports from certain Foreign Service officers in the field denouncing the Kuomintang, praising the Communists and recommending a course of action directly contrary to the one we were pursuing. And the fact that some of our official observers whose reports later influenced changes in policy completely failed to recognize the nature and character of the Communist movement only served to compound the complications already inherent in the situation.

A review of our mistakes of the past is pertinent now only to the extent that it helps us to evaluate the present and possibly avoid similar mistakes in planning for the future. What justification is there for saying that we unwittingly weakened our friends and strengthened our enemies? . . .

Chiang Kai-shek responded to our friendship. When the outlook seemed blackest for him, he reputedly spurned a glamorous offer to sell out to the Japanese, thus freezing upon the continent of Asia large, well-equipped Japanese forces which would otherwise have been freed to oppose our struggle up the Pacific. In this one action he made a significant, if indirect, contribution to victory which saved untold numbers of American lives.

Against this background, the deal at Yalta respecting Manchuria seems incredible. In February, 1945, with our forces mopping up the Philippines far ahead of schedule, it was deemed necessary to bring Russia into the war to hasten the victory already in sight. Russia's price was Manchuria. We granted it without China's knowledge or consent. We granted it despite the renouncement of extraterritoriality by ourselves and other allies, despite the specific pledges made in Cairo, despite the fact that China had been fighting for eight years in the hope of recovering these same rich northeastern provinces from the Japanese, despite the fact that we ourselves had been plunged into a terrible war protesting the Japanese in Manchuria as a threat to our national interests and an infringement upon the sovereignty of China.

What happened is an all-too-familiar story. On August 9, the day after the second atomic bomb was dropped on Nagasaki, Russia declared war on Japan. The Japanese surrendered on August 14. Russia, five days in the war, swept in and took full military possession of Manchuria. Firmly entrenched, they began a systematic looting of its magnificent industrial plants, the only industrial production left in China. They vitiated the Potsdam declarations by refusing the Chinese use of their own ports and railroads to take over surrender of the Japanese. They denied us, the victors in the war, permission even to send in our consular representatives. They finally capitalized our ill-fated efforts at mediation as an opportunity for abandoning to the Chinese Communists large areas of Manchurian territory and large quantities of Japanese arms and equipment. In a footnote to the Sino-Soviet Treaty, the Russians had pledged themselves to evacuate Manchuria within three months after V-J Day. Actually, three months after V-J Day no Chinese troops had been able to get into Manchuria to take over either territory or Japanese surrender.

It was in the summer of 1945, immediately following V-J Day, that China was desperately in need of economic assistance if collapse was to be avoided. Eight years of war had destroyed communications, paralyzed industry and commerce, devastated agricultural lands and brought to the brink of disaster an economy which is only a pauper economy at best. The Russian rape of Manchuria had removed the sole industrial production left intact by the war. Without prompt outside relief gigantic inflation and economic collapse was inevitable. From every standpoint of our own interest, it would seem that there was just as compelling a reason for a loan to "strengthen China's position as regards her internal economy"[2] in 1945 as there had been in 1942.

But by this time the Communist propaganda machine with loud echoes in the American press, was in full swing, giving voice to the same views that some of our Foreign Service officers had been proclaiming. So with victory now seemingly assured, we suddenly reversed our policy towards the National Government. We took the position that "a China disorganized and divided either by foreign aggression . . . or by internal strife is an undermining influence to world stability and peace" (China had been so disorganized and divided for some 20 years); that "a strong, united and democratic China is of the utmost importance to the success of the United Nations organization" (China was neither strong, united nor democratic when she was designated a great power and given a seat on the Security Council, nor has she ever been in her 4,000-year-old history); that "as China moves towards peace and unity . . . the United States would be prepared to assist the National Government in every reasonable way to rehabilitate the country, improve the agrarian and industrial economy and establish a military organization capable of discharging China's national and international responsibilities . . .," that "in furtherance of such assistance the United States would be prepared to give favorable consideration to Chinese requests for credit and loans under reasonable conditions . . .," etc.

If the Chinese Government could have fulfilled this counsel of perfection it would have needed little of American assistance. And so through this ominously critical period, with economic forces inexorably approaching the brink of disaster, we withheld our help, exercising instead our prestige and power to bring about a coalition with the Communists. In Europe we poured out our millions to prevent economic collapse to keep the Communists out. In China we withheld assistance at the only time it probably had any chance of being effective to force the Communists in. Once this opportunity

2 Quoted phrases are from a statement by Truman; see document 6, below.

was lost, the economic, political and military collapse which followed was inevitable. Much stress has been laid upon our so-called 2-billion-dollar aid since V-J Day. An analysis of the character and timing of such aid is striking evidence of the lack of a positive and co-ordinated policy which served either Chinese or American interests.

Our position now would be ludicrous were it not so tragic and ominous. Having fought and won the war at terrific sacrifice, we see our brilliant victory turned into bitter defeat and find ourselves confronted with a situation far more menacing to our interests than that which existed before we fired a shot, killed a son or spent a dollar of our resources.

What should our objectives now be and what methods should be employed to realize them?

In a world of tottering economies and social unrest, of ideological hatred, of Russian intrigue and power, a global situation involving unknown but probably staggering demands upon our already over-burdened economy, I assume that our objectives in China and elsewhere must of necessity be primarily concerned with the preservation of ourselves and that nebulous thing we call our world. If this be true, policies and commitments in any given area would depend solely upon that area's relative importance to our over-all security. Obviously these are questions not for the layman or specialist but rather for policy makers, diplomatic, military and economic, at the highest level of Government. One cannot see the contents of a room by peeping through the keyhole.

I feel in no way qualified to pass upon the question, but I am strongly of the opinion that recognition of the Communist regime would not be to the best interests either of China's suffering millions or of ourselves. The Communists will almost certainly make ingra-tiating overtures to obtain recognition. Strong pressure will no doubt be brought from our trade interests in favor of it. There would be obvious advantages to us in being able to maintain diplomatic repre-sentation in Communist territory for such reporting as might be per-mitted. On the other hand, if the Communists were allowed to stew in their own juice for a time, they would, in my opinion, soon begin to be confronted with the same overwhelming economic and social problems which contributed so largely to the downfall of the National Government. Recognition would bring re-establishment of trade and possibly economic assistance, both vitally necessary to the permanent maintenance of any semblance of economic stability. It would also bring tremendous prestige to the Communist movement throughout Asia.

China's ignorant masses are not concerned with ideologies. They know when they are hungry; they know when they are cold; they know when there is scant margin left over from the tax collector to show for their unceasing labors; they know when their sons are conscripted from the fields. There is logical reason to assume that once they experience the ruthless exploitation and regimentation of Communist power, as surely they will experience it, they will again be restive to follow any leadership which promises relief. There are good men in China, as well as venal men, who are opposed to the Communists. We have to work in China with what is there, not what we should like to have there. Withholding recognition would seem to offer the Chinese people some hope of eventually escaping Communist domination and control. And, important from our standpoint, it would seem to offer the best hope of re-establishing American prestige and influence in the Pacific.

Of one fact we can be certain. The leaders of the Communist movement in China are zealous consecrated Marxists intense in their loyalty to Moscow and haters of everything we are and stand for.

YALTA AGREEMENT ON FAR EAST

3 ◄§ CRITICISM OF U.S. FAR EASTERN POLICY customarily begins with an attack on the agreements relating to Asia that Roosevelt and Stalin concluded at Yalta in February 1945. The protocols on the Far East follow:[3]

The leaders of the three Great Powers—the Soviet Union, the United States of America and Great Britain—have agreed that in two or three months after Germany has surrendered and the war in Europe has terminated the Soviet Union shall enter into the war against Japan on the side of the Allies on condition that:

1. The *status quo* in Outer-Mongolia (The Mongolian People's Republic) shall be preserved;

2. The former rights of Russia violated by the treacherous attack of Japan in 1904 shall be restored, viz:

[3] Excerpts reprinted from Department of State, *Foreign Relations of the United States: The Conferences at Malta and Yalta, 1945* (Washington, D.C., 1955), p. 984.

(a) the southern part of Sakhalin as well as all the islands adjacent to it shall be returned to the Soviet Union,

(b) the commercial port of Dairen shall be internationalized, the preeminent interests of the Soviet Union in this port being safeguarded and the lease of Port Arthur as a naval base of the USSR restored,

(c) the Chinese-Eastern Railroad and the South-Manchurian Railroad which provides an outlet to Dairen shall be jointly operated by the establishment of a joint Soviet-Chinese Company it being understood that the preeminent interests of the Soviet Union shall be safeguarded and that China shall retain full sovereignty in Manchuria; . . .

3. The Kuril islands shall be handed over to the Soviet Union.

It is understood, that the agreement concerning Outer-Mongolia and the ports and railroads referred to above will require concurrence of Generalissimo Chiang Kai Shek. The President will take measures in order to obtain this concurrence on advice from Marshal Stalin.

The Heads of the three Great Powers have agreed that these claims of the Soviet Union shall be unquestionably fulfilled after Japan has been defeated.

For its part the Soviet Union expresses its readiness to conclude with the National Government of China a pact of friendship and alliance between the USSR and China in order to render assistance to China with its armed forces for the purpose of liberating China from the Japanese yoke.

MACARTHUR'S VIEWS ON JAPAN

4 ◄§ ONE OF THE MAJOR OBJECTIVES of the Americans at Yalta was to hasten the end of the war against Japan. The views of General MacArthur, American Far Eastern commander, on how this could be done best are described in the following summaries of conversations that he had with American officers in the winter of 1945. On February 13, 1945, Colonel Paul F. Freeman, Jr., an operations officer in the War Department, wrote a letter to General Marshall, then the American Chief of Staff, summarizing an hour and a half of conversation with MacArthur:[4]

[4] Excerpt reprinted from Department of Defense, *The Entry of the Soviet Union into the War Against Japan: Military Plans, 1941–1945* (Washington, D.C., 1955), pp. 51–2.

General MacArthur then elaborated on his concept of operations for the ultimate defeat of Japan. He was in thorough agreement that the only means of defeating Japan was by the invasion of the industrial heart of Japan. He stressed the potency of the Japanese army and stated that when we entered Japan we must be prepared to reckon with the Japanese army in far greater strength than is now there. He was apprehensive as to the possibility of the movement of the bulk of the Manchurian army and other Japanese forces from China to the defense of the homeland. He emphatically stated that we must not invade Japan proper unless the Russian army is previously committed to action in Manchuria. He said that this was essential, and that it should be done without the three month's delay upon the conclusion of the defeat of Germany as intimated by Marshal Stalin to the President. He said that it was only necessary for action to commence in Manchuria to contain that force of Japanese in order to make possible our invasion of Japan and the rapid conclusion of the war. He understands Russia's aims; that they would want all of Manchuria, Korea and possibly part of North China. This seizure of territory was inevitable; but the United States must insist that Russia pay her way by invading Manchuria at the earliest possible date after the defeat of Germany.

a. He understood that the Navy still favored a plan whereby they would ring Japan proper with air bases and naval bases and eventually blockade and bombard them into submission. He said that this never would be effective. (I informed him that that was the opinion of the JCS [Joint Chiefs of Staff—Eds.] and was agreed upon at Sextant [Code name for Cairo Conference, November-December 1943]).

b. General MacArthur agreed that the Tokyo Plain was the proper place to invade Japan and he was fully conversant with the restrictions of seasons. He believed it would be a mistake to make a prior landing in Japan, either in Kyushu or Hokkaido. He felt that proper timing, in conjunction with a move by the Russians and the strategic surprise to be gained, would be a far greater advantage in landing initially in the heart of Japan whereby the enemy force could be split, rather than to tip our hand by first landing at some other remote part of the Japanese islands.

ATTITUDE OF MACARTHUR TOWARD RUSSIA

5 ⤶ ON MARCH 8, 1945, General George A. Lincoln, chief of Strategy and Policy Group, Operations Division, War De-

partment, sent a memorandum to General Marshall summarizing some of MacArthur's views:[5]

As to Russia, General MacArthur pointed out that politically they want a warm water port which would be Port Arthur. He considered that it would be impracticable to deny them such a port because of their great military power. Therefore, it was only right they should share the cost in blood in defeating Japan. From the military stand-point we should make every effort to get Russia into the Japanese war before we go into Japan, otherwise we will take the impact of the Jap divisions and reap the losses, while the Russians in due time advance into an area free of major resistance. General MacArthur stated he considered the President should start putting pressure on the Russians now.

PRESIDENTIAL STATEMENT ON U.S. POLICY

6 ⋖§ THE MAJOR UNDERTAKING of U.S. policy in China during the postwar period was General Marshall's mission to recon-cile, if possible, the Nationalists and the Communists. The story of that mission is told in the documents that follow. On December 15, 1945, President Truman made a statement on U.S. policy toward China:[6]

It is the firm belief of this Government that a strong, united and democratic China is of the utmost importance to the success of this United Nations organization and for world peace. A China disorgan-ized and divided either by foreign aggression, such as that undertaken by the Japanese, or by violent internal strife, is an undermining influ-ence to world stability and peace, now and in the future. The United States Government has long subscribed to the principle that the management of internal affairs is the responsibility of the peoples of the sovereign nations. Events of this century, however, would indicate that a breach of peace anywhere in the world threatens the peace of the entire world. It is thus in the most vital interest of the United States and all the United Nations that the people of China overlook no opportunity to adjust their internal differences promptly by means of peaceful negotiation.

The Government of the United States believes it essential:

[5] Ibid., p. 51.
[6] Excerpt reprinted from United States Relations with China, pp. 607–9.

(1) That a cessation of hostilities be arranged between the armies of the National Government and the Chinese Communists and other dissident Chinese armed forces for the purpose of completing the return of all China to effective Chinese control, including the immediate evacuation of the Japanese forces.

(2) That a national conference of representatives of major political elements be arranged to develop an early solution to the present internal strife—a solution which will bring about the unification of China.

The United States and the other United Nations have recognized the present National Government of the Republic of China as the only legal government in China. It is the proper instrument to achieve the objective of a unified China.

The United States and the United Kingdom by the Cairo Declaration in 1943 and the Union of Soviet Socialist Republics by adhering to the Potsdam Declaration of last July and by the Sino-Soviet Treaty and Agreements of August 1945, are all committed to the liberation of China, including the return of Manchuria to Chinese control. These agreements were made with the National Government of the Republic of China.

In continuation of the constant and close collaboration with the National Government of the Republic of China in the prosecution of this war, in consonance with the Potsdam Declaration, and to remove possibility of Japanese influence remaining in China, the United States has assumed a definite obligation in the disarmament and evacuation of the Japanese troops. Accordingly the United States has been assisting and will continue to assist the National Government of the Republic of China in effecting the disarmament and evacuation of Japanese troops in the liberated areas. The United States Marines are in North China for that purpose.

The United States recognizes and will continue to recognize the National Government of China and cooperate with it in international affairs and specifically in eliminating Japanese influence from China. The United States is convinced that a prompt arrangement for a cessation of hostilities is essential to the effective achievement of this end. United States support will not extend to United States military intervention to influence the course of any Chinese internal strife.

The United States has already been compelled to pay a great price to restore the peace which was first broken by Japanese aggression in Manchuria. The maintenance of peace in the Pacific may be jeopardized, if not frustrated, unless Japanese influence in China is wholly removed and unless China takes her place as a unified, democratic and peaceful nation. This is the purpose of the maintenance for the time being of United States military and naval forces in China.

The United States is cognizant that the present National Government of China is a "one-party government" and believes that peace, unity and democratic reform in China will be furthered if the basis of this Government is broadened to include other political elements in the country. Hence, the United States strongly advocates that the national conference of representatives of major political elements in the country agree upon arrangements which would give those elements a fair and effective representation in the Chinese National Government. It is recognized that this would require modification of the one-party "political tutelage" established as an interim arrangement in the progress of the nation toward democracy by the father of the Chinese Republic, Doctor Sun Yat-sen.

The existence of autonomous armies such as that of the Communist army is inconsistent with, and actually makes impossible, political unity in China. With the institution of a broadly representative government, autonomous armies should be eliminated as such and all armed forces in China integrated effectively into the Chinese National Army.

In line with its often expressed views regarding self-determination, the United States Government considers that the detailed steps necessary to the achievement of political unity in China must be worked out by the Chinese themselves and that intervention by any foreign government in these matters would be inappropriate. The United States Government feels, however, that China has a clear responsibility to the other United Nations to eliminate armed conflict within its territory as constituting a threat to world stability and peace—a responsibility which is shared by the National Government and all Chinese political and military groups.

As China moves toward peace and unity along the lines described above, the United States would be prepared to assist the National Government in every reasonable way to rehabilitate the country, improve the agrarian and industrial economy, and establish a military organization capable of discharging China's national and international responsibilities for the maintenance of peace and order. In furtherance of such assistance, it would be prepared to give favorable consideration to Chinese requests for credits and loans under reasonable conditions for projects which would contribute toward the development of a healthy economy throughout China and healthy trade relations between China and the United States.

TRUMAN'S LETTER TO MARSHALL

7 ◆§ ON DECEMBER 15, 1945, President Truman wrote to the Special Representative of the President to China, General Marshall:[7]

The fact that I have asked you to go to China is the clearest evidence of my very real concern with regard to the situation there. Secretary Byrnes and I are both anxious that the unification of China by peaceful, democratic methods be achieved as soon as possible. It is my desire that you, as my Special Representative, bring to bear in an appropriate and practicable manner the influence of the United States to this end.

Specifically, I desire that you endeavor to persuade the Chinese Government to call a national conference of representatives of the major political elements to bring about the unification of China and, concurrently, to effect a cessation of hostilities, particularly in north China.

It is my understanding that there is now in session in Chungking a People's Consultative Council [Political Consultative Conference —Eds.] made up of representatives of the various political elements, including the Chinese Communists. The meeting of this Council should furnish you with a convenient opportunity for discussions with the various political leaders.

Upon the success of your efforts, as outlined above, will depend largely, of course, the success of our plans for evacuating Japanese troops from China, particularly north China, and for the subsequent withdrawal of our own armed forces from China. I am particularly desirous that both be accomplished as soon as possible.

In your conversations with Chiang Kai-shek and other Chinese leaders you are authorized to speak with the utmost frankness. Particularly, you may state, in connection with the Chinese desire for credits, technical assistance in the economic field, and military assistance (I have in mind the proposed U.S. military advisory group which I have approved in principle), that a China disunited and torn by

---

[7] Excerpt, *ibid.*, pp. 605–6.

civil strife could not be considered realistically as a proper place for American assistance along the lines enumerated.

I am anxious that you keep Secretary Byrnes and me currently informed of the progress of your negotiations and of obstacles you may encounter. You will have our full support and we shall endeavor at all times to be as helpful to you as possible.

LETTER OF TRUMAN TO CHIANG KAI-SHEK

8 ✑ THE TEMPORARY COALITION was never formed, and the meeting of the National Assembly to draft a new constitution was postponed until November. By July 1946 full-scale fighting had resumed, and the irreconcilable nature of the conflict was becoming obvious. The following exchange of August 1946 suggests the extent of the political and diplomatic disintegration. Truman wrote to Chiang Kai-shek on August 10, 1946:[8]

I have followed closely the situation in China since I sent General Marshall to you as my Special Envoy. It is with profound regret that I am forced to the conclusion that his efforts have seemingly proved unavailing.

In his discussions with you, I am certain that General Marshall has reflected accurately the overall attitude and policy of the American Government and of informed American public opinion also.

The rapidly deteriorating political situation in China, during recent months, has been a cause of grave concern to the American people. While it is the continued hope of the United States that an influential and democratic China can still be achieved under your leadership, I would be less than honest if I did not point out that latest developments have forced me to the conclusion that the selfish interests of extremist elements, both in the Kuomintang and the Communist Party, are obstructing the aspirations of the people of China.

A far sighted step toward the achievement of national unity and democracy was acclaimed in the United States when the agreements were reached on January 31st by the Political Consultative Conference. Disappointment over failure to implement the agreements of the PCC by concrete measures is becoming an important factor in the American outlook with regard to China.

In the United States, there now exists an increasing school of

8 *Ibid.*, p. 652.

thought which maintains that our whole policy toward China must be re-examined in the light of spreading strife, and notably by evidence of the increasing trend to suppress the expression of liberal views among intellectuals as well as freedom of the press. The assassinations of distinguished Chinese liberals at Kunming recently have not been ignored. Regardless of where responsibility may lie for these cruel murders, the result has been to cause American attention to focus on the China situation, and there is increasing belief that an attempt is being made to resort to force, military or secret police rather than democratic processes to settle major social issues.

American faith in the peaceful and democratic aspirations of the Chinese people has not been destroyed by recent events, but has been shaken. The firm desire of the people of the United States and of the American Government is still to help China achieve lasting peace and a stable economy under a truly democratic government. There is an increasing awareness, however, that the hopes of the people of China are being thwarted by militarists and a small group of political reactionaries who are obstructing the advancement of the general good of the nation by failing to understand the liberal trend of the times. The people of the United States view with violent repugnance this state of affairs.

It cannot be expected that American opinion will continue in its generous attitude towards your nation unless convincing proof is shortly forthcoming that genuine progress is being made toward a peaceful settlement of China's internal problems. Furthermore, it will be necessary for me to redefine and explain the position of the United States to the people of America.

I earnestly hope that in the near future I may receive some encouraging word from you which will facilitate the achievement of our mutually declared aims.

CHIANG'S REPLY TO TRUMAN

9 ⋅✑ ON AUGUST 28, 1946, Chiang Kai-shek answered the President's letter:[9]

Referring to your message of August 10, I wish to thank you cordially for your expressions of genuine concern for the welfare of my country.

General Marshall has labored most unsparingly to achieve our

9 *Ibid.*

common objective; namely, peace and democracy in China, since his arrival. Despite all obstacles, I, too, have done my utmost to cooperate with him in the accomplishment of his task.

The desire for peace has to be mutual, therefore, it means the Communists must give up their policy to seize political power through the use of armed force, to overthrow the government and to install a totalitarian regime such as those with which Eastern Europe is now being engulfed.

The minimum requirement for the preservation of peace in our country is the abandonment of such a policy. The Communists attacked and captured Changchun in Manchuria and attacked and captured Tehchow in Shantung after the conclusion of the January agreement. In June, during the cease-fire period, they attacked Tatung and Taiyuan in Shansi and Hsuchow in northern Kiangsu. They have opened a wide offensive on the Lunghai railway in the last few days, with Hsuchow and Kaifeng as their objectives.

Mistakes have also been made by some subordinates on the government side, of course, but compared to the flagrant violations on the part of the Communists, they are minor in scale. We deal sternly with the offender whenever any mistake occurs on our Government side.

In my V-J Day message on August 14, I announced the firm policy of the government to broaden speedily the basis of the Government by the inclusion of all parties and non-partisans, amounting to the effectuation of the program of peaceful reconstruction adopted on January 13 by the political consultation conference. It is my sincere hope that our views will be accepted by the Chinese Communist party. On its part, the Government will do the utmost in the shortest possible time to make peace and democracy a reality in this country.

I am cooperating with General Marshall with all my power in implementing that policy which has as its aim our mutually declared objective. Success must depend upon the sincerity of the Communists in response to our appeals. I am depending on your continued support in the realization of our goal.

PRESIDENT ON U.S. POLICY

10 ◄§ BY THE END OF 1946 the policy of mediation had obviously failed. On December 18 Truman made a statement on the administration's policy toward China:[10]

[10] Excerpts, *ibid.*, pp. 689–94.

I asked General Marshall to go to China as my representative. We had agreed upon my statement of the United States Government's views and policies regarding China as his directive. He knew full well in undertaking the mission that halting civil strife, broadening the base of the Chinese Government and bringing about a united, democratic China were tasks for the Chinese themselves. He went as a great American to make his outstanding abilities available to the Chinese.

During the war, the United States entered into an agreement with the Chinese Government regarding the training and equipment of a special force of 39 divisions. That training ended V-J Day and the transfer of the equipment had been largely completed when General Marshall arrived.

The United States, the United Kingdom and the Union of Soviet Socialist Republics all committed themselves to the liberation of China, including the return of Manchuria to Chinese control. Our Government had agreed to assist the Chinese Government in the reoccupation of areas liberated from the Japanese, including Manchuria, because of China's lack of shipping and transport planes. Three armies were moved by air and eleven by sea, to central China, Formosa, north China and Manchuria. Most of these moves had been made or started when General Marshall arrived.

The disarming and evacuation of Japanese progressed slowly—too slowly. We regarded our commitment to assist the Chinese in this program as of overwhelming importance to the future peace of China and the whole Far East. Surrendered but undefeated Japanese armies and hordes of administrators, technicians, and Japanese merchants, totalling about 3,000,000 persons, had to be removed under the most difficult conditions. At the request of the Chinese Government we had retained a considerable number of American troops in China, and immediately after V-J Day we landed a corps of Marines in north China. The principal task of these forces was to assist in the evacuation of Japanese. Only some 200,000 had been returned to Japan by the time General Marshall arrived.

General Marshall also faced a most unpropitious internal situation on his arrival in China. Communications throughout the country were badly disrupted due to destruction during the war and the civil conflicts which had broken out since. This disruption was preventing the restoration of Chinese economy, the distribution of relief supplies, and was rendering the evacuation of Japanese a slow and difficult process. The wartime destruction of factories and plants, the war-induced inflation in China, the Japanese action in shutting down the economy of occupied China immediately after V-J Day, and finally the destruction of communications combined to paralyze the economic life of the country, spreading untold hardship to millions, robbing the victory over the Japanese of significance to most Chinese and seriously aggravating all the tensions and discontents that existed in China.

Progress toward solution of China's internal difficulties by the Chinese themselves was essential to the rapid and effective completion of most of the programs in which we had already pledged our assistance to the Chinese Government. General Marshall's experience and wisdom were available to the Chinese in their efforts to reach such solutions.

Events moved rapidly upon General Marshall's arrival. With all parties availing themselves of his impartial advice, agreement for a country-wide truce was reached and announced on January 10th. A feature of this agreement was the establishment of a unique organization, the Executive Headquarters in Peiping. It was realized that due to poor communications and the bitter feelings on local fronts, generalized orders to cease fire and withdraw might have little chance of being carried out unless some authoritative executive agency, trusted by both sides, could function in any local situation.

The Headquarters operated under the leaders of three commissioners—one American who served as chairman, one Chinese Government representative, and one representative of the Chinese Communist Party. Mr. Walter S. Robertson, Charge d'Affaires of the American Embassy in China, served as chairman until his return to this country in the fall. In order to carry out its function in the field, Executive Headquarters formed a large number of truce teams, each headed by one American officer, one Chinese Government officer, and one Chinese Communist officer. They proceeded to all danger spots where fighting was going on or seemed impending and saw to the implementation of the truce terms, often under conditions imposing exceptional hardships and requiring courageous action. The degree of cooperation attained between Government and Communist officers in the Headquarters and on the truce teams was a welcome proof that despite two decades of fighting, these two Chinese groups could work together.

Events moved forward with equal promise on the political front.

On January 10th, the Political Consultative Conference began its sessions with representatives of the Kuomintang or Government Party, the Communist Party and several minor political parties participating. Within three weeks of direct discussion these groups had come to a series of statesmanlike agreements on outstanding political and military problems. The agreements provided for an interim government of a coalition type with representation of all parties, for revision of the Draft Constitution along democratic lines prior to its discussion and adoption by a National Assembly and for reduction of the Government and Communist armies and their eventual amalgamation into a small modernized truly national army responsible to a civilian government.

In March, General Marshall returned to this country. He reported on the important step the Chinese had made toward peace and unity in arriving at these agreements. He also pointed out that these agreements could not be satisfactorily implemented and given substance unless China's economic disintegration were checked and particularly unless the transportation system could be put in working order. Political unity could not be built on economic chaos. This Government had already authorized certain minor credits to the Chinese Government in an effort to meet emergency rehabilitation needs as it was doing for other war devastated countries throughout the world. A total of approximately $66,000,000 was involved in six specific projects, chiefly for the purchase of raw cotton, and for ships and railroad repair material. But these emergency measures were inadequate. Following the important forward step made by the Chinese in the agreements as reported by General Marshall, the Export-Import Bank earmarked a total of $500,000,000 for possible additional credits on a project by project basis to Chinese Government agencies and private enterprises. Agreement to extend actual credits for such projects would obviously have to be based upon this Government's policy as announced December 15, 1945. So far, this $500,000,000 remains earmarked, but unexpended. . . .

Before General Marshall arrived in China for the second time, in April, there was evidence that the truce agreement was being disregarded. The sincere and unflagging efforts of Executive Headquarters and its truce teams have succeeded in many instances in preventing or ending local engagements and thus saved thousands of lives. But fresh outbreaks of civil strife continued to occur, reaching a crisis of violence in Manchuria with the capture of Changchun by the Communists and where the presence of truce teams had not been fully agreed to by the National Government.

A change in the course of events in the political field was equally disappointing. Negotiations between the Government and the Communists have been resumed again and again, but they have as often broken down. Although hope for final success has never disappeared completely, the agreements made in January and February have not been implemented, and the various Chinese groups have not since that time been able to achieve the degree of agreement reached at the Political Consultative Conference.

There has been encouraging progress in other fields, particularly the elimination of Japanese from China. The Chinese Government was responsible under an Allied agreement for the disarmament of all Japanese military personnel and for the repatriation of all Japanese civilians and military personnel from China, Formosa and French Indo China north of the sixteenth degree of latitude. Our Government agreed to assist the Chinese in this task. The scope of the job was tremendous. There were about 3,000,000 Japanese, nearly one-half of them Army or Navy personnel to be evacuated. Water and rail transportation had been destroyed or was immobilized. Port facilities were badly damaged and overcrowded with relief and other supplies. The Japanese had to be disarmed, concentrated and then transported to the nearest available port. In some instances this involved long distances. At the ports they had to be individually searched and put through a health inspection. All had to be inoculated. Segregation camps had to be established at the ports to cope with the incidence of epidemic diseases such as Asiatic cholera. Finally, 3,000,000 persons had to be moved by ship to Japan.

American forces helped in the disarmament of Japanese units. Executive Headquarters and its truce teams were able to make the complicated arrangements necessary to transfer Japanese across lines and through areas involved in civil conflict on their way to ports of embarkation. American units also participated in the inspections at the port, while American medical units supervised all inoculation and other medical work. Finally, American and Japanese ships under the control of General MacArthur in Japan, and a number of United States Navy ships under the Seventh Fleet transported this enormous number of persons to reception ports in Japan.

At the end of last year, approximately 200,000 Japanese had been repatriated. They were leaving Chinese ports at a rate of about 2,500 a •day. By March of this year, rapidly increased efforts on the part of the American forces and the Chinese authorities involved had increased this rate to more than 20,000 a day. By November, 2,986,438 Japanese had been evacuated and the program was considered completed. Except for indeterminate numbers in certain parts of Manchuria, only war criminals and technicians retained on an emergency basis by the Chinese Government remain. That this tremendous undertaking has been accomplished despite conflict, disrupted communications and other difficulties will remain an outstanding example of successful American-Chinese cooperation toward a common goal.

Much has been said of the presence of United States armed forces in China during the past year. Last fall these forces were relatively large. They had to be. No one could prophesy in advance how well the Japanese forces in China would observe surrender terms. We had to provide forces adequate to assist the Chinese in the event of trouble. When it became obvious that the armed Japanese would not be a problem beyond the capabilities of the Chinese Armies to handle, redeployment was begun at once.

The chief responsibility of our forces was that of assisting in evacuation of Japanese. This task was prolonged by local circumstances. Provision of American personnel for the Executive Headquarters and in its truce teams has required a fairly large number of men, particularly since the all important network of radio and other communications was provided entirely by the United States. The Executive Headquarters is located at Peiping, a hundred miles from the sea and in an area where there was the possibility of local fighting. Hence, another responsibility was to protect the line of supply to and from Headquarters. Another duty our forces undertook immediately upon the Japanese surrender was to provide the necessary protection so that coal from the great mines northeast of Tientsin could reach the sea for shipment to supply the cities and railroads of central China. This coal was essential to prevent the collapse of this industrial area. Our Marines were withdrawn from this duty last September. Other units of our forces were engaged in searching for the bodies or graves of American soldiers who had died fighting the Japanese in China. Still others were required to guard United States installations and stores of equipment, and to process these for return to this country or sale as surplus property. . . .

Thus during the past year we have successfully assisted in the repatriation of the Japanese and have subsequently been able to bring most of our own troops home. We have afforded appropriate assistance in the reoccupation of the country from the Japanese. We have undertaken some emergency measures of economic assistance to prevent the collapse of China's economy and have liquidated our own wartime financial account with China.

It is a matter of deep regret that China has not yet been able to achieve unity by peaceful methods. Because he knows how serious the problem is, and how important it is to reach a solution, General Marshall has remained at his post even though active negotiations have been broken off by the Communist Party. We are ready to help China as she moves toward peace and genuine democratic government.

The views expressed a year ago by this Government are valid today. The plan for political unification agreed to last February is sound. The plan for military unification of last February has been made difficult of implementation by the progress of the fighting since last April, but the general principles involved are fundamentally sound.

China is a sovereign nation. We recognize that fact and we recognize the National Government of China. We continue to hope that the Government will find a peaceful solution. We are pledged not to interfere in the internal affairs of China. Our position is clear. While avoiding involvement in their civil strife, we will persevere with our policy of helping the Chinese people to bring about peace and economic recovery in their country.

As ways and means are presented for constructive aid to China, we will give them careful and sympathetic consideration. An example of such aid is the recent agricultural mission to China under Dean Hutchison of the University of California sent at the request of the Chinese Government. A joint Chinese-American Agricultural Collaboration Commission was formed which included the Hutchison mission. It spent over four months studying rural problems. Its recommendations are now available to the Chinese Government, and so also is any feasible aid we can give in implementing those recommendations. When conditions in China improve, we are prepared to consider aid in carrying out other projects, unrelated to civil strife, which would encourage economic reconstruction and reform in China and which, in so doing, would promote a general revival of commercial relations between American and Chinese businessmen.

We believe that our hopes for China are identical with what the

Chinese people themselves most earnestly desire. We shall therefore continue our positive and realistic policy toward China which is based on full respect for her national sovereignty and on our traditional friendship for the Chinese people and is designed to promote international peace.

MARSHALL ON CHINA MISSION

11 ⤳ THE SPECIAL REPRESENTATIVE of the President, Marshall, made a personal statement on January 7, 1947:[11]

The President has recently given a summary of the developments in China during the past year and the position of the American Government toward China. Circumstances now dictate that I should supplement this with impressions gained at first hand.

In this intricate and confused situation, I shall merely endeavor here to touch on some of the more important considerations—as they appeared to me—during my connection with the negotiations to bring about peace in China and a stable democratic form of government.

In the first place, the greatest obstacle to peace has been the complete, almost overwhelming suspicion with which the Chinese Communist Party and the Kuomintang regard each other.

On the one hand, the leaders of the Government are strongly opposed to a communistic form of government. On the other, the Communists frankly state that they are Marxists and intend to work toward establishing a communistic form of government in China, though first advancing through the medium of a democratic form of government of the American or British type.

The leaders of the Government are convinced in their minds that the Communist-expressed desire to participate in a government of the type endorsed by the Political Consultative Conference last January had for its purpose only a destructive intention. The Communists felt, I believe, that the government was insincere in its apparent acceptance of the PCC resolutions for the formation of the new government and intended by coercion of military force and the action of secret police to obliterate the Communist Party. Combined with this mutual deep distrust was the conspicuous error by both parties of ignoring the effect of the fears and suspicions of the other party in estimating the reason for proposals or opposition regard-

11 *Ibid.*, pp. 686–7.

ing the settlement of various matters under negotiation. They each sought only to take counsel of their own fears. They both, therefore, to that extent took a rather lopsided view of each situation and were susceptible to every evil suggestion or possibility. This complication was exaggerated to an explosive degree by the confused reports of fighting on the distant and tremendous fronts of hostile military contact. Patrol clashes were deliberately magnified into large offensive actions. The distortion of the facts was utilized by both sides to heap condemnation on the other. It was only through the reports of American officers in the field teams from Executive Headquarters that I could get even a partial idea of what was actually happening and the incidents were too numerous and the distances too great for the American personnel to cover all of the ground. I must comment here on the superb courage of the officers of our Army and Marines in struggling against almost insurmountable and maddening obstacles to bring some measure of peace to China.

I think the most important factors involved in the recent breakdown of negotiations are these: On the side of the National Government, which is in effect the Kuomintang, there is a dominant group of reactionaries who have been opposed, in my opinion, to almost every effort I have made to influence the formation of a genuine coalition government. This has usually been under the cover of political or party action, but since the Party was the Government, this action, though subtle or indirect, has been devastating in its effect. They were quite frank in publicly stating their belief that cooperation by the Chinese Communist Party in the government was inconceivable and that only a policy of force could definitely settle the issue. This group includes military as well as political leaders.

On the side of the Chinese Communist Party there are, I believe, liberals as well as radicals, though this view is vigorously opposed by many who believe that the Chinese Communist Party discipline is too rigidly enforced to admit of such differences of viewpoint. Nevertheless, it has appeared to me that there is a definite liberal group among the Communists, especially of young men who have turned to the Communists in disgust at the corruption evident in the local governments—men who would put the interest of the Chinese people above ruthless measures to establish a Communist ideology in the immediate future. The dyed-in-the-wool Communists do not hesitate at the most drastic measures to gain their end as, for instance, the destruction of communications in order to wreck the economy of China and produce a situation that would facilitate the overthrow or collapse of the Government, without any regard to the immediate suffering of the people involved. They completely distrust the leaders of the Kuomintang and appear convinced that every Government proposal is designed to crush the Chinese Communist Party. I must say that the quite evidently inspired mob actions of last February and March, some within a few blocks of where I was then engaged in completing negotiations, gave the Communists good excuse for such suspicions.

However, a very harmful and immensely provocative phase of the Chinese Communist Party procedure has been in the character of its propaganda. I wish to state to the American people that in the deliberate misrepresentation and abuse of the action, policies and purposes of our Government this propaganda has been without regard for the truth, without any regard whatsoever for the facts, and has given plain evidence of a determined purpose to mislead the Chinese people and the world and to arouse a bitter hatred of Americans. It has been difficult to remain silent in the midst of such public abuse and wholesale disregard of facts, but a denial would merely lead to the necessity of daily denials; an intolerable course of action for an American official. In the interest of fairness, I must state that the Nationalist Government publicity agency has made numerous misrepresentations, though not of the vicious nature of the Communist propaganda. Incidentally, the Communist statements regarding the Anping incident which resulted in the death of three Marines and the wounding of twelve others were almost pure fabrication, deliberately representing a carefully arranged ambuscade of a Marine convoy with supplies for the maintenance of Executive Headquarters and some UNRRA supplies, as a defence against a Marine assault. The investigation of this incident was a tortuous procedure of delays and maneuvers to disguise the true and privately admitted facts of the case.

WEDEMEYER SECRET REPORT

12 ᥟᥬ AFTER THE FAILURE of the Marshall mission the administration became convinced that further aid to Chiang would only be wasted and that in any case, the Nationalists were not yet in serious trouble. In spite of these convictions, in 1947 the administration continued to extend small amounts of aid in order to appease its Republican critics. As a further concession to the Republicans, General Marshall, now Secretary of State, dis-

patched General Wedemeyer to China in July on a fact-finding mission. (Significantly, Representative Walter Judd of Minnesota, a Republican critic of the administration's China policy, suggested this move.) Wedemeyer made his secret report to the President on September 19, 1947:[12]

Notwithstanding all the corruption and incompetence that one notes in China, it is a certainty that the bulk of the people are not disposed to a Communist political and economic structure. Some have become affiliated with Communism in indignant protest against oppressive police measures, corrupt practices and mal-administration of National Government officials. Some have lost all hope for China under existing leadership and turn to the Communists in despair. Some accept a new leadership by mere inertia.

Indirectly, the United States facilitated the Soviet program in the Far East by agreeing at the Yalta Conference to Russian re-entry into Manchuria, and later by withholding aid from the National Government. There were justifiable reasons for these policies. In the one case we were concentrating maximum Allied strength against Japanese in order to accelerate crushing defeat and thus save Allied lives. In the other, we were withholding unqualified support from a government within which corruption and incompetence were so prevalent that it was losing the support of its own people. Further, the United States had not yet realized that the Soviet Union would fail to cooperate in the accomplishment of world-wide plans for post-war rehabilitation. Our own participation in those plans has already afforded assistance to other nations and peoples, friends and former foes alike, to a degree unparalleled in humanitarian history.

Gradually it has become apparent that the World War II objectives for which we and others made tremendous sacrifices are not being fully attained, and that there remains in the world a force presenting even greater dangers to world peace than did the Nazi militarists and the Japanese jingoists. Consequently the United States made the decision in the Spring of 1947 to assist Greece and Turkey with a view to protecting their sovereignties, which were threatened by the direct or inspired activities of the Soviet Union. Charges of unilateral action and circumvention of the United Nations were made by members of that organization. In the light of its purposes and principles such criticisms seemed plausible. The United

[12] Excerpts, *ibid.*, pp. 766–75.

States promptly declared its intention of referring the matter to the United Nations when that organization would be ready to assume responsibility.

It follows that the United Nations should be informed of contemplated action with regard to China. If the recommendations of this report are approved, the United States should suggest to China that she inform the United Nations officially of her request to the United States for material assistance and advisory aid in order to facilitate China's post-war rehabilitation and economic recovery. This will demonstrate that the United Nations is not being circumvented, and that the United States is not infringing upon China's sovereignty, but contrarywise is cooperating constructively in the interest of peace and stability in the Far East, concomitantly in the world.

The situation in Manchuria has deteriorated to such a degree that prompt action is necessary to prevent that area from becoming a Soviet satellite. The Chinese Communists may soon gain military control of Manchuria and announce the establishment of a government. Outer Mongolia, already a Soviet satellite, may then recognize Manchuria and conclude a "mutual support agreement" with a de facto Manchurian government of the Chinese Communists. In that event, the Soviet Union might accomplish a mutual support agreement with Communist-dominated Manchuria, because of her current similar agreement with Outer Mongolia. This would create a difficult situation for China, the United States and the United Nations. Ultimately it could lead to a Communist-dominated China.

The United Nations might take immediate action to bring about cessation of hostilities in Manchuria as a prelude to the establishment of a Guardianship or Trusteeship. The Guardianship might consist of China, Soviet Russia, the United States, Great Britain and France. This should be attempted promptly and could be initiated only by China. Should one of the nations refuse to participate in Manchurian Guardianship, China might then request the General Assembly of the United Nations to establish a Trusteeship, under the provisions of the Charter.

Initially China might interpret Guardianship or Trusteeship as an infringement upon her sovereignty. But the urgency of the matter should encourage a realistic view of the situation. If these steps are not taken by China, Manchuria may be drawn into the Soviet orbit, despite United States aid, and lost, perhaps permanently, to China.

The economic deterioration and the incompetence and corruption in the political and military organizations in China should be considered against an all-inclusive background lest there be disproportionate emphasis upon defects. Comity requires that cognizance be taken of the following:

Unlike other Powers since V-J Day, China has never been free to devote full attention to internal problems that were greatly confounded by eight years of war. The current civil war has imposed an overwhelming financial and economic burden at a time when resources and energies have been dissipated and when, in any event, they would have been strained to the utmost to meet the problems of recovery.

The National Government has consistently, since 1927, opposed Communism. Today the same political leader and same civil and military officials are determined to prevent their country from becoming a Communist-dominated State or Soviet satellite.

Although the Japanese offered increasingly favorable surrender terms during the course of the war, China elected to remain steadfast with her Allies. If China had accepted surrender terms, approximately a million Japanese would have been released for employment against American forces in the Pacific.

I was assured by the Generalissimo that China would support to the limit of her ability an American program for the stabilization of the Far East. He stated categorically that, regardless of moral encouragement or material aid received from the United States, he is determined to oppose Communism and to create a democratic form of government in consonance with Doctor Sun Yat-sen's principles. He stated further that he plans to make sweeping reforms in the government including the removal of incompetent and corrupt officials. He stated that some progress has been made along these lines but, with spiraling inflation, economic distress and civil war, it has been difficult to accomplish fully these objectives. He emphasized that, when the Communist problem is solved, he could drastically reduce the Army and concentrate upon political and economic reforms. I retain the conviction that the Generalissimo is sincere in his desire to attain these objectives. I am not certain that he has today sufficient determination to do so if this requires absolute overruling of the political and military cliques surrounding him. Yet, if realistic United States aid is to prove effective in stabilizing the situation in China and in coping with the dangerous expansion of Communism, that determination must be established.

Adoption by the United States of a policy motivated solely toward stopping the expansion of Communism without regard to the continued existence of an unpopular repressive government would render any aid ineffective. Further, United States prestige in the Far East would suffer heavily, and wavering elements might turn away from the existing government to Communism.

In China [and Korea], the political, economic and psychological problems are inextricably mingled. All of them are complex and are becoming increasingly difficult of solution. Each has been studied assiduously in compliance with your directive. Each will be discussed in the course of this report. However, it is recognized that a continued global appraisal is mandatory in order to preclude disproportionate or untimely assistance to any specific area.

The following three postulates of United States foreign policy are pertinent to indicate the background of my investigations, analyses and report:

The United States will continue support of the United Nations in the attainment of its lofty aims, accepting the possible development that the Soviet Union or other nations may not actively participate.

Moral support will be given to nations and peoples that have established political and economic structures compatible with our own, or that give convincing evidence of their desire to do so.

Material aid may be given to those same nations and peoples in order to accelerate post-war rehabilitation and to develop economic stability, provided:

That such aid shall be used for the purposes intended.

That there is continuing evidence that they are taking effective steps to help themselves, or are firmly committed to do so.

That such aid shall not jeopardize American economy and shall conform to an integrated program that involves other international commitments and contributes to the attainment of political, economic and psychological objectives of the United States.

Political

Although the Chinese people are unanimous in their desire for peace at almost any cost, there seems to be no possibility of its realization under existing circumstances. On one side is the Kuomintang, whose reactionary leadership, repression and corruption have caused a loss of popular faith in the Government. On the other side, bound ideologically to the Soviet Union, are the Chinese Communists, whose eventual aim is admittedly a Communist state in China. Some reports indicate that Communist measures of land reform have gained for them the support of the majority of peasants in areas under their control, while others indicate that their ruthless tactics of land distribution and terrorism have alienated the majority of such peasants. They have, however, successfully organized many rural areas against the National Government. Moderate groups are caught between Kuomintang misrule and repression and ruthless Communist totalitarianism. Minority parties lack dynamic leadership and sizable following. Neither the moderates, many of whom are in the Kuomintang, nor the minority parties are able to make their influence felt because of National Government repression. Existing provincial opposition leading to possible separatist movements would probably crystallize only if collapse of the Government were imminent.

Soviet actions, contrary to the letter and spirit of the Sino-Soviet Treaty of 1945 and its related documents, have strengthened the Chinese Communist position in Manchuria, with political, economic and military repercussions on the National Government's position both in Manchuria and in China proper, and have made more difficult peace and stability in China. The present trend points toward a gradual disintegration of the National Government's control, with the ultimate possibility of a Communist-dominated China.

Steps taken by the Chinese Government toward governmental reorganization in mid-April 1947 aroused hopes of improvement in the political situation. However, the reorganization resulted in little change. Reactionary influences continue to mold important policies even though the Generalissimo remains the principal determinative force in the government. Since the April reorganization, the most significant change has been the appointment of General Chen Cheng to head the civil and military administration in Manchuria. Projected steps include elections in the Fall for the formation of a constitutional government, but, under present conditions, they are not expected to result in a government more representative than the present regime.

Economic

Under the impact of civil strife and inflation, the Chinese economy is disintegrating. The most probable outcome of present trends would be, not sudden collapse, but a continued and creeping paralysis and consequent decline in the authority and power of the National Government. The past ten years of war have caused serious deterioration of transportation and communication facilities, mines, utilities and industries. Notwithstanding some commendable efforts and large amounts of economic aid, their overall capabilities are scarcely half those of the pre-war period. With disruption of transportation facilities and the loss of much of North China and Manchuria, important resources of those rich areas are no longer available for the rehabilitation and support of China's economy.

Inflation in China has been diffused slowly through an enormous population without causing the immediate dislocation which would have occurred in a highly industrialized economy. The rural people, 80 per cent of the total Chinese population of 450 million, barter food-stuffs for local handicraft products without suffering a drastic cut in living standards. Thus, local economies exist in many parts of China, largely insulated from the disruption of urban industry. Some local economies are under the control of Communists, and some are loosely under the control of provincial authorities.

The principal cause of the hyper-inflation is the long-continued deficit in the national budget. Present revenue collections, plus the profits of nationalized enterprises, cover only one-third of governmental expenditures, which are approximately 70 per cent military, and an increasing proportion of the budget is financed by the issuance of new currency. In the first six months of 1947 note-issue was tripled but rice prices increased seven-fold. Thus prices and governmental expenditures spiral upwards, with price increases occurring faster than new currency can be printed. With further price increases, budget revisions will undoubtedly be necessary. The most urgent economic need of Nationalist China is a reduction of the military budget.

China's external official assets amounted to $327 million (US) on July 30, 1947. Privately-held foreign exchange assets are at least $600 million and may total $1500 million, but no serious attempt has been made to mobilize these private resources for rehabilitation purposes. Private Chinese assets located in China include probably $200 million in gold, and about $75 million in US currency notes. Although China has not exhausted her foreign official assets, and probably will not do so at the present rates of imports and exports until early 1949, the continuing deficit in her external balance of payments is a serious problem. . . .

Under inflationary conditions, long-term investment is unattractive for both Chinese and foreign capital. Private Chinese funds tend to go into short-term advances, hoarding of commodities, and capital flight. The entire psychology is speculative and inflationary, preventing ordinary business planning and handicapping industrial recovery.

Foreign business enterprises in China are adversely affected by the inefficient and corrupt administration of exchange and import controls, discriminatory application of tax laws, the increasing role of government trading agencies and the trend towards state ownership of industries. The Chinese Government has taken some steps toward improvement but generally has been apathetic in its efforts. Between 1944 and 1947, the anti-inflationary measure on which the Chinese Government placed most reliance was the public sale of gold borrowed from the United States. The intention was to absorb paper currency, and thus reduce the effective demand for goods. Under the circumstance of continued large deficits, however, the only effect of the gold sales program was to retard slightly the price inflation and dissipate dollar assets. . . .

On August 1, 1947, the State Council approved a "Plan for Economic Reform." This appears to be an omnibus of plans covering all phases of Chinese economic reconstruction but its effectiveness cannot yet be determined.

Social—Cultural

Public education has been one of the chief victims of war and social and economic disruption. Schoolhouses, textbooks and other equipment have been destroyed and the cost of replacing any considerable portion cannot now be met. Teachers, like other public servants, have seen the purchasing power of a month's salary shrink to the market value of a few days' rice ration. This applies to the entire educational system, from primary schools, which provide a medium to combat the nation's grievous illiteracy, to universities, from which must come the nation's professional men, technicians and administrators. The universities have suffered in an additional and no less serious respect—traditional academic freedom. Students participating in protest demonstrations have been severely and at times brutally punished by National Government agents without pretense of trial or public evidence of the sedition charged. Faculty members have often been dismissed or refused employment with no evidence of professional unfitness, patently because they were politically objectionable to government officials. Somewhat similarly, periodicals have been closed down "for reasons of military security" without stated charges, and permitted to reopen only after new managements have been imposed. Resumption of educational and other public welfare activities on anything like the desired scale can be accomplished only by restraint of officialdom's abuses, and when the nation's economy is stabilized sufficiently to defray the cost of such vital activities.

Military

The overall military position of the National Government has deteriorated in the past several months and the current military situation favors Communist forces. The Generalissimo has never wavered in his contention that he is fighting for national independence against forces of an armed rebellion nor has he been completely convinced that the Communist problem can be resolved except by force of arms. Although the Nationalist Army has a preponderance of force, the tactical initiative rests with the Communists. Their hit-and-run tactics, adapted to their mission of destruction at points or in areas of their own selection, give them a decided advantage over Nationalists, who must defend many critical areas including connecting lines of communication. Obviously large numbers of Nationalist troops involved in such defensive roles are immobilized whereas Communist tactics permit almost complete freedom of action. The Nationalists' position is precarious in Manchuria, where they occupy only a slender finger of territory. Their control is strongly disputed in Shantung and Hopei Provinces where the Communists make frequent dislocating attacks against isolated garrisons.

In order to improve materially the current military situation, the Nationalist forces must first stabilize the fronts and then regain the initiative. Further, since the Government is supporting the civil war with approximately seventy per cent of its national budget, it is evident that steps taken to alleviate the situation must point toward an improvement in the effectiveness of the armed forces with a concomitant program of social, political and economic reforms, including a decrease in the size of the military establishment. Whereas some rather ineffective steps have been taken to reorganize and revitalize the command structure, and more sweeping reforms are projected, the effectiveness of the Nationalist Army requires a sound program of equipment and improved logistical support. The present industrial potential of China is inadequate to support military forces effectively. Chinese forces under present conditions cannot cope successfully with

internal strife or fulfill China's obligations as a member of the family
of nations. Hence outside aid, in the form of munitions (most urgently
ammunition) and technical assistance, is essential before any plan of
operations can be undertaken with a reasonable prospect of success.
Military advice is now available to the Nationalists on a General Staff
level through American military advisory groups. The Generalissimo
expressed to me repeatedly a strong desire to have this advice and
supervision extended in scope to include field forces, training centers
and particularly logistical agencies.

Extension of military aid by the United States to the National
Government might possibly be followed by similar aid from the
Soviet Union to the Chinese Communists, either openly or covertly—
the latter course seems more likely. An arena of conflicting ideologies
might be created as in 1935 in Spain. There is always the possibility
that such developments in this area, as in Europe and in the Middle
East, might precipitate a third world war. . . .

A China dominated by Chinese Communists would be inimical to
the interests of the United States, in view of their openly expressed
hostility and active opposition to those principles which the United
States regards as vital to the peace of the world. . . .

Recommendations

It is recommended:

That the United States Government provide as early as practicable
moral, advisory, and material support to China in order to contribute
to the early establishment of peace in the world in consonance with
the enunciated principles of the United Nations, and concomitantly
to protect United States strategic interests against militant forces
which now threaten them.

That United States policies and actions suggested in this report be
thoroughly integrated by appropriate government agencies with other
international commitments. It is recognized that any foreign assistance
extended must avoid jeopardizing the American economy.

China

That China be advised that the United States is favorably disposed
to continue aid designed to protect China's territorial integrity and
to facilitate her recovery, under agreements to be negotiated by
representatives of the two governments, with the following stipulations:

That China inform the United Nations promptly of her request to the United States for increased material and advisory assistance.

That China request the United Nations to take immediate action to bring about a cessation of hostilities in Manchuria and request that Manchuria be placed under a Five-Power Guardianship or, failing that, under a Trusteeship in accordance with the United Nations Charter.

That China make effective use of her own resources in a program for economic reconstruction and initiate sound fiscal policies leading to reduction of budgetary deficits.

That China give continuing evidence that the urgently required political and military reforms are being implemented.

That China accept American advisors as responsible representatives of the United States Government in specified military and economic fields to assist China in utilizing United States aid in the manner for which it is intended.

TRUMAN'S REQUEST FOR CHINA AID

13 ✍ THE ADMINISTRATION regarded Wedemeyer's suggestions and others like them as mere palliatives. But in February 1948, to secure the support of the China bloc in Congress for the Marshall Plan for Europe, Truman found it necessary to request a large appropriation to aid China. The economy-minded Eightieth Congress provided only $463 million, although the President had requested $570 million on February 18:[13]

The continued deterioration of the Chinese economy is a source of deep concern to the United States. Ever since the return of General Marshall from China, the problem of assistance to the Chinese has been under continuous study. We have hoped for conditions in China that would make possible the effective and constructive use of American assistance in reconstruction and rehabilitation. Conditions have not developed as we had hoped, and we can only do what is feasible under circumstances as they exist.

We can assist in retarding the current economic deterioration and thus give the Chinese Government a further opportunity to initiate the measures necessary to the establishment of more stable economic conditions. But it is, and has been, clear that only the Chinese Government itself can undertake the vital measures necessary to provide

[13] Excerpt, *ibid.*, pp. 981-3.

the framework within which efforts toward peace and true economic recovery may be effective.

In determining the character and dimensions of the program which might be suited to this purpose, we have had to take into account a number of diverse and conflicting factors, including the other demands on our national resources at this time, the availability of specific commodities, the dimensions and complexities of the problems facing the Chinese Government, and the extent to which these problems could be promptly and effectively alleviated by foreign aid. United States assistance to China, like that provided to any other nation, must be adapted to its particular requirements and capacities.

In the light of these factors, I recommend that the Congress authorize a program for aid to China in the amount of $570,000,000 to provide assistance until June 30, 1949.

The program should make provision for the financing, through loans or grants, of essential imports into China in the amount of $510,000,000. This estimate is based upon prices as of January 1, 1948, since it is impossible at present to predict what effect current price changes may have on the program. Revised dollar estimates can be presented in connection with the request for appropriations if necessary. The essential imports include cereals, cotton, petroleum, fertilizer, tobacco, pharmaceuticals, coal, and repair parts for existing capital equipment. The quantities provided for under this program are within the limits of available supplies. The financing of these essential commodity imports by the United States would permit the Chinese Government to devote its limited dollar resources to the most urgent of its other needs.

The program should also provide $60,000,000 for a few selected reconstruction projects to be initiated prior to June 30, 1949. There is an urgent need for the restoration of essential transportation facilities, fuel and power operations, and export industries. This work could be undertaken in areas sheltered from military operations and could help in improving the supply and distribution of essential commodities.

As in the case of aid to European recovery, the conduct of this program of aid should be made subject to an agreement between China and the United States setting forth the conditions and procedures for administering the aid. The agreement should include assurances that the Chinese Government will take such economic, financial, and other measures as are practicable, looking toward the ultimate goal of economic stability and recovery. The United States would, of course, reserve the right to terminate aid if it is determined that the assistance provided is not being handled in accordance with the agreement or that the policies of the Chinese Government are inconsistent with the objective of using the aid to help achieve a self-supporting economy.

Pending establishment of the agency which is to be set up for the administration of the European recovery program, the assistance to China should be carried forward under the existing machinery now administering the foreign-relief programs. Legislation authorizing the Chinese program should make possible transfer of the administration of the Chinese program to the agency administering our aid to European recovery. The need for authority in the administering agency to make adjustments in the program from time to time will be as great here as in the European recovery program.

ACHESON ON FURTHER AID TO CHINA

14 ᴇᏣ   THE ADMINISTRATION's position in 1949 on further aid to Chiang is summarized in a letter of March 14, 1949, from Secretary of State Acheson to Senator Tom Connally, Democrat from Texas:[14]

Despite the present aid program authorized by the last Congress, together with the very substantial other aid extended by the United States to China since VJ-day, aggregating over $2,000,000,000, the economic and military position of the Chinese Government has deteriorated to the point where the Chinese Communists hold almost all important areas of China from Manchuria to the Yangtze River and have the military capability of expanding their control to the populous areas of the Yangtze Valley and of eventually dominating south China. The national government does not have the military capability of maintaining a foothold in south China against a determined Communist advance. The Chinese Government forces have lost no battles during the past year because of lack of ammunition and equipment, while the Chinese Communists have captured the major portion of military supplies, exclusive of ammunition, furnished the Chinese Government by the United States since VJ-day. There is no evidence that the furnishing of additional military matériel

---

[14] Excerpt reprinted from *Congressional Record*, Eighty-first Congress, first session, pp. 4914–15.

would alter the pattern of current developments in China. There is, however, ample evidence that the Chinese people are weary of hostilities and that there is an overwhelming desire for peace at any price. To furnish solely military matériel and advice would only prolong hostilities and the suffering of the Chinese people and would arouse in them deep resentment against the United States. Yet, to furnish the military means for bringing about a reversal of the present deterioration and for providing some prospect of successful military resistance would require the use of an unpredictably large American armed force in actual combat, a course of action which would represent direct United States involvement in China's fratricidal warfare and would be contrary to our traditional policy toward China and the interests of this country.

In these circumstances, the extension of as much as $1,500,000,000 of credits to the Chinese Government, as proposed by the bill, would embark this Government on an undertaking the eventual cost of which would be unpredictable but of great magnitude, and the outcome of which would almost surely be catastrophic. The field supervision of United States military aid, the pledging of revenue of major Chinese ports in payment of United States aid, United States administration and collection of Chinese customs in such ports, and United States participation in Chinese tax administration, all of which are called for by the bill, would without question be deeply resented by the Chinese people as an extreme infringement of China's sovereignty and would arouse distrust in the minds of the Chinese people with respect to the motives of the United States in extending aid. While the use of up to $500,000,000 in support of the Chinese currency, as proposed in the bill, would undoubtedly ease temporarily the fiscal problem of the Chinese Government, stabilization of the Chinese currency cannot be considered feasible so long as the government's monetary outlays exceed its income by a large margin. After the first $500,000,000 had been expended the United States would find it necessary to continue provision of funds to cover the Chinese Government's budgetary deficit if the inflationary spiral were not to be resumed. That China could be expected to repay United States financial, economic, and military aid of the magnitude proposed, which the bill indicates should all be on a credit basis, cannot be supported by realistic estimates of China's future ability to service foreign debts even under conditions of peace and economic stability.

The United States has in the past sought to encourage the Chinese

Government to initiate those vital measures necessary to provide a basis for economic improvement and political stability. It has recognized that in the absence of a Chinese Government capable of initiating such measures and winning popular support, United States aid of great magnitude would be dissipated and United States attempts to guide the operations of the Chinese Government would be ineffective and probably lead to direct involvement in China's fratricidal warfare. General Marshall reflected these considerations when he stated in February 1948 that an attempt to underwrite the Chinese economy and the Chinese Government's military effort represented a burden on the United States economy and a military responsibility which he could not recommend as a course of action for this Government.

Despite the above observations, it would be undesirable for the United States precipitously to cease aid to areas under the control of the Chinese Government which it continues to recognize. Future developments in China, including the outcome of political negotiations now being undertaken, are uncertain. Consideration is being given, therefore, to a request for congressional action to extend the authority of the China Aid Act of 1948 to permit commitment of unobligated appropriations for a limited period beyond April 2, 1949, the present expiration date of the act. If during such a period, the situation in China clarifies itself sufficiently, further recommendations might be made.

Because of the urgency of the matter this letter has not been cleared by the Bureau of the Budget, to which copies are being sent.

PRESIDENT'S STATEMENT ON FORMOSA

15 ►§ ON DECEMBER 8, 1949, the Nationalist government moved to the island of Formosa. On December 30 Senator Robert A. Taft of Ohio, the leader of the Republican conservatives in Congress, suggested that, if necessary, the U.S. Navy should be used to keep Formosa out of Communist hands. On December 31, in a letter to Republican Senator William F. Knowland, Herbert Hoover proposed the same course of action. The administration was attempting to enunciate a policy for Formosa when the President made a statement on January 5, 1950:[15]

---

[15] Reprinted from *Department of State Bulletin*, January 16, 1950, p. 79.

The United States Government has always stood for good faith in international relations. Traditional United States policy toward China, as exemplified in the open-door policy, called for international respect for the territorial integrity of China. This principle was recently reaffirmed in the United Nations General Assembly resolution of December 8, 1949, which, in part, calls on all states—

> To refrain from (a) seeking to acquire spheres of influence or to create foreign controlled regimes within the territory of China; (b) seeking to obtain special rights or privileges within the territory of China.

A specific application of the foregoing principles is seen in the present situation with respect to Formosa. In the joint declaration at Cairo on December 1, 1943, the President of the United States, the British Prime Minister, and the President of China stated that it was their purpose that territories Japan had stolen from China, such as Formosa, should be restored to the Republic of China. The United States was a signatory to the Potsdam declaration of July 26, 1945, which declared that the terms of the Cairo declaration should be carried out. The provisions of this declaration were accepted by Japan at the time of its surrender. In keeping with these declarations, Formosa was surrendered to Generalissimo Chiang Kai-shek, and for the past 4 years, the United States and the other Allied Powers have accepted the exercise of Chinese authority over the Island.

The United States has no predatory designs on Formosa or on any other Chinese territory. The United States has no desire to obtain special rights or privileges or to establish military bases on Formosa at this time. Nor does it have any intention of utilizing its armed forces to interfere in the present situation. The United States Government will not pursue a course which will lead to involvement in the civil conflict in China.

Similarly, the United States Government will not provide military aid or advice to Chinese forces on Formosa. In the view of the United States Government, the resources on Formosa are adequate to enable them to obtain the items which they might consider necessary for the defense of the Island. The United States Government proposes to continue under existing legislative authority the present ECA [Economic Cooperation Administration—Eds.] program of economic assistance.

16 &s AFTER THE PRESIDENT's statement of the morning, Secretary
Acheson held a press conference:[16]

I am having this conference this afternoon at the request and at
the direction of the President for the purpose of going into the
background of the statement which he made this morning on the
subject of Formosa.

I should like to make a few remarks on this subject for the purpose
of trying to put it in its setting for you, and then we will get down
into such details as you want to get into.

Why was the statement made at this particular time? That is a
question that arises in all of your minds and I want to recall to you
that I have said very often in these meetings that the foreign policy
of the United States is determined not merely by what the State
Department says, or not even by what the President says, and not
even by what the Congress says, but reflects the sum total of the
activities, thoughts, and speech of the American people. For the
past week or 10 days, this subject of Formosa has become one of the
foremost subjects of discussion throughout the country.

The ordinary processes of life in this town of Washington have
made their contribution. We have had leak and counterleak, gossip
and countergossip. We have had the contributions of distinguished
statesmen in the debate. We have had a great deal of talk in the
press and on the radio. Much of that is good and much of that is
desirable, and all of it has to go on to make the United States the
democracy that it is. But we slide very easily from discussion to the
statement of fact. I have here a distinguished foreign newspaper
dated Friday last [December 30] which announces as a fact that
President Truman has decided, et cetera, and et cetera, giving something which President Truman had not decided and had not intended
to decide. Therefore, what has occurred is that we have gotten a great
deal of confusion in the minds of our own people. We have gotten
a great deal of confusion in the minds of foreign people. We have
stirred up a good deal of speculation, all of which, if allowed to continue, would be highly prejudicial to the interests of the United
States of America. And therefore, it was the President's desire to

16 *Ibid.*, pp. 79–81.

clarify the situation. He was not primarily concerned in stating anything new, and you will find very little which is new in the statement. What he was interested in doing was bringing clarity out of confusion.

That, I think, gives you the background as to why it was necessary to make the statement at the present time. It would have been desirable from our point of view if the whole question of the Far East, and all of the parts of the Far East and of Formosa, which after all is a small part of the great question of the Far East, could have been discussed very fully with members of both parties on the Hill before any statement was made. But one has to choose in this life, and it was more important to clarify thinking than it was to go on and have the most desirable of all possible things which is consultation.

Now, getting down to this statement, let's be clear about one or two things. There has been a great deal of amateur military strategy indulged in in regard to this matter of Formosa. The underlying factors in the decision are not in that area. They have to do with the fundamental integrity of the United States and with maintaining in the world the belief that when the United States takes a position it sticks to that position and does not change it by reason of transitory expediency or advantage on its part. If we are going to maintain the free nations of the world as a great unit opposed to the encroachment of communism and other sorts of totalitarian aggression, the world must believe that we stand for principle and that we are honorable and decent people and that we do not put forward words, as propagandists do in other countries, to serve their advantage only to throw them overboard when some change in events makes the position difficult for us.

We believe in integrity in our foreign relations. We believe also in respect of the integrity of other countries. That is a view not held by some other countries with respect to China.

It is important that our position in regard to China should never be subject to the slightest doubt or the slightest question.

Now, what has that position been? In the middle of the war, the President of the United States, the Prime Minister of Great Britain, and the President of China agreed at Cairo that among the areas stolen from China by Japan was Formosa and Formosa should go back to China.

As the President pointed out this morning, that statement was incorporated in the declaration at Potsdam and that declaration at

Potsdam was conveyed to the Japanese as one of the terms of their surrender and was accepted by them, and the surrender was made on that basis.

Shortly after that, the Island of Formosa was turned over to the Chinese in accordance with the declarations made and with the conditions of the surrender.

The Chinese have administered Formosa for 4 years. Neither the United States nor any other ally ever questioned that authority and that occupation. When Formosa was made a province of China nobody raised any lawyers' doubts about that. That was regarded as in accordance with the commitments.

Now, in the opinion of some, the situation is changed. They believe that the forces now in control of the mainland of China, the forces which undoubtedly will soon be recognized by some other countries, are not friendly to us, and therefore they want to say, "Well, we have to wait for a treaty." We did not wait for a treaty on Korea. We did not wait for a treaty on the Kuriles. We did not wait for a treaty for the islands over which we have trusteeship.

Whatever may be the legal situation, the United States of America, Mr. Truman said this morning, is not going to quibble on any lawyers' words about the integrity of its position. That is where we stand.

Therefore, the President says, we are not going to use our forces in connection with the present situation in Formosa. We are not going to attempt to seize the Island. We are not going to get involved militarily in any way on the Island of Formosa. So far as I know, no responsible person in the Government, no military man has ever believed that we should involve our forces in the island.

I do not believe that is new policy. It would be new policy if we decided to do that. The President is affirming what so far as I know has been the view of his Administration, and the unquestioned view ever since I have known about it.

The President goes on to say that we do not intend to give military assistance or advice, that is matériel and military people, to the forces on Formosa, and he says why. He says that there are resources on that Island which are adequate to enable those on the island to obtain whatever necessary military supplies they believe they have to have. That is against a background of very considerable gifts on our part at a time when the Government on Formosa was recognized by everybody as the Government of China and was in control of a very large part of China. We gave vast amounts of military equipment to that government after the war up until 1948. In 1948 another act of Congress was passed, and 125 million dollars of military equipment was turned over.

That is not where the difficulty lies in maintaining the Island by the forces on it. It is not that they lack rifles or ammunition or that, if they do have any deficiencies in any of those, they cannot purchase what they need. That is not the trouble. The trouble lies elsewhere, and it is not the function of the United States nor will it or can it attempt to furnish a will to resist and a purpose for resistance to those who must provide for themselves.

That is the background of this statement. The President goes on to say that in regard to economic assistance which we have been furnishing, we will furnish it for as long as the legislation that Congress has passed permits us to. Whether that legislation will be extended or not, I don't wish to prejudice this afternoon. That is a matter for discussion with the leaders, and for action by the Congress.

We have been, through the ECA, conducting programs one of which has resulted in all the fertilizer necessary for the spring crop on the Island of Formosa. Others have been the purchase of necessary oil for refining on the Island and for running the power plants and other things on the Island. Other programs have had to do with keeping their power plants and other factories in repair and in operation. Those are going forward.

Now those are the main statements of background which I wish to make. I am informed by Mr. McDermott that some of you wish me to say what if any significance is to be attached to the sentence in the next-to-last paragraph of the statement which says, "The United States has no desire to obtain special rights or privileges or to establish military bases on Formosa at this time." The question is, what does that phrase "at this time" mean. That phrase does not qualify or modify or weaken the fundamental policies stated in this declaration by the President in any respect. It is a recognition of the fact that, in the unlikely and unhappy event that our forces might be attacked in the Far East, the United States must be completely free to take whatever action in whatever area is necessary for its own security.

17 ◆§ MANY AMERICANS came to view the State Department as criminally negligent in its conduct of China policy. As a consequence, the administration had to spend considerable time and energy in defending the Foreign Service. That the attackers were not always Republicans is illustrated by the following statement of John F. Kennedy on January 30, 1949:[17]

Over these past few days we have learned the extent of the disasters befalling China and the United States. Our relationship with China since the end of the Second World War has been a tragic one, and it is of the utmost importance that we search out and spotlight those who must bear the responsibility for our present predicament.

When we look at the ease with which the Communists have overthrown the National Government of Chiang Kai-shek, it comes as somewhat of a shock to remember that on November 22, 1941, our Secretary of State, Cordell Hull, handed Ambassador Namuru an ultimatum to the effect that: (1) Government of Japan will withdraw all military, naval, air, and police forces from China and Indochina; (2) the United States and Japan will not support militarily, politically, economically, any government or regime in China other than the National Government of the Republic of China.

It was clearly enunciated that the independence of China and the stability of the National Government was the fundamental object of our far eastern policy.

That this and other statements of our policies in the Far East led directly to the attack on Pearl Harbor is well known. And it might be said that we almost knowingly entered into combat with Japan to preserve the independence of China and the countries to the south of it. Contrast this policy which reached its height in 1943 when the United States and Britain agreed at Cairo to liberate China and return to that country at the end of the war Manchuria and all Japanese-held areas, to the confused and vacillating policy which we have followed since that day.

In 1944 Gen. "Vinegar Joe" [Joseph W.—Eds.] Stilwell presented

[17] Reprinted from Congressional Record, Eighty-first Congress, first session, p. A993.

a plan to arm 1,000,000 Chinese Communists, who had been carefully building their resources in preparation for a post-war seizure of power, and with them to capture Shanghai and clear the Yangtze. This plan was supported by some State Department officials, including Ambassador Clarence Gauss. Chiang Kai-shek refused to cooperate with this plan, which would have presented the Chinese Communists with an easy coup. Chiang requested that Stilwell be recalled, which caused such bitter comment in this country; and Gauss resigned. From this date on our relations with the National Government declined.

At the Yalta Conference in 1945 a sick Roosevelt, with the advice of General Marshall and other Chiefs of Staff, gave the Kurile Islands as well as the control of various strategic Chinese ports, such as Port Arthur and Dairen, to the Soviet Union.

According to former Ambassador [William C.—Eds.] Bullitt, in Life magazine in 1947, "Whatever share of the responsibility was Roosevelt's and whatever share was Marshall's the vital interest of the United States in the independent integrity of China was sacrificed, and the foundation was laid for the present tragic situation in the Far East."

When the armies of Soviet Russia withdrew from Manchuria they left Chinese Communists in control of this area and in possession of great masses of Japanese war matériel.

During this period began the great split in the minds of our diplomats over whether to support the government of Chiang Kai-shek, or force Chiang Kai-shek as the price of our assistance to bring Chinese Communists into his government to form a coalition.

When Ambassador Patrick Hurley resigned in 1945 he stated, "Professional diplomats continuously advised the Chinese Communists that my efforts in preventing the collapse of the national government did not represent the policy of the United States. The chief opposition to the accomplishment of our mission came from American career diplomats, the embassy at Chungking, and the Chinese Far Eastern divisions of the State Department."

With the troubled situation in China beginning to loom large in the United States, General Marshall was sent at the request of President Truman as special emissary to China to effect a compromise and to bring about a coalition government.

In Ambassador Bullitt's article in Life, he states, and I quote: "In early summer of 1946 in order to force Chiang Kai-shek to take

Communists into the Chinese Government, General Marshall had the Department of State refuse to give licenses for export of ammunition to China. Thus from the summer of 1946 to February 1948 not a single shell or a single cartridge was delivered to China for use in its American armament. And in the aviation field Marshall likewise blundered, and as a result of his breaking the American Government's contract to deliver to China planes to maintain eight and one-third air groups, for 3 years no combat or bombing planes were delivered to China—from September 1946 to March 1948. As Marshall himself confessed in February 1948 to the House Committee on Foreign Affairs, this "was in effect an embargo on military supplies."

In 1948 we appropriated $468,000,000 for China, only a fraction of what we were sending to Europe, and out of this $468,000,000 only $125,000,000 was for military purposes. The end was drawing near; the assistance was too little and too late; and the nationalist government was engaged in a death struggle with the on-rushing Communist armies.

On November 20, 1948, former Senator D. Worth Clark, who had been sent on a special mission to China by the Senate Committee on Appropriations, in his report to that committee said, "Piecemeal aid will no longer save failing China from communism. It is now an all-out program or none, a fish or cut bait proposition."

Clark said this conclusion was confirmed by Ambassador J. Leighton Stuart and top American Army officers in China.

On November 25, 1948, 3 years too late, the New York Times said: "Secretary of State George Marshall said today the United States Government was considering what assistance it could properly give to the Chinese Government in the present critical situation."

On December 21 a Times headline was: "ECA Administrator [Paul G.—Eds.] Hoffman, after seeing Truman, discloses freezing of $70,-000,000 program in China in view of uncertain war situation."

The indifference, if not the contempt, with which the State Department and the President treated the wife of the head of the nationalist government, who was then fighting for a free China—Madame Chiang Kai-shek—was the final chapter in this tragic story.

Our policy in China has reaped the whirlwind. The continued insistence that aid would not be forthcoming unless a coalition government with the Communists was formed, was a crippling blow to the national government. So concerned were our diplomats and their advisers, the [Owen—Eds.] Lattimores and the [John K.—Eds.]

Fairbanks, with the imperfections of the diplomatic system in China after 20 years of war, and the tales of corruption in high places, that they lost sight of our tremendous stake in a non-Communist China.

There were those who claimed, and still claim, that Chinese communism was not really communism at all but merely an advanced agrarian movement which did not take directions from Moscow.

Listen to the words of the Bolton report: "Its doctrines follow those of Lenin and Stalin. Its leaders are Moscow-trained (of 35 leading Chinese Communist political leaders listed in the report, over a half either spent some time or studied in Moscow). Its policies and actions, its strategy and tactics are Communist. The Chinese Communists have followed faithfully every zigzag of the Kremlin's line for a generation."

This is the tragic story of China whose freedom we once fought to preserve. What our young men had saved, our diplomats and our President have frittered away.

6 · Loyalty and Security

In the 1930's members of the Communist party made important inroads into a few areas of American life, notably in the labor movement and among intellectuals. They also penetrated the federal bureaucracy, in which a group of strategically placed conspirators engaged in passing secret documents to Russian agents, a form of espionage that persisted into the war period. But during World War II the government began to take measures to protect itself against disloyalty. Before the war, in 1939, Congress made it unlawful for any federal employee "to have membership in any political party . . . which advocates the overthrow of our constitutional form of government" and in 1941 appropriated $100,000 for an FBI investigation of employees "who are members of subversive organizations." In April 1942 the Attorney General appointed an Interdepartmental Committee on Investigations to advise government agencies on procedures for examining employee loyalty and to prepare reports on so-called front groups. In 1943 President Roosevelt replaced this committee with an interdepartmental advisory board that was "to consider cases of subversive action on the part of employees." In the next three years this board heard 726 cases, twenty-four of which resulted in dismissals from the federal service. Ultimate responsibility for the government's loyalty and security programs, however, rested with the individual agency chiefs, whose standards and procedures varied widely, sometimes to the detriment of employees, sometimes to the harm of the government.

In 1945 and afterward, revelations of espionage seriously disturbed Congress and the public and focused critical attention on the government's loyalty and security programs. Early in 1945 the Office of Strategic Services discovered that important OSS documents had fallen into the hands of the editor of Amerasia, a pro-Communist monthly magazine established to influence American Far Eastern policies. A raid on the Amerasia offices uncovered reams of stolen government documents, and subsequent investigation established a link between Amerasia's editor and foreign Communists. Even more frightening was the 1946 report of the Canadian Royal Commission on Soviet espionage. The commission concluded that the Canadian Communist party was an arm of the Soviet government, that several Soviet spy rings had been operating in Canada, and that at least twenty-three Canadians "in positions of trust" had aided in transmitting atomic secrets to Moscow.

In response to rising congressional insistence that the American government's loyalty procedures be tightened, President Truman in 1947 issued an executive order revamping the entire program. The President's order did not satisfy conservatives, antagonized liberals, and failed to calm the public. In time, with results again controversial and unsatisfying, Congress and the Supreme Court addressed themselves to the problem of how an open society ought to deal with a minority whom it believes to be totalitarian and disloyal.

In the next few years evidence of treason continued to accumulate. As in the case of Alger Hiss, most of the revelations concerned alleged espionage in the 1930's, but in two instances betrayal was more recent. On March 4, 1949, FBI agents captured Judith Coplon, an employee of the Department of Justice, in the act of passing documents to a Russian spy. And in February 1950 the British government arrested Klaus Fuchs, a scientist who had worked on the Los Alamos project, and charged him with having passed secrets to the Russians between 1943 and 1947. Fuchs's subsequent interrogation implicated a group of Americans, including Julius and Ethel Rosenberg, who were eventually executed for their espionage. The sad irony is that while these events were feeding public anxieties about internal subversion, the actual menace of domestic Communism was vanishing. Thrown on the defensive by the Cold War, the American Communist party suffered a sharp decline in membership, was driven from the labor movement, and lost its influence on the loyal American left. By the time the danger had entirely disappeared, disloyalty became a political issue that almost wrecked the Truman administration. In 1950 McCarthyism burst upon the country and soon poisoned political discourse, disrupted parts of the civil service, and impaired public confidence in the executive branch of the government.

EXECUTIVE ORDER ON LOYALTY

1 ◆§ ON NOVEMBER 25, 1946, President Truman established a Temporary Commission on Loyalty, composed of repre-

sentatives from the departments of Justice, State, Treasury, War, and Navy and from the Civil Service Commission. On the basis of the report of this commission, President Truman, on March 21, 1947, issued an executive order (No. 9835) prescribing uniform procedures for the government's loyalty program:[1]

WHEREAS each employee of the Government of the United States is endowed with a measure of trusteeship over the democratic processes which are the heart and sinew of the United States; and

WHEREAS it is of vital importance that persons employed in the Federal service be of complete and unswerving loyalty to the United States; and

WHEREAS, although the loyalty of by far the overwhelming majority of all Government employees is beyond question, the presence within the Government service of any disloyal or subversive person constitutes a threat to our democratic processes; and

WHEREAS maximum protection must be afforded the United States against infiltration of disloyal persons into the ranks of its employees, and equal protection from unfounded accusations of disloyalty must be afforded the loyal employees of the Government:
NOW, THEREFORE . . .

PART I—INVESTIGATION OF APPLICANTS

1. There shall be a loyalty investigation of every person entering the civilian employment of any department or agency of the executive branch of the Federal Government.

a. Investigations of persons entering the competitive service shall be conducted by the Civil Service Commission, except in such cases as are covered by a special agreement between the Commission and any given department or agency.

b. Investigations of persons other than those entering the competitive service shall be conducted by the employing department or agency. Departments and agencies without investigative organizations shall utilize the investigative facilities of the Civil Service Commission.

2. The investigations of persons entering the employ of the executive branch may be conducted after any such person enters upon actual employment therein, but in any such case the appointment of such person shall be conditioned upon a favorable determination with respect to his loyalty.

[1] Excerpts reprinted from *Federal Register*, XII (March 25, 1947), 1935-8.

a. Investigations of persons entering the competitive service shall be conducted as expeditiously as possible; provided, however, that if any such investigation is not completed within 18 months from the date on which a person enters actual employment, the condition that his employment is subject to investigation shall expire, except in a case in which the Civil Service Commission has made an initial adjudication of disloyalty and the case continues to be active by reason of an appeal, and it shall then be the responsibility of the employing department or agency to conclude such investigation and make a final determination concerning the loyalty of such person.

3. An investigation shall be made of all applicants at all available pertinent sources of information and shall include reference to:

a. Federal Bureau of Investigation files.

b. Civil Service Commission files.

c. Military and naval intelligence files.

d. The files of any other appropriate government investigative or intelligence agency.

e. House Committee on un-American Activities files.

f. Local law-enforcement files at the place of residence and employment of the applicant, including municipal, county, and State law-enforcement files.

g. Schools and colleges attended by applicant.

h. Former employers of applicant.

i. References given by applicant.

j. Any other appropriate source.

4. Whenever derogatory information with respect to loyalty of an applicant is revealed a full field investigation shall be conducted. A full field investigation shall also be conducted of those applicants, or of applicants for particular positions, as may be designated by the head of the employing department or agency, such designations to be based on the determination by any such head of the best interests of national security.

PART II—INVESTIGATION OF EMPLOYEES

1. The head of each department and agency in the executive branch of the Government shall be personally responsible for an effective program to assure that disloyal civilian officers or employees are not retained in employment in his department or agency.

a. He shall be responsible for prescribing and supervising the loyalty determination procedures of his department or agency, in accordance with the provisions of this order, which shall be considered as providing minimum requirements.

b. The head of a department or agency which does not have an investigative organization shall utilize the investigative facilities of the Civil Service Commission.

2. The head of each department and agency shall appoint one or more loyalty boards, each composed of not less than three representatives of the department or agency concerned, for the purpose of hearing loyalty cases arising within such department or agency and making recommendations with respect to the removal of any officer or employee of such department or agency on grounds relating to loyalty, and he shall prescribe regulations for the conduct of the proceedings before such boards.

a. An officer or employee who is charged with being disloyal shall have a right to an administrative hearing before a loyalty board in the employing department or agency. He may appear before such board personally, accompanied by counsel or representative of his own choosing, and present evidence on his own behalf, through witnesses by affidavit.

b. The officer or employee shall be served with a written notice of such hearing in sufficient time, and shall be informed therein of the nature of the charges against him in sufficient detail, so that he will be enabled to prepare his defense. The charges shall be stated as specifically and completely as, in the discretion of the employing department or agency, security considerations permit, and the officer or employee shall be informed in the notice (1) of his right to reply to such charges in writing within a specified reasonable period of time, (2) of his right to an administrative hearing on such charges before a loyalty board, and (3) of his right to appear before such board personally, to be accompanied by counsel or representative of his own choosing, and to present evidence on his behalf, through witness or by affidavit.

3. A recommendation of removal by a loyalty board shall be subject to appeal by the officer or employee affected, prior to his removal, to the head of the employing department or agency or to such person or persons as may be designated by such head, under such regulations as may be prescribed by him, and the decision of the department or agency concerned shall be subject to appeal to the Civil Service Commission's Loyalty Review Board, hereinafter provided for, for an advisory recommendation.

4. The rights of hearing, notice thereof, and appeal therefrom shall be accorded to every officer or employee prior to his removal on grounds of disloyalty, irrespective of tenure, or of manner, method, or nature of appointment, but the head of the employing department or agency may suspend any officer or employee at any time pending a determination with respect to loyalty.

5. The loyalty boards of the various departments and agencies shall furnish to the Loyalty Review Board, hereinafter provided for, such reports as may be requested concerning the operation of the loyalty program in any such department or agency.

PART III—RESPONSIBILITIES OF CIVIL SERVICE COMMISSION

1. There shall be established in the Civil Service Commission a Loyalty Review Board of not less than three impartial persons, the members . . . shall be officers or employees of the Commission. . . .

2. There shall also be established and maintained in the Civil Service Commission a central master index covering all persons on whom loyalty investigations have been made by any department or agency since September 1, 1939. Such master index shall contain the name of each person investigated, adequate identifying information concerning each such person, and a reference to each department and agency which has conducted a loyalty investigation concerning the person involved. . . .

3. The Loyalty Review Board shall currently be furnished by the Department of Justice the name of each foreign or domestic organization, association, movement, group or combination of persons which the Attorney General, after appropriate investigation and determination, designates as totalitarian, fascist, communist or subversive, or as having adopted a policy of advocating or approving the commission of acts of force or violence to deny others their rights under the Constitution of the United States, or as seeking to alter the form of government of the United States by unconstitutional means. . . .

PART IV—SECURITY MEASURES IN INVESTIGATIONS

1. At the request of the head of any department or agency of the executive branch an investigative agency shall make available to such head, personally, all investigative material and information collected by the investigative agency concerning any employee or prospective employee of the requesting department or agency, or shall make such

material and information available to any officer or officers designated by such head and approved by the investigative agency.

2. Notwithstanding the foregoing requirement, however, the investigative agency may refuse to disclose the names of confidential informants, provided it furnishes sufficient information about such informants on the basis of which the requesting department or agency can make an adequate evaluation of the information furnished by them, and provided it advises the requesting department or agency in writing that it is essential to the protection of the informants or to the investigation of other cases that the identity of the informants not be revealed. Investigative agencies shall not use this discretion to decline to reveal sources of information where such action is not essential.

3. Each department and agency of the executive branch should develop and maintain, for the collection and analysis of information relating to the loyalty of its employees and prospective employees, a staff specially trained in security techniques, and an effective security control system for protecting such information generally and for protecting confidential sources of such information particularly.

PART V—STANDARDS

1. The standard for the refusal of employment or the removal from employment in an executive department or agency on grounds relating to loyalty shall be that, on all the evidence, reasonable grounds exist for belief that the person involved is disloyal to the Government of the United States.

2. Activities and associations of an applicant or employee which may be considered in connection with the determination of disloyalty may include one or more of the following:

a. Sabotage, espionage, or attempts or preparations therefor, or knowingly associating with spies or saboteurs;

b. Treason or sedition or advocacy thereof;

c. Advocacy of revolution or force or violence to alter the constitutional form of government of the United States;

d. Intentional, unauthorized disclosure to any person, under circumstances which may indicate disloyalty to the United States, of documents or information of a confidential or non-public character obtained by the person making the disclosure as a result of his employment by the Government of the United States;

e. Performing or attempting to perform his duties, or otherwise acting, so as to serve the interests of another government in preference to the interests of the United States.

f. Membership in, affiliation with or sympathetic association with any foreign or domestic organization, association, movement, group or combination of persons, designated by the Attorney General as totalitarian, fascist, communist, or subversive, or as having adopted a policy of advocating or approving the commission of acts of force or violence to deny other persons their rights under the Constitution of the United States, or as seeking to alter the form of government of the United States by unconstitutional means.

PART VI—MISCELLANEOUS

1. Each department and agency of the executive branch, to the extent that it has not already done so, shall submit, to the Federal Bureau of Investigation of the Department of Justice, either directly or through the Civil Service Commission, the names (and such other necessary identifying material as the Federal Bureau of Investigation may require) of all of its incumbent employees.

a. The Federal Bureau of Investigation shall check such names against its records of persons concerning whom there is substantial evidence of being within the purview of paragraph 2 of Part V hereof, and shall notify each department and agency of such information.

b. Upon receipt of the above-mentioned information from the Federal Bureau of Investigation, each department and agency shall make, or cause to be made by the Civil Service Commission, such investigation of those employees as the head of the department or agency shall deem advisable.

CONSERVATIVE CRITICISM OF PLAN

2 ◆◊ "LOOPHOLES IN LOYALTY PLAN," by Rex Collier, published in *The Washington Star*, is an example of conservative objections to the President's loyalty order:[2]

Although President Truman's program for ridding the Government pay roll of Communists and other subversive elements is a bold move in the right direction, there are serious loopholes in the plan. They are loopholes which should be plugged if the movement to root out

[2] From *The Washington Star*, April 6, 1947, p. 12. Reprinted by permission of *The Washington Star*.

all potentially disloyal Federal employees is to meet with any reasonable degree of success.

In the first place, the Executive order setting up the new loyalty program draws a distinction between applicants for Government employment and employees already in the service. In the case of applicants, an investigation is compulsory. The language of the order is explicit in that respect. In the case of employees already on the rolls, however, the wording of the order is so ambiguous as to leave the way open for indifferent compliance or evasions that could circumvent the intent of the order altogether.

APPLICANT SCREENING SPECIFIED

For example, Part I of the order states unequivocally that there "shall be a loyalty investigation of every person entering the civilian employment of any department or agency of the executive branch of the Government." Moreover, the same section specifies the type of investigation that shall be conducted. It must cover "all available pertinent sources of information," including the files of the Federal Bureau of Investigation, the Civil Service Commission, Army and Navy Intelligence, the House Committee on Un-American Activities, State and local police records, former places of employment, educational institutions attended, etc. If these records produce any "derogatory information with respect to loyalty of an applicant," a full field investigation must be made by the Civil Service Commission.

Given sufficient funds and adequate personnel, the Civil Service Commission can do a highly effective job of exposing and turning back any applicant whose loyalty to the United States is a matter of serious doubt.

DISCRETIONARY ENFORCEMENT

Compare the positive phraseology pertaining to applicants with this directive regarding investigation of employees already inside the Government gates: "The head of each department and agency in the executive branch of the Government shall be personally responsible for an effective program to assure that disloyal civilian officers or employees are not retained in employment in his department or agency." Furthermore, the head of the department or agency is given the responsibility of "prescribing and supervising the loyalty determination procedures of his department or agency, in accordance with the provisions of this order, which shall be considered as providing minimum requirements."

By thus placing on department heads the responsibility for investigating their own employees and of establishing procedures, the order could be interpreted by some administrators as leaving matters pretty much to their own discretion. It is no secret that some departmental officials, including some personnel officers, have evidenced in the past a complete lack of sympathy with respect to loyalty inquiries. This apathetic, if not antagonistic attitude, may account for the fact that during the past year, when the departments were supposed to take over the investigative job relinquished by the Civil Service Commission for lack of funds, no effort whatever was made by some personnel officers to carry out their new responsibilities.

COMMUNISTS IGNORE OATHS

The President's Loyalty Commission, of which A. Devitt Vanech, special assistant to the attorney general, was chairman and Civil Service Commissioner Harry B. Mitchell a member, found that most of the agencies have been content to accept the oath of office taken by the employee as prima facie evidence of his loyalty. Yet Canada learned that Communists and fellow travelers have no qualms about violating oaths of allegiance when occasion requires.

Another weakness in the new plan for checking on employees already in the civil service is the failure to provide for anything more thorough than a "name check" by the FBI. Director J. Edgar Hoover has made it clear that such a check is far from conclusive. The fact that the FBI may have little or no evidence in its files against a particular employee does not mean that the FBI is willing to guarantee the loyalty of that person. Under the order the FBI has no authority to do more than report to a department head whether the employee has a record at the FBI.

Even if the FBI should report that the employee has a bad record, it is still discretionary with the department head as to whether action under the loyalty order should be initiated. And, as Mr. Hoover told the House Committee on Un-American Activities recently, there have been instances in the past when such discretion operated to permit a Communist to remain in office.

FINDING A SOLUTION

While these defects in the loyalty program are known to be worrying some of the officials concerned with safeguarding the security of the Government, no one pretends as yet to have a complete solution for what is admittedly a tough problem. The FBI, largest of Federal investigative agencies, has neither funds nor facilities to undertake the huge task of conducting a "full field investigation" of every Government worker. Even the limited screening provided in the Executive order will entail large additional appropriations and the hiring of many new employees by the Civil Service Commission.

A compromise arrangement that would immensely strengthen the proposed program, with little extra expense, would be to direct the Civil Service Commission to supervise and periodically check on the administration of the loyalty order within the various departments. If the Commission found that some agency was not doing an effective job the dereliction should be reported to the President. Such pressure from higher up might have a salutary effect on indifferent or reluctant administrative officers.

LIBERAL CRITICISM OF PROGRAM

3 THE BEST LIBERAL CRITIQUE of Truman's loyalty program is in Francis Biddle's *Fear of Freedom*, published in 1951. As U.S. Attorney General during World War II, Biddle appointed in 1942 the Interdepartmental Committee on Investigations, which made the first attempt to suggest procedures for loyalty investigations. Excerpts from his book follow:[3]

Charges under the loyalty procedure must be specific—but only as specific as "security considerations will permit." The employee (and the Government) is permitted to introduce evidence—but only "such evidence as the board may deem proper in the particular case." He may appear by counsel and cross-examine—but not cross-examine the informants. He may call witnesses—but cannot subpoena them. Nonconfidential informants may be called at the hearings and cross-examined, but their names are not in the notice of charges or interrogatories. Testimony is under oath—but not the testimony of informants. The proceedings "are in the nature of an investigation and not of a prosecution"—yet it is suggested that "the head of the agency provide for each hearing before its board, a representative of the agency (a legal officer, if practicable), who, subject to the direction of the board, will assist in the preparation of the charges and

---

[3] From *Fear of Freedom* by Francis Biddle, copyright 1951 by Francis Biddle. Pages 210–11, 214–15, 217–18, 238–41, reprinted by permission of Doubleday & Company, Inc.

in the presentation of the case to the board." A written record is made of the hearings before the department loyalty board and the Loyalty Review Board; but confidential information—and one would suppose that most evidence of subversive activities is confidential—does not get into the record to which the employee has access.

There are indeed two records, one for the Government, one for the employee. The record which on appeal goes to the Review Board is complete, with "all reports of investigation or other inquiry . . . all memoranda analyzing the evidence or setting forth conclusions, findings, recommendations, determinations, decisions . . . and all affidavits, supporting documents, correspondence, or memoranda in connection with the investigation, determination, [and] decision." But this record is not available to the employee. He is entitled only to a copy of the evidence given before the loyalty boards.

Although the Loyalty Review Board is made up of individuals holding no other government position, each agency and department prosecutes loyalty cases before boards chosen from its own employees, thus doing violence to the principle that the prosecutor and the body making the decision should be separated.

There is no requirement as to what sort of "determination" the loyalty boards shall render, no provision for a discussion of the evidence, or for a statement of the reasons for dismissal, or for findings of fact. The regulations provide that "the determination . . . shall be made in writing and . . . shall state merely the action taken." It has been said that requirements for specific findings are for the purpose of setting the issue before a court for review, and that this is not necessary, since there is no court review. But the Loyalty Review Board acts like a court. And the value of requiring findings tends to make the deciding body stick to a precise issue. The very vagueness of the "subversive" standards—"disloyal to the Government," "sympathetic association"—makes it particularly desirable that the facts on which the decision is made should be set forth in detail as part of the determination. . . .

The President's Temporary Commission on Employee Loyalty pointed out that "the action taken by a federal department or agency to remove an employee is administrative in character and a hearing conducted for such purpose is an administrative hearing and not a judicial proceeding." The employee has committed no crime, nor is he accused of any. He is not being deprived of property, since he has no vested right in his job and due process does not apply. He is not being prevented from holding ideas or preaching them, from joining any association he likes, from being a fellow traveler, or a Communist, if he chooses. But clearly the Government has then the right to get rid of him.

These arguments seem to me legalistic and directed at an artificial and unreal distinction. Where a man is accused of a crime—of theft, of treason—our Constitution and laws protect him so far as possible with the strength of objective and impartial procedure; a court independent of the State, a jury trial, definite charges, no hearsay evidence, an open public proceeding, the presumption of innocence. He is treated thus because so much is at stake—his livelihood, his freedom, his good name.

All these considerations are present in the loyalty cases. There is little difference, in the opinion of the world, between being treacherous and being disloyal, between being a traitor and a subversive. This is a brand of shame—*disloyal to the Government of the United States.* That is the standard and the *only* standard, the broad basis for dismissal. "The standard for the refusal of employment or the removal from employment in an executive department or agency" —so reads the President's executive order—"on grounds relating to loyalty shall be that, on all the evidence, reasonable grounds exist for belief that the person involved is disloyal to the Government of the United States." The future holds no chance for such an individual. His country will not employ him again, or his state, or his city. He will not be given an opportunity to teach at a university or in any school. Private employers will not be eager to use him. A convict who has gone astray once, has stolen or forged or embezzled, often gets another chance. But a man who has been disloyal to his own country . . . Do you think I am exaggerating? Would you employ him? I would not. He is a man without a country. Perhaps eventually, when he has tried all other doors and found them closed, some fellow traveler will let him in, some Communist outfit will welcome him. Let him go back where he came from. . . .

I doubt whether much hysteria exists among clerical employees throughout the vast spread of the government departments and agencies. Most clerks are the same everywhere, and take what comes, rather indifferently, for they do not wish to break a lance for causes, to make policies or to change them. They are content with the routine direction of their work and of their lives. But that is not true of the men and women who do not accept the commonplace as inevitable, the individuals of imagination, who think of their work as something humane and creative. I am tempted to think that they have felt the walls close around them.

And what has the system done to the future of those about whose loyalty the boards have felt a doubt existed, a doubt which, under the regulations, cannot be resolved in their favor? A few—a very few—have been discharged, branded as quasi-traitors, for always, it would seem.

And a very few applicants for positions have been turned down on the ground of possible disloyalty. But the prevailing atmosphere is hardly calculated to attract economists or students of foreign relations to a public career. In many departments they no longer are protected from summary dismissal.* They face not only a slow and elaborate personal investigation, necessarily distasteful even if they are ultimately cleared, but also the possibility of being reinvestigated at any time, and of also being subjected to the cruel notoriety of a congressional inquisition.

The existing situation necessarily makes more cautious the employing official. One applicant, technically equipped for the special job for which he had applied, was finally cleared. But he was not employed. There had been an intensive investigation because his wife in 1938 had sent money to an organization that was helping the Republican government of Spain. The head of the bureau shrugged when he told me this. "The only man for the job," he said, and added: "But what would Congress have done to my appropriation?" . . .

The Loyalty Review Board reported as of July 31, 1950, that of the 8288 cases adjudicated by the loyalty boards (presumably cases in which derogatory information was filed) in the combined incumbent and appointee program, only two hundred and forty-six had been finally dismissed or refused employment as a result of ineligible determination.

Out of the two hundred and forty-six no spies were discovered, no indictments filed. They were considered bad risks, or at least doubtful risks, since all presumptions are resolved in favor of the Government. We do not know if any were Communists, how many

---

* In August 1950, legislation was adopted giving the heads of eleven government agencies the right to fire employees summarily for security reasons, and empowering the President to extend its provisions to any other federal agency. The departments were State, Defense, Army, Navy, Air Force, Treasury (Coast Guard), Commerce, Justice, Atomic Energy Commission, National Securities Resources Board, and the National Advisory Committee for Aeronautics.

fellow travelers there were, how many were simply unstable individuals. But if we assume that they were all Communists, we come out with the comforting knowledge that, of the cases considered worth an intensive investigation, only .03 per cent were thought questionable enough to involve unfavorable action.

This percentage applies to those employees in which an intensive investigation was considered advisable, for both incumbents and applicants. But all government employees (within the scope of the President's order), and all new applicants were checked. Of the incumbents one hundred and thirty-nine were dismissed as a result of ineligible determinations—one hundred and thirty-nine out of approximately two million employees. Those dismissed for possible disloyalty, therefore, numbered about .000069 of the total. . . .

On April 4, 1950, Mr. [Seth W.—Eds.] Richardson, the chairman of the Loyalty Review Board at that time, testified before the Senate subcommittee investigating Senator McCarthy's charges of Communist infiltration in the State Department that the loyalty investigations had not produced "one single case" of espionage or turned up any evidence "directing toward espionage."

Far more serious than any waste of money is the stultifying waste of human effort and energy, and the resulting discouragement to applicants. It is shocking to think that more than eight thousand employees had to be put through this test before the boards when so few of them were serious cases. In the same report it appears that fourteen hundred and eighty-four employees left the service during investigation, and eleven hundred and twenty-five prior to the adjudication. It would be interesting to know how many resigned from a fear of being ultimately branded as disloyal, and how many because they felt unable to put up with the psychological and financial strain. . . .

Assuming that all of the one hundred and thirty-nine are Communists, I do not believe that their attempt to spread Marxian dialectic among the balance of the two million constitutes a serious threat to the Government of the United States. I suspect, moreover, that if they had tried to make converts they would very soon have been reported and fired. It would be interesting to know whether any of them was in a position to exercise influence on the formation of policy within the Government. An analysis of their jobs and their activities would, I believe, show that this was not the case. It would then be clear that the problem should be considered solely as one of security, and that the program of intensive investigation should be limited to cover sensitive positions and areas.

TRUMAN LETTER ON SECURITY PROGRAMS

4 ⋅∕§ IN ADDITION to weeding out disloyal employees, certain sensitive agencies of the government also developed security programs to eliminate those whose personal weaknesses might make them dupes of spies. Beginning in 1947, after the State Department had used its authority to make several arbitrary dismissals, the relevant agencies usually extended the same protections to security as to loyalty cases, though security risks could not appeal outside their agency to the Loyalty Review Board. In most agencies the same panel heard both kinds of cases. On July 14, 1951, President Truman wrote the following letter to James S. Lay, the executive secretary of the National Security Council, expressing his anxieties about the government's security programs:[4]

I have become seriously concerned by a number of reports I have heard recently concerning the administration of the provisions of existing laws which authorize the heads of the various departments and agencies to discharge government employees, or to refuse Government employment to applicants, on the ground that they are poor security risks.

If these provisions of law are to achieve their purpose of protecting the security of the Government without unduly infringing on the rights of individuals, they must be administered with the utmost wisdom and courage. We must never forget that the fundamental purpose of our Government is to protect the rights of individual citizens and one of the highest obligations of the Government is to see that those rights are protected in its own operations.

The present situation does not make for good administration. There are no uniform standards or procedures to be followed in the different departments and agencies concerned. Neither is there any provision for review at a central point as there is in the case of the Government employee loyalty program. This is a problem that falls within the scope of the work which I have asked to have undertaken by the Commission on Internal Security and Individual Rights. However,

[4] Reprinted from Commission on Government Security, *Report of the Commission on Government Security* (Washington, D.C., 1957), pp. 10–11.

the work of that Commission has been delayed because of the failure of the Senate Committee on the Judiciary to report legislation which would exempt the members and staff of the Commission from the conflict-of-interest statutes.

I believe that the present problems involved in the administration of the Government employee security program are so acute that they should be given at least preliminary consideration without waiting further for the Commission on Internal Security and Individual Rights. Consequently, I should like the National Security Council, utilizing its Interdepartmental Committee on Internal Security, and with the participation of the Civil Service Commission, to make an investigation of the way this program is being administered, and to advise me what changes are believed to be required. In particular, I should like consideration given to whether provision should be made for uniform standards and procedures and for central review of the decisions made in the various departments and agencies.

When the Commission on Internal Security and Individual Rights is able to resume its work, it would, of course, have the benefit of the work done pursuant to this request.

I am asking each of the departments and agencies concerned to cooperate fully in this study.

HISS-CHAMBERS CONFRONTATION

5 ᴇᴈ   CONGRESSIONAL COMMITTEES played a large role in keeping the problem of subversion before the public eye. Indeed it was the House Un-American Activities Committee that first uncovered the most famous espionage case of all—the strange case of Alger Hiss. Hiss had come into government service in the 1930's, seemed then a model New Deal civil servant, and in time rose to a position of considerable responsibility in the State Department. In 1947 he left the government to assume the presidency of the Carnegie Endowment for World Peace. Then on August 3, 1948, Whittaker Chambers appeared before the House committee and testified that in the thirties he had collected Communist-party dues from, among others, Alger Hiss. Hiss immediately requested and received an opportunity to appear before the committee to deny these charges and stated further that he had never heard of Whittaker Chambers. Chambers returned two days later to assure the committee in executive session that he had made no mistake and offered a wealth of information about Hiss to corroborate his story.

Maybe, said Hiss in his next appearance before the committee, Chambers, whom he had not yet seen, was George Crosley, a casual acquaintance of Hiss's in the thirties, a man to whom Hiss had once sublet his apartment. Finally on August 17, 1948, in a hotel room in New York City, the committee brought Hiss and Chambers face to face in a memorable encounter.

After Hiss instituted libel proceedings against Chambers, Chambers produced documentary evidence purporting to prove that Hiss had passed secret government papers to him in the thirties. (Chambers had previously sworn to the House committee that he had no such evidence.) On December 15, 1948, a New York City grand jury indicted Hiss for perjury for having denied these allegations of espionage. The real charge against Hiss was, of course, treason, but the statute of limitations protected Hiss from a trial for that crime. After one jury failed to reach agreement, a second found Hiss guilty, and he was sentenced to five years in prison. Most historians have agreed with this verdict.

Among the papers Chambers produced were some copies of secret State Department documents that had been typed on a typewriter once owned by Mrs. Alger Hiss. Failure to account for this singular fact was the major weakness in Hiss's defense. Because Hiss had once seemed so typical of the bright young men who had gone to Washington to serve the New Deal, the accusation against him took on, for some, a symbolic significance that made the case one of the major events of the whole Truman era. Below is the record of the confrontation of Hiss and Chambers before the House Un-American Activities Committee on August 17, 1948:[5]

The first witness will be Mr. Alger Hiss.

Mr. Hiss, will you please take the oath.

Do you solemnly swear the testimony you shall give this committee will be the truth, the whole truth and nothing but the truth, so help you God?

Mr. HISS. I do.

Mr. [Robert E.—Eds.] STRIPLING. [Chief of the committee's staff —Eds.] The purpose of the meeting is for the committee to continue to determine the truth or falsity of the testimony which has been

[5] Excerpts reprinted from House Committee on Un-American Activities, *Hearings Regarding Communist Espionage in the United States Government*, Eightieth Congress, second session, pp. 975–1000.

given by Mr. Whittaker Chambers. Do you want to proceed, Mr. [Richard M.—Eds.] Nixon?

Mr. NIXON. Yes. It is quite apparent at this stage in the testimony, as you indicated yesterday, that the case is dependent upon the question of identity. We have attempted to establish the identity through photographs of Mr. Chambers and that has been inadequate for that purpose. Today, we thought that since you had in your testimony raised the possibility of a third party who might be involved in this case in some way and had described him at some length to the committee that it would be well to, at the earliest possible time, determine whether the third party is different from the two parties or the same one, and so consequently we have asked Mr. Chambers to be in New York at the same time so that you can have the opportunity to see him and make up your own mind on that point. . . .

Mr. HISS. May I also make a statement before you begin?

Mr. [John—Eds.] McDOWELL. Certainly.

Mr. HISS. I would like the record to show that on my way downtown from my uptown office, I learned from the press of the death of Harry White [former Assistant Secretary of the Treasury—Eds.], which came as a great shock to me, and I am not sure that I feel in the best possible mood for testimony. I do not for a moment want to miss the opportunity of seeing Mr. Chambers. I merely wanted the record to show that.

I would like to make one further comment. Yesterday, I think I witnessed—in any event, I was told that those in the room were going to take an oath of secrecy. I made some comments before I answered certain questions of Mr. Nixon which I had not intended as a reflection on the committee, but which some members of the committee thought implied that. I was referring merely to the possibility of leakage of information. I would like this record to show at this stage that the first thing I saw in the morning paper, the Herald Tribune, was a statement that the committee yesterday had asked me if I would submit to a lie-detector test. . . .

Mr. McDOWELL. The Chair would like to say something. I, too, was greatly disturbed when I read the morning paper. Obviously, there was a leak, because the story that appeared in the various papers I read was part of the activities of yesterday afternoon. I have no idea how this story got out. In my own case, I very carefully guarded myself last night, saw and talked to no one except my wife in Pittsburgh. It is regrettable and unfortunate.

Further than that, I don't know what else to say other than if it was an employee of the committee, and I should discover it, he will no longer be an employee of the committee. As a member of Congress, there is nothing I can do about that. It is a regrettable thing, and I join you in feeling rather rotten about the whole thing.

Mr. Hiss. I didn't mean to make any charges but meant to state certain facts which have occurred which I think have a bearing on the reason I made the statements I made to the committee yesterday before I went on with certain parts of my testimony. . . .

Mr. Nixon. Mr. [Louis J.—Eds.] Russell [an investigator for the committee—Eds.], will you bring Mr. Chambers in?

Mr. Russell. Yes.

(Mr. Russell leaves room and returns accompanied by Mr. Chambers.)

Mr. Nixon. Sit over here, Mr. Chambers.

Mr. Chambers, will you please stand?

And will you please stand, Mr. Hiss?

Mr. Hiss, the man standing here is Mr. Whittaker Chambers. I ask you now if you have ever known that man before.

Mr. Hiss. May I ask him to speak?

Will you ask him to say something?

Mr. Nixon. Yes.

Mr. Chambers, will you tell us your name and your business?

Mr. Chambers. My name is Whittaker Chambers.

(At this point, Mr. Hiss walked in the direction of Mr. Chambers.)

Mr. Hiss. Would you mind opening your mouth wider?

Mr. Chambers. My name is Whittaker Chambers.

Mr. Hiss. I said, would you open your mouth?

You know what I am referring to, Mr. Nixon.

Will you go on talking?

Mr. Chambers. I am senior editor of Time magazine.

Mr. Hiss. May I ask whether his voice, when he testified before, was comparable to this?

Mr. Nixon. His voice?

Mr. Hiss. Or did he talk a little more in a lower key?

Mr. McDowell. I would say it is about the same now as we have heard.

Mr. Hiss. Would you ask him to talk a little more?

Mr. Nixon. Read something, Mr. Chambers. I will let you read from——

Mr. HISS. I think he is George Crosley, but I would like to hear him talk a little longer.

Mr. McDOWELL. Mr. Chambers, if you would be more comfortable, you may sit down.

Mr. HISS. Are you George Crosley?

Mr. CHAMBERS. Not to my knowledge. You are Alger Hiss, I believe.

Mr. HISS. I certainly am.

Mr. CHAMBERS. That was my recollection. (Reading:)

Since June——

Mr. NIXON (interposing). Just one moment. Since some repartee goes on between these two people, I think Mr. Chambers should be sworn.

Mr. HISS. That is a good idea.

Mr. McDOWELL. You do solemnly swear, sir, that the testimony you shall give this committee will be the truth, the whole truth, and nothing but the truth, so help you God?

Mr. CHAMBERS. I do.

Mr. NIXON. Mr. Hiss, may I say something? I suggested that he be sworn, and when I say something like that I want no interruptions from you.

Mr. HISS. Mr. Nixon, in view of what happened yesterday, I think there is no occasion for you to use that tone of voice in speaking to me, and I hope the record will show what I have just said.

Mr. NIXON. The record shows everything that is being said here today.

Mr. STRIPLING. You were going to read.

Mr. CHAMBERS (reading from Newsweek magazine):

Tobin for Labor. Since June, Harry S. Truman had been peddling the labor secretaryship left vacant by Lewis B. Schwellenbach's death in hope of gaining the maximum political advantage from the appointment.

Mr. HISS. May I interrupt?

Mr. McDOWELL. Yes.

Mr. HISS. The voice sounds a little less resonant than the voice that I recall of the man I knew as George Crosley. The teeth look to me as though either they have been improved upon or that there has

Truman at start of non-political campaign, Pittsburgh, June 4, 1948
(*Wide World*)

Progressive party candidates Henry A. Wallace (*left*) and Glen H. Taylor, Philadelphia convention, July 24, 1948 (*Wide World*)

Truman at Union Station, St. Louis, celebrating unpredicted victory, Nov. 5, 1948 (*Wide World*)

Truman taking oath of office, Jan. 1949 (*UPI*)

The President and members of cabinet, Jan. 9, 1948; *left to right:* Secretary of the Interior Julius A. Krug; Commerce, W. Averell Harriman; Federal Works Administrator Philip B. Fleming; Assistant to the President John R. Steelman; Labor, Lewis B. Schwellenbach; Agriculture, Clinton P. Anderson; Postmaster-General Jesse M. Donaldson; Defense, James V. Forrestal; State, George C. Marshall; Truman; Treasury, John W. Snyder; Attorney General Tom C. Clark (*UPI*)

The President and members of cabinet, Aug. 25, 1950; *left to right:* Secretary of Commerce Charles S. Sawyer; presidential assistants Harriman and Steelman; Vice President Alben W. Barkley; Labor, Maurice J. Tobin; chairman, National Resources Security Board, Stuart H. Symington; Agriculture, Charles F. Brannan; Postmaster-General Donaldson; Defense, Louis A. Johnson; State, Dean Acheson; Truman; Treasury, Snyder; Attorney General J. Howard McGrath; Interior, Oscar L. Chapman (*Wide World*)

U.S. Supreme Court, Jan. 1947; seated, left to right: Felix Frankfurter, Hugo L. Black, Chief Justice Fred M. Vinson, Stanley F. Reed, William O. Douglas; standing: Wiley B. Rutledge, Frank Murphy, Robert H. Jackson, Harold H. Burton (UPI)

nominee for President may

I shall not be a candidate for re-election. I have served my country long and I think efficiently and honestly. I shall not accept a renomination. I do not feel that it is my duty to spend another four years in the White House.

teadily,

and women and children

the things

eat.

and keep it foremost in service to the people.

Truman's notes for Jefferson-Jackson Day dinner, March 29, 1952 (*UPI*)

Robert A. Taft, candidate for nomination, New York City, May 9, 1952 (*Wide World*)

Dwight D. Eisenhower and Richard M. Nixon, GOP convention, Chicago, July 11, 1952 (*Wide World*)

Truman and Adlai E. Stevenson after discussing presidential campaign, Aug. 12, 1952 (*Wide World*)

been considerable dental work done since I knew George Crosley, which was some years ago.

I believe I am not prepared without further checking to take an absolute oath that he must be George Crosley.

Mr. NIXON. May I ask a question of Mr. Chambers?

Mr. HISS. I would like to ask Mr. Chambers, if I may.

Mr. NIXON. I will ask the questions at this time.

Mr. Chambers, have you had any dental work since 1934 of a substantial nature?

Mr. CHAMBERS. Yes; I have.

Mr. NIXON. What type of dental work?

Mr. CHAMBERS. I have had some extractions and a plate.

Mr. NIXON. Have you had any dental work in the front of your mouth?

Mr. CHAMBERS. Yes.

Mr. NIXON. What is the nature of that work?

Mr. CHAMBERS. That is a plate in place of some of the upper dentures.

Mr. NIXON. I see.

Mr. HISS. Could you ask him the name of the dentist that performed these things? Is that appropriate?

Mr. NIXON. Yes. What is the name?

Mr. CHAMBERS. Dr. Hitchcock, Westminster, Md.

Mr. HISS. That testimony of Mr. Chambers, if it can be believed, would tend to substantiate my feeling that he represented himself to me in 1934 or 1935 or thereabout as George Crosley, a free lance writer of articles for magazines.

I would like to find out from Dr. Hitchcock if what he has just said is true, because I am relying partly, one of my main recollections of Crosley was the poor condition of his teeth.

Mr. NIXON. Can you describe the condition of your teeth in 1934?

Mr. CHAMBERS. Yes. They were in very bad shape.

Mr. NIXON. The front teeth were?

Mr. CHAMBERS. Yes; I think so.

Mr. HISS. Mr. Chairman.

Mr. NIXON. Excuse me. Before we leave the teeth, Mr. Hiss, do you feel that you would have to have the dentist tell you just what he did to the teeth before you could tell anything about this man?

Mr. HISS. I would like a few more questions asked.

I didn't intend to say anything about this, because I feel very strongly that he is Crosley, but he looks very different in girth and in other appearances—hair, forehead, and so on, particularly the jowls.

Mr. NIXON. What was Crosley's wife's name?

Mr. HISS. I don't think I recall.

Mr. NIXON. You did testify that she on several occasions was in your home overnight.

Mr. HISS. That is right.

Mr. NIXON. And that you have ridden with her in a car as well as with him.

Mr. HISS. I don't recall testifying to that.

Mr. NIXON. Do you testify she didn't?

Mr. HISS. I don't recall.

Mr. NIXON. But she did stay overnight in your home on several occasions?

Mr. HISS. She did. I don't think I said several occasions.

Mr. NIXON. How many times did you say?

Mr. HISS. My recollection is that at the time George Crosley sub-rented my apartment on Twenty-ninth Street his wife and he and infant spent two or three or four consecutive nights in my house because the van had not come with their furniture, and we left only certain pieces of furniture behind to accommodate them.

Mr. NIXON. In regard to the rental agreement that was entered into with Mr. Crosley, do you recall approximately the rental that was charged and agreed to?

Mr. HISS. My recollection is that I said I would be glad to let him have the apartment for the cost to me. It was a rather moderate rental.

Mr. NIXON. Could you say within certain limits?

Mr. HISS. My recollection—I can't remember just what I paid for the apartment that far back—my recollection is it was under $75 a month. It was a very reasonable rental. That is one of the reasons I had taken it.

Mr. NIXON. For how long was this rental agreement?

Mr. HISS. I think I went into this yesterday in the testimony. Sometime in the spring, according to my recollection, of 1934.

Mr. NIXON. Or did you say 1935?

Mr. HISS. I am looking at notes I made, trying to remember the dates. Sometime in the spring of 1935 I leased the house on P Street. Having both a house and an apartment on my hands, I was looking for a way of disposing of the apartment on sublease, and [on—Eds.] the occasion of one of the talks I had with Crosley, he said he was planning to spend the summer in Washington carrying on the researches he had been doing in the field of the Munitions Committee [Nye Committee—Eds.] investigations.

I asked him if he would like to sublet my apartment during that period of time, that it was not too cool, but that it was up on a hill and had a very decent location as Washington goes, that I would let him have it for the cost to me. In the course of the negotiation he referred to the fact that he also wanted an automobile. . . .

Mr. STRIPLING. Mr. Hiss, you say that person you knew as George Crosley, the one feature which you must have to check on to identify him is the dentures.

Mr. HISS. May I answer that my own way rather than just "Yes" or "No"?

Mr. STRIPLING. Well, now, I would like to preface whatever you are going to say by what I say first.

I certainly gathered the impression when Mr. Chambers walked in this room and you walked over and examined him and asked him to open his mouth, that you were basing your identification purely on what his upper teeth might have looked like.

Now, here is a person that you knew for several months at least. You knew him so well that he was a guest in your home.

Mr. HISS. Would you——

Mr. STRIPLING. I would like to complete my statement—that he was a guest in your home, that you gave him an old Ford automobile, and permitted him to use, or you leased him your apartment and in this, a very important confrontation, the only thing that you have to check on is this denture; is that correct?

There is nothing else about this man's features which you could definitely say, "This is the man I knew as George Crosley," that you have to rely entirely on this denture; is that your position?

Mr. HISS. Is your preface through? My answer to the question you have asked is this:

From the time on Wednesday, August 4, 1948, when I was able to get hold of newspapers containing photographs of one Whittaker Chambers, I was struck by a certain familiarity in features. When I testified on August 5 and was shown a photograph by you, Mr. Stripling, there was again some familiarity [in—Eds.] features. I could not be sure that I had never seen the person whose photograph you showed me. I said I would want to see the person.

The photographs are rather good photographs of Whittaker Chambers as I see Whittaker Chambers today. I am not given on important occasions to snap judgments or simple, easy statements. I am confident that George Crosley had notably bad teeth. I would not call George Crosley a guest in my house. I have explained the circumstances. If you choose to call him a guest, that is your affair.

Mr. STRIPLING. I am willing to strike the word "guest." He was in your house.

Mr. HISS. I saw him at the time I was seeing hundreds of people. Since then I have seen thousands of people. He meant nothing to me except as one I saw under the circumstances I have described.

My recollection of George Crosley, if this man had said he was George Crosley, I would have no difficulty in identification. He denied it right here.

I would like and asked earlier in this hearing if I could ask some further questions to help in identification. I was denied that.

Mr. STRIPLING. I think you should be permitted——

Mr. HISS. I was denied that right. I am not, therefore, able to take an oath that this man is George Crosley. I have been testifying about George Crosley. Whether he and this man are the same or whether he has means of getting information from George Crosley about my house, I do not know. He may have had his face lifted.

Mr. STRIPLING. The witness says he was denied the right to ask this witness questions. I believe the record will show you stated "at this time." I think he should be permitted to ask the witness questions now or any other motion should be granted which will permit him to determine whether or not this is the individual to whom he is referring.

Mr. HISS. Right. I would be very happy if I could pursue that. Do I have the Chair's permission?

Mr. McDOWELL. The Chair will agree to that.

Mr. HISS. Do I have Mr. Nixon's permission.

Mr. NIXON. Yes.

Mr. McDOWELL. Here is a very difficult situation. . . .

Mr. HISS. That is my recollection. I have a rather good visual memory, and my recollection of his spelling of his name is C-r-o-s-l-e-y. I don't think that would change as much as his appearance.

Mr. STRIPLING. You will identify him positively now?

Mr. HISS. I will on the basis of what he has just said positively identify him without further questioning as George Crosley.

Mr. STRIPLING. Will you produce for the committee three people who will testify that they knew him as George Crosley?

Mr. HISS. I will if it is possible. Why is that a question to ask me? I will see what is possible. This occurred in 1935. The only people that I can think of who would have known him as George Crosley with certainty would have been the people who were associated with me in the Nye committee. . . .

Mr. NIXON. Mr. Hiss, another point that I want to be clear on, Mr. Chambers said he was a Communist and that you were a Communist.

Mr. HISS. I heard him.

Mr. NIXON. Will you tell the committee whether or not during this period of time that you knew him, which included periods of 3 nights, or 2 or 3 nights, in which he stayed overnight and one trip to New York, from any conversation you ever had any idea that he might be a Communist?

Mr. HISS. I certainly didn't.

Mr. NIXON. You never discussed politics?

Mr. HISS. Oh, as far as I recall his conversations—and I may be confusing them with a lot of other conversations that went on in 1934 and 1935—politics were discussed quite frequently.

May I just state for the record that it was not the habit in Washington in those days, when particularly if a member of the press called on you, to ask him before you had further conversation whether or not he was a Communist. It was a quite different atmosphere in Washington then than today. I had no reason to suspect George Crosley of being a Communist. It never occurred to me that he might be or whether that was of any significance to me if he was. He was a press representative and it was my duty to give him information, as I did any other member of the press.

It was to the interest of the committee investigating the munitions industry, as its members and we of its staff saw it, to furnish guidance and information to people who were popularizing and writing about its work.

I would like to say that to come here and discover that the ass under the lion's skin is Crosley, I don't know why your committee didn't pursue this careful method of interrogation at an earlier date before all the publicity. You told me yesterday you didn't know he was going to mention my name, although a lot of people now tell me that the press did know it in advance. They were apparently more effective in getting information than the committee itself. That is all I have to say now.

Mr. McDOWELL. Well, now, Mr. Hiss, you positively identify——

Mr. HISS. Positively on the basis of his own statement that he was in my apartment at the time when I say he was there. I have no further question at all. If he had lost both eyes and taken his nose off, I would be sure.

Mr. McDOWELL. Then, your identification of George Crosley is complete?

Mr. HISS. Yes, as far as I am concerned, on his own testimony.

Mr. McDOWELL. Mr. Chambers, is this the man, Alger Hiss, who was also a member of the Communist Party at whose home you stayed?

Mr. NIXON. According to your testimony.

Mr. McDOWELL. You make the identification positive?

Mr. CHAMBERS. Positive identification.

(At this point, Mr. Hiss arose and walked in the direction of Mr. Chambers.)

Mr. HISS. May I say for the record at this point, that I would like to invite Mr. Whittaker Chambers to make those same statements out of the presence of this committee without their being privileged for suit for libel. I challenge you to do it, and I hope you will do it damned quickly.

I am not going to touch him [addressing Mr. Russell]. You are touching me.

Mr. RUSSELL. Please sit down, Mr. Hiss.

Mr. HISS. I will sit down when the chairman asks me.

Mr. Russell, when the chairman asks me to sit down——

Mr. RUSSELL. I want no disturbance.

Mr. HISS. I don't——

Mr. McDOWELL. Sit down, please.

Mr. HISS. You know who started this.

Mr. McDOWELL. We will suspend testimony here for a minute or two, until I return.

(Short recess.)

Mr. HISS. Mr. Chairman, would you be good enough to ask Mr. Chambers for the record his response to the challenge that I have just made to him?

Mr. McDOWELL. That has nothing to do with the pertinency of

the matter that the committee is investigating, and I don't feel I should.

Mr. HISS. I thought the committee was interested in ascertaining truth.

Mr. STRIPLING. What is the challenge?

Mr. McDOWELL. That he, Mr. Chambers, would make those statements he has made before the committee in public where they would not be privileged under congressional immunity. That I would take it would be strictly a matter up to Mr. Chambers and Mr. Hiss, but I don't feel the committee has any proper or parliamentary right to ask such a question. . . .

Mr. McDOWELL. Did you ever meet this man in the presence of Harold Ware?

Mr. HISS. I did not.

Mr. McDOWELL. Or J. Peters?[6]

Mr. HISS. I did not.

Mr. STRIPLING. Also known as Isidor Boorstein.

Mr. McDOWELL. Or Isidor Boorstein?

Mr. HISS. I did not. I have never heard of Isidor Boorstein.

Mr. McDOWELL. Or Alexander Stevens?

Mr. HISS. I did not, never heard the name of Alexander Stevens before. . . .

The CHAIRMAN. Completing my statement, I instruct the chief investigator to serve a subpena on both Mr. Hiss and Mr. Chambers to appear on that date.

Mr. HISS. May I make a statement at this point for the record?

The CHAIRMAN. Just a minute.

Mr. HISS. Oh, yes.

(There was a short pause.)

Mr. HISS. Has the minute passed yet, Mr. Chairman?

The CHAIRMAN. Make it 2 minutes, then. Wait until we get through, please.

Mr. HISS. I have been waiting some time. I was told this would take 15 minutes. You now want me to take 2 minutes.

The CHAIRMAN. Do you have anything further?

Mr. STRIPLING. I just want to make the subpena out.

The CHAIRMAN. Go ahead.

[6] Peters was identified by Chambers as the head of the Communist underground in the United States. He was also known as Alexander Stevens and Isidor Boorstein, but his real name was Alexander Goldberger.

Mr. HISS. I would like to say the service of a subpena is quite unnecessary on me. I would be very happy to appear and I told the committee yesterday if they asked me to appear without talking about subpenas, I, of course, would be there. I was asked yesterday also by the committee—and since the committee seems to change its mind so quickly and frequently, I would like to get it clear—I was asked yesterday to make arrangements for Mrs. Hiss to come down from Vermont to meet in executive session with a subcommittee.

As I mentioned earlier, I was told it would be without publicity. That was volunteered by the committee, although I read about it in the papers this morning. Does the committee still desire to hear Mrs. Hiss in executive session or have you changed your mind?

The CHAIRMAN. Can she be in Washington on Monday morning?

Mr. HISS. God, she just made arrangements, if she succeeded at all, to get somebody to stay with the kid 2 or 3 nights.

The CHAIRMAN. You don't know whether she has made arrangements or not?

Mr. HISS. I believe so.

The CHAIRMAN. You don't know; you just believe so.

Mr. NIXON. I will stay over tonight. There is no objection to this. Just let us know. I don't want to stay a week.

Mr. HISS. I don't want her to stay a week. Where can I reach you tonight?

Mr. NIXON. You can reach me at this hotel; and if you will simply let me know if she will be here any time tomorrow, I am perfectly willing to be here.

Mr. HISS. Vermont trains are unpredictable. May I ask if she is privileged to have anybody with her?

Mr. NIXON. Absolutely.

Mr. HISS. May I come with her?

Mr. McDOWELL. Yes.

Mr. HISS. Thank you. Am I dismissed?

Is the proceeding over?

The CHAIRMAN. Any more questions to ask of Mr. Hiss?

Mr. NIXON. I have nothing.

The CHAIRMAN. That is all. Thank you very much.

Mr. HISS. *I don't reciprocate.*

The CHAIRMAN. Italicize that in the record.

Mr. HISS. I wish you would.

(Whereupon, at 7:15 p.m., the subcommittee adjourned.)

TRUMAN'S "RED HERRING" STATEMENT

6 ⋅ᢒ IN THE MIDST of the furor occasioned by Chambers' testimony, President Truman, on August 5, 1948, made the
following remarks to the press:[7]

Q. Mr. President, do you think that the Capitol Hill spy scare is
a "red herring" to divert public attention from inflation?

THE PRESIDENT. Yes, I do, and I will read you another statement
on that, since you brought it up. [*Laughter*]

[*Reading*] "In response to written requests from congressional
groups for information relating to the employment of individuals,
the department or agency may forward to the committee all unclas
sified routine papers, such as Civil Service Form 57, records of promotion, efficiency ratings, letters of recommendation, etc.

"No information of any sort relating to the employee's loyalty, and
no investigative data of any type, whether relating to loyalty or other
aspects of the individual's record, shall be included in the material
submitted to a congressional committee. If there is doubt as to
whether a certain document or group of documents should be supplied, the matter should be referred to the White House.

"No information has been revealed by these committees' investigations that has not long since been presented to a Federal grand
jury.

"No information has been disclosed in the past few days by the
congressional committees that has not long been known to the FBI.

"The Federal grand jury found this information insufficient to
justify indictment of the Federal employees involved.

"All but two of the employees involved have left the Federal
Government, and these two have been placed on leave without pay
before the congressional hearings started.

"The public hearings now under way are serving no useful purpose.
On the contrary, they are doing irreparable harm to certain people,
seriously impairing the morale of Federal employees, and undermining
public confidence in the Government."

And they are simply a "red herring" to keep from doing what they
ought to do.

Q. Don't you think the American public is entitled to this
information?

[7] Excerpt reprinted from the *Truman Papers*, 1948, pp. 432–3.

THE PRESIDENT. What information?

Q. That has been brought out in these investigations?

THE PRESIDENT. What useful purpose is it serving when we are having this matter before a grand jury where action has to take place, no matter what this committee does? They haven't revealed anything that everybody hasn't known all along, or hasn't been presented to the grand jury. That is where it has to be taken, in the first place, if you are going to do anything about it. They are slandering a lot of people that don't deserve it.

Q. Mr. President, could we use a part of the quote there, that last: they are simply a "red herring," etc?

THE PRESIDENT. Using this as a "red herring" to keep from doing what they ought to do.

VETO OF INTERNAL SECURITY ACT

7 ᥱᥱ᫕ THE MAJOR STATUTORY CONTRIBUTION of Congress in the battle against subversion was the Internal Security Act, passed in September 1950. The act required all Communist organizations, including so-called front groups, to register with the Attorney General and to furnish him with lists of their members. "Substantially" contributing to the establishment of a totalitarian dictatorship within the United States became a crime under the terms of the act, but membership in a Communist organization was not in itself to be considered unlawful. The act barred Communists from employment in defense plants, denied them passports for travel, and made them subject to internment in case of war. Aliens who belonged to Communist organizations or "who advocate the economic, international, and governmental doctrines of any other form of totalitarianism" could not gain admittance to the country. Moreover, naturalized citizens who joined Communist organizations within five years of acquiring citizenship could have their papers revoked. To assist the Attorney General in designating Communist organizations, the act created a bipartisan Subversive Activities Control Board. On September 22, 1950, Truman vetoed the bill, but the veto was easily overridden in Congress. Excerpts from the veto message follow:[8]

[8] Reprinted from Congressional Record, Eighty-first Congress, second session, pp. 15629–32.

I return herewith, without my approval, H. R. 9490, the proposed "Internal Security Act of 1950."

I am taking this action only after the most serious study and reflection and after consultation with the security and intelligence agencies of the Government. The Department of Justice, the Department of Defense, the Central Intelligence Agency, and the Department of State have all advised me that the bill would seriously damage the security and intelligence operations for which they are responsible. They have strongly expressed the hope that the bill would not become law. . . .

H. R. 9490 would not hurt the Communists. Instead, it would help them. . . .

In brief, when all the provisions of H. R. 9490 are considered together, it is evident that the great bulk of them are not directed toward the real and present dangers that exist from communism. Instead of striking blows at communism, they would strike blows at our own liberties and at our position in the forefront of those working for freedom in the world. . . .

Most of the first 17 sections of H. R. 9490 are concerned with requiring registration and annual reports. . . .

The idea of requiring Communist organizations to divulge information about themselves is a simple and attractive one. But it is about as practical as requiring thieves to register with the sheriff. Obviously, no such organization as the Communist Party is likely to register voluntarily.

Under the provisions of the bill, if an organization which the Attorney General believes should register does not do so, he must request a five-man Subversive Activities Control Board to order the organization to register. The Attorney General would have to produce proof that the organization in question was in fact a Communist-action or a Communist-front organization. To do this he would have to offer evidence relating to every aspect of the organization's activities. The organization could present opposing evidence. Prolonged hearings would be required to allow both sides to present proof and to cross-examine opposing witnesses. . . .

Thus the net result of the registration provision of this bill would probably be an endless chasing of one organization after another. . . .

Insofar as the bill would require registration by the Communist Party itself, it does not endanger our traditional liberties. However, the application of the registration requirements to so-called Communist-front organizations can be the greatest danger to freedom of speech, press, and assembly, since the Alien and Sedition Laws of 1798. This danger arises out of the criteria or standards to be applied in determining whether an organization is a Communist-front organization.

There would be no serious problem if the bill required proof that an organization was controlled and financed by the Communist Party before it could be classified as a Communist-front organization. However, recognizing the difficulty of proving those matters, the bill would permit such a determination to be based solely upon the extent to which the positions taken or advanced by it from time to time on matters of policy do not deviate from those of the Communist movement.

This provision could easily be used to classify as a Communist-front organization any organization which is advocating a single policy or objective which is also being urged by the Communist Party or by a Communist foreign government. In fact, this may be the intended result, since the bill defines "organization" to include "a group of persons permanently or temporarily associated together for joint action on any subject or subjects." Thus, an organization which advocates low-cost housing for sincere humanitarian reasons might be classified as a Communist-front organization because the Communists regularly exploit slum conditions as one of their fifth-column techniques.

It is not enough to say that this probably would not be done. The mere fact that it could be done shows clearly how the bill would open a Pandora's box of opportunities for official condemnation of organizations and individuals for perfectly honest opinions which happen to be stated also by Communists.

The basic error of these sections is that they move in the direction of suppressing opinion and belief. This would be a very dangerous course to take, not because we have any sympathy for Communist opinions, but because any governmental stifling of the free expression of opinion is a long step toward totalitarianism.

There is no more fundamental axiom of American freedom than the familiar statement: In a free country, we punish men for the crimes they commit, but never for the opinions they have. . . .

We can and we will prevent espionage, sabotage, or other actions endangering our national security. But we would betray our finest traditions if we attempted, as this bill would attempt, to curb the simple expression of opinion. . . .

And what kind of effect would these provisions have on the normal expression of political views? Obviously, if this law were on the statute books, the part of prudence would be to avoid saying anything that might be construed by someone as not deviating sufficiently from the current Communist propaganda line. And since no one could be sure in advance what views were safe to express, the inevitable tendency would be to express no views on controversial subjects.

The result could only be to reduce the vigor and strength of our political life—an outcome that the Communists would happily welcome, but that free men should abhor.

We need not fear the expression of ideas—we do need to fear their suppression.

Our position in the vanguard of freedom rests largely on our demonstration that the free expression of opinion, coupled with government by popular consent, leads to national strength and human advancement. Let us not, in cowering and foolish fear, throw away the ideals which are the fundamental basis of our free society.

Not only are the registration provisions of this bill unworkable and dangerous, they are also grossly misleading in that all but one of the objectives which are claimed for them are already being accomplished by other and superior methods—and the one objective which is not now being accomplished would not in fact be accomplished under this bill either.

It is claimed that the bill would provide information about the Communist Party and its members. The fact is, the FBI already possesses very complete sources of information concerning the Communist movement in this country. If the FBI must disclose its sources of information in public hearings to require registration under this bill, its present sources of information, and its ability to acquire new information, will be largely destroyed. . . .

It is claimed that this bill would deny passports to Communists. The fact is that the Government can and does deny passports to Communists under existing law. . . .

Section 4 (a) of the bill, like its registration provisions, would be ineffective, would be subject to dangerous abuse, and would seek to accomplish an objective which is already better accomplished under existing law.

This provision would make unlawful any agreement to perform

any act which would substantially contribute to the establishment within the United States of a foreign-controlled dictatorship. Of course, this provision would be unconstitutional if it infringed upon the fundamental right of the American people to establish for themselves by constitutional methods any form of government they choose. To avoid this, it is provided that this section shall not apply to the proposal of a constitutional amendment. If this language limits the prohibition of the section to the use of unlawful methods, then it adds nothing to the Smith Act, under which 11 Communist leaders have been convicted, and would be more difficult to enforce. Thus, it would accomplish nothing. Moreover, the bill does not even purport to define the phrase, unique in a criminal statute, "substantially contribute." A phrase so vague raises a serious constitutional question.

Sections 22 and 25 of this bill are directed toward the specific questions of who should be admitted to our country, and who should be permitted to become a United States citizen. I believe there is general agreement that the answers to those questions should be: We should admit to our country, within the available quotas, anyone with a legitimate purpose who would not endanger our security, and we should admit to citizenship any immigrant who will be a loyal and constructive member of the community. Those are essentially the standards set by existing law. Under present law, we do not admit to our country known Communists, because we believe they work to overthrow our Government, and we do not admit Communists to citizenship, because we believe they are not loyal to the United States. . . .

Until now, no one has suggested that we should abandon cultural and commercial relations with a country merely because it has a form of government different from ours. Yet section 22 would require that. As one instance, it is clear that under the definitions of the bill the present Government of Spain, among others, would be classified as "totalitarian." As a result, the Attorney General would be required to exclude from the United States all Spanish businessmen, students, and other nonofficial travelers who support the present Government of their country. I cannot understand how the sponsors of this bill can think that such an action would contribute to our national security.

Moreover, the provisions of section 22 of this bill would strike a serious blow to our national security by taking away from the Government the power to grant asylum in this country to foreign diplomats who repudiate Communist imperialism and wish to escape its reprisals. It must be obvious to anyone that it is in our national interest to persuade people to renounce communism, and to encourage their defection from Communist forces. Many of these people are extremely valuable to our intelligence operations. Yet under this bill the Government would lose the limited authority it now has to offer asylum in our country as the great incentive for such defection. . . .

Section 22 is so contrary to our national interests that it would actually put the Government into the business of thought control by requiring the deportation of any alien who distributes or publishes, or who is affiliated with an organization which distributes or publishes, any written or printed matter advocating (or merely expressing belief in) the economic and governmental doctrines of any form of totalitarianism.

This provision does not require an evil intent or purpose on the part of the alien, as does a similar provision in the Smith Act. Thus, the Attorney General would be required to deport any alien operating or connected with a well-stocked bookshop containing books on economics or politics written by supporters of the present government of Spain, of Yugoslavia or any one of a number of other countries. Section 25 would make the same aliens ineligible for citizenship. There should be no room in our laws for such hysterical provisions. The next logical step would be to "burn the books. . . ."

Earlier this month, we launched a great Crusade for Freedom designed, in the words of General Eisenhower, to fight the big lie with the big truth. I can think of no better way to make a mockery of that crusade and of the deep American belief in human freedom and dignity which underlie it than to put the provisions of H. R. 9490 on our statute books.

COURT OPINION ON DENNIS CASE

8 ⊷§ IN 1948, AS PART of its crackdown on Communism, the Truman administration obtained indictments against eleven high-ranking Communist-party leaders for conspiracy, in violation of the Smith Act, to teach the violent overthrow of the government. After a trial of nine months a jury found the defendants guilty, and the case went to the Supreme Court. The case of *Dennis et al. v. United States* was decided on June 4, 1951. One of the most

important opinions in the history of the Supreme Court, the majority decision written by Chief Justice Fred M. Vinson, upheld the convictions:[9]

... We granted certiorari ... limited to the following two questions: (1) Whether either § 2 or § 3 of the Smith Act, inherently or as construed and applied in the instant case, violates the First Amendment and other provisions of the Bill of Rights; (2) whether either § 2 or § 3 of the Act, inherently or as construed and applied in the instant case, violates the First and Fifth Amendments because of indefiniteness.

Sections 2 and 3 of the Smith Act ... provide as follows:

SEC. 2. (a) It shall be unlawful for any person—

(1) to knowingly or willfully advocate, abet, advise, or teach the duty, necessity, desirability, or propriety of overthrowing or destroying any government in the United States by force or violence, or by the assassination of any officer of any such government;

(2) with intent to cause the overthrow or destruction of any government in the United States, to print, publish, edit, issue, circulate, sell, distribute, or publicly display any written or printed matter advocating, advising, or teaching the duty, necessity, desirability, or propriety of overthrowing or destroying any government in the United States by force or violence;

(3) to organize or help to organize any society, group, or assembly of persons who teach, advocate, or encourage the overthrow or destruction of any government in the United States by force or violence; or to be or become a member of, or affiliate with, any such society, group, or assembly of persons, knowing the purposes thereof. . . .

SEC. 3. It shall be unlawful for any person to attempt to commit, or to conspire to commit, any of the acts prohibited by the provisions of this title.

The indictment charged the petitioners with willfully and knowingly conspiring (1) to organize as the Communist Party of the United States of America a society, group and assembly of persons who teach and advocate the overthrow and destruction of the Government of the United States by force and violence, and (2) knowingly and willfully to advocate and teach the duty and necessity of overthrowing and destroying the Government of the United States

[9] Excerpts reprinted from 341 U.S. 494 (1951).

by force and violence. The indictment further alleged that § 2 of the Smith Act proscribes these acts and that any conspiracy to take such action is a violation of § 3 of the Act. . . .

The obvious purpose of the statute is to protect existing Government, not from change by peaceable, lawful and constitutional means, but from change by violence, revolution and terrorism. That it is within the power of the Congress to protect the Government of the United States from armed rebellion is a proposition which requires little discussion. Whatever theoretical merit there may be to the argument that there is a "right" to rebellion against dictatorial governments is without force where the existing structure of the government provides for peaceful and orderly change. We reject any principle of governmental helplessness in the face of preparation for revolution, which principle, carried to its logical conclusion, must lead to anarchy. No one could conceive that it is not within the power of Congress to prohibit acts intended to overthrow the Government by force and violence. The question with which we are concerned here is not whether Congress has such power, but whether the means which it has employed conflict with the First and Fifth Amendments to the Constitution. . . .

The very language of the Smith Act negates the interpretation which petitioners would have us impose on that Act. It is directed at advocacy, not discussion. Thus, the trial judge properly charged the jury that they could not convict if they found that petitioners did "no more than pursue peaceful studies and discussions or teaching and advocacy in the realm of ideas." He further charged that it was not unlawful "to conduct in an American college or university a course explaining the philosophical theories set forth in the books which have been placed in evidence." Such a charge is in strict accord with the statutory language, and illustrates the meaning to be placed on those words. Congress did not intend to eradicate the free discussion of political theories, to destroy the traditional rights of Americans to discuss and evaluate ideas without fear of governmental sanction. Rather Congress was concerned with the very kind of activity in which the evidence showed these petitioners engaged.

But although the statute is not directed at the hypothetical cases which petitioners have conjured, its application in this case has resulted in convictions for the teaching and advocacy of the overthrow of the Government by force and violence, which, even though coupled with the intent to accomplish that overthrow, contains an element of speech. For this reason, we must pay special heed to the demands of the First Amendment marking out the boundaries of speech.

We pointed out in *Douds, supra*, that the basis of the First Amendment is the hypothesis that speech can rebut speech, propaganda will answer propaganda, free debate of ideas will result in the wisest governmental policies. It is for this reason that this Court has recognized the inherent value of free discourse. An analysis of the leading cases in this Court which have involved direct limitations on speech, however, will demonstrate that both the majority of the Court and the dissenters in particular cases have recognized that this is not an unlimited, unqualified right, but that the societal value of speech must, on occasion, be subordinated to other values and considerations.

No important case involving free speech was decided by this Court prior to *Schenck v. United States*, 249 U.S. 47 (1919). Indeed, the summary treatment accorded an argument based upon an individual's claim that the First Amendment protected certain utterances indicates that the Court at earlier dates placed no unique emphasis upon that right. It was not until the classic dictum of Justice Holmes in the *Schenck* case that speech *per se* received that emphasis in a majority opinion. That case involved a conviction under the Criminal Espionage Act, 40 Stat. 217. The question the Court faced was whether the evidence was sufficient to sustain the conviction. Writing for a unanimous Court, Justice Holmes stated that the "question in every case is whether the words used are used in such circumstances and are of such a nature as to create a clear and present danger that they will bring about the substantive evils that Congress has a right to prevent." . . .

In this case we are squarely presented with the application of the "clear and present danger" test, and must decide what that phrase imports. We first note that many of the cases in which this Court has reversed convictions by use of this or similar tests have been based on the fact that the interest which the State was attempting to protect was itself too insubstantial to warrant restriction of speech. . . . Overthrow of the Government by force and violence is certainly a substantial enough interest for the Government to limit speech. Indeed, this is the ultimate value of any society, for if a society cannot protect its very structure from armed internal attack, it must follow that no subordinate value can be protected. If, then, this interest may be protected, the literal problem which is presented is what has been meant by the use of the phrase "clear and present danger" of the utterances bringing about the evil within the power of Congress to punish.

Obviously, the words cannot mean that before the Government may act, it must wait until the *putsch* is about to be executed, the plans have been laid and the signal is awaited. If Government is aware that a group aiming at its overthrow is attempting to indoctrinate its members and to commit them to a course whereby they will strike when the leaders feel the circumstances permit, action by the Government is required. The argument that there is no need for Government to concern itself, for Government is strong, it possesses ample powers to put down a rebellion, it may defeat the revolution with ease needs no answer. For that is not the question. Certainly an attempt to overthrow the Government by force, even though doomed from the outset because of inadequate numbers or power of the revolutionists, is a sufficient evil for Congress to prevent. The damage which such attempts create both physically and politically to a nation makes it impossible to measure the validity in terms of the probability of success, or the immediacy of a successful attempt. In the instant case the trial judge charged the jury that they could not convict unless they found that petitioners intended to overthrow the Government "as speedily as circumstances would permit." This does not mean, and could not properly mean, that they would not strike until there was certainty of success. What was meant was that the revolutionists would strike when they thought the time was ripe. We must therefore reject the contention that success or probability of success is the criterion.

Likewise, we are in accord with the court below, which affirmed the trial court's finding that the requisite danger existed. The mere fact that from the period 1945 to 1948 petitioners' activities did not result in an attempt to overthrow the Government by force and violence is of course no answer to the fact that there was a group that was ready to make the attempt. The formation by petitioners of such a highly organized conspiracy, with rigidly disciplined members subject to call when the leaders, these petitioners, felt that the time had come for action, coupled with the inflammable nature of world conditions, similar uprisings in other countries, and the touch-and-go nature of our relations with countries with whom petitioners were in the very least ideologically attuned, convince us that their convictions were justified on this score. And this analysis disposes of the contention that a conspiracy to advocate as distinguished from the advocacy itself, cannot be constitutionally restrained, because it comprises only the preparation. It is the existence of the conspiracy which creates the danger. . . . If the ingredients of the reaction are present, we cannot bind the Government to wait until the catalyst is added. . . .

There remains to be discussed the question of vagueness—whether the statute as we have interpreted it is too vague, not sufficiently advising those who would speak of the limitations upon their activity. It is urged that such vagueness contravenes the First and Fifth Amendments. This argument is particularly nonpersuasive when presented by petitioners, who, the jury found, intended to overthrow the Government as speedily as circumstances would permit. . . .

We agree that the standard as defined is not a neat, mathematical formulary. Like all verbalizations it is subject to criticism on the score of indefiniteness. But petitioners themselves contend that the verbalization "clear and present danger" is the proper standard. We see no difference, from the standpoint of vagueness, whether the standard of "clear and present danger" is one contained *in haec verba* within the statute, or whether it is the judicial measure of constitutional applicability. We have shown the indeterminate standard the phrase necessarily connotes. We do not think we have rendered that standard any more indefinite by our attempt to sum up the factors which are included within its scope. We think it well serves to indicate to those who would advocate constitutionally prohibited conduct that there is a line beyond which they may not go—a line which they, in full knowledge of what they intend and the circumstances in which their activity takes place, will well appreciate and understand. . . . Where there is doubt as to the intent of the defendants, the nature of their activities, or their power to bring about the evil, this Court will review the convictions with the scrupulous care demanded by our Constitution. But we are not convinced that because there may be borderline cases at some time in the future, these convictions should be reversed because of the argument that these petitioners could not know that their activities were constitutionally proscribed by the statute.

We hold that §§ 2 (a) (1), 2 (a) (3) and 3 of the Smith Act do not inherently, or as construed or applied in the instant case, violate the First Amendment and other provisions of the Bill of Rights, or the First and Fifth Amendments because of indefiniteness. Petitioners intended to overthrow the Government of the United States as speedily as the circumstances would permit. Their conspiracy to organize the Communist Party and to teach and advocate the overthrow of the Government of the United States by force and violence created a "clear and present danger" of an attempt to overthrow the Government by force and violence. They were properly and constitutionally convicted for violation of the Smith Act. The judgments of conviction are

Affirmed.

DISSENT ON DENNIS CASE

9 ⋙ JUSTICES HUGO BLACK AND WILLIAM DOUGLAS each wrote vigorous dissenting opinions to the *Dennis* decision. Parts of Justice Douglas' dissent follow:[10]

If this were a case where those who claimed protection under the First Amendment were teaching the techniques of sabotage, the assassination of the President, the filching of documents from public files, the planting of bombs, the art of street warfare, and the like, I would have no doubts. The freedom to speak is not absolute; the teaching of methods of terror and other seditious conduct should be beyond the pale along with obscenity and immorality. This case was argued as if those were the facts. The argument imported much seditious conduct into the record. That is easy and it has popular appeal, for the activities of Communists in plotting and scheming against the free world are common knowledge. But the fact is that no such evidence was introduced at the trial. There is a statute which makes a seditious conspiracy unlawful. Petitioners, however, were not charged with a "conspiracy to overthrow" the Government. They were charged with a conspiracy to form a party and groups and assemblies of people who teach and advocate the overthrow of our Government by force or violence and with a conspiracy to advocate and teach its overthrow by force and violence. It may well be that indoctrination in the techniques of terror to destroy the Government would be indictable under either statute. But the teaching which is condemned here is of a different character.

So far as the present record is concerned, what petitioners did was to organize people to teach and themselves teach the Marxist-Leninist doctrine contained chiefly in four books: Stalin, Foundations of

[10] Reprinted from 341 U.S. 581 (1951).

Leninism (1924); Marx and Engels, Manifesto of the Communist Party (1848); Lenin, The State and Revolution (1917); History of the Communist Party of the Soviet Union (B.) (1939).

Those books are to Soviet Communism what *Mein Kampf* was to Nazism. If they are understood, the ugliness of Communism is revealed, its deceit and cunning are exposed, the nature of its activities becomes apparent, and the chances of its success less likely. That is not, of course, the reason why petitioners chose these books for their classrooms. They are fervent Communists to whom these volumes are gospel. They preached the creed with the hope that some day it would be acted upon.

The opinion of the Court does not outlaw these texts nor condemn them to the fire, as the Communists do literature offensive to their creed. But if the books themselves are not outlawed, if they can lawfully remain on library shelves, by what reasoning does their use in a classroom become a crime? It would not be a crime under the Act to introduce these books to a class, though that would be teaching what the creed of violent overthrow of the Government is. The Act, as construed, requires the element of intent—that those who teach the creed believe in it. The crime then depends not on what is taught but on who the teacher is. That is to make freedom of speech turn not on *what is said*, but on the *intent* with which it is said. Once we start down that road we enter territory dangerous to the liberties of every citizen. . . .

Intent, of course, often makes the difference in the law. An act otherwise excusable or carrying minor penalties may grow to an abhorrent thing if the evil intent is present. We deal here, however, not with ordinary acts but with speech, to which the Constitution has given a special sanction. . . .

Free speech has occupied an exalted position because of the high service it has given our society. Its protection is essential to the very existence of a democracy. The airing of ideas releases pressures which otherwise might become destructive. When ideas compete in the market for acceptance, full and free discussion exposes the false and they gain few adherents. Full and free discussion even of ideas we hate encourages the testing of our own prejudices and preconceptions. Full and free discussion keeps a society from becoming stagnant and unprepared for the stresses and strains that work to tear all civilizations apart.

Full and free discussion has indeed been the first article of our faith. We have founded our political system on it. It has been the safeguard of every religious, political, philosophical, economic, and racial group amongst us. We have counted on it to keep us from embracing what is cheap and false; we have trusted the common sense of our people to choose the doctrine true to our genius and to reject the rest. This has been the one single outstanding tenet that has made our institutions the symbol of freedom and equality. We have deemed it more costly to liberty to suppress a despised minority than to let them vent their spleen. We have above all else feared the political censor. We have wanted a land where our people can be exposed to all the diverse creeds and cultures of the world.

There comes a time when even speech loses its constitutional immunity. Speech innocuous one year may at another time fan such destructive flames that it must be halted in the interests of the safety of the Republic. That is the meaning of the clear and present danger test. When conditions are so critical that there will be no time to avoid the evil that the speech threatens, it is time to call a halt. Otherwise, free speech which is the strength of the Nation will be the cause of its destruction.

Yet free speech is the rule, not the exception. The restraint to be constitutional must be based on more than fear, on more than passionate opposition against the speech, on more than a revolted dislike for its contents. There must be some immediate injury to society that is likely if speech is allowed. . . .

The nature of Communism as a force on the world scene would, of course, be relevant to the issue of clear and present danger of petitioners' advocacy within the United States. But the primary consideration is the strength and tactical position of petitioners and their converts in this country. On that there is no evidence in the record. If we are to take judicial notice of the threat of Communists within the nation, it should not be difficult to conclude that as a *political party* they are of little consequence. Communists in this country have never made a respectable or serious showing in any election. I would doubt that there is a village, let alone a city or county or state, which the Communists could carry. Communism in the world scene is no bogeyman; but Communism as a political faction or party in this country plainly is. Communism has been so thoroughly exposed in this country that it has been crippled as a political force. Free speech has destroyed it as an effective political party. It is inconceivable that those who went up and down this country preaching the doctrine of revolution which petitioners espouse would have any success. In days of trouble and confusion, when bread lines were long, when the unemployed walked the streets, when people were starving, the advocates of a short-cut by revolution might have a chance to gain adherents. But today there are no such conditions. The country is not in despair; the people know Soviet Communism; the doctrine of Soviet revolution is exposed in all of its ugliness and the American people want none of it.

How it can be said that there is a clear and present danger that this advocacy will succeed is, therefore, a mystery. Some nations less resilient than the United States, where illiteracy is high and where democratic traditions are only budding, might have to take drastic steps and jail these men for merely speaking their creed. But in America they are miserable merchants of unwanted ideas; their wares remain unsold. The fact that their ideas are abhorrent does not make them powerful.

The political impotence of the Communists in this country does not, of course, dispose of the problem. Their numbers; their positions in industry and government; the extent to which they have in fact infiltrated the police, the armed services, transportation, stevedoring, power plants, munitions works, and other critical places—these facts all bear on the likelihood that their advocacy of the Soviet theory of revolution will endanger the Republic. But the record is silent on these facts. If we are to proceed on the basis of judicial notice, it is impossible for me to say that the Communists in this country are so potent or so strategically deployed that they must be suppressed for their speech. I could not so hold unless I were willing to conclude that the activities in recent years of committees of Congress, of the Attorney General, of labor unions, of state legislatures, and of Loyalty Boards were so futile as to leave the country on the edge of grave peril. To believe that petitioners and their following are placed in such critical positions as to endanger the Nation is to believe the incredible. It is safe to say that the followers of the creed of Soviet Communism are known to the F.B.I.; that in case of war with Russia they will be picked up overnight as were all prospective saboteurs at the commencement of World War II; that the invisible army of petitioners is the best known, the most beset, and the least thriving of any fifth column in history. Only those held by fear and panic could think otherwise.

MCCARTHY'S FIRST ATTACK ON STATE DEPARTMENT

10 ◄§   THE MAN WHO DID MOST to turn the concern about domestic Communism into a form of national hysteria was Wisconsin's junior senator, Joseph R. McCarthy. With four undistinguished years in Washington behind him, McCarthy traveled to Wheeling, West Virginia, on February 9, 1950, to charge that the State Department was currently employing 205 Communists. On February 20, 1950, McCarthy read into the *Congressional Record* a version of the Wheeling speech that moderated the accusation and reduced the number of alleged Communists to fifty-seven. The version that he read into the *Record* follows:[11]

Today we are engaged in a final, all-out battle between communistic atheism and Christianity. The modern champions of communism have selected this as the time. And, ladies and gentlemen, the chips are down—they are truly down. . . .

Ladies and gentlemen, can there be anyone here tonight who is so blind as to say that the war is not on? Can there be anyone who fails to realize that the Communist world has said, "The time is now"— that this is the time for the show-down between the democratic Christian world and the Communist atheistic world?

Unless we face this fact, we shall pay the price that must be paid by those who wait too long.

Six years ago, at the time of the first conference to map out the peace—Dumbarton Oaks—there was within the Soviet orbit 180,000,-000 people. Lined up on the antitotalitarian side there were in the world at that time roughly 1,625,000,000 people. Today, only 6 years later, there are 800,000,000 people under the absolute domination of Soviet Russia—an increase of over 400 percent. On our side, the figure has shrunk to around 500,000,000. In other words, in less than 6 years the odds have changed from 9 to 1 in our favor to 8 to 5 against us. This indicates the swiftness of the tempo of Communist victories and American defeats in the cold war. As one of our outstanding historical figures once said, "When a great democracy is destroyed, it will not

[11] Reprinted from *Congressional Record*, Eighty-first Congress, second session, pp. 1954, 1956, 1957.

be because of enemies from without, but rather because of enemies from within."

The truth of this statement is becoming terrifyingly clear as we see this country each day losing on every front.

At war's end we were physically the strongest nation on earth and, at least potentially, the most powerful intellectually and morally. Ours could have been the honor of being a beacon in the desert of destruction, a shining living proof that civilization was not yet ready to destroy itself. Unfortunately, we have failed miserably and tragically to arise to the opportunity.

The reason why we find ourselves in a position of impotency is not because our only powerful potential enemy has sent men to invade our shores, but rather because of the traitorous actions of those who have been treated so well by this Nation. It has not been the less fortunate or members of minority groups who have been selling this Nation out, but rather those who have had all the benefits that the wealthiest nation on earth has had to offer—the finest homes, the finest college education, and the finest jobs in Government we can give.

This is glaringly true in the State Department. There the bright young men who are born with silver spoons in their mouths are the ones who have been worst.

Now I know it is very easy for anyone to condemn a particular bureau or department in general terms. Therefore, I would like to cite one rather unusual case—the case of a man who has done much to shape our foreign policy.

When Chiang Kai-shek was fighting our war, the State Department had in China a young man named John S. Service. His task, obviously, was not to work for the communization of China. Strangely, however, he sent official reports back to the State Department urging that we torpedo our ally Chiang Kai-shek and stating, in effect, that communism was the best hope of China.

Later, this man—John Service—was picked up by the Federal Bureau of Investigation for turning over to the Communists secret State Department information. Strangely, however, he was never prosecuted. However, Joseph Grew, the Under Secretary of State, who insisted on his prosecution, was forced to resign. Two days after Grew's successor, Dean Acheson, took over as Under Secretary of State, this man—John Service—who had been picked up by the FBI and who had previously urged that communism was the best hope of China, was not only reinstated in the State Department but promoted.

And finally, under Acheson, placed in charge of all placements and promotions.

Today, ladies and gentlemen, this man Service is on his way to represent the State Department and Acheson in Calcutta—by far and away the most important listening post in the Far East.

Now, let's see what happens when individuals with Communist connections are forced out of the State Department. Gustave Duran, who was labeled as (I quote) "a notorious international Communist," was made assistant to the Assistant Secretary of State in charge of Latin American affairs. He was taken into the State Department from his job as a lieutenant colonel in the Communist International Brigade. Finally, after intense congressional pressure and criticism, he resigned in 1946 from the State Department—and, ladies and gentlemen, where do you think he is now? He took over a high-salaried job as Chief of Cultural Activities Section in the office of the Assistant Secretary General of the United Nations. . . .

Then there was a Mrs. Mary Jane Kenny, from the Board of Economic Warfare in the State Department, who was named in an FBI report and in a House committee report as a courier for the Communist Party while working for the Government. And where do you think Mrs. Kenny is—she is now an editor in the United Nations Document Bureau.

Another interesting case was that of Julian H. Wadleigh, economist in the Trade Agreements Section of the State Department for 11 years and was sent to Turkey and Italy and other countries as United States representative. After the statute of limitations had run so he could not be prosecuted for treason, he openly and brazenly not only admitted but proclaimed that he had been a member of the Communist Party * * * that while working for the State Department he stole a vast number of secret documents * * * and furnished these documents to the Russian spy ring of which he was a part.

You will recall last spring there was held in New York what was known as the World Peace Conference—a conference which was labeled by the State Department and Mr. Truman as the sounding board for Communist propaganda and a front for Russia. Dr. Harlow Shapley was the chairman of that conference. Interestingly enough, according to the news release put out by the Department in July, the Secretary of State appointed Shapley on a commission which acts as liaison between UNESCO and the State Department. . . .

This, ladies and gentlemen, gives you somewhat of a picture of the type of individuals who have been helping to shape our foreign policy. In my opinion the State Department, which is one of the most important government departments, is thoroughly infested with Communists.

I have in my hand 57 cases of individuals who would appear to be either card carrying members or certainly loyal to the Communist Party, but who nevertheless are still helping to shape our foreign policy.

One thing to remember in discussing the Communists in our Government is that we are not dealing with spies who get 30 pieces of silver to steal the blueprints of a new weapon. We are dealing with a far more sinister type of activity because it permits the enemy to guide and shape our policy.

In that connection, I would like to read to you very briefly from the testimony of Larry E. Kerley, a man who was with the counter espionage section of the FBI for 8 years. And keep in mind as I read this to you that at the time he is speaking, there was in the State Department Alger Hiss, the convicted Alger Hiss; John Service, the man whom the FBI picked up for espionage— . . . Julian Wadleigh, who brazenly admitted he was a spy and wrote newspaper articles in regard thereto, plus hundreds of other bad security risks.

The FBI, I may add, has done an outstanding job, as all persons in Washington, Democrats and Republicans alike, agree. If J. Edgar Hoover had a free hand, we would not be plagued by Hisses and Wadleighs in high positions of power in the State Department. The FBI has only power to investigate.

Here is what the FBI man said.

In accordance with instructions of the State Department to the FBI, the FBI was not even permitted to open an espionage case against any Russian suspect without State Department approval.

Mr. [RICHARD—Eds.] ARENS. Did the State Department ever withhold from the Justice Department the right to intern suspects?

Mr. KERLEY. They withheld the right to get out process for them which, in effect, kept them from being arrested, as in the case of Schevchenko and others.

Mr. ARENS. In how many instances did the State Department decline to permit process to be served on Soviet agents?

Mr. KERLEY. Do you mean how many Soviet agents were affected?

Mr. ARENS. Yes.

Mr. KERLEY. That would be difficult to say because there were so many people connected in one espionage ring, whether or not they were directly conspiring with the ring.

Mr. ARENS. Was that order applicable to all persons?

Mr. KERLEY. Yes; all persons in the Soviet-espionage organization.

Mr. ARENS. What did you say the order was as you understood it or as it came to you?

Mr. KERLEY. That no arrests of any suspects in the Russian-espionage activities in the United States were to be made without the prior approval of the State Department.

Now the reason for the State Department's opposition to arresting any of this spy ring is made rather clear in the next question and answer.

Senator [HERBERT R.—Eds.] O'CONOR. Did you understand that that was to include also American participants?

MR. KERLEY. Yes; because if they were arrested that would disclose the whole apparatus, you see. . . .

In other words they could not afford to let the whole ring which extended into the State Department be exposed. . . .

This brings us down to the case of one Alger Hiss who is important not as an individual any more, but rather because he is so representative of a group in the State Department. It is unnecessary to go over the sordid events showing how he sold out the Nation which had given him so much. Those are rather fresh in all of our minds.

However, it should be remembered that the facts in regard to his connection with this international Communist spy ring were made known to the then Under Secretary of State [Adolph A.—Eds.] Berle 3 days after Hitler and Stalin signed the Russo-German alliance pact. At that time one Whittaker Chambers—who was also part of the spy ring—apparently decided that with Russia on Hitler's side, he could no longer betray our Nation to Russia. He gave Under Secretary of State Berle—and this is all a matter of record—practically all, if not more, of the facts upon which Hiss' conviction was based.

Under Secretary Berle promptly contacted Dean Acheson and received word in return that Acheson (and I quote) "could vouch for Hiss absolutely"—at which time the matter was dropped. And this, you understand, was at a time when Russia was an ally of Germany. This condition existed while Russia and Germany were invading and dismembering Poland, and while the Communist groups here were screaming "warmonger" at the United States for their support of the allied nations.

Again in 1943, the FBI had occasion to investigate the facts surrounding Hiss' contacts with the Russian spy ring. But even after that FBI report was submitted, nothing was done.

Then late in 1948—on August 5—when the Un-American Activities Committee called Alger Hiss to give an accounting, President Truman at once issued a Presidential directive ordering all Government agencies to refuse to turn over any information whatsoever in regard to the Communist activities of any Government employee to a congressional committee.

Incidentally, even after Hiss was convicted— . . . it is interesting to note that the President still labeled the exposé of Hiss as a "red herring."

If time permitted, it might be well to go into detail about the fact that Hiss was Roosevelt's chief adviser at Yalta when Roosevelt was admittedly in ill health and tired physically and mentally * * * and when, according to the Secretary of State, Hiss and Gromyko drafted the report on the conference. . . .

According to the then Secretary of State Stettinius, here are some of the things that Hiss helped to decide at Yalta. (1) The establishment of a European High Commission; (2) the treatment of Germany —this you will recall was the conference at which it was decided that we would occupy Berlin with Russia occupying an area completely circling the city, which, as you know, resulted in the Berlin airlift which cost 31 American lives; (3) the Polish question; (4) the relationship between UNRRA and the Soviet; (5) the rights of Americans on control commissions of Rumania, Bulgaria, and Hungary; (6) Iran; (7) China—here's where we gave away Manchuria; (8) Turkish Straits question; (9) international trusteeships; (10) Korea.

Of the results of this conference, Arthur Bliss Lane of the State Department had this to say: "As I glanced over the document, I could not believe my eyes. To me, almost every line spoke of a surrender to Stalin."

As you hear this story of high treason, I know that you are saying to yourself, "Well, why doesn't the Congress do something about it?" Actually, ladies and gentlemen, one of the important reasons for the graft, the corruption, the dishonesty, the disloyalty, the treason in high Government positions—one of the most important reasons why this continues is a lack of moral uprising on the part of the 140,000,000

American people. In the light of history, however, this is not hard to explain.

It is the result of an emotional hang-over and a temporary moral lapse which follows every war. It is the apathy to evil which people who have been subjected to the tremendous evils of war feel. As the people of the world see mass murder, the destruction of defenseless and innocent people, and all of the crime and lack of morals which go with war, they become numb and apathetic. It has always been thus after war.

However, the morals of our people have not been destroyed. They still exist. This cloak of numbness and apathy has only needed a spark to rekindle them. Happily, this spark has finally been supplied.

As you know, very recently the Secretary of State proclaimed his loyalty to a man guilty of what has always been considered as the most abominable of all crimes—of being a traitor to the people who gave him a position of great trust. The Secretary of State in attempting to justify his continued devotion to the man who sold out the Christian world to the atheistic world, referred to Christ's Sermon on the Mount as a justification and reason therefor, and the reaction of the American people to this would have made the heart of Abraham Lincoln happy.

When this pompous diplomat in striped pants, with a phony British accent, proclaimed to the American people that Christ on the Mount endorsed communism, high treason, and betrayal of a sacred trust, the blasphemy was so great that it awakened the dormant indignation of the American people.

He has lighted the spark which is resulting in a moral uprising and will end only when the whole sorry mess of twisted, warped thinkers are swept from the national scene so that we may have a new birth of national honesty and decency in Government.

TYDINGS COMMITTEE REPORT

11 ◄§ ON FEBRUARY 22, 1950, as a result of McCarthy's accusations, the Senate directed its Committee on Foreign Relations to investigate disloyalty in the State Department. Under the chairmanship of Senator Millard Tydings, Democrat of Maryland, a subcommittee of the Committee on Foreign Relations held hearings over a period of four months and reported back to the Senate in the summer. All three Democratic members signed the

committee report, but the two Republicans refused their assent. Senator Henry Cabot Lodge, Republican of Massachusetts, filed a separate statement giving his own views of the subcommittee's work. Excerpts from the majority report follow:[12]

REVIEW OF LOYALTY FILES

Of the 81 alleged State Department employees, only 40 were found to be employed by the State Department at the time of the review. Seven of the so-called 81 were never employed by the State Department and the remaining 33 are no longer in the Department, having been separated either through resignation, termination, or reduction in force. Specifically, of the 33 former employees, 3 were separated in 1949; 16, in 1948; 12, in 1947; and 2, in 1946. . . .

With the foregoing considerations in mind, we have carefully and conscientiously reviewed each and every one of the loyalty files relative to the individuals charged by Senator McCarthy. In no instance was any one of them now employed in the State Department found to be a "card-carrying Communist," a member of the Communist Party, or "loyal to the Communist Party." Furthermore, in no instance have we found in our considered judgment that the decision to grant loyalty and security clearance has been erroneously or improperly made in the light of existing loyalty standards. Otherwise stated, we do not find basis in any instance for reversing the judgment of the State Department officials charged with responsibility for employee loyalty; or concluding that they have not conscientiously discharged their duties. . . .

We are fully satisfied, therefore, on the basis of our study of the loyalty files, that the State Department has not knowingly retained in its employ individuals who have been disloyal. Manifestly, of course, the State Department or any other department or agency of government cannot be charged with responsibility for what it does not know concerning an employee or for what may be developed at some future time relative to him. Conceivably, derogatory information revealing the employee as disloyal may be developed at some future time concerning any one of the employees whose files we reviewed, or others. This self-evident fact is necessarily beside the point since, as

[12] Reprinted from Senate Committee on Foreign Relations, "State Department Employee Loyalty Investigation," *Senate Report No. 2108*, Eighty-first Congress, second session.

indicated, no man may be held responsible for facts which he does not know.

What the State Department knows concerning an employee's loyalty is to be found in its loyalty and security files. These files contain all information bearing on loyalty, obtained from any and all sources, including, of course, the reports of full field investigations by the FBI. Interestingly, in this regard, no sooner had the President indicated that the files would be available for review by the subcommittee than Senator McCarthy charged they were being "raped," altered, or otherwise subjected to a "housecleaning." This charge was found to be utterly without foundation in fact. The files were reviewed by representatives of the Department of Justice, and the Department has certified that all information bearing on the employee's loyalty as developed by the FBI appears in the files which were reviewed by the subcommittee. . . .

GENERAL OBSERVATIONS

In concluding our report, we are constrained to make observations which we regard as fundamental.

It is, of course, clearly apparent that the charges of Communist infiltration of and influence upon the State Department are false. This knowledge is reassuring to all Americans whose faith has been temporarily shaken in the security of their Government by perhaps the most nefarious campaign of untruth in the history of our Republic. . . .

We have seen the character of private citizens and of Government employees virtually destroyed by public condemnation on the basis of gossip, distortion, hearsay, and deliberate untruths. By the mere fact of their associations with a few persons of alleged questionable proclivities an effort has been made to place the stigma of disloyalty upon individuals, some of whom are little people whose only asset is their character and devotion to duty and country. This has been done without the slightest vestige of respect for even the most elementary rules of evidence or fair play or, indeed, common decency. Indeed, we have seen an effort not merely to establish guilt by association but guilt by accusation alone. The spectacle is one we would expect in a totalitarian nation where the rights of the individual are crushed beneath the juggernaut of statism and oppression; it has no place in America where government exists to serve our people, not to destroy them.

We have seen an effort to inflame the American people with a wave of hysteria and fear on an unbelievable scale in this free Nation. . . .

In this situation, we appreciate anew the indispensable nature of a free press as a necessary handmaiden of freedom. One cannot but shudder at the contemplation of a controlled press treating the distortions and fabrications inherent in the charges that have been made. It is to a free press that the American people are indebted for a balanced treatment of our proceedings, even though we, as members of the subcommittee, were powerless until now to reveal the truth.

Communism represents the most diabolical concept ever designed to enslave mankind. Its stock and trade are deception, falsehood, and hate. The one hope of communism's success is to divide our people at home and our allies abroad. The false charges made in this case have succeeded in accomplishing to a great degree what the Communist themselves have been unable to do. These charges have created distrust and suspicion at home and raised serious doubts abroad.

We can never hope to preserve for posterity the American dream of freedom by adopting totalitarian methods as an excuse to preserve that freedom. Our greatest weapon against communism is truth. . . .

FINDINGS AND CONCLUSIONS . . .

4. We find that in making a speech on the Senate floor on February 20, 1950, Senator McCarthy read what purported to be the speech delivered by him at Wheeling, W. Va.; that the purported speech as read to the Senate was identical with the speech delievered at Wheeling except that he withheld from the Senate the statement actually made, as set forth in conclusion 1 above, and substituted in lieu thereof the following:

> I have in my hand 57 cases of individuals who would appear to be either card-carrying members or certainly loyal to the Communist Party, but who nevertheless are still helping to shape our foreign policy.

The substitution of the foregoing terminology constituted a misrepresentation of the true facts to the Senate.

5. We find that in making his speech on February 20, 1950, which occasioned the passage of Senate Resolution 231, Senator McCarthy left the unmistakable inference that he had but recently obtained from unrevealed sources in the State Department the information which he was presenting to the Senate.

Our investigation establishes that the material presented in this speech was data developed in 1947 by the Republican-controlled Eightieth Congress; and that representations indicating it had recently come from "loyal" State Department employees misled and deceived the Senate.

6. We find that the information presented to the Senate on February 20, 1950, by Senator McCarthy, concerning "81" individuals identified by him only by numbers, was a colored and distorted version of material developed by investigators of the House Appropriations Committee in 1947 during the Eightieth Congress.

To the extent that the information was colored and distorted and the source thereof concealed, the Senate was deceived.

7. We find that four separate committees of the Eightieth Congress, controlled by Senator McCarthy's own party, formally considered the same information relative to the "81" individuals, as that utilized in the Senator's speech, and did not regard such information as sufficiently significant to prepare a report relative to the matter or to cite a single employee of the State Department as disloyal.

In suggesting on February 20, 1950, that the situation as reflected by his information was so gravely disturbing that he felt it his immediate duty to expose it, Senator McCarthy misled the Senate.

8. We find that Senator McCarthy failed to cooperate with the subcommittee or to supply further information concerning the "81" individuals mentioned in his speech of February 20, 1950, after having assured the Senate that he would "be willing, happy, and eager to go before any committee and give the names and all the information available."

Our investigation establishes that the only logical reason for the Senator's noncooperation and failure to supply further information was the fact that he had no information to supply.

9. We find that Senator McCarthy asserted the proof to sustain his charges against the "81" individuals would be found in the loyalty files concerning them.

Our review of these files reveals that they do not contain proof to support the charges. . . .

20. We have found that the complaint of Senator McCarthy concerning disloyalty in the State Department, which precipitated our investigation, is false and have fully assured ourselves that the existing agencies and facilities for meeting the problem of security are doing their jobs efficiently and conscientiously. . . .

21. We furthermore find that public congressional inquiries on the question of disloyalty, particularly in view of the fact that the standard for judgment is necessarily highly subjective, tend inevitably to prejudice unfairly and with complete immunity and impunity the reputations, careers, and very livelihood of many innocent people. . . .

24. At a time when American blood is again being shed to preserve our dream of freedom, we are constrained fearlessly and frankly to call the charges, and the methods employed to give them ostensible validity, what they truly are: A fraud and a hoax perpetrated on the Senate of the United States and the American people. . . . In such a disillusioning setting, we appreciate as never before our Bill of Rights, a free press, and the heritage of freedom that has made this Nation great.

REPUBLICAN DECLARATION OF CONSCIENCE

12 ◦§   NOT ALL REPUBLICANS welcomed the accusations of treason
         that were hurled against the Democratic administration.
On June 1, 1950, Margaret Chase Smith of Maine, joined by six other Republican senators, signed a Declaration of Conscience that was an unmistakable repudiation of McCarthyism. Mrs. Smith's speech on issuing the declaration follows:[13]

Mr. President, I would like to speak briefly and simply about a serious national condition. It is a national feeling of fear and frustration that could result in national suicide and the end of everything that we Americans hold dear. It is a condition that comes from the lack of effective leadership either in the legislative branch or the executive branch of our Government. That leadership is so lacking that serious and responsible proposals are being made that national advisory commissions be appointed to provide such critically needed leadership.

I speak as briefly as possible because too much harm has already been done with irresponsible words of bitterness and selfish political opportunism. I speak as simply as possible because the issue is too great to be obscured by eloquence. I speak simply and briefly in the hope that my words will be taken to heart.

Mr. President, I speak as a Republican. I speak as a woman. I speak as a United States Senator. I speak as an American.

[13] Reprinted from Congressional Record, Eighty-first Congress, second session, pp. 7894–5.

The United States Senate has long enjoyed world-wide respect as the greatest deliberative body in the world. But recently that deliberative character has too often been debased to the level of a forum of hate and character assassination sheltered by the shield of congressional immunity.

It is ironical that we Senators can in debate in the Senate, directly or indirectly, by any form of words, impute to any American who is not a Senator any conduct or motive unworthy or unbecoming an American—and without that non-Senator American having any legal redress against us—yet if we say the same thing in the Senate about our colleagues we can be stopped on the grounds of being out of order.

It is strange that we can verbally attack anyone else without restraint and with full protection, and yet we hold ourselves above the same type of criticism here on the Senate floor. Surely the United States Senate is big enough to take self-criticism and self-appraisal. Surely we should be able to take the same kind of character attacks that we "dish out" to outsiders.

I think that it is high time for the United States Senate and its Members to do some real soul searching and to weigh our consciences as to the manner in which we are performing our duty to the people of America and the manner in which we are using or abusing our individual powers and privileges.

I think it is high time that we remembered that we have sworn to uphold and defend the Constitution. I think it is high time that we remembered that the Constitution, as amended, speaks not only of the freedom of speech but also of trial by jury instead of trial by accusation.

Whether it be a criminal prosecution in court or a character prosecution in the Senate, there is little practical distinction when the life of a person has been ruined.

Those of us who shout the loudest about Americanism in making character assassinations are all too frequently those who, by our own words and acts, ignore some of the basic principles of Americanism—

The right to criticize.

The right to hold unpopular beliefs.

The right to protest.

The right of independent thought.

The exercise of these rights should not cost one single American citizen his reputation or his right to a livelihood nor should he be in danger of losing his reputation or livelihood merely because he happens to know someone who holds unpopular beliefs. Who of us does not? Otherwise none of us could call our souls our own. Otherwise thought control would have set in.

The American people are sick and tired of being afraid to speak their minds lest they be politically smeared as Communists or Fascists by their opponents. Freedom of speech is not what it used to be in America. It has been so abused by some that it is not exercised by others.

The American people are sick and tired of seeing innocent people smeared and guilty people whitewashed. But there have been enough proved cases, such as the Amerasia case, the Hiss case, the Coplon case, the Gold case, to cause Nation-wide distrust and strong suspicion that there may be something to the unproved, sensational accusations.

As a Republican, I say to my colleagues on this side of the aisle that the Republican Party faces a challenge today that is not unlike the challenge which it faced back in Lincoln's day. The Republican Party so successfully met that challenge that it emerged from the Civil War as the champion of a united nation—in addition to being a party which unrelentingly fought loose spending and loose programs.

Today our country is being psychologically divided by the confusion and the suspicions that are bred in the United States Senate to spread like cancerous tentacles of "know nothing, suspect everything" attitudes. Today we have a Democratic administration which has developed a mania for loose spending and loose programs. History is repeating itself—and the Republican Party again has the opportunity to emerge as the champion of unity and prudence.

The record of the present Democratic administration has provided us with sufficient campaign issues without the necessity of resorting to political smears. America is rapidly losing its position as leader of the world simply because the Democratic administration has pitifully failed to provide effective leadership.

The Democratic administration has completely confused the American people by its daily contradictory grave warnings and optimistic assurances, which show the people that our Democratic administration has no idea of where it is going.

The Democratic administration has greatly lost the confidence of the American people by its complacency to the threat of communism here at home and the leak of vital secrets to Russia through key officials of the Democratic administration. There are enough proved cases to make this point without diluting our criticism with unproved charges.

Surely these are sufficient reasons to make it clear to the American people that it is time for a change and that a Republican victory is necessary to the security of the country. Surely it is clear that this Nation will continue to suffer so long as it is governed by the present ineffective Democratic administration.

Yet to displace it with a Republican regime embracing a philosophy that lacks political integrity or intellectual honesty would prove equally disastrous to the Nation. The Nation sorely needs a Republican victory. But I do not want to see the Republican Party ride to political victory on the Four Horsemen of Calumny—fear, ignorance, bigotry, and smear.

I doubt if the Republican Party could do so, simply because I do not believe the American people will uphold any political party that puts political exploitation above national interest. Surely we Republicans are not so desperate for victory.

I do not want to see the Republican Party win that way. While it might be a fleeting victory for the Republican Party, it would be a more lasting defeat for the American people. Surely it would ultimately be suicide for the Republican Party and the two-party system that has protected our American liberties from the dictatorship of a one-party system.

As members of the minority party, we do not have the primary authority to formulate the policy of our Government. But we do have the responsibility of rendering constructive criticism, of clarifying issues, of allaying fears by acting as responsible citizens.

As a woman, I wonder how the mothers, wives, sisters, and daughters feel about the way in which members of their families have been politically mangled in Senate debate—and I use the word "debate" advisedly.

As a United States Senator, I am not proud of the way in which the Senate has been made a publicity platform for irresponsible sensationalism. I am not proud of the reckless abandon in which unproved charges have been hurled from this side of the aisle. I am not proud of the obviously staged, undignified countercharges which have been attempted in retaliation from the other side of the aisle.

I do not like the way the Senate has been made a rendezvous for villification, for selfish political gain at the sacrifice of individual reputations and national unity. I am not proud of the way we smear outsiders from the floor of the Senate and hide behind the cloak of congressional immunity and still place ourselves beyond criticism on the floor of the Senate.

As an American, I am shocked at the way Republicans and Democrats alike are playing directly into the Communist design of "confuse, divide, and conquer." As an American, I do not want a Democratic administration white wash or cover up any more than I want a Republican smear or witch hunt.

As an American, I condemn a Republican Fascist just as much as I condemn a Democrat Communist. I condemn a Democrat Fascist just as much as I condemn a Republican Communist. They are equally dangerous to you and me and to our country. As an American, I want to see our Nation recapture the strength and unity it once had when we fought the enemy instead of ourselves.

It is with these thoughts that I have drafted what I call a Declaration of Conscience. I am gratified that the Senator from New Hampshire [Mr. (Charles W.—Eds.) Tobey], the Senator from Vermont [Mr. (George D.—Eds.) Aiken], the Senator from Oregon [Mr. (Wayne L.—Eds.) Morse], the Senator from New York [Mr. (Irving M.—Eds.) Ives], the Senator from Minnesota [Mr. (Edward J.—Eds.) Thye], and the Senator from New Jersey [Mr. (Robert C.—Eds.) Hendrickson] have concurred in that declaration and have authorized me to announce their concurrence.

The declaration reads as follows:

STATEMENT OF SEVEN REPUBLICAN SENATORS

1. We are Republicans. But we are Americans first. It is as Americans that we express our concern with the growing confusion that threatens the security and stability of our country. Democrats and Republicans alike have contributed to that confusion.

2. The Democratic administration has initially created the confusion by its lack of effective leadership, by its contradictory grave warnings and optimistic assurances, by its complacency to the threat of communism here at home, by its oversensitiveness to rightful criticism, by its petty bitterness against its critics.

3. Certain elements of the Republican Party have materially added to this confusion in the hopes of riding the Republican Party to victory through the selfish political exploitation of fear, bigotry, ignorance, and intolerance. There are enough mistakes of the Democrats for

Republicans to criticize constructively without resorting to political smears.

4. To this extent, Democrats and Republicans alike have unwittingly, but undeniably, played directly into the Communist design of "confuse, divide, and conquer."

5. It is high time that we stopped thinking politically as Republicans and Democrats about elections and started thinking patriotically as Americans about national security based on individual freedom. It is high time that we all stopped being tools and victims of totalitarian techniques—techniques that, if continued here unchecked, will surely end what we have come to cherish as the American way of life.

TRUMAN'S DEFENSE OF ADMINISTRATION

13 ‿§ THE PRESIDENT'S most notable attempt to defend his administration against Senator McCarthy was a speech that he delivered to an American Legion convention on August 15, 1951:[14]

In the preamble to the Legion's constitution, its members pledged themselves—among other things—to "uphold and defend the Constitution of the United States * * * to foster and perpetuate a 100-percent Americanism * * * to safeguard and transmit to posterity the principles of justice, freedom, and democracy."

At the present time, it is especially important for us to understand what these words mean and to live up to them.

The keystone of our form of government is the liberty of the individual. The Bill of Rights, which protects our individual liberties, is the most fundamental part of our Constitution. . . .

When the Legion pledged itself to uphold the Constitution, and to foster 100-percent Americanism, it pledged itself to protect the rights and liberties of all our citizens.

Real Americanism means that we will protect freedom of speech—we will defend the right of people to say what they think, regardless of how much we may disagree with them.

Real Americanism means freedom of religion. It means that we will not discriminate against a man because of his religious faith.

Real Americanism means fair opportunities for all our citizens. It means that none of our citizens should be held back by unfair discrimination and prejudice.

[14] Excerpts, *ibid.*, Eighty-second Congress, first session, pp. 10051-2.

Real Americanism means fair play. It means that a man who is accused of a crime shall be considered innocent until he has been proved guilty. It means that people are not to be penalized and persecuted for exercising their constitutional liberties.

Real Americanism means also that liberty is not license. There is no freedom to injure others. The Constitution does not protect free speech to the extent of permitting conspiracies to overthrow the Government. Neither does the right of free speech authorize slander or character assassination. These limitations are essential to keep us working together in one great community.

Real Americanism includes all these things. And it takes all of them together to make 100-percent Americanism—the kind the Legion is pledged to support.

I'm glad the Legion has made that pledge. For true Americanism is under terrible attack today. True Americanism needs defending— here and now. It needs defending by every decent human being in this country.

Americanism is under attack by communism, at home and abroad. We are defending it against that attack. We are protecting our country from spies and saboteurs. We are breaking up the Communist conspiracy in the United States. We are building our defenses and making our country strong and helping our allies to help themselves.

If we keep on doing these things—if we put our best into the job —we can protect ourselves from the attack of communism.

But Americanism is also under another kind of attack. It is being undermined by some people in this country who are loudly proclaiming that they are its chief defenders. These people claim to be against communism. But they are chipping away our basic freedoms just as insidiously and far more effectively than the Communists have ever been able to do.

These people have attacked the basic principle of fair play that underlies our Constitution. They are trying to create fear and suspicion among us by the use of slander, unproved accusations, and just plain lies.

They are filling the air with the most irresponsible kinds of accusations against other people. They are trying to get us to believe that our Government is riddled with communism and corruption —when the fact is that we have the finest and most loyal body of civil servants in the world. These slandermongers are trying to get us so hysterical that no one will stand up to them for fear of being called a Communist.

Now, this is an old Communist trick in reverse. Everybody in Russia lives in terror of being called an anti-Communist. For once that charge is made against anybody in Russia—no matter what the facts are—he is on the way out.

In a dictatorship everybody lives in fear and terror of being denounced and slandered. Nobody dares stand up for his rights.

We must never let such a condition come to pass in this country.

Yet this is exactly what the scaremongers and hatemongers are trying to bring about. Character assassination is their stock in trade. Guilt by association is their motto. They have created such a wave of fear and uncertainty that their attacks upon our liberties go almost unchallenged. Many people are growing frightened—and frightened people don't protest.

Stop and think. Stop and think where this is leading us.

The growing practice of character assassination is already curbing free speech and it is threatening all our other freedoms. I daresay there are people here today who have reached the point where they are afraid to explore a new idea. How many of you are afraid to come right out in public and say what you think about a controversial issue? How many of you feel that you must "play it safe" in all things—and on all occasions?

I hope there are not many, but from all that I have seen and heard, I am afraid of what your answers might be.

For I know you have no way of telling when some unfounded accusation may be hurled at you, perhaps straight from the Halls of Congress.

Some of you have friends or neighbors who have been singled out for the pitiless publicity that follows accusations of this kind—accusations that are made without any regard for the actual guilt or innocence of the victim.

That is not playing fair. That is not Americanism. It is not the American way to slur the loyalty and besmirch the character of the innocent and the guilty alike. We have always considered it just as important to protect the innocent as it is to punish the guilty.

We want to protect the country against disloyalty—of course we do. We have been punishing people for disloyal acts, and we are going to keep on punishing the guilty whenever we have a case against them. But we don't want to destroy our whole system of justice in the process. We don't want to injure innocent people. And yet the scurrilous work of the scandalmongers gravely threatens the whole idea of protection for the innocent in our country today.

Perhaps the Americans who live outside of Washington are less aware of this than you and I. If that is so I want to warn them all. Slander, lies, character assassination—these things are a threat to every single citizen everywhere in this country. When even one American —who has done nothing wrong—is forced by fear to shut his mind and close his mouth, then all Americans are in peril.

It is the job of all of us—of every American who loves his country and his freedom—to rise up and put a stop to this terrible business. This is one of the greatest challenges we face today. We have got to make a fight for real 100-percent Americanism.

You Legionnaires, living up to your Constitution as I know you want to do, can help lead the way. You can set an example of fair play. You can raise your voices against hysteria. You can expose the rotten motives of those people who are trying to divide us and confuse us and tear up the Bill of Rights.

No organization ever had the opportunity to do a greater service for America. No organization was ever better suited or better equipped to do the job.

I know the Legion. I know what a tremendous force for good it can be.

Now go to it.

And God bless you.

MCCARTHY ATTACK ON STEVENSON

14 > THROUGHOUT 1952 McCarthy continued his assault on the Truman administration. Now a major figure in his party, the senator received a hero's welcome when he appeared before the Republican national convention that nominated Eisenhower. During the campaign, on October 27, 1952, McCarthy went on national television to deliver a characteristic attack on Adlai E. Stevenson, the Democratic nominee for the presidency. The distrust and fear sown by McCarthy since 1950 contributed to the decisive repudiation of the Democrats on Election Day. Excerpts from McCarthy's attack on Stevenson follow:[15]

15 Reprinted from *The New York Times*, October 28, 1952, p. 26.

Thank you, fellow Americans. I am deeply grateful, very deeply grateful to all of you who have made this night possible.

We are at war tonight—a war which started decades ago, a war which we did not start, a war which we cannot stop except by either victory or death. The Korean war is only one phase of this war between international atheistic communism and our free civilization.

And we've been losing, we've been losing that war since the shooting part of World War II ended, losing it at an incredibly fantastic rate of 100,000,000 people a year.

And for the past two and a half years I've been trying to expose and force out of high positions in Government those who are in charge of our deliberate planned retreat from victory.

Now this fight, this fight against international communism, should not be a contest between America's two great political parties. Certainly, after all the millions of Americans who've long voted the Democratic ticket are just as loyal, they love America just as much, they hate communism just as much as the average Republican.

Unfortunately, the millions of loyal Democrats no longer have a party in Washington. And tonight, tonight I shall give you the history of the Democratic candidate for the Presidency who endorsed and could continue the suicidal Kremlin-directed policies of the nation.

Now I'm not going to give you a speech tonight. Tonight I'm a lawyer giving you the facts on the evidence in the case of Stevenson vs. Stevenson.

Let me make it clear that I'm only covering his history in so far as it deals with his aid to the Communist cause and the extent, the extent to which he is part and parcel of the Acheson-Hiss-Lattimore group. Now I perform the unpleasant task because the American people are entitled to have the coldly-documented history of this man who says, "I want to be your President." . . .

I shall now try to fit together the jigsaw puzzle of the man who wants to be President on the Truman-Acheson ticket. And I don't call it Democratic ticket because it would be a great insult to all the good Democrats in this nation. . . .

Now these facts, my good friends, cannot be answered—cannot be answered by screams of smears and lies. These facts can only be answered by facts. And we call upon Adlai of Illinois to so answer those facts.

The time is short, so let me get about the task of looking at his record. The Democratic candidate has said, and I quote him verbatim.

He said, "As evidence of my direction I have established my head-quarters here in Springfield with people of my own choosing." In other words he says, judge me, judge me by the advisers whom I have selected. Good, let's do that. Let's examine a few of those advisers first.

First is Wilson Wyatt, his personal manager. Now Wilson Wyatt is a former head of the left-winger A.D.A., the Americans for Democratic Action. The A.D.A. has five major points in its program. Listen to these and remember them if you will.

Point No. 1. Repeal of the Smith Act, which makes it a crime to conspire to overthrow this Government,

No. 2. Recognition of Red China,

No. 3. Opposition to the loyalty oath,

No. 4. Condemnation of the F.B.I. for exposing traitors like Coplon and Gubitchev, and

No. 5. Continuous all-out opposition to the House Committee on Un-American Activities.

Let me speak to you about that platform. They publish it day after day.

Now, according to an article in The New York Times, and I have that which I hold in my hand—the Democratic candidate's campaign manager Wyatt condemns the Government's loyalty program and here's the proof—it condemns the loyalty program in the most vicious terms. Strangely Alger—I mean Adlai—Adlai in 1952, now that he's running for President, says, I will dig out the Communists using as my weapon the loyalty program which my campaign manager damns and condemns.

Next, and perhaps the key figure in the Stevenson camp is his speech writer, Arthur Schlesinger Jr., former vice chairman of the same A.D.A. Now, Schlesinger has been a writer, incidentally, for The New York Post—New York Post whose editor and his wife admit, admit that they were members of the Young Communist League.

Now in 1946, Stevenson's speech writer wrote that the present system in the United States makes, and I quote. Listen to this, here's his speech writer, he says, "The present system in the United States makes even freedom-loving Americans look wistfully at Russia." I wonder if there's anyone in the audience tonight who's looking wist-fully at Russia. And I wonder, also, if some calamity would happen and Stevenson would be elected, what job this man would have.

Perhaps the most revealing article written by Stevenson's speech writer appeared in the The New York Times on Dec. 11, 1949, on Page 3, and listen to this if you will. I quote, he says, "I happen to believe that the Communist party should be granted the freedom of political action and that Communists should be allowed to teach in universities."

Nothing secret, nothing's secret about it, it's in The New York Times, Dec. 11, 1949. Stevenson's speech writer saying I think that Communists should be allowed to teach your children, my good friends. And he says, Oh but judge me, judge me by the advisers whom I select.

Now let's see how Stevenson's speech writer feels on the subject of religion. The answer is given in his review of the book of Whittaker Chambers. Whittaker Chambers, the man whose testimony convicted Alger Hiss. Chambers in his book, as you know, maintained that a belief in God was the hope of the free world—the feeling which most Americans have regardless of whether they're Protestant, Jewish or Catholic. Well, Schlesinger wrote about that. What did he say?

He says this—let me quote him verbatim. He says: "The whole record, the whole record of history, indeed gives proof that a belief in God has created human vanity as overweening and human arrogance as intolerable as the vanity and arrogance of . . . Communists." . . .

Stevenson says, judge me by the people I choose as my advisers. Here you have the philosophy of his chief adviser, the philosophy of his speech writer, laid bare. This idea of course that religion should be ridiculed is one of the basic principles of the Communist party. Now if you couple—couple this ridicule of religion with his statement that Communists should be allowed to teach your children and you have a fairly clear portrait of the man. . . .

The next—one of the men selected by Stevenson as one of his ghost writers—is a man Jim, James Wechsler. Wechsler and his wife both admit—both admit having been members of the Young Communist League, and I hold in my hand an article from The New York Times which states that Wechsler's the man who helped Stevenson write the speech, here it is, helped Stevenson write the speech in which Stevenson ridiculed anti-Communists as men who hunt for Communists in the Bureau of Wildlife and Fisheries.

That's a speech also in which he condemned—condemned my exposure of Communists as low comedy.

Now I just doubt whether the mothers and wives of the 120,000 Korean casualties consider it low comedy. I think they may possibly consider it a high tragedy. I'd like to call Mr. Stevenson's attention to that.

Some light is shed on the importance of this man in the Stevenson camp by the list of long-distance phone calls between the Governor's office in Springfield and this man who says "I belonged to the Young Communist League" Wechsler. Here's a list of the phone calls between Wechsler and the Governor's mansion.

I will not read it all over but it's available to the press. One of these calls particularly is important. I think this might be called the "trigger call," the "trigger phone call" made just before Wechsler and two others unleashed the smear attack upon Richard Nixon.

Another of the men in the Democratic candidate's camp is Archibald MacLeish. Stevenson's biography, on Page 77, states that MacLeish was the man who brought him into the State Department—it's his own biography. Now Stevenson has him as an adviser.

Well, how does this man MacLeish—he's got that—the longest record of affiliation with Communist fronts of any man that I have ever named in Washington. And Adlai says, Judge me by the friends I select. To that I say, "Amen, Adlai, amen."

The time is running out, and I'd like to give you more about the people who are guiding Stevenson, but let's go on to other things.

In Stevenson's biography—and here's something which I especially call to your attention—in Stevenson's biography on Page 73 we find that in the summer of 1943, this is his own biography, the summer of 1943 after Mussolini's government had fallen, Stevenson was given the task of formulating America's post-war policy in Italy.

On Page 75 we find the statement that his recommendations were followed in Italy. And Truman was before you in a crowd in New York (thank you), New York on Columbus Day and he confirmed the fact that Stevenson was the man as would, he said, sow the seeds for the immediate post-war policy in Italy.

Well, Gen. Bedell Smith, a fine American, in his testimony and in his book has told what that foreign policy established by Stevenson was—listen to this if you will—he says that foreign policy, here's his testimony, Page 35 and 37, he says that foreign policy was to "connive," to "connive" to bring Communists into the Italian Government and to bring the Italian Communist leader, [Palmiro—Eds.] Togliatti, back from Moscow.

You get the picture of that, my friends, Stevenson says I was the man who formulated the policy. Truman says, Yes he did. And the head of the Central Intelligence Agency says the policy then was to "connive" to put Communists into the Italian Government, "connive" and to bring Togliatti, the Communist leader, back from Moscow, which they did.

Keep in mind that [Walter—Eds.] Bedell Smith had nothing to do with this program—he was just testifying as to what it was. . . .

Now let us pick up another piece of the jigsaw puzzle of Stevenson's history. On Sept. 23 of this year Admiral [Adolphus—Eds.] Station, who is a holder of the Medal of Honor, signed a statement for us, signed a statement covering his experience with Stevenson after he, Station, had been assigned to the task of enforcing Public Law 151 and removing the Communists from the radios aboard our ships.

Well, Stevenson was a special assistant at that time in the Navy Department. He called Admiral Station to his office and here's the affidavit given to us by Station about that meeting.

It hasn't been used until tonight. Let me read just one paragraph. He says, "On arrival Stevenson told me that he had received six or eight of the Communist cases which my board had recommended for removal and that he wanted to discuss them with me."

Still quoting the Admiral: "Stevenson said that he could not see that we had anything against them and stated that we should not be hard on the Communists. The conference ended with Stevenson disagreeing with our recommendations to fire the Communists."

This was in 1943, my good friends, and two or three days ago Stevenson went on the air and said, but he said, "Oh, in 1943 I was warning about the danger of Communism in the Mediterranean."

Now immediately after, Station appeared at Stevenson's office and said, Mr. Stevenson get rid of those Communists. The law provides you must. And he said no. What happened to Station? He was retired to inactive duty.

And another part of the jigsaw puzzle of Stevenson's history is his membership over many years on the Central Committee of the World Citizens Association.

Now I know that you may find some good people in that organization. You may even find some good Republicans, but Stevenson was not merely a member of the group. Stevenson was one of the twelve-man policy forming committee.

And this is quite an outfit, really quite an outfit, and the time is so short I'll cover Point 5 in their platform. I hold that platform in my hand. Keep in mind that the twelve men including Stevenson drafted this platform.

Let me read plank No. 5. "National states must be subordinate to world civilization; their jurisdiction must be limited by world law, and any local legislation contrary to world law must be null and void."

Now what does this mean, my good friends, what does this mean to the 150,000,000 American people? It means that a world organization such as the United Nations could veto any state or Federal law or any part of our Constitution. This becomes doubly significant in view of the recent revelation that twelve of the men who were recommended by the State Department to the United Nations have been dropped because they refused to say under oath whether or not they were or had been members of the Communist party.

Twelve of the men in this world organization that should have the power to veto your laws. Well, while Stevenson's own office has been stating that he was a member of this unusual organization for only 1941, I have here a copy of Who's Who which he gives in a signed statement admitting that he was a member until 1945. I have a copy of the letterhead of this organization, February, 1948, carrying Stevenson not as a member but as part of the Central Committee twelve-man governing body.

Why is this significant? Simply my friends, simply because you're asked to elect a Presidential candidate who proposed to fly the flag of a super-world government over the Stars and Stripes.

But let me go on to another piece of the jigsaw puzzle.

While you think, while you may think that there could be no connection between the debonair Democratic candidate and a dilapidated Massachusetts barn, I want to show you a picture of this barn and explain the connection. Here's the outside of a barn. Give me a picture showing the inside of the barn.

Here's the outside of a barn up at Lee, Mass. Looks like it couldn't house a farmer's cow or goat from the outside. Here's the inside. A beautifully paneled conference room with maps of the Soviet Union. Now in what way does Stevenson tie up with this?

My investigators went up and took pictures of this barn after we had been tipped off about what was in it, tipped off that there was in this barn all of the missing documents from the Communist front I.P.R. [Institute of Pacific Relations], the I.P.R. which has been named by the McCarran Committee [a subcommittee of Senate

Judiciary Committee; investigated administration of Internal Security Act and other internal-security laws—Eds.], named before the Mc-Carran Committee as a cover shop for Communist espionage. We went up and we found in the room adjoining this conference room 200,000—200,000 of the missing I.P.R. documents. The hidden files showing the vouchers, among other things, showing money from Moscow. Men—a group of Communists.

We now come to the much-discussed testimony by Adlai Stevenson in the trial of Alger Hiss. Now, my good friends, I haven't considered, I have not considered this part standing alone as overly important in the Stevenson record. It is only a link in the chain of events that proves a case in Stevenson vs. Stevenson.

Now what does impress me, however, is the deathly fear that Governor Stevenson displays when additional links tying him to Alger Hiss are brought forth. We find that he very cleverly attempts to imply that his knowledge of Hiss was casual, remote and that he is not vouching for Hiss' character at the trial.

And I hold in my hand a petition which has never been made public before, either in the New York courts, a petition by the Hiss lawyers when they asked the court to admit Stevenson's statement. You will recall Stevenson said, I will sign a statement but I will not go to New York and run the risk of being put under cross-examination.

And Senator McCarran's committee, unanimously found that the I.P.R. was Communist-controlled. Communist-dominated and shaping our foreign policy.

Now let's take a look at a photostat of a document taken from that Massachusetts barn. One of those documents that was never supposed to see the light of day, rather interesting it is, this is the document that shows that Alger Hiss and Frank Coe recommended Adlai Stevenson to the Mont Tremblant conference which was called for the purpose of establishing foreign policy—post-war foreign policy in Asia.

Now as you know Alger Hiss is a convicted traitor. Frank Coe was the man [named] under oath before Congressional committees seven times as a member of the Communist party. Why, why do Hiss and Coe find that Adlai Stevenson is the man they want representing them at this conference. I don't know, perhaps Adlai knows.

Let me read this one small section of this affidavit to you, and the entire affidavit's available to the press. Here's the affidavit of the Hiss lawyer:

"Gov. Adlai Stevenson of Illinois has been closely associated with Alger Hiss in the course of certain international diplomatic undertakings. They were together at the San Francisco conference of the United Nations at which the Charter of the United Nations was adopted and they were together at the London conference which preceded and prepared the agenda for the San Francisco conference."

They say this: "The testimony of Governor Stevenson would be of great importance to Alger Hiss." Now I want you to examine closely the statement Governor Stevenson made at Cleveland, Ohio, about two days ago, the twenty-third, in which he attempted to defend his support of the reputation of Hiss—Hiss, the arch-traitor of our times. Stevenson said this last Thursday. I quote him. He said: "I said his reputation was good. I did not say that his reputation was very good."

Now here we have a man who says I want to be your President, saying that Hiss' reputation was good but not very good.

Now I say, my good friends, that if he had such misgivings he should not have vouched for Hiss at all. There are no degrees of loyalty in the United States. A man is either loyal or he's disloyal. There is no such thing—there is no such thing as being a little bit disloyal or being partly a traitor.

Now I note that the television man is holding up a sign, saying thirty seconds to go—I have much, much more of the documentation here. I'm sorry we can't give it to our television audience and I want our audience to know it was not the fault of the television station—we've only arranged for half an hour and that half an hour's about up.

But with your permission my good friends, when we go off the air I would like to complete for this audience the documentation.

7 · The Korean War

*B*ecause of its strategic location, Korea had long been a cause of international animosity. In 1894–95 Japan had fought one war to end Chinese claims of suzerainty over the peninsula and in 1904–05 fought another to end Russian influence in Korean affairs. In 1910 Korea fell under the tight control of Japan, where it remained until the Allied victory of 1945. In 1943 at Cairo, Roosevelt, Churchill, and Chiang Kai-shek issued a vague declaration proclaiming their determination "that in due course Korea shall be free and independent," a pronouncement Stalin endorsed at Potsdam.

At the end of the war, as a military arrangement, Russia moved into Korea to accept the surrender of all Japanese troops above the 38th parallel, and American forces occupied Korea south of that line. The Americans looked upon this arbitrary division as temporary and for the next two years strived to negotiate an agreement with the Russians that would lead to the creation of a democratic, united, and independent Korean state. In 1947, having been frustrated in its efforts, the United States referred the Korean problem to the United Nations; in November the General Assembly authorized the UN Temporary Commission on Korea to supervise nationwide elections for a constituent assembly. Barred by the Russians from North Korea, the commission conducted elections in the South, and in August 1948 the Republic of Korea was established there, with Syngman Rhee as its first president. In 1949 the Russians created the Democratic People's Republic of Korea and shortly thereafter withdrew their occupation troops. That same year the last American combat soldier also departed Korea. In June 1950 the North Korean armies invaded the South, precipitating the greatest crisis of the postwar era.

The U.S. administration took bold steps to repel the aggressor, and for a brief time the nation united behind the President. But the eventual intervention of the Red Chinese precipitated a quarrel between the administration and its field commander, General Douglas MacArthur, which provoked a great Republican outburst against the foreign policies of the Democrats, led to widespread disillusionment with the doctrine of containment, and left the country even more deeply divided.

ACHESON SPEECH ON FAR EAST

1 ⅙   ON JANUARY 12, 1950, Secretary of State Acheson delivered a major foreign-policy speech on the subject of the Far East. Important at the time because it frankly discussed U.S. intentions toward China, Acheson's remarks later became the center of great political controversy for other reasons. According to the opponents of the administration, this speech, by placing Korea outside the American defensive perimeter, had invited North Korean aggression. The decision to exclude Korea from the sphere of American strategic concern had been made by the Joint Chiefs of Staff, with MacArthur's concurrence, in September 1947. Believing that any future war would be worldwide, the Joint Chiefs had discounted the military significance of Korea, and in view of the dangerously small size of the peacetime U.S. Army, regarded the maintenance of U.S. forces on that peninsula as an unnecessary dilution of military strength. Accordingly, in 1949 the United States withdrew its last remaining troops of occupation. The question of whether Acheson's remarks in early 1950 really contributed to the Communists' decision to launch an invasion has still to be answered. MacArthur himself had once publicly proclaimed the same defensive perimeter, and U.S. actions had already made it clear that Korea did not fit into the administration's military plans.

Excerpts from Secretary Acheson's address appear below:[1]

. . . I am frequently asked: Has the State Department got an Asian policy? And it seems to me that that discloses such a depth of ignorance that it is very hard to begin to deal with it. The people of Asia are so incredibly diverse and their problems are so incredibly diverse that how could anyone, even the most utter charlatan, believe that he had a uniform policy which would deal with all of them. On the other hand, there are very important similarities in ideas and in problems among the peoples of Asia, and so what we come to, after we understand these diversities and these common attitudes of mind, is

[1] Reprinted from Congressional Record, Eighty-first Congress, second session, pp. 672–5.

the fact that there must be certain similarities of approach and there must be very great dissimilarities in action.

To illustrate this only a moment: If you will consider as an example of the differences in Asia the subcontinent of India and Pakistan you will find there an area which is roughly comparable in size and population to Europe. You will find that the different states and provinces of that subcontinent are roughly comparable in size to the nations of Europe, and yet you will find such differences in race, in ideas, in languages and religion and culture that, compared to that subcontinent, Europe is almost one homogeneous people.

Or take the difference, for instance, between the people and problems of Japan and Indonesia, both in the same Asian area. In Japan, you have a people far advanced in the complexities of industrial civilization, a people whose problems grow out of overpopulation on small islands and the necessity of finding raw materials to bring in and finding markets for the finished goods which they produce. In Indonesia, you find something wholly different—a people on the very threshold of their experience with these complexities and a people who live in an area which possesses vast resources which are awaiting development. Now, those are illustrations of complexities.

Let's come now to the matters which Asia has in common. There is in this vast area what we might call a developing Asian consciousness, and a developing pattern, and this, I think, is based upon two factors which are pretty nearly common to the entire experience of all these Asian people.

One of these factors is a revulsion against the acceptance of misery and poverty as the normal condition of life. Throughout all of this vast area, you have that fundamental revolutionary aspect in mind and belief. The other common aspect that they have is the revulsion against foreign domination. Whether that foreign domination takes the form of colonialism or whether it takes the form of imperialism, they are through with it. They have had enough of it and they want no more.

These two basic ideas which are held so broadly and commonly in Asia tend to fuse in the minds of many Asian peoples, and many of them tend to believe that if you could get rid of foreign domination, if you could gain independence, then the relief from poverty and misery would follow almost in course. It is easy to point out that that is not true, and, of course, they are discovering that it is not true. But underneath that belief there was a very profound understanding of a basic truth, and it is the basic truth which underlies all our democratic belief and all our democratic concept. That truth is that just as no man and no government is wise enough or disinterested enough to direct the thinking and the action of another individual, so no nation and no people are wise enough and disinterested enough very long to assume the responsibility for another people or to control another people's opportunities.

That great truth they have sensed, and on that great truth they are acting. They say and they believe that from now on they are on their own. They will make their own decisions. They will attempt to better their own lot, and on occasion they will make their own mistakes. But it will be their mistakes, and they are not going to have their mistakes dictated to them by anybody else.

The symbol of these concepts has become nationalism. National independence has become the symbol both of freedom from foreign domination and freedom from the tyranny of poverty and misery. . . .

Now, may I suggest to you that much of the bewilderment which has seized the minds of many of us about recent developments in China comes from a failure to understand this basic revolutionary force which is loose in Asia. The reasons for the fall of the Nationalist Government in China are preoccupying many people. All sorts of reasons have been attributed to it. Most commonly it is said in various speeches and publications that it is the result of American bungling, that we are incompetent, that we did not understand, that American aid was too little, that we did the wrong things at the wrong time. Other people go on and say: "No, it is not quite that, but that an American general did not like Chiang Kai-shek and out of all that relationship grows the real trouble." And they say: "Well, you have to add to that there are a lot of women fooling around in politics in China."

Nobody, I think, says that the Nationalist Government fell because it was confronted by overwhelming military force which it could not resist. Certainly no one in his right mind suggests that. Now, what I ask you to do is to stop looking for a moment under the bed and under the chair and under the rug to find out these reasons, but rather to look at the broad picture and see whether something doesn't suggest itself.

The broad picture is that after the war, Chiang Kai-shek emerged as the undisputed leader of the Chinese people. Only one faction, the Communists, up in the hills, ill-equipped, ragged, a very small military force, was determinedly opposed to his position. He had overwhelming military power, greater military power than any ruler had ever had in the entire history of China. He had tremendous economic and military support and backing from the United States. He had the acceptance of all other foreign countries, whether sincerely or insincerely in the case of the Soviet Union is not really material to this matter. Here he was in this position and 4 years later what do we find? We find that his armies have melted away. His support in the country has melted away. His support largely outside the country has melted away and he is a refugee on a small island off the coast of China with the remnants of his forces.

As I said, no one says that vast armies moved out of the hills and defeated him. To attribute this to the inadequacy of American aid is only to point out the depth and power of the forces which were miscalculated or ignored. What has happened, in my judgment, is that the almost inexhaustible patience of the Chinese people in their misery ended. They did not bother to overthrow this government. There was really nothing to overthrow. They simply ignored it throughout the country. They took the solution of their immediate village problems into their own hands. If there was any trouble or interference with the representatives of the government, they simply brushed them aside. They completely withdrew their support from this government and when that support was withdrawn, the whole military establishment disintegrated. Added to the grossest incompetence ever experienced by any military command was this total lack of support both in the armies and in the country, and so the whole matter just simply disintegrated.

The Communists did not create this. The Communists did not create this condition. They did not create this revolutionary spirit. They did not create a great force which moved out from under Chiang Kai-shek. But they were shrewd and cunning to mount it, to ride this thing into victory and into power.

That, I suggest to you, is an explanation which has certain roots and realism and which does not require all this examination of intricate and perhaps irrelevant details. . . .

Now, I stress this, which you may think is a platitude, because of a very important fact: I hear almost everyday someone say that the real interest of the United States is to stop the spread of communism. Nothing seems to me to put the cart before the horse more completely than that. Of course we are interested in stopping the spread of communism. But we are interested for a far deeper reason than any conflict between the Soviet Union and the United States. We are interested in stopping the spread of communism because communism is a doctrine that we don't happen to like. Communism is the most subtle instrument of Soviet foreign policy that has ever been devised and it is really the spearhead of Russian imperialism which would, if it could, take from these people what they have won, what we want them to keep and develop which is their own national independence, their own individual independence, their own development of their own resources for their own good and not as mere tributary states to this great Soviet Union. . . .

Now, let me come to another underlying and important factor which determines our relations and, in turn, our policy with the peoples of Asia. That is the attitude of the Soviet Union toward Asia and particularly toward those parts of Asia which are contiguous to the Soviet Union, and with great particularity this afternoon, to north China.

The attitude and interest of the Russians in north China, and in these other areas as well, long antedates communism. This is not something that has come out of communism at all. It long antedates it. But the Communist regime has added new methods, new skills, and new concepts to the thrust of Russian imperialism. These communistic concepts and techniques have armed Russian imperialism with a new and most insidious weapon of penetration. Armed with these new powers, what is happening in China is that the Soviet Union is detaching the northern provinces [areas] of China from China and is attaching them to the Soviet Union. This process is complete in Outer Mongolia. It is nearly complete in Manchuria and I am sure that in Inner Mongolia and in Sinkiang, there are very happy reports coming from Soviet agents to Moscow. This is what is going on. It is the detachment of these whole areas, vast areas—populated by Chinese—the detachment of these areas from China and their attachment to the Soviet Union.

I wish to state this and perhaps sin against my doctrine of non-dogmatism, but I should like to suggest at any rate that this fact that the Soviet Union is taking the four northern provinces of China is the single most significant, most important fact, in the relation of any foreign power with Asia.

What does that mean for us? It means something very, very significant. It means that nothing that we do and nothing that we say must be allowed to obscure the reality of this fact. All the efforts of propaganda will not be able to obscure it. The only thing that can obscure it is the folly of ill-conceived adventures on our part which easily could do so and I urge all who are thinking about these foolish adventures to remember that we must not seize the unenviable position which the Russians have carved out for themselves. We must not undertake to deflect from the Russians to ourselves the righteous anger and the wrath and the hatred of the Chinese people which must develop. It would be folly to deflect it to ourselves. We must take the position we have always taken that anyone who violates the integrity of China is the enemy of China and is acting contrary to our own interest. That, I suggest to you this afternoon, is the first and the greatest rule in regard to the formulation of American policy toward Asia. . . .

Now, let's, in the light of that, consider some of these policies. First of all, let's deal with the question of military security. I deal with it first because it is important and because, having stated our policy in that regard, we must clearly understand that the military menace is not the most immediate.

What is the situation in regard to the military security of the Pacific area and what is our policy in regard to it?

In the first place, the defeat and the disarmament of Japan has placed upon the United States the necessity of assuming the military defense of Japan so long as that is required, both in the interest of our security and in the interests of the security of the entire Pacific area and in all honor in the interest of Japanese security. We have American and there are Australian troops in Japan. I am not in a position to speak for the Australians, but I can assure you that there is no intention of any sort of abandoning or weakening the defenses of Japan and that whatever arrangements are to be made, either through permanent settlement or otherwise, that defense must, and shall be, maintained.

This defensive perimeter runs along the Aleutians to Japan and then goes to the Ryukyus. We hold important defense positions in the Ryukyu Islands and those we will continue to hold. In the interest of the population of the Ryukyu Islands, we will at an appropriate time offer to hold these islands under trusteeship of the United Nations. But they are essential parts of the defensive perimeter of the Pacific and they must, and will be, held.

The defensive perimeter runs from the Ryukyus to the Philippine

Islands. Our relations, our defensive relations with the Philippines, are contained in agreements between us. Those agreements are being loyally carried out and will be loyally carried out. Both peoples have learned by bitter experience the vital connections between our mutual defense requirements. We are in no doubt about that and it is hardly necessary for me to say an attack on the Philippines could not and would not be tolerated by the United States. But I hasten to add that no one perceives the imminence of any such attack.

So far as the military security of other areas in the Pacific is concerned, it must be clear that no person can guarantee these areas against military attack. But it must also be clear that such a guarantee is hardly sensible or necessary within the realm of practical relationship. Should such an attack occur—one hesitates to say where such an armed attack could come from—the initial reliance must be on the people attacked to resist it and then upon the commitments of the entire civilized world under the Charter of the United Nations which so far has not proved a weak reed to lean on by any people who are determined to protect their independence against outside aggression. But it is a mistake, I think, in considering Pacific and far-eastern problems to become obsessed with military considerations. Important as they are, there are other problems that press and these other problems are not capable of solution through military means. These other problems arise out of the susceptibility of many areas and many countries in the Pacific area to subversion and penetration. That cannot be stopped by military means.

That leads me to the other thing that I wanted to point out and that is the limitation of effective American assistance. American assistance can be effective when it is the missing component in a situation which might otherwise be solved. The United States cannot furnish all these components to solve the question. It cannot furnish determination, it cannot furnish the will and it cannot furnish the loyalty of a people to its Government. But if the will and if the determination exists and if the people are behind their Government, then, and not always then, is there a very good chance. In that situation American help can be effective and it can lead to an accomplishment which could not otherwise be achieved. . . .

So after this survey, what we conclude, I believe, is that there is a new day which has dawned in Asia. It is a day in which the Asian peoples are on their own and know it and intend to continue on their own. It is a day in which the old relationships between east and west are gone, relationships which at their worst were exploitation and which at their best were paternalism. That relationship is over and the relationship of east and west must now be in the Far East one of mutual respect and mutual helpfulness. We are their friends. Others are their friends. We and those others are willing to help but we can help only where we are wanted and only where the conditions of help are really sensible and possible. So what we can see is that this new day in Asia, this new day which is dawning, may go on to a glorious noon or it may darken and it may drizzle out. But that decision lies within the countries of Asia and within the power of the Asian people. It is not a decision which a friend or even an enemy from the outside can decide for them.

Thank you very much.

TRUMAN'S STATEMENT ON KOREA

2 ☙ ON JUNE 24, 1950, at 9:26 P.M., Washington, D.C., time, news reached the United States that the North Korean armies had invaded South Korea. The next afternoon the Security Council of the United Nations unanimously condemned the invasion and called for the withdrawal of the aggressor to the 38th parallel. Since January, Russia had been boycotting the Council to protest UN refusal to grant Communist China a Council seat and so was not present to veto this resolution. On June 27 President Truman issued the following statement:[2]

In Korea the Government forces, which were armed to prevent border raids and to preserve internal security, were attacked by invading forces from North Korea. The Security Council of the United Nations called upon the invading troops to cease hostilities and to withdraw to the thirty-eighth parallel. This they have not done, but on the contrary have pressed the attack. The Security Council called upon all members of the United Nations to render every assistance to the United Nations in the execution of this resolution. In these circumstances I have ordered United States air and sea forces to give the Korean Government troops cover and support.

The attack upon Korea makes it plain beyond all doubt that communism has passed beyond the use of subversion to conquer inde-

[2] Reprinted from Senate Foreign Relations and Armed Services Committees, *Hearings, Military Situation in the Far East,* Eighty-second Congress, first session, p. 3369.

pendent nations and will now use armed invasion and war. It has defied the orders of the Security Council of the United Nations issued to preserve international peace and security. In these circumstances the occupation of Formosa by Communist forces would be a direct threat to the security of the Pacific area and to United States forces performing their lawful and necessary functions in that area.

Accordingly I have ordered the Seventh Fleet to prevent any attack on Formosa. As a corollary of this action I am calling upon the Chinese Government on Formosa to cease all air and sea operations against the mainland. The Seventh Fleet will see that this is done. The determination of the future status of Formosa must await the restoration of security in the Pacific, a peace settlement with Japan, or consideration by the United Nations.

I have also directed that United States forces in the Philippines be strengthened and that military assistance to the Philippine Government be accelerated.

I have similarly directed acceleration in the furnishing of military assistance to the forces of France and the associated states in Indochina and the dispatch of a military mission to provide close working relations with those forces.

I know that all members of the United Nations will consider carefully the consequences of this latest aggression in Korea in defiance of the Charter of the United Nations. A return to the rule of force in international affairs would have far-reaching effects. The United States will continue to uphold the rule of Law.

I have instructed Ambassador [Warren R.—Eds.] Austin, as the representative of the United States to the Security Council, to report these steps to the Council.

UN RESOLUTION

3 ⋙ ON JUNE 30 President Truman committed American ground troops to the struggle, acting in accordance with the Second United Nations Security Council Resolution, of June 27, 1950:[3]

Resolution concerning the complaint of aggression upon the Republic of Korea, adopted at the four hundred and seventy-fourth meeting of the Security Council, on June 27, 1950:

The Security Council,

Having determined that the armed attack upon the Republic

[3] *Ibid.*, p. 3371.

of Korea by forces from North Korea constitutes a breach of the peace,

Having called for an immediate cessation of hostilities, and

Having called upon the authorities of North Korea to withdraw forthwith their armed forces to the 38th parallel, and

Having noted from the report of the United Nations Commission for Korea that the authorities in North Korea have neither ceased hostilities nor withdrawn their armed forces to the 38th parallel and that urgent military measures are required to restore international peace and security, and

Having noted the appeal from the Republic of Korea to the United Nations for immediate and effective steps to secure peace and security,

Recommends that the Members of the United Nations furnish such assistance to the Republic of Korea as may be necessary to repel the armed attack and to restore international peace and security in the area.

(*Voting for the resolution:* United States, United Kingdom, France, China, Norway, Ecuador, and Cuba. *Voting against:* Yugoslavia. *Abstention:* Egypt, India (2 days later India accepted the resolution). *Absent:* Soviet Union.)

TAFT'S ENDORSEMENT OF INTERVENTION

4 ᴼ᷄ THE CRISIS brought on by the North Korean invasion briefly quieted the conservative Republican attack on American Far Eastern policies. Senator Taft's speech of June 28, 1950, gave reluctant endorsement of Truman's decision to intervene in Korea:[4]

Mr. President, I desire to speak with reference to the Korean crisis. . . .

Early on Sunday morning, June 25, the Communist-dominated Republic of North Korea launched an unprovoked aggressive military attack on the Republic of Korea, recognized as an independent nation by the United Nations. . . .

The attack did not cease, and on Tuesday, June 27, the President issued a statement announcing that he had "ordered United States air and sea forces to give the Korean Government troops cover and support." He also announced that he had ordered the Seventh Fleet

[4] Excerpts reprinted from *Congressional Record*, Eighty-first Congress, second session, pp. 9319–23.

to prevent any attack on Formosa, and that he had directed that United States forces in the Philippines be strengthened, and that military assistance to the Philippine Government and the forces of France and the associated states in Indochina be accelerated. . . .

No one can deny that a serious crisis exists. The attack was as much a surprise to the public as the attack at Pearl Harbor, although, apparently, the possibility was foreseen by all our intelligence forces, and should have been foreseen by the administration. We are now actually engaged in a de facto war with the northern Korean Communists. That in itself is serious, but nothing compared to the possibility that it might lead to war with Soviet Russia. It is entirely possible that Soviet Russia might move in to help the North Koreans and that the present limited field of conflict might cover the entire civilized world. Without question, the attack of the North Koreans is an outrageous act of aggression against a friendly independent nation, recognized by the United Nations, and which we were instrumental in setting up. The attack in all probability was instigated by Soviet Russia. We can only hope that the leaders of that country have sufficient judgment to know that a world war will result in their own destruction, and will therefore refrain from such acts as might bring about such a tragic conflict.

Mr. President, Korea itself is not vitally important to the United States. It is hard to defend. We have another instance of communism picking out a soft spot where the Communists feel that they can make a substantial advance and can obtain a moral victory without risking war. From the past philosophy and declarations of our leaders, it was not unreasonable for the North Koreans to suppose that they could get away with it and that we would do nothing about it.

The President's statement of policy represents a complete change in the programs and policies heretofore proclaimed by the administration. I have heretofore urged a much more determined attitude against communism in the Far East, and the President's new policy moves in that direction. It seems to me that the time had to come, sooner or later, when we would give definite notice to the Communists that a move beyond a declared line would result in war. That has been the policy which we have adopted in Europe. Whether the President has chosen the right time or the right place to declare this policy may be open to question. He has information which I do not have.

It seems to me that the new policy is adopted at an unfortunate time, and involves the attempt to defend Korea, which is a very difficult military operation indeed. I sincerely hope that our Armed Forces may be successful in Korea. I sincerely hope that the policy thus adopted will not lead to war with Russia. In any event, I believe the general principle of the policy is right, and I see no choice except to back up wholeheartedly and with every available resource the men in our Armed Forces who have been moved into Korea.

If we are going to defend Korea, it seems to me that we should have retained our Armed Forces there and should have given, a year ago, the notice which the President has given today. With such a policy, there never would have been such an attack by the North Koreans. In short, this entirely unfortunate crisis has been produced first, by the outrageous, aggressive attitude of Soviet Russia, and second, by the bungling and inconsistent foreign policy of the administration.

I think it is important to point out, Mr. President, that there has been no pretense of any bipartisan foreign policy about this action. The leaders of the Republican Party in Congress have never been consulted on . . . Chinese policy or Formosa or Korea or Indochina. . . .

Furthermore, it should be noted that there has been no pretense of consulting the Congress. No resolution has ever been introduced asking for the approval of Congress for the use of American forces in Korea. I shall discuss later the question of whether the President is usurping his powers as Commander in Chief. My own opinion is that he is doing so; that there is no legal authority for what he has done. But I may say that if a joint resolution were introduced asking for approval of the use of our Armed Forces already sent to Korea and full support of them in their present venture, I would vote in favor of it.

I have said that the present crisis is produced by the bungling and inconsistent policies of the administration.

First, at Yalta and at Potsdam we agreed to the division of Korea along the thirty-eighth parallel, giving the Russians the northern half of the country, with most of the power and a good deal of the industry, and leaving a southern half which could not support itself, except on an agricultural basis. . . .

Second, the Chinese policy of the administration gives basic encouragement to the North Korean aggression. If the United States was not prepared to use its troops and give military assistance to Nationalist China against Chinese Communists, why should it use its troops to defend Nationalist Korea against Communists? . . .

Mr. President, in my opinion, we should long ago have declared a definite policy. In certain areas we may have to undertake an actual defense with American troops. In other areas we can perhaps undertake only to furnish arms. . . .

I welcome the indication of a more definite policy, and I strongly hope that having adopted it the President may maintain it intact.

In the President's statement there is a direct repudiation of the policies of Secretary Acheson declared in January of this year. . . .

The President now says that the determination of the future status of Formosa must await the restoration of security in the Pacific, a peace settlement with Japan, or consideration by the United Nations. This is a direct overruling of Secretary Acheson's position on January 5 to the effect that it was wholly unnecessary to wait for a treaty with Japan because Formosa's position had been definitely settled by the Cairo and Potsdam agreements. . . .

Mr. President, since I approve of the changes now made in our foreign policy, I approve of the general policies outlined in the President's statement. I feel that we must back up our troops, where they have been sent by the President, with unstinted support. Whether the President chose the right time for his new policy, or the right place, can be discussed in the future. I suggest, however, that any Secretary of State who has been so reversed by his superiors and whose policies have precipitated the danger of war, had better resign and let someone else administer the program to which he was, and perhaps still is, so violently opposed.

[Applause on the floor and in the galleries.]

MESSAGE FROM MACARTHUR

5 ⚭ EARLY IN THE WAR differences between the administration and its Far Eastern commander, General MacArthur, developed over American policy toward Formosa. On June 29 Chiang Kai-shek offered 30,000 of his Nationalist troops to the UN command in Korea. The Joint Chiefs of Staff in Washington, with MacArthur's support, recommended rejection of Chiang's offer on military grounds. The State Department agreed with this conclusion of the military, for it feared that close links with the reactionary regime on Formosa would hurt the United States throughout the

rest of Asia. Furthermore, the department hoped to keep Communist China out of the war and wished to keep alive the possibility of an eventual accommodation with Mao Tse-tung. On July 31 the administration dispatched MacArthur to Formosa to explain to Chiang the military reasons for the government's decision. At the conclusion of this conference MacArthur issued a communiqué extravagantly praising Chiang and announcing that arrangements for coordinating Chinese and American forces in case of an attack on Formosa had been made. Alarmed by the political overtones of MacArthur's statement, Truman sent his trusted adviser, W. Averell Harriman, to Japan to explain his policies to MacArthur. For a time the storm quieted. Then, on August 20, 1950, MacArthur sent a message to the Veterans of Foreign Wars that almost provoked Truman to relieve the General of his command:[5]

In view of misconceptions currently being voiced concerning the relationship of Formosa to our strategic potential in the Pacific, I believe it in the public interest to avail myself of this opportunity to state my views thereon to you, all of whom, having fought overseas, understand broad strategic concepts.

To begin with, any appraisal of that strategic potential requires an appreciation of the changes wrought in the course of the past war. Prior thereto the western strategic frontier of the United States lay on the littoral line of the Americas with an exposed island salient extending out through Hawaii, Midway, and Guam to the Philippines.

That salient was not an outpost of strength but an avenue of weakness along which the enemy could and did attack us. The Pacific was a potential area of advancement for any predatory force intent upon striking at the bordering land areas.

All of this was changed by our Pacific victory. Our strategic frontier then shifted to embrace the entire Pacific Ocean, which has become a vast moat to protect us as long as we hold it.

Indeed, it acts as a protective shield to all of the Americas and all free lands of the Pacific Ocean area we control to the shores of Asia by a chain of islands extending in an arc from the Aleutians to the Marianas held by us and our free Allies. From this island chain we can dominate with air power every Asiatic port from Vladivostock to Singapore and prevent any hostile movement into the Pacific.

---

[5] Reprinted from Hearings, Military Situation in the Far East, pp. 3477-80.

Any predatory attack from Asia must be an amphibious effort. No amphibious force can be successful with our control of the sea lanes and the air over these lanes in its avenue of advance. With naval and air supremacy and modern ground elements to defend bases, any major attack from continental Asia toward us or our friends of the Pacific would come to failure.

Under such conditions the Pacific no longer represents menacing avenues of approach for a prospective invader—it assumes instead the friendly aspect of a peaceful lake. Our line of defense is a natural one and can be maintained with a minimum of military effort and expense.

It envisions no attack against anyone nor does it provide the bastions essential for offensive operations, but properly maintained would be an invincible defense against aggression. If we hold this line we may have peace—lose it and war is inevitable.

The geographic location of Formosa is such that in the hand of a power unfriendly to the United States it constitutes an enemy salient in the very center of this defensive perimeter, 100 to 150 miles closer to the adjacent friendly segments—Okinawa and the Philippines—than any point in continental Asia.

At the present time there is on Formosa a concentration of operational air and naval bases which is potentially greater than any similar concentration of the Asiatic mainland between the Yellow Sea and the Strait of Malacca. Additional bases can be developed in a relatively short time by an aggressive exploitation of all World War II Japanese facilities.

An enemy force utilizing those installations currently available could increase by 100 per cent the air effort which could be directed against Okinawa as compared to operations based on the mainland and at the same time could direct damaging air attacks with fighter-type aircraft against friendly installations in the Philippines, which are currently beyond the range of fighters based on the mainland. Our air supremacy at once would become doubtful.

As a result of its geographic location and base potential, utilization of Formosa by a military power hostile to the United States may either counter-balance or overshadow the strategic importance of the central and southern flank of the United States front line position.

Formosa in the hands of such a hostile power could be compared to an unsinkable aircraft carrier and submarine tender ideally located to accomplish offensive strategy and at the same time checkmate defensive or counter-offensive operations by friendly forces based on Okinawa and the Philippines.

This unsinkable carrier-tender has the capacity to operate from ten to tweny air groups of types ranging from jet fighters to B-29 type bombers as well as to provide forward operating facilities for short-range coastal submarines.

In acquiring this forward submarine base, the efficacy of the short-range submarine would be so enormously increased by the additional radius of activity as to threaten completely sea traffic from the south and interdict all set lanes in the Western Pacific. Submarine blockade by the enemy with all its destructive ramifications would thereby become a virtual certainty.

Should Formosa fall and bases thereafter come into the hands of a potential enemy of the United States, the latter will have acquired an additional "fleet" which will have been obtained and can be maintained at an incomparably lower cost than could its equivalent in aircraft carriers and submarine tenders.

Current estimates of air and submarine resources in the Far East indicate the capability of such a potential enemy to extend his forces southward and still maintain an imposing degree of military strength for employment elsewhere in the Pacific area.

Nothing could be more fallacious than the threadbare argument by those who advocate appeasement and defeatism in the Pacific that if we defend Formosa we alienate continental Asia.

Those who speak thus do not understand the Orient. They do not grant that it is in the pattern of the Oriental psychology to respect and follow aggressive, resolute and dynamic leadership—to quickly turn on a leadership characterized by timidity or vacillation—and they underestimate the Oriental mentality. Nothing in the last five years has so inspired the Far East as the American determination to preserve the bulwarks of our Pacific Ocean strategic position from future encroachment, for few of its people fail accurately to appraise the safeguard such determination brings to their free institutions.

To pursue any other course would be to turn over the fruits of our Pacific victory to a potential enemy. It would shift any future battle area 5,000 miles eastward to the coasts of the American continents, our own home coast; it would completely expose our friends in the Philippines, our friends in Australia and New Zealand, our friends in Indonesia, our friends in Japan, and other areas, to the lustful thrusts of those who stand for slavery against liberty, for atheism as against God.

The decision of President Truman on June 27 lighted into flame a lamp of hope throughout Asia that was burning dimly toward extinction. It marked for the Far East the focal and turning point in this area's struggle for freedom. It swept aside in one great monumental stroke all of the hypocrisy and the sophistry which has confused and deluded so many people distant from the actual scene.

TRUMAN-MACARTHUR CONFERENCE AT WAKE ISLAND

6 ⋘ ON SEPTEMBER 15, 1950, MacArthur sent the marines into Inchon harbor and by this one brilliant stroke reversed the military course of the war. As he had predicted, the North Korean armies collapsed and fled across the 38th parallel. On October 7 the UN General Assembly recommended that (1) "All appropriate steps be taken to ensure conditions of stability throughout Korea," and that (2) "All constituent acts be taken including the holding of elections, under the auspices of the UN for the establishment of a unified independent and democratic government in the sovereign state of Korea." UN forces then crossed the 38th parallel in force. In the meantime the Red Chinese were issuing warnings that they would not stand by while North Korea was invaded. On October 15 President Truman flew to Wake Island to confer with the famous general whom he had never before met. Truman hoped that in the crucial last stages of the war he and MacArthur could reach a cordial understanding.

The following transcript of the second meeting of the two men at Wake Island is itself a subject of controversy. Without authorization, a secretary beyond the sight of the conferees, and without MacArthur's knowledge, made a stenographic record of this famous conversation:[6]

Gen. MacArthur:
It [rehabilitation of Korea—Eds.] cannot occur until the military operations have ended. I believe that formal resistance will end throughout North and South Korea by Thanksgiving. There is little

[6] Excerpts reprinted from *Substance of Statements Made at Wake Island Conference on October 15, 1950*, compiled by Omar N. Bradley and released by the Senate committees on the Armed Services and on Foreign Relations, Eighty-second Congress, first session (Washington, D.C., 1951)', pp. 1–8.

resistance left in South Korea—only about 15,000 men—and those we do not destroy, the winter will. We now have about 60,000 prisoners in compounds.

In North Korea, unfortunately, they are pursuing a forlorn hope. They have about 100,000 men who were trained as replacements. They are poorly trained, led and equipped, but they are obstinate and it goes against my grain to have to destroy them. They are only fighting to save face. Orientals prefer to die rather than to lose face.

I am now driving with the 1st Cavalry Division up the line to Pyongyang. I am thinking of making up a tank and truck column and sending it up the road to take Pyongyang directly. It depends on the intelligence we get in the next forty-eight hours. We have already taken Wonsan. I am landing the X Corps, which will take Pyongyang in one week. The North Koreans are making the same mistake they have made before. They have not deployed in depth. When the gap is closed the same thing will happen in the North as happened in the South.

It is my hope to be able to withdraw the 8th Army to Japan by Christmas. That will leave the X Corps, which will be reconstituted, composed of the 2d and 3d Divisions and U.N. detachments. I hope the U.N. will hold elections by the first of the year. Nothing is gained by military occupation. All occupations are failures. (The President nodded agreement.) After elections are held I expect to pull out all occupying troops. Korea should have about ten divisions with our equipment, supplemented by a small but competent air force and also by a small but competent navy. If we do that, I will not only secure Korea but it will be a tremendous deterrent to the Chinese Communists moving south. . . . a threat that cannot be laughed off. . . .

The President: What are the chances for Chinese or Soviet interference?

Gen. MacArthur: Very little. Had they interfered in the first or second months it would have been decisive. We are no longer fearful of their intervention. We no longer stand hat in hand. The Chinese have 300,000 men in Manchuria. Of these probably not more than 100/125,000 are distributed along the Yalu River. Only 50/60,000 could be gotten across the Yalu River. They have no air force. Now that we have bases for our Air Force in Korea, if the Chinese tried to get down to Pyongyang there would be the greatest slaughter.

With the Russians it is a little different. They have an air force in Siberia and a fairly good one, with excellent pilots equipped with some jets and B-25 and B-29 planes. They can put 1,000 planes in the air with some 2/300 more from the 5th and 7th Soviet fleets. They are probably no match for our Air Force. The Russians have no ground troops available for North Korea. They would have difficulty in putting troops into the field. It would take six weeks to get a division across, and six weeks brings the winter. The only other combination would be Russian air support of Chinese ground troops. Russian air is deployed in a semicircle through Mukden and Harbin, but the co-ordination between the Russian air and the Chinese ground would be so flimsy that I believe Russian air would bomb the Chinese as often as they would bomb us. Ground support is a very difficult thing to do. Our Marines do it perfectly. They have been trained for it. Our own air and ground forces are not as the Marines, but they are effective. Between untrained air and ground forces an air umbrella is impossible without a lot of joint training. I believe it just wouldn't work with Chinese Communist ground and Russian air. We are the best.

MACARTHUR COMMUNIQUÉ ON CHINESE INTERVENTION

7 ✍ ON OCTOBER 30 UN troops took Chinese prisoners of war, and by November 4 MacArthur conceded that full-scale Chinese intervention was a "distinct possibility." Convinced, however, that the Chinese did not really intend to risk the military wrath of the United States, MacArthur launched an offensive on November 24 that would for "all practical purposes end the war." On November 28 he issued the following grim communiqué:[7]

Enemy reactions developed in the course of our assault operations of the past four days disclose that a major segment of the Chinese continental armed forces in army, corps and divisional organization of an aggregate strength of over 200,000 men is now arrayed against the United Nations forces in North Korea.

There exists the obvious intent and preparation for support of these forces by heavy reinforcements now concentrated within the privileged sanctuary north of the international boundary and constantly moving forward.

Consequently, we face an entirely new war. This has shattered the high hopes we entertained that the intervention of the Chinese was only of a token nature on a volunteer and individual basis as

---

[7] Reprinted from *Hearings, Military Situation in the Far East*, p. 3495.

publicly announced, and that therefore the war in Korea could be brought to a rapid close by our movement to the international boundary and the prompt withdrawal thereafter of United Nations forces, leaving Korean problems for settlement by the Koreans themselves.

It now appears to have been the enemy's intent, in breaking off contact with our forces some two weeks ago, to secure the time necessary surreptitiously to build up for a later surprise assault upon our lines in overwhelming force, taking advantage of the freezing of all rivers and roadbeds which would have materially reduced the effectiveness of our air interdiction and permitted a greatly accelerated forward movement of enemy reinforcements and supplies. This plan has been disrupted by our own offensive action, which forced upon the enemy a premature engagement.

General MacArthur later issued this additional paragraph to the communiqué:

This situation, repugnant as it may be, poses issues beyond the authority of the United Nations military council—issues which must find their solution within the councils of the United Nations and chancelleries of the world.

MESSAGE FROM JOINT CHIEFS TO MACARTHUR

8 ⤙ ON DECEMBER 29, 1950, amid a deteriorating military situation in Korea, the Joint Chiefs sent MacArthur a message, the official paraphrase of which follows:[8]

Chinese Communists now appear, from estimates available, capable of forcing evacuation by forces of UN. By committing substantial United States forces which would place other commitments, including safety of Japan, in serious jeopardy, or by inflicting serious losses on him, enemy might be forced to abandon exercise of his capability. If with present UN strength successful resistance at some position in Korea without our incurring serious losses could be accomplished and apparent military and political prestige of Chinese Communists could be deflated, it would be of great importance to our national interests. In the face of increased threat of general war JCS believe commitment of additional United States ground forces in Korea should not be made, since our view is that major war should not be fought in Korea.

[8] *Ibid.*, pp. 2179–80.

Not considered practicable to obtain at this time significant additional forces from other United Nations. Therefore in light of present situation your basic directive, of furnish to ROK [Republic of Korea—Eds.] assistance as necessary to repel armed attack and restore to the area security and peace, is modified. Your directive now is to defend in successive positions, subject to safety of your troops as your primary consideration, inflicting as much damage to hostile forces in Korea as is possible.

In view of continued threat to safety of Japan and possibility of forced withdrawal from Korea it is important to make advance determination of last reasonable opportunity for orderly evacuation. It appears here—that if Chinese Communists retain force capability of forcing evacuation after having driven UN forces to rear it would be necessary to direct commencement of your withdrawal. Request your views on these conditions which should determine evacuation. You should consider your mission of defending Japan and limitation on troops available to you. Definite directive on conditions for initiation of evacuation will be provided when your views are received.

For the present—this message which has been handled with ultimate security should be known only to your chief of staff and to Ridgway and his chief of staff.

MACARTHUR'S STRATEGY RECOMMENDATIONS

9 ⮜§ ON DECEMBER 30, 1950, MacArthur cabled to the Joint Chiefs recommendations that in his view would prevent an evacuation of Korea and eventually culminate in a UN victory:[9]

Any estimate of relative capabilities in the Korean campaign . . . appears to be dependent upon political-military policies yet to be formulated vis-à-vis Chinese military operations being conducted against our forces. It is quite clear now that the entire military resource of the Chinese nation, with logistic support from the Soviet, is committed to a maximum effort against the United Nations command. In implementation of this commitment a major concentration of Chinese force in the Korean-Manchurian area will increasingly leave China vulnerable in areas whence troops to support Korean operations have been drawn. Meanwhile, under existing restrictions, our naval

---

[9] From Courtney Whitney, MacArthur: His Rendezvous with History (New York: Alfred A. Knopf, 1956), pp. 432–4. Reprinted by permission of Alfred A. Knopf, Inc.

and air potential are being only partially utilized and the great potential of Chinese Nationalist force on Formosa and guerrilla action on the mainland are being ignored. Indeed, as to the former, we are preventing its employment against the common enemy by our own naval force.

Should a policy determination be reached by our government or through it by the United Nations to recognize the state of war which has been forced upon us by the Chinese authorities and to take retaliatory measures within our capabilities, we could: (1) blockade the coast of China; (2) destroy through naval gun fire and air bombardment China's industrial capacity to wage war; (3) secure reinforcements from the Nationalist garrison in Formosa to strengthen our position in Korea if we decided to continue the fight for that peninsula; and (4) release existing restrictions upon the Formosan garrison for diversionary action (possibly leading to counter-invasion) against vulnerable areas of the Chinese mainland.

I believe that by the foregoing measures we could severely cripple and largely neutralize China's capability to wage aggressive war and thus save Asia from the engulfment otherwise facing it. I believe furthermore that we could do so with but a small part of our overall military potential committed to the purpose. There is no slightest doubt but that this action would at once release the pressure upon our forces in Korea, whereupon determination could be reached as to whether to maintain the fight in that area or to affect a strategic displacement of our forces with the view to strengthening our defense of the littoral island chain while continuing our naval and air pressure upon China's military potential. I am fully conscious of the fact that this course of action has been rejected in the past for fear of provoking China into a major war effort, but we must now realistically recognize that China's commitment thereto has already been fully and unequivocally made and that nothing we can do would further aggravate the situation as far as China is concerned.

Whether defending ourselves by way of military retaliation would bring in Soviet military intervention or not is a matter of speculation. I have always felt that a Soviet decision to precipitate a general war would depend solely upon the Soviet's own estimate of relative strengths and capabilities with little regard to other factors. . . . If we are forced to evacuate Korea without taking military measures against China proper as suggested in your message, it would have the most adverse affect upon the people of Asia, not excepting the Japanese, and a material reinforcement of the forces now in this theater would be mandatory if we are to hold the littoral defense chain against determined assault.

Moreover, it must be borne in mind that evacuation of our forces from Korea under any circumstances would at once release the bulk of the Chinese forces now absorbed by that campaign for action elsewhere—quite probably in areas of far greater importance than Korea itself. . . .

I understand thoroughly the demand for European security and fully concur in doing everything possible in that sector, but not to the point of accepting defeat anywhere else—an acceptance which I am sure could not fail to insure later defeat in Europe itself. The preparations for the defense of Europe, however, by the most optimistic estimate are aimed at a condition of readiness two years hence. The use of forces in the present emergency in the Far East could not in any way prejudice this basic concept. To the contrary, it would ensure thoroughly seasoned forces for later commitment in Europe synchronously with Europe's own development of military resources.

MACARTHUR ON THE WAR

10 ⋘ BY THE END OF JANUARY General Matthew Ridgway, commander of the U.S. Eighth Army, succeeded in halting the Chinese thrust and in launching a limited offensive. As it became clear that American troops were not going to be driven from Korea, MacArthur's recommendations for expanding the war lost their urgency. But he contrived in many different ways to bring his case before the public. An example of the kind of statement that his superiors in Washington found objectionable is that of March 7, 1951:[10]

Progress of the campaign continues to be satisfactory, with all three services—Army, Navy and Air—performing well their completely coordinated tactical missions. Designed to meet abnormal military inhibitions, our strategic plan, involving constant movement to keep the enemy off balance with a corresponding limitation upon his initiative, remains unaltered.

Our selection of the battle area furthermore has forced him into the military disadvantage of fighting far from his base and permitted greater employment of our air and sea arms against which he has

[10] Reprinted from Hearings, Military Situation in the Far East, pp. 3540–1.

little defense. There has been a resultant continuing and exhausting attrition upon both his manpower and supplies. There should be no illusions in this matter, however. In such a campaign of maneuver, as our battle lines shift north the supply position of the enemy will progressively improve, just as inversely the effectiveness of our air potential will progressively diminish, thus in turn causing his numerical ground superiority to become of increasing battlefield significance.

Assuming no diminution of the enemy's flow of ground forces and matériel to the Korean battle area, a continuation of the existing limitation upon our freedom of counter-offensive action, and no major additions to our organizational strength, the battle lines cannot fail in time to reach a point of theoretical military stalemate. Thereafter our further advance would militarily benefit the enemy more than it would ourselves.

The exact place of stabilization is of necessity a fluctuating variable dependent upon the shifting relative strengths of forces committed and will constantly move up or down. Even now there are indications that the enemy is attempting to build up from China a new and massive offensive for the spring. These are the salient factors which must continue to delimit strategical thinking and planning as the campaign proceeds.

This does not alter the fact, however, that the heavy toll we have taken of the enemy's military power since its commitment to war in Korea cannot fail to weaken his hold upon the Chinese nation and people and materially dampen his ardor for engaging in other aggressive adventures in Asia.

Even under our existing conditions of restraint it should be clearly evident to the Communist foes now committed against us that they cannot hope to impose their will in Korea by military force. They have failed twice—once through North Korean forces, and now through the military might of the army of Communist China. Theirs was the aggression in both cases. Theirs has been the double failure. That they should continue this savage slaughter despite an almost hopeless chance of ultimate military success is a measure of wanton disregard of international decencies and restraints and displays a complete contempt for the sanctity of human life.

No longer is there even a shallow pretense of concern for the welfare of the Korean nation and people, now being so ruthlessly and senselessly sacrificed. Through endless blood it is apparently hoped to enforce either international banditry or blackmail.

Vital decisions have yet to be made—decisions far beyond the scope [of a theater commander—Eds.] which are neither solely political nor solely military, but which must provide on the highest international levels an answer to the obscurities which now becloud the unsolved problems raised by Red China's undeclared war in Korea.

LETTER OF JOSEPH MARTIN TO MACARTHUR

11 ⋖§ BY MARCH 1951 UN troops had fought their way back to the 38th parallel. The administration then decided to call for a cease-fire and for negotiations to settle the Korean problem. Aware of the impending announcement of this decision, on March 24 MacArthur issued an unauthorized statement of his own calling for an end of the war on UN terms and offering to confer himself with the enemy commander to achieve this end. A few days later House Republican Leader Joseph W. Martin, Jr., made public an exchange of letters between himself and the General that again made clear MacArthur's unwillingness to accept administration policies. In Truman's view the time had come to recall his Far Eastern commander. The first letter, of March 8, 1951, was from Martin to MacArthur:[11]

MY DEAR GENERAL: In the current discussions on foreign policy and overall strategy many of us have been distressed that, although the European aspects have been heavily emphasized, we have been without the views of yourself as Commander in Chief of the Far Eastern Command.

I think it is imperative to the security of our Nation and for the safety of the world that policies of the United States embrace the broadest possible strategy and that in our earnest desire to protect Europe we not weaken our position in Asia.

Enclosed is a copy of an address I delivered in Brooklyn, N.Y., February 12, stressing this vital point and suggesting that the forces of Generalissimo Chiang Kai-shek on Formosa might be employed in the opening of a second Asiatic front to relieve the pressure on our forces in Korea.

I have since repeated the essence of this thesis in other speeches, and intend to do so again on March 21, when I will be on a radio hook-up.

[11] *Ibid.,* p. 3543.

I would deem it a great help if I could have your views on this point, either on a confidential basis or otherwise. Your admirers are legion, and the respect you command is enormous. May success be yours in the gigantic undertaking which you direct.

MACARTHUR'S REPLY TO MARTIN'S LETTER

12 ◄ঌ   MACARTHUR REPLIED on March 20, 1951:[12]

DEAR CONGRESSMAN MARTIN: I am most grateful for your note of the 8th forwarding me a copy of your address of February 12. The latter I have read with much interest, and find that with the passage of years you have certainly lost none of your old-time punch.

My views and recommendations with respect to the situation created by Red China's entry into war against us in Korea have been submitted to Washington in most complete detail. Generally these views are well known and clearly understood, as they follow the conventional pattern of meeting force with maximum counter-force as we have never failed to do in the past. Your view with respect to the utilization of the Chinese forces on Formosa is in conflict with neither logic nor this tradition.

It seems strangely difficult for some to realize that here in Asia is where the Communist conspirators have elected to make their play for global conquest, and that we have joined the issue thus raised on the battlefield; that here we fight Europe's war with arms while the diplomats there still fight it with words; that if we lose the war to communism in Asia the fall of Europe is inevitable, win it and Europe most probably would avoid war and yet preserve freedom. As you pointed out, we must win. There is no substitute for victory.

TRUMAN EXPLANATION OF MACARTHUR DISMISSAL

13 ◄ঌ   ON APRIL 10, 1951, Truman ordered General MacArthur to turn over his command to General Ridgway. The public outcry against Truman's action was immediate, emotional, and rancorous. On April 11 the President made a radio address to explain his policy to the nation:[13]

I want to talk plainly to you tonight about what we are doing in Korea and about our policy in the Far East.

[12] Excerpt, *ibid.*, pp. 3543–4.
[13] *Ibid.*, pp. 3547–51.

In the simplest terms, what we are doing in Korea is this:

We are trying to prevent a third world war.

I think most people in this country recognized that fact last June. And they warmly supported the decision of the Government to help the Republic of Korea against the Communist aggressors. Now, many persons, even some who applauded our decision to defend Korea, have forgotten the basic reason for our action.

It is right for us to be in Korea. It was right last June. It is right today.

I want to remind you why this is true.

The Communists in the Kremlin are engaged in a monstrous conspiracy to stamp out freedom all over the world. If they were to succeed, the United States would be numbered among their principal victims. It must be clear to everyone that the United States cannot—and will not—sit idly by and await foreign conquest. The only question is: When is the best time to meet the threat and how is the best way to meet it?

The best time to meet the threat is in the beginning. It is easier to put out a fire in the beginning when it is small than after it has become a roaring blaze.

And the best way to meet the threat of aggression is for the peace-loving nations to act together. If they don't act together, they are likely to be picked off, one by one.

If they had followed the right policies in the 1930's—if the free countries had acted together, to crush the aggression of the dictators, and if they had acted in the beginning, when the aggression was small—there probably would have been no World War II.

If history has taught us anything, it is that aggression anywhere in the world is a threat to peace everywhere in the world. When that aggression is supported by the cruel and selfish rulers of a powerful nation who are bent on conquest, it becomes a clear and present danger to the security and independence of every free nation.

This is a lesson that most people in this country have learned thoroughly. This is the basic reason why we joined in creating the United Nations. And, since the end of World War II, we have been putting that lesson into practice—we have been working with other free nations to check the aggressive designs of the Soviet Union before they can result in a third world war.

That is what we did in Greece, when that nation was threatened by the aggression of international communism.

The attack against Greece could have led to general war. But this country came to the aid of Greece. The United Nations supported Greek resistance. With our help, the determination and efforts of the Greek people defeated the attack on the spot.

Another big Communist threat to peace was the Berlin blockade. That too could have led to war. But again it was settled because free men would not back down in an emergency.

The aggression against Korea is the boldest and most dangerous move the Communists have yet made.

The attack on Korea was part of a greater plan for conquering all of Asia.

I would like to read to you from a secret intelligence report which came to us after the attack. It is a report of a speech a Communist army officer in North Korea gave to a group of spies and saboteurs last May, one month before South Korea was invaded. The report shows in great detail how this invasion was a part of a carefully prepared plot. Here is part of what the Communist officer, who had been trained in Moscow, told his men: "Our forces," he said, "are scheduled to attack South Korean forces about the middle of June * * * the coming attack on South Korea marks the first step toward liberation of Asia."

Notice that he uses the world "liberation." That is Communist double-talk meaning "conquest."

I have another secret intelligence report here. This one tells what another Communist officer in the Far East told his men several months before the invasion of Korea. Here is what he said: "In order to successfully undertake the long awaited world revolution, we must first unify Asia. * * * Java, Indo-China, Malaya, India, Tibet, Thailand, Philippines, and Japan are our ultimate targets * * * the United States is the only obstacle on our road for the liberation of all countries in southeast Asia. In other words, we must unify the people of Asia and crush the United States."

That is what the Communist leaders are telling their people, and that is what they have been trying to do.

Again, "liberation" in Commie language, means "conquest."

They want to control all Asia from the Kremlin.

This plan of conquest is in flat contradiction to what we believe. We believe that Korea belongs to the Koreans. We believe that India belongs to the Indians. We believe that all the nations of Asia should be free to work out their affairs in their own way. This is the basis of peace in the Far East and it is the basis of peace everywhere else.

The whole Communist imperialism is back of the attack on peace in the Far East. It was the Soviet Union that trained and equipped the North Koreans for aggression. The Chinese Communists massed 44 well-trained and well-equipped divisions on the Korean frontier. These were the troops they threw into battle when the North Korean Communists were beaten.

The question we have had to face is whether the Communist plan of conquest can be stopped without general war. Our Government and other countries associated with us in the United Nations believe that the best chance of stopping it without general war is to meet the attack in Korea and defeat it there.

That is what we have been doing. It is a difficult and bitter task. But so far it has been successful.

So far, we have prevented World War III.

So far, by fighting a limited war in Korea, we have prevented aggression from succeeding, and bringing on a general war. And the ability of the whole free world to resist Communist aggression has been greatly improved.

We have taught the enemy a lesson. He has found out that aggression is not cheap or easy. Moreover, men all over the world who want to remain free have been given new courage and new hope. They know now that the champions of freedom can stand up and fight and that they will stand up and fight.

Our resolute stand in Korea is helping the forces of freedom now fighting in Indo-China and other countries in that part of the world. It has already slowed down the time-table of conquest.

In Korea itself, there are signs that the enemy is building up his ground forces for a new mass offensive. We also know that there have been large increases in the enemy's available air forces.

If a new attack comes I feel confident it will be turned back. The United Nations fighting forces are tough and able and well equipped. They are fighting for a just cause. They are proving to all the world that the principle of collective security will work. We are proud of all these forces for the magnificent job they have done against heavy odds. We pray that their efforts may succeed, for upon their success may hinge the peace of the world.

The Communist side must now choose its course of action. The Communist rulers may press the attack against us. They may take further action which will spread the conflict. They have that choice, and with it the awful responsibility for what may follow. The Communists also have the choice of a peaceful settlement which could lead to a general relaxation of tensions in the Far East. The decision is theirs, because the forces of the United Nations will strive to limit the conflict if possible.

We do not want to see the conflict in Korea extended. We are trying to prevent a world war—not to start one. The best way to do that is to make it plain that we and the other free countries will continue to resist the attack.

But you may ask why can't we take other steps to punish the aggressor. Why don't we bomb Manchuria and China itself? Why don't we assist Chinese Nationalist troops to land on the mainland of China?

If we were to do these things [we—Eds.] would be running a very grave risk of starting a general war. If that were to happen, we would have brought about the exact situation we are trying to prevent.

If we were to do these things, we would become entangled in a vast conflict on the continent of Asia and our task would become immeasurably more difficult all over the world.

What would suit the ambitions of the Kremlin better than for our military forces to be committed to a full scale war with Red China?

It may well be that, in spite of our best efforts, the Communists may spread the war. But it would be wrong—tragically wrong—for us to take the initiative in extending the war.

The dangers are great. Make no mistake about it. Behind the North Koreans and Chinese Communists in the front lines stand additional millions of Chinese soldiers. And behind the Chinese stand the tanks, the planes, the submarines, the soldiers, and the scheming rulers of the Soviet Union.

Our aim is to avoid the spread of the conflict.

The course we have been following is the one best calculated to avoid an all-out war. It is the course consistent with our obligation to do all we can to maintain international peace and security. Our experience in Greece and Berlin shows that it is the most effective course of action we can follow.

First of all, it is clear that our efforts in Korea can blunt the will of the Chinese Communists to continue the struggle. The United Nations forces have put up a tremendous fight in Korea and have inflicted very heavy casualties on the enemy. Our forces are stronger now than they have been before. These are plain facts which may discourage the Chinese Communists from continuing their attack.

Second, the free world as a whole is growing in military strength every day. In the United States, in western Europe, and throughout the world, free men are alert to the Soviet threat and are building their defenses. This may discourage the Communist rulers from continuing the war in Korea—and from undertaking new acts of aggression elsewhere.

If the Communist authorities realize that they cannot defeat us in Korea, if they realize it would be foolhardy to widen the hostilities beyond Korea, then they may recognize the folly of continuing their aggression. A peaceful settlement may then be possible. The door is always open.

Then we may achieve a settlement in Korea which will not compromise the principles and purposes of the United Nations.

I have thought long and hard about this question of extending the war in Asia. I have discussed it many time with the ablest military advisers in the country. I believe with all my heart that the course we are following is the best course.

I believe that we must try to limit the war to Korea for these vital reasons: To make sure that the precious lives of our fighting men are not wasted, to see that the security of our country and the free world is not needlessly jeopardized and to prevent a third world war.

A number of events have made it evident that General MacArthur did not agree with that policy. I have, therefore, considered it essential to relieve General MacArthur so that there would be no doubt or confusion as to the real purpose and aim of our policy.

It was with the deepest personal regret that I found myself compelled to take this action. General MacArthur is one of our greatest military commanders. But the cause of world peace is more important than any individual.

The change in commands in the Far East means no change whatever in the policy of the United States. We will carry on the fight in Korea with vigor and determination in an effort to bring the war to a speedy and successful conclusion.

The new commander, Lieut. Gen. Matthew Ridgway, has already demonstrated that he has the great qualities of leadership needed for this task.

We are ready, at any time, to negotiate for a restoration of peace in the area. But we will not engage in appeasement. We are only interested in real peace.

Real peace can be achieved through a settlement based on the following factors:

One: The fighting must stop.

Two: Concrete steps must be taken to insure that the fighting will not break out again.

Three: There must be an end to the aggression.

A settlement founded upon these elements would open the way for the unification of Korea and the withdrawal of all foreign forces.

In the meantime, I want to be clear about our military objective. We are fighting to resist an outrageous aggression in Korea. We are trying to keep the Korean conflict from spreading to other areas. But at the same time we must conduct our military activities so as to insure the security of our forces. This is essential if they are to continue the fight until the enemy abandons its ruthless attempt to destroy the Republic of Korea.

That is our military objective—to repel attack and to restore peace.

MACARTHUR STATEMENT TO CONGRESS

14 ◄§ ON MACARTHUR'S RETURN HOME, the public accorded him a hero's welcome. On April 19, 1951, amid thunderous applause, he delivered a speech to a joint session of Congress:[14]

Mr. President, Mr. Speaker, and distinguished Members of the Congress, I stand on this rostrum with a sense of deep humility and great pride—humility in the wake of those great American architects of our history who have stood here before me, pride in the reflection that this forum of legislative debate represents human liberty in the purest form yet devised. [Applause.] Here are centered the hopes, and aspirations, and faith of the entire human race.

I do not stand here as advocate for any partisan cause, for the issues are fundamental and reach quite beyond the realm of partisan consideration. They must be resolved on the highest plane of national interest if our course is to prove sound and our future protected. I trust, therefore, that you will do me the justice of receiving that which I have to say as solely expressing the considered viewpoint of a fellow American. I address you with neither rancor nor bitterness in the

[14] Reprinted from *Congressional Record*, Eighty-second Congress, first session, pp. 4123–5.

fading twilight of life with but one purpose in mind—to serve my country. [Applause.]

The issues are global and so interlocked that to consider the problems of one sector, oblivious to those of another, is but to court disaster for the whole.

While Asia is commonly referred to as the gateway to Europe, it is no less true that Europe is the gateway to Asia, and the broad influence of the one cannot fail to have its impact upon the other.

There are those who claim our strength is inadquate to protect on both fronts—that we cannot divide our effort. I can think of no greater expression of defeatism. [Applause.] If a potential enemy can divide his strength on two fronts, it is for us to counter his effort.

The Communist threat is a global one. Its successful advance in one sector threatens the destruction of every other sector. You cannot appease or otherwise surrender to communism in Asia without simultaneously undermining our efforts to halt its advance in Europe. [Applause.]

Beyond pointing out these general truisms, I shall confine my discussion to the general areas of Asia. Before one may objectively assess the situation now existing there, he must comprehend something of Asia's past and the revolutionary changes which have marked her course up to the present. Long exploited by the so-called colonial powers, with little opportunity to achieve any degree of social justice, individual dignity, or a higher standard of life such as guided our own noble administration of the Philippines, the peoples of Asia found their opportunity in the war just past to throw off the shackles of colonialism, and now see the dawn of new opportunity, a heretofore unfelt dignity and the self-respect of political freedom.

Mustering half of the earth's population and 60 percent of its natural resources, these peoples are rapidly consolidating a new force, both moral and material, with which to raise the living standard and erect adaptations of the design of modern progress to their own distinct cultural environments. Whether one adheres to the concept of colonization or not, this is the direction of Asian progress and it may not be stopped. It is a corollary to the shift of the world economic frontiers, as the whole epicenter of world affairs rotates back toward the area whence it started. In this situation it becomes vital that our own country orient its policies in consonance with this basic evolutionary condition rather than pursue a course blind to the reality that the colonial era is now past and the Asian peoples covet the right to shape their own free destiny. What they seek now is friendly guidance, understanding, and support, not imperious direction [applause]; the dignity of equality, not the shame of subjugation. Their prewar standard of life, pitifully low, is infinitely lower now in the devastation left in the war's wake. World ideologies play little part in Asian thinking and are little understood. What the peoples strive for is the opportunity for a little more food in their stomachs, a little better clothing on their backs, a little firmer roof over their heads, and the realization of the normal nationalist urge for political freedom. These political-social conditions have but an indirect bearing upon our own national security, but do form a backdrop to contemporary planning which must be thoughtfully considered if we are to avoid the pitfalls of unrealism.

Of more direct and immediate bearing upon our national security are the changes wrought in the strategic potential of the Pacific Ocean in the course of the past war. Prior thereto, the western strategic frontier of the United States lay on the littoral line of the Americas with an exposed island salient extending out through Hawaii, Midway, and Guam to the Philippines. That salient proved not an outpost of strength but an avenue of weakness along which the enemy could and did attack. The Pacific was a potential area of advance for any predatory force intent upon striking at the bordering land areas.

All this was changed by our Pacific victory. Our strategic frontier then shifted to embrace the entire Pacific Ocean which became a vast moat to protect us as long as we hold it. Indeed, it acts as a protective shield for all of the Americas and all free lands of the Pacific Ocean area. We control it to the shores of Asia by a chain of islands extending in an arc from the Aleutians to the Marianas held by us and our free allies.

From this island chain we can dominate with sea and air power every Asiatic port from Vladivostok to Singapore and prevent any hostile movement into the Pacific. Any predatory attack from Asia must be an amphibious effort. No amphibious force can be successful without control of the sea lanes and the air over those lanes in its avenue of advance. With naval and air supremacy and modest ground elements to defend bases, any major attack from continental Asia toward us or our friends of the Pacific would be doomed to failure. Under such conditions the Pacific no longer represents menacing avenues of approach for a prospective invader—it assumes instead the friendly aspect of a peaceful lake. Our line of defense is a natural one and can be maintained with a minimum of military effort and expense. It envisions no attack against anyone nor does it provide the bastions essential for offensive operations, but properly maintained would be an invincible defense against aggression.

The holding of this littoral defense line in the western Pacific is entirely dependent upon holding all segments thereof, for any major breach of that line by an unfriendly power would render vulnerable to determined attack every other major segment. This is a military estimate as to which I have yet to find a military leader who will take exception. [Applause.]

For that reason I have strongly recommended in the past as a matter of military urgency that under no circumstances must Formosa fall under Communist control. [Applause.] Such an eventuality would at once threaten the freedom of the Philippines and the loss of Japan, and might well force our western frontier back to the coasts of California, Oregon, and Washington.

To understand the changes which now appear upon the Chinese mainland, one must understand the changes in Chinese character and culture over the past 50 years. China up to 50 years ago was completely nonhomogeneous, being compartmented into groups divided against each other. The war-making tendency was almost nonexistent, as they still followed the tenets of the Confucian ideal of pacifist culture. At the turn of the century, under the regime of Chan So Lin, efforts toward greater homogeneity produced the start of a nationalist urge. This was further and more successfully developed under the leadership of Chiang Kai-shek, but has been brought to its greatest fruition under the present regime, to the point that it has now taken on the character of a united nationalism of increasingly dominant aggressive tendencies. Through these past 50 years, the Chinese people have thus become militarized in their concepts and in their ideals. They now constitute excellent soldiers with competent staffs and commanders. This has produced a new and dominant power in Asia which for its own purposes is allied with Soviet Russia, but which in its own concepts and methods has become aggressively imperialistic with a lust for expansion and increased power normal to this type of imperialism. There is little of the ideological concept either one way or another in the Chinese make-up. The standard of living is so low and the capital accumulation has been so thoroughly dissipated by war that the masses are desperate and avid to follow any leadership which seems to promise the alleviation of local stringencies. I have from the beginning believed that the Chinese Communists' support of the North Koreans was the dominant one. Their interests are at present parallel to those of the Soviet, but I believe that the aggressiveness recently displayed not only in Korea, but also in Indochina and Tibet and pointing potentially toward the south, reflects predominantly the same lust for the expansion of power and which has animated every would-be conqueror since the beginning of time. [Applause.]

The Japanese people since the war have undergone the greatest reformation recorded in modern history. With a commendable will, eagerness to learn, and marked capacity to understand, they have, from the ashes left in war's wake, erected in Japan an edifice dedicated to the primacy of individual liberty and personal dignity, and in the ensuing process there has been created a truly representative government committed to the advance of political morality, freedom of economic enterprise and social justice. [Applause.] Politically, economically and socially Japan is now abreast of many free nations of the earth and will not again fail the universal trust. That it may be counted upon to wield a profoundly beneficial influence over the course of events in Asia is attested by the magnificent manner in which the Japanese people have met the recent challenge of war, unrest, and confusion surrounding them from the outside, and checked communism within their own frontiers without the slightest slackening in their forward progress. I sent all four of our occupation divisions to the Korean battle front without the slightest qualms as to the effect of the resulting power vacuum upon Japan. The results fully justified my faith. [Applause.] I know of no nation more serene, orderly, and industrious—nor in which higher hopes can be entertained for future constructive service in the advance of the human race. [Applause.]

Of our former wards, the Philippines, we can look forward in confidence that the existing unrest will be corrected and a strong and healthy nation will grow in the longer aftermath of war's terrible destructiveness. We must be patient and understanding and never fail them, as in our hour of need they did not fail us. [Applause.] A Christian nation, the Philippines stand as a mighty bulwark of Christianity in the Far East, and its capacity for high moral leadership in Asia is unlimited.

On Formosa, the Government of the Republic of China has had the opportunity to refute by action much of the malicious gossip which so undermined the strength of its leadership on the Chinese mainland. [Applause.] The Formosan people are receiving a just and enlightened administration with majority representation on the organs of government; and politically, economically and socially they appear to be advancing along sound and constructive lines.

With this brief insight into the surrounding areas I now turn to the Korean conflict. While I was not consulted prior to the President's decision to intervene in support of the Republic of Korea, that decision, from a military standpoint, proved a sound one [applause] as we hurled back the invaders and decimated his forces. Our victory was complete and our objectives within reach when Red China intervened with numerically superior ground forces. This created a new war and an entirely new situation—a situation not contemplated when our forces were committed against the North Korean invaders —a situation which called for new decisions in the diplomatic sphere to permit the realistic adjustment of military strategy. Such decisions have not been forthcoming. [Applause.]

While no man in his right mind would advocate sending our ground forces into continental China and such was never given a thought, the new situation did urgently demand a drastic revision of strategic planning if our political aim was to defeat this new enemy as we had defeated the old. [Applause.]

Apart from the military need as I saw it to neutralize the sanctuary protection given the enemy north of the Yalu, I felt that military necessity in the conduct of the war made mandatory:

1. The intensification of our economic blockade against China;
2. The imposition of a naval blockade against the China coast;
3. Removal of restrictions on air reconnaissance of China's coast areas and of Manchuria [applause];
4. Removal of restrictions on the forces of the Republic of China on Formosa with logistical support to contribute to their effective operations against the common enemy. [Applause.]

For entertaining these views, all professionally designed to support our forces committed to Korea and bring hostilities to an end with the least possible delay and at a saving of countless American and Allied lives, I have been severely criticized in lay circles, principally abroad, despite my understanding that from a military standpoint the above views have been fully shared in the past by practically every military leader concerned with the Korean campaign, including our own Joint Chiefs of Staff. [Applause, the Members rising.]

I called for reinforcements, but was informed that reinforcements were not available. I made clear that if not permitted to destroy the build-up bases north of the Yalu; if not permitted to utilize the friendly Chinese force of some 600,000 men on Formosa; if not permitted to blockade the China coast to prevent the Chinese Reds from getting succor from without; and if there were to be no hope of major reinforcements, the position of the command from the military standpoint forbade victory. We could hold in Korea by constant maneuver and at an approximate area where our supply line advantages were in balance with the supply line disadvantages of the enemy, but we could hope at best for only an indecisive campaign, with its terrible and constant attrition upon our forces if the enemy utilized his full military potential. I have constantly called for the new political decisions essential to a solution. Efforts have been made to distort my position. It has been said, in effect, that I am a warmonger. Nothing could be further from the truth. I know war as few other men now living know it, and nothing to me is more revolting. I have long advocated its complete abolition as its very destructiveness on both friend and foe has rendered it useless as a means of settling international disputes. Indeed, on the 2d of September 1945, just following the surrender of the Japanese Nation on the battleship *Missouri,* I formally cautioned as follows:

"Men since the beginning of time have sought peace. Various methods through the ages have been attempted to devise an international process to prevent or settle disputes between nations. From the very start, workable methods were found insofar as individual citizens were concerned, but the mechanics of an instrumentality of larger international scope have never been successful. Military alliances, balances of power, leagues of nations, all in turn failed, leaving the only path to be by way of the crucible of war. The utter destructiveness of war now blots out this alternative. We have had our last chance. If we will not devise some greater and more equitable system, Armageddon will be at our door. The problem basically is theological and involves a spiritual recrudescence and improvement of human character that will synchronize with our almost matchless advances in science, art, literature, and all material and cultural developments of the past 2,000 years. It must be of the spirit if we are to save the flesh." [Applause.]

But once war is forced upon us, there is no other alternative than to apply every available means to bring it to a swift end. War's very object is victory—not prolonged indecision. [Applause.] In war, indeed, there can be no substitute for victory. [Applause.]

There are some who for varying reasons would appease Red China. They are blind to history's clear lesson. For history teaches with unmistakable emphasis that appeasement but begets new and bloodier war. It points to no single instance where the end has justified that means—where appeasement has led to more than a sham peace. Like blackmail, it lays the basis for new and successively greater demands, until, as in blackmail, violence becomes the only other alternative. Why, my soldiers asked me, surrender military advantages to an enemy in the field? I could not answer. [Applause.] Some may say to avoid spread of the conflict into an all-out war with China; others, to avoid Soviet intervention. Neither explanation seems valid. For China is already engaging with the maximum power it can commit and the Soviet will not necessarily mesh its actions with our moves. Like a cobra, any new enemy will more likely strike whenever it feels that the relativity in military or other potential is in its favor on a world-wide basis.

The tragedy of Korea is further heightened by the fact that as military action is confined to its territorial limits, it condemns that nation, which it is our purpose to save, to suffer the devastating impact of full naval and air bombardment, while the enemy's sanctuaries are fully protected from such attack and devastation. Of the nations of the world, Korea alone, up to now, is the sole one which has risked its all against communism. The magnificence of the courage and fortitude of the Korean people defies description. [Applause.] They have chosen to risk death rather than slavery. Their last words to me were "Don't scuttle the Pacific." [Applause.]

I have just left your fighting sons in Korea. They have met all tests there and I can report to you without reservation they are splendid in every way. [Applause.] It was my constant effort to preserve them and end this savage conflict honorably and with the least loss of time and a minimum sacrifice of life. Its growing bloodshed has caused me the deepest anguish and anxiety. Those gallant men will remain often in my thoughts and in my prayers always. [Applause.]

I am closing my 52 years of military service. [Applause.] When I joined the Army even before the turn of the century, it was the fulfillment of all my boyish hopes and dreams. The world has turned over many times since I took the oath on the plain at West Point, and the hopes and dreams have long since vanished. But I still remember the refrain of one of the most popular barrack ballads of that day which proclaimed most proudly that—

"Old soldiers never die; they just fade away."

And like the old soldier of that ballad, I now close my military career and just fade away—an old soldier who tried to do his duty as God gave him the light to see that duty.

Good-by.

TESTIMONY OF MACARTHUR

15 ⋖§ MACARTHUR'S RECALL inspired a great national debate over the policy of limited war. The major forum for the controversy was a room in the Senate Office Building in which the Senate Foreign Relations and Armed Services committees conducted hearings on the administration's Far East policies. The first witness was General MacArthur, who in three days of testimony, beginning on May 3, 1951, ably presented his case:[15]

Senator [Leverett—Eds.] SALTONSTALL. Now, on April 15, the Assistant Secretary of State, Dean Rusk, in a television and press broadcast, stated, in part—and this is the pertinent part of his speech, as I read it:

> What we are trying to do is to maintain peace and security without a general war. We are saying to the aggressors, "You will not be allowed to get away with your crime. You must stop it."
> At the same time, we are trying to prevent a general conflagration which would consume the very things we are now trying to defend.

I would appreciate it very much, with your knowledge of the Far East, if you will give me your opinion of that statement, and if that is a practical policy.

General MACARTHUR. That policy, as you have read it, seems to me to introduce a new concept into military operations—the concept of appeasement, the concept that when you use force, you can limit that force.

The concept that I have is that when you go into war, you have

---

[15] Excerpts reprinted from *Hearings, Military Situation in the Far East*, pp. 39–40, 42–3, 66–9, 74–7, 81–3.

exhausted all other potentialities of bringing the disagreements to an end.

As I understand what you read, that we would apply to the military situation in Korea certain military appeasements—that is, that we would not use our Air Forces to their maximum extent, only to the limited area of that Korea; that we would not use our Navy, except along the border lines of Korea.

To me, that would mean that you would have a continued and indefinite extension of bloodshed, which would have limitless—a limitless end.

You would not have the potentialities of destroying the enemy's military power, and bringing the conflict to a decisive close in the minimum of time, and with a minimum of loss.

It seems to me the worst possible concept, militarily, that we would simply stay there, resisting aggression, so-called, although I do not know what you mean by "resisting aggression."

The very term of "resisting aggression," it seems to me that you destroy the potentialities of the aggressor to continually hit you.

If that is the concept of a continued and indefinite campaign in Korea, with no definite purpose of stopping it until the enemy gets tired or you yield to his terms, I think that introduces into the military sphere a political control such as I have never known in my life or have ever studied.

Senator SALTONSTALL. In other words, you feel that the Korean situation, having gone into an armed conflict, it should be brought to an end in the quickest possible way through a military victory.

General MACARTHUR. I do, Senator, exactly; and I believe if you do not do that, if you hit soft, if you practice appeasement in the use of force, you are doomed to disaster.

I believe that if you continue that way, you are inviting the very thing that you desire to stop—the spread of the conflict. . . .

The only way I know, when a nation wars on you, is to beat her by force. I do not know of any argument that will bring an end to this thing.

War, in itself, is the application of superior force, and as we chose that path, and have entered upon that path, it seems to me that we must end it in some way.

Now, there are only three ways that I can see, as I said this morning: Either to pursue it to victory; to surrender to an enemy and end it on his terms; or, what I think is the worst of all choices, to go on indefinitely and indefinitely, neither to win nor lose, in that stalemate; because what we are doing is sacrificing thousands of men while we are doing it.

If you could just say that this line stops aggression, and we didn't lose the men, that would be a different thing; but every day over there you have this terrific and savage conflict, the most savage I ever fought in; and you are losing the very flower of our youth, and if you keep on month after month, and month after month, why, these losses are going to mount up to figures which would stagger the imagination.

Now, in that third process of merely continuing, as has been projected in some circles, that leads to an indefinite sacrifice of lives.

Senator [Wayne L.—Eds.] MORSE. Will the general let me say that——

General MACARTHUR. Now, war never before in the history of the world has been applied in a piecemeal way, that you make half war, and not whole war.

Now, that China is using the maximum of her force against us is quite evident; and we are not using the maximum of ours against her, in reply.

The result is—we do not even use, to the maximum, the forces at our disposal, the scientific methods, and the result is that for every percentage you take away in the use of the Air and the Navy, you add a percentage to the dead American infantrymen.

It may seem emotional for me to say that, but I happen to be the man that had to send them into it. The blood, to some extent, would rest on me; and with the objectives, I believe I could stop them—it seems terrific to me that we should not attempt something.

The inertia that exists. There is no policy—there is nothing, I tell you, no plan, or anything.

When you say, merely, "we are going to continue to fight aggression," that is not what the enemy is fighting for.

The enemy is fighting for a very definite purpose—to destroy our forces in Korea.

We constantly, every day, run that risk, without the potential of defeating him, and stopping him—to come again.

He attacks today. We resist it. We fall back. We form a new line, and we surge back.

Then, he is right back, within a week, maybe, up to the battle front with his inexhaustible supply of manpower. He brings in another hundred thousand, or another half-million men, and tosses them at these troops constantly.

That is a new concept in war.

That is not war—that is appeasement. . . .

Senator [Theodore—Eds.] GREEN. What I would like to ask is a question which seems to me to go to the basis of the whole difference that has been developed. It is this:

The theory that we could win a quick victory in China simply by lending logistic support to the Chinese troops now in Formosa and in bombarding the coast cities and in establishing blockage would, in the first place, would it not, indicate we would proceed alone and not with any help from the other United Nations?

General MACARTHUR. I can give you no testimony about the United Nations, Senator.

Senator GREEN. What would be your expectation?

General MACARTHUR. My hope would be of course that the United Nations would see the wisdom and utility of that course, but if they did not, I still believe that the interest of the United States being the predominant one in Korea, would require our action.

Senator GREEN. Alone?

General MACARTHUR. Alone, if necessary. If the other nations of the world haven't got enough sense to see where appeasement leads after the appeasement which led to the Second World War in Europe, if they can't see exactly the road that they are following in Asia, why then we had better protect ourselves and go it alone. . . .

Senator [Brien—Eds.] McMAHON. . . . You see, General, what I want to find out from you is this—that if you happen to be wrong this time and we go into all-out war, I want to find out how you propose in your own mind to defend the American Nation against that war.

General MACARTHUR. That doesn't happen to be my responsibility, Senator. My responsibilities were in the Pacific, and the Joint Chiefs of Staff and the various agencies of this Government are working day and night for an over-all solution to the global problem.

Now I am not familiar with their studies. I haven't gone into it. I have been desperately occupied over on the other side of the world, and to discuss in detail things that I haven't ever superficially touched doesn't contribute in any way, shape, or manner to the information of this committee or anybody else.

Senator McMAHON. General, I think you make the point very well that I want to make; that the Joint Chiefs of Staff and the President of the United States, the Commander in Chief, has to look at this thing on a global basis and a global defense.

You as a theater commander by your own statement have not made that kind of a study, and yet you advise us to push forward with a course of action that may involve us in that global conflict.

General MacARTHUR. Everything that is involved in international relationships, Senator, amount to a gamble, risk. You have to take risks.

Senator McMAHON. I couldn't agree with you more.

General MacARTHUR. What I faced in the Pacific wasn't something that was speculative in the future. It's right now. What are you going to do to stop the slaughter in Korea? Are you going to let it go on? Does your global plan for defense of this United States against war consist of permitting war indefinitely to go on in the Pacific? What is your plan or what is the other plan to stop the war there in the Pacific?

It is there. There is no sophistry of talk when you see thousands of battle casualties every month; you can't talk those off that there is no war. There is a savage war there.

If you are not going to bring the war to a decisive conclusion, what does the preparedness mean? You are faced with a fact in Asia.

You are speculating about what takes place in the rest of the global parts of the world. I assume that the plans that are being made are to meet the contingencies that may arise.

Otherwise the whole force of the United States would be poured into Korea.

Senator McMAHON. General, the purpose of this hearing certainly is not for any Senator and certainly not one who is ill-equipped as I am, to argue this question with you this time.

My purpose is to try to develop information that will be helpful to me in reaching my final conclusions on the matter. General, are you aware of what our atomic preparedness situation is today?

General MacARTHUR. Only in a very general way, sir.

Senator McMAHON. I am not asking you for numbers, but do you know the numbers in our stockpile?

General MacARTHUR. I do not. I have no more information on that than the average officer would have. It's confined to a very select circle, you know.

Senator McMahon. Have you ever asked about that? Have you ever asked for information on it, General?

General MacArthur. On the atomic thing?

Senator McMahon. Yes.

General MacArthur. I have discussed it, but I have never attempted to pry into matters which I regarded as beyond my own authority.

Senator McMahon. In the course of your conduct of your duties in the Far East, as a theater commander, did you ever make inquiry of the Joint Chiefs of Staff about our atomic situation?

General MacArthur. I have made inquiries as to what might be the potentialities and possibilities of the use of the atomic bomb in my own theater. I know what that is.

Senator McMahon. Have you at any time advocated the use of the atomic bomb in your theater?

General MacArthur. Of the atomic bomb?

Senator McMahon. Yes.

General MacArthur. The limit of——

Senator McMahon. Pardon me?

General MacArthur. The limit of what I did was to ask for information as to whether there were any plans to use the atomic bomb in the Far East.

Senator McMahon. Did you recommend its use?

General MacArthur. I did not. As I understand it, the use of the atomic bomb has, by fiat and order, been limited to the decision of the President of the United States.

Senator McMahon. That is true. Of course, I wondered whether you made any recommendations.

General MacArthur. Why should I, Senator? . . .

General MacArthur. . . . I shrink—I shrink with a horror that I cannot express in words—at this continuous slaughter of men in Korea.

The battle casualties in Korea today probably have passed the million-man mark. Our own casualties, American casualties, have passed 65,000. The Koreans have lost about 140,000. Our losses, on our side, are a quarter of a million men. I am not talking of the civilian populations, who must have lost many, many, many times that.

The enemy probably has lost 750,000 casualties. There are 145,000 of them that are now in our prison bull pens, prisoners, so they might be excepted from that figure because they live; but a million men in less than 11 months of fighting, in less than 11 months of this conflict, have already gone and it grows more savage every day.

I just cannot brush that off as a Korean skirmish. I believe that is something of such tremendous importance that it must be solved, and it cannot be solved by the nebulous process of saying "Give us time, and we will be prepared; or we will be in a better shape 2 years from now"—which is argumentative.

I don't know whether we will, or not; and neither do you, because you do not know, and none of us know the capacity of the enemy.

He may build faster than we do. I couldn't tell you.

I don't know that, you are gambling on chances; but I say there is no chance in Korea, because it is a fact—you have lost a million men now. You will lose more than a million if you go on another year; if you go on until 1953, you will lose another million.

What are you trying to protect?

The war in Korea has already almost destroyed that nation of 20,000,000 people.

I have never seen such devastation.

I have seen, I guess, as much blood and disaster as any living man, and it just curdled my stomach, the last time I was there. After I looked at that wreckage and those thousands of women and children and everything, I vomited.

Now, are you going to let that go on, by any sophistry of reasoning, or possibilities? They may be there, but this is a certainty.

What are you going to do? Once more, I repeat the question, What is the policy in Korea?

If you go on indefinitely, you are perpetuating a slaughter such as I have never heard of in the history of mankind.

Now, what I am trying to do is to find some reasonable and honorable way to stop that slaughter. It is not to conquer this country, or China, or anything else.

It is to bring this thing to an honorable end.

If you go on, you are going to destroy not only the casualties that I speak of, which are military, but you are going to destroy that people.

Now, I just cannot bring myself to analyze it with that shrewdness of legal capacity that you enunciate in your argument, which is an argument, to let it by.

Your entire drift has been not to do anything, just keep on fighting, losing and bleeding there; and I think we should make some extraordinary effort to bring it to an end.

GENERAL BRADLEY'S TESTIMONY

16 ⋅≈§   GENERAL OMAR N. BRADLEY, head of the Joint Chiefs of Staff, was perhaps the most effective of the administration's witnesses, in his testimony during the Senate hearings:[16]

The fundamental military issue that has arisen is whether to increase the risk of a global war by taking additional measures that are open to the United States and its allies. We now have a localized conflict in Korea. Some of the military measures under discussion might well place the United States in the position of responsibility for broadening the war and at the same time losing most if not all of our allies.

General MacArthur has stated that there are certain additional measures which can and should be taken, and that by so doing no unacceptable increased risk of global war will result.

The Joint Chiefs of Staff believe that these same measures do increase the risk of global war and that such a risk should not be taken unnecessarily. At the same time we recognize the military advantages that might accrue to the United Nations' position in Korea and to the United States position in the Far East by these measures. While a field commander very properly estimates his needs from the viewpoint of operations in his own theater or sphere of action, those responsible for higher direction must necessarily base their actions on broader aspects, and on the needs, actual or prospective, of several theaters. The Joint Chiefs of Staff, in view of their global responsibilities and their perspective with respect to the world-wide strategic situation, are in a better position than is any single theater commander to assess the risk of general war. Moreover, the Joint Chiefs of Staff are best able to judge our own military resources with which to meet that risk.

In order that all may understand the strategy which the Joint Chiefs of Staff believe the United States must pursue, I would like to discuss in broad terms this perspective in which we view our security problems.

As a background to our consideration of global strategy, we must realize that human beings have invented a great variety of techniques

[16] Excerpt, *ibid.*, pp. 729–34, 742–3.

designed to influence other nations. Right now, nations are being subjected to persuasion by propaganda and coercion by force of arms. It is my conviction that broad and comprehensive knowledge of the strength, aims, and the policies of nations is basic to understanding the problem of security in a world of tension.

We must understand—as we conduct our foreign affairs and our military affairs—that while power and nationalism prevail, it is up to us to gain strength through cooperative efforts with other nations which have common ideals and objectives with our own. At the same time, we must create and maintain the power essential to persuasion, and to our own security in such a world. We must understand the role and nature, including the limitations, of this power if we are to exercise it wisely.

One of the great power potentials of this world is the United States of America and her allies. The other great power in this world is Soviet Russia and her satellites. As much as we desire peace, we must realize that we have two centers of power supporting opposing ideologies.

From a global viewpoint—and with the security of our Nation of prime importance—our military mission is to support a policy of preventing communism from gaining the manpower, the resources, the raw materials, and the industrial capacity essential to world domination. If Soviet Russia ever controls the entire Eurasian land mass, then the Soviet-satellite imperialism may have the broad base upon which to build the military power to rule the world.

Three times in the past 5 years the Kremlin-inspired imperialism has been thwarted by direct action.

In Berlin, Greece, and Korea, the free nations have opposed Communist aggression with a different type of action. But each time the power of the United States has been called upon and we have become involved. Each incident has cost us money, resources, and some lives.

But in each instance we have prevented the domination of one more area, and the absorption of another source of manpower, raw materials, and resources.

Korea, in spite of the importance of the engagement, must be looked upon with proper perspective. It is just one engagement, just one phase of this battle that we are having with the other power center in the world which opposes us and all we stand for. For 5 years this "guerrilla diplomacy" has been going on. In each of the actions in which we have participated to oppose this gangster conduct, we have risked world war III. But each time we have used methods short of total war. As costly as Berlin and Greece and Korea may be, they are less expensive than the vast destruction which would be inflicted upon all sides if a total war were to be precipitated.

I am under no illusion that our present strategy of using means short of total war to achieve our ends and oppose communism is a guarantee that a world war will not be thrust upon us. But a policy of patience and determination without provoking a world war, while we improve our military power, is one which we believe we must continue to follow.

As long as we keep the conflict within its present scope, we are holding to a minimum the forces we must commit and tie down.

The strategic alternative, enlargement of the war in Korea to include Red China, would probably delight the Kremlin more than anything else we could do. It would necessarily tie down additional forces, especially our sea power and our air power, while the Soviet Union would not be obliged to put a single man into the conflict.

Under present circumstances, we have recommended against enlarging the war. The course of action often described as a "limited war" with Red China would increase the risk we are taking by engaging too much of our power in an area that is not the critical strategic prize.

Red China is not the powerful nation seeking to dominate the world. Frankly, in the opinion of the Joint Chiefs of Staff, this strategy would involve us in the wrong war, at the wrong place, at the wrong time, and with the wrong enemy.

There are some other considerations which have tended to obscure this main issue. Some critics have not hesitated to state that the policy our Government is following, and its included strategy, is not that which has been recommended by the Joint Chiefs of Staff.

Statements have been made that the President, as Commander in Chief, and the Secretary of State and the Secretary of Defense, have a policy all their own, and that the Joint Chiefs of Staff have been overridden.

This is just not so. The Joint Chiefs of Staff have continually given their considered opinion—always from a military viewpoint—concerning our global capabilities and responsibilities and have recommended our present strategy in and for Korea. This has been the course of action which the Secretary of Defense and the Commander in Chief have adopted as far as practicable.

I pointed out earlier that many times the international policy considerations, including the views of our allies, are also considered and in some instances modify the course of action.

In other instances, even after the international considerations and the views of our allies have been considered, the proposed military strategy has not been altered.

Our over-all policy has been one of steadfast patience and determination in opposing Communist aggression without provoking unnecessarily a total war.

There are many critics who have become impatient with this strategy and who would like to call for a show-down. From a purely military viewpoint, this is not desirable. We are not in the best military position to seek a show-down, even if it were the Nation's desire to forfeit the chances for peace by precipitating a total war.

Undoubtedly, this statement will be misconstrued by some critics who will say, "Why are the Joint Chiefs of Staff advertising the fact that we are not militarily in a position to have a show-down?"

I can assure those critics that with the methods we must pursue in a democracy in order to support a military establishment—including this present investigation of our strategy in the Far East—our capabilities are not unknown to the Communists.

They are apt students of military power, and fully realize that although we are not prepared to deliver any ultimatum, we could hurt them badly if they attacked us or our friends.

They also know that with our potential, and the strength of our allies, in the long run they could not win a war with a United States that is alert, and continuously prepared.

I would not be a proponent of any policy which would ignore the military facts and rush us headlong into a show-down before we are ready. It is true that this policy of armed resistance to aggression, which we pursue while we are getting stronger, often risks a world war. But so far we have taken these risks without disastrous results.

I think our global strategy is paying off and I see no reason to let impatience alter it in the Far East. Certainly the course of action we are pursuing has avoided a total war which could only bring death and destruction to millions of Americans, both in the United States and on the battlefield. Our present course of action has at the same time won us respect and admiration everywhere in the world, both inside and outside the iron curtain.

There are also those who deplore the present military situation in

Korea and urge us to engage Red China in a larger war to solve this problem. Taking on Red China is not a decisive move, does not guarantee the end of the war in Korea, and may not bring China to her knees. We have only to look back to the five long years when the Japanese, one of the greatest military powers of that time, moved into China and had almost full control of a large part of China, and yet were never able to conclude that war successfully. I would say that from past history one would only jump from a smaller conflict to a larger deadlock at greater expense. My own feeling is to avoid such an engagement if possible because victory in Korea would not be assured and victory over Red China would be many years away. We believe that every effort should be made to settle the present conflict without extending it outside Korea. If this proves to be impossible, then other measures may have to be taken.

In my consideration of this viewpoint, I am going back to the basic objective of the American people—as much peace as we can gain without appeasement.

Some critics of our strategy say if we do not immediately bomb troop concentration points and airfields in Manchuria, it is "appeasement." If we do not immediately set up a blockade of Chinese ports—which to be successful would have to include British and Russian ports in Asia—it is "appeasement." These same critics would say that if we do not provide the logistical support and air and naval assistance to launch Chinese Nationalist troops into China it is "appeasement."

These critics ignore the vital questions:

Will these actions, if taken, actually assure victory in Korea?

Do these actions mean prolongation of the war by bringing Russia into the fight?

Will these actions strip us of our allies in Korea and in other parts of the world?

From a military viewpoint, appeasement occurs when you give up something, which is rightfully free, to an aggressor without putting up a struggle, or making him pay a price. Forsaking Korea—withdrawing from the fight unless we are forced out—would be an appeasement to aggression. Refusing to enlarge the quarrel to the point where our global capabilities are diminished, is certainly not appeasement but is a militarily sound course of action under the present circumstances.

It is my sincere hope that these hearings will encourage us as a

Nation to follow a steadfast and determined course of action in this world, which would deny any free nation to Soviet imperialism, and at the same time preserve the peace for which so many men died in World War I, World War II, and in Greece, Indochina, Malaya, and Korea.

GENERAL VANDENBERG'S TESTIMONY

17 ☙ GENERAL HOYT S. VANDENBERG, Chief of Staff of the Air Force, explained to the committee the military grounds on which he opposed MacArthur's proposals:[17]

Chairman [Richard B.—Eds.] RUSSELL. Did you participate in any meetings of the Joint Chiefs of Staff when restrictions were placed upon the bombing of the Chinese installations and bases and troop concentrations north of the Yalu River in Manchuria?

General VANDENBERG. Yes, sir.

Chairman RUSSELL. Did you approve of these orders which prohibited the Air Force in the Far East from attacking north of the Yalu?

General VANDENBERG. Yes, sir.

Chairman RUSSELL. Well, you are the Chief of Staff of the Air Force, General, and of course one of the stanchest champions of air power as a weapon of war. Why did you conclude that it should not be used north of the Yalu River?

General VANDENBERG. Mr. Chairman, the application of air power is not very well understood in this country by people in general, in my opinion. While I was and am today against bombing across the Yalu, it does not mean by any stretch of the imagination that I might not be for it tomorrow, a month from now, or 6 months from now.

Air power, and especially the application of strategic air power, should go to the heart of the industrial centers to become reasonably efficient. Now, the source of the matériel that is coming to the Chinese Communists and the North Koreans is from Russia. Therefore, hitting across the Yalu, we could destroy or lay waste to all of Manchuria and the principal cities of China if we utilized the full power of the United States Air Force. However, in doing that——

Senator MORSE. Did you say we could or could not?

General VANDENBERG (continuing). We could. In doing that,

[17] *Ibid.*, pp. 1378-9.

however, we are bound to get attrition. If we utilize less than the full power of the United States Air Force, in my opinion it might not and probably would not be conclusive.

And even if we utilized it and laid waste to it there is a possibility that it would not be conclusive. But the effect on the United States Air Force, with our start from approximately 40 groups, would fix it so that, should we have to operate in any other area with full power of the United States Air Force, we would not be able to.

The fact is that the United States is operating a shoestring air force in view of its global responsibilities.

Starting from a forty-odd-group Air Force, the aircraft industry is unable until almost 1953 to do much of a job toward supplying the airplanes that we would lose in war against any major opposition.

In my opinion, the United States Air Force is the single potential that has kept the balance of power in our favor. It is the one thing that has, up to date, kept the Russians from deciding to go to war.

In my opinion, we cannot afford to, what I would like to call, peck at the periphery as long as we have a shoestring Air Force.

While we can lay the industrial potential of Russia today waste, in my opinion, or we can lay the Manchurian countryside waste, as well as the principal cities of China, we cannot do both, again because we have got a shoestring Air Force. We are trying to operate a $20 million business with about $20,000.

Chairman RUSSELL. You base it then on purely military grounds rather than political considerations that it might bring Russia into the war or is that a military consideration?

General VANDENBERG. From my point of view, Mr. Chairman, I am looking at it from the point of view of the United States Air Force and the potential that it has that has kept the peace so far. If I may go on just a minute to enlarge a little bit—

Chairman RUSSELL. I did not intend to interrupt you, General. I did not know whether you were through or not.

General VANDENBERG. Today the United States is relatively safe from air attack. Tomorrow in my opinion we will not be. Because we are relatively safe from air attack today, an air force of a certain size can protect the United States and keep the balance of power in our favor.

Today we only have one job that we would have to do if we got into a major war with Russia, and that is to lay waste the industrial potential of that country. Tomorrow when they have developed their long-range air force and they have more atomic weapons, we have two jobs.

EISENHOWER'S CAMPAIGN SPEECH ON KOREA

18 ⌇ LATE IN JUNE 1951, after the failure of two massive Chinese offensives, the Communists agreed to engage in discussions to bring about a cease-fire and an armistice providing for the mutual withdrawal of forces from the 38th parallel. Truce negotiations began on July 10 but soon became bogged down in disputes on boundaries and then on forcible repatriation of prisoners of war. In the meantime American military efforts became largely defensive in character. In October 1952, after more than a year of fruitless talks, the Chinese temporarily broke off negotiations. By that time Korea had become the major issue in a bitterly fought contest for the U.S. presidency. The years of frustrating and bloody struggle, which had already cost the administration much politically, in combination with the magnetic personality of Dwight Eisenhower, assured a Republican victory in 1952.

Eisenhower, whose administration would finally negotiate the Korean truce, made his major campaign pronouncement on the subject of the war on October 24, 1952:[18]

In this anxious autumn for America, one fact looms above all others in our people's mind. One tragedy challenges all men dedicated to the work of peace. One word shouts denial to those who foolishly pretend that ours is not a nation at war.

This fact, this tragedy, this word is: Korea.

A small country, Korea has been, for more than two years, the battleground for the costliest foreign war our nation has fought, excepting the two world wars. It has been the burial ground for 20,000 American dead. It has been another historic field of honor for the valor and skill and tenacity of American soldiers.

All these things it has been—and yet one thing more. It has been a symbol—a telling symbol—of the foreign policy of our nation.

It has been a sign—a warning sign—of the way the Administration has conducted our world affairs.

It has been a measure—a damning measure—of the quality of leadership we have been given.

Tonight I am going to talk about our foreign policy and of its

[18] Excerpts reprinted from *The New York Times*, October 25, 1952, p. 8.

supreme symbol—the Korean war. I am not going to give you elaborate generalizations—but hard, tough facts. I am going to state the
unvarnished truth.

What, then, are the plain facts?

The biggest fact about the Korean war is this: It was never inevitable, it was never inescapable, no fantastic fiat of history decreed
that little South Korea—in the summer of 1950—would fatally tempt
Communist aggressors as their easiest victim. No demonic destiny
decreed that America had to be bled this way in order to keep South
Korea free and to keep freedom itself self-respecting.

We are not mute prisoners of history. That is a doctrine for
totalitarians, it is no creed for free men.

There is a Korean war—and we are fighting it—for the simplest of
reasons: Because free leadership failed to check and to turn back
Communist ambition before it savagely attacked us. The Korean war
—more perhaps than any other war in history—simply and swiftly
followed the collapse of our political defenses. There is no other
reason than this: We failed to read and to outwit the totalitarian
mind. . . .

Then, one week later [after the U.S. government announced that
it would not provide military aid to Chinese forces on Formosa—Eds.],
the Secretary of State announced his famous "defense perimeter"—
publicly advising our enemies that, so far as nations outside this
perimeter were concerned, "no person can guarantee these areas
against military attack." Under these circumstances, it was cold
comfort to the nations outside this perimeter to be reminded that
they could appeal to the United Nations.

These nations, of course, included Korea. The armies of communism, thus informed, began their big build-up. Six months later they
were ready to strike across the Thirty-eighth Parallel. They struck
on June 25, 1950.

On that day, the record of political and diplomatic failure of this
Administration was completed and sealed.

The responsibility for this record cannot be dodged or evaded.
Even if not a single Republican leader had warned so clearly against
the coming disaster, the responsibility for the fateful political decisions
would still rest wholly with the men charged with making those
decisions—in the Department of State and in the White House.
They cannot escape that responsibility now or ever.

When the enemy struck, on that June day of 1950, what did America do? It did what it always has done in all its times of peril. It appealed to the heroism of its youth.

This appeal was utterly right and utterly inescapable. It was inescapable not only because this was the only way to defend the idea of collective freedom against savage aggression. That appeal was inescapable because there was now in the plight into which we had stumbled no other way to save honor and self-respect.

The answer to that appeal has been what any American knew it would be. It has been sheer valor—valor on all the Korean mountainsides that, each day, bear fresh scars of new graves.

Now—in this anxious autumn—from these heroic men there comes back an answering appeal. It is no whine, no whimpering plea. It is a question that addresses itself to simple reason. It asks: Where do we go from here? When comes the end? Is there an end?

These questions touch all of us. They demand truthful answers. Neither glib promises nor glib excuses will serve. They would be no better than the glib prophecies that brought us to this pass.

To these questions there are two false answers—both equally false. The first would be any answer that dishonestly pledged an end to war in Korea by any imminent, exact date. Such a pledge would brand its speaker as a deceiver.

The second and equally false answer declares that nothing can be done to speed a secure peace. It dares to tell us that we, the strongest nation in the history of freedom, can only wait—and wait—and wait. Such a statement brands its speaker as a defeatist.

My answer—candid and complete—is this:

The first task of a new administration will be to review and reexamine every course of action open to us with one goal in view: To bring the Korean war to an early and honorable end. That is my pledge, to the American people.

For this task a wholly new Administration is necessary. The reason for this is simple. The old Administration cannot be expected to repair what it failed to prevent.

Where will a new Administration begin?

It will begin with its President taking a simple, firm resolution. That resolution will be: To forego the diversions of politics and to concentrate on the job of ending the Korean war—until that job is honorably done.

That job requires a personal trip to Korea.

I shall make that trip. Only in that way could I learn how best to serve the American people in the cause of peace.

I shall go to Korea.

That is my second pledge to the American people.

Carefully, then, this new Administration, unfettered by past decisions and inherited mistakes, can review every factor—military, political and psychological—to be mobilized in speeding a just peace.

Progress along at least two lines can instantly begin. We can—first—step up the program of training and arming the South Korean forces. Manifestly, under the circumstances of today, United Nations forces cannot abandon that unhappy land. But just as troops of the Republic of Korea covet and deserve the honor of defending their frontiers, so should we give them maximum assistance to insure their ability to do so.

Then, United Nations forces in reserve positions and supporting roles would be assurance that disaster would not again strike.

We can—secondly—shape our psychological warfare program into a weapon capable of cracking the Communist front.

Beyond all this we must carefully weigh all interrelated courses of action. We will, of course, constantly confer with associated free nations of Asia and with the cooperating members of the United Nations. Thus we could bring into being a practical plan for world peace.

That is my third pledge to you.

As the next Administration goes to work for peace, we must be guided at every instant by that lesson I spoke of earlier. The vital lesson is this: To vacillate, to appease, to placate is only to invite war—vaster war—bloodier war. In the words of the late Senator [Arthur H.] Vandenberg, appeasement is not the road to peace; it is only surrender on the installment plan.

I will always reject appeasement.

And that is my fourth pledge to you.

A nation's foreign policy is a much graver matter than rustling papers and bustling conferences. It is much more than diplomatic decisions and trade treaties and military arrangements.

A foreign policy is the face and voice of a whole people. It is all that the world sees and hears and understands about a single nation. It expresses the character and the faith and the will of that nation. In this, a nation is like any individual of our personal acquaintance;

the simplest gesture can betray hesitation or weakness, the merest inflection of voice can reveal doubt or fear.

It is in this deep sense that our foreign policy has faltered and failed.

For a democracy, a great election, such as this, signifies a most solemn trial. It is the time when—to the bewilderment of all tyrants —the people sit in judgment upon the leaders. It is the time when these leaders are summoned before the bar of public decision. There they must give evidence both to justify their actions and explain their intentions.

In the great trial of this election, the judges—the people—must not be deceived into believing that the choice is between isolationism and internationalism. That is a debate of the dead past. The vast majority of Americans of both parties know that to keep their own nation free, they bear a majestic responsibility for freedom through all the world. As practical people, Americans also know the critical necessity of unimpaired access to raw materials on other continents for our own economic and military strength.

Today the choice—the real choice—lies between policies that assume that responsibility awkwardly and fearfully—and policies that accept that responsibility with sure purpose and firm will. The choice is between foresight and blindness, between doing and apologizing, between planning and improvising.

In rendering their verdict, the people must judge with courage and with wisdom. For—at this date—any faltering in America's leadership is a capital offense against freedom.

In this trial, my testimony, of a personal kind, is quite simple. A soldier all my life, I have enlisted in the greatest cause of my life —the cause of peace.

I do not believe it a presumption for me to call the effort of all who have enlisted with me—a crusade.

I use that word only to signify two facts. First: We are united and devoted to a just cause of the purest meaning to all humankind. Second: We know that—for all the might of our effort—victory can come only with the gift of God's help.

In this spirit—humble servants of a proud ideal—we do soberly say: This is a crusade.

Bibliography

The literature on the Truman years is already huge. Though there is no scholarly history of the administration, Alfred Steinberg, *The Man from Missouri: The Life and Times of Harry S. Truman* (New York, 1962), briefly discusses Truman's presidency. Herbert Agar, *The Price of Power* (Chicago, 1957), Eric Goldman, *The Crucial Decade: America, 1945–1955* (New York, 1956), and Walter Johnson, *1600 Pennsylvania Avenue: Presidents and People Since 1929* (Boston, 1960), survey the period. Truman's eight years also receive considerable attention in Oscar Barck, Jr., *A History of the United States Since 1945* (New York, 1965); Frank Freidel, *America in the Twentieth Century* (New York, 1960); Arthur Link, with the assistance of William Catton, *American Epoch: A History of the United States Since the 1890's* (2nd ed.; New York, 1963); Henry B. Parkes and Vincent Carosso, *Recent America*, Vol. II (New York, 1963); David Shannon, *Twentieth Century America: The United States Since the 1890s* (Chicago, 1963); and William Zornow, *America at Mid-Century* (Cleveland, 1959). Probably the best summary of events and discussion of the bibliography on Truman's government is the forthcoming, but still untitled, volume edited by Richard Kirkendall.

Truman's *Memoirs*, 2 vols. (Garden City, L.I., 1955), and the still unfinished series *Public Papers of the Presidents: Harry S. Truman, 1945–1951*, 7 vols. (Washington, D.C., 1961–1966), are essential to any serious study of the administration. Congressional hearings and reports, as well as the *Congressional Record*, are invaluable sources of information for domestic and foreign policies. Reports by departments and agencies also constitute an important record of, and guide to, federal activities.

For foreign affairs the major primary sources are *Department of State Bulletin*; Senate Foreign Relations Committee, *Decade of American Foreign Policy: Basic Documents*, Eighty-first Congress, first session, Senate Document 123; and a shorter version, Francis Wilcox and Thorsten Kalijarvi, eds., *Recent American Foreign Policy: Basic Documents, 1941–1951* (New York, 1952); and the Department of State, *Foreign Relations Series*, which, at the time of writing, has not progressed beyond the Potsdam Conference. Useful summaries of foreign affairs are available in the Council of Foreign Relations, *The United States in World Affairs*, and the Royal Institute of International Affairs, *Survey of International Relations*. Among the available studies of postwar foreign policy are Denna F. Fleming, *The Cold War and Its Origins*, 2 vols. (Garden City, 1961); Norman Graebner, *Cold War Diplomacy* (New York, 1962); John Lukacs, *History of the Cold War* (New York, 1961); and John Spanier, *American Foreign Policy Since World War II* (New York, 1962). The best sources for bibliography on foreign affairs are Henry Roberts, *Foreign Affairs Bibliography: A Selected and Annotated List of Books on International Relations, 1942–1952* (New York, 1955), and his *Foreign Affairs Bibliography, 1952–1962* (New York, 1964).

For students wishing to read further in the topics included in this volume, the following selective bibliography will serve as a beginning.

1. The A-Bomb Decision

Alperovitz, Gar. *Atomic Diplomacy: Hiroshima and Potsdam*. New York, 1965.

Arnold, Henry. *Global Mission*. New York, 1949.

Atomic Energy Commission. *In the Matter of J. Robert Oppenheimer*. Washington, D.C., 1954.

Baldwin, Hanson. *Great Mistakes of the War*. New York, 1950.

Batchelder, Robert. *The Irreversible Decision*. Boston, 1962.

Baxter, James. *Scientists Against Time*. Boston, 1946.

Butow, Robert. *Japan's Decision to Surrender*. Stanford, 1954.

Byrnes, James. *Speaking Frankly*. New York, 1947.

Churchill, Winston. *The Second World War*, Vol. VI. Boston, 1953.

Compton, Arthur H. *Atomic Quest*. New York, 1956.

Compton, Karl. "If the Atomic Bomb Had Not Been Used," *Atlantic Monthly*, December 1946.

Cousins, Norman, and Thomas Finletter. "A Beginning for Sanity," *Saturday Review*, June 15, 1946.

Department of Defense. *The Entry of the Soviet Union into the War Against Japan; Military Plans, 1941–1945*. Washington, D.C., 1955.

Eisenhower, Dwight. *Crusade in Europe*. New York, 1947.

Feis, Herbert. *Between War and Peace: The Potsdam Conference*. Princeton, 1960.

———. *Japan Subdued: The Atomic Bomb and the End of the War in the Pacific*. Princeton, 1961.

Giovannitti, Len, and Frederick Freed. *The Decision to Drop the Bomb*. New York, 1965.

Grew, Joseph. *Turbulent Era*, Vol. II. Boston, 1952.

Groves, Leslie. *Now It Can Be Told: The Story of the Manhattan Project*. New York, 1962.

Hewlett, Richard, and Oscar Anderson, Jr. *The New World*, Vol. I. University Park, Pa., 1962.

"Ike on Ike," *Newsweek*, November 11, 1963.

Kase, Toshikazu. *Journey to the Missouri*. New Haven, 1950.

Kawai, Kazuo. "Mokusatsu, Japan's Response to the Potsdam Declaration," *Pacific Historical Review*, November 1950.

King, Ernest, and Walter Whitehill. *Fleet Admiral King*. New York, 1962.

Knebel, Fletcher, and Charles Bailey. "The Fight Over the A-Bomb," *Look*, August 13, 1963.

———. *No High Ground*. New York, 1960.

Leahy, William. *I Was There*. New York, 1950.

McCloy, John. *The Challenge to American Foreign Policy*. Cambridge, Mass., 1963.

Morison, Elting. *Turmoil and Tradition: The Life and Times of Henry L. Stimson*. Boston, 1960.

Morton, Louis. "The Decision to Use the Atomic Bomb," in *Command Decisions*, ed. Kent Roberts Greenfield. Washington, D.C., 1958.

Neumann, William. *Making the Peace, 1941–1945*. Washington, D.C., 1950.

Smith, Alice K. *A Peril and a Hope: The Scientists' Movement in America: 1945–47*. Chicago, 1965.

Stimson, Henry. "The Decision to Use the Atomic Bomb," *Harper's Magazine*, February 1947.

——— and McGeorge Bundy. *On Active Service in Peace and War*. New York, 1958.

Strauss, Lewis. *Men and Decisions*. New York, 1962.

"Was A-Bomb on Japan a Mistake?" *U.S. News and World Report*, August 15, 1960.

2. Inflation and Politics, 1945–1946

Abbot, Charles. *The Federal Debt: Structure and Impact*. New York, 1953.

Alinsky, Saul. *John L. Lewis: An Unauthorized Biography*. Chicago, 1956.

Bailey, Stephen. *Congress Makes a Law: The Story Behind the Employment Act of 1946*. New York, 1950.

Bernstein, Barton. "The Postwar Famine and Price Control, 1946," *Agricultural History*, October 1964.

————. "The Removal of War Production Board Controls on Business, 1944–1946," *Business History Review*, Summer 1965.

————. "The Truman Administration and Its Reconversion Wage Policy," *Labor History*, Fall 1965.

————. "The Truman Administration and the Steel Strike of 1946," *Journal of American History*, March 1966.

————. "Walter Reuther and the UAW-GM Strike of 1945–46," *Michigan History*, September 1965.

Bureau of the Budget. *United States at War*. Washington, D.C., 1946.

Byrnes, James. *All in One Lifetime*, New York, 1958.

Calkins, Fay. *The CIO and the Democratic Party*. Chicago, 1952.

Chandler, Lester. *Inflation in the United States, 1940–1948*. New York, 1951.

Coffin, This. *Missouri Compromise*. Boston, 1947.

Daniels, Jonathan. *The Man From Independence*. Philadelphia, 1950.

Eccles, Marriner. *Beckoning Frontiers: Personal and Public Recollections*. New York, 1951.

Fesler, James, et al. *Industrial Mobilization for War*. Washington, D.C., 1947.

Fforde, J. S. *The Federal Reserve System*. New York, 1954.

Friedman, Milton, and Anna Schwartz. *A Monetary History of the United States*. Princeton, 1963.

Galbraith, John. *A Theory of Price Control*. Cambridge, Mass., 1952.

Glasser, Carrie. "Union Wage Policy in Bituminous Coal," *Industrial and Labor Relations*, July 1948.

Hagen, Everett. "The Reconversion Period: Reflections of a Forecaster," *Review of Economics and Statistics*, May 1947.

Hickman, Bert. *Growth and Stability in the Postwar Economy*. Washington, D.C., 1961.

Holmans, A. E. *United States Fiscal Policy, 1945–1959*. New York, 1961.

Knipe, James. *The Federal Reserve and the American Dollar: Problems and Policies, 1946–1964*. Chapel Hill, N.C., 1965.

Lubell, Samuel. *The Future of American Politics*. New York, 1952.

Murphy, Henry. *The National Debt in War and Transition*. New York, 1950.

Neustadt, Richard. "Congress and the Fair Deal: A Legislative Balance Sheet," in *Public Policy*, eds. Carl Friedrich and John Galbraith. Vol. V, 1954.

Seidman, Joel. *American Labor from Defense to Reconversion*. Chicago, 1953.

Somers, Herman. *Presidential Agency: The Office of War Mobilization and Reconversion*. Cambridge, Mass., 1950.

Warne, Colston, et al., eds. *Labor in Postwar America*. New York, 1949.

3. The Fair Deal, 1945–1953

Abels, Jules. *Out of the Jaws of Victory.* New York, 1959.

Abrams, Charles. *Forbidden Neighbors: A Study of Prejudice in Housing.* New York, 1955.

Adelman, M. A. "The Measurement of Industrial Concentration," *Review of Economics and Statistics,* November 1951.

Ader, William. "Why the Dixiecrats Failed," *Journal of Politics,* August 1953.

Allen, Robert, and William Shannon. *The Truman Merry-Go-Round.* New York, 1950.

Bell, Daniel. *The End of Ideology.* Glencoe, Ill., 1960.

——, ed. *The New American Right.* New York, 1955.

——. "Taft-Hartley, Five Years Old," *Fortune,* July 1952.

Benedict, Murray. *Farm Policies of the United States, 1790–1950.* New York, 1953.

Berelson, Bernard, Paul Lazarsfeld, and William McPhee. *Voting.* Chicago, 1954.

Berger, Morroe. *Equality by Statute.* New York, 1952.

Blaustein, Albert, and Clyde Ferguson. *Desegregation and the Law.* New Brunswick, 1957.

Brock, Clifton. *Americans for Democratic Action: Its Role in National Politics.* Washington, D.C., 1962.

Calkins, Fay. *The CIO and the Democratic Party.* Chicago, 1952.

Campbell, Angus, Gerald Gurin, and Warren Miller. *The Voter Decides.* Evanston, 1954.

Carleton, William. "The Dilemma of the Democrats," *Virginia Quarterly Review,* July 1948.

—— "The Fate of Our Fourth Party," *Yale Review,* Spring 1949.

Carr, Robert. *The Federal Protection of Civil Rights.* Ithaca, 1947.

Christenson, Reo. *The Brannan Plan: Farm Politics and Policy.* Ann Arbor, 1959.

Daniels, Jonathan. *The Man from Independence.* Philadelphia, 1950.

Davies, Richard. *Housing Reform During the Truman Administration.* Columbia, Mo., 1966.

Einaudi, Mario. *The Roosevelt Revolution.* New York, 1959.

Eldersveld, Samuel. "The Influence of Metropolitan Party Pluralities in Presidential Elections Since 1920: A Study of Twelve Key Cities," *American Political Science Review,* December 1949.

Garfinkel, Herbert. *When Negroes March: The March on Washington Movement in the Organizational Politics for FEPC.* Glencoe, 1959.

Gregory, C. O. *Labor and the Law.* New York, 1958.

Hartley, Fred A., Jr. Our New National Labor Party. New York, 1958.

Hendrix, W. E. "The Brannan Plan in the Cotton South," Journal of Farm Economics, August 1949.

Hofstadter, Richard. "What Happened to the Anti-Trust Movement? Notes on the Evolution of a Creed," in The Business Establishment, ed. Earl Cheit. New York, 1965.

Kesselman, Louis. The Social Politics of FEPC. Chapel Hill, 1948.

Key, V. O. Southern Politics in State and Nation. New York, 1949.

Konvitz, Milton. The Constitution and Civil Rights. New York, 1947.

Lee, R. Alton. "Federal Assistance to Depressed Areas in Postwar Recessions," Western Economic Journal, Fall 1963.

————. "The Turnip Session of the Do-Nothing Congress: Presidential Campaign Strategy," Southwestern Social Science Quarterly, December 1963.

Lemmon, S. M. "Ideology of the Dixiecrat Movement," Social Forces, December 1951.

Lewis, Wilfred. Federal Fiscal Policy in the Postwar Recessions. Washington, D.C., 1962.

Longaker, Richard. The Presidency and Individual Liberty. Ithaca, 1961.

Lubell, Samuel. The Future of American Politics. New York, 1952.

MacDougall, Curtis. Gideon's Army. 3 vols., 1965-1966.

McConnell, Grant. The Decline of Agrarian Democracy. Berkeley, 1953.

McNaughton, Frank, and Walter Hehmeyer. Harry Truman: President. New York, 1958.

McWilliams, Carey. Brothers Under the Skin. Rev. ed. New York, 1951.

Maslow, Will. "FEPC—A Case History in Parliamentary Maneuver," University of Chicago Law Review, June 1946.

Millis, Harry, and Emily Brown. From the Wagner Act to Taft-Hartley. Chicago, 1950.

Moon, Henry. Balance of Power: The Negro Vote. New York, 1948.

Neustadt, Richard. "Congress and the Fair Deal: A Legislative Balance Sheet," in Public Policy, eds. Carl Friedrich and John Galbraith. Vol. V, 19

Nichols, Lee. Breakthrough on the Color Front. New York, 1954.

Nourse, Edwin. Economics in the Public Service: Administrative Aspects of the Employment Act. New York, 1953.

Pomper, Gerald. "Labor and Congress: The Repeal of Taft-Hartley," Labor History, Fall 1961.

President's Committee on Civil Rights. To Secure These Rights. Washington, D.C., 1947.

President's Committee on Equality of Treatment and Opportunity in the Armed Services. Freedom to Serve. Washington, D.C., 1950.

Riddick, F. M. "The Eighty-first Congress," *Western Political Quarterly,* March 1951.

————. "The Eighty-second Congress," *Western Political Quarterly,* March 1952.

Ruchames, Louis. *Race, Jobs and Politics.* New York, 1953.

Schmidt, Karl. *Henry Wallace: Quixotic Crusade.* Syracuse, 1960.

Schnapper, Morris, ed. *The Truman Program.* Washington, D.C., 1949.

Shannon, J. B. "Presidential Politics in the South," *Journal of Politics,* August 1948.

Steiner, George. *The Government's Role in Economic Life.* New York, 1953.

Sutton, Francis, *et al. The American Business Creed.* Cambridge, Mass., 1956.

Taft, Philip. *The A.F. of L. from the Death of Gompers to the Merger.* New York, 1959.

Truman, Harry. *Freedom and Equality,* ed. David Horton. Columbia, Mo., 1960.

Van Auken, Cecelia. "The Negro Press in the 1948 Election," *Journalism Quarterly,* December 1949.

White, Walter. *A Man Called White.* New York, 1948.

————. *How Far the Promised Land.* New York, 1955.

White, William S. *The Taft Story.* New York, 1954.

Whitney, Simon. *Antitrust Policies: American Experience in Twenty Industries.* 2 vols. New York, 1958.

Woodward, C. Vann. *The Strange Career of Jim Crow.* 2nd rev. ed. New York, 1966.

4. The Cold War, 1945–1953

Acheson, Dean. *The Pattern of Responsibility,* ed. McGeorge Bundy. Boston, 1952.

Almond, Gabriel. *The American People and Foreign Policy.* New York, 1950.

Bailey, Thomas. *America Faces Russia: Russian American Relations from Early Times to Our Day.* Ithaca, 1950.

Barnet, Richard, and Marcus Raskin. *After 20 Years: Alternatives to the Cold War in Europe.* New York, 1965.

Bechhoefer, Bernard. *Postwar Negotiations for Arms Control.* Washington, D.C., 1961.

Bell, Coral. Negotiation from Strength. New York, 1963.

Bradley, Omar. A Soldier's Story. New York, 1951.

Bryant, Arthur. Triumph in the West: A History of the War Years (based on the diaries and autobiographical notes of Field-Marshal Viscount Lord Alanbrooke).

Byrnes, James. All in One Lifetime. New York, 1958.

Carr, Albert. Truman, Stalin and Peace. New York, 1950.

Ciechanowski, Jan. Defeat in Victory. New York, 1947.

Clark, Mark. Calculated Risk. New York, 1950.

Clay, Lucius. Decision in Germany. New York, 1950.

Connally, Tom. My Name is Tom Connally. New York, 1954.

Current, Richard N. Secretary Stimson. New Brunswick, N.J., 1954.

Curry, George. "James F. Byrnes," in American Secretaries of State and Their Diplomacy, ed. Robert Ferrell. Vol. XIV, New York, 1966.

Dallin, Alexander. Soviet Conduct in World Affairs. New York, 1960.

Davison, W. Phillips. The Berlin Blockade. Princeton, 1958.

Deane, John. The Strange Alliance: The Story of Our Efforts at Wartime Cooperation with Russia. New York, 1947.

DeGaulle, Charles. War Memoirs, Vol. III. New York, 1960.

Dennett, Raymond, and J. E. Johnson, eds. Negotiating with the Russians. Boston, 1951.

Department of State. American Foreign Policy, 1950–1955. 2 vols. Washington, D.C., 1957.

———. Documents on Disarmament, 1945–1960. 3 vols. Washington, D.C., 1960–61.

———. In Quest of Peace and Security: Selected Documents. Washington, D.C., 1951.

———. Making of Peace Treaties, 1941–1947. Washington, D.C., 1947.

———. Paris Peace Conference, 1946: Selected Documents. Washington, D.C., 1954.

———. Participation in International Conferences, July 1, 1947 . . . June 30, 1950. 3 vols. Washington, D.C., 1949–50.

Deutscher, Isaac. The Great Contest: Russia and the West. New York, 1960.

———. Russia: What Next? New York, 1953.

———. Stalin, A Political Biography. New York, 1950.

Djilas, Milovan. Conversations with Stalin. New York, 1963.

Dulles, John Foster. War or Peace. New York, 1950.

Eden, Anthony. The Memoirs of Anthony Eden, Vols. II and III. Boston, 1960, 1965.

Epstein, Leon. Britain—Uneasy Ally. Chicago, 1954.

Feis, Herbert. *Churchill, Roosevelt, Stalin: The War They Waged and the Peace They Sought.* Princeton, 1953.

Fenno, Richard, ed. *The Yalta Conference.* New York, 1955.

Ferrell, Robert. "George C. Marshall," in *American Secretaries of State and Their Diplomacy,* ed. Robert Ferrell. Vol. XV, New York, 1966.

Forrestal, James. *The Forrestal Diaries,* ed. Walter Millis. New York, 1955.

Goodrich, Leland. *The United Nations.* New York, 1959.

Graebner, Norman. *The New Isolationism.* New York, 1956.

Grosser, Alfred. *The Colossus Again: Western Germany from Defeat to Rearmament.* New York, 1955.

Hammond, Paul. "Directives for the Occupation of Germany: The Washington Controversy," in *American Civil-Military Relations,* ed. Harold Stein. Birmingham, 1963.

Harriman, W. Averell. *Peace with Russia?* New York, 1959.

Healey, Denis, ed. *The Curtain Falls.* London, 1951.

Herz, Martin. *Beginnings of the Cold War.* Bloomington, Ind., 1966.

Hillman, William, ed. *Mr. President.* New York, 1952.

Horowitz, David. *The Free World Colossus: A Critique of American Foreign Policy in the Cold War.* New York, 1965.

Hoskins, Halford. *The Atlantic Pact.* Washington, D.C., 1949.

Huntington, Samuel. *The Common Defense: Strategic Programs in National Politics.* Princeton, 1961.

Ismay, Hastings. *The Memoirs of Lord Ismay.* London, 1960.

Jones, Joseph. *The Fifteen Weeks.* New York, 1955.

Kecskemeti, Paul. *Strategic Surrender: The Politics of Victory and Defeat.* Stanford, 1958.

Kennan, George F. *American Diplomacy, 1900–1950.* Chicago, 1951.

———. *Russia, the Atom, and the West.* New York, 1957.

Kousoulas, Dimitrios. *Revolution and Defeat: The Story of the Greek Communist Party.* New York, 1965.

Lane, A. *I Saw Poland Betrayed.* Indianapolis, 1959.

Lilienthal, David. *Journals of David E. Lilienthal,* Vol. II. New York, 1964.

Lippmann, Walter. *The Cold War: A Study in U.S. Foreign Policy.* New York, 1947.

Lukacs, John. *Decline and Rise of Europe.* Garden City, 1965.

———. *The Great Powers and Eastern Europe.* New York, 1953.

Lynd, Staughton. "How the Cold War Began," *Commentary,* November 1960.

McNeill, William. *America, Britain and Russia, Their Cooperation and Their Conflict.* New York, 1953.

————. *Greece: American Aid in Action, 1947–1956.* New York, 1956.

Martin, Laurence. "The American Decision to Rearm Germany," in *American Civil-Military Relations,* ed. Harold Stein. Birmingham, 1963.

Merkl, Peter. *The Origins of the West-German Republic.* New York, 1963.

Mikolajczyk, Stanislaw. *The Rape of Poland: Pattern of Soviet Aggression.* New York, 1948.

Morgenthau, Hans. *The Impasse of American Foreign Policy.* Chicago, 1962.

————. *In Defense of the National Interest.* New York, 1951.

Morray, J. P. *From Yalta to Disarmament.* New York, 1961.

Mosely, Philip. *The Kremlin and World Politics.* New York, 1960.

Murphy, Robert. *Diplomat Among Warriors.* New York, 1964.

Nettl, John. *The Eastern Zone and Soviet Policy in Germany, 1945–50.* New York, 1951.

Nogee, Joseph. *Soviet Policy Toward International Control of Atomic Energy.* South Bend, 1961.

Opie, Redvers, et al. *The Search for Peace Settlements.* Washington, D.C., 1951.

Osgood, Robert. *NATO: The Entangling Alliance.* Chicago, 1963.

Papandreou, Georgios. *The Third War.* Athens, 1948.

Penrose, Ernest. *Economic Planning for the Peace.* Princeton, 1953.

Price, Harry. *The Marshall Plan and Its Meaning.* Ithaca, 1955.

Rogow, Arnold. *James Forrestal.* New York, 1964.

Rostow, Walt W. *Dynamics of Soviet Society.* New York, 1952.

————. *United States in the World Arena.* New York, 1960.

Rozek, Edward. *Allied Wartime Diplomacy: A Pattern in Poland.* New York, 1958.

Russell, Ruth. *A History of the United Nations Charter.* New York, 1958.

Schilling, Warner. "The H-Bomb Decision: How to Decide without Actually Choosing," *Political Science Quarterly,* March 1961.

———— et al. *Strategy, Politics and Defense Budgets.* New York, 1962.

Schuman, Frederic. *The Cold War: Retrospect and Prospect.* Baton Rouge, 1962.

Senate Foreign Relations Committee. *Documents on Germany, 1944–1959.* Washington, D.C., 1959.

Seton-Watson, Hugh. *Neither War Nor Peace.* New York, 1963.

Sherwood, Robert. *Roosevelt and Hopkins: An Intimate History.* New York, 1950.

Shulman, Marshall. *Stalin's Foreign Policy Reappraised.* Cambridge, Mass., 1963.

Smith, Gaddis. *American Diplomacy During the Second World War, 1941–1945.* New York, 1965.

Smith, Jean. *The Defense of Berlin.* Baltimore, 1963.

Smith, Walter B. *My Three Years in Moscow.* New York, 1950.

Snell, John, et al., eds. *The Meaning of Yalta: Big Three Diplomacy and the New Balance of Power.* Baton Rouge, 1956.

————. *Wartime Origins of the East-West Dilemma Over Germany.* New Orleans, 1958.

Stalin, Joseph. *Stalin's Correspondence with Churchill, Attlee, Roosevelt and Truman, 1941–45.* Moscow, 1957.

Stettinius, Edward, Jr. *Roosevelt and the Russians: The Yalta Conference,* ed. Walter Johnson. New York, 1951.

Taft, Robert. *A Foreign Policy for Americans.* New York, 1951.

Thomas, Lewis, and Richard Frye. *The United States and Turkey and Iran.* Cambridge, Mass., 1953.

Vandenberg, Arthur. *The Private Papers of Senator Vandenberg,* ed. Arthur Vandenberg, Jr., New York, 1952.

Walker, Richard. "E. R. Stettinius, Jr.," in *The American Secretaries of State and Their Diplomacy,* ed. Robert Ferrell. Vol. XIV, New York, 1965.

Wallace, Henry. *Toward World Peace.* New York, 1948.

Warburg, James. *Germany, Key to Peace.* Cambridge, Mass., 1953.

Westerfield, H. Bradford. *Foreign Policy and Party Politics: Pearl Harbor to Korea.* New Haven, 1955.

Williams, William A. *American-Russian Relations, 1781–1947.* New York, 1952.

————. *The Tragedy of American Diplomacy.* Rev. ed. New York, 1962.

Winant, John. *Letter from Grosvenor Square.* New York, 1947.

Wolff, Robert. *The Balkans in Our Time.* Cambridge, Mass., 1956.

Woodhouse, C. M. *British Foreign Policy Since the Second World War.* New York, 1962.

World Peace Foundation. *European Peace Treaties After World War II.* Boston, 1954.

Xydis, Stephen. *Greece and the Great Powers, 1944–1947.* Thesaloniki, 1963.

Zink, Harold. *The United States in Germany, 1944–1955.* Princeton, 1957.

5. China Policy, 1945–1950

Beloff, Max. *Soviet Policy in the Far East.* London, 1953.

Bullitt, William. "Report to the American People on China," *Life,* October 13, 1947.

De Jaegher, Raymond, and Irene Kuhn. *The Enemy Within*. New York, 1952.

Department of State. *United States Relations with China*. Washington, D.C., 1949.

Fairbank, John K. *The United States and China*. Rev. ed. Cambridge, Mass., 1958.

Feis, Herbert. *The China Tangle*. Princeton, 1953.

Latourette, Kenneth S. *The American Record in the Far East, 1945–1951*. New York, 1953.

North, Robert C. *Moscow and the Chinese Communists*. 2nd ed. Stanford, 1963.

Senate Committee on Armed Services and Committee on Foreign Relations. *Hearings, Military Situation in the Far East*. Washington, D.C., 1951.

Stilwell, Joseph. *The Stilwell Papers*, ed. Theodore White. New York, 1948.

Tsou, Tang. *America's Failure in China. 1941–1950*. Chicago, 1963.

Utley, Freda. *The China Story*. Chicago, 1951.

Wedemeyer, General Albert C. *Wedemeyer Reports!* New York, 1958.

Westerfield, H. Bradford. *Foreign Policy and Party Politics*. New Haven, 1955.

Young, Arthur. *China and the Helping Hand, 1937–1945*. Cambridge, Mass., 1963.

6. Loyalty and Security

American Civil Liberties Union. *From War to Peace: American Civil Liberties, 1945–46*. New York, 1947.

———. *Our Uncertain Liberties, 1947–48*. New York, 1949.

Anderson, Jack, and R. W. May. *McCarthy*. Boston, 1952.

Barth, Alan. *The Loyalty of Free Men*. New York, 1951.

Bell, Daniel, ed. *The New American Right*. New York, 1955.

Biddle, Francis. *The Fear of Freedom*. New York, 1951.

Bontecou, Eleanor. *The Federal Loyalty and Security Program*. Ithaca, 1953.

Brown, Ralph. *Loyalty and Security*. New Haven, 1958.

Buckley, William, Jr., and L. Brent Bozell. *McCarthy and His Enemies*. Chicago, 1954.

Budenz, Louis. *Men Without Faces*. New York, 1950.

Carr, Robert. *The House Committee on Un-American Activities, 1945–1950*. Ithaca, 1952.

Chafee, Zechariah. *The Blessings of Liberty*. Philadelphia, 1956.

———. *Free Speech in the United States*. Cambridge, Mass., 1946.

Chambers, Whittaker. *Witness*. New York, 1956.

Chase, Harold. Security and Liberty: The Problem of Native Communists, 1947–1955. Garden City, N.Y., 1955.

Cook, Fred. The Unfinished Story of Alger Hiss. New York, 1958.

Cooke, Alistair. A Generation on Trial: U.S.A. vs. Alger Hiss. New York, 1950.

Coser, Louis, and Irving Howe. The American Communist Party. New York, 1957.

Cushman, Robert. Civil Liberties in the United States. Ithaca, 1956.

Davis, Elmer. But We Were Born Free. New York, 1952.

Donovan, William, and Mary Jones. "Program for a Democratic Counter-Attack to Communist Penetration of Government Service," Yale Law Journal, July 1949.

Emerson, Thomas, and David Haber. Political and Civil Rights in the United States. Buffalo, 1952.

——— and David Helfeld. "Loyalty Among Government Employees," Yale Law Journal, December 1948.

Ernst, Morris, and David Loth. Report on the American Communist. New York, 1952.

Fraenkel, Oswald. The Supreme Court and Civil Liberties. Rev. ed. New York, 1952.

Gellhorn, Walter. "Report on a Report of the House Committee on Un-American Activities," Harvard Law Review, October 1947.

———. Security, Loyalty and Science. Ithaca, 1950.

Hicks, Granville. Where We Came Out. New York, 1954.

Hiss, Alger. In The Court of Public Opinion. New York, 1957.

Hoover, J. Edgar. "Loyalty Among Government Employees," Yale Law Journal, February 1949.

Jowitt, Earl. The Strange Case of Alger Hiss. New York, 1953.

Kahn, Gordon. Hollywood on Trial. New York, 1948.

Lasswell, Harold. National Security and Individual Freedom. New York, 1950.

Lattimore, Owen. Ordeal By Slander. Boston, 1950.

Longaker, Richard. The Presidency and Individual Liberties. Ithaca, 1961.

McCarthy, Joseph. McCarthyism, The Fight for America. New York, 1952.

McWilliams, Carey. Witch Hunt: The Revival of Heresy. Boston, 1950.

O'Brian, John Lord. "Loyalty Tests and Guilt by Association," Harvard Law Review, April 1948.

———. "New Encroachments on Individual Freedom," Harvard Law Review, November 1952.

Polsby, Nelson. "Towards an Explanation of McCarthyism," Political Studies, October 1960.

Pritchett, C. H. Civil Liberties and the Vinson Court. Chicago, 1954.

Record, Wilson. *The Negro and the Communist Party*. Chapel Hill, 1951.

Rovere, Richard. *Senator Joe McCarthy*. New York, 1959.

Schlesinger, Arthur, Jr. *The Vital Center*. Cambridge, Mass., 1949.

Shannon, David. *The Decline of American Communism*. New York, 1959.

Shils, Edward. *The Torment of Secrecy*. New York, 1956.

Stouffer, Samuel. *Communism, Conformity, and Civil Liberties*. New York, 1955.

Sutherland, Arthur. "Freedom and Internal Security," *Harvard Law Review*, January 1951.

Toledano, Ralph de, and Victor Lasky. *Seeds of Treason: The True Story of the Hiss-Chambers Tragedy*. New York, 1950.

Trow, Martin. "Small Businessmen, Political Tolerance, and Support for McCarthy," *American Journal of Sociology*, November 1958.

Weyl, Nathaniel. *Battle Against Disloyalty*. New York, 1951.

Wilcox, Clair, ed. *Civil Liberties Under Attack*. Philadelphia, 1951.

Wrong, Dennis. "Theories of McCarthyism—a Survey," *Dissent*, Autumn, 1954.

7. The Korean War

Allen, Richard. *Korea's Syngman Rhee: An Unauthorized Portrait*. Rutland, Vt., 1960.

Appleman, Roy. *United States Army in the Korean War: South to the Nektong, North to the Yalu*. Washington, D.C., 1961.

Berger, Carl. *The Korea Knot*. Philadelphia, 1964.

Clark, Mark M. *From the Danube to the Yalu*. New York, 1954.

Department of State, *United States Policy in the Korean Crisis*. Washington, D.C., 1950.

Fehrenbach, T. R. *This Kind of War; a Study in Unpreparedness*. New York, 1963.

Goodrich, Leland M. *Korea: A Study of U.S. Policy in the United Nations*. New York, 1956.

Halperin, Morton. *Limited War in the Nuclear Age*. New York, 1963.

Higgins, Trumbull. *Korea and the Fall of MacArthur*. New York, 1960.

Joy, C. Turner. *How Communists Negotiate*. New York, 1955.

Leckie, Robert. *Conflict: The History of the Korean War, 1950–53*. New York, 1962.

MacArthur, Douglas. *Reminiscences*. New York, 1964.

Marshall, S. L. A. *The Military History of the Korean War*. New York, 1963.

Neustadt, Richard. *Presidential Power: The Politics of Leadership*. New York, 1960.

Panikkar, K. M. *In Two Chinas*. London, 1955.

Rees, David. *Korea: The Limited War.* New York, 1964.

Reeve, W. D. *The Republic of Korea.* New York, 1963.

Rovere, Richard, and Arthur M. Schlesinger Jr. *The General and the President.* New York, 1951.

Senate Committee on Armed Services and Committee on Foreign Relations. *Hearings, Military Situation in the Far East.* Washington, D.C., 1951.

Snyder, Richard, and Glenn Paige. "The United States Decision to Resist Aggression in Korea: The Application of an Analytical Scheme," in *Foreign Policy Decision-Making: An Approach to the Study of International Politics,* eds. Richard Snyder et al. New York, 1962.

Spanier, J. W. *The Truman-MacArthur Controversy and the Korean War.* Cambridge, Mass., 1959.

Whiting, Allen. *China Crosses the Yalu: The Decision to Enter the Korean War.* New York, 1960.

Whitney, Courtney. *MacArthur: His Rendezvous with History.* New York, 1950.

Index

ABOUT THE EDITORS

Barton J. Bernstein and Allen J. Matusow have been gathering materials on the Truman administration for several years. They have done research in most of the major collections—the Truman Library, the National Archives, the papers of Henry Stimson, James Forrestal, Julius Krug, and Lewis Schwellenbach, and of the Farmers Union and the United Mine Workers. They have had access to the private papers of Chester Bowles and Clinton Anderson, and have interviewed approximately fifty of the important members of the administration, including former President Truman, Clinton Anderson, Charles Brannan, and Chester Bowles.

Both men, each of whom was in grammar school when Truman became President, received their Ph.D.'s from Harvard University, where they wrote their dissertations on aspects of the Truman administration. They first conceived of their project in 1963, when they realized how few studies of the Truman administration were available and decided to put together a collection of the most important documents of the period. Barton Bernstein is now an assistant professor of history at Stanford University; Allen Matusow is assistant professor of history at Rice University.

71 72 73 74   12 11 10 9 8 7 6 5 4 3

COLOPHON BOOKS ON AMERICAN HISTORY

*In Preparation